SECRET SHAKESPEARE

Published in our
centenary year

≈ **2004** ≈

MANCHESTER

SECRET SHAKESPEARE

Studies in theatre, religion and resistance

RICHARD WILSON

MANCHESTER UNIVERSITY PRESS

MANCHESTER AND NEW YORK

distributed exclusively in the USA by Palgrave

Copyright © Richard Wilson 2004

The right of Richard Wilson to be identified as the author of this work has been asserted by him in accordance with the Copyright, Designs and Patents Act 1988

Published by Manchester University Press
Oxford Road, Manchester M13 9NR, UK
and Room 400, 175 Fifth Avenue, New York, NY 10010, USA
www.manchesteruniversitypress.co.uk

Distributed exclusively in the USA by
Palgrave, 175 Fifth Avenue, New York, NY 10010, USA

Distributed exclusively in Canada by
UBC Press, University of British Columbia, 2029 West Mall, Vancouver, BC,
Canada V6T 1Z2

British Library Cataloguing-in-Publication Data
A catalogue record for this book is available from the British Library

Library of Congress Cataloging-in-Publication Data applied for

ISBN 0 7190 7024 4 *hardback*
     0 7190 7025 2 *paperback*

First published 2004

13 12 11 10 09 08 07 06 05 04   10 9 8 7 6 5 4 3 2 1

Typeset in Aldus
by Koinonia, Manchester
Printed in Great Britain
by Bell & Bain Ltd, Glasgow

FOR MARK

Ever-fixed and never shaken

Gone are the days when we could enjoy *Hamlet* and not interest ourselves in Shakespeare. All of us tend to seek out not only the writer, who by definition expresses himself in his books, but also the individual, always necessarily manifold, contradictory and changeable, hidden in some places and visible in others, and finally – perhaps more than the other two – the *persona*, that reflection or shadow which sometimes the man himself projects as a defence or out of bravado, but behind which the human being of flesh and blood lived and died in that impenetrable mystery which is part of everyday life.

Marguerite Yourcenar, *Mishima: A Vision of the Void*, trans. Alberto Manguel (University of Chicago Press, 2001), pp. 4–5

Contents

Acknowledgements

Secret Shakespeare is a book about the real historical conditions of Shakespeare's art. Its argument is that Shakespeare's plays were written out of a profound engagement with the Europe of the Counter-Reformation, but that, if the dramatist can be aligned with any party, what he called 'our fashion' was the *politique* one of those moderate Catholics who reacted against the suicidal violence of the fanatics with a project of freedom of conscience and mutual toleration. Shakespeare's plays were shaped as critiques of martyrdom, I argue, by '*resistance* to the resistance' into which he had been born, and by his *politique* respect for the secrecy of the human heart. It was in France, and the essays of Montaigne, that this programme, which has lessons for our age of religious terrorism and sectarian hatred, first evolved. So, it is apt that much of this book on 'politic Shakespeare' was first given to French conferences and seminars during a year as Visiting Professor at the Institut du Monde Anglophone in Paris at the invitation of my colleague, friend and inspiration, François Laroque. There I was also able to benefit from the enthusiastic engagement with my ideas of Frank Lessay, André Topia and Gisèle Venet, for which I am extremely grateful. On a number of occasions Robert Ellrodt commented on my thoughts with a magisterial authority, and I count myself privileged to have been given the chance to air them so often through the indefatigable leadership of Marie-Thérèse Jones-Davies. Margaret Jones-Davies and Michel Lucazeau gave me startling new perspectives, and Jean-Michel Deprats offered me wry encouragement. My view of Elizabethan politics was enriched by conversations with Dominique Goy-Blanquet, while Adolphe Haberer, Pierre Iselin, Anne Lecercle, Liliane Louvel, Jean-Marie Maguin, Jean Pironon, Frédéric Regard, Wendy Ribeyrol, Isabelle Schwarz-Gastaing and Charles Whitworth were among those who generously invited me to give parts of this book as lectures which they organised. My sense that this is a golden moment for Shakespeare studies in France was confirmed by the informed criticism I received from students when I presented my work at the universities of Amiens, Caen, Clermont-Ferrand, Creteil (Paris XII), Lyons (II), Montpellier, Nanterre (Paris X), Poitiers, the Sorbonne (Paris IV), the Sorbonne Nouvelle (Paris III) and Tours, and at the Ecole Normale Supérieure at Lyon and Saint-Cloud. Chapters were also given at the Universities of Berlin (Free), Helsinki, Munich (Ludwig-Maximilian) and Valencia, and I am grateful to my hosts on those occasions. My most recent intellectual debt to Tobias Doering, Sonja Feilitz,

Andreas Hofele, Manfred Pfister and Wolfgang Weiss is the signpost, I hope, towards even wider involvement in the project of Shakespeare and Europe.

An earlier version of Chapter 2 was published in *The Times Literary Supplement*, 19 December 1997, and in *Histoire et secret à la Renaissance*, edited by François Laroque (Paris: Presses de la Sorbonne Nouvelle, 1997); of Chapter 6 in *Religion and the Arts*, 5 (2001); of Chapter 7 in *L'Oisiveté au Temps de la Renaissance*, edited by Marie-Thérèse Jones-Davies (Paris: Presses de l'Université de Paris-Sorbonne, 2002); of Chapter 10 in *The Lancashire Witches*, edited by Robert Poole (Manchester: Manchester University Press, 2002); of Chapter 11 in *English Literary History (ELH)*, 64 (1997); of Chapter 12 in *Shakespeare's Late Plays*, edited by Jennifer Richards and James Knowles (Edinburgh: Edinburgh University Press, 1999); and of Chapter 13 in *Le Détour*, edited by Liliane Louvel (Poitiers: Maison des Sciences de l'Homme et de la Société, 2000).

NOTE ON TEXTS

All quotations of Shakespeare are from the Oxford Edition as published in *The Norton Shakespeare* (New York: Norton, 1997), ed. Stephen Greenblatt, Walter Cohen, Jean Howard and Katharine Maus, and quotations of *King Lear* are from the conflated text.

Introduction

THIS is a book about what Shakespeare did not write. In view of the number of books published on what he did, this might seem perverse, but for the fact that Shakespeare's silence has become, in one respect, a focus of current interpretations of his life and work. The silence in question is his total effacement of the religious politics of his age. Previous generations had noticed this omission, but were able to believe, as did Graham Greene, that this 'vast vacuum' resulted from the fact that Shakespeare never personally confronted the 'Bloody Question' of religious loyalty which split his contemporaries between the Pope and Queen: for if he had sat 'across the board' from the Elizabethan martyrs, and passed judgement on them, there would have slipped into his 'smooth and ambiguous' plays 'a more profound doubt than Hamlet's, a love greater than Romeo's'.[1] Shakespeare's silence on the sectarian violence of his time has become all the more resounding, therefore, when set against mounting evidence that he did in fact sit where the novelist would like to have placed him – side-by-side with the persecuted – as a member of one of the most militant recusant families in a town which was a bastion of Elizabethan papist resistance. Local studies and biographies have now converged, that is to say, to situate young Shakespeare at the epicentre of the English Counter-Reformation culture which has itself been a recent rediscovery of historians such as John Bossy, Eamon Duffy, Christopher Haigh and Michael Questier. The debate over whether he lived or 'died a papist' has a long history; but this latest research on his Catholic contexts presents a different, and more interesting, problem, which is why, given so much pressure to break his silence on the 'Bloody Question', and a background that might even have made him a great religious poet, William Shakespeare remained, in this respect alone, so dumb.

'The first thing to remember ... is that he was a Catholic; the second that he betrayed his faith': the opening of John Carey's study of Donne describes not only the apostasy of a poet, but the tragedy of an entire generation of Elizabethan writers born into families which had prospered until 1558 under the Catholic Mary, and to query what this has to do with their writing is as reasonable as 'to demand what the Nazi persecution of Jews had to do with a writer in Germany in the 1930s. Donne was born into a terror, and formed by it'.[2] This book is therefore about how Shakespeare's muteness on the persecution of his family and friends relates to the conditions in which he wrote, when, as Bossy argues in his account of one of the many Catholic plots that originated in the dramatist's backyard, the division was not between Protestants and Catholics but between the silent ones and zealots such as the Throckmortons, who were politicised into suicidal resistance by the arrival among them in 1580 of the mission of the Jesuits Edmund Campion and Robert Parsons.[3] Its theme is that the question which in fact resonates through Shakespeare's plays, of whether 'To be or not to be' was prompted by the existential crisis of this moment, when it would have been impossible for him not to share Hamlet's predicament: 'Whether 'tis nobler in the mind to suffer / The slings and arrows of outrageous fortune, / Or to take arms against a sea of troubles, / And, by opposing, end them' (*Hamlet*, 3.1.59–62). Shakespeare started, I propose, as what his distant relative the poet and martyr Robert Southwell apparently called him, one of the 'finest wits' of Catholic England, but survived to become instead the most secret writer of his age.[4] Critics are edging towards the implications of the revelation that, as Stephen Greenblatt concludes in his book *Hamlet in Purgatory*, Shakespeare 'was probably brought up in a Roman Catholic household in a time of official suspicion and persecution of recusancy', and are teasing out the textual traces that reveal how much he was 'haunted by the spirit of his Catholic father'.[5] Shakespeare's theatre suddenly seems to echo with the ghosts of his Catholic past. But this book is about why, apart from these fading voices from the grave, 'The rest is silence' (5.2.300).

'Man speaks by being silent': Heidegger's sly aphorism is a reminder that the breach of the taboo on historicist criticism of Shakespeare has coincided with the discrediting of the modernist doxa of impersonality that was all too convenient for those who needed to separate the writer from the work.[6] To be sure, there is no equivalence between Shakespeare's silence on Catholic persecution and Heidegger's notorious silence on the Jews. But there is a parallel between current interest in the dramatist's reticence about the historical tragedy he witnessed and the suspicion of those deniers of history, like Paul de Man, whose cult of indeterminacy is now seen to have served as a timely alibi for political amnesia. The question of Shakespeare's silence would never have arisen so urgently without the scepticism towards all such gaps, omissions, suppressions and evasions which has been one result of the metacritical moment when deconstruction imploded to disclose its own ideological roots. So, it cannot be chance that the sharpest ridicule of the 'Catholic turn' in Shakespeare studies comes from modernist specialists who insist that 'the details available can be made to point in different directions', so it is impossible to construct any analysis which puts the author into his cultural space: the 'complicated web of circumstantial detail' is like the delusion of Macaulay's vicar who had been so long in the sun 'he could prove Napoleon was the Beast of the Apocalypse'.[7] As the 'details' of history dismissed with such lofty scorn include Campion's minutely documented mission, the anti-Catholic terror, Essex's Revolt and the Gunpowder Plot, it is not hard to see that the reason the idea of the Bard's invisibility persists is that those literary mystifiers who depend upon it remain oblivious to the revolution in post-Reformation historiography which has transformed the ways in which Shakespeare's texts, and textual remains, now need to be read. The rediscovery of the English Counter-Reformation provides a context for locating the dramatist's legendary inaccessibility, however, analogous to the sinister one which Michel Foucault offered for his own modernist desire, as a child of Vichy France, to write without a face:

> I think that any child educated in a Catholic milieu just before or during the Second World War had the experience that there were many different ways of speaking as well as many forms of silence … Maybe this appreciation of silence is related to the obligation of speaking. I lived as a child in a petit-bourgeois, provincial milieu in France and the obligation of speaking was for me both very strange and very boring. I often wondered why people had to speak.[8]

If Shakespeare's silence has been exemplary for theorists of the death of the author it has ironically also made possible one of the most naive myths of literary biography, which is that of the dramatist as a hero of Protestant England and favourite of the Queen. As Michael Dobson and Nicola Watson recount in their hilarious history of this popular fantasy, 'the illogical end-point of the claim that Shakespeare was Elizabeth's protégé was reached by those conspiracy theorists who argued that "Shakespeare" was, in fact, her pseudonym', and that the portrait on the Folio title-page 'was itself merely a disguised likeness of the Queen'.[9] But the media myth incarnated when Judi Dench's Gloriana takes the stage at the climax of *Shakespeare in Love* locks into an academic illusion which is equally pervasive, of the playwright as an Anglican spokesman, who 'recreates the Reformation image of Roman religion' to 'make his audience into more committed Protestants'.[10] Like the film, the construction of a Shakespeare in love with Protestant empire serves the ideological function of annexing the plays to the dominant Anglo-Saxon discourses of populism and individualism, and so to globalisation and American hegemony. It is easy to see why a 'global Shakespeare' who prefigures a republican politics, consumerism and the public sphere by articulating what Annabel Patterson calls 'the Popular Voice' of Protestant London should be consecrated in the transatlantic university system.[11] Likewise, there is no surprise that the shrillest response to the 'Catholic Shakespeare' thesis comes from critics scandalised that 'this version of the Bard provides the perfect excuse not to engage with Shakespeare in terms of Protestant, Reformed and Calvinist doctrine – that is, of the orthodox beliefs of his time'.[12] Hostile over-reaction to the conference on Shakespeare's Catholic contexts held at Lancaster University in 1999 was the pique of the current critical establishment, deeply invested in building a Protestant canon centred on Spenser, Middleton and Milton, which remains, long after the world turned round again in Tudor historiography, a last redoubt of the Whig–Marxist version of English history. For this Panglossian consensus, inflated by its professed association with Habermas, it is as if the Foucauldian critique of the Enlightenment had never taken place. But as Alison Shell remarks in her path-breaking book *Catholicism, Controversy and the English Literary Imagination, 1558–1660,* opposition to the recovery of Elizabethan recusant culture arises in the contemporary academy from some very impure motives:

> Responses to current Catholicism seem to determine whether one welcomes or shuns it as a subject for historical enquiry. If one thinks of it as inordinately powerful and unconscionably conservative under John Paul II, one's sympathy for its persecuted representatives in early modern Britain is likely to be diminished; and thence there arises a secularised anti-popery ... When non-Catholics consider early modern Catholicism, their attitude is inevitably coloured by their views on Catholicism now.[13]

There is an inherent paradox, as Shell admits, about researching Elizabethan Catholic resistance as a corrective to the domination of the academic WASP patriarchy, given that the Vatican is such a repressive tyranny, with its medieval doctrines on women, contraception and divorce. One would want to add to this litany of hate the Church's murderous bigotry on gay rights, before accepting, as Shell does, that early modern Catholics can be co-opted by a dissident criticism in the belief that 'a "politically correct" attitude ... will result in a careful and loving study of the reactionary, not as an enemy, but as an indispensable co-actor'.[14] Yet although I began this book hoping that a recusant Shakespeare would be useful, through affiliation with a dangerous and subversive freedom movement, in disrupting the worship of the patriotic Bard of Stratford, I soon discovered that the issues were not so simple or polarised. Crucially, I encountered the complication that, as the leading authority on Puritanism, Patrick Collinson, writes, if the notion of his family's conformity 'rests on mistaken, anachronistic perspectives of Elizabethan religious life', Shakespeare appears to have lived the schizophrenia of his era, with a father who was 'a Catholic of the old stamp' and 'an impeccable Jacobean Protestant' for a son-in-law. Thus, the poet looks representative, according to Collinson, of a community where 'the majority of those in the church were "church papists", [who] if not "rank papists" retained "still a smack and savour of popish principles"'.[15] In this confessional twilight, which has been spotlit by Alexandra Walsham, the split, Bossy claims, was between the gentleman, 'pragmatic, anti-heroic, old-fashioned in politics', and the priest: 'intellectual, radical, idealist and politically activist'.[16] But new research shows that the gentry of the Elizabethan Midlands were more implicated in the treason of their clerks than they ever dared admit.[17] Thus, it must be telling that in play after play by Shakespeare there is an anti-Jesuit subtext. In this game of gentlemen and

Jesuits it seems as if the dramatist takes a stand in resistance to resistance. And yet, towards the end, he buys the very Blackfriars Gatehouse which had for years been a hive of Jesuit conspiracy. So, Shakespeare's faith is like some Escher drawing, or perhaps his own Blackfriars property, with its secret passageways and priest-holes built to defy the grandest inquisitions.

'This papist and his poet, of like conscience for lies, the one ever feigning and the other ever falsifying the truth': John Speed's 1611 outing of Shakespeare as a co-conspirator with Parsons makes the professional equivocation of priest and playwright interchangeable.[18] Indeed, recent critics of Shakespeare's stage are intrigued by John Stow's report, in his 1598 *Survey of London*, that 'Of late time … certain public places, as the Theatre, the Curtain, &c., have been erected' precisely 'in place of' the city's suppressed religious institutions.[19] Thus, Louis Montrose contends that audiences found 'a substitute for the metaphysical aid of the medieval church' in 'a visit to the theatre'; while Greenblatt asserts that the actors took over 'more than a cut-price wardrobe' when they bought ecclesiastical costumes: 'they acquired the tarnished but potent charisma that clung to the old vestments'.[20] In these New Historicist readings, it is no accident that the players colonised the actual lots left vacant by demolition of London's monasteries.[21] But the question they raise, of course, is 'What happens when the piece of cloth is passed from the church to the playhouse', or when the consecrated space is appropriated for theatre?[22] What was the exact relationship between the papist and the poet if the playhouse was, in fact, literally a place of spilled religion? A fascinating answer is offered by Jeffrey Knapp in *Shakespeare's Tribe*, where he takes seriously Ben Jonson's remark that his 'tribe' consisted of 'Priests and Poets', to propose that when Shakespeare's company acquired Blackfriars property in 1596, and the poet bought the Gatehouse, 'not only did theatre people literally take the place of friars, they also seem to have felt a professional camaraderie with them'.[23] So while Greenblatt decides that Shakespeare's workplace was merely 'haunted' by Catholic rituals that had been 'emptied out',[24] Knapp's thesis is that a foothold in the Liberty once occupied by the Black Friars gave him licence to preach, as the Dominicans had done, a more accommodationist creed than 'the other Catholic clergy'. With authority from the good friars to disavow the zealots, Shakespeare 'conceived that the players could unite audiences through a shared examination of human frailty', Knapp concludes, in the ecumenicist spirit he gave to the clown of *All's Well That Ends Well*:

> For young Chairebonne the puritan and old Poisson the papist,
> howsome'er their hearts are severed in religion, their heads are
> both one: they may jowl horns together like any deer i'th'herd. (1.3.45–7)

'The most convenient place … For such receipt of learning is the Blackfriars' (*Henry VIII*, 2.2.137–8): when Shakespeare and his Protestant collaborator John Fletcher restaged the English Reformation in the very chamber at

Blackfriars where Katherine of Aragon had been divorced, they did so, if Knapp is correct, as a ritual act of religious reconciliation.[25] The idea would have appealed to the editors of *The Times* who later sat on the same site and were also dubbed the Black Friars for preaching Appeasement. But Knapp's portrait of the playwright as a lay-preacher, ever mindful that, as his fools jest, '*Cucullus non facit monachum*' (*Twelfth Night*, 1.5.48; *Measure*, 5.1.259) – the cowl does not make the monk – highlights the fact that his 'negative capability' – the ability to tolerate 'uncertainties, Mysteries, doubts', with which Keats credited him – and the elusiveness of his personality, 'signal more than his diplomacy on religious issues', since, as the Victorian critic Richard Simpson noted, the very opposition to sectarianism was itself, in a Protestant state, a developed Catholic position.[26] So, if reluctance to preach Christian doctrine was, as Knapp writes, 'a mark not of secularism, but of fears regarding the divisiveness of his religious beliefs'; and if, as Frank Brownlow infers, this reticence was shaped by his childhood experience of persecution, which taught him 'that belief was a private matter to be kept to oneself', the writer would have found such quietism sanctioned by a school of tolerant, or *politique*, Catholic thinking that was rooted in enclaves such as Blackfriars and the houses of nobles such as the Montagues.[27] Knapp likens him to Sir John Harington, who described himself as 'neither Papist, Protestant, nor Puritan, or a protesting Catholic Puritan' (Jesuit); and the comparison puts Shakespeare squarely among those politic Catholics ('schismatics' to the Jesuits) who hoped, in the words of Sir John's 1602 *Tract on the Succession to the Crown*, that 'neither the burning used in Queen Mary's time, nor the hanging used in this ... might be used in the next Prince's time ... but all good means for a reconcilement and pacification'.[28] That such a 'golden time' remained, within Shakespeare's Blackfriars, as much a dream as restoration of the city's 'convents' (*Twelfth Night*, 5.1.369), was itself the proof of how, far from being evacuated in the *via media* of art, the unforgiving passions of sectarian violence continued to swirl around his stage.

On 25 October 1598, at the Bell Inn, a hundred yards from the Blackfriars Gatehouse, and beside the royal Wardrobe that operated, under the control of the Catholic Fortescues, as an illicit Mass-centre,[29] his Stratford friend Richard Quiney wrote the only surviving letter to William Shakespeare, begging '£30 upon Mr Bushell's and my security'.[30] Here, in the oasis of licence where another Stratfordian, Richard Field, had printed, among works by *politiques* like Harington, his debut, *Venus and Adonis*, Quiney's business was to link Shakespeare with men at the heart of Catholic hopes, as the Bushells, Thomas and Edward (whose sister married Quiney's son), were former agents of the Stanleys in the core of the Essex Plot. We do not know whether the poet did trust Thomas Bushell's word, but the Earl would be condemned on Edward's, when the brother, himself incriminated in a 1594 plot to asssassinate the Queen, testified to the contents of a 'black bag' that included the list of conspirators.[31]

And a year later, on 3 May 1602, Quiney would himself be stabbed to death by assassins hired by Stratford's Puritans.[32] Thus, a thin web of textuality ties the owner of the Gatehouse to the desperate politics of resistance in the last days of Elizabeth. The evidence, as it stands, shows how the idea of the dramatist as a secularising figure is as false as the picture of him as a Roman Catholic spy. Secret Shakespeare turns out, instead, to resemble the *politique* Montaigne who praised Julian the Apostate, in his essay 'On freedom of conscience', as a model for the rulers of multi-confessional societies, who, if they cannot impose belief, can at least pretend that acts of toleration, such as the Edict of Nantes, are what they always wished.[33] This is not what I expected to write. But then, I never looked to be writing about Shakespeare and Catholicism at all, since I come from a part of England, near Lewes in Sussex, where on 5 November they still burn effigies of the Pope. It is just that, as Dympna Callaghan reports, the question of his relation to Catholic beliefs and practices now seems as unavoidable as the 'long-held assumption about Shakespeare as the Protestant national poet' appears 'wide of the mark'.[34] And the return of fundamentalism has taught us never again to conflate spirituality with humanism, or to euphemise Protestantism, in the old Left tradition, as 'hardly religion at all, but a kind of anti-Christian anarchy'.[35] We know so much more about religious violence than critics before 11 September 2001. For as I write this, on the site of Shakespeare's Gatehouse, the 'Ring of Steel' around Blackfriars and the City, first erected to counter the Catholic IRA, is being reinforced, to seal the precinct even more securely from a world elsewhere.

NOTES

1 Graham Greene, 'Introduction', *John Gerard: The Autobiography of an Elizabethan*, trans. Philip Caraman (London: Longmans, 1951), pp. x–xi.

2 John Carey, *John Donne: Life, Mind and Art* (London: Faber and Faber, 1981), pp. 15 and 18.

3 John Bossy, *Under the Molehill: An Elizabethan Spy Story* (New Haven: Yale University Press, 2001), p. 31.

4 Robert Southwell, 'Saint Peter's Complaint: The Author to the Reader', 13–18, in *Poems of Robert Southwell, S.J.*, ed. James McDonald and Nancy Pollard Brown (Oxford: Oxford University Press, 1967), p. 75; Christopher Devlin, *The Life of Robert Southwell, Poet and Martyr* (London: Longmans, 1956), pp. 262–5.

5 Stephen Greenblatt, *Hamlet in Purgatory* (Princeton: Princeton University Press, 2001), p. 249.

6 Martin Heidegger, 'What Is Called Thinking?' For a commentary see Berel Lang, *Heidegger's Silence* (Ithaca: Cornell University Press, 1996).

7 David Ellis, 'Biography and Shakespeare: An Outsider's View', *The Cambridge Quarterly*, 29:4 (2000), pp. 302–3.

8 Michel Foucault, 'An Interview with Stephen Riggins', in *Michel Foucault: The Essential Works: 1: Ethics*, ed. Paul Rabinow (London: Allen Lane, 1997), pp. 121–2.

9 Michael Dobson and Nicola Watson, *England's Elizabeth* (Oxford: Oxford University Press, 2002), p. 137.

10 Robert Watson, '*Othello* as Protestant Propaganda', in Claire McEachern and Debora

Shuger (eds), *Religion and Culture in Renaissance England* (Cambridge: Cambridge University Press, 1997), pp. 234–7. See also Brian Crockett, *The Play of Paradox: Stage and Sermon in Renaissance England* (Philadelphia: Pennsylvania University Press, 1995); Huston Diehl, *Staging Reform, Reforming the Stage: Protestantism and Popular Theater in Early Modern England* (Ithaca: Cornell University Press, 1997); John King, *English Reformation Literature* (Princeton: Princeton University Press, 1982); Peggy Munoz Simonds, *Myth, Emblem, and Music in Shakespeare's 'Cymbeline'* (Newark: New Jersey University Press, 1992); and Paul Whitfield White, *Theatre and Reformation: Protestantism, Patronage, and Playing in Tudor England* (Cambridge: Cambridge University Press, 1993).

11 Annabel Patterson, *Shakespeare and the Popular Voice* (Oxford: Basil Blackwell, 1989). See also Walter Cohen, *Drama of a Nation: Public Theater in Renaissance England and Spain* (Ithaca: Cornell University Press, 1985).

12 Michael Davies, 'On This Side Bardolatry: The Canonisation of the Catholic Shakespeare', *Cahiers Elisabethans*, 58 (2000), p. 39.

13 Alison Shell, *Catholicism, Controversy and the English Literary Imagination, 1558–1660* (Cambridge: Cambridge University Press, 1999), pp. 8–9.

14 Ibid., p. 6; quoting Virgil Nemoianu, 'Literary History: Some Roads Not (Yet) Taken', in Marshall Brown (ed.), *The Uses of Literary History* (Durham: Duke University Press, 1995), pp. 18–19.

15 Patrick Collinson, 'William Shakespeare's Religious Heritage', in *Elizabethan Essays* (London: Hambledon Press, 1994), pp. 230 and 250–2.

16 Ibid., p. 234; Alexandra Walsham, *Church Papists: Catholicism, Conformity and Confessional Polemic in Early Modern England* (Woodbridge: Boydell and Brewer, 1993); John Bossy, 'The Character of Elizabethan Catholicism', *Past and Present*, 21 (1962), pp. 39–59. See also Christopher Haigh, 'The Fall of a Church or the Rise of a Sect? Post-Reformation Catholicism in England', *Historical Journal*, 21 (1978), pp. 181–6; and 'From Monopoly to Minority: Catholicism in Early Modern England', *Transactions of the Royal Historical Society*, 5th series, 31 (1981), pp. 129–48.

17 Sandeep Kaushak, 'Resistance, Loyalty and Recusant Politics: Sir Thomas Tresham and the Elizabethan State', *Midland History*, 21 (1996), pp. 37–72. For an earlier version of this thesis see Peter Holmes, *Resistance and Compromise: The Political Thought of Elizabethan Catholics* (Cambridge: Cambridge University Press, 1982, pp. 6–7 and 176–85.

18 E.K. Chambers, *The Elizabethan Stage* (4 vols, Oxford: Oxford University Press, 1923), vol. 2, p. 217; John Speed, *History of Great Britain* (London: 1611), bk 9: 15.

19 John Stow, *A Survey of London*, ed. Henry Morley (London: Routledge, 1890), p. 119.

20 Louis Montrose, *The Purpose of Playing: Shakespeare and the Cultural Politics of the Elizabethan Theatre* (Chicago: Chicago University Press, 1996), pp. 30–1; Stephen Greenblatt, *Learning to Curse: Essays in Early Modern Culture* (London: Routledge, 1990), p. 162.

21 See Stephen Mullaney, *The Place of the Stage: License, Play, and Power in Renaissance England* (Chicago: Chicago University Press, 1988), pp. 43–5.

22 Stephen Greenblatt, *Shakespearean Negotiations: The Circulation of Social Energy in Renaissance England* (Oxford: Clarendon Press, 1988), p. 113.

23 Ben Jonson, 'To the Immortal Memory and Friendship of That Noble Pair, Sir Lucius Cary and Sir H. Morrison', 82, in *Ben Jonson*, ed. C.H. Herford and Percy and Evelyn Simpson (11 vols, Oxford: Oxford University Press, 1925–52), vol. 8, p. 245; Jeffrey Knapp, *Shakespeare's Tribe: Church, Nation, and Theater in Renaissance England* (Chicago: Chicago University Press, 2002), pp. 53 and 169.

24 Greenblatt, op. cit. (note 22), p. 119.

25 Irwin Smith, *Shakespeare's Blackfriars Playhouse: Its History and Design* (New York: New York University Press, 1964), pp. 20–1, 102–9 and 320–5.

26 Richard Simpson, 'The Political Use of the Stage in Shakespeare's Time', *The New*

Shakespere Society's Transactions, 2 (1874), pp. 393–4; Knapp, op. cit. (note 23), pp. 51–2; John Keats, *The Letters of John Keats*, ed. Hyder E. Rollins, (2 vols, Cambridge, Mass.: Harvard University Press, 1958), vol. 1, pp. 193–4.

27 Knapp, op. cit. (note 23), p. 51; Frank Brownlow, 'John Shakespeare's Recusancy: New Light on an Old Document', *Shakespeare Quarterly*, 40 (1989), p. 191.

28 Sir John Harington, *A Tract on the Succession to the Crown*, ed. Clement Markham (London: J.B. Nichols, 1880), pp. 108–9.

29 For the way the Fortescues 'turned a blind eye to what was going on' in the Wardrobe and the Gatehouse see Christopher Devlin, *The Life of Robert Southwell, Poet and Martyr* (London: Longmans, 1956), pp. 216–17.

30 The letter is reproduced in Samuel Schoenbaum, *William Shakespeare: A Documentary Life* (Oxford: Oxford University Press, 1975), pp. 180–1.

31 G.B. Harrison, *The Life and Death of Robert Devereux, Earl of Essex* (London: Cassell, 1937), pp. 303–4; *Calendar of State Papers Domestic, 1591–94*, vol. 249, nos 64, 89 and 103. On Edward Bushell's terrorist activities see Charles Nicholl, *A Cup of News: The Life of Thomas Nashe* (London: Routledge and Kegan Paul, 1984), pp. 190 and 196.

32 Mark Eccles, *Shakespeare in Warwickshire* (Madison: University of Wisconsin Press, 1963), pp. 98–9.

33 Michel de Montaigne, 'On Freedom of Conscience', in *The Complete Essays of Michel de Montaigne*, trans. M.A. Screech (London: Allen Lane, 1991), p. 763.

34 Dympna Callaghan, 'Shakespeare and Religion', *Textual Practice*, 15 (2001), pp. 1–4.

35 Shell, op. cit. (note 13), p. 55. Shell is objecting to the idealisation of Protestantism by Jonathan Dollimore and Alan Sinfield in their edition of *The Selected Plays of John Webster* (Cambridge: Cambridge University Press, 1983), p. xvi; in Dollimore's *Radical Tragedy* (Brighton: Harvester, 1983); and in Sinfield's *Literature in Protestant England* (London: Croom Helm, 1983).

1

Wrapped in a player's hide

Shakespeare's secret history

Night and silence. Who is here? (*A Midsummer Night's Dream*, 2.2.76)

'WHO's there? / Nay, answer me. Stand and unfold yourself': friend or foe; the opening of *Hamlet* sets the scene for the world's greatest spy story as a challenge to its interpreters to reveal the identity of the mystery figure who precedes the words. But the only thing everyone knows about the actual man who wrote them is that we know nothing about him. This is the paradox of the Shakespeare phenomenon: that the most applauded of all plays were produced from a life of such apparent secrecy. Yet it is precisely this contradiction, between the eloquence and brilliance of a spectacular stage and the darkness and silence of a secret self, that has become for many contemporary critics the central subject of his plays, and the obsessiveness with which these texts seem to return to it might itself provide a key to the enigma of Shakespeare's difference. For the fact is that we now know more about the life of this absconding author than that of almost any other Elizabethan except the Queen herself; but that what we know seems in such contradiction to the works. And this cannot be by chance. A life lived so much in the shadows of an art staged so much in the light must have been the result of some very specific historical circumstances, though it was to become a justification for our modern doctrine of the separation of the writer from his words. The great irony of this author's life and career, therefore, is that he has become universally celebrated for his invisibility. As the theatre director Peter Brook observes, 'What makes Shakespeare unique is precisely his refusal to put himself in the foreground. There are few authors with such a need to conceal themselves. Shakespeare used all his art to prevent his life becoming visible'.[1] This is not at all the same argument as the conventional suspicion that 'the mystery had to be invented in order to account for the genius'.[2] Instead, it will be the theme of *Secret Shakespeare* that while it may have been historically determined and perpetuated, this author's vanishing act was a deliberate function of his work: that Shakespeare wrote his plays with the conscious intention of secreting himself.

'Evidently, he dreams of a world in which he would be *exempt from meaning* (as one is from military service)': it is easy to see why Shakespeare's absence from his texts has become such an article of faith for a criticism transfixed with the mystique of 'The Death of the Author', and why his legendary impersonality should be valorised as the ultimate vindication of Roland Barthes's theory that literature is a utopia exempted from authorial intention. For if he had not existed, the invisible Bard would surely have had to be invented by an aesthetic which maintains as its dogma the modernist mystification that 'discretion – reserve – is the place of literature'.[3] The 'divine incognito' is privileged by such a criticism because his disinterestedness legitimates the project 'to write in order to have no face'. Yet it was Michel Foucault, who confessed this desire, who also acknowledged how in reality 'the eraser marks intended to attain the anonymous indicate more surely than any ostentatious penholder the signature of a name'.[4] Likewise, it was Barthes, the champion of textual disinheritance, who turned back in his last lectures to 'the work as volition', and who conceded that those most reassured by the disappearance of the author are purveyors of 'common sense', who have 'no love of meaning (for which intellectuals are held responsible)'.[5] Thus, even the author of 'The Death of the Author' recognised that it is a naive essentialism which is reinforced by myths such as the one still persistently recycled in the mass media, that 'all that is known with certainty concerning Shakespeare' (as George Steevens swore in 1780) 'is that he was born in Stratford-upon-Avon, married and had children there, went to London, where he commenced an actor, and wrote poems and plays, returned to Stratford, made his will, died, and was buried'.[6] The meaning of Shakespeare's disinterestedness, by contrast, begins with the material certainties of *what we do not know* about him: as, for instance, that (barring a single letter for which he was the addressee, and that may not even have been sent) he left behind no correspondence; nor (except for one scene of a collaboration) any manuscripts of his plays; nor registration of education at any school or university; nor evidence of attendance at, or absence from, any church; nor professional accounts; nor diary; nor records of any table-talk. No wonder, then, that the commonsense historian Blair Worden is sufficiently bemused by this chronicle of immaculate absenteeism to imagine that, while the relationship between an artist's life and work is always problematic, 'there can be no other writer since the invention of printing for whom we are unable to demonstrate any relationship at all'.[7] But it cannot be an accident that it was just this contrast between public success and private secrecy which first attracted comment from Shakespeare's own sceptical rivals and suspicious contemporaries.

'There is an upstart crow, beautified with our feathers': the playwright Robert Greene's dying curse on young Shakespeare introduced him to the London stage in terms that would stick on him the 'vile phrase, "beautified"'

(*Hamlet*, 2.2.111), as a gatecrashing imposter whose facile professionalism concealed something dark and deadly underneath.[8] For whether a rival was here tarring him implicitly with the Catholics of Tyburn, through the stock caricature of Jesuits as 'massing crows' who flocked about the scaffold,[9] the black legend of the dramatist as a fellow-traveller of hooded treason persisted long enough for the Puritan historian John Speed to out him in 1611, alongside the Jesuit Robert Parsons, as 'this papist and his poet, of like conscience for lies, the one ever feigning, the other ever falsifying the truth'.[10] In fact, the picture of the Jesuit 'black-robe' as a carrion crow was one which Shakespeare would himself use to dissociate from papist terrorism, when he wrote of the evil hour when 'the crow / Makes wing to th' rooky wood' (*Macbeth*, 3.3.51–2) in denunciation of the Masses hosted by the conspirator Ambrose Rookwood at Clopton House, near Stratford, in the darkening days before the Gunpowder Plot.[11] 'Night's black agents' (54) was then Shakespeare's term for such ill-omened 'birds' winging to his own backyard. Yet according to the latest research, it was one of the corvine priests who made for Rookwood's safe-house, and was executed for his part in the Plot, whom the poet welcomed, in his 1601 elegy *The Phoenix and the Turtle*, among those he called 'our mourners' grieving for the Catholic dead. Born in 1555, the Jesuit Henry Garnet, whom the Porter abuses in *Macbeth* as 'an equivocator that could swear in both the scales against either scale' (2.3.8–9), is identified as the 'treble-dated crow' saluted in the poem for his unique power to generate his 'sable gender' with the breath he gives and takes (18–19). Garnet's licence to admit applicants into the Society of Jesus *in extremis* without noviceship was, indeed, a special faculty to bestow the kiss of death; and it was granted on the occasion the poem, it now emerges, was composed to celebrate, which was the internment with 'great decorum' of the remains of the Jesuits' matron, Anne Line, with those of her husband, after she was hanged in the wake of the Essex Revolt.[12] Set to music by 'the bird of loudest lay' – that 'Herald sad and trumpet' of Elizabethan recusancy, the lay-priest William Byrd himself – Shakespeare's avian obsequy thus places him, despite later protestations, in the very midst of those 'crows' who hid their soutanes beneath plumes, in a scenario of secret rites in country houses, like the mansion beside the Thames at Marlow of Richard Bold from Prescot in Lancashire, where his Stratford contemporary, the doomed Robert Debdale, was the chaplain and master of ceremonies:

> On reaching this gentlemen's house, we were received with every attention and courtesy. Indeed, the place was most suitable to our ministrations, not merely for the reason that it was remote ... but also because it possessed a chapel, set aside for the celebration of the Church's offices. The gentleman was a skilled musician, and had an organ and musical instruments, and choristers, male and female, members of his household. So, during those days it was just as if we were celebrating an uninterrupted octave of some great feast. Mr Byrd, the very famous musician and organist, was among the company. Earlier he had been attached to the Queen's chapel, where he had gained a great reputation.

But he had sacrificed everything for the faith – his position, the court, and all those aspirations common to men who seek preferment in royal circles.

Father Garnet sang Mass, and we had with us the domestic chaplain, a man who deserved well of this distinguished and saintly family, for not long afterwards he became a most illustrious martyr.[13]

'Cucullus non facit monachum': twice, in scenes of Jesuitical parody, Shakespeare quotes the proverb that the cowl does not make the monk (Twelfth Night, 1.5.48; Measure, 5.1.259). And the evidence accumulates which places him, alongside the Byrd he partners in The Phoenix and the Turtle, in the encrypted culture of seigneurial Catholicism, with its Masses and madrigals sung in defiance of the 'shrieking harbinger' – the pursuivant – and 'Every fowl of tyrant wing' (5–10). Yet this very proximity to the composer who 'sacrificed everything for faith' emphasises how much the poet's story differed from the narrative that might have been predicted for him: of social ostracism in a censored art. Shakespeare, by contrast with the rest of the choir who sing 'the anthem' (21) of outlawed religion in his Aesopian poem, seems like an Elizabethan Shostakovich. For this was a man who could also deplore how 'crows are fatted with the murrain flock' (Dream, 2.1.97) in a sour pun on Jesuit infiltration of the church for which More had died. But then, Greene's warning about Shakespeare secreting a 'Tiger's heart wrapped in a player's hide' does seem to identify him among those survivors, like Parsons, who could hide truth in equivocation as plausibly as they disguised vestments under an actor's cloak: 'dressed up', as the Catholic hero Edmund Campion joked, 'like a peacock, such a swaggerer a man must needs have sharp eyes to catch a glimpse of holiness beneath such a garb, such a look, such a strut'.[14] As historians remind us, it was because the English Jesuit was, 'by necessity, a man playing a role, often the appealing one of a gentleman', that such 'beautified crows' were so feared, for 'the hiddenness of their commitment was as disturbing as their faith'.[15] When Henry Chettle printed it in 1592, the 'upstart crow' aspersion cut so near the bone, in any case, that 'divers of worship', who may have included the crypto-Catholic Lords Montague, Southampton and Strange, swore to Shakespeare's 'uprightness of dealing', pressuring the publisher to retract the imputation with a testimonial to the poet's honesty: 'because myself have seen his demeanor no less civil than he excellent in the quality [acting] he professes'. This tribute to an actor's truth had, of course, the status of the paradox of the Cretan liar. So, thereafter, the writer who mocked himself as 'our bending author' on the one occasion, in the Epilogue to Henry V, when he took a bow, deferred to those who might detect the 'offence' of Catholic bias, as they did in his travesty of the Protestant hero, Sir John Oldcastle,[16] by effacing his own presence behind an innocuous persona like that of 'good Peter Quince' (Dream, 1.2.7), whose very name seems to hint at some strategy to sugar a bitter aftertaste with euphemistic gloss.

Shakespeare minimised himself, according to Jonathan Bate, in the 'deliciously ironic' characters called William in *As You Like It* and *The Merry Wives of Windsor*: a country bumpkin and a cheeky schoolboy.[17] But if 'honey-tongu'd' Shakespeare did smother his true tartness with such an inoffensive syrup, to make the bitter pill go down with Elizabeth's regime, 'in those danger-ous times, when words and even thoughts might make a man a traitor', as the Victorian Catholic critic Richard Simpson inferred, this 'honey-flowing vein' may have been cloying enough to its creator to provoke Pandarus's saccharine homage to Helen as his 'Sweet Queen, sweet Queen, a sweet Queen … my sweet Queen, my very very sweet Queen' (*Troilus*, 3.1.65–73).[18] For despite the fact that, as William Empson archly pointed out, one of the reasons why 'Shakespeare did not love dogs as he should', was that he associated them with the nauseating sycophancy of court spaniels salivating over candy,[19] the poet's literary image quickly became one of sickening sugariness. Praised *ad nauseam* as 'honey-tongued', by 1598 it was clear that, as Francis Meres drooled, 'The sweet and witty soul of Ovid lives in mellifluous and honey-tongued Shakespeare, witness … his sugared sonnets to his private friends'.[20] 'Melicert' was what Chettle sneeringly called him, and that there was something in this dulcified reputation more strategic than fashion is suggested, by the sentimental stickiness which also clung to Shakespeare's personality. His distant relative the martyr and poet Robert Southwell paid him a backhand compliment as one of the gentry who did not fear 'Of mirth to make a trade'.[21] But despite class anxiety about making himself 'a motley to the view', and permitting his quality to be 'subdued / To what it works in, like the dyer's hand' (Sonnet 110, 111), what underwrote Shakespeare's true integrity, according to John Davies of Hereford, was indeed his anodyne disinterestedness: for 'though the stage doth stain pure gentle blood, / Yet generous are ye in mind and spirit'.[22] Spenser, if Ernst Honigmann is correct, specifically attributed the 'large streams of honey and sweet nectar' that flowed from the 'gentle spirit' of 'our pleasant Willy' to his emotionally 'deaded' aloofness from the 'boldness' of the 'base-born'.[23] Thus, a portrait of 'gentle Shakespeare, the sweet swan of Avon'[24] emerged as a sign of a paradoxical mode of self-fashioning, whereby the author's public personality only ever registered because it was asserted 'as gently as any sucking dove' (*Dream*, 2.1.67). 'Sweet and witty' Shakespeare was present in his social and professional relations, it seems, in strict proportion to the detachment of what Jonson called his 'gentle expressions', and 'Good Will' of the Mermaid Tavern, whose 'right happy and copious industry' made him 'so worthy a friend and fellow' to his colleagues,[25] was fashioned, like his Folio publication itself, 'without ambition either of self-profit or fame', or so Davies vouched, from a lifetime of exemption from social contest and abstention from political intent:

> Some say, good Will, which I in sport do sing,
> Hadst thou not played some kingly parts in sport,
> Thou hadst been a companion for a King,
> And been a King among the meaner sort.[26]

The dissolution of Shakespeare's personality into his art, theorised T.S. Eliot, was the measure of his greatness; as for Stephen Greenblatt it remains precisely his disinterestedness that determines his 'limitless talent for entering into the consciousness of another'.[27] Likewise, for Borges, he was a void, or 'everything and nothing', since 'There was no one in him ... only a bit of coldness, a dream dreamt by no one'.[28] But, as Gary Taylor objects, 'That blank – the blank check that underwrites Shakespeare's reputation – is an illusion', for 'Nature, after all, abhors a vacuum; vacuums have to be carefully constructed and maintained', and 'any act so bizarre and sustained' as Shakespeare's 'apparent invisibility is not a simple fact, it is an *act*. Which is to say, is it a motivated action and a performance'.[29] The most obvious material precondition of this author's disappearing trick was, after all, his use of the recusant tactic of dual residence, allowing him to slip between parish pump and state intelligence as habitually as his own characters go 'To liberty, and not to banishment' (*As You Like It*, 1.3.132). And it may be that this alternation of different locations, and the constant recourse in his plays to some estranged 'world elsewhere' (*Coriolanus*, 3.3.139), are indeed clues to the negative capability which Greenblatt honours as Shakespeare's unique genius for inhabiting the identities of others through the extinction of his own. Good Will's sweetness begins, in other words, to seem less like holy idiocy and more like the signifier of the tactically 'split personality' of Elizabethan Catholicism, which is defined by recent critics as just such a 'curious mix of self-assertion and self-cancellation', by virtue of its mutually incompatible models of a transcendent subjectivity, all-powerful in relation to others, and an alienated subjectivity constituted by its abnegation to power. As Ronald Corthell has observed, in the cases of martyrs like Campion and Southwell this ideological double-bind led to the 'literally death-defying feat' of defending loyalty to Rome while denying political intent; but since their community was so intensely 'observed, interrogated, and persecuted', self-abasement, and even self-annihilation, came to seem a suicidal 'consummation / Devoutly wished' (*Hamlet*, 3.1.65), for an entire generation of Catholic Elizabethans born 'to serve two masters, even as each made it impossible to serve the other'.[30] It cannot, therefore, be complete coincidence that in Shakespeare's boyhood the intellectual foundations of this Counter-Reformation cult of self-effacement were being laid close to Stratford, in the Catholic households of the Warwickshire Forest of Arden.

'He was so gentle and affable, even to the lowest sort of people, and he arrived at such a low estimate of himself, that he who most excelled others thought himself inferior to all': if there was a prototype of the self-negating subject of recusant discourse it was the heir to Coughton, the mansion of the Throckmorton family, six miles from Stratford. And if young Shakespeare looked for a mentor in the fashioning of self-denial, he had to go no further than this cousin through his mother, Mary Arden, whose short life – as eulogised by their mutual kinsman, Southwell – was a *reductio ad absurdum* of the negative identity which the dramatist would reputedly make his own, and a performance of *noli me tangere* at once so self-consuming and self-dramatising, so deeply 'bizarre and sustained', that 'all the neighbouring gentry held him up as an example of piety for their sons to imitate'.[31] Two years older than Shakespeare, Edward Throckmorton left Stratford for Rome in 1580, and died there in the English College at the age of twenty; but 'this angelical boy ... distinguished for his perfection in every kind of virtue requisite for constituting a saintly youth, left behind him', according to his supervisors, 'a model for the imitation of all future comers from England'.[32] He did this by organising an unofficial seminary in the Forest of Arden, which Christopher Devlin describes as 'the Counter-Reformation in miniature', and which started when 'after school he used to go a great part of the way home with those who lived at a distance, urging them to piety, and exhorting them that if they were required to act against their faith, they should steadfastly refuse'.[33] Because Coughton was under the envious watch of the Puritan priest-hunter Sir Thomas Lucy, Throckmorton had been sent to be tutored himself deeper in the Forest at Park Hall, the seat of Edward Arden, the 'old religious uncle' (*As You Like It*, 3.2.311) he shared with Shakespeare; and it was there that under his influence 'other youths flocked from all parts of the county for education as well in letters as in virtue'. Whether or not the lovers of *As You Like It* retrace these steps when they too go to join an 'uncle in the Forest of Arden', after hearing how 'young gentlemen flock to him every day', Throckmorton's tactics were certainly those of 'the old Robin Hood' (1.1.101; 1.3.101) when 'he went to neighbouring houses, asking parents to send their sons to him on feast days', and wherever there was parental opposition, 'went to his uncle with whom he lodged', and arranged for 'the boy to run away from home', so that he would 'stay with him, and be educated in the same house as himself'.[34] It was at Park Hall, evidently, that the identification of Warwickshire Arden with the Ardennes of the seminaries – Douai and Saint-Omer – first became irresistible to Stratford students, and there, under the fanatical tutelege of an adolescent zealot, that they were first taught to speak those negative dialectics of self-control and 'Sweet ... adversity' (2.1.12), the virtual invisibility that by tradition Shakespeare would make his own:

> If ever he found any of his companions offending against modesty, he rebuked him sharply, and declared that he would avoid him in future unless he was more guarded. He was so remarkable for the gravity of his manners and innocence of his life that many people, and those not of the lowest class, begged earnestly of the uncle with whom he lived that their children might be admitted into Edward's service, with the intention that they should be instructed by him, and moulded according to his own character. Hence it appears with what sanctity and gentleness he was endowed, being so faithful to the service of God as to win for himself the good will of all to an extent which seemed to forbode already the position he was afterwards to gain above the rest

of his kinsmen … He attracted all hearts to himself by his charming affability, sweetness, and sedateness of manner, combined with sprightliness of countenance and conversation. But though these things may appear surprising to men of the world, they will not do so to those who can appreciate the interior delight of his heart, and know the sweetness of the heavenly food wherewith his soul was nourished.[35]

'Saints are well worth the attention of historians', as Peter Burke remarks in 'How to be a Counter-Reformation Saint', because they reflect the values that the culture currently holds most dear. And if the teenage Shakespeare was one of the 'co-mates and brothers in exile' who found his religious uncle's 'woods / More free from peril than the envious' Coughton (2.1.1–4), he would have been indoctrinated into the heady pietistic decorum of the Counter-Reformation not only through the fanatical Throckmorton but also through the young priests who regularly arrived at Park Hall from Europe, and who included Campion and Parsons.[36] In fact, Shakespeare's paradoxical mixture of superiority and selflessness exactly parallels the aristocratism of Campion, who was likewise adulated for both his 'mild behaviour', and his 'rare and virtuous will'. A personality in which 'nature's flowers' were said to be 'mixed with herbs of grace', and 'A lowly mind' in 'learned place', the Jesuit hero came to Stratford from Prague, where, according to Katherine Duncan-Jones, Philip Sidney had been 'all but persuaded' by his 'sugared speech' to convert to Rome.[37] In reality, Campion's performance of a Christ-like humility and hauteur had been honed ever since his days as a famous infant prodigy at Oxford, where he had been lionised by mobs of teenage 'Campionists', who imitated not only his studied dress, speech and manner, but even his abstemious diet.[38] And en route to England in June 1580 his mission had conferred for eight days in Milan with the supreme exemplar of this Jesuitical art of self-consuming sanctity, the zealot prelate-prince Carlo Borromeo. 'He had most learned and godly speeches with us', enthused Parsons of this briefing, 'tending to contempt of this world and perfect zeal of Christ's service, whereof we saw so rare an example in himself, being nothing, in effect, but skin and bone, through continual pains, fasting and penance'.[39] The cardinal armed Campion's mission with the Testament of faith he had devised during a plague in 1578, and which Shakespeare's father John, it seems, would be one of the very first to sign. So, when they distributed this pledge to 'the crowd of gentry' who greeted them,[40] the Jesuits were putting the boy's relatives into contact with the latest machinery of Tridentine Catholicism, and with a new concept of self-government organised around the invention that John Bossy, Foucault and others see as a inaugurating a 'Copernican Revolution' in the history of the soul: Borromeo's confession box.

'For a long time an individual was vouched for by reference to others', observes Foucault of Borromeo's techniques of self-invigilation, but 'now he was authenticated by the truth he was obliged to pronounce concerning himself. Western man had become a confessing animal.'[41] Initially constructed around 1550, the confession box was first made mandatory in Milan in 1576, when Borromeo's specifications – for a miniature Baroque theatre, partitioned in two by a grille with mesh 'the size of pea' no finger could penetrate – abruptly terminated the medieval practice of confession as a collective sacrament, solemnised by a public laying-on of hands, and instituted a modern disciplinary economy in which responsibility was internalised.[42] For as Bossy explains, the impact of this *camera obscura*, and the 'proliferation of forms, files, receipts and regulations' with which the Counter-Reformation bureaucratised the soul, was to turn culture 'away from objective social relations to interiorised discipline', by 'suggesting sin was essentially something that occurred in the mind. The new confessional technology was an instrument of intimate self-examination available to the average man.'[43] Recent studies have developed Foucault's thesis of the dark twinship between this private proscenium of self-interrogation and the torture chamber, considering how the effect of the confessional regime was to constitute the confessant as subject of a deep and guilty sexuality. Certainly, its beauty for Borromeo was that it made confession a form of judicial inquisition, where the priest spoke 'like a judge from the seat of judgement'; or as Cardinal William Allen explained (just a year after he is supposed to have taught at Stratford Grammar School himself), like a new type of prince who had power to bind not the body but 'the very soul'.[44] But what historians also notice is the social effect of this chamber of secrets on the confessor himself, which was to install him in a godlike detachment, at the price, however, of the sealed repression of his subjective interest: the whispered privacy, impossibility of touching, imperative of confidentiality, and above all, the mutual invisibility, all combined to obliterate his personality as totally as that of the overseer of Bentham's Panopticon. The confession cubicle, in other words, was a theatrical mechanism for fabricating in its masochistic young stage managers precisely the type of impersonality so desired by English recusants: all-seeing in relation to others by virtue of its own concealment. Thus, when he arrived from Milan, Campion did not only bring the Shakespeares, father and son, Borromeo's Testament; he brought them news of an invention to generate exactly the 'disinterest effect' which critics now attribute to the omniscient dramatist: a machine for manufacturing a human vacuum.

'He was, indeed, honest and of an open and free disposition':[45] Shakespeare's mysterious vacuousness – the impression he made on contemporaries of transparency and disinterestedness – may come to be interpreted not so much as the signifier of unique genius but as the historically conditioned self-fashioning of one born and educated at the violent epicentre of the Elizabethan Counter-Reformation. For as soon as this 'mellifluous and honey-tongued' author is returned to the conflicted world of Catholic resistance, his 'civil demeanour … generous mind and spirit' and 'gentle expressions' begin to look like the studied and conscious performance of just that style of self-discipline which was exemplified by his own confessors. When he abandoned the prospect of the pulpit for the playhouse, wrapping his 'tiger's heart in a player's hide', gentle Shakespeare, meek and mild, might, therefore, have been simply the most triumphant of all the representatives of that strategy of 'beautification' recommended by his 'Campionist' teachers as the means to preserve inwardness and conscience. The risk with this dissimulation, Bossy notes, was always that 'the disguise would absorb the personality';[46] and it could be that Shakespeare's limitless talent for entering the consciousness of others was an ultimate function, in this sense, of Catholic England's greatest act of ventriloquising self-forgetfulness. Perhaps that was what the papist Ben Jonson meant, when he insinuated that his rival was always at risk of overdoing the performance, and that before he gave himself away entirely and said too much, 'sometimes it was necessary he should be stopped'.[47] In any event, like Campion's aristocratism, the 'sweet and witty soul' of Shakespeare can be historicised, in light of what is being discovered about his Jesuit influences, as the classic instance of what Pierre Bourdieu has analysed as the *faux-naif* vision of *calculated disinterestedness* which dates from the crisis of traditional society, when 'the most holy actions – ascetism or extreme devotion – may be suspected of being inspired by a search for the symbolic profit of saintliness'. Bourdieu relates this performance of disinterestness specifically to the late sixteenth-century Wars of Religion, the fatal moment when sectarian thinking 'slipped into the aristocratic apple', and began to whisper that 'aristocratic attitudes are the supreme forms of calculation'.[48] Likewise, Lucien Goldmann attributed the tragic vision of Baroque drama to the instant when Catholic intellectuals withdrew from a world in which, they suddenly perceived, it was impossible to live without interest.[49] Shakespeare's famous impersonality clearly belonged to such a juncture, when the nation state first required its subjects to declare their interest, whilst, in Foucault's formulation, the Counter-Reformation Catholic Church demanded obedience, and two opposing hemispheres converged:

> How to govern oneself, how to be be governed, how to become the best possible governor – all these problems, which seem to be characteristic of the sixteenth century, lie at the crossroads of two processes: the one which leads to the establishment of the nation states; and that totally different movement which, with the Counter-Reformation, raises the issue of how one must be ruled and led on this earth in order to achieve eternal salvation … And it is at the intersection of these two tendencies that the problem comes to pose itself with this peculiar intensity: of how to be ruled, by whom, and to what end.[50]

On 8 August 1588, at the hour of greatest crisis for her regime, Queen Elizabeth had herself strapped on to a warhorse to inspect the army assembled to repel the Spanish Armada along the banks of the Thames. The militia had mustered there from across southern England, and 'It was a pleasant sight to behold the soldiers', according to the official account, 'as they marched towards

Tilbury', with their 'cheerful countenances, courageous words and gestures, dancing and leaping wheresoever they came'. Such was the festive humour defiantly adopted that morning by the Queen herself, as she 'passed like some Amazon empress through all her army', explaining how she had come as a king in the disguise 'of a weak and and feeble woman ... not for my recreation and disport, but being resolved to live and die amongst you all'.[51] The New Historicism has reminded us that 'Elizabeth's exercise of power was bound up with her use of fictions' of romantic love;[52] and even this dire emergency was like some courtship game, she insinuated, since though 'we have been persuaded by some that are careful of our safety, to take heed how we commit ourselves to armed multitudes, for fear of treachery ... I do not desire to distrust my faithful and loving people. Let tyrants fear. I have always so behaved myself that I have ever placed my chiefest strength and safeguard in the loyal hearts of my subjects'.[53] Certainly, Elizabeth's challenge to her subjects to 'stand and unfold', and to demonstrate the faithfulness of their 'loyal hearts' by acting out their love, did seem to be vindicated when the troops paraded before her, and – according to a secret report alleged to have been smuggled out from an enemy spy to Bernardino Mendoza, the Spanish Ambassador in Paris – the very 'first that showed his bands to the Queen' was none other than England's foremost Catholic peer: 'that noble, virtuous, and honourable man, the Viscount Montague', who had stoutly led his regiment up to Tilbury from Sussex:

> and now came, though he was very sickly and in age, with a full resolution to live and die in defence of the Queen, and of his country, against all invaders, whether it were pope, king, or potentate whatsoever; and in that quarrel he would hazard his life, his children, his lands, and his goods. And to show his mind agreeably thereto, he came personally himself before the Queen with his band of horsemen, being almost two hundred; the same being led by his own sons, and with them a very young child, very comely, seated on horseback, being the heir of his house, that is, the eldest son of his son and heir: a matter much noted of many, whom I heard to commend the same, to see a grand-father, father, and son, at one time on horseback, afore a Queen for her services; though, in truth, I was sorry to see our adversaries so greatly pleased therewith.[54]

It was the spectacle of the aged Lord Montague, 'this great Roman Catholic', putting his loving allegiance on display to his sovereign, and thus 'perilling his whole house in the expected conflict', which convinced observers, according to the Spanish informant, of the patriotism of Elizabeth's Catholic subjects.[55] No wonder, therefore, that the government rushed the so-called *Letter to Mendoza* into print immediately it was said to have been found in the hiding-place of a seminary priest named Richard Leigh, executed a month after the Armada, for as Burghley's biographer, Conyers Read, observes, its tear-jerking portrait of 'an English Catholic, loyal to his faith, paying tribute to England's war-effort, to the English nobility, to the gallant Queen, and most of all to the national loyalty of the English Catholics', made a mockery of claims of papal omniscience and Spanish invincibility.[56] This was a script that Elizabeth's chief minister might have devised himself specifically to dramatise the ultimate affiliation of England's Catholic community. And, as a matter of fact, he did, since historians are now convinced that the famous *Letter to Mendoza* was forged by his secretaries, and that 'of all his contributions to the literature of propaganda', this sentimental tableau of the oath-taking of the Montagues was Burghley's fictional masterpiece.[57] In reality, Lord Montague was excused leading his troops to Tilbury because of his 'indisposition', before being put under house arrest on 25 August; and when his men were finally pressed into a battle, a year later in France, they proved so 'ill-chosen and badly armed' that they 'went to all lengths of excuse and desertion rather than serve', whilst uttering 'most slanderous speeches of Her Majesty's service and entertainment'.[58] So, whether historians are right to doubt that the picturesque scene in which the old 'Roman' pledged to fight for Queen and country against the Pope ever, in fact, took place,[59] what Burghley's wishful-thinking fantasy highlights is the vital importance to the Elizabethan regime not only of the nominal acquiescence of its Catholic subjects but of a public protestation of their 'faithful and loving' hearts. And it cannot, therefore, be chance that a comparable test of love and loyalty, within the same scenario of enforced affection and false festivity, or seduction and compulsion, should be a mainspring of Shakespearean drama, which is initiated, in text after text, by some prince's repetition of Queen Elizabeth's oppressive question to her 'faithful and loving people': 'Which of you shall we say doth love us most?' (*Lear*, 1.1.49).

From the coronation of Tamora in *Titus Andronicus* – when the Queen of the Goths plots to 'enchant the old Andronicus' into submission (*Titus*, 1.1.333–40; 4.4.89) – to the christening of Elizabeth in *Henry VIII* – when the Queen of England is at last named as she who must be both 'lov'd and fear'd' (5.4.30) – Shakespeare's political dramas can be read as a series of variations on Burghley's theatre of allegiance, in which the Tudor despot does seem to figure as the sinister paragon Cranmer proclaims her in the play: 'A pattern to all princes', through her alternation of 'Peace, plenty, love' and 'truth' with 'terror' (47). In words given to the Protestant Archbishop, the Queen's coercive ploy would be to ensure that while 'her own shall bless her; / Her foes shall shake like a field of beaten corn, / And hang their heads in sorrow' (30–2); and in these stories it is as if the Armada choice is reenacted over and over, in response to this ultimatum to a 'shaken' people. Whether it is Theseus, segregating 'The pale companion' of sedition from 'the Athenian youth' with 'merriments' that 'Turn melancholy forth to funerals' (*Dream*, 1.1.12–15); or Caesar, preferring 'fat, / Sleek-headed men, and such as sleep a-nights', to the 'lean and hungry look' of dissent (*Julius*, 1.2.189–92), the recurring project of Shakespeare's rulers is the Elizabethan one of divide and rule, as Tamora schemes to neutralise the Andronici: 'With words more sweet, and yet more dangerous, / Than baits to fish, or honey-stalks to sheep, / When as the one is wounded with the bait, / The other rotted with delicious feed' (*Titus*, 4.4.90–4). *Titus Andronicus* may well have been acted under the patronage of the Montagues, or their young heir, Southampton, and its group-portrait of the old Roman nobility at the court of the Caesars, with barbarians at the gates, seems to sum up the historical predicament of Shakespeare's Catholic patrons in the empire of the Tudors, waiting on the Protestant 'Goths'.[60] For as Francis Barker wrote, the paradigmatic scene of Shakespearean history is situated in that great hall 'aptly named the *presence* chamber', where 'knots of courtiers are gathered beneath the dais, some fawning, others gravely keeping their own counsel', and as 'servants move among the throng with sweet wine and honey cakes', the Queen challenges 'the one great exception to the rule of this world' – the sombre prince, who 'stands apart from all the others, his head bowed in thought' – and orders this 'pale companion' to 'unfold' himself with some public performance of his loyalty and love:[61]

> Good Hamlet, cast thy nighted colour off,
> And let thine eye look like a friend on Denmark.
> Do not for ever with thy vailed lids
> Seek for thy noble father in the dust.
>   (*Hamlet*, 1.2.68–71)

Hamlet's reply to his sovereign's appeal to 'throw to earth' his 'unprevailing woe' (106) – that he has 'that within which passes show' (86) – has become probably the single most discussed literary passage in contemporary criticism, the occasion of sharp debate over claims of humanists such as Harold Bloom, who celebrate in it 'Shakespeare's greatest invention, the internalization of the self', the inauguration of 'a new kind of human being', as 'authentically unsponsored' as self-aware, and proof, therefore, that while for Foucault 'the self is fashioned, for Shakespeare it is given'.[62] Against this traditional affirmation of Hamlet's lines as the instant of 'the invention of the human', theoretically informed critics such as Terry Eagleton counter that 'Hamlet has no "essence" of being, no inner sanctum to be safeguarded … His "self" consists simply in the range of gestures with which he resists available definitions, not in a radical alternative beyond their reach.'[63] They do so because of the objection that, as Catherine Belsey explains, to seek to 'pluck out the heart' of Hamlet's mystery (3.2.356) is to impose upon the text an anachronistic modern concept of self-presence, when, in fact, 'Hamlet cannot be present to himself or to the audience in his own speeches and *this* is the heart of his mystery, his essence, his interiority'.[64] Obedient to Foucault's maxim that what we term 'the soul is the effect of political arrangements',[65] these critics assert that the rhetoric of inwardness and self-possession which defines the sovereign self originated only in the later seventeenth century, and that, as Jonathan Goldberg comments, in the English Renaissance 'the individual derived a sense of self largely from external matrices'.[66] For New Historicism, therefore, it has become axiomatic that in Shakespearean England 'one's place in the world was identical to one's self-definition', and that 'the supposed "private" sphere could be imagined only through its dissimilarities to the public world'. Yet, as Barker admits, Hamlet's refusal to emote or 'unfold' himself does seem to gesture towards 'an essential interiority', for 'a separation has already opened up' in his resistance 'between the inner reality of the subject and an inauthentic exterior'.[67] And it is just this startlingly 'premature' conception of a secretive and personal inwardness in Shakespearean theatre which has been related directly to the Elizabethan question of allegiance in the work of the most recent historicist interpreters.

'No one knew better how to handle the alternation of withholding and imparting secrets than Shakespeare', observes William Slights in a study of 'secret places in Renaissance drama', as he 'played off scenes of public ceremony against scenes of private conference'. Yet compared to his rivals, for whom 'nothing remains hidden', and *all* the dirty linen gets hung out to view', in Shakespeare 'secrets both tear apart and bind together institutions', so his 'signals concerning secrecy are extraordinarily mixed'.[68] And, as other critics note, Shakespeare's ambivalence can, in fact, be keyed to the secret place of the subject in the very architecture of the late-Renaissance state. For whereas in modern society 'the "public" can be sensed only through the private', writes Patricia Fumerton, 'Elizabethans were in the inverse habit of representing private experience as inescapably public', and yet this public self 'was forever loath to give itself up … forever creating its very sense of self through acts of withholding full assent to publicness'. Secrecy, according to this theory, was itself, therefore, the essence of Elizabethan subjectivity, which 'always withheld for itself some "secret" room, cabinet, case or other recess locked away', for within its innermost recesses, 'further recesses, cabinets, or cases kept opening up'.[69] Thus, it must be significant that Shakespeare grew up in the labyrinth of priest-holes, attic chapels and underground passages that honeycombed houses of the Warwickshire gentry, as the material determinants of an entire lifestyle of self-concealment. Many of these hiding-places, like the 'Martyrs' Chamber' at Mancetter Manor, near Atherstone, were constructed by persecuted Protestants during the reign of Mary.[70] But the most complicated were those inserted by Jesuit engineers into the mansions of Catholic neighbours and relations of the Shakespeares, such as the maze of tunnels at Hindlip, the home of the Habingtons; the Mass chamber behind panels at Huddington, the base of the Winters; the stack of hides in the Tower at Coughton, the Throckmorton seat; or the roof chapel at Clopton, the house, in the 1600s, of the Rookwoods. All these hideaways were used to conceal priests or conspirators in the Gunpowder Plot, and so became the focus for romantic fiction. But recent historians have begun to revisit their design, often the work of that 'worthy pioneer' (1.5.165), Nicholas Owen, known as 'Little John', as expressions of the Counter-Reformation mentality, a new type of perspectival 'thinking in three dimensions', which was contrived to ensure that 'the searcher cannot stand still and keep a sense of direction', and the very invisibility of which was proof that 'in no other form of craftsmanship was originality such a virtue'.[71]

Spliced into solid brickwork or insinuated in stairwells, the Jesuit hiding-places built by 'Little John' have been likened to the ciphered Masses of Byrd that were sung in the same places, and analysed as the architectural deter-minants of 'a kind of schizophrenic existence' endured by a closeted society or counter-culture, which secreted its real intentions and true identity behind illusionistic surfaces, deceptive contours, false walls and trap-doors.[72] They are the most extreme representations of the aristocratic form of self-consciousness discussed by John Archer in his study of 'Spying and Court Culture in the English Renaissance', the means by which an elite which found itself under continual observation, by pursuivants, messengers, militia, spies and watches, 'attempted to deflect the gaze of the monarch', as 'at the moment of its con-stitution, subjectivity was threatened with annihilation by the gaze – not its own gaze, but a gaze that was outside of it'. Archer diagnoses this secretive society as clinically paranoid.[73] So, it may not be coincidental that the teenage Shakespeare is said to have worked as a secretary in the library at Billesley, the manor house, near Shottery, of his cousin, the crypto-Catholic literary executor and publisher of Southwell, Thomas Trussell, where a priest-hole is concealed behind the panelling.[74] For whatever the truth of this tradition, it is clear that the young poet wrote literally a wall away from the secret cavities of a clandestine faith, and that, however studiously detached, no one who worked in such dangerous proximity to the treasonable politics of Catholic resistance could have remained oblivious to the tactics of survival adopted by the hosts of those fugitives crouching in adjoining rooms, or simply rumoured, like Edgar in disguise, to 'Lurk, lurk' (*Lear*, 3.6.108). For there is a Shakespearean *trompe l'oeil* about the refusal of Midlanders such as Lord Vaux, Sir William Catesby and Sir Thomas Tresham, 'to swear they had not harboured Campion the Jesuit', on the grounds that, if the priest had been as well hidden as alleged, they could not vouch for certain that he had not been living among them unsuspected by themselves.[75] And sensational escapes like the one recorded by the Jesuit Gerard at Baddesley Clinton, the Ferrars mansion near Warwick, must have schooled the author of so many hermeneutic puzzles and games of hide-and-seek into a precocious awareness of the anxieties of discovery and the histrionics of concealment, programming him to think in terms of a politic diversion or dissimulation when confronted at his secretaire by an authority which, as Cloten warns while hunting for Imogen, 'will have this secret from thy tongue or rip / Thy heart to find it' (*Cymbeline*, 3.5.86–7):

> It was five o'clock in the morning … Father Southwell was beginning Mass and the rest were at prayer, when suddenly I heard a great uproar outside. It was the priest-hunters, with swords drawn, and they were battering at the door … The ruffians were bawling and yelling, but the servants held the door

fast. This gave us time to stow ourselves and all our belongings into a very cleverly built sort of cave. At last these leopards were let in. They tore madly through the whole house, searched everywhere, pried with candles into the darkest corners. They took four hours over the work, but chanced on nothing. All they did was show how dogged and spiteful they could be, and how forbearing the Catholics were. In the end, they made off, but only after they had got paid for their trouble ... When they had gone a good way, so that there was no danger of their turning back, a lady came and called us out of our den, not one but several Daniels. The hiding-place was below ground level; the floor was covered with water and I was standing with my feet in it all the time. Father Garnet was there; also Father Southwell and Father Oldcorne, Father Stanney and myself, two secular priests and two or three laymen. So we were all saved that day.[76]

It is tempting to imagine a 'secretary Shakespeare' within the occulted writing regime studied by Goldberg; where the secrecy of the secretary was that of the keeper of consoles, keys, and safes; and where, as Richard Rambuss reveals, Spenser's 'secret designs' incubated literally 'in cabinet', to the point where, Annabel Patterson decides, the poet employed the figure of the cabinet to 'reveal *by failing to reveal* the mysteries of the text'.[77] For many Elizabethan hiding-places have been detected only in the last few years, or are suspected only from literary sources. But Renaissance secrecy, as John Kerrigan quips in an essay on secrecy and 'the cubiculo' in *Twelfth Night* (3.2.44), 'is no longer quite as secret as it was', since we are starting to have a better understanding of how the discretion of the secretarial pen could produce, in Lois Potter's phrase, 'secret rites and secret writing', while 'in Foucauldian accounts, Renaissance espionage is analysed afresh ... a line of enquiry which leads back to the civilised dissimulation advocated by Castiglione, but also to the politic ruthlessness of "l'art machiavélien d'être secret"'. And it is in this analysis of the material foundation of secrecy, and the way in which Renaissance culture instituted novel ideas about privacy 'by building and exploring secluded chambers and closets', that Kerrigan finds clues to the emergent mentality he traces in Shakespeare's ambivalent staging of 'exhibitionistic secrecy', and his characters' ironic yet ostentatious 'appeal to privy space'.[78] For while identity, according to historians, was shaped by the new 'refuges of intimacy' in early modern Europe, and by all those alcoves and *kunstkammers*, the carrels, commodes and cubicles that made social separation and professional discretion for the first time physical possibilities,[79] it is within an interplay of secrecy and disclosure, the transparent and occluded, that Shakespeare's drama in fact unfolds. Thus, the dialectic in his plays between opacity and exposure, mystery and revelation, or openness and closure, can be connected to 'the epistemology of the closet' that has been outlined by Eve Kosofsky Sedgwick in her book of that title developed from D.A. Miller's thesis, in his reading of 'Secret Subjects, Open Secrets', that secrecy – 'the subjective practice in which oppositions of public / private, inside / outside, subject / object are established' – is a mode of being whose ultimate meaning lies in the subject's formal yet self-protective revelation that 'he is radically inaccessible to the culture that would otherwise determine him'.[80]

The power of the secret, according to the sociologist Georg Simmel, depends on display, for 'one appears as noteworthy precisely through what one conceals'.[81] Likewise, for Sedgwick, writing of modern gay identity, the architectural metaphor of the closet defines a type of secrecy which is ironically affirmed as such, and which is articulated through 'the relations of the known and unknown, the explicit and the inexplicit'. Thus, in her analysis, the closet 'is made available as a publicly intelligible signifier only by the difference made by coming out'.[82] This perception is the inspiration for Alan Stewart's excavation of the 'inglenook' of sodomy in early modern England, which follows Fumerton in proposing that 'the early modern closet is associated with the construction of a new modern subjectivity', in that its position in the architecture of the early modern house made it evident to those 'in the know', and so indicative of what Fumerton calls 'the paradox of being locked away (in full view)'.[83] Likewise, Bruce R. Smith contends that the first modern homosexual identity is actually advertised in the 'secret sharing' of Shakespeare's Sonnets 'among his private friends';[84] an analysis the poet seems to demand, since in his texts privacy is the preserve of those who 'enjoy [their] private' (Twelfth, 3.4.89) as a flagrant self-assertion. Thus, when Achilles claims 'strong reasons' for 'this my privacy' in withdrawing into his tent, he does so in defiance of the conventional wisdom that, as Ulysses protests, ''gainst your privacy the reasons are more potent and heroical' (Troilus, 3.3.184–6). This inside/outside collusion is built into the most closeted of chamber plays, where so much hinges on an actual closet scene, and on Polonius's scheme to 'convey' himself 'Behind the arras', when Hamlet is 'going to his mother's closet' (Hamlet, 3.3.27–8). As Patricia Parker insists, the tension between secrecy and discovery is gendered in Hamlet 'in relation to the sexual "privity" of women', as 'a hidden matrix to be opened, dilated, and displayed', and thus 'the business of detection and informing, of espial and bringing "privy secrets" before the eyes', of unlocking of 'things done "privily" or in secret, in the confessional, the secret chamber of the heart, or the "closet" of the monarch', is 'keyed' to 'the sense that secrets, or the hid, will finally out'.[85] So, it also figures in terms of penetration, as when Cassius posts writings 'in at [the] windows' of Brutus's closet (Julius, 1.2.310; 2.1.35); or Edmund claims to find a letter 'thrown in at the casement of my closet' (Lear, 1.2.58). The closet is unlike the cabinet, then, in being shut and open. And, tellingly, Stewart relates the evolution of 'closet sexuality' as a strategic gesture specifically to the thresholds and intermediate zones, the lobbies, anterooms, cubbyholes, partitions, galleries and gazebos of the Elizabethan Catholic house:

> As the architectural historian Mark Girouard writes, the closet 'was essentially … a room for private devotions, for private study and business' … But this

clear-cut model needs to be examined … 'Closet' was also used to designate private chapels … particularly in the early sixteenth century … Significantly, the experience of a worshipper in this closet is not solitary (the lord being accompanied by his entourage) and the closet works in a complex relationship with wider society: it is placed 'like a gallery at one end of, or looking down into, a two-storey chapel. The family and guests attended services up in the closet, and everyone else down in the body of the chapel', the lord's family taking part in the social event, while remaining aloof from it. To describe this as 'private devotion', when the devotion takes place apart from general society but still and deliberately in public view, begs the question: what is being constituted as 'private' here?[86]

Stewart's reading of the closet as 'a politically crucial transactive space' is exemplary for a criticism which 'rejects the search for the secret subject in favour of an interrogation of secret spaces and relationships', and seems a model for the materialist analysis of Shakespeare.[87] For at places like the Montague seat at Battle, where the dramatist's patrons 'assembled and pre-served a visible church or company of Catholics' of eighty or more throughout the reign of Elizabeth, in a chapel with stairs leading up to 'a choir for singers and a pulpit for the priests', the open secret of recusant impunity was keyed to the indeterminate status of aristocratic space in a society that still looked upon 'every man possessed of a great estate as a kind of petty prince'.[88] Shakespeare's fascination with nobles who strive for 'Rome indeed, and room enough' (*Julius*, 1.2.157), had its origin, it might seem, in his sponsors' efforts to save for themselves a 'Little Rome' at Battle, or in the Montague compound beside the theatres on Bankside. For, as the historian Roger Manning comments, there seems to be 'a very definite connection between the strength of Catholicism … and the proximity' of these Montague households, 'which were able to main-tain autonomy with regard to religious worship' because their owners were so careful to screen 'the spiritual aspects of post-Tridentine Catholicism from its political overtones'.[89] Thus, the precondition of Catholic existence was one of compartmentalised buildings and withdrawing rooms, as these Montagues played cat-and-mouse with their pursuers by literally retreating, over the course of generations, according to Bossy, from their great halls into crannies and attics.[90] Their retreat into a 'Godly Garret' ensured that 'the issues were blurred', just as their clerics 'provided official sacraments in churches and Catholic ones in secret'.[91] Likewise, the decoy design of Catholic hideaways in the Shakespearean Midlands, according to their archivist Michael Hodgetts, was typically that of a nest of Chinese boxes constructed in stages, as the raids became more probing and 'Little John' 'did much strive to make his hides of several fashions in several places, that on being taken, one might give no light to the discovery of the other'.[92] This was an architecture, in short, of outward concession and inward reservation, a self-immurement painstakingly con-structed to permit 'the man that dwelleth among the wicked', in the words of the Montague chaplain, Alban Langdale, to 'withdraw from trouble as a peaceable child of the church, not seeking to provoke ire'.[93] A 'catacomb culture', according to Alison Shell, 'defined by secret or discreet worship', Elizabethan Catholicism was none the less visible to the world, for these sequestered 'Catholics did not spend their whole lives underground'.[94] So, the great question for Shakespeare's generation of English Catholics, as Alexandra Walsham shows, was one that he stages again and again, of the limits of sequestration, and the precise occasion of 'coming out':[95]

> Whether 'tis nobler in the mind to suffer
> The slings and arrows of outrageous fortune,
> Or to take arms against a sea of troubles
> And by opposing, end them.
>   (*Hamlet*, 3.1.59–62)

'What shall de honest man do in my closet? Dere is no honest man dat shall come in my closet' (*Merry Wives*, 1.4.64–5): Doctor Caius's affront at discovering an intruder in his closet introduces the terror of the St Bartholomew's Day Massacre (from which he has, perhaps, fled) into a Windsor where, as Falstaff learns when starting to 'creep up into the chimney', a vigilante like Frank Ford sees to it that 'there is no hiding in the house', since 'Neither press, coffer, chest, trunk, well, vault, but he hath an abstract for the remembrance of such places, and goes to them by his note' (4.2.43–50). Thus, even in Shakespeare's most domestic comedy, the action consists of the interplay between the fear of exposure and the mania for discovery, as the gossips of the royal town test the dictum that an Englishman's home is his castle, before accepting that in their society 'secrecy shall be a tailor to thee, and shall make thee a new doublet and hose' (3.3.25–6). The paranoia of the French physician is a topical reminder, moreover, of the stakes in this game, which might easily end with throats cut 'in de Park' (1.4.96). But if this is a scenario in which it is still possible to 'go home' at the close, 'And laugh this sport o'er by a country fire' (5.5.218–19), that says much about the relaxed religious politics of a dramatist who lodged with a family of French Huguenot refugees in London, and whose own daughter, Susanna, married a physician trained in the Huguenot citadel of Montpellier.[96] Robert Ellrodt has made the affinity, indeed, between Shakespeare and Montaigne a starting-point for considering the emergence in the plays of 'a form of self-consciousness which implies simultaneous awareness of experience and the experiencing self', the relativism, also discussed by Jonathan Dollimore, which arises, in both writers, from their sensation of the contingency of beliefs.[97] So, while Greenblatt points out that self-fashioning in Montaigne meant withdrawal into the ultimate Renaissance closet, the study in his tower, while Shakespeare became the master of the prototype mass medium,[98] it is suggestive that it was in the circle of Shakespeare's Montague patrons, where Montaigne's translator, John Florio, was Southampton's tutor, that the dream of religious toleration associated with the French essayist first took root in England. This was the idea – keyed to Montaigne's defence of privacy, and the solitude he found in gardens, bedrooms and even privies[99] – of those moderate Catholics known as the *Politiques*, that since fundamentalism assumed certainty where certainty can never be attained, 'the forcing of consciences is never justified':

> The *Politiques* believed not only that religious persecution was morally indefensible, but that it was also tactically mistaken. While they valued religious uniformity, they did not think it worth preserving at the cost of the commonwealth. Religious uniformity was not essential to the well-being of [the state], and the only sane policy was to give up religious unity for the sake of domestic peace.[100]

'A plague o' both your houses' (*Romeo*, 3.1.108): there is a striking correlation between Shakespeare's staging of sectarianism and Montaigne's neutralism, and it must be significant that the only book we think we know came from his library was *The Life of Catherine de Medici*, the Queen of *Politiques*, by Henri Estienne.[101] Thus, when Montaigne is described as 'a Catholic from the most intransigent wing', with 'many friends prominent in the extreme Catholic faction'; who mocked the Reform religion, and always 'implied there is a right side', even if 'its motives and actions are discreditable'; but who used his knowledge of fanaticism to 'suggest in a veiled way that if Protestants are bad' the Catholic ultras are worse, that 'any opinion is powerful enough to make martyrs', and that Christianity is not worth 'the rivers of blood which flow to maintain it';[102] when, in short, he is categorised as (in Gide's phrase) 'a Catholic but not a Christian', who never mentioned Christ,[103] this could, in fact, be one of the best summaries of Shakespeare's position, as an 'insider outside' the Elizabethan Catholic extreme. For if his works arose from any agenda, it was surely that of the *politique* party, the English branch of which was led by Lord Montague. In *Romeo and Juliet*, for instance, old Montague's fate, to be 'early up / To see [his] son and heir now early down' (5.3.207), seems to reflect the grief of his namesake at the death, in suspicious circumstances, of his son and heir in June 1592, when the poet may have been at the funeral, and seen 'summer's green all girded up in sheaves / Borne on the bier with white and bristly beard' (Sonnet 12).[104] Muriel Bradbrook thought the play was, in fact, put on in connection with a blood-feud involving the Viscount and his grandson, Southampton, through association with *politique* aides of Henri IV of France.[105] But whether or not acted at his Bankside palace, the tragedy does illustrate the line Montague took, as the only Catholic in the House of Lords and a nephew of Thomas More, when he predicted a civil war unless both sides co-existed, 'all rites remained inviolate, both of praying, preaching and sacrifice', and no one was 'forced to leave the same', which was 'contrary to nature and reason, as not being offered to the Jews'. Montague lectured the Lords that 'we have no authority to treat upon such matters, and therefore I most humbly wish that we intermeddle no further therein'.[106] But in *Romeo and Juliet*, which opens with Capulets blackening Montagues as 'colliers', or 'moors', who will be 'pushed from the wall' that immures them, or have necks drawn 'out of collar' like More (*Romeo*, 1.1.1–28), his attempts to turn two 'households' rancour to pure love' (2.2.92) seem to be caricatured in Friar Laurence, who looks like a portrait of his chaplain, Langdale.[107] So, the Prince's lines may express Shakespeare's own rueful conclusion, that the demolition of the wall between such 'Jewliets' – or Protestants – and the tribe of More would depend upon the Crown:

> Capulet, Montague,
> See what a scourge is laid upon your hate,
> That heaven finds means to kill your joys with love.
> And I, for winking at your discords, too
> Have lost a brace of kinsman. All are punished.
> (*Romeo*, 5.3.290–4)

Like Tudor London, Shakespeare's Verona is a city where, until its Prince imposes peace, 'civil brawls' are 'bred of an airy word' (1.1.82). What that word might be is spelled out when Romeo swears Juliet 'hangs upon the cheek of night / As a rich jewel in an Ethiop's ear', and he is given away 'by his voice' (1.5.42–51), as Tybalt instantly detects the 'moorish' code of Roman worship Shakespeare also wove around the name of More – 'the black word death' (3.3.27) – in *A Midsummer Night's Dream*, *The Merchant of Venice* and *Othello*.[108] So, as a diagnosis of the ills of Zion, Shakespeare's 'Mount-ague' play suggests there can be no return to 'Belmont' until the Prince frees the love that dare not speak its word. This had been the theme, indeed, of a petition for freedom of religion drafted in 1585 by Montague, which was thrust into the Queen's hand 'as she walked in her park at Greenwich' by his kinsman Richard Shelley, with the result that the petitioner was 'promptly thrown into prison by Walsingham and left there to die'.[109] The incident haunted the English Catholic imagination, and may have inspired not only Southwell's *Humble Supplication*, printed by the Montagues in Southwark but the savage episode in *Titus Andronicus* when Titus sends a similar 'supplication' by means of a 'Clown' bringing doves to the Emperor, who simply reads the appeal and orders the guards to 'take him away, and hang him presently' (4.3.98; 4.4.44).[110] Like Titus's crazed attempt to 'solicit heaven and move the gods / To send down justice for to wreak our wrongs' with arrows shot into the sky (4.3.51–2), these Montague petitions therefore merely served to confirm the futility of begging for toleration to the Crown, which in the words of Shakespeare's old Roman, 'were as good [as] to shoot against the wind' (58). As such, they provide a precise discursive context for the secretive self which critics see as Shakespeare's premature version of modern subjectivity, the Catholic counterpart of the Puritan discourse of self-assertion in which Simon Shepherd locates one of the earliest determinants of interiority, with its awareness that 'There is in man a double speech' (in the words of Philippe de Mornay translated by Philip Sidney), 'the one in the mind, which they call the inward speech … the other which is uttered by our mouth and is termed the speech of the voice'.[111] They suggest that if the soul is indeed the effect of political arrangements, then Shakespeare's dramatisation of Hamlet's silence or Cordelia's refusal was indeed grounded in specific circumstances, and the compromise desired by his patrons, to suffer outrageous fortune in return, as Montague pleaded, for release from the order to heave their hearts into their mouths (*King Lear*, 1.1.91):

> What man is there so without courage and stomach, or void of all honour, that can consent or agree to receive an opinion and new religion by force and compulsion, or will swear that he thinketh the contrary to what he thinketh? To be still and dissemble may be borne and suffered for a time; to keep his reckoning with God alone; but to be compelled to lie and swear, or else to die therefore, are things that no man ought to suffer and endure.[112]

'Loath to seem unto you to frame myself a conscience', Montague claimed in his appeal to the House of Lords, 'I am two ways much afraid, the one by speaking to offend those whom I most desire to please, the other and chief, by not speaking to offend my Conscience, and thereby God himself'.[113] Thus, the inability of the Shakespearean private self to 'stand and unfold itself' (*Hamlet*, 1.1.2), and the gap the dramatist places between private subjectivity and public identity, in contrast to those 'scenes of visibility and knowability' staged by his rivals,[114] have a historical equivalent in the 'madness of discourse that cause sets up against itself' experienced by Catholics in the writer's circle forced to swear the Elizabethan Oath of Supremacy, and so torn between the 'bifold authority' (*Troilus*, 5.2.143–4) of the state and Rome. But as Donna Hamilton has argued, the privileging of Protestantism, which has led critics to neglect the English Catholic situation, results in an almost total obliviousness towards the debate over the oaths of allegiance exacted by Tudor and Stuart sovereigns, even though this may have moulded Shakespeare's characters and plots.[115] Debora Shuger concurs that consideration of the impact of the oaths on Shakespeare's dramaturgy is long overdue, given that the pressure of the controversy, which was most acute after the Gunpowder Plot, 'can be felt throughout the Tudor-Stuart period': on the one hand, in claims made for the state over religion, 'on the other, in attempts to draw a line between politics and religion (or outward conformity and private belief) that would keep the state from making windows in men's souls'.[116] Editors from Dowden onwards have been intrigued by Shakespeare's Pinteresque silences, the gaps 'placed against the dominant eloquence', like Isabella's reaction to the Duke's marriage offer, Gertrude's alienation from Claudius or 'the tremendously significant reticences of Cordelia and Hermione' that punctuate the action with 'pregnant' pauses, without noticing how often what Alwin Thaler termed this 'artistry of silence' comes into play not only in scenes of sexual coercion but also in stand-offs between the dissident subject and the state which exacts allegiance.[117] Yet as recent critics have noted, hidden persuasion and secret wisdom were prized in the *arcana* of Renaissance politics, where silence was golden, and the icon of the finger pressed to lips imaged the power of 'eloquent silence'.[118] There was 'a language of silence', we are reminded, 'in which Elizabeth was fluent', so when she required her subjects to produce their love in a discourse of submission, they could model their resistance on the 'prone and speechless dialect' (*Measure*, 1.2.160) of one who herself demonstrated 'language in her eye, her cheek, her lip, / Nay, her very foot', and 'every joint and motion of her body' (*Troilus*, 4.6.56–8):

> If the silent language of the most powerful figure of her time could be multidirectional, that of her subjects was necessarily more circumspect, and that of the dissidents among them subtle and even more constrained. Yet all types found silent language an effective mode of communication … Non-verbal communication was more prudent than words: safer for Sir Thomas Tresham to build his lodge in the significant shape of a triangle than to confess [his true loyalty] in literal Romanist terms.[119]

'The period was one of enforced silence', concludes Belsey, in her study of Elizabethan subjectivity, 'producing an order which still bears the marks of conflict and violence, and of the silence too'.[120] Yet it was also a period which understood Foucault's wisdom that where speech is compulsory, 'silences – the things one declines to say – are an integral part of the strategies of discourse'.[121] That being so, it is not surprising how the problem of oath-taking dominates the action of Shakespeare's political plays and even his comedies, reflecting the confessional panic in which Campion's secret pledge of Roman faith was trumped by the government's 1584 Bond of Association; a resort, according to legal historians, to 'Texan justice' and 'lynch law', and 'a naked appeal to the most primitive instincts of its signatories', but an oath which was solemnly administered in every English church, parishioners kneeling at the altar six at a time to swear to defend the Queen's life.[122] But what is impressive about Shakespeare's intervention in this mass hysteria is the legitimacy it gives to oath-*breaking*, confirming that, as William Kerrigan points out, 'oaths were never really trusted … most people merely mouthed the words', and the common attitude, articulated by John Selden, was that 'there is no oath scarcely but we swear to things we are ignorant of, for example the Oath of Supremacy'.[123] For with the stalwart Earl of Salisbury rationalising how it is a 'greater sin to keep a sinful oath' (2 *Henry VI*, 5.1.181); foresters breaking their oaths to arrest Henry VI (3 *Henry VI*, 3.1.72–97); Stanley betraying Richard III (*Richard III*, 4.4.424); York remaining 'neuter' between Richard II and rebel invaders (*Richard II*, 2.3.158); and the good soldier Williams problematising his loyalty to Henry V (*Henry V*, 4.1.123–9), the Histories drive home the implication of *Love's Labour's Lost*, that the precedent of *Politiques* such as Henri IV – the Protestant King of Navarre who won Paris with a Mass – determined the shape of a drama in which the faithful break their oaths to save themselves, on the principle that 'It is religion to be thus forsworn … Or else we lose ourselves to keep our oaths' (5.1.335–7). But as Brutus explains, in a refusal which sums up the tactics of Elizabethan Catholic resistance, such 'secret Romans' will, in fact, do everything they can to avoid making any public declaration of the 'sufferance' of their 'souls':

> No, not an oath. If not the face of men
> The sufferance of our souls, the time's abuse –
> If these be motives weak, break off betimes,
> And every man hence to his idle bed.
> So let high-handed tyranny range on
> Till each man drop by lottery. But if these,
> As I am sure they do, bear fire enough
> To kindle cowards and to steel with valour
> The melting spirits of women, then, countrymen,
> What need we any spur but our own cause
> To prick us to redress? What other bond
> Than secret Romans, that hath spoke the word.
>
> (Julius, 2.1.113–24)

If secrecy is power, as Elias Canetti observes,[124] it is also, in Shakespeare as in Foucault, resistance. Thus, 'Swear priests and cowards', Brutus exclaims, 'and men cautelous, / Old feeble carrions, and such suffering souls as welcome wrongs'; and his tarring of oath-takers with those that 'unto bad causes swear' (128–30) makes total sense as a reaction to pressure on such 'secret Romans' to declare their faith. Loyalty tests, such as the 'Bloody Question' put to suspect papists after Campion's mission, of whether, in an invasion, they would support the Pope or Queen, did split English Catholics along the lines drawn by Brutus, with twenty priests listed between 1581 and 1603 saying they would 'take the Queen's part', as opposed to 'fourteen people who would support the Pope, nine who would decide when the time came, one who would support neither', and fifty-nine who refused to speak at all or gave evasive answers.[125] Likewise, the 1606 Oath of Allegiance 'caused utter chaos' in the Catholic community, according to Michael Questier, as it was intended to do, by fracturing opinion not only between Jesuit militants, who denounced 'the godless oath' as 'a horrendous invasion of Catholic consciences', and the secular clergy, who might be expected to comply, but across the whole spectrum of the sixteen thousand summoned to take it in the first ten years.[126] As David Jones recounts, in his history of the state oath in early modern England, this was the point at which the Jesuits first systematically resorted to the casuistical technique of equivocation, or mental reservation, tried a decade earlier by Southwell, so as to 'swear without actually intending to perform what they had sworn'. But it was also a crisis in which Shakespeare's neighbours, like the Stonors of Oxfordshire, simply absented themselves from their houses when justices called, 'because they would not take the oath'; and when other conformists, like John Donne, found themselves 'divided within themselves', accepting that non-compliance was a 'pseudo-martyrdom' whilst resenting the loyalty test as an intrusion into 'the secret recesses of the heart'. By the second decade of the seventeenth century, Jones shows, 'most Protestant Englishmen considered state oaths central to their conception of allegiance'; but in the case of the Catholic conscience, 'the competing claims of pope and king, made vivid by performance or refusal of an oath, volatized questions of selfhood', as 'the Anglo-Catholic self' shattered into responses that ranged from those of the martyr, pseudo-martyr, Jesuit, and loyalist, to that of the apostate.[127] And Shakespeare, who had the Jesuit 'equivocator that could swear in both the scales against either scale' mocked as a pseudo-martyr at this moment in *Macbeth* (2.3.8–9), reflected just this fragmentation, when he almost simultaneously staged the refusal of the 'true heart' to do more for the king than what was required by the Bond of Association, or 'Love, and be silent':

> Then poor Cordelia!
> And yet not so; since, I am sure, my love's
> More ponderous than my tongue ...
> Unhappy that I am, I cannot heave
> My heart into my mouth. I love your majesty
> According to my bond, no more nor less.
> (*Lear*, 1.1.60; 75–7; 90–2)

'Swear ... Swear ... Swear': if the old 'fellow in the cellarage', the 'true-penny' (*Hamlet*, 1.5.151–62) who compels the student of Lutheran Wittenburg and his fellow scholars to swear 'Never to speak' of what they have seen and heard to the king to whom they owe allegiance, is indeed 'a distinctly Catholic ghost', then what is at stake, as Greenblatt argues, is a 'deliberate forcing together' of radically incompatible voices of authority, and of opposing responses which 'challenge each other, clashing and sending shock waves through the play'. Shakespeare's tragic vision thus appears to be intimately bound up with the political situation of the Catholic elite into which he was born, and the problem of 'divided duty' (*Othello*, 1.3.180) that he stages repeatedly as a genera-tional or domestic drama, to be tied to his own subject position, conflicted between the twin tests of Jesuit confession and Protestant truth. As Greenblatt writes, to infer this is not to enter into 'the long-standing critical game' of whether Hamlet's apparition – and, by implication, the author's true commit-ment – 'is "Catholic" or "Protestant" ... as if these were questions that could be decisively answered, if only we were somehow clever enough'.[128] But it is to recognise how the systematic inconclusiveness that characterises Shakespearean theatre was related to the fracture of the Anglo-Catholic world within which, so these discourses suggest, its creator wrote. The resistance to interpretation that Shakespeare's conspirator asserts, when he warns the spies that they will never 'pluck out the heart' of his mystery (*Hamlet*, 3.2.336), may not be a marker of authorial intention, any more than a signifier of 'an essential subjectivity fully realised';[129] yet it is, as Alan Sinfield notes, the sign of a fault-line in early modern culture, when 'people were beginning to experience them-selves' volitionally, a gap opened between the inner reality of the subject and an inauthentic exterior, and an 'awareness of interiority' became, in certain places, possible.[130] And all the evidence suggests that this fault-line was never more acute or problematic for Shakespeare's generation than when it ran through the fortress of a beleaguered Catholicism. Donne's 'crime', for instance, as a 'double-crossing' apostate, is what constituted the 'secrecy' of his poetry, according to Thomas Docherty, and related it to 'other modes of criminality requiring secrecy or covering up' from the 'epistemological sleuth'.[131] Thus, to historicise Shakespearean secrecy is not to claim that its author was a Roman Catholic, Anglo-Catholic or Catholic loyalist. But it is to perceive how much the construction of this 'secret self' was the historically determined precondition of writing in the universe of those, like the Stonors of Henley-on-Thames, who were simply 'not at home' when the inspectors called. For as the historian Perez Zagorin concludes, in his book *Ways of Lying*, theirs was a culture of alternating persecution and conformity in which a strategic opacity, or dissimulation, was so well rationalised and so extensive that it was like some 'submerged continent'.[132]

'He begins by seductively inviting the spectator to read him', but his paintings 'repeatedly initiate the conditions under which a visual field more or less urgently solicits and resists its own symbolization'. The brilliant critique of the other great artistic tease of the Counter-Reformation by Leo Bersani and Ulysse Dutoit, in their study of *Caravaggio's Secrets*, offers an interpretative itinerary for reading Shakespeare's equally compelling yet frustrating game.[133] For the playwright who imagined the players hanged for their pains (*Dream*, 2,1,64; 5.2.343) shared the painter's paranoid fascination with the penalties of self-exposure, and drew the same analogy between castration or decapitation and interpretation, when he had his Prince threaten to send the murdered Marlowe's *Dido* 'to the barber's' along with its spectator's 'beard' (*Hamlet*, 2.2.479). So, when Bersani and Dutoit write that in Caravaggio's pictures, where again and again 'the subject performs a secret, which is not to say that he or she has any knowledge of it', it is as if 'we were being solicited by a desire determined to remain hidden', they additionally provide an insight into *Hamlet*. For what gives these works originality is indeed 'their intractably enigmatic quality', and what makes Shakespeare's characters as seductive as Caravaggio's boys is precisely 'a provocative unreadability: identities, however probable, deprive these works of their emotional charge'.[134] In Caravaggio, of course, the question *posed* is homosexuality, just as the cliché query with Shakespeare was once whether he was 'gay'. But, as the history of the closet implies, and Dympna Callaghan points out, there are, in fact, 'parallels between the issues that confront us when we address Shakespeare's religion and sexuality', and the lesson of the sexuality debate, 'that identity does not come in neat packages in any era', now needs to be applied to the 'Bloody Question' of religious choice.[135] Since sodomy and heresy were both capital offences, it is no surprise that the two deviations should be closeted together, as what Bersani and Dutoit term the 'sexy secrets' for which a *provocateur* such as Marlowe might well 'lose his head'. Like the Roman artist, then, what Shakespeare seems to represent, over and over, is not so much a secret that dares not speak its name, as the conditions of representation itself, in a scenario suspended between the dictate that 'If it be love indeed, tell me how much', and the objection that 'There's beggary in the love that can be reckoned' (*Antony*, 1.1.14–15). Thus, just as in *The Calling of St Matthew* Caravaggio problematises the archetypal interpellation by depicting the confusion of the chosen one and the bafflement of his companions, who 'appear to be looking elsewhere, beyond Peter and Jesus, to another source of light', so in Shakespeare's equally fascinated repetitions of the primal instant of interrogation we are confronted by the same epistemological puzzle, of a self 'at once presenting and withdrawing itself', in a space which is illuminated not by certainty or knowledge, but always by multiple sources of light.[136]

Secret Shakespeare wrote, as Parker observes, in 'an England that included not only a secret service as the dispersed eyes and ears of state, but networks of secretaries who conveyed and enfolded secrets … an England that had recourse to the language of the chamber and closet as the cover for the hidden and open secret'. It is for this reason, Parker concludes, that far from mystifying secrecy 'by separating Shakespeare artificially from history', we need to attend not only to the secret history of the plays, but to the history they secrete.[137] So, in our post-theoretical moment, with its return to real bodies in social sites, this means a revival of the very question posed by the interrogators and priest-hunters, of the intention secreted by the author; an intention understood, moreover, as Elizabeth's torturers understood it, not as the free determination of a lone individual, but as a fabric of 'sustaining collaborations', which is to say, as a conspiracy.[138] Then, 'the book even of his secret soul' (*Twelfth*, 1.4.14) may well be found to be implicated in the schemes of the authors of those other texts presented at the Elizabethan and Jacobean courts, the petitions that aimed, as historians now see, 'too high', like Titus's arrows, by reaching for the sky of royal mercy and religious toleration.[139] It may be that archival research, or the thickening plot of circumstantial evidence, will associate Shakespeare's plays even more definitely with the dream of religious freedom – when the Puritan is pacified and 'golden time convents' (5.1.369) – his Catholic contemporaries indulged. Yet, in the meantime, as Graham Greene complained, 'in Shakespeare's world of comedy and despair' there is 'one portrait one sadly misses', since while 'the kings speak, the adventurers speak, the madmen and the lovers, the soldiers and the poets, the martyrs are quite silent. We come out of the world of the pilgrims into the silence of Hamlet's court'.[140] Other Catholic commentators, such as Simpson, infer that this silence speaks, reasoning that 'the repudiation of all politics, in that dangerous time, was itself political'.[141] But for all its necessity, this is a silence that cannot help but seem expedient, when it is the refusal to speak that constitutes the play. There is a secrecy here that is all too politic. This is an artist who, in the words of Bersani and Dutoit, 'entered the historical order as witness in order to prevent us from reading his work *as* history'.[142] For as Taylor objects, any account of Shakespeare which ignores the religious passions of his life and world is a falsification, and yet 'that falsification, that misrepresentation, begins with Shakespeare himself'.[143] We are reminded of how, when the leader of the *Politiques* was asked to speak to save Campion, on the day of his execution, the future Henri III was about to begin a game of tennis at Whitehall:

> His confessor, an abbé, came with the petitioners. They exposed their case. The martyr would only suffer in body, but the duke's fame and honour would be lost if he permitted this foul tragedy to proceed. The duke stood hesitating, like a man just awakened from a deep sleep, stroking his face with his left hand. After a while he raised his right hand with the racket in it, and said to his companion, 'Play!' That was all the answer the petitioners could get.[144]

NOTES

1 Peter Brook, 'Sharing Shakespeare with the World', *Guardian*, 2 November 1990.

2 Jonathan Bate, *The Genius of Shakespeare* (London: Picador, 1997), p. 5.

3 Roland Barthes, *Roland Barthes by Roland Barthes*, trans. Richard Howard (London: Macmillan, 1977), p. 87; Maurice Blanchot, *L'Amitié* (Paris: Gallimard, 1971), p. 194, quoted in Leslie Hill, *Blanchot: Extreme Contemporary* (London: Routledge, 1997), p. 5.

4 Michel Foucault, 'What Is An Author?' trans. Donald Bouchard and Sherry Simon (eds), *Language, Counter-Memory, Practice* (Ithaca: Cornell University Press, 1977), p. 115; interview with Raymond Bellour, 1967, in Sylvère Lotringer (ed.), *Foucault Live* (New York: Semiotext(e), 1989), p. 28.

5 Barthes, op. cit. (note 3), p. 87; unpublished lecture series, Collège de France, 1979/80, quoted in Jonathan Culler, *Barthes: A Very Short Introduction* (Oxford: Oxford University Press, 2002), p. 113.

6 Quoted in Samuel Schoenbaum, *Shakespeare's Lives* (Oxford: Clarendon Press, 1970), p. 174.

7 Blair Worden, 'Shakespeare and Politics', *Shakespeare Survey*, 44 (1992), p. 2.

8 Quoted in Schoenbaum, op. cit. (note 6), p. 50.

9 See, for example, the picture of the seminarians who flock to worship in Rome 'as massed crows seek dead bodies' in John Clapham's *Narcissus*, a poem originating from Lord Burghley's office: reproduced in Charles Martindale and Colin Borrow, 'Clapham's *Narcissus*: A Pre-Text for Shakespeare's *Venus and Adonis*?', *English Literary Renaissance*, 22 (Spring 1992), p. 163, l. 58–62.

10 John Speed, *The Theatre of the Empire of Great Britain* (London: 1611), vol. 2, bk 9, p. 637; cited in John Munro (ed.), *The Shakespeare Allusion Book*, 2 vols (London: Chatto and Windus, 1909), vol. 1, pp. 224–5.

11 Antonia Fraser, *The Gunpowder Plot: Terror and Faith in 1605* (London: Weidenfeld and Nicolson, 1996), pp. 145 and 175.

12 John Finnis and Patrick Martin, 'Another Turn for the Turtle: Shakespeare's Intercession for Love's Martyr', *Times Literary Supplement*, 18 April 2003, pp. 12–14. The identification of 'the bird of loudest lay' with William Byrd was initially proposed by Claire Asquith in 'A Phoenix for Palm Sunday: Was Shakespeare's Poem a Requiem for Catholic martyrs?', *Times Literary Supplement*, 13 April 2001, pp. 14–15. For Garnet's special faculty to admit new members to the Society of Jesus without noviceship see Philip Caraman, *Henry Garnet, 1555–1606, and the Gunpowder Plot* (London: Longmans, 1964), p. 271.

13 William Weston, *The Autobiography of an Elizabethan*, trans. Philip Caraman (London: Longman, 1955), pp. 71–2.

14 Quoted in Bernard Basset, S.J., *The English Jesuits: From Campion to Martindale* (London: Burns and Oates, 1967), p. 43.

15 Ronald Corthell, '"The Secrecy of Man": Recusant Discourse and the Elizabethan Subject', *English Literary Renaissance*, 19 (1989), pp. 274 and 287.

16 Richard James, Bodleian Library, James MS, 34; see Gary Taylor, 'William Shakespeare, Richard James, and the House of Cobham', *Review of English Studies*, 38 (1987), pp. 334–54.

17 Bate, op. cit. (note 2), pp. 7–8.

18 Richard Simpson, 'The Political Use of the Stage in Shakespere's Time', *New Shakespere Society Transactions* (1874), pp. 371–95; Richard Barnfield and John Weever quoted in Schoenbaum, op. cit. (note 6), p. 53.

19 William Empson, *The Structure of Complex Words* (London: Chatto and Windus, 1951), p. 176.

20 John Weever, Epigram 22, *Epigrams*, repr. in Ernst Honigmann, *John Weever* (Manchester: Manchester University Press, 1987), p. 110; Meres quoted in Schoenbaum, op. cit. (note 6), p. 54.

21 Robert Southwell, *Saint Peter's Complaint and Saint Mary Magdalen's Funeral Tears* (Saint-Omer: Society of Jesus, 1616), A4.

22 Quoted in Schoenbaum, op. cit. (note 6), p. 55.

23 Edmund Spenser, 'The Tears of the Muses' (1591), quoted in Ernst Honigmann, *Shakespeare: The 'Lost Years'* (Manchester: Manchester University Press, 1985), pp. 71–2.

24 Ibid., p. 59.

25 Ben Jonson, John Webster, John Heminges and Henry Condell, quoted, ibid., p. 57.

26 Quoted, ibid., pp. 55 and 57.

27 Stephen Greenblatt, *Renaissance Self-Fashioning: From More to Shakespeare* (Chicago: Chicago University Press, 1980), p. 252.

28 Jorge Luis Borges, 'Everything and Nothing', *Labyrinths: Selected Stories and Other Writings*, trans. James Irby (Harmondsworth: Penguin, 1970), p. 284.

29 Gary Taylor, 'Forms of Opposition: Shakespeare and Middleton', *English Literary Renaissance*, 24 (1994), pp. 313–14.

30 Corthell, op. cit. (note 15), pp. 272, 277–9, 283 and 289–90.

31 'The Life of Brother Edward Throckmorton', Stonyhurst manuscript attributed to Robert Southwell, ed. Henry Foley, *Records of the English Province of the Society of Jesus* (London: Burns and Oates, 1878), vol. 4, pp. 299 and 311.

32 Ibid., p. 288.

33 Ibid., p. 293; Christopher Devlin, *The Life of Robert Southwell, Poet and Martyr* (London: Longmans, 1956), p. 19.

34 Foley, op. cit. (note 31), pp. 293–4.

35 Ibid., pp. 299, 313–14 and 318.

36 Peter Burke, *The Historical Anthropology of Early Modern* Italy (Cambridge: Cambridge University Press, 1987), p. 48; Herbert Thurston, *The Month*, November 1911, vol. 108, p. 487; and Devlin, op. cit. (note 33), p. 263.

37 Henry Walpole (attr.), 'Verses Made by a Catholic in Praise of Campion', in Emrys Jones (ed.), *New Oxford Book of Sixteenth Century Verse* (Oxford: Oxford University Press, 1991), p. 333, ll. 26–8; Katherine Duncan-Jones, *Sir Philip Sidney: Courtier Poet* (London: Hamish Hamilton, 1991), pp. 124–7.

38 Richard Simpson, *Edmund Campion* (London: John Hodges, 1896), p. 6.

39 Quoted ibid., p. 157.

40 Foley, op. cit. (note 31), p. 298.

41 Michel Foucault, *The History of Sexuality*, trans. Robert Hurley, 3 vols (Harmondsworth: Penguin, 1981), vol. 1, Introduction, p. 59.

42 John Bossy, 'The Social History of Confession in the Age of the Reformation', *Transactions of the Royal Historical Society*, 25 (1975), pp. 21–38, esp. pp. 27–33.

43 Ibid., pp. 21, 27, 29 and 33.

44 Borromeo quoted ibid., p. 30; William Allen, *A Treatise Made in Defence of the Lawful Power of Priests to Remit Sins* (Louvain: 1567), pp. 73–4. See also Elizabeth Hanson, *Discovering the Subject in Renaissance England* (Cambridge: Cambridge University Press, 1998), pp. 49–50; and Jeremy Tambling, *Confession: Sexuality, Sin, the Subject* (Manchester: Manchester University Press, 1990) pp. 67–9 and 84–5.

45 Ben Jonson, quoted in Schoenbaum, op. cit. (note 6), p. 58.

46 John Bossy, 'The Character of Elizabethan Catholicism', *Past and Present*, 21 (1962), pp. 51–2.

47 Jonson quoted in Schoenbaum, op. cit. (note 6), p. 58.

48 Pierre Bourdieu, *Practical Reason: On the Theory of Action*, trans. Randal Johnson (Cambridge: Polity Press, 1998), pp. 86–7.

49 Lucien Goldmann, *The Hidden God: A Study of the Tragic Vision in the 'Pensées' of Pascal and the Tragedies of Racine*, trans. Philip Thody (London: Routledge and Kegan Paul), 1964, esp. p. 105.

50 Michel Foucault, 'Governmentality', trans. Colin Gordon, in Graham Burchell, Colin Gordon and Peter Miller (eds), *The Foucault Effect: Studies in Governmentality* (Hemel Hempstead: Harvester, 1991), pp. 87–8.

51 J.E. Neale, *Queen Elizabeth* (London: Jonathan Cape, 1934), p. 297.

52 Greenblatt, op. cit. (note 27), p. 166.

53 Neale, op. cit. (note 51), pp. 297–8.

54 'Copy of a Letter to Mendoza the Spanish Ambassador in France, dated London, September 1588, and Found in the Chamber of a Seminary Priest in England', *BL Harleian Miscellany*, 1, p. 149.

55 Quoted in Sibbald David Scott, 'A Book of Orders and Rules of Anthony Viscount Montague in 1595', *Sussex Archaeological Collections*, 7:1 (1869), pp. 180–1.

56 Conyers Read, 'William Cecil and Elizabethan Politics', in S.T. Bindoff, J. Hurstfield and C.H. Williams (eds), *Elizabethan Government and Society* (London: Athlone Press, 1961), pp. 45–7.

57 Ibid., p. 46.

58 *Calendar of State Papers Domestic, 1581–1590*, p. 510; *Acts of the Privy Council*, 16 (1588), pp. 174–8, 194, 232 and 249–50; *Calendar of State Papers Spanish, 1587–1603*, p. 420; Edward Cheyney, *A History of England from the Defeat of the Armada to the Death of Elizabeth* (London: Longman, 1914), pp. 210, 238, 259 and 284.

59 For the sceptical view see, for instance, Roger B. Manning, 'Anthony Browne, lst Viscount Montague: The Influence in County Politics of an Elizabethan Catholic Nobleman', *Sussex Archaeological Collections*, 106:1 (1968), pp. 106–7.

60 For the identification of the Goths with the Lutheran reformers of the Roman religion see Jonathan Bate, '"*Lucius*, the Severely Flawed Redeemer of *Titus Andronicus*": A Reply', *Connotations*, 63 (1997), p. 332.

61 Francis Barker, *The Tremulous Private Body: Essays on Subjection* (London: Routledge, 1984), pp. 25–6 and 35.

62 Harold Bloom, *Shakespeare: The Invention of the Human* (London: Fourth Estate, 1999), pp. 409–11 and 418.

63 Terry Eagleton, *William Shakespeare* (Oxford: Basil Blackwell, 1986), p. 72.

64 Catherine Belsey, *The Subject of Tragedy: Identity and Difference in Renaissance Drama* (London: Methuen, 1985), p. 50.

65 Michel Foucault, *Discipline and Punish: The Birth of the Prison*, trans. Alan Sheridan (Harmondsworth: Penguin, 1977), p. 30.

66 Jonathan Goldberg, *James I and the Politics of Literature* (Baltimore: Johns Hopkins University Press, 1983), p. 86.

67 Kay Stockholder, '"Yet Can He Write": Reading the Silences in *The Spanish Tragedy*',

American Imago, 47 (1990), pp. 3–124; Ann Rosalind Jones and Peter Stallybrass, 'The Politics of *Astrophil and Stella*', *Studies in English Literature*, 24 (1984), p. 54; Barker, op. cit. (note 61), p. 35.

68 William Slights, *Ben Jonson and the Art of Secrecy* (Toronto: Toronto University Press, 1994), pp. 24–5 and 28.

69 Patricia Fumerton, *Cultural Aesthetics: Renaissance Literature and the Practice of Social Ornament* (Chicago: Chicago University Press, 1991), p. 69; see also pp. 109 and 130.

70 Allan Fea, *Rooms of Mystery and Romance* (London: Hutchinson, 1931), pp. 87–8.

71 Michael Hodgetts, 'Elizabethan Priest-Holes: Dating and Chronology', *Recusant History*, 11 (1972), pp. 281 and 290.

72 Ibid., p. 279; Fraser, op. cit. (note 11), pp. 34–5.

73 John Michael Archer, *Sovereignty and Intelligence: Spying and Court Culture in the English Renaissance* (Stanford: Stanford University Press, 1993), pp. 4–10.

74 Granville Squiers, *Secret Hiding Places* (London: Stanley Paul, 1934), pp. 38–9; Clara Longworth De Chambrun, *Shakespeare: A Portrait Restored* (London: Hollis and Carter, 1957), pp. 25–6.

75 Anthony Petti (ed.), *Recusant Documents from the Ellesmere Manuscripts* (London: Catholic Record Society, 1968), pp. 5–13.

76 John Gerard, *The Autobiography of an Elizabethan*, trans. Philip Caraman (London: Longman, Green and Co, 1951), pp. 41–2.

77 Jonathan Goldberg, *Writing Matters* (Stanford: Stanford University Press, 1990), esp. pp. 265–72; Richard Rambuss, *Spenser's Secret Career* (Cambridge: Cambridge University Press, 1993), esp. pp. 48–62; Annabel Patterson, 'Re-Opening the Green Cabinet: Clement Marot and Edmund Spenser', *ELR*, 16 (1986), p. 69. See also Jonathan Crewe's reading of Philip Sidney's Sonnets as encrypted poems in *Hidden Designs: The Critical Profession and Renaissance Literature* (London: Methuen, 1986), pp. 76–9.

78 John Kerrigan, 'Secrecy and Gossip in *Twelfth Night*', in François Laroque (ed.), *Histoire et secret à la Renaissance* (Paris: Presses de la Nouvelle Sorbonne, 1997), pp. 179–80 and 194–5.

79 See Orest Ranum, 'The Refuges of Intimacy', in Roger Chartier (ed.), *Passions of the Renaissance: A History of Private Life, III*, trans. Arthur Goldhammer (Cambridge, Mass.: Harvard University Press, 1989), p. 207.

80 D.A. Miller, *The Novel and the Police* (Berkeley: University of California Press, 1988), pp. 195 and 207.

81 Georg Simmel, 'The Role of the Secret in Social Life', in *The Sociology of Georg Simmel*, trans. and ed. Kurt H. Wolff (Glencoe, Ill.: The Free Press, 1950), p. 335.

82 Eve Kosofsky Sedgwick, *Epistemology of the Closet* (Berkeley: University of Calfornia Press, 1990), pp. 3 and 14.

83 Fumerton, op. cit. (note 69), p. 77.

84 Bruce R. Smith, *Homosexual Desire in Shakespeare's England: A Cultural Poetics* (Chicago: Chicago University Press, 1991), chap. 7.

85 Patricia Parker, *Shakespeare From the Margins: Language, Culture, Context* (Chicago: Chicago University Press, 1996), p. 234.

86 Alan Stewart, *Close Readers: Humanism and Sodomy in Early Modern England* (Princeton: Princeton University Press, 1997), p. 167; Mark Girouard, *Life in the English Country House* (New Haven: Yale University Press, 1978), p. 56.

87 Ibid., p. 163.

88 A.C. Southern (ed.), *An Elizabethan Recusant House: The Life of Lady Magdalen Viscountess Montague, Translated from the Original Latin of Dr Richard Smith by Cuthbert Fursdon, O.S.B., in the Year 1627* (London: Sands, 1954), pp. 39 and 43; the Catholic gentleman Stephen Tempest, quoted in John Bossy, *The English Catholic Community* (London: Darton, Longman and Todd, 1975), pp. 174–5.

89 Roger B. Manning, *Religion and Society in Elizabethan Sussex* (Leicester: Leicester University Press, 1969), pp. 158–9.

90 Bossy, op. cit. (note 88), p. 127.

91 John Bossy, 'The Continuity of English Catholicism', *Past and Present*, 93 (1981), pp. 40–1.

92 Hodgetts, op. cit. (note 71), p. 286.

93 Quoted in Alexandra Walsham, *Church Papists: Catholicism, Conformity and Confessional Polemic in Early Modern England* (Woodbridge: Boydell and Brewer, 1993), p. 53.

94 Alison Shell, *Catholicism, Controversy and he English Literary Imagination, 1558–1660* (Cambridge: Cambridge University Press, 1999), p. 16.

95 Walsham, op. cit. (note 93).

96 For the Huguenot religion of the Mountjoy family, with whom Shakespeare lodged in London, see Park Honan, *Shakespeare: A Life* (Oxford: Oxford University Press, 1998), pp. 325–9; and for the Puritanism of the dramatist's son-in-law, Dr John Hall, see pp. 357–8.

97 Robert Ellrodt, 'Self-Consciousness in Montaigne and Shakespeare', *Shakespeare Survey*, 28 (1975), p. 42; Jonathan Dollimore, *Radical Tragedy: Religion, Ideology and Power in the Drama of Shakespeare and His Contemporaries* (Hemel Hempstead: Harvester Wheatsheaf, 1984), pp. 14–21 and 173–4.

98 Greenblatt, op. cit. (note 27), p. 253. For an epistemology of Montaigne's tower see also Theodore Ziolkowski, *The View from the Tower: Origins of an Antimodern Image* (Princeton: Princeton University Press, 1998), pp. 22–3, 33, 39 and 167–8.

99 For a discussion of Montaigne's ideas about the different definitions of privacy and solitude see Philip Hallie, *The Scar of Montaigne: An Essay in Personal Philosophy* (Middleton, Conn.: Wesleyan University Press, 1966), pp. 138–40.

100 R.J. Knecht, *The French Wars of Religion, 1559–1598* (Harlow: Longman, 1996), p. 57.

101 Samuel Schoenbaum, *William Shakespeare: A Documentary Life* (Oxford: Oxford University Press, 1975), p. 249.

102 R.A. Sayce, *The Essays of Montaigne: A Critical Exploration* (London: Northwestern University, 1972), pp. 214–17.

103 Quoted ibid., p. 217.

104 R.J.C. Wait, *The Background of Shakespeare's Sonnets* (London: Chatto and Windus, 1972), pp. 23–4.

105 Muriel Bradbrook, *Shakespeare: The Poet in His World* (London: Weidenfeld and Nicolson, 1978), pp. 98–101. The violent background to the possible first performance of *Romeo and Juliet*, marking Southampton's coming-of-age in October 1594, involved a blood-feud between the Montague-affiliated Danvers brothers and the family of Sir Walter Long, who were clients of the Cecils. See also Lawrence Stone, *The Crisis of the Aristocracy, 1558–1641* (Oxford: Clarendon Press, 1965), pp. 224, 229 and 236–7.

106 Timothy McCann, 'The Parliamentary Speech of Viscount Montague Against the Act of Supremacy, 1559', *Sussex Archaeological Collections*, 108 (1970), pp. 53 and 55

107 For Langdale as a type of Friar Laurence see Walsham, op. cit. (note 93), pp. 50–5.

108 For Shakespeare's systematic punning on the name of More see Patricia Parker, 'What's in a Name: and More', *Sederi XI: Revista de la Sociedad Española de Estudios Renascentistas Ingleses* (Huelva: Universidad de Huelva, 2002), pp. 128–45.

109 R.C. Bald (ed.), *An Humble Supplication to Her Majesty by Robert Southwell* (Cambridge: Cambridge University Press, 1953), p. 72.

110 See John Klause, 'Politics, Heresy, and Martyrdom in Sonnet 124 and *Titus Andronicus*', in James Schiffer (ed.), *Shakespeare's Sonnets: Critical Essays* (New York: Garland, 1999), pp. 225–6.

111 Simon Shepherd, *Marlowe and the Politics of Elizabethan Theatre* (Hemel Hempstead: Harvester, 1986), p. 79.

112 Quoted in Manning, op. cit. (note 59), p. 105.

113 Quoted in McCann, op. cit. (note 106), p. 52.

114 Paul Yachnin, *Stage-Wrights: Shakespeare, Jonson, Middleton and the Making of Theatrical Value* (Philadelphia: University of Pennsylvania Press, 1997), pp. 114–15.

115 Donna Hamilton, *Shakespeare and the Politics of Protestant England* (Lexington: University of Kentucky Press, 1992), pp. 128–9.

116 Debora Shuger, *Political Theologies in Shakespeare's England: The Sacred and the State in 'Measure for Measure'* (London: Palgrave, 2001), pp. 111–12.

117 Edward Dowden and Algernon Swinburne (eds), *Shakespeare's Complete Works* (2 vols. Oxford: Oxford University Press, 1924), vol. 1, pp. 72–3; Shepherd, op. cit. (note 111), p. 20; Alwin Thaler, *Shakespeare's Silences* (Cambridge, Mass.: Harvard University Press, 1929), p. 4.

118 Slights, op. cit. (note 68), p. 96; and see Raymond B. Waddington, 'The Iconography of Silence and Chapman's Hercules', *Journal of the Warburg and Courtauld Institutes*, 33 (1970), pp. 248–63.

119 Mary Hazard, *Elizabethan Silent Language* (Lincoln: University of Nebraska Press, 2000), pp. 5–8.

120 Belsey, op. cit. (note 64), p. 222.

121 Foucault, op. cit. (note 41), p. 27.

122 John Black, *The Reign of Elizabeth, 1558–1603* (Oxford: Clarendon Press, 1959), p. 377; John Neale, *Queen Elizabeth I* (London: Jonathan Cape, 1957), p. 274; Alison Plowden, *Danger to Elizabeth: The Catholics under Elizabeth I* (New York: Stein and Day, 1973), p. 204. See also David Cressy, 'Binding the Nation: Bonds of Association, 1584 and 1696', in Dellroyd Guth and John McKenna (eds), *Tudor Rule and Revolution* (Cambridge: Cambridge University Press, 1982), pp. 218–19 and 222–4.

123 William Kerrigan, *Shakespeare's Promises* (Baltimore: Johns Hopkins University Press, 1999), pp. 38–9; John Selden, quoted ibid., p. 39. See also Frances Shirley, *Swearing and Perjury in Shakespeare's Plays* (London: Allen and Unwin, 1985), esp. pp. 20–1 and 78–81.

124 Elias Canetti, *Crowds and Power* (Harmondsworth: Penguin, 1966), pp. 290–6.

125 Patrick McGrath, 'The Bloody Question Reconsidered', *Recusant History*, 20 (1991), p. 313.

126 Michael Questier, 'Loyalty, Religion and State Power in Early Modern England: English Romanism and the Jacobean Oath of Allegiance', *The Historical Journal*, 40 (1997), pp. 313–15.

127 David Martin Jones, *Conscience and Allegiance in Seventeenth Century England: The Political Significance of Oaths and Engagements* (Rochester, N.Y.: University of Rochester Press, 1999), pp. 45–51.

128 Stephen Greenblatt, *Hamlet in Purgatory* (Princeton: Princeton University Press, 2001), pp. 239–40.

129 Barker, op. cit. (note 61), pp. 36–8.

130 Alan Sinfield, *Faultlines: Cultural Materialism and the Politics of Dissident Reading* (Oxford: Oxford University Press, 1992), pp. 61–2.

131 Thomas Docherty, *John Donne Undone* (London: Methuen, 1986), p. 5.

132 Perez Zagorin, *Ways of Lying: Dissimulation, Persecution, and Conformity in Early Modern Europe* (Cambridge, Mass.: Harvard University Press, 1990), p. 14.

133 Leo Bersani and Ulysse Dutoit, *Caravaggio's Secrets* (Cambridge, Mass.: MIT Press, 1998), p. 2.

134 Ibid., pp. 8–9 and 13.

135 Dympna Callaghan, 'Shakespeare and Religion', *Textual Practice*, 15:1 (2001), pp. 1–4.

136 Bersani and Dutoit, op. cit. (note 133), pp. 8–9 and 18–20.

137 Parker, op. cit. (note 85), p. 271.

138 David Scott Kastan, *Shakespeare After Theory* (London: Routledge, 2001), p. 40. For the theoretical context of a restoration of the question of intentionality see also Hal Foster, *The Return of Reality* (Cambridge, Mass.: MIT Press, 1996).

139 Peter Holmes, *Resistance and Compromise: The Political Thought of the Elizabethan Catholics* (Cambridge: Cambridge University Press, 1982), p. 62.

140 Graham Greene, 'Introduction' to *John Gerard: The Autobiography of an Elizabethan*, trans. and ed. Philip Caraman (London: Longmans and Green, 1951), p. x.

141 Simpson, op. cit. (note 18), pp. 393–4.
142 Bersani and Dutoit, op. cit. (note 133), p. 91.
143 Gary Taylor, 'The Cultural Politics of Maybe', in Richard Dutton, Alison Findlay and Richard Wilson (eds), *Lancastrian Shakespeare: Theatre and Religion* (Manchester: Manchester University Press, 2003), p. 256.
144 Simpson, op. cit. (note 38), p. 447.

2

Ghostly fathers

Shakeshafte and the Jesuits

WILLIAM Cecil, Lord Burghley, was obsessed with visual aids. In his London chambers, Queen Elizabeth's Lord Treasurer was equipped with the latest graphic techniques to represent panoptic power, and educated his nephew, Francis Bacon, in the moral of the modern prince: that 'the greatness of a state in bulk and territory doth fall under measure and its finances under computation. Population may appear by musters and the number and greatness of cities by maps and cards.'[1] With his clocks, globes, charts of France, and murals of European towns, Cecil was the grey eminence of this new science of invisible surveillance, and power at a remove was the darker purpose of the project that he sponsored between 1574 and 1579: Christopher Saxton's cartographic survey of English counties, which he assembled in proof and personally annotated for his secretariat. With their unprecedented combination of field observation and typographic detail, Saxton's charts amply justify Marshall McLuhan's thesis that in the age of Mercator 'the map was the key to a new vision of the peripheries of power';[2] but in 1590 the spymaster commanded his cartographer to sharpen focus on one of the most remote of all limits of Elizabethan empire. The map of Lancashire he commissioned from Saxton that year plotted a mental as well as geographical divide, since it pinpointed the houses of all potential traitors in the most Catholic of English counties. Here in diagrammatic form, historians believe, Cecil imagined his worst nightmare, 'with one arrow stretching from Spain to Ireland, a second from Ireland to Lancashire, and a third from Lancashire to London'.[3] As he sat in his clockwork planetarium, the old minister therefore scored with an ominous cross the name of every Catholic under suspicion; but in the centre, at Hoghton Tower, he wrote only that its owner, Thomas Hoghton, was 'the fugitive'. The legend of this outlaw from a Protestant state is significant, because it was in his mansion, with its fenced and forested park, that the young Shakespeare is said to have passed some of his mysterious 'lost years':[4]

> At Hoghton high, which is a bower
>   Of sports and lordly pleasure,
> I wept and left the lofty tower
>   Which was my chiefest treasure.
> To save my soul and lose the rest
>   It was my true pretence:
> Like frighted bird, I left my nest
>   To keep my conscience.[5]

The legend of Thomas Hoghton, who saved his soul but lost the world, is told in a Lancashire ballad, 'The Blessed Conscience,' ascribed to his loyal steward, Roger Anderton. In fact, Anderton was a prolific printer of recusant texts, and his relationship to Hoghton, who was a kinsman, may have been as publisher of the earliest version of his story. This tells how 'the fugitive' sailed from the Ribble during the last Catholic rebellion, the doomed rising of the northern earls, in the winter of 1569. A sponsor of the English seminary at Douai, Thomas died at Liège in 1580, and was buried there by the Jesuits in sumptuous state. But his fame lived on in Lancashire (along with that of his son, a priest, also called Thomas, executed in Salford gaol) as a model of the pure in heart: 'His life a mirror was to all, / His death without offence; / Confessor, then, let us him call, / Of blessed conscience.' Hoghton's 'blessed conscience' in fact reflected the militancy of the Counter-Reformation, expounded by his cousin and guest at Hoghton, the first President of Douai, Cardinal William Allen, when he asserted that while an earthly prince has power to bind the body, only the priest has power to bind 'the very soul'.[6] The first to defy the Elizabethan regime with this doctrine was the jurist Edmund Plowden, who on the eve of the rising refused the endorsement of the Prayer Book demanded by ministers as a test of loyalty, pleading 'scruple of conscience'.[7] Forged between the Catholic confessional and Protestant Prayer Book, Hoghton's 'blessed conscience' thus confirms Stephen Greenblatt's dating of English self-fashioning to the clash of these two rival systems of inwardness, when a modern subjectivity is being conditioned even as the 'traditional examination of conscience by virtue of the Church's power of the keys is bitterly renounced'.[8] By fleeing his castle and county for the continent and confessional, Hoghton was prostrating before a papal absolutism that would in 1570 declare Elizabeth deposed and excommunicated; but he left a perilous predicament for his heirs. In the words of the ballad, it 'made his conscience sad' when his family paid lawyers a fortune to ensure he 'should not come home again'; but their excuse was Cecil's plan to 'attaint and try' those guilty of the crime of 'fugacy', so 'the Queen shall have forfeit of their land'.[9] Thus, the trustees of 'Thomas the Builder' resorted to the tactics of Catholic survival, for in the absence of 'the fugitive' Hoghton Tower remained locked in legal limbo, the true loyalty of its custodians an enigma to the Crown:

> At Hoghton where I used to rest
>   Of men I had great store,
> Full twenty gentlemen at least,
>   Of yeomen good three score!
> And of them all, I brought but two
>   With me, when I came thence.
> I left them, all the world knows how,
>   To keep my conscience.

Thomas Hoghton's conscience was famously 'blessed' precisely because he was so conspicuous amongst his peers. As the historian of Tudor Lancashire, Christopher Haigh, has written, what was notable about the county was that in 1569 it did *not* follow this saintly nobleman into resistance but took its lead instead from its overlord, the Earl of Derby, who 'played a game at which he excelled, waiting to gauge the strength of the opposing forces before throwing in his lot with the stronger'.[10] So, though the Spanish ambassador predicted that the whole county would rise up since it was so Catholic, and the Queen herself declared that its disaffection was such 'as we hear not of the like in any other parts,[11] it was the very conservatism of Lancashire which assured the status quo. Outside the purview of the Council of the North, the palatinate of Lancaster was an anomalous appendage of the English nation-state, the patrimony of John of Gaunt, which preserved semi-independence, with a separate legal system and a homage structure that invested power in a handful of feudal lords who still bore the names of their landholdings and gave them to their clans. It was this seigneurialism which fuelled the perpetual turf-wars of a shire with the largest number of private armies in England, where 'those at the top of the hierarchy maintained their authority by violence and intimidation', and, as the Earl of Derby himself warned the central administration in 1581, a dynasty like the Hoghtons was 'so great in kindred ... and so stored with friends, that if they should be burned in the hand' they would create 'such a ceaseless and dangerous quarrel as any county hath these many years contained'.[12] And it was also their feudal society which made Lancastrians 'this so unbridled and bad an handful of England', as Derby's son, Lord Strange, depicted his countrymen in 1583, since 'the detestable crimes of adultery, incest and fornication' were as intrinsic to its extended families as child-marriages. Thomas Hoghton's own father had typified this 'blindness and whoredom' in keeping four mistresses at a time and siring numerous bastards who shared in his estate;[13] so when Elizabeth's ministers looked north-west in the 1570s what they had to fear was not so much 'the fugitive' as their reliance on his kin.

'Where be thy tenants and thy followers? ... / Are they not now upon the western shore, / Safe-conducting the rebels from their ships' (*Richard III*, 4.5.411–13): Richard's doubts about Derby before the Battle of Bosworth condense in one of Shakespeare's earliest texts the misgivings over the

Lancashire clan system of successive English governments. For if the dramatist exaggerated the role of the Stanleys as king-makers, what he grasped was the equivocalness of the Duchy's magnates towards a regime they would aid, in 1485, in the 1536 Pilgrimage of Grace, and in 1569, only 'to their best advantage', lurking not 'too forward' but on the side, in each 'doubtful shock of arms' (4.4.480–2; 5.3.93–5). Burghley's map expresses this marginality by turning the suspect 'western shore' to the top, so defining the coastal delta as the most benighted of all 'dark corners of the land'. Again, it was 'the power of the gentry', in Bacon's view, that was 'a chief danger of the good subject here', since it was where feudal social relations held that Catholicism survived.[14] Economically primitive, sparsely populated, and legally exempt from the Queen's writ, the wetlands of west Lancashire, in particular, had resisted the Reformation more stubbornly than any other English region, and were identified in London – as well as Madrid – as the beachhead for any invading force. In the words of a 1574 Privy Council memorandum, this was 'the very sink of popery, where more unlawful acts are committed and more unlawful persons held secret than in any other part of the realm'. Here Mass had long been sung in private chapels and statues dressed at lonely shrines by an underground of 'popish and perverse priests', the Marian or Old clergy, who 'misliking true religion', it was reported in 1564, 'have forsaken the ministry to live in corners, being kept in gentlemen's houses, and held in great esteem by the people'.[15] In 1571 over fifty of these Old priests were still practicing 'predictions, divinations, sorceries, charmings and enchantments' in the area, of whom eighteen were presented for drunkenness or lechery. A 'dicer, carder, hawker and hunter', the Old priest remained a folk hero in Lancashire, and the charisma of the vicar of Whalley, near Hoghton, who taught that Anglican communion was to be cheerfully received as a dole of free bread and wine, explains why he outraged the reformers:

> A common drunkard, and such an ale-knight as the like is not in our parish, who in the night when most men be in bed is in the alehouse with a company like himself, but not one of whom can match him in ale-house tricks, for he will, when he cannot discern black from blue, dance with a full cup on his head, far surpassing all the rest.[16]

While Thomas Hoghton bared his confessing soul, his Lancashire neighbours were happy to dance behind their priest with a tankard on his head. Protected by such leaders, theirs was a religion of outward observance, where piety was manifested collectively with bells, candles, rushbearing or holy water, and villagers were used to 'signing themselves with the cross in every action, even when they gape'.[17] As reformers bemoaned, this north-country popular Catholicism was impervious to southern evangelism, because 'Those that seem to be reformed behave so unconformably: withdrawing to the farthest part of the church in private prayers; talking … and departing when Service is half done; crossing their breast with beads closely handled, or remaining in the churchyard, from whence stones are thrown and many a clamorous noise given out to the disquieting of the congregation'.[18] In these deep backwoods, where altar cloths, plate and icons were hidden in so many homes, open recusancy was never necessary, Haigh shows, as 'Those who did not appreciate the Anglican services could stuff their ears with wool and concentrate on their rosaries', or signify defiance by bellowing Latin psalms at the tops of their voices.[19] Lancashire was the heartland, that is to say, of the church papists, first characterised in a puritan polemic of 1582 as 'Papists who keep their conscience to themselves and yet go to church;' and in a recent survey as those 'who responded prudently to the re-established Church of England' by nominal attendance while 'adhering tenaciously to the faith in which they had been baptised'.[20] Such were the squires who avoided church 'except for one Sunday before the assizes', or the labourers who caused 'notorious disorder' with their 'tumultuous' appearance once a year at Easter. But they were also the temporizing majority of Lancastrians, according to informers, whose lip-service was paid with a 'scornful laughing countenance'.[21] If rebellion was futile, the two-faced natives of 'the uttermost skirts of the North' could still chant their 'spells and charms' while the organ drowned out the preacher, as ignorant of the true god, according to one M.P., as 'the Indians of Virginia'.[22]

Shakespearean Lancashire was infamous as the poorest and most primitive county in England, a wild west which was 'lamentable to behold', in the eyes of southerners, because of the violence and immorality of its people.[23] Yet what made this rain-washed coastline such a challenge to London was not so much its lawlessness as its potential as a bridgehead for the Counter-Reformation, and it was as such a European half-way house that Lancashire may have figured in Shakespeare's intellectual formation, since he travelled there as young as the age of sixteeen, according to E.K. Chambers, around 1580. The theory – first propounded in 1937 by Oliver Baker, and restated by Chambers in 1944 – that the dramatist spent the 1580s intermittently in Lancashire, as a servant in a chain of Catholic households, and that he is identifiable with William Shakeshafte, a player kept by the Hoghtons, was expanded by Ernst Honigmann in his 1985 book Shakespeare: The 'Lost Years', and now appears substantiated. It does so because of Honigmann's discovery that John Cottam, the Stratford schoolmaster from 1579 to 1581, belonged to Lancashire gentry who were neighbours, relatives and tenants of the Hoghtons;[24] but what neither Honigmann, Chambers, nor any of the other proponents of the 'Lancashire Shakespeare' have been able to explain is what tied Hoghton Tower to Stratford, and why, if Shakespeare was Shakeshafte, it should have remained such a secret. The reason they were not able to do so is that no one explored the specific Catholic context; but it is, in fact, a famous Jesuit mission of 1580/1 which connects the two places, provides an itinerary for Shakespeare's 'lost years' and suggests a solution to the puzzle of Shakeshafte's vanishing. Above all, it is the tragic story of the Jesuits' doomed children's crusade which confirms, beyond reasonable doubt, the identification of the Stratford boy with the servant at Hoghton.

The document which brings together Shakespeare's Stratford world and the drama of Hoghton Tower is an exhaustive will in the Lancashire County Records office at Preston. There Alexander Hoghton, the acting head of the family, named both Cottam and Shakeshafte his legatees when he disposed of his estate on 3 August 1581, bequeathing his stock of theatre costumes and musical instruments to his brother, and in the next breath enjoining a neighbour, Sir Thomas Hesketh of Rufford, 'to be friendly unto Fulke Gillam and William Shakeshafte now dwelling with me, and either take them into his service or help them to some good master'. An independent tradition has long connected Shakespeare with Rufford Old Hall; but though Hesketh did retain Gillam, Honigmann conjectures that he recommended Shakeshafte to the Stanleys, and that it was in their livery, as one of Ferdinando, Lord Strange's, and then Lord Derby's Men, that Shakespeare launched his career about 1590 in London, where his earliest admirers included the Lancashire poet John Weever, a relation and protégé of the Hoghtons.[25] That there was a pattern of recruitment from the Midlands into these Lancastrian households is suggested by the career of Sir Edward Bushell (whose brother stood surety for a loan the dramatist made to their friend Richard Quiney, and whose sister married Quiney's elder son three years before the younger one married Judith Shakespeare), who started out at Knowsley in 1591 as a retainer of Ferdinando.[26] Bushell, who became Gentleman Usher to the Earl of Essex, was a cousin of the Gunpowder Plotters, the Winters, and, on his mother's side, a Throckmorton. But such is also the increasingly accepted trajectory of Shakespeare's 'lost years', though the questions it raises are why an ambitious and talented young Midlander should have beaten a path to such a poverty-striken backwater as the wetlands of west Lancashire; and why, if he did make his way to this remote desert country near the sea, it should have been under the name of William Shakeshafte.

If William Shakespeare assumed the name of Shakeshafte, commentators infer, he was reverting to the style of his fathers, as this had been one variant used by his grandfather Richard. A motive for the change to the older form was perhaps the crisis which hit his actual father after 1576, when he suddenly ceased to attend Stratford corporation meetings and, in the words of 1592 depositions, 'obstinately refused to resort to the church', pleading 'fear of process of debt'.[27] For four hundred years John Shakespeare's financial alibi was swallowed by most scholars, until research in the Exchequer records revealed in 1984 that the Stratford businessman remained rich to the end and active as a banker.[28] What did grip Warwickshire in the late 1570s, however, was not an economic but a religious fever, for it was then the first seminary priests began to arrive from Douai (funded partly by the Hoghtons), after 'long and dangerous travel', in Spenser's account, 'knowing peril of death awaited them, and no reward nor riches were to be found'.[29] In Stratford they were drawn, none the less, to a place Patrick Collinson describes as 'essentially a Catholic stronghold down to the middle of the sixteenth century'; Antonia Fraser as the 'town at the centre of the recusant map of England'; and John Neale as a bastion of middle-class church papists encircled by Calvinist landowners such as the Lucys and Grevilles.[30] Peter Milward has suggested that their President, William Allen, may have been the master named Allen paid by John Shakespeare for 'teaching the children' at Stratford in 1564/5 (sponsored, we can assume, by his Hoghton cousins);[31] and biographers agree that one of their first recruits was the man who taught the dramatist from the ages of seven to eleven: Simon Hunt, who enrolled at Douai in 1575, and followed the Jesuit Robert Parsons as director of penance at the English College in Rome.[32] But it was Hunt's successor, John Cottam, who could have fixed their safe-house in Stratford, as the 1580 mission under Parsons and Edmund Campion included his brother Thomas, who was returning from Poland when he was arrested at Dover. Whether or not the teacher hid Parsons on his journey through the Midlands, Campion, we know, lodged in September at Sir William Catesby's Lapworth Park, just north of Stratford. So it was there – in a house later a setting for the Gunpowder Plot – that the text was likely signed by Shakespeare's father which sheds most light on his son's Lancashire detour: the Spiritual Testament the Jesuits had brought from Milan, where it had been presented to them by no less an authority than soon-to-be St Carlo Borromeo.

Ever since it was uncovered by workmen in the roof of his Henley Street house in 1757, John Shakespeare's Spiritual Testament has been an embarrass-ment to the Shakespeare establishment. Malone, who printed it, but then lost the original, was finally persuaded that 'it could not have been the composition of any one of our poet's family'; while Sir Sidney Lee dismissed it as a forgery.[33] Its authenticity was established, however, along with its forgotten provenance, with the discovery of a 1661 Spanish version in 1923, and of another English one in 1966. In fact, its discovery parallels that of similar recusant documents, such as the *Agnus Dei* of Gregory XIII hidden in joists of the roof by Campion before his arrest at Lyford in 1581, and found there by workmen as late as 1959. Yet it continues to dumbfound Shakespeareans, who prefer to retreat, like Samuel Schoenbaum, into 'a secular agnosticism' in face of such evidence.[34] According to Parsons, however, the meetings at which this Testament were distributed were so emotional precisely because they were so covert, being convened in houses 'we entered as kinsfolk of some person within, where putting ourselves in priest's apparel, we had secret view and conference with all the Catholics that might come, whom we caused to be that night late for Confession, and next morning very early we had Mass and after an exhortation'.[35] Such was the fervour in which Shakespeare's father appears to have put his name to Borromeo's text, confessing to be an 'abominable and grievous sinner'; vowing to 'patiently endure and suffer violence of pain and agony', rather than renounce the 'Catholic, Roman and Apostolic Church'; beseeching his 'friends and kinsfolk, by the bowels of our Saviour', to celebrate the Dirige, or Office of the Dead, for him; bequeathing his soul to be 'entombed in the sweet and amorous coffin of the side of Jesus Christ … there to bless for ever and ever that direful Iron of the Lance'; and appointing 'the glorious and everVirgin Mary', together with his own patron saints, as 'chief Executress' of his will.[36] By the spring of 1581, copies of this Testament were printed in their thousands, but John Shakespeare's was one of the early select handwritten versions, so it can be dated exactly to the autumn days of the Stratford mission, when the testator must have signed it, 'in presence of the Blessed Virgin Mary, my Angel Guardian, and all the Celestial Court as Witnesses', with an irrevocable sense of privilege and commitment. Certainly, the inculcation of such commitment was the document's express intent:

> The devout person who will make use of this spiritual writing, for the good of his soul let him read or hear it read often, especially when he hopes that he is in a state of grace after Confession. And let him keep it in some place of note and near unto him: when he goeth on any journey, let him carry the same always with him to have it ready upon all occasions. And when he shall fall sick, let him renew by reading, or hearing read, this Testament in presence of others, confirming finally what he hath formerly at all times promised and bequeathed for the good of his soul.[37]

The binding words of John Shakespeare's pseudo-contractual Testament invite us to believe that they were indeed 'read often' in his household, and that his family were, as it says, enjoined to participation. That may explain why, in a scene overwrought with ghosts of father-figures, Old Hamlet appears to echo the testator's hope that, if 'by reason of my sins, I be to pass a long stay in Purgatory', his descendants 'will vouchsafe to assist and succour me with holy prayers', when he reports how he is 'Doom'd for a certain term to walk the night, / And for the day confin'd to fast in fires, / Till the foul crimes done in my days of nature / Are burnt and purg'd away' (*Hamlet*, 1.5.10–13). As John Henry de Groot remarked, this ghostly father is 'no folklore spirit, but a soul returned from the realm of Catholic immortality';[38] and his compact with his son to 'Remember me' (90) places the entire recollection in the context of an eternal undertaking. It is, in fact, recent work by Catholic historians such as Alexandra Walsham which situates the sworn Testament in relation to the alderman's church absence and his son's Lancashire itinerary. For, as she shows, Anglican observance would have been intolerable to the signatory of such a text, which Borromeo had drafted deliberately to enforce resistance to churchgoing, seen as a violation of conscience. In answer to the question, then, which must have haunted John Shakespeare when he hid his Testament in his attic – 'Why did spokesmen of the Counter-Reformation choose the permanance, indelibility, and illegality' of texts 'to expound the ideology of recusancy?'

– Walsham argues that such formularies 'aimed to stiffen those faint-hearted not in fidelity to the hereditary faith of their forefathers, but in their inner resolve to suffer for it'. Addressed to 'persons whose very possession and perusal of prohibited reading material was … an act of defiance, an assertion of identity, and a self-consciously pious gesture',[39] John Shakespeare's Spiritual Will and Testament was designed to be remembered, as his son seemed to affirm from the gallery of the Globe, precisely for its indelible compulsion:

> Remember thee?
> Ay, thou poor ghost, whiles memory holds a seat
> In this distracted globe. Remember thee?
> Yea, from the table of my memory
> I'll wipe away trivial fond records,
> All saws of books, all forms, all pressures past
> That youth and observation copied there,
> And thy commandment all alone shall live
> Within the book and volume of my brain,
> Unmix'd with baser matter.
>
> (*Hamlet*, 1.5.95–104)

It was professions of militant commitment like John Shakespeare's which split English Catholicism between resistance and the conformity of those, like the Catholic nobles who petitioned Elizabeth in 1585, who protested their allegiance; but to prove 'the only gain they covet is souls', even the Jesuits were forbidden by Rome to 'mix in affairs of state, to write about political matters, or allow others to speak against the Queen'.[40] So Campion insisted at his trial that he was 'forbidden to deal with matters of state, as those things appertain not to my vocation'; and the intention of this self-denying ordinance was to give Catholics the moral advantage of 'martyrs who suffered for conscience, innocent of anything that could be called treason'.[41] This was the net that was to entangle Thomas Cottam, who, having been freed on bail, 'conceived some scruple', and 'went with a merry countenance to the Star in New Fish Street, and offered himself a prisoner to Lord Cobham, who carried him to the Tower'.[42] At Dover he had held in his possession a letter from Shakespeare's Stratford contemporary and possible second cousin, Robert Debdale, a seminarian in Rome, in which he 'commended Cottam to his parents at Shottery', and sent militant tokens of Catholic faith for them and their neighbours. It seems likely that Debdale, who would follow Cottam to the gallows in 1586, had been recruited for Rome by his teacher Hunt, so that, as T.W. Baldwin inferred, Stratford Grammar school operated under a succession of masters as virtually a cell for these suicide missions.[43] And as well as confirming the missionaries' plan to converge on Stratford, it is Debdale's part in this macabre relay race which supplies a possible clue to the strange diversion now taken by his Stratford kinsman. For if Chambers and Honigmann are correct, Shakespeare rode north at exactly the same time as another journey linked Stratford and

Hoghton Tower, when Campion himself departed Lapworth, and left behind the knot of Midland gentry who would shortly seal the Throckmorton Plot.

'Commend thy grievance to my holy prayers, / For I will be thy beadsman, Valentine' (*Two Gents*, 1.1.17): Proteus's farewell to his schoolfriend, *en route* for Milan, suggests the pious fervour with which these young seminarians quit Shakespeare's Stratford. And in his biography of one of them – Edward Throckmorton, who died in Rome in 1582, aged twenty – Robert Southwell relates a story straight out of some early Shakespearean play, in which the heir to Coughton, near Stratford, is sent by his outwardly conforming father to be educated at Park Hall in the Forest of Arden by Edward Arden, recusant head of the Arden family, and an uncle he shared with Shakespeare. As Christopher Devlin observed, Edward Arden's mansion became a headquarters of the Counter-Reformation during Shakespeare's teenage years, when the Park Hall tutor, 'who combined learning with ardent Catholicism', inspired boys from the distruct to regiment themselves into an ultramontane club of 'young gentlemen of zeal and forwardness', whose 'joy and alacrity' in vowing chastity and poverty, and Jesuitical schemes to 'pry into corners and inveigle youths to fly overseas to seminaries', mimicked the French Catholic League: 'They pledged themselves to suffer all sorts of tortures rather than take part in Protestant services, canvassed neighbours and tenants to discover other boys who attended only for fear … and would arrange for boys to escape from their homes and live in hiding elsewhere.'[44] This was, in fact, the moment when the suicidal militancy of St Bartholomew's Day crossed the Channel, and, with both his father and teacher so close to this so-called Sodality, it would be surprising if the sixteen-year-old pupil of Stratford Grammar School were *not* pressed to join 'boys who for this cause have separated from their parents', as Campion enthused, in emotional scenes like that laid on for young Throckmorton:

> It is wonderful how many of his old school-fellows and of the common people and gentry assembled both to bid farewell to the object of their singular esteem, and congratulate him on his departure to a Catholic country. What tears started to the eyes of relations! What lamentations there were of servants, male and female! What weeping and grief of all! Each one bewailed the great loss which he foresaw he would suffer by the departure; and as though about to be deprived forever of one whom they held so dear, they accompanied him upon his way as if in a funeral procession, with many sad tokens of their deep affection.[45]

Jesuits should follow the example of Christ, Ignatius Loyola ordained, 'when He remained in the Temple, leaving His adoptive father and His natural Mother to attend to the service of His eternal Father'; and a recent study of the sixteenth-century Order confirms that novices were expected to abandon their families, which was why affluent candidates were preferred, so they could 'say they have no parents, but *had* them'.[46] It was in this spirit of self-abnegation that the first seminarists were also trained to submerge their identities by assuming aliases and, if necessary, disguise. As Peter Holmes has shown, much ingenuity was spent on defending the adoption of false names and appearances in reply to Protestant critics, with Allen citing the precedent of David's feigned madness or Christ's escape from the Jews. The entire strategy of equivocation, which would later damn the Jesuits in the eyes of adversaries, began, therefore, with the arrival at Dover in June 1580 of Parsons in the role of a sea captain and Campion of an Irish merchant, subterfuges they excused as 'not tantamount to lying, but rather as "dissimulation", for which there were good precedents', since 'it was common practice to change names when entering religion'.[47] Contrary to the assumption of critics who argue against the 'Lancashire theory' on the grounds that if Shakespeare wanted to change his identity he would thought of a better alias than 'Shakeshaft', for the Jesuits the adoption of a new name was never simply a matter of disguise. Campion, who admitted that his borrowed clothes and names often seemed 'very ridiculous', considered an alias less an evasion tactic, in fact, than a form of personal sacrifice, since the 'new soldiers' he recruited *give up their names*', he rejoiced, 'as veterans offer their blood, by which oblations God will be pleased'.[48] So, it was actually incumbent on all those who joined the mission to take some symbolic *nom de guerre*, as Parsons became Doleman; Campion, Hastings; and Debdale, Palmer: the name of the grandfather he is thought to have shared with Shakespeare. It may well be significant therefore, that, if Shakespeare was Shakeshafte, he varied the word so little – perhaps thereby registering an equivocation about equivocation – when, as Campion declared at his trial, the assumption of the new name was such a matter of Jesuit commitment:

> We read of sundry shifts whereto Paul betook himself to shun persecution; but especially the changing of his name, whereby, as occasion administered, he termed himself now Paul, now Saul; neither was he of opinion always to be known, but sometimes thought it expedient to be hidden, lest being discovered, persecution should ensue … If these shifts were then approved in Paul, why are they now reproved in me? The same cause was common to us both. I saw if I were known I should be apprehended. I changed my name; I kept secretly; I imitated Paul.[49]

From warlike 'Shakespeare' to priestly 'Shakeshafte': if the Warwickshire boy did give up his name for a Lancashire variant, it needed only a slight shift – like Paul's – to satisfy the rules of his cause. But then, it was only ever 'a short step', Gary Taylor contends, 'from Parsons, Allen and Southwell to Shakespeare';[50] and just how short a step is underlined by the text which prompts most current discussion of the playwright's Catholic sympathies: Samuel Harsnett's savage Anglican polemic, *A Declaration of Egregious Popish Impostures*, where the 'strange new names' of exorcised devils, echoed by Shakespeare in *King Lear*, are said to 'take their fashion from our wandering Jesuits' themselves, 'who to dissemble have always three or four odd conceited names in their budget'.[51] In 1610, *King Lear* would be staged along with *Pericles*, in a season of miracle plays toured through the Yorkshire Dales by a troupe of recusant actors, and it is easy to see how Edgar's 'popish imposture' as Poor Tom might resonate in that country of secret tunnels, priest-holes and hidden chapels. Yet, as Stephen Greenblatt complains, the connection of Shakespeare's play of assumed identities to the drama of Catholic survival 'has remained inert, locked in the pieties of source study that ... reduce history to a decorative setting'.[52] What is now clear, however, is that no account of *King Lear* can ignore the implication that what drew Shakespeare to Harsnett's satire on Jesuit exorcisms was that these had been instigated by his relative, Debdale himself, in a family, at Denham in Buckinghamshire, closely tied to Lancashire gentry; and that, when the possessed supposedly vomited up the 'uncouth non-significant names' which Shakespeare borrowed, of 'Frateratto, Hoberdidance and Fliberdigibbet' (3.6.6; 3.6.30; 3.4.112), they did so after the exorcist 'crammed' Campion's amputated thumb into their mouths or summoned up the spirit of Thomas Cottam. Shakespeare evidently read *Popish Impostures* because of its attacks on the memory of his own 'ghostly fathers', for if he was Shakeshafte, he had himself been one of those very 'children of pride' who acted a part for these Jesuits, who 'made them so giddy-headed with their holy charms and dreadful fumigations', or so Harsnett jeered, that 'They gave themselves giddy names to go current among themselves, as the Gipsies do of gibberish, which none but themselves can read without spectacles'.[53]

'Though, as Ben Jonson said of him, he had but little Latin and less Greek, he understood Latin pretty well, for he had been in his younger years a schoolmaster in the country':[54] John Aubrey's anecdote has always been a starting-point for discussion of Shakespeare's education, but it is Catholic resistance which may offer a key to mysterious omissions from his *curriculum vitae*. For as John Dover Wilson recognised in 1932, if 'John Shakespeare fell into trouble about 1580 due to being a member of the "old religion" who refused to attend church ... as an ardent Catholic he might well seek other means for his son's education in the service of a Catholic nobleman'.[55] And it is recusancy which supplies the clue to one salient fact about the Stratford writer, which is that, of all Elizabethan and Stuart dramatists, he alone emerged from outside the golden academic triangle of London and the universities. Thus, Beaumont, Cartwright, Chapman, Daniel, Davenant, Ford, Lyly, Marmion, Marston, Massinger, Middleton, Nabbes, Peele, Sackville and Shirley all attended Oxford; and Clapthorpe, Day, Fletcher, Gascoigne, Greene, Heywood, Marlowe, May, Norton and Randolph Cambridge; while Kyd, Lodge and Webster went to Merchant Taylors' School; Field to St Paul's; and Jonson to Westminster. The Londoners Chettle and Munday were apprenticed to printers; and ties with the guilds or Inns of Court can be inferred for Dekker, Rowley, Thatham, Tourneur and Wilson; but the only dramatist whose provenance resembles Shakespeare's is his Warwickshire contemporary, Drayton, who came to London as a page in Leicester's circle. So, if Chambers and Honigmann are right, it was a detour to the recusant North that took Shakespeare in a clear opposite direction to the social logic of his professional field and constituted his freakish statistical difference. It was a Lancashire affiliation that may, therefore, have made Shakespeare, as Anne Barton notes, almost unique among contemporary dramatists in persistently rejecting London settings with plays that are 'filled with evasions of the urban'.[56] It may also have made him the outstanding example of what Pierre Bourdieu termed the academic heretic, whose cultural power arises from being marginal to metropolitan institutions and so 'liberated from the privileges and constraints of the ordinary intellectual'.[57] If so, it was northern Catholicism which differentiated Shakespeare from the roster of all who wrote for the London playhouses, as in fact the least a Londoner.

While every other dramatist gravitated towards the metropolitan centre, research suggests that Shakespeare made his isolated way through the Marches to the wildest corner of the Tudor kingdom. Even Honigmann is at a loss 'why Shakespeare should have been sent so far from home', speculating that it was to distance him from Anne Hathaway.[58] But then he underrates the dire force of Catholic circumstance, as when he merely notes that, if the boy was retained by the Hoghtons in late 1580, 'their Catholic sympathies are important, as it is unlikely such a family would employ, at a time so dangerous to recusants, a servant who was not a practising Catholic'.[59] In fact, we know that Campion himself took the same road that autumn accompanied by a picked escort of young 'subseminarians' or 'conductors', sworn to 'content themselves with the bare necessities for the good of the cause'; and that he stayed in the North with the Hoghtons and their neighbours until 15 May 1581, writing his book *Ten Reasons* to arm recusants with arguments to 'refuse' the Anglican Church. According to his biographer, Richard Simpson, 'Lancashire was chosen because it was furthest from London and best affected to the Catholic religion, but also because there was more hope to find there the books to help him answer the heretics'. For before retreating north, Campion had issued his famous 'brag' to ministers, to 'avow our Catholic Church by proofs invincible', and at Hoghton he was equipped with all the 'scriptures, fathers, councils, histories, and works of natural and moral reason' needed to prepare for public debate. No wonder that as late as 1660 locals recalled how 'many persons of quality spent whole nights in barns so they might be early next day to his sermon on the King who went a journey'.[60] As Evelyn Waugh enthused, 'the rich rhetoric that had stirred the lecture halls of Oxford and Douai, Rome, Prague and Rheims, now rang through the summer dawn'.[61] If Shakespeare was Shakeshafte, he was a member of a household which was for six months, it seems, nothing less than the secret headquarters of the English Counter-Reformation.

'The day is too short, and the sun must run a greater circumference', Campion boasted, before he could 'number all the Epistles, Homilies, Volumes and Disputations' he amassed at Hoghton. It was this library which would infuriate his prosecutors, who ordered a series of posses to Lancashire to root out contraband texts 'dispersed in that shire' by his hosts. But as their prisoner taunted, it was 'in vain that the houses of Catholics, with their trunks, boxes, and private receptacles, were violently broken open', for no seditious pamphlet told against Anglicanism more eloquently than the classics, and 'as long as these Monuments of Learning were sold, so long in vain were our books forbidden to be read'. Campion's learning was not worn lightly, but it was his catalogue of esoterica – from Athanasius to Zozomene – which caused him to mock those who 'learn some few Greek words and will seem literate'.[62] It would be strange if some of these tomes were not carted away by the boy named Shakeshafte when the priest's library was broken up. But, whatever their destination, their collection at Hoghton adds new substance to the view that 'Shakespeare's rhetoric was grandson to Campion's'. Baldwin based that insight on the fact that Thomas Jenkins, John Cottam's predecessor as Stratford schoolmaster, was another of Campion's contacts, having been tutored by him in at St John's, Oxford, where his friend was yet another Jesuit martyr, William Hartley, whose execution Shakespeare would record in *The Comedy of Errors*. As Baldwin deduced, the poet's 'small Latin' and Greek were acquired in a milieu dominated by 'Campionists', as four of the five Stratford masters who might have taught him were linked with Jesuits, and 'though outwardly conformist, there is a great deal to show their sympathies were all Catholic'. It is this 'significant background' which for Baldwin accounts for the fact that four of the five were also Lancastrians.[63] And when Campion's princely library is also considered, it explains the otherwise improbable connection between the Midland market town and the wilds of Hoghton. In this environment, all roads led literally to Lancashire.

It is in the light of Campion's northern retreat that the story of Shakespeare's country schoolteaching acquires significance. For, of all counties, Lancashire was where 'The youth of both the gentry and common sort' were reckoned to be most 'noseled up in Popery by Popish schoolmasters fostered in gentlemen's houses'.[64] And if the playwright was one of those so 'fostered' by the Hoghtons, he would have been recruited to a system that historians describe as 'the most dangerous device of Catholic resistance and the most important means of maintaining priests'.[65] To be such a schoolmaster in Lancashire was to be automatically suspect, since as the official 'Regulations for Schools' calculated, 'three out of four papists were not twelve years old when the Queen came to her crown, but have learnt it in her reign from corrupt schoolmasters in private houses'. In 1592 an apostate priest listed ten leading Catholic gentry in the county as keeping 'recusants as schoolmasters', including Alexander Hoghton himself, his cousin Richard, who had 'this twenty years had one after another', his brother-in-law Bartholomew Hesketh and Vivian Haydock, a kinsman of the Cottams.[66] All were related, the informer noted, to Cardinal Allen, and it was this dynasty which ensured that 'one-sixth of those who entered Douai by 1584 came from Lancashire'.[67] It was no accident, then, that nine of the twenty-one Catholic schoolmasters executed under Elizabeth were Lancastrians. With thirty-two Catholic schools, the county was a springboard for missionaries such as Thomas Hoghton and Thomas Cottam, who both taught there before sailing to Douai; or John Finch, hanged at Lancaster in 1584 for operating a liaison chain between recusant houses while ostensibly a tutor.[68] The son of the Stratford recusant had models for such a vocation in his master, Hunt, and schoolmate, Debdale; but if he was also Shakeshafte he had run between the two most active resistance cells in Catholic England. For if Shakespeare was Shakeshafte, he would by 1581 have had glittering prospects, such as Allen envisaged when he founded his continental alternative to Oxford and Cambridge for 'youths (Gentlemen's sons especially)' from 'Grammar Schools in all parts of the Realm':

> To draw into this College the best wits out of England, that were either Catholicly bent or desirous of a more exact education than is these days in either of the Universities (where there is no art, holy or profane, thoroughly studied, and some not touched at all); or that had scruple of conscience to take the oath of the Queen's Supremacy in causes Ecclesiastical (which gave us diverse, not only Catholics but others, out of both the Universities, where it tormenteth the conscience of many that seem pure Protestants), or that misliked to be forced to the Ministry, as the use is in diverse Colleges ... or that were doubtful whether of the two religions were true.[69]

A 'young scholar, that hath been long studying at Rheims; as cunning in Greek, Latin, and other languages, as ... in music and mathematics', is the role adopted by Lucentio in *The Taming of the Shew* to gain entrance, with a 'small packet of Greek and Latin books', as tutor to Bianca (2.1.80; 100); and from this it seems that Shakespeare knew as much about Jesuit education as about its association with disguise. In particular, this tribute to the Rheims curriculum raises the intriguing possibility that he was familiar with the Jesuit use of drama as a teaching aid, which has been described by Alison Shell as the occasion of 'some of the most powerfully subversive texts ever to come from English pens', infused by writers 'who were unequivocally opposed to the Tudor regime' with 'a Catholic fury which would have been, quite simply, unstageable' in a legitimate English playhouse. At colleges in northern France, such as Douai, Saint-Omer, and Rheims, the pupils and seminarians were drilled to perform plays written by masters on subjects that 'hardly figure, for obvious reasons, in English mainland drama: stories from the persecuted early Church, from Byzantium during the period of the Iconoclast controversy, and from Christianity's embattled beginnings in pagan Britain'. Typically, Jesuit dramaturgy hinged on tragic martyrdom, but Shell points out that English students specialised instead in tragi-comedy as a genre with unique relevance to their own Catholic compatriots, currently caged in a tyrannical prison, yet promised 'an ending of unspeakable happiness'. Thus, the theme of miraculous renewal which characterised this exiled theatre expressed 'the 'potency of nostalgia to English Catholics', and the 'resilience … within the seminaries that trained priests to return to England'.[70] Robert Miola has argued that this Jesuit college drama, with its 'tragi-comedies that ended in repentance … left an indelible impression on European writers', such as Calderón, Corneille, Goldoni, Lope de Vega and Molière.[71] It may be that Shakespeare should be added to this list, and that, if he began his career in Campion's circle, he too acquired from the performance of Catholic conversion a template for his own theatre of restoration, where so much in the Ardennes likewise turns on news that the tyrant, 'meeting with an old religious man':

> After some question with him, was converted
> Both from his enterprise and from world,
> His crown bequeathing to his banish'd brother,
> And all their lands restor'd to them again
> That were with him exil'd.
> *(As You Like It, 5.4.1509–4)*

Carol Enos has recently proposed that the dream of the émigrés' return, with 'all their lands restor'd', makes *As You Like It* and the other plays in which it recurs especially apt for the Hoghtons, so many of whom went into exile in the Ardennes.[72] If so, then it may have been at their Tower that Shakespeare absorbed the principle of hope he shared with the Jesuits that 'The saddest birds a season find to sing'.[73] When it was first reproduced by Chambers in 1923, Alexander Hoghton's will simply struck historians as a window on to the cultural life of the northern nobility, and a glimpse of the route by which performers might be passed from one patron to another.[74] But knowing now that Campion had been staying at Hoghton, we can also read this document as indicating that the theatrical performances he personally directed as recently as the previous summer in Bohemia continued to be part of his curriculum. By the time of his mission, Shell relates, Campion had developed his own tragi-comedic dramaturgy, involving resurrection of saints and salvage of lost fortunes, and it must have seemed right to his hosts that the endings of his six plays were, 'in worldly terms, brilliantly optimistic'.[75] But though written for schoolboys, these theatricals were technically ambitious and composed in Latin. To stage any of them at Hoghton would have required at least some of the resources Campion had exploited in the Prague of Rudolf II, where his drama about King Saul enacted the story of the tyrant and his player, David, to an audience that included the Queen of France, over a span of six hours.[76] So, this could be why Fulke Gillam and his brother Thomas were added to the household some time after July 1580 (when Alexander drafted an earlier list of servants which did not mention them). For we know enough about them to be certain that these young actors from Chester had no reason to be added to the staff at Hoghton except as masters of revels.

In the light of Campion's plays, it is worth considering what it may suggest about William Shakeshafte to be listed in Alexander Hoghton's will alongside Fulke and Thomas Gillam. For the Gillams were from a well-documented family firm of costumiers and pageant masters, who organised Chester mystery plays and civic shows for generations under the patronage of the Earls of Derby, and one of whose relations became the foremost Jacobean authority on heraldry. Their father Hugh was 'paid for dancing at Midsummer' in the Chester Treasurer's accounts yearly from 1563. Another brother, Jasper, was Yeoman of Apprentices, Captain of the Watch, and head of the city's 'waitmen' in the Midsummer Show from 1587 to 1632; while Thomas was himself one of the townsmen paid 'for their morris dancing', or later 'for music on Midsummer eve', from 1576 until 1622.[77] The next person listed in Hoghton's will was 'William Ashcroft, *alias* Ormshaw', from a Rufford family who were bear-wardens, no less, to the Heskeths and Stanleys.[78] And Campion's theatrical demands might be why another 'servant' rewarded in the will was the Stratford schoolmaster, John Cottam. His Latin would be invaluable for coaching actors in Jesuit plays. In any case, during these weeks when Hoghton became home to a famous dramatist, a team of stage technicians, and a dedicated Catholic educator, the household furnished them with musical instruments, 'all manner of play clothes', and 'an ideal place for performances', Honigmann notes, in its Great Hall, with 'a minstrel's gallery for upper stage, and an acting area below'.[79] Designed like a college, Hoghton had waited for such use since the exile of its builder. But if it now saw a production of a 'comedy' such as Campion's *Ambrosia*, that may have been according to his wishes. For when he died Thomas Hoghton left £100 to found a music library in Preston.[80] His brother Alexander's will, in which he bequeathed 40 shillings a year to each of the players, showed how he shared the same educational aims. So, an attempt by the Stratford archivist Robert Bearman to explode the 'Lancastrian' theory, on the grounds that Shakeshafte was a common Preston name (but this begs the question why, if local, Shakeshafte was 'now living' with the Hoghtons), and that Alexander's bequest was too generous for a seventeen-year-old, misses the point, by ignoring both Campion and the Gillams, of the Hoghton cultural programme.[81] In fact, Shakeshafte received exactly the same bequest as Fulke and Thomas, who must have been born in the 1560s, to become, respectively, a Freeman of Chester in 1596, and 'Captain at Midsummer' in 1610. Of course, if Bearman is correct, Thomas Gillam could have had a child, as he did in 1605, aged over seventy, and danced through the streets of Chester into his nineties.[82] But it seems more likely that in 1581 he was still a teenager, and endowed, like Shakeshafte, with the means to continue the Campion project. Touted as a definitive answer to the 'Lancashire Shakespeare', Bearman's case does not itself survive examination.

On 16 December 1580 the Privy Council issued an order aimed at putting a stop to the 'education of young gentlemen in parts beyond sea, where they are accustomed and nourished in papistry'. The order gave sponsors of 'papist pupils' three months 'for calling home their sons or friends', and one of those commanded to cease smuggling boys 'under their charge beyond seas' was Alexander Hoghton. Even as Shakespeare may have travelled to Lancashire, officers were on his tracks to prevent his going further.[83] But the possibility that the dramatist was among the youths recruited to this system answers one objection to the Hoghton Tower theory, which is that, as Peter Levi demurs, someone whose 'talent was so enormous and obvious' would never have 'drifted shiftlessly into a troop of ragged players or taken private service in obscure Lancashire'.[84] In fact, far from such obscurity, the aristocratic Catholicism harboured behind walls at a mansion such as Hoghton was the advance guard of the Baroque, according to Judith Hook, since this was the one English community where contact with Europe was all-important: 'Culturally dependent on countries that could provide an orthodox education for Catholic children', families like the Hoghtons became as familiar with Rome, Paris or Madrid 'as any place in England', while 'the vast majority of Catholics educated abroad came back ... helping to maintain cultural links with the outside Catholic world'.[85] This was a culture, then, much like Shakespeare's earliest plots in flitting between home and abroad, and the oaths and aliases subscribed by the Sodality had the arrogance of those assumed by the 'little academe' of zealots in *Love's Labour's Lost* who 'war against ... the huge army of the world' (1.1.9–13). In her study of the Gunpowder Plot, Antonia Fraser describes this 'small world' of 'perpetual aliases', in which 'everyone was related to everyone else', as 'schizophrenic' in its oscillation between the glittering light where prizes were won and the spectral darkness of a forbidden religion;[86] but to the brightest and best who signed up for Campion's crusade, the prospect would have seemed like that of Shakespeare's two gentlemen of Verona, who would rather 'see the wonders of the world abroad' than 'Wear out youth in shapeless idleness' (*Two Gents*, 1.1.6–8). Cottam, who carried letters from Italy to Shottery like some Valentine or Proteus, had lodged in Rome with the composer Victoria; and Lawrence Stone confirms that the provincial geography of Elizabethan Catholicism was liberating, not limiting, for its chosen protégés, who received 'shelter, encouragement, protection and financial backing' from the patronage network of great houses on their way to universities abroad.[87] English Catholicism would later shrink into quietist isolation, but in 1580 the way through Lancashire still led on to the continent, and the militant culture of what might have been Shakespeare's Belmont was a window on the world.

'Their sugared tongues and power-attractive beauty', wrote John Weever of Shakespeare's early works, 'Say they are Saints ... For thousands vows to them subjective duty.'[88] The Lancashire writer noticed, it seems, an affinity between Catholic beliefs and the stage where Titus shoots at Virgo after the true goddess of justice flees the earth (*Titus*, 4.3.4–64); Romeo kisses Juliet like a 'holy shrine' (*Romeo*, 1.5.91), and uses Friar Laurence as his 'sin-absolver' and 'ghostly confessor' (3.3.49); Richard III is haunted by spirits on All Soul's

Eve; an Abbess appears from 'sanctuary' in *The Comedy of Errors*, to redeem 'The place of death and sorry execution / Behind the ditches of the Abbey' with her 'holy prayers' (5.1.104–22); Petruchio swears he loves Kate, 'By God's wounds', so loud the priest lets fall the book (*Shrew*, 3.2.158); Fairies 'consecrate … each several chamber' of Theseus's palace with their sacred 'dew' (*Dream*, 5.1.401); Claudio vows to 'the goddess of the night' a 'yearly rite' at Hero's tomb (*Much Ado*, 5.3.12–23); 'Mistress Mall's picture' is dusted down in the house where Olivia, with her 'sweet Roman hand', is 'catechized' as 'madonna' (*Twelfth*, 1.3.124; 1.5.60; 3.4.29); and the King of Navarre departs, like Jaques, 'To some forlorn and naked hermitage, / Remote from the pleasures of the world' (*Love's*, 5.2.787). No wonder that in the Civil War, 'Shakespeare's works' were excoriated by Puritans as 'prelatical trash such as clergymen spend their canonical hours on', nor that they became the favourite reading of the imprisoned Charles I;[89] for critics have marshalled ample internal evidence of their author's Catholic set of mind. When the priest-hunter Anthony Munday exposed the clay feet of Thomas More, Shakespeare made the Catholic hero a lawabiding Church papist; and, when Munday heroised the Lollard John Oldcastle, Shakespeare travestied him as the hypocritical Falstaff. In *King John* he toned down an anti-Catholic source; and in *Henry V* promoted the loyality of England's papist subjects through the scrupulosity of the soldier Michael Williams. Richard Dutton has established how indebted the Histories are to Parson's 1595 *Conference on the Succession*, advocating the Catholic claimants of the House of Lancaster;[90] and though research still remains to be done on Alan Keen's fifty-year-old discovery of a copy of *Hall's Chronicle* traceable to the Hoghton library – with historical scenes annotated from a Catholic point of view in a hand he believed was Shakespeare's[91] – what is already striking is the stark difference from all other English drama of this Gothic theatre of dark towers, moated granges and silent convents, where statues weep in secret chapels, and friars emerge from hiding-places to resolve each plot. However long he studied in their 'little academe' in Lancashire, Shakespeare's 'ghostly fathers' had clearly left their mark.

On 4 August 1581 – the very day after Alexander commended Shakeshafte to his neighbour Thomas Hesketh in his will – the Privy Council commanded a search for 'certain books and papers which Edmund Campion has confessed he left at the house of one Richard Hoghton in Lancashire'.[92] Campion had been hurrying north to safeguard his library when he had been persuaded to say Mass at a Lyford in Berkshire, where on 16 July he was ambushed. From there he was taken in parodic cavalcade to the Tower, where on 31 July he was racked to discover 'at whose houses had he been received? Who had assisted him? At whose houses had he said Mass? Whose confessions had he heard, where did they live, and what had they talked about?'[93] Very soon, Burghley could crow that 'We have gotten from Campion knowledge of all his peregrinations and have sent for his hosts'. As his biographer admits, 'By August 2 the government had suddenly acquired a flood of light about his doings. They knew where he had lodged in Lancashire and where he had hidden his library'; enough to order the arrest of Richard Hoghton and his wife, a sister of one of the other captured priests, Bartholomew Hesketh, and everyone suspected of concealing Campion or his books. They knew enough also to detain Sir William Catesby at Lapworth, and put Parsons's Warwickshire Arden and Throckmorton hosts under surveillance.[94] So, it cannot be chance that this was the moment when John Cottam relinquished his Stratford teaching post and retired to Lancashire (where he remained for thirty years a business associate of the Hoghtons). Nor that he was then replaced by yet another Lancastrian, Alexander Aspinall from Clitheroe, five miles from Hoghton Tower, and a family long connected to the Hoghtons and Heskeths, who maintained ties with the firmly Catholic town, even nominating its constable in 1618, while schoolmaster at Stratford.[95] Nor that Alexander Hoghton then made his will, for another who did so before his arrest on 4 August was Campion's London sponsor, the Earl of Southampton, who would die in equally suspicious circumstances, at the age of thirty-six, on 4 October.[96] Honigmann deduced that, when he hurriedly signed his will, Alexander 'may have hoped to disperse family property to forestall confis-cation',[97] but even he does not seem to have grasped the dire emergency in which, among more desperate measures, Shakeshafte was protected: on the very day between Campion's forced confession and the raids on the Hoghton estates. Even as the master of Hoghton Tower helped his servants to new identities, in the Tower of London Campion was being tortured for their names.

On 21 August 1581 the Lancashire magistrates were thanked by the Privy Council for apprehending Campion's hosts, together 'with certain papers, in Hoghton House'.[98] And 'indeed, they are searchers of secrets', concurred Thomas Cottam from the Tower, 'for they would needs know of me what my sins were for which penance was enjoined me. Whereupon they sore tormented me, but I persisted that I would not answer, though they tormented me to death.'[99] As Campion himself understood, torture and confession were what Foucault calls the 'dark twins' of Counter-Reformation government, for 'the secrets he would not "confess" to the authorities were those that had been confessed to him';[100] so it is ironic that Shakespeare's interpreters are now driven by the same rage to discover the hidden truth about his circle as the inquisitors, and that Campion should have been tortured to reveal, among such secrets, the identity of William Shakeshafte. For critics know that, while other Renaissance dramatists reassure spectactors 'by putting privacy on display', Shakespeare's difference is that in his plays the 'obsessive desire to spy out secrets' is offset by 'a sense of opacity – of what could not, even on stage, be brought to "show"'.[101] And, as Gary Taylor argues, it was precisely his forma-tion within a culture of paranoid circumspection, like that of England's Catholics, which determined Shakespeare's celebrated invisibility: the illusion that 'Wherever we look in his writings', in Dutton's words, 'he is self-effacing to the point of anonymity'. For such a vacuum, Taylor insists, has to be carefully constructed and maintained: 'There may be many motives for self-erasure, but the desire to protect yourself from those who would "pluck out the heart" of your mystery is most understandable in adherents of a religion that was defined as treason'.[102] Such was Campion's desire when, having admitted to divulging names, he protested that 'I never discovered any secrets, to the revealing whereof I will not be brought, come Rack, come Rope'; and it remained Cottam's even on the scaffold, where he was still harried to 'confess the grievous sin he committed in the market long ago', until a bystander 'affirmed it was not Father Cottam but his brother John who had committed the offence'.[103] Whatever the crime committed in Cheapside by the Stratford school-master, it was certain that even at Tyburn the interrogators would not relent until they had indeed plucked out the heart from Shakespeare's world.

'He died a papist': the presumption of Shakespeare's Catholicism is no new theory, but dates from the Restoration, when Richard Davies, a chaplain at Oxford, recorded the testimony of surviving witnesses.[104] In the nineteenth century, Richard Simpson explored the recusancy of Tudor Stratford, tracing Shakespeare's nostalgia for the 'Bare ruined choirs where late the sweet birds sang' (Sonnet 73) to the influence of the town's Guild of the Holy Cross and the Arden legacy. In 1946, John Henry de Groot compiled a magisterial dossier on the loyalty of the Shakespeares to 'the old faith'; and in 1958 Robert Stevenson made the crucial deduction that it was his Lancashire sojourn that conditioned the dramatist's cultural marginality, on the 'religious frontier' of Elizabethan England. That conditioning has been made probable by the research of E.K. Chambers, Leslie Hotson and Ernst Honigmann, and indefatigably publicised by Father Peter Milward. Recent biographers, such as Ian Wilson, Park Honan and Anthony Holden, have all added significant new pieces to the overwhelming mass of circumstantial evidence which links the young Shakes-peare to Stratford Catholicism and the Hoghton resistance.[105] But what has not been explained is the connection between the Midland market town and the northern household. Though Campion's itinerary is famous, it has never been linked with the shifts that transformed Shakespeare into Shakeshafte, and then 'the only Shakescene in a country'.[106] It was the 1580 mission, however, which not only tied Stratford to Hoghton directly but necessitated the adoption of aliases by everyone involved. There were many Lancashire Shakeshaftes, it has been objected; but none had reason to lodge at Hoghton Tower like the boy educated, under Hoghton tutelage, by recusant schoomasters at Stratford. Their tuition accounts for Shakespeare's presence at Hoghton in August 1581, and his silence in the ensuing decade of persecution, when both his Warwick-shire cousins and his Lancashire patrons would be decimated for their alleged treason. Campion's rhetoric has been thought Shakespearean; but, if it was his campaign that took his converts north, it was also his catastrophe which spared the playwright the penalties of priesthood. Biographers hunting for the 'smoking gun' – to confirm the identity of Shakeshafte – possessed it all along, had they but noticed the coincidence of Campion's confession, in the date of the will of his harassed host at Hoghton.

Alexander Hoghton's will was proved shortly after his death on 12 September 1581. Like so many in Shakespeare's Catholic world – his patron, Ferdinando Stanley; his friend's father, the Earl of Southampton; his cousin, the would-be regicide, John Somerville – he died in circumstances that suggest a government murder. Edmund Campion, likewise, was hanged on 1 December, and so it might have been at this time that John Shakespeare first hid his Spiritual Testament beneath the tiles of his house, where it was to remain, a dusty secret from his son's admirers, for so long. The Stratford burgess had come very close indeed to the ordeal of truth which would take his co-signatories to the gallows, but he had not, in the end, honoured his suicidal promise to carry the document 'continually about with me', so as to be sure to be 'finally buried with it' after death. And if his son was Shakeshafte, he too flinched, it seems, from a faith that would send so many of his 'ghostly fathers' to their violent ends. In Lancashire the young 'subseminarian' would have encountered instead an older folk religion, which, as historians have shown, did not lead automatically to recusancy, and put more faith in charms and rosaries than moral invigilation. It was to envangelise this popular Catholicism that Campion had preached at Hoghton; and, when he returned north, John Cottam similarly continued to 'receive into his charge youths to be educated' as late as 1604, and to 'send catechisms and books' to 'other gentlemen of Lancashire and certain priests'.[107] His most famous pupil must have disappointed the master, therefore, by slipping from the pulpit to the playhouse. For some time after the raid on Hoghton, Shakeshafte vanished into the interstices of a state that preferred, in Queen Elizabeth's phrase, *not* to make windows in men's souls, to re-emerge transformed, with his 'tiger's heart wrapped in a player's hide',[108] from a papist to a poet. Campion's arrest had cut short the brilliant career that should have propelled the Stratford boy, with all the ardour of his martyred mentors, from the schoolroom to the scaffold. And though the historian John Speed would publicly brand him with Robert Parsons as two of a kind, both being 'Papists and his Poets, of like conscience for lies',[109] what Shakespeare learned from his fathers, it seems, was that conscience makes not heroes but cowards of us all. For in an age which demanded visibility and unformity, he produced a world of difference from a secrecy darker even than the priest-hole or confession.

NOTES

1 Francis Bacon, 'Of the True Greatness of Kingdoms and Estates', *The Essays*, ed. John Pitcher (Harmondsworth: Penguin, 1985), p. 148.
2 Ifor Evans and Heather Lawrence, *Christopher Saxton: Elizabethan Map-Maker* (Wakefield: Wakefield Historical Publications, 1979), pp. 9–11, 40–1; Marshall McLuhan,

The Gutenberg Galaxy: The Making of Typographic Man (Toronto: University of Toronto Press, 1962), p. 11; B.W. Beckingsale, *Burghley: Tudor Statesman* (London: Macmillan, 1967), pp. 222–5, 259–60.

3 A.G. Dickens, *The English Reformation* (London: Batsford, 1964), p. 312.

4 Joseph Gillow, *Lord Burghley's Map of Lancashire in 1590* (London: Arden Press and Catholic Records Society, 1907), p. 4.

5 Joseph Gillow, *The Haydock Papers: A Glimpse into English Catholic Life* (London: Burns and Oates, 1888), pp. 10–15; F.O. Blundell, *Old Catholic Lancashire*, 2 vols (London: Burns, Oates and Washbourne, 1925), vol. 1, pp. 131–3.

6 William Allen, *A Treatise Made in Defence of the Lawful Power and Authority of Priesthood to Remit Sins* (Louvain, 1567), pp. 73–4. See also Arnold Pritchard, *Catholic Loyalism in Elizabethan England* (London: Scolar Press, 1979), pp. 4–15.

7 Quoted Elliot Rose, *Cases of Conscience: Alternatives Open to Recusants and Puritans under Elizabeth I and James I* (Cambridge: Cambridge University Press, 1975), p. 38.

8 Stephen Greenblatt, *Renaissance Self-Fashioning: From More to Shakespeare* (Chicago: Chicago University Press, 1980), p. 85.

9 Beckingsale, op. cit. (note 2), p. 126.

10 Christopher Haigh, *Reformation and Resistance in Tudor Lancashire* (Cambridge: Cambridge University Press, 1975), p. 126.

11 Ibid., pp. 222–3.

12 Ibid., pp. 52–3. The County Palatine retained its separate legal system until 1856.

13 Ibid., pp. 46–7.

14 Francis Bacon, *The Works of Francis Bacon*, ed. James Spedding, 14 vols (London: Macmillan, 1857–74), vol. 10, p. 381; quoted J.E.C. Hill, 'The Puritans and the "Dark Corners of the Land"', *Transactions of the Royal Historical Society*, 5th series, 13 (1963), p. 99. See also Haigh, op. cit. (note 10), p. 97; John Bossy, 'The Character of Elizabethan Catholicism', *Past and Present*, 21 (1962), pp. 50 and 66.

15 *Acts of the Privy Council*, vol. 8, pp. 276–7; Adrian Morley, *The Catholic Subjects of Elizabeth I* (London: Allen and Unwin, 1878), pp. 44–5.

16 Quoted Haigh, op. cit. (note 10), pp. 240–1.

17 Ibid., pp. 219 and 222.

18 F.R. Raines (ed.), *A Description of the State, Civil and Ecclesiastical, of the County of Lancaster about the Year 1590* (London: Chetham Society, 1875), pp. 3–4.

19 Haigh, op. cit. (note 10), pp. 219 and 248.

20 George Gifford, *A Dialogue between a Papist and a Protestant, applied to the capacity of the unlearned* (London: 1582); quoted in Alexandra Walsham, *Church Papists: Catholicism, Conformity and Confessional Polemic in Early Modern England* (Woodbridge: Boydell and Brewer, 1993), p. 1.

21 Raines, op. cit. (note 18), p. 4.

22 Sir Benjamin Rudyerd speaking in the House of Commons in 1628, quoted Hill, op. cit. (note 14), pp. 96–7.

23 Haigh, op. cit. (note 10), p. 265.

24 Oliver Baker, *Shakespeare's Warwickshire and the Unknown Years* (London: Simpkin Marshall, 1937); E.K. Chambers, 'William Shakeshafte', *Shakespearean Gleanings* (Oxford: Oxford University Press, 1944); E.A.J. Honigmann, *Shakespeare: The 'Lost Years'* (Manchester: Manchester University Press, 1985).

25 Ibid., pp. 3–4 and passim. For John Weever see chap. 5.

26 Leslie Hotson, *I, William Shakespeare* (London: Jonathan Cape, 1937), pp. 141–9.

27 Samuel Schoenbaum, *William Shakespeare: A Documentary Life* (Oxford: Clarendon Press, 1975), p. 38.

28 D.L. Thomas and N.E. Evans, 'John Shakespeare in the Exchequer', *Shakespeare Quarterly*, 15 (1984), pp. 315–18.

29 Edmund Spenser, *A View of the Present State of Ireland*, ed. W.I. Renwick (Oxford: Oxford University Press, 1925), p. 162. Spenser was himself resident in Lancashire and

near Hoghton from 1576 to 1577, when the first Douai priests began to arrive there, a fact which may have influenced his contrast in *The Shepherd's Calendar* between good and suspect pastors.

30 Henry Bowden, *The Religion of Shakespeare, Chiefly from the Writings of the Late Mr Richard Simpson* (London: John Hodges, 1899), p. 63; Patrick Collinson, 'William Shakespeare's Religious Inheritance and Environment', *Elizabethan Essays* (London: Hambledon Press, 1994), pp. 246–7; J.E. Neale, *The Elizabethan House of Commons* (Harmondsworth: Penguin, 1963), p. 241.

31 Peter Milward, *Shakespeare's Religious Background* (London: Sidgwick and Jackson, 1973), p. 41.

32 John Henry de Groot, *The Shakespeares and 'The Old Faith'* (New York: Crown Press, 1946), pp. 135–40.

33 Schoenbaum, op. cit. (note 27), pp. 41–3; Sir Sidney Lee, *A Life of William Shakespeare* (London: John Murray, 1915; rev. ed.), p. 647.

34 For the Lyford discovery see Michael Hodgetts, 'Elizabethan Priest-Holes', *Recusant History*, 11 (1972), p. 282; Schoenbaum, op. cit. (note 27), p. 46.

35 Quoted Richard Simpson, *Edmund Campion: A Biography* (London: John Hodges, 1896; rev. ed.), p. 233.

36 The Spiritual Testament is reproduced in Schoenbaum, op. cit. (note 27), pp. 44–5.

37 Ibid., p. 45.

38 De Groot, op. cit. (note 32), p. 176.

39 Op. cit. (note 20), p. 26.

40 Arnold Oscar Meyer, *England and the Catholic Church under Queen Elizabeth*, trans. J.R. McKee (London: Routledge and Kegan Paul, 1967), pp. 142–4.

41 Pritchard, op. cit. (note 6), p. 38.

42 Simpson, op. cit. (note 35), p. 191.

43 T.W. Baldwin, *William Shakspere's Small Latine and Lesse Greeke* (2 vols, Urbana: University of Illinois Press, 1944), vol. 1, pp. 483–5. Edgar Fripp suggested that Debdale's great-aunt was Shakespeare's maternal grandmother, Mrs Robert Arden, née Palmer (Debdale's alias): *Shakespeare's Haunts Near Stratford* (Oxford: Oxford University Press, 1929), pp. 33 and 53.

44 Christopher Devlin, *The Life of Robert Southwell, Poet and Martyr* (London: Longmans and Green, 1956), pp. 18–19; Simpson, op. cit. (note 35), 205, 222–3.

45 Quoted Devlin, op. cit. (note 44), p. 21.

46 A. Lynn Martin, *The Jesuit Mind: The Mentality of an Elite in Early Modern France* (Ithaca: Cornell University Press, 1988), p. 187.

47 Peter Holmes, *Resistance and Compromise: The Political Thought of the Elizabethan Catholics* (Cambridge: Cambridge University Press, 1982), p. 118.

48 Evelyn Waugh, *Edmund Campion* (Oxford: Campion Hall, 1935), p. 113; De Groot, op. cit. (note 32), p. 87.

49 Edmund Campion quoted in Simpson, op. cit. (note 35), p. 414.

50 Gary Taylor, 'Forms of Opposition: Shakespeare and Middleton', *English Literary Renaissance (ELR)*, 24 (Spring 1994), pp. 283–314, esp. p. 306.

51 Samuel Harsnett, *A Declaration of Egregious Popish Impostures to withdraw the Hearts of Her Majesty's Subjects from their Allegiance* (London, 1603), p. 46; quoted in Frank Brownlow, *Shakespeare, Harsnett, and the Devils of Denham* (Newark: University of Delaware Press, 1993), pp. 294–5.

52 Stephen Greenblatt, *Shakespearean Negotiations: The Circulation of Social Energy in Renaissance England* (Oxford: Clarendon Press, 1990), pp. 94–5.

53 Brownlow, op. cit. (note 51), p. 294.

54 John Aubrey, *Brief Lives*, ed. Oliver Lawson Dick (Harmondsworth: Penguin, 1962), p. 438.

55 John Dover Wilson, *The Essential Shakespeare* (Cambridge: Cambridge University Press, 1932), pp. 40–1.

56 Anne Barton, 'London Comedy and the Ethos of the City, *London Journal*, 4 (1978), p. 160. And see also Gail Kern Paster, *The Idea of the City in the Age of Shakespeare* (Athens: University of Georgia Press, 1985), p. 178: 'Shakespeare's evident disinclination to place comic action in contemporary London sets him apart from other major comic dramatists of his time ... Moreover, Shakespeare tends to ruralize his comic cities ... [which] lack almost all nitty-gritty traces of urban habitation but the name'.

57 Pierre Bourdieu, *Homo Academicus*, trans. Peter Collier (Cambridge: Polity Press, 1988), p. xix.

58 Honigmann, op. cit. (note 24), pp. 129–30.

59 Ibid., p. 9.

60 Simpson, op. cit. (note 35), pp. 222, 226, 252, 266.

61 Evelyn Waugh, *Edmund Campion* (Oxford: Oxford University Press, 1935), p. 127.

62 Simpson, op. cit. (note 35), p. 107.

63 Baldwin, op. cit. (note 43), p. 486.

64 Raines, op. cit. (note 18), p. 3; Haigh, op. cit. (note 10), p. 291.

65 C.P. Beales, *Education under Penalty: English Catholic Education from the Reformation to the Fall of James II, 1547–1689* (London: Athlone Press, 1963), p. 74.

66 Ibid., pp. 74–5 and 78–9.

67 Ibid., pp. 74–5, 78–9 and 83; Haigh op. cit (note 10), pp. 278–9 and 291–3. For the importance of the relationship to William Allen see also Historic Manuscripts Commission, 9: Salisbury Mss, p. 13: a letter to the government from Richard Hesketh detailing Allen's influence in west Lancashire.

68 Beales, op. cit. (note 65), p. 78.

69 William Allen, *An Apology and True Declaration of the Insititution and Endeavours of the Two English Colleges* (Menston: Scolar Press, 1971), pp. 12–13.

70 Alison Shell, *Catholicism, Controversy and the English Literary Imagination, 1558–1660* (Cambridge: Cambridge University Press, 1999), pp. 173–5 and 194–5.

71 Robert Miola, 'Jesuit Drama in Early Modern England', in Richard Dutton, Alison Findlay and Richard Wilson (eds), *Lancastrian Shakespeare: Essays on Theatre and Religion* (Manchester: Manchester University Press, 2003), pp. 94–120.

72 Carol Enos, 'Catholic Exiles and *As You Like It*: Or What if You Don't Like It at All?', ibid., pp. 185–201.

73 Robert Southwell, 'Times Go By Turns', in James H. McDonald and Nancy Pollard Brown, *The Poems of Robert Southwell* (Oxford: Clarendon Press, 1967), pp. 57–8.

74 E.K. Chambers, *The Elizabethan Stage* (4 vols, Oxford: Oxford University Press, 1923), vol. 1, p. 280.

75 Shell, op. cit. (note 70), p. 112.

76 Simpson, op. cit. (note 35), p. 117.

77 Rupert Morris, *Chester in the Plantagenet and Tudor Reigns* (Chester: Privately Published, 1887), pp. 218 and 287; *Dictionary of National Biography*; 'Records of the Chester Midsummer Day Pageant', in J.H.E. Bennett, *The Rolls of the Freemen of the City of Chester* (Chester: Chester Corporation, 1906); Mark Eccles, *Shakespeare in Warwickshire* (Madison: University of Wisconsin Press, 1961), p. 74; Alan Keen, correspondence, *Times Literary Supplement*, 18 November 1955, p. 689; Lawrence Clopper (ed.), *Records of Early English Drama: Chester* (Toronto: Toronto University Press, 1979), pp. 70, 74, 84, 96, 120, 151, 154, 155, 162, 165–6, 170, 209, 222, 264 and 348.

78 David George (ed.), *Records of Early English Drama: Lancashire* (Toronto: Toronto University Press, 1991), pp. 97–8.

79 Honigmann, op. cit. (note 24), p. 27.

80 George Miller, *Hoghton Tower* (Preston: Guardian Press, 1948), p. 154.

81 Robert Bearman, '"Was William Shakespeare William Shakeshafte?" Revisited?', *Shakespeare Quarterly*, 53 (2002), pp. 82–94.

82 L.M. Farrall (ed.), *Parish Register of the Holy and Undivided Trinity in the City of*

Chester, 1532–1837 (Chester: G.R. Griffith, 1914), p. 12 'August 22 1605: Luke Gillam son to Thomas Gillam, Embroiderer'; p. 82, 'December 21 1615: Grace, wife to Thomas Gillam, buried in church yard'; Eccles, op. cit. (note 77), p. 74; Clopper, op. cit. (note 77), p. 264.

83   Ibid., p. 157.

84   Peter Levi, *The Life and Times of William Shakespeare* (London: Macmillan, 1988), p. 42.

85   Judith Hook, *The Baroque Age in England* (London: Thames and Hudson, 1976), p. 126.

86   Antonia Fraser, *The Gunpowder Plot: Treason and Faith in 1605* (London: Weidenfeld and Nicolson, 1996), pp. 22 and 35.

87   Lawrence Stone, *The Crisis of the Aristocracy* (Oxford: Oxford University Press, 1965), p. 373.

88   John Weever, 'Epigram 22; 4th Week', in E.A.J. Honigmann, *John Weever: A Biography of a Literary Associate of Shakespeare with a Photographic Facsimile of Weever's 'Epigrammes' (1595)* (Manchester: Manchester University Press, 1987), pp. 110 and 124.

89   *Mercurius Britannicus*, 2 September 1644, quoted in Ernest Sirluck, 'Shakespeare and Jonson among the Pamphleteers of the First Civil War: Some Unreported Seventeenth-Century Allusions', *Modern Philology*, 53 (1955), p. 94.

90   Richard Dutton, *William Shakespeare: A Literary Life* (London: Macmillan, 1989), p. 9.

91   Alan Keen and Roger Lubbock, *The Annotator* (London: Putnam, 1954), pp. 93–4.

92   Simpson, op. cit. (note 35), p. 343.

93   Ibid., pp. 341–2.

94   Ibid., pp. 343–4; Christopher Devlin, *Hamlet's Divinity and Other Essays* (London: Rupert Hart-Davis, 1963), p. 14.

95   J.H. Lumby (ed.), *De Hoghton Deeds and Papers* (Manchester: Lancashire and Cheshire Records Society, 1936), pp. 98–9; William Weeks (ed.), *Clitheroe in the Seventeenth Century* (Clitheroe: Advertiser and Times, 1887), pp. 11, 62, and passim. In 1594 Aspinall married Anne Shaw, who lived next door to John Shakespeare's Henley Street house, and so became stepfather of the overseer of Shakespeare's will, Julius Shaw. The poet gave him a pair of gloves, accompanied by a ribald rhyme, for a wedding present. Aspinall was sponsored at Oxford by Alexander Nowell, a relation of the Heskeths: see Keen and Lubbock, op. cit. (note 91), pp. 195–8.

96   G.P.V. Akrigg, *Shakespeare and the Earl of Southampton* (London: Hamish Hamilton, 1968), pp. 14–18; A.L. Rowse, *Shakespeare's Southampton* (London: Macmillan, 1965), p. 40.

97   Honigmann, op. cit. (note 24), p. 23.

98   Simpson, op. cit. (note 35), p. 355.

99   Quoted William Allen, *A Defence of English Catholics*, ed. Robert M. Kingdon (Ithaca: Cornell University Press, 1965), p. 72.

100 Michel Foucault, *The History of Sexuality*, trans. Robert Hurley, 3 vols (Harmondsworth: Penguin, 1981), vol. 1: *Introduction*, p. 59; Elizabeth Hanson, *Discovering the Subject in Renaissance England* (Cambridge: Cambridge University Press, 1998), p. 48.

101 Katharine Eisaman Maus, 'Proof and Consequence: Inwardness and its Exposure in the English Renaissance', *Representations*, 34 (Spring 1991), p. 46; Patricia Parker, '*Othello* and *Hamlet*: Dilation, Spying, and the "Secret Place" of Woman', *Representations*, 44 (Fall 1993), p. 84.

102 Taylor, op. cit. (note 50), p. 314.

103 Quoted Hanson, op. cit. (note 100), p. 48; and Allen, op. cit. (note 99), p. 72. For an incisive commentary on this episode see Scott Wilson, 'Racked on the Tyrant's Bed: The Politics of Pleasure and Pain and the Elizabethan Sonnet Sequence', *Textual Practice*, 3:2 (Summer 1989), pp. 244–7.

104 Quoted Schoenbaum, op. cit. (note 27), p. 47.

105 Robert Stevenson, *Shakespeare's Religious Frontier* (London; Routledge, 1958); Ian Wilson, *Shakespeare: The Evidence* (London: Headline, 1993); Park Honan, *Shakespeare:*

A Life (Oxford: Oxford University Press, 1998); Anthony Holden, *William Shakespeare: His Life and Work* (London: Little, Brown and Co., 1999).

106 Robert Greene quoted in Schoenbaum, op. cit. (note 27), p. 115. Greene was Shakespeare's rival for the patronage of Ferdinando Stanley.

107 Historic Manuscripts Commission, 9: Salisbury Mss, vol. 16, p. 33: 30 January 1604. For Lancashire folk religion see Haigh, op. cit. (note 10), p. 321.

108 Robert Greene quoted in Schoenbaum, op. cit. (note 27), pp. 115–16.

109 John Munro, ed., *The Shakespeare Allusion Book* (London: Chatto and Windus, 1909), pp. 224–5.

3

Secret as a dumb man

Two comedies of Italy and
the genesis of secrecy

JUST before dawn on 25 June 1580 Edmund Campion landed beneath Dover Cliff, and 'climbing a great rock, fell upon his knees to commend to God his cause and his coming' to restore the faith to England. The night before, he wrote from Calais that the wind was set fair for his mission by 'the incredible comfort' it had received in Milan from Carlo Borromeo, so 'I think we are now safe, unless we are betrayed in these sea-side places'. The grand narrative of Catholic return seemed about to be fulfilled. In fact, we know Campion's movements had been relayed to Lord Burghley, from the day he set foot in Italy from Prague in the Emperor's coach, by a ring of spies, who included the double agent Anthony Munday. This playwright and informer would always remain on his tail. But disguised as a Dublin 'jewel merchant', who had for sale 'a pearl of great price', like the one in Matthew, the Jesuit was waved on by the Mayor of Dover, to join his partner Robert Parsons, before setting off on their crusade to politicise English Catholics into resistance, which first took them from the London home of Sir William Catesby to his house at Lapworth Park, near Stratford.[1] There, during September, the 'pious terrorists' gave out copies of a Testament of faith they had themselves been given by Borromeo,[2] and as one of the first to sign, we think, was John Shakespeare, it seems vital to consider what this mission from Milan might have meant to his son, whose career would start, in *The Two Gentlemen of Verona*, with a broken journey to the city, and end, in *The Tempest*, with hope of finally arriving there, where 'Every third thought' shall be a grave (5.1.312). Certainly, the blessing from Milan was mixed, as the Testament, composed by Borromeo to stiffen opposition to Protestantism, compounded the reputation of his diocese as more fundamentalist than even its nominal Duke, Philip II of Spain. The charismatic and fanatic Cardinal was distrusted in Madrid, indeed, as a rival to the occupying Hapsburgs, who might even 'provoke a revolt in Milan to chase the Spaniards out'.[3] Borromeo's subsidy of the missionaries, and offer to 'receive with all charity' any recruits sent to him,[4] might support Campion's claim to be innocent of Spanish intrigues, therefore, but suggests that one reason why Milan stayed in Shakespeare's imagination as a far-off goal and destination was because of its association with this poisoned chalice: the first and last of all those places in his plays which lie beyond the horizon of the text; spaces of total revelation, so utopian that they retain the transcendence of 'a pearl of great price'.

In 1580, Campion and his missionaries evidently made for Stratford as the end of a line of communication which stretched there from Milan. But one of those who did not arrive from the continent was Thomas Cottam, the younger brother of the town's Grammar School master, who had been described by Munday in such detail that he was arrested at Dover, with the result that the entire itinerary of the mission was soon known to the authorities.[5] He had in his pocket, most disastrously, a letter from Robert Debdale, a seminarian in Rome and, since January, Rheims, addressed to his 'right well-beloved parents' at Shottery, the hamlet a mile west of Stratford, enclosing 'certain tokens' of Counter-Reformation faith: 'a gilt crucifix and medal' for his father, rosaries for his mother and sister Joan, a Roman coin for his sister Alice, French ones for his brother Richard and his brother-in-law John Pace, and two other strings of rosary beads 'to be divided' amongst his friends.[6] With ghoulish irony, it would be the grisly relics of Cottam and Campion themselves that Debdale would later use in the lurid exorcisms which made him notorious, and which haunted Shakespeare long enough for them to inspire Edgar's desperate antics in *King Lear*, after the Jesuit had himself followed his mentors to the scaffold. As Frank Brownlow comments, Shakespeare's biographers have been astonishingly reluctant to explore the connection; but one reason why Debdale's sensational story continued to fascinate the dramatist is that they may have shared great-grandparents, as Shakespeare's grandmother, Mrs Robert Arden, née Palmer (Debdale's alias), is thought to have been the exorcist's great-aunt.[7] Another reason is the more immediate closeness of these two Stratford contemporaries and probable cousins, since the priest had grown up a next-door neighbour to Anne Hathaway, whose father was the regular business associate of Pace. And when Debdale went on, in his letter, 'commending my especial friend Mr Cottam, who hath been unto me the half of my life', for 'his loving kindness showed and bestowed upon me', an intimate link is revealed between Shakespeare's Warwickshire milieu and the Lancashire Ribble Valley of the Cottams, where the future dramatist may himself shortly afterwards have stayed. So, if Shakespeare attended Stratford Grammar School, where the master surely waited in anxiety for news of his absent brother, this mission from Milan would have marked any adventure of young gentlemen in Italy with danger, and given real urgency to that 'underlying opposition between England and Italy' which critics now see as a mainspring of his plots.[8]

The interrogators would delay six months before applying torture instruments to the brother of the Stratford teacher, but his absence from the feast when Campion distributed the Testament from Milan must have overshadowed the event, and put Shakespeare's own path towards Rome in fiction under a sinister sign. In what looks like a reference to the mission, Debdale had cryptically enjoined his relations to 'take counsel' from Cottam 'in matters of great weight'. The priest had presumably arranged to lodge with them at Shottery, but, when the other missionaries arrived without him, these 'great matters' suddenly became truly grave. For Shakespeare's relatives and teacher never would, of course, receive news of the two 'special friends' in Italy until it was too late. And so, while these Jesuits might have planted an image of ultramontane Milan as, in the words of a recent historian, so 'rationalized, bureaucratized, hierarchized, officered, and submissive' as to be 'the single most developed cultural space in Europe',[9] they must also have terrified these Midlanders with an impression of this theocratic city as the capital of confession and a final repository of all their secrets, like that copy of the Milanese Testament that John Shakespeare was wise – or frightened – enough to hide between his roof-tiles. No wonder then, that if *The Two Gentlemen of Verona* is Shakespeare's earliest work, as editors presume, it should be not only a play about betrayal and broken faith but a text which is itself so evasive in meeting narrative expectations about its ultimate destination and design. For at Stratford in 1580 Campion's appearance from central Europe in his tragic motley must have seemed like that of a latter-day Pied Piper, charming the youth of the town to follow him to a far-away country about which they knew so little, but 'from whose bourn / No traveller returns' (*Hamlet*, 3.1.81–2). Certainly, the starting-point of Shakespeare's first drama is that for both travellers and those they leave behind at home the temptation of such a continental journey is the occasion for prayers and fears:

> Wilt thou be gone? Sweet Valentine, adieu.
> Think on thy Proteus when thou haply seest
> Some rare noteworthy object in thy travel.
> Wish me partaker in thy happiness
> When thou dost meet good hap; and in thy danger –
> If ever danger do environ thee –
> Commend thy grievance to my holy prayers;
> For I will be thy beadsman, Valentine.
> (*Two Gents*, 1.1.11–18)

'To Milan let me hear from thee by letters', Proteus urges his friend, 'And I likewise will visit thee with mine' (1.1.57); but their incriminating mail must have a delayed delivery, because, after being reported to have 'parted to embark for Milan' (71), the next we learn of him is that the 'youthful Valentine / Attends the Emperor in his royal court' (1.3.26); and soon Proteus has heard how he is 'daily graced by the Emperor' (58), and is himself joining one Don Alphonso with 'other gentlemen journeying to salute the Emperor', and 'commend their service to his will' (39–42), while even the servant Launce is 'going with Sir Proteus to the Imperial's court' (2.3.4). Editors have offered various explanations for this detour 'to the Emperor's court' (1.3.38): proposing that Milan and the empire are one place; that references to a spectral Emperor come from a source; or that scenes have been cut. Tantalisingly, though, when he rejoins Valentine, Proteus has earned 'commendation from great potentates' which testify how fit he is 'to be an emperor's counsellor' (2.4.70–9). And it is these credentials that suggest why the royal road to the emperor might offer an alternative path, not taken in this text, towards a different end. For there were, Bossy explains, two roads to Rome Elizabethan Catholics could choose. Both met in Milan, but, unless the Netherlands were blocked by war, the French was less used than the 'imperial route', via a quick crossing to Antwerp, along the postal road to Augsberg and Prague, then into Italy by the Brenner Pass. As if alarmed by the implications, *The Two Gentlemen* seems to recoil from this trans-Alpine choice, which would lead, Bossy shows, to a split among English Catholics between supporters of Habsburg and Stuart claimants to the throne.[10] For it is, of course, the Hispanic company of 'Don Alfonso' which points to the court of King Philip's nephew, Rudolf II, in Prague, as a lost location in this play, and the English College in Rome, under its Rector Alphonso Agazzari, as the final destination for those émigrés who intend to serve the Emperor. In 1577 Campion had written from Prague to Robert Arden, a Jesuit, later Canon of Toledo, operating in Warwickshire and possibly related to Shakespeare's mother, that his 'abundant harvest' of recruits should be told of the hospitality awaiting them if the storms of persecution swept them towards 'the pleasant and blessed shore' of Bohemia.[11] Arden returned to Prague in 1580; but one of the young gentlemen of Stratford who followed him there, *en route* to Italy, was Arthur Throckmorton, the twenty-three-year-old lord of the manor of Alderminster (which he later rented to Shakespeare's friend Thomas Russell), whose diary recorded the opportunities that drove so many Midlanders to seek a haven on the metaphorical coast of Bohemia:

> January 3 [1581]. At the disputations at the Jesuits' college, where proceeded six Bachelors of Arts, having seven questions: two of metaphysics, three of physics, and two of logic, beginning at one in the afternoon. Georgius Warus, an Englishman [George Ware, a former Fellow of Oriel College, Oxford], Moderator and Reader, in that house, of Philosophy … January 4. Saw a dialogue of the birth of Our Lord Jesus Christ … Gave a dollar to Father Robert [Arden] the Jesuit.[12]

'Behold the Jesuits', exclaimed Sir Edward Sandys, after a European tour in 1599, 'the great politicians and orators of the world … In all places wherever they plant nests, they open free schools for all studies of humanity. To these flock the best wits and principal men's sons … and in truth, such is their diligence and dexterity in instructing, that even Protestants send their sons unto their schools'.[13] So, when Shakespeare opens *The Two Gentlemen of Verona* with Valentine's concern that 'My father at the road / Expects my coming, there to see me shipp'd' (1.1.53–4); and with 'sad talk' of Proteus's uncle 'in the cloister' about the boy's reluctance to be 'put forth' to 'the wars' or 'studious universities' (1.3.1–10), he may be reviving a memory of family pressure to conform to the model of local contemporaries such as Throckmorton, by travelling towards Rome, via an education in Bohemia. In particular, the anxiety that surrounds the separation of the friends perhaps registers the dilemma presented to English Catholics when Campion left Oxford, and (after helping plan Trinity College Dublin) founded the School of Rhetoric in 1574 at the Clementinum, the Jesuit Academy in Prague. As Alison Shell notes, visits to the colleges at Saint-Omer, Douai and Rome were forbidden by Elizabethan travel licences;[14] but, since it was situated in a predominantly Protestant city, the new Czech University offered Englishmen the chance to experience Jesuit teaching without falling foul of the law. Yet visitors such as Throckmorton would be exposed there to plays the priests staged as part of their pedagogy: dramas of discovery and revelation with themes of exile or rebirth, like Campion's own *Ambrosia*, that made them, to English eyes, among 'the most powerfully subversive texts' of the age.[15] As Sandys commented, Jesuit education aimed 'to plant with great exactness and skill, an extreme detestation of the other party ... For which cause, I have seem them in their disputations inflame their scholars with such fierceness, as to seem to be at the point of flying each in other's face, to the amazement of strangers who had never seen the like before.'[16] It was the intensity of this intellectual vortex which attracted a brilliant coterie of English emigres to Rudolfine Bohemia, ranging fron the alchemist John Dee to the poetess Elizabeth Weston.[17] But given Prague's volatility as a bearpit of competing faiths, it is highly suggestive for Shakespeare's development, that having set out so hopefully for the Emperor's 'studious universities', neither Valentine nor Proteus once mentions the city of Rudolf again. In *The Two Gentlemen of Verona* the Counter-Reformation wind that blows towards Bohemia remains unexploited; yet not before it has carried the protagonists off route, as it may have taken their creator himself far away from Oxford.

Like Shakespeare's aspiring courtiers, after reeling from Campion's Academy, the squire of Alderminster travelled south to Italy, where he was welcomed in the ultra circles of his uncle Michael Throckmorton, the secretary of Cardinal Pole, who had retired to die in Mantua. Catholic links between Mantua and Prague were strong, and Italians had funded the Clementinum.[18] But in both Italy and Bohemia this young gentleman of Stratford was feeling his way with an opportunism which seems equivalent to the fickleness of Shakespeare's plot. Thus, in Prague on 3 February. 'we heard how Lord Arundel and others conspire to kill her Majesty and other lords of the Council in a masque', he recorded. So, he 'sent home letters to the Queen' reporting the tip-off, but also to Lord Henry Windsor, a Catholic conspirator.[19] Throckmorton would ultimately disown his family's papist politics; but in 1581 his tour was as speculative as that of another, more illustrious, young visitor to Prague, Philip

Sidney. In his biography of the poet, Alan Stewart details the precautions, involving study of Livy, for Sidney's official mission 'to salute the Emperor', prompted by the need for intelligence at a time when it looked as if 'the Holy Roman Empire was in the hands of Spaniards: Catholic counsellors and cardinals who had the ear of the new emperor and were pouring into it the "poison of the Roman court"'.[20] Sidney reported to Walsingham that Rudolf was likely to confirm these fears, being 'sullen, very secret, resolute ... and extremely Spaniolated'.[21] But this did not deter him from accompanying the saturnine monarch to the Clementinum, where they were both spellbound by Campion's lectures. Sidney had been chosen as ambassador to appeal to the student prince as a contemporary; but his superiors might not have authorised the initiative with which he also insinuated himself into the Jesuit's quarters for a meeting which, according to Parsons, was fraught with dangers, since 'Sir Philip was afraid of spies set and sent about him by the English Council'.[22] For whether or not he was becoming a closet Catholic, his kinship with the papist Shelleys and his own father's help, while Viceroy of Ireland, in Campion's escape, explain why the Jesuit was so excited by the possibility that Sidney might slip his minders and defect.[23] Yet Campion's over-excited relay of their talks to Nicholas Saunders, at that moment organising the invasion of Ireland, is sensational enough to suggest why the young Emperor's Jesuitical court remained only a hypothetical terminus in *The Two Gentlemen of Verona*, as Shakespeare veered away from such a self-incriminating association, to offer his characters a different fate:

> Now listen to my news. The Emperor Rudolf, a prudent, brave, and good youth, and a sincere son of the Church, has fixed upon himself the eyes and hearts of the Germans and Bohemians. If he lives, great things are expected of him. The Empress Dowager, Maximilian's widow and a sister of Philip of Spain, is living in Prague. A few months ago Philip Sidney came from England to Prague magnificently provided. He had much conversation with me, I hope not in vain, for to all appearance he was most eager. I commend him to your sacrifices, for he asked for the prayers of all good men. Tell this to Dr Nicholas Saunders, because if any one of the labourers sent into the vineyard from the Douai seminary has an opportunity of watering this plant, he may watch the occasion for helping a poor wavering soul. If this young man, so wonderfully beloved and admired by his countrymen, chances to be converted, he will astonish his father, the Deputy of Ireland, his uncles the Dudleys, Cecil himself, and all young courtiers. Let it be kept secret.[24]

In the castle of secrets, Campion was sure he had extracted the envoy's inner truth. In fact, Sidney was probably playing the Jesuit at his own game, the equivocation Shakespeare also seems to have seen as the Habsburg element from the start. Rudolf II's 'mad, fantastical trick to steal from the state' and abandon Vienna in 1583 for a secretive 'beggary he was not born to' may have prompted the dramatist, for instance, in a game aborted in *Two Gentlemen*, but perfected with the ludic Duke in *Measure for Measure*, of having some 'ghostly father' shadow his plot, while 'Some say he is with the Emperor of Russia; and other some, he is in Rome' (3.2.88; 4.3.48). Recently, David Scott Kastan has claimed that the reclusive Emperor, who was finally deposed in 1610, ghosts *The Tempest*, too, as a double of the Duke of Milan who is likewise 'transported / And rapt in secret studies' (1.2.76).[25] What Shakespeare learned from Prague missionaries was the gamesmanship, perhaps, of occupying at least two places at once. So, if even the Bohemian diversion of *The Winter's Tale* can be glimpsed in the aborted Czech detour of the early play, that is because the author seems there, as its editors complain, to want to visit so many places at once. This play may originally have had just two settings, but, from the moment Valentine enters to exit, and 'see the wonders of the world abroad', rather than stay 'dully sluggardised at home' (1.1.6), Shakespeare's technical need to keep his dangerous liaisons moving, so the travellers can write to one another, seems to complement his own quest for 'enfranchisement' (2.4.90; 3.1.151). Thus, although almost the entire plot consists of scenes of farewell, no one is certain where they are going, or whether they have arrived at Milan, back in Verona, or even in Padua. This hesitation may well express the writer's own misgivings about an ultramontane future, for there is something sinister in the Duke of Milan's patronage of 'heaven-bred poesy' – after Proteus tells him 'Orpheus' lute was strung with poets' sinews' (3.2.71–7) – seeing how 'the Thracian singer' who looked into the abyss had been ripped to pieces by the 'Bacchanals' (*Dream*, 5.1.48). Tridentine Milan may have been a papist parnassus for the 'exquisite detail' with which its artists were super-vised,[26] but from the day his teacher, Simon Hunt, left in 1576, Shakespeare witnessed a generation of scholars depart Stratford for Italy, only to die there or at Tyburn. He was perhaps among the 'school-fellows and common people', for instance, who saw off Throckmorton's saintly and self-righteous cousin Edward, the heir to Coughton, in 1580, bound for early death in Rome, amid 'the tears of relations and lamentations of servants, as if in a funeral procession'.[27] But, if so, he distanced himself from such hysteria with Crab's dogged refusal to 'shed one tear', when, according to Launce, 'A Jew would have wept to see our parting' (*Two Gents*, 2.3.1–32). Instead, a text by the most famous of murdered poets, Christopher Marlowe, prefaces *The Two Gentlemen of Verona* with an epigraph suggesting that the gift of a martyr's education is more profound in fiction than in fact:

> PROTEUS: Upon some book of love I'll pray for thee.
> VALENTINE: That's on some shallow story of deep love,
> How young Leander cross'd the Hellespont.
> PROTEUS: That's a deep story, of a deeper love,
> For he was more than over shoes in love.
> VALENTINE: 'Tis true; for you are over boots in love,
> And yet you never swum the Hellespont.
> (1.1.20–6)

With its schizoid splitting of boats and boots, or ships and sheep, and fretting over the parental impatience to see sons 'shipp'd' (53–6), Shakespeare's earliest comedy condenses all the uneasiness of an enforced Elizabethan journey to Milan, but, notoriously, *by sea*. This is a play, in other words, that seems so evasive in its geography because it encodes the reluctance of one who (we can assume) 'never swum the Hellespont' to take that passage to the capital of the Counter-Reformation that carried so many English martyrs to their deaths, 'blasting ... in the prime', as Valentine grieves, 'all the fair effects of future hopes' (1.1.47–50). Luckily, the only victim in this particular mad Italian escapade is not even the dog Crab, but another little dog 'stol'n ... by the hangman boys in the market place' (4.4.56); and, if the travellers never do quite arrive in Milan, that is because the Duke's daughter reveals a secret exit which provides an alternative to this murderous public space, when Silvia foils her father's 'spies' by escaping 'Out at the postern by the abbey wall', intending, she claims, to confess later on 'at Friar Patrick's cell' (5.1.3–9). *Friar Patrick* was, in fact, the alias of Campion, adopted at Lough Derg in Ireland, where St Patrick had supposedly discovered the mouth of Purgatory. It is significant, therefore, that it is 'by Saint Patrick' that Hamlet swears to the Ghost (*Hamlet*, 1.5.136), since, as Stephen Greenblatt reminds us, the 'vast unreal space' of Purgatory invoked in Borromeo's Testament as a court of ultimate truth, and by the Prince as a cellar where souls are bound to walk, was one of the most terrifying reinventions of the Counter-Reformation Baroque. So, the mere mention of 'confession / At Patrick's cell' (5.3.40) opens up a gaping chasm beneath Shakespeare's text.[28] Nor was this abyss merely theological, for, as Parsons admitted, the embarrassment of Campion's militant alias was one for which he would die, since his adoption of the name Patrick and an Irish accent inevitably reminded the English authorities of the one incontrovertible fact which continues (even among Catholic historians) to stain his martyrdom with the taint of treason, that his mission coincided so suspiciously with the long-planned Spanish invasion of Ireland:

> (We) wanted to call Campion Peter; but he, remembering how well he had escaped from Ireland under St. Patrick's patronage, would take no other name but his old one of Patrick, albeit when we were to enter into England ... the name, being Irish, might bring him in question; for Ireland at that time was noised to be in trouble by the arrival of Dr. Saunders with some soldiers from the Pope for the assistance of certain Catholic noblemen in arms for their religion, as they said.[29]

When Duke Theseus condemns Hermia, in *A Midsummer Night's Dream*, either to be executed or 'in shady cloister mewed' (1.1.71), he seems to concede that power does meet its terminus in Shakespearean drama, in the shadows 'underneath that consecrated roof' (*Twelfth*, 4.3.25), which is the sanctum of those who forsake 'the full stream of the world to live in a nook merely monastic' (*As You Like It*, 3.2.375): where Romeo is 'hid at Friar Laurence' cell', Juliet helped by Friar John (*Romeo*, 3.2.141;5.2.1); Hero 'secretly kept' by Friar Francis (*Much Ado*, 4.1.202); Olivia married by an unnamed Friar (*Twelfth*, 5.1.149); and the Duke of Vienna, as Friar Lodowick, given 'secret harbour' by Friar Thomas, before returning with Friar Peter (*Measure*, 1.3.4; 5.1.151). So, as Jean Howard wryly notes of the incident that now occurs in *The Two Gentlemen of Verona*, when, instead of waiting 'At Friar Patrick's cell', Silvia meets yet another Friar Laurence, 'As he in penance wandered thtough the forest', who may or may not be the mysterious 'brother in the cloister' who started the action with his 'sad talk' urging Proteus to emigrate (1.3.2; 4.3.43; 5.3.35–40), the headache for the editor is that at any one time in Shakespeare there may always be 'more than one friar in the forest',[30] about to emerge from some priest-hole or mere monastic nook. But, tellingly, the lovers of *The Two Gentlemen* never do meet up at Friar Patrick's ominous cell, preferring to return home with outlaws, who look reassuringly like actors. Evidently, that ancient tunnel through the Abbey provided a bolt-hole not only from the Duke's spies but also from sectarian extremes. So, what the writer rivals called a Jesuitical 'upstart crow'[31] seems to re-enact in the forest scenes of this proto-type of all his works is how he changed confession for performance and a clerical black for player's plumes, as he groped for a way out of his liaison with those real Jesuit outlaws who followed 'Friar Patrick' from Milan. Yet by evading the piazza with those cruel hangman boys, and rerouting its lovers around the derelict Abbey and 'St Gregory's well' (4.2.84), *The Two Gentle-men of Verona* also reveals how his proximity to Campion's mission might have shaped Shakespeare's entire dramatic strategy, which in an age of violent confessional extremes seems terrorised into resisting the petrifying spaces of the Baroque, and into endlessly deferring the arrival in an absolutist Milan, by seeking refuge in some secluded retreat – half-way between Canterbury and Rome – such as a ruined convent, moated grange, abandoned cave or wayside shrine. Like those two attendant lords expecting merely to 'swell a progress, start a scene or two' by acting, in Tom Stoppard's comi-tragedy, when spotlit by the brilliance of the Counter-Reformation, it seems that Shakespeare's young gentlemen just 'want to go home'.[32]

It was to ease his passage home from Catholic Italy, according to his own account, and prove he had never 'forsaken his native country, to live, contrary to the law, beyond the seas, under the Pope's obedience', that Anthony Munday turned over to Burleigh and Walsingham the information he claimed he had collected on Campion's mission deliberately to 'undermine them and sift out their purposes!' And when the Jesuit was ambushed on 16 July 1581, whilst preaching to a congregation of recusants and Oxford undergraduates at Lyford, it was this spy who rushed out *A Brief Discourse of the Taking of Edmund Campion Gathered by A.M.* as a supposed eyewitness report on the 'dragging forth of the priests from a cramped little den walled-up over the stairs'.[33] Thus, it was Munday's part in this catastrophe which makes it so significant that when Shakespeare wrote his play about the journey to Milan, which opens with Proteus commending Valentine to 'holy prayers' and piously pledging with his rosary to be his 'beadsman' (*Two Gents*, 1.1.18), he should model it, as Giorgio Melchiori has pointed out, on the informer's comedy of *The Two Italian Gentlemen: Fedele and Fortunio*.[34] For the eighteen-year-old Munday had travelled to Milan in 1578 himself, side by side with another young student named Thomas Nowell, who was heir to one of the great Lancashire recusant families, for all the world like two gentlemen out of a romantic comedy. Dining in the Cardinal's palace on Christmas Day, they were regaled by Hugh Griffin, a Welsh priest 'notorious as an agitator',[35] with details of how their co-religionists in the North of England would shortly be led to 'overrun the island at their pleasure, and make all Catholics "Kings and Dukes and Earls"'.[36] Munday instantly reported this advance notice of a papal invasion to his controllers in London. For though he would later claim to have been recruited by Catholic 'persuaders', eager to supply 'any young gentleman that is willing to travel' with 'sufficiency of money' and 'letters for his entertainment' in continental seminaries, 'that he shall not only be welcomed gratefully, but also esteemed equal with any other', he was, in fact, operating from the start as a mole and informer for (but also against) his long-time patron, Edward de Vere, Earl of Oxford, the son-in-law of Lord Burghley.[37]

'Favour comes by conformity', observed Munday of his Italian journey, 'and death by obstinacy'; so, 'humbly manifesting his willingness to learn', according to his biographer, 'he incidentally picked up the locations of half a dozen houses in London' where Mass was said, 'along with such remarks as that Elizabeth was a "usurping Jezebel", which he filed for future use', and which proved more useful to his governmental career than all his poetry and plays.[38] No wonder, therefore, that Shakespeare answered this Protean role-player with a drama which at first seems destined to reach 'All happiness in Milan' (1.1.61), but then side-steps any such incriminating disclosure. For while Donna Hamilton has recently argued that, because Oxford might have been a crypto-Catholic, Munday probably began his Italian adventure as a *sincere* 'Romanist dissenter', before he realised he was 'truly in danger and switched sides to save his life',[39] what is striking about all his writing, Tracey Hill remarks, is its inquisitorial mania for discovery and mastery of the total truth. Munday was indeed sincere, Hill concludes: but as a 'Cretan Liar', who shared with his masters in Burghley's office the desperation 'to uphold a complete dichotomy between truth and falsity', and to grasp at such 'hysterical assertions of credibility' that these could never disguise the falsehoods and betrayals on which his survival hinged.[40] As Cardinal Allen noticed, whenever a death sentence on one of his former brothers was in doubt, 'Munday was ready with oath and testimony to help at a pinch'; so, it may have been intended as a barb when Francis Meres praised this avid practiser, in his 1598 review of English stage, as 'our best plotter'.[41] 'The facility would serve him well',

Charles Nicholl dryly confirms, in espionage as much as entertainment.[42] Thus, his *Two Italian Gentlemen* is in the grip of the informer's law, that the last laugh will belong to those who 'Unseen by any, yet viewing all, / A pretty scout set to take a knave in a pitfall' (2.1.86), and its action depends on the watch committee's motto that 'visibility is a trap'.[43] Technically virtuosic, its panopticism thereby initiated what William Slights terms the 'multi-perspectivism' of Elizabethan theatre, where, in a world of spies, intelligencers and searchers, it is impossible 'to locate any private space or sanctuary' from exposure.[44] For it cannot be chance that the plays written by Munday and the other informers in the pay of Elizabethan intelligence, though fixated on disguise and dissimulation, should be locked into a scenario of discovery and disclosure, nor that their characters are all, by light of day, revealed to be such *observed* observers:

> In this drama of 'observers' and 'observed', at the core of which are spying and secrecy, we the spectators lend ourselves to a scenario in which the characters on stage reflect on the disparity between illusion and reality. Any observer is, in turn, observed. This seems to be the underlying pattern. Observation is linked to experience. Thus, the study of physiognomy is matched by an ability to read the psychic complexity of the observed. Here the idea of outer appearance relating to inner qualities is fundamental. Even plays like Middleton's, Ford's, and Webster's echo the premises of Elizabethan physio-psychology, in which observation leads to knowledge.[45]

In Shakespeare's shadow, no one struggled more for light than 'Judas Munday',[46] the eclipsed rival mocked for his Italian exploits as 'pageant-poet to the city of Milan'.[47] There is an anecdote which epitomises his exhibitionism and might stand for the self-destruction of all those who fought, in Shakespearean London, to steal the limelight. In 1580 Munday had just returned from Italy to perform '*extempore*, like the Italian comedians', on themes suggested by his audience, when 'those gentlemen which were present, being weary of his folly, hissed him from the stage'.[48] Evidently, the barrackers were Catholics, provoked by the performer's betrayals, since we owe the story to Thomas Pound, an uncle of Shakespeare's patron, the Earl of Southampton, and a priest (who had himself been applauded for his acting before the Queen at Kenilworth) who spent many years in gaol on allegations of such informers.[49] And it was this catastrophic scene of self-debasement, his biographer claims, that stung the actor into accepting a fee from the Corporation of London to sound his *Blast of Retreat from Plays and Theatres*, disowning the theatre and villifying the performers as 'brawlers, roisterers, loiterers, and ruffians, as variable in heart as in their parts', and the Bankside playhouses as 'chapels of Satan' infested with priests disguised in gentlemen's livery, who came to say Mass before or after the performance. It had been during the Roman Carnival of 1579 that Munday studied the *commedia dell'arte* and marvelled at a theatre state where 'gentlemen attire themselves in diverse forms of apparel, some like

Women, others like Turks, and everyone in contrary order of disguising'.[50] But now, he protested, 'the Lord of His goodness had called him home' from that land of 'impurity and abomination', like the recognition scene in one of his plays, and so his stripping of the stage climaxed with an anthem to the solar enlightenment of the Church of England: 'The Lord look upon us and open our eyes', the pamphlet prayed, 'that we may see our sin and loathe it in ourselves.' And in a citation recalling the author's recent exposure, the polemic ended with paranoid aggression from St. Paul: 'All things, when they are reproved of the light, are manifest. / For it is the light that maketh all things manifest.'[51]

New Historicism has alerted critics to the theatricality that destabilises anti-theatrical rhetoric; but when Munday returned to the stage soon after this anti-theatrical tirade, 'like a dog', Pound said, 'to his vomit', it was anti-theatrical rhetoric which destabilised his theatre, and inaugurated an enlightenment drama for London fatally committed to the iconoclasm he quoted from St Paul: 'For ye were in darkness, but now are ye the light of the Lord. Walk as children of light, and have no fellowship with the works of darkness. For it is a shame even to speak of those things are done in secret.'[52] It was the same Letter St Paul addressed to the 'nimble jugglers that deceive the eye, / Dark-working sorcerers that change the mind, / Soul-killing witches that deform the body, / Disguised cheaters' and 'prating mountebanks' of Ephesus which Shakespeare ironised in *The Comedy of Errors* (1.2.97–102). But one reason why Munday remained in Shakespeare's shadow was the consistency with which this spying intelligencer's dramaturgy would follow the Pauline faith of his *Retreat from Plays*: that 'the eyes are two open windows to the soul. Nothing entereth more effectually into memory than that which cometh of seeing. Things heard pass lightly away, but the tokens of that which we have seen stick fast in us, whether we will or no.'[53] Howard has described such anti-theatrical discourse as 'feudal' in its esentialist belief that 'appearances falsify a *true* identity';[54] but its valorisation of sight implies a relation to the ideals of the Baroque. For Munday's credo, that 'light makes all things manifest', anticipates the Baroque visuality discussed by Martin Jay in his study of ocularcentrism, where fear of 'being an object of another's look created a theater of resentment in which being seen was less a mark of glory than shame', and 'brightness of daylight signalled more than visibility: it meant as well the absolute gaze, the judging eye of God or the sun'. Jay locates the birth of a modern culture of surveillance, with its oscillation between visual security and anxiety, precisely, that is to say, in the absolutist court that Munday made his home, and where 'the insatiable desire and unresolvable dread that accompanies visual experience' for modernity originated in a systematic employment of spies, decipherers, *agents provocateurs*, inquisitors and torturers: the new political order that was 'bewildering to outsiders but legible to those who knew how to read its meaning'.[55] What made Munday's 'theatre of resentment' so un-Shakespearean, in other words, was its faith in the transparency of the self: a paranoid delusion enacted in the

Prologue of his first play (which Shakespeare would so need to rewrite) when it was staged at court in 1584. before the supposedly radiant and omniscient Elizabeth:

> On every side wherein I this instant gaze,
> The glimpse of honour dims my dazzled eye,
> Which sight may set a stouter in amaze,
> And chiefly him that penned this comedy …
> He shoots at mirth, yet if he miss that white,
> Your Highness' pardon he doth humbly crave:
> Will wanted not to send his arrow right.
> But sith you please to see what mirth we have,
>   With Phoebus cast your fiery blaze aside,
>   That meaner men your presence may abide.[56]

In his study of 'Spying and Court Culture in the English Renaissance', *Sovereignty and Intelligence*, John Archer diagnoses Elizabethan courtiers as suffering from Schreber's Syndrome, named by Freud after a judge who feared penetration by the gaze of a castrating female. And Archer's characterisation of the English court as a scopic regime terrorised by a 'knowing woman who produced deep ambivalence in the men who surrounded her', seems apt for the narcissistic anxieties of the intelligencer and telltale whose alias was Antonius Auleus – Anthony the Courtier – self-styled son of a Staffordshire Catholic gentleman, whom those who knew him to be a Holborn printer's apprentice called 'cogging Munday'.[57] Acted under the eye of a sovereign saluted as both the source of light and the sun who sees everything, *Fidele and Fortunio* reveals the Protestant truth beneath Catholic appearances through the exposure of Munday's fall-guy, Captain Crackstone, whose very name ('Frangipietra' in the source) deconstructs to reveal the flawed champion of St Peter's rock – or Campion. A 'crafty knave' who runs rings round the pursuivants by his ability to 'nick them of their measure and the soldiers beguile', until 'One calls [him] Captain Cheese, another Captain Crust, / Another brave Crackstone, take which name ye list' (2.1.52), and who swaggers like one of the Jesuits in uniform stolen from a real dead Captain, spouting malapropisms and dog Latin, Munday's anti-hero is said to be an original of Falstaff.[58] If so, it would confirm identification of the fat knight as a hypocritical Puritan, constructed in retaliation for this gross travesty of a Catholic martyr.[59] For the driving force of *Fidele and Fortunio* is the surveillance system that breaks the Captain's aliases and disguises, as he 'braves it with the best in every company, / And knows where every gallant loves, and sees the remedy' (21). This is truly the inception of a drama, therefore, where power equals light and, as Slights says, 'someone always seems to be watching' to ensure that, 'secrets being too good not to be shared, suspenseful concealment is followed by exciting revelation', and 'by eavesdropping, skulking characters gain knowledge, often sexual or political, in full view of the audience but unobserved by anyone on stage'.[60] It can be no accident, in fact, that Munday's best-known text was a lyric on Diana and Actaeon, where 'wanton thoughts enticed [his] eye / To see what was forbidden', as the poet dreamed he 'Seem'd to see' the mysteries of the goddess.[61] For by inviting Elizabeth, as omnipotent spectator, to imitate the sun-god, and discard her 'fiery blaze', he was appealing for a blind eye to be turned not only to his counter-insurgency but to a whole economy of ghost writers and double agents in secret service of the Protestant light:

> If Apollo, the very brother of Diana, and Jupiter's son,
> For the love of a lady that was hard to be won,
> Thought it no shame in a shepherd's weed
> Himself to debase, the sooner to speed,
> Should I, that am not worthy to bear out Apollo's chamber pot, think any scorn,
> That these rascally rags by me should be worn ...
> Therefore, god Apollo, whose example I take,
> Vouchsafe to stay thy chariot awhile for my sake.
> Suffer not thy horses to hasten the day,
> But prolong the night, as when Jupiter thy father with Alcmena lay.
>
> (3.2.59–72)

Yearning to steal away the night-soil of the great, Munday's affiliation was truly with Hermes, 'god of going-between the living and the dead', the anal and violent thief on whom nothing is lost, since he is also the genie of interpretation.[62] But by 1594. when he wrote *The Terrors of the Night*, Thomas Nashe could scoff that a Munday-esque noctambulism was so pervasive that no plot was complete unless 'to add some credence unto it, the poet beginneth to tell how it was dark night when it was done, and how cheerful light had quite abandoned the firmament'.[63] *Fidele and Fortunio* sets the penumbral scene with a clockwork reflex of this tic: 'Soft, it is night' (2.1.1); 'Now it is the stillest time of night' (2.2.29); 'Content, for it is night' (4.2.32); 'It is night' (4.1.31); ''Tis now midnight' (5.1.14). But a clanging chime of 'night' on 'sight' also keeps the faith awake that 'light' will come, as day must follow dark: 'Soon at night / I will lay my meaning open before your sight' (1.2.34); 'We must withdraw ourselves and work it out of sight: the sun is set and now begins the night' (1.3.93); 'Be you here about the midst of night, / That when I come, you both of me have sight' (3.2.45); 'They shall play, if they will, from morning to night, / During which time they shall not come in my sight' (3.2.79); and 'We shall go batfowling this night / That of this pretty sport we may have sight' (4.5.22). This counterpoint upon the sight/blindness dyad is Munday's elaboration of his source, an Italian tragi-comedy of 1576 by Luigi Pasquaglio, which melo-dramatised the old story of a groom tricked by false accusations into slandering his bride. For what Munday adds to the plot is the paranoid politics that 'Justice's palace stands above the skies / And angry gods look down into our lives' (3.1.54). As his editor objects, the problem with this Baroque transparency is that it simplifies the Mannerism of the original, where a vendetta is justified precisely because truth is so opaque.[64] But Munday brought Pasquaglio's text from Rome, and it is easy to see why his shady Italians are no threat, by night or day, to English audiences. Here the popish idols of the witch Medusa are demystified as garbage; just as icons and relics were denigrated as 'crafty kind of cosenage, whereby ignorant people are beguiled', in Munday's anti-papist polemic, *The English Roman Life*.[65] When Crackstone is 'discovered' in the holy of holies, rising from a shrine of bones 'with one candle in his mouth and in each hand', the iconoclasm is, in fact, that of the Protestant vandal, Munday himself, towards the 'monstrous blindness' all such 'Romish Relics':

> In all these churches there be diverse relics, which make them haunted by multitudes, whereby the lazy friars get more riches … For at the altar where the relics be there standeth a basin, and the people cast money therein with great liberality. And there standeth a friar with a forked stick in his hand, and thereupon he taketh everybody's beads and wipes them along a great propor-tioned thing of crystal and gold wherein are a number of rotten old bones, which people credit to be the bones of saints; so wiping them along the outside of this tabernacle, the beads steal a terrible deal of holiness out of those bones, and God knows, the people think they do good service in it: Oh, monstrous blindness![66]

When in 1580 Munday wrote a version of the legend which Shakespeare would adapt in *The Merchant of Venice*, it was indicative that the pledge staked by yet another pair of his 'Noble Gentlemen of Italy' was not the pound of flesh of every other analogue, but an eye.[67] It is vision which is next to godliness in this Puritan heliopolitics, and night holds no terror in *Fidele and Fortunio* compared to daylight, when 'every eye our folly then doth see' (1.3.28). Munday's *Two Gentlemen* is the paradigm for later metropolitan drama in its devotion to such social transparency: the same dedication, its author claimed, that led him and his fellow-agent Charles Sledd to emerge into the sunshine with 'witness sound and plain' about Campion's missionaries: 'Myself a witness, Sledd, and all the rest / Who had their treasons noted in our book, / Account ourselves of God most highly blest, / Who gave us grace at such attempts to look'.[68] Nothing therefore disempowers the heroine more in the play's economy of being and seeing than refusing means 'To make you go invisible', on the grounds that 'these things are not for a mistress fit, / For if she be invisible, what profits it? / She shall behold the man she delighteth most to see, / But, being hid, she never can enjoy his company' (1.3.74). For what Munday's women learn, of course, is just how visibility entraps, when their two gentlemen contrive to 'shroud ourselves the while, that standing out of sight' (in the imperative rhyme), 'We may perceive what lovers haunt Victoria's house by night' (4.2.4). Fidele's threat to 'blaze' his lover 'out to every gazer's eye' (2.4.66), and Fortunio's to make her 'a mirror to this town, / A pointing stock to everyone that passeth up and down' (4.2.17), expresses the paranoia, therefore, that engulfs all Munday's characters, until it is displaced on to

Crackstone, when he is carted 'With mirth and glee about the town, to put him to shame' (4.6,19), for courting Victoria himself. So, if the temptation of women occupies the symbolic place in this play of the blinding seduction of Rome, it is with Crackstone's exposure that the work comes closest to the visual anxieties of its author, the despised object of all 'gazers' eyes' (5.4.71), himself 'hissed' ignominiously off stage. *Fidele and Fortunio* is contemporary with another of Munday's counter-espionage commissions, *A Watchword to England to Beware Traitors*, and the glare in which the watch nets the Captain recapitulates his own 'best plot': his part in the capture and exhibition of the real 'glorious Captain' with whom he may briefly once have identified: the Jesuit commander, paraded through the streets of London 'in mock triumph, with a paper stuck in his hat with his title written, "Campion the Seditious Priest," the mob gazing with delight'.[69] For Munday returned from the Roman carnival with a Baroque sense of theatre as the space of revelation, and he stage-managed the ambush and executions of his travelling companions with what he imagined to be a genius for comic timing:

> When Campion, their glorious Captain, looked dead in the face as soon as he saw the place, and remained quaking and trembling unto death. Sherwood ran down the ladder when death should arrest him. Shert, who would have the people think he feared not death, yet catched hold of the halter when the cart was drawn away. Kirbie, quaking when he felt the cart go away, looked still how near the end of it he was, till he was quite beside. And Cottam, dismaying, died trembling and in great fear. These are the martyrs of the Romish Church, dismaying, trembling and fearful, as the eyewitnesses can bear me record.[70]

In Shakespeare's shadow, no one came nearer to exposing him to light than Munday, the messenger of death for so many 'gentlemen of Stratford'. For it was the rival dramatist who lurked behind another torturing playwright, the author of *Gorboduc* and Rackmaster, Thomas Norton (who saluted him as 'a man who wants no sort of wit'), taking notes, when, to extract names of his hosts, Cottam was subjected to 'a machine which made the rack seem child's play': the Scavenger's Daughter, an iron hoop to bend a prisoner over, and 'from excess of compression cause him to bleed profusely from the nostrils, or from the extremities of hands and feet'.[71] Munday's mercurial rise as a priest-hunter in the guise of a Messenger of Her Majesty's Chamber was explained by such victims as a psychopathic case of guilt displacement, fuelled by his terror of his own exposure as a committed seminarian in Rome, and the books he wrote to exculpate himself have been discounted by historians for 'a savagery and bigotry, which no scribe of the Inquisition could surpass'.[72] Yet what made even Holinshed quote Munday as the last word on Catholic prosecutions was his own certainty of manifest truth, and the supposedly spontaneous discovery scenes he staged at Tyburn – when he stepped out of the crowd to denounce and harass his former comrades as they stood in the noose – suggest why contemporaries found no contradiction between his histrionics and his histories. All were driven by the same discovery scenario that made the denouement of *Fidele and Fortunio* as predictable as its rhyme, and that inspired both the sameness of his imitators and Shakespeare's difference. In Shakespeare's shadow, it was to be the pursuivant's fate to dog his prey with challenges. So, when Munday exposed the clay feet of the Catholic martyr, Shakespeare's additions to *The Play of Thomas More* inserted into More's mouth the loyalty of an Elizabethan church papist; and when Munday heroised the Lollard John Oldcastle, that was because Shakespeare traduced the proto-Puritan as Falstaff. When Munday desacralised folk customs in *John a Kent*, Shakespeare restored them to mystery in *A Midsummer Night's Deam*. Likewise, when one writer set the Robin Hood story, with *As You Like It*, in a Forest which might be taken for the Ardennes of the seminaries, the other reassigned the legend to the family tree of the Earl of Huntingdon, a Protestant claimant to Elizabeth's crown. In art and life, no one shadowed Shakespeare closer than the Queen's so-called Messenger. Yet the quarry turned to confront his pursuer only once in print. Shakespeare's sole quotation of the recusant-hunter is a phrase which reeks, however, of the torture-chamber. And it pointedly occurs in the tragedy of treason, *Macbeth*, which remembers Munday's tell-tale image, from *The Death of Robert Earl of Huntingdon*, as if marking the mass murderer with the indelible stigma of his crimes, of 'multitudes of seas died red with blood'.[73]

In Munday's version of Robin Hood, Marion's father feigns blindness to hide his identity from his daughter, but 'the dramatist, concentrating on the blindness, forgot that he invented it for a particular purpose', when the old man continues to act blind, even after his identity is known, until he meets the king.[74] The mistake underlines the ocularcentrism of this master of the pat 'catastrophe of the old comedy' (*Lear*, 1.2.123). So, when Munday, the poet of public exposure, translated a treatise on silence, Stephen Mullaney points out, it was to counter the secrecy of confession, on the lines of the opening of *Fidele and Fortunio*: 'He that discloseth the secrets of his mind / Doth rob himself of liberty.' Yet after uttering this maxim, Fidele immediately gives himself away to initiate the plot. Torturer and confessor had more in common with each other than with their victims. And Shakespeare, the playwright of private enclosure, made this resemblance the starting-point for the work of his which is most focused on secret treason and false disclosure, and which constitutes a decisive rebuttal of the theatre of suspicion instigated by his rival. For *Much Ado About Nothing* gives the definitive twist to the tale of slander that Munday made his own, announcing with its title a dissociation from the entire Elizabethan culture of surveillance and denunciation. Benedick's pledge at the outset that he can be as 'secret as a dumb man' about Claudio's love for Hero, propels a plot which will unfold, so he predicts, 'like the old tale: "It is not so, nor 'twas not so: but indeed, God forbid it should be so!"', without yielding the truth (*Much Ado*, 1.1.169–76). The allusion is to the English variant of the

Bluebeard story, in which the facts emerge only when the serial killer is finally faced with the irrefutable evidence of a severed hand. Known to folklorists as 'Mr Fox', the tale therefore provides a chilling threshold to Shakespeare's comedy of spying, concealment and symbolic murder, as its mise-en-scène is eerily close to the house of horror where Munday and his masters so craftily dismembered and obliterated the body parts of the Catholic captives they ensnared. *Much Ado About Nothing*, the sinister citation of 'Bluebeard' implies, is also about everything staged in that 'theatre of cruelties' where 'Hero' meant more than just a name:[75]

> Mr Fox frequently invited Lady Mary to come and see his house. So, one day that her brothers were absent … she determined to go thither, and set out unattended. When she arrived and knocked at the door no one answered. At length she opened it and went in. Over the portal was written, "Be bold, be bold, but not too bold." She advanced; over the staircase was the same inscription. She went up; over the entrance of a gallery, the same. She proceeded; over the door of a chamber, "Be bold, be bold, but not too bold, lest that your heart's blood run cold." She opened it; it was full of skeletons and tubs filled with blood.[76]

In Catholic martyrology, 'Mr Fox' was synonymous with the lying hypocrisy of 'Fox the martyrmonger', with his 'brainsick book' of Protestant martyrs.[77] So, accused of murder, the English Bluebeard smiles, '"It is not so, nor it was not so, and God forbid it should be so," which he repeats at every turn of the dreadful story, till Lady Mary retorts, "But it is so, and it was so, and here the hand I have to show," at the same time producing the hand from her lap, whereupon, her brothers drew their swords and cut Mr Fox into a thousand pieces.' The name of the intended victim may be coincidence, but Elizabethans might easily have decoded this gruesome scenario as an allegory of the plight of English Catholics, prey to a system of state violence whose perpetrators insisted 'It is not so, was not so, and God forbid it should be so', even as they twisted the rack. For the grim irony of Elizabethan torture (which, Elizabeth Hanson points out, was rationalised by one of its most enthusiastic practitioners, the Attorney General, Francis Bacon, as a method of investiga-tion comparable to scientific discovery)[78] is that an operation ostensibly con-ducted in quest of the hidden truth should itself be subject to such denials and lies. Thus, the torturers shared with the tortured, whose deniability they strove to penetrate, the same equivocation, when they protested, as Burghley did, that a suspect was racked only when it was evident 'by former detections, confess-ions and otherwise that the party tortured was guilty and did know, and could deliver truth, of the things wherewith he was charged'; or even, as rackmen such as Sir Edward Coke vouched, that 'the torment used in other countries … to make a malefactor confess himself … is not used in England', since 'there is no law to warrant tortures in this land'.[79] Hanson stresses that such weasel words were not hypocrisy; but the fact that torture supervised by Topcliffe was moved from the Tower to his residence in Bridewell reveals the obfuscation in face of the equally disingenuous claims by Catholics, such as the Jesuit Robert Southwell, that as political innocents, they suffered for their religion, the truth of which was thereby confirmed: 'Go on you Good Magistrates, rack us, torture us, yea grind us: your iniquity is proof of our faith'.[80] Each side in this deadly inquisitorial game being convinced of the truth of its bare-faced lies, the title of *Much Ado About Nothing* thus seems to refer to a confessional practice which (since it did not officially exist) created a world of difference *ex nihilo*; as Benedick jokes when Don Pedro orders him to 'speak his thought', and he swears – 'by my two faiths and troths' – that his own 'opinion' is of such secrecy 'that fire cannot melt out of me; I will die in it at the stake' (1.1.208–15):

DON PEDRO: What secret held you here, that you followed not to Leonato's?
BENEDICK: I would your grace would constrain me to tell.
DON PEDRO: I charge thee on thy allegiance.
BENEDICK: You hear, Count Claudio; I can be secret as a dumb man, I would have you think so; but, on my allegiance, mark you this, on my allegiance.

(1.1.190–95)

'On my allegiance, mark you': if *Much Ado About Nothing* is indeed Shakespeare's 'Bluebeard', then the Prince's challenge to the 'obstinate heretic' (216), Benedick, to disclose his secret *on his allegiance* situates this raillery in the same terrifying juridico-political zone as those tragedies which likewise originate with the sovereigns' tyrannical craving to possess their subjects' hearts, the despotic drive to 'find / Where truth is hid, though it were indeed / Within the centre' (*Hamlet*, 2.2.157–9). Turning the slander plot, therefore, back upon its evil genius, Shakespeare's updating of the story of the defamed bride associates Hero directly with Munday's victims, who all disappeared on his false testimony into that mysterious chamber of horrors at Bridewell, 'full of skeletons and tubs of blood'. In the earlier comedy, Proteus had repeated Munday's apostasy, when he changed faith in Milan and pledged to 'forget that Julia is alive' (*Two Gents*, 2.6.27); but in this later version the symbolic murder of the heroine is far closer to being literalised, and the substitution of the 'former Hero! Hero that is dead' with 'another Hero' (5.4.62–5) is nearer to the homicidal seriality of 'Bluebeard'. Yet, as Jonathan Bate has recently argued, the seriousness of Shakespeare's second Italian comedy comes not only from its sombre story but also from its sanguinary setting, which in the 1590s was the Mediterranean base of the Spanish fleet and the arsenal of Habsburg power.[81] To alarmist Londoners, the Messina of *Much Ado*, with its Spanish garrison, would have been more like the enemy camp, therefore, than even Borromean Milan. And, of course, Shakespeare further aggravated this anxiety by assigning his villain the very name of the English bogeyman, Don John, illegitimate half-brother of Philip II, and a prime agitator, during the author's boyhood, for a Protestant holocaust.

Morose at his 'imagined victimisation by his royal brother', the real Don John was an obvious model for the bastard of the play, since he was famous not only as a man who saw himself as King of England but as the victor of Lepanto, who sailed from Messina to rout the Turks.[82] Evidently, the location of this play of misplaced suspicion inside the Spanish citadel was far from casual. And if Don John also shares with Iago and Iachimo an association with the St Iago heroised by the Jesuits for conquering the Moors, his refusal to 'frame the season' for his 'harvest', and resolve to 'rather be a canker in a hedge than a rose' (1.3.23–5), affiliates him (and in their own imagery of 'weeds or flowers' (Sonnet 124)) with English recusants, likewise determined not to 'sing like birds i'the'cage' (*Lear*, 5.3.9), as he puts it, or to allow themselves to be 'enfranchised with a clog' (1.3.51). Such topicality seems further implicit in the anglicisation of the Governor of Messina, Leonato, and the Spanish occupiers, who talk more like the Lord Lieutenant and militia of some English Midland county than any Habsburg commandants. In this dialectic of mutual distrust, those who slander others are the bogeys themselves, therefore, of Puritan scaremongers, yet, as the doubles of English gentry, the least likely to be 'suspected' (3.3.48; 4.2.72) of treason. So, if Bate is right about the significance of the Hispanic setting, the moral of the 'Bluebeard' story for Shakespeare's audience would be just as Marina Warner suggests it was for Perrault's readers: as 'a warning against trespass' into forbidden knowledge, and a reminder that it was curiosity which killed the cat, yet one in which 'Eve is allowed to get away with it, and no one for once heaps blame on Pandora'.[83] Such a displacement of the great 'ado' about Elizabethan 'noting' would have been apt for the hermeneutic crisis generated, Katherine Maus explains, by the moral panic over the politicisation of English Catholics, when the assumption that outward conformity is 'all a queen can reasonably require' was suddenly transformed into the paranoid anxiety that 'good outward behaviour was merely the cloak for subversive conspiracies':

> This anxiety was only exacerbated by the willingness of Catholic casuists ... to exploit the hiddenness of the interior realm by resorting to various forms of equivocation. So, violating common law, Elizabeth's government begins to subject Catholics to torture, using bodily compulsions as a way to discover the truths of the soul. The demarcation between inside and outside, covert and obvious, soul and body, God and Caesar, persuasion and coercion, then threatens to collapse, even though those distinctions had been made earlier by Elizabeth's government.[84]

In *Much Ado* the violence that surrounds the Spaniards is displaced by a 'merry war' of words, and the 'skirmish of wit between them' defers the horror that lurks behind locked doors (1.1.50–1). None the less, as Greenblatt points out, in this drama language may be an alternative to violence, but it is violent itself, for what we glimpse in the symbolic murder of Hero is 'not only the malign power of slander, but the aggressive potential of even playful speech'.[85]

Thus, Leonato tells Claudio his 'slander hath gone through and through her heart, / And she lies buried ... in a tomb' (5.1.68–70); and when Beatrice orders Benedick to 'Kill Claudio' in revenge (4.1.285) the duel which then impends brings the comedy very close indeed to the atrocious termination of 'Mr Fox'. 'The more one attends to the language of *Much Ado*', writes Greenblatt, 'the more it seems saturated ... with references to war, plague, betrayal, heresy, burning at the stake, blinding, hanging, poisoning.' Yet, though 'recalled again and again by threat of disaster, by symbolic death, by public shaming ... these horrors are not realized, they are present as mere jokes'.[86] Thus, as Benedick quips, what this play clips is the violent signifier of foreign virility, the 'Great Cham's' (for which read King of Spain's) beard, so pulled by the Elizabethans privateers (2.1.233). It cannot be coincidence, therefore, that the work should date from a season of peace negotiations in 1598/9, when the claims of Philip II's daughter, the Infanta Isabella, to inherit the English crown as the latest Lancastrian contender, pushed by Parsons in *A Conference on the Succession*, were subjected to a frenzy of 'impossible slanders' by Protestants, and 'honest slanders' by Catholics keen to align her with their dream of a bloody settling of scores (2.1.124; 3.184).[87] The commission for a text which allays suspicions of a Spanish heiress, shows her father to be a toothless lion, and then disarms Aragonese troops as more ardent 'pipers' than conquistadores (5.4.126), might well have come from those with most to gain from discrediting the 'black legend' of Inquisitorial Spain. Even the historical setting of the play, following the 'action' airbrushed at the start as a rebellion by Don John, and a matter of 'but few' casualties (1.1.5–6) – which was, in fact, the fatal Sicilian Vespers of 1283?. when the Spaniards and citizens of Messina rose up at Easter to slaughter the French – seems chosen to defuse alarmist memories of the St Bartholomew's Day Massacre of Huguenots by the Catholic League in France, which took place during the celebrations of what was likewise supposed to be a religious peace-making, at the wedding of Margaret Valois and Henry of Navarre. For in Shakespeare's re-enactment of the dance of the veils, what the 'dancing afterward' (5.4.118) will mercifully go to show is the saving grace of *not* prying into the identity of those who arrive as '*Ladies masked*' (SD, 52).

'Be bold, bold, but not too bold': if the dark secret of a play that stages the malacious falsehood of Protestant libels against the Catholic enemy is sectarian violence, the drama cuts both ways, none the less, in hinting at the perils, since 'care killed a cat' (5.1.131), of Catholic accusations against the Protestant state. Benedick (whose origin in Padua, at the other end of Italy, places him, in the fine gradations of the play, near the *politique* position of the religious sceptic) challenges 'Lord Lackbeard' (185) in this tale, therefore, with all the weary fatalism of the Wars of Religion, when Beatrice utters her fanatical command. And the play avoids the bloodbath of the Bluebeard solution only because the chamber of horrors in which the body of the bride is supposedly interred turns out to be not a tomb but an empty cenotaph. Thus, Hero – a 'virgin knight' whose name denotes iconic status in Christian martyrology – seems to stand for all those slain in the cause of the 'goddess of the night' on whom 'the wolves have preyed' in Tudor fact. Certainly, Claudio's prayer at her graveside – 'Now, unto thy bones good night! / Yearly will I do this rite' (11–23) – is far from iconoclasm, and suggests that what 'mourning ostentation' (4.1.203) would expect to find in Hero's chapel are indeed the bones and blood of some Counter-Reformation saint. So, the secret Benedick keeps, 'As secretly and justly as your soul / Should with your body', despite his 'inwardness and love' being 'unto the Prince', is that 'every lovely organ of her life' will indeed 'come apparelled in more precious habit', after the martyr has been 'secretly kept in' and dedicated by the Friar to 'some reclusive and religious life, / Out of all eyes, tongues, minds, and injuries' (224–47). Thus, if Hero's final *unmasking* (SD, 5.4.59) does not quite amount to the unveiling of the relics of some 'virgin knight', the ritual with which her 'every lovely organ' is 'apparelled' does bring the play very close to those clandestine ceremonies with which recusants preserved the remains of Tyburn victims, as well as to the militancy of Lady Mary in the tale, triumphantly refuting Mr Fox's denials with miraculous proof: 'It is so, it was so, and here the hand I have to show'. For the body parts with which English Catholics did proclaim the truth of the executioner's bloody chamber included, of course, as Munday recorded, the actual hands and fingers of the young gentlemen from Italy, pulled from the scene of the crime with all the grim determination of Lady Mary wrenching the grisly remainder from Mr Fox:

> While Campion was being chopped to pieces, the Catholic gentlemen who stood around were contriving in some guise to steal some relics from him; but the greatest precautions were taken to prevent it. A young man who dropped a handkerchief into the blood on the ground was taken and committed. In the tumult that ensued another was quick enough to cut off a finger and carry it away. The loss was quickly discovered, but the thief could not be found.[88]

'A saint-like face', Munday conceded Campion, 'but such a devilish heart / As spared no travail for his country's smart ... His nature's flowers were mix'd with honey gall ... A climbing mind, rejecting wisdom's call.' Just as much as those Catholics who smuggled grisly remnants of the author of *Ambrosia* from his execution, the writer of *Fidele and Fortunio* was sure 'this man had made a perfect discovery of himself' at Tyburn, where, however, it was the 'visor of vanity' which had fallen to reveal the truth: 'His lewd behaviour, enemy to skill; / A sugar'd tongue, to shroud a vicious will; / A pregnant wit, I grant, to treachery; / A lusty man, detesting chastity ... A graceless imp, sprung up of basest kind, / A simple man, to bear a lofty mind.' The torturer counted himself 'of God most highly blessed, / Who gave us grace at such attempts to look', since he had seen through the priests' protestations of political innocence, 'Who had their treasons noted in our book'.[89] Likewise, in *Much Ado*, Claudio is appalled 'what authority and show of truth / Can cunning sin cover itself withal!' when he denounces Hero in terms that similarly combine accusations of political and sexual betrayal: 'O Hero! What a Hero hadst thou been, / If half thy outward graces had been placed / About thy thoughts and counsels of thy heart!' (4.1.33–4; 98–100). The religious fervour of Claudio's repudiation of 'pure impiety and impious purity' (102) echoes the Judas' kiss of Campion's betrayers. So, it is very much to the point that when the bride returns as if from the charnel house, in this version of 'Bluebeard', her 'killers' are left in the dark as to the evidence of their own eyes, assured there is 'Nothing certainer' than that she is 'Another Hero!' but also that this is, in fact, 'The former Hero! Hero that is dead!' since 'She died ... but whiles her slander lived' (5.4.62–6). For contrary to those critics who assume that 'Claudio discovers Leonato's "niece" to be Hero herself',[90] the accusers never do uncover the 'truth' about the salvaged body in *Much Ado*, which is presented to them as simply the latest of the 'practices' on which the plot revolves. Instead, in an evasion just short of the deliberate deception of his audience with the statement that 'Hermione hath suffer'd death' in *The Winter's Tale* (3.3.41), and in which, as Slights says, to combat secret treachery, 'Hero's supporters have recourse to a secret of their own', as 'one set of supposes supplants another',[91] Shakespeare finesses the ending by withholding the evidence from the characters into the secrecy of an ambiguously religious doubt. As the Friar says:

> All this amazement can I qualify,
> When, after that the holy rites are ended,
> I'll tell you largely of fair Hero's death.
> Meantime, let wonder seem familiar,
> And to the chapel let us presently.
>
> (5.4.67–71)

In *Much Ado About Nothing* 'amazement' will only be 'qualified' by truth after an act of faith in 'holy rites'. Yet, like the status of this Friar Francis, 'The supposition of the Lady's death' (4.1.236) carries a disturbing implication for co-religionists forced from necessity, like Beatrice, Benedick and Leonato, to conspire in such a 'Popish imposture', which is that they know this 'strange cure' (250) to be a fraud. Their consent perhaps reflects the connivance of Elizabethan Catholics in the cures and exorcisms staged by Jesuits with relics on their behalf. But whatever the context, it is with these scenes that the dramatist refines the practice which he began in *The Merchant of Venice*, of ensuring that neither characters nor audience can be 'satisfied / Of these events' (5.1.295). For, by withholding information, Shakespeare from now on leaves questions to 'qualify' in play after play. Thus, in *As You Like It* it will be for Jaques to pursue the 'matter to be heard and learned' (5.4.174) about Duke Frederick's conversion on which the happy end depends. In *Twelfth Night* a resolution hangs upon facts that only the Puritan Malvolio possesses about the 'durance' of Viola's captain, but his co-operation is as likely as a return of the 'golden time' of 'convents' (5.1.269; 369). In *Measure for Measure* the Duke's marriage proposal to Isabella is as contingent as the consent of his other subjects on 'a willing ear incline[d]' to his report of 'What's yet behind that's meet you all should know' (5.1.528–9). In *All's Well That Ends Well*, whose very title ironises finality, while 'All yet seems well', nothing is ended until Helena lets the other characters 'from point to point [her] story know' (5.3.321–30). In *Pericles* the facts of how the 'dead queen re-lives' are promised by Cerimon, 'No needful thing omitted', but celebrations are suspended until he can 'deliver' all: 'we do our longing stay / To hear the rest untold' (22.86–107). Likewise, in *The Winter's Tale*, whose title again problematises desire for closure, truth will be pieced together only when the actors repeat the plot: when 'we may leisurely / Each one demand and answer to his part / Performed in this wide gap of time since first / We were dissevered' (5.3.153–6). And in *The Tempest* the tautology is complete with Prospero's pledge to tell 'the story of my life, / And the particular accidents gone by / Since I came to this isle' – which, of course, constitute the play – before he frees his hostages (5.1.308–11). After the hermeneutic crisis of *Much Ado*, it seems as if Shakespeare's characters can never escape from a fiction that begins again the moment it is supposed to end. Earlier plays repel interpretation by claiming to be 'no more yielding than a dream' (*Dream*, Epi, 6), 'or worthless fancy' (*Shrew*, Ind, 1.40), like 'the songs of Apollo' (*Love's*, 5.2.903). But from this point, Shakespeare's 'qualified' endings do not merely erase the play as 'an improbable fiction' (*Twelfth*, 3.4.115). Far from foreclosing interpretation in this way, they beg for it by deferring a truth too violent to be ignored to some indefinite later disclosure, outside the endless circle of the story, like the torture of Don John:

> MESSENGER: My lord, your brother John is ta'en in flight,
> And brought with armed men back to Messina.
> BENEDICK: Think not on him till tomorrow, I'll devise thee
> Brave punishments for him. Strike up pipers.
> (*Much Ado*, 5.4.119–22)

'Let us go in, / And charge us there upon inter'gatories', advises Portia, in her last act as a lawyer in *The Merchant of Venice*, 'And we will answer all things faithfully' (5.1.296–8). The suggestion to 'go in' is indicative of the self-concealing way these plays gesture towards truth yet resist its symbolisation. In later Shakespearean comedy, the whole truth sworn under oath will be discovered only at some future date, behind locked doors, by characters off stage. Truth, they thus imply, can never be an object of knowledge. Moreover, it is precisely pursuit of truth to a bitter end that generates Shakespearean tragedy: when Hamlet is to his own 'self true' (*Hamlet*, 1.3.78); Troilus vows to 'Let all untruths stand' by Cressida's name (*Troilus*, 5.3.178); Othello rushes 'directly to the door of truth' (*Othello*, 3.3.412); Timon despairs that 'a man be true' (*Timon*, 4.3.457); Cordelia takes 'truth' as a 'dower' (*Lear*, 1.1.108); Macbeth imagines 'The instruments of darkness tell us truths' (*Macbeth*, 1.3.122); Coriolanus clings to his 'own truth' (*Coriolanus*, 3.3.121); and Posthumus thinks ''Tis true … 'tis true' that Imogen is false (*Cymbeline*, 2.4.123). In *Much*

Ado, therefore, where a reconciliation depends on *not* unlocking the bolted door to the vault where the body of the murdered bride is supposed to be interred (but that contains *nothing* at all), Munday's paranoid watch is disarmed, malopropism and all, into an English constabulary whose function is not to recover the facts, but, as Howard writes, to disabuse the Puritan dream of a society 'where good and evil are transparent to the eye'.[92] Thus, the Watchman's identification of Don John's agent as 'Deformed ... 'a wears a lock' (3.3.163), and Dogberry and Verges's order that Borachio and Conrade 'be opinioned ... in the hands' (4.2.64–5), discredits (like the dog-burying name) the reformers' hunt for some essential truth recoverable beneath a world of clues and signs. When Shakespeare returned to Munday's story, in *Othello*, it was to confound both pursuivant and priest with the lesson that, as Iago smirks, the truth of 'an essence that's not seen' can never be substantiated through the 'ocular proof' of tortured bodies or their bloody relics, such as handkerchiefs and hearts: 'You cannot, if my heart were in your hands' (3.3.16; 365; 4.1.16). In that play, disaster occurs when the Moor forces 'the door of truth' and kills the thing inside. But the tragedy merely takes to a conclusion the logic of *Much Ado* (again, inscribed in the name that had become synonymous with massacre) that whatever 'studied torments ... wheels, racks, fires.. flaying, boiling / In leads and oil ... old or new torture' (*Winter's Tale*, 3.2.173–5) may be devised to 'ope your lips' in that *don john* of the Inquisition, there will never be torture enough to 'pluck out the heart' of the mystery of the self (*Hamlet*, 3.2.336), for the reason that there is *nothing* there to hide:

> Demand me nothing. What you know, you know.
> From this time forth I never will speak word.
> (*Othello*, 5.2.309–12)

Between a Puritan mania to expose the hidden meaning, and the Jesuit obsession with the secret self, *Much Ado About Nothing* shows truth to be nothing but a charade, and identity itself a mask, like the 'counterfeit' Antonio performs so badly he receives ironic compliments: 'You could never do him so ill-well unless you were the very man' (2.1.99). In this theatrical society, where everyone dons a mask to dance, Don John's plain-speaking declaration that 'I cannot hide what I am. I must be sad when I have cause, and smile at no man's jests' (1.2.12), therefore places him beside such spoil-sports and truth-tellers as Brutus, Hamlet, Cordelia and Coriolanus, whose conceit that they have 'that within which passeth show' (*Hamlet*, 1.2.85) makes them cleave so truly to their own selfhood that they can be true to no one else: 'As if a man were author of himself / And knew no other kin' (*Coriolanus*, 5.3.36). Their 'reluctance to enter the symbolic order' is based, it is said, on a sense of 'personal identity as private, autonomous and non-exchangeable', but it would be a mistake to attribute this self-validation automatically to Protestantism.[93] A more historically specific criticism might see the non-cooperation of these aristocratic *refuseniks* as imaging instead the isolation imposed by politicised

Catholic upon themselves, and the plays that they initiate as variations on the conflict within the dramatist's world, between the conformist and the 'true heart' who states, with Cordelia, that 'I cannot heave / My heart into my mouth' (*Lear*, 1.1.69; 90). Such a reading would answer the problem that Don John's melancholy, arrogance, duplicity and spite are endemic in Messina, where, feminists remark, the lie about Hero passes so easily because the other characters fear that it expresses an essential truth.[94] Thus, Don John's rebellion would figure the politics of the 'party of massacre' who looked to his namesake for help.[95] Then, the irony of this play would be that the biggest lie spread about recusants, in their own eyes, was one they had done everything to justify by their abetting of Don John: the slander that killed their 'hero' Mary Stuart and stained the Infanta, that a Catholic succession would bring in Spanish troops and a final bloody settling of accounts:

> Done to death by slanderous tongues
> Was the Hero that here lies.
> Death in guerdon of her wrongs
> Gives her fame that never dies.
> So the life that died with shame
> Lives in death with glorious fame.
>
> (5.3.3–8)

'Strike up pipers!' (5.4.122): *Much Ado* draws a discreet veil across the skeleton in the sectarian cupboard with festivities, though, according to the evidence of Munday at Campion's trial, the secret he had learned in Milan was that it had been the Jesuit plot to lure the Queen to just such a masque, and blow her up with fireworks 'when she were on the Thames in her barge', which would be the signal for a massacre, when 'whosoever had not the watchword, "Jesus Maria," should be slain'.[96] In oral variants of 'Bluebeard', however, the violent climax of the story is postponed when 'the heroines delay their executions by insisting on donning bridal clothes, and prolong the possibility of rescue by recounting each and every item of clothing' for their weddings. Shakespeare may be closer to these early tales, therefore, than to Perrault, who has his heroine 'ask for time to say her prayers, thus becoming a model of devout piety', when he too defers entry into the bloody chamber with a folkloric ceremony of robing, which seems to have no other function than to distance Hero from those previous brides who carried Catholic hopes into the house of death.[97] Beginning with her rejection of the ominous Spanish 'rebato', or gigantic starched ruff, suggested for her neck by the treacherous Margaret; and her selection of a headdress the servant thinks not 'brown' (or Brownist, which is to say, Puritan) enough; Hero's choice of wedding-dress is an exercise in religious balancing. But it is with her drapes that this bride disavows most explicitly her disastrous predecessors, when she puts on a garment that makes 'the Duchess of Milan's gown that they praise so' seem 'but a nightgown' in comparison. The maid, who says she saw it worn, remembers the Milanese clothes as a true Bronzino creation, consisting of 'cloth o'gold, and cuts, and lac'd with silver, set with pearls, down-sleeves, side-sleeves, and skirts, round underborne with a bluish tinsel'. To an English audience, however, there had only ever been one Duchess of Milan, and her wedding-dress was indeed enskyed with the 'bluish tinsel' of Marian symbolism, when she had been married in popish pomp at Winchester cathedral, in a ceremony during which her father-in-law had solemnly bestowed the Milanese duchy on the groom and bride. But when this one and only Duchess of Milan had afterwards been buried in that same ill-fated Italian 'nightgown', the hopes of England's Catholics for a *Te Deum* at Westminster Abbey had been interred with it as well; for she was, of course, the childless daughter-in-law of the Emperor Charles V and wife of Philip II, whom her Protestant subjects would for ever hate as 'Bloody Mary' Tudor.[98] No wonder, then, that though Hero is restored to life, like faith reborn, we see that her bridal dress, 'worth ten' of the Duchess's 'for a fine, quaint, graceful, and excellent fashion' (3.4.1–24), has been deliberately designed to outshine that bloodstained signifier, and to evade another reign of terror like that of the barren Duchess of Milan.

'I Pandulf, of fair Milan Cardinal ... Do ... religiously demand / Why thou against the Church, our Holy Mother, / So wilfully dost spurn': if, as editors note, Shakespeare altered the title of the papal legate in *King John* (3.1.138–42) to make him the 'holy lord of Milan' (5.2.120), that may be because the city of Borromeo had come, through Campion's disaster, to signify the illusoriness of any such alternative to the Church of England. So while it comes as no shock that the failure of the 'good father cardinal' (5.2.120) to broker English subjection was censored from the text in the 1640s by the Holy Office,[99] this does not mean, Gary Taylor notes, that 'Shakespeare was not a Catholic, only that like most English Catholics in the late sixteenth century [he] did not agree with papal policies'.[100] Thus, with his pledge to 'canonise and worship as a saint' any assassin of the excommunicated English monarch (3.1.177), the Borromean Archbishop becomes a figurehead, in *King John*, for gifts for ever spurned. 'He who gives dominates', remarks Fernand Braudel in his history of the Mediterranean, and in the age of Philip II what Milan gave the world was the violence of the Counter-Reformation and the art of the Baroque. So, as the historian suggests, contrary to the myth of a decadent Italy, what the Stratford boy would have encountered with the Jesuit mission from Borromeo was 'a superior force' and 'a new light' which brought 'more lurid colours to the landscapes of western Europe'. But critics who detect Baroque tendencies in Shakespearean drama might pause at Braudel's reminder that the battle fought from Milan was a ferocious one, for all that it was 'waged with intelligence', and that 'the civilization it carried forward was a militant one', with an art that was 'merely one more means to an end: an art done to order ... with all the disadvantages that order implies'.[101] For the Baroque order of 'absolute Milan', which had come so menacingly close to Shakespeare's England, is, indeed, what the open endings of his plays seem constructed to avoid (*Tempest*, 1.2.109), as poised between the confessional extremes of London and Rome, they dedicate 'Every third thought' to arriving at last, though always tomorrow, in what Prospero so prudently designates instead as 'my Milan' (5.1.311). In 1610 'poor Milan' had, indeed, been on the eve of just such a solution, as the champion of the *politique* middle way, Henri IV of France, had been about to liberate 'The dukedom yet unbowed' (1.2.115), when he was assassinated by a Jesuit-inspired fanatic.[102] This failure to free the dukedom ensured, however, that, up to the last moment in *The Tempest*, Milan would remain what Prospero envisions: a final destination and last resort, the shining city over the mountains, for ever receding, as the characters troop into the darkness of his cell, beyond the horizon of the stage.

'Who is Silvia? What is she, / That all our swains commend her?' (*Two Gents*, 4.2.37–8): dressed as 'some well-reputed page', Julia has arrived in Milan after her 'longing journey', hoping to rest 'as after much turmoil / A blessed soul doth in Elysium', when she overhears her lover Proteus betray her and Valentine, and deceive his patrons, the Host, Thurio and the Duke, by courting Silvia with 'composed rhymes … full-fraught with serviceable vows' (2.7,37; 85; 3.2.69). Critics note the 'stair-stepped structure' of this scene, where Julia, who 'left Verona in ignorance, is raised to our level of awareness', because she 'now knows all'.[103] Yet Milan proves to be the location not of promised plenitude but of disillusion, and what 'this page' (5.4.161) suffers is, in fact, the prime instance of a betrayal repeated over and again in Shakespeare's theatre, when unobserved observers 'overpeer the petty traffickers' (*Merchant*, 1.1.12) on stage. For far from being empowering, recent commentators maintain, the scenario initiated by this girlish boy's arrival in Milan is a model for the audience precisely because it enacts the impotence of the voyeur who 'watches from a hidden place, his gaze unreturned by those he views'. In situations like those when Hortensio spies on Bianca; Claudio bugs Hero; Frank Ford hounds his wife; Troilus stalks Cressida; Hamlet harasses Gertrude; Iachimo ogles Imogen; or Leontes peers at Hermione; the correspondence between the voyeur and the spectator is not merely that they share Othello's craving to be 'the supervisor, grossly gape on', and 'Behold her topped', but that they suffer a peeping Tom's castration, his failure ever to obtain 'ocular proof' (*Othello*, 3.3.357; 401). Thus, if the discovery scenario instigated by Munday provided Shakespeare with his primal comedic scene – in which a man looks on while he is betrayed – what made his versions so different from those of the paid informer was the way they turned spying on the spy, by presenting such 'noting' as a form of blindness.[104] True 'searchers of secrets', Cottam called the authors of *Gorboduc* and *Fidele and Fortunio*, when they applied the 'intolerable torment of the rack' until he confessed to them what he had confessed to his actual confessors.[105] Shakespeare, who could recognise in the empty rhymes of these two torturing playwrights, Norton and Munday, the 'serviceable vows' of Judas, took the Queen of torturers at her own word, however, and refused to perform what both she and Borromeo so much craved, which was 'to make windows into men's hearts and secret thoughts'.[106]

NOTES

1   Richard Simpson, *Edmund Campion: A Biography* (London: John Hodges, 1896), pp. 171, 176, 224 and 251–2.

2   For the missionary priests as 'pious terrorists' see John Bossy, *Under the Molehill: An Elizabethan Spy Story* (New Haven: Yale University Press, 2001), pp. 31f.

3   Agostino Borromeo, 'Archbishop Carlo Borromeo and the Ecclesiastical Policy of Philip II in the State of Milan', in John M. Headley and John B. Tomaro (eds), *San Carlo Borromeo: Catholic Reform and Ecclesiastical Politics in the Second Half of the Sixteenth Century* (Washington: Folger Books, 1988), p. 95.

4   Letter to Alphonsus Agazzari, 30 June 1580; quoted in Simpson, op. cit. (note 1), p. 157.

5   Simpson, op. cit. (note 1), pp. 190–1.

6   The letter is printed in Edgar Fripp, *Shakespeare: Man and Artist* (Oxford: Oxford University Press, 1938), pp. 181–2.

7   See Edgar Fripp, *Shakespeare's Haunts Near Stratford* (Oxford: Oxford University Press, 1929), pp. 33 and 53; and Frank Brownlow, *Shakespeare, Harsnett, and the Devils of Denham* (Newark: University of Delaware Press, 1993), pp. 108–10.

8   Fripp, op. cit. (note 6), p. 181; Manfred Pfister, 'Shakespeare and Italy, or, the Law of Diminishing Returns', in Michelle Marrapodi, A.J. Hoenslaars, Marcello Cappuzzo and L. Falzon Santucci (eds), *Shakespeare's Italy: Functions of Italian Locations in Renaissance Drama* (Manchester: Manchester University Press, 1997), p. 300.

9   Marc Venard, 'The Influence of Carlo Borromeo on the Church of France', in Headley and Tomaro, op. cit. (note 2), p. 221.

10 John Bossy, 'Rome and the Elizabethan Catholics: A Question of Geography', *The Historical Journal*, 7:1 (1964), pp. 135–42; and see also Peter Guilday, *The English Catholic Refugees on the Continent, 1558–1795* (London: Longmans and Green, 1914), pp. 95–6.

11 6 August 1577; quoted Simpson, op. cit. (note 1), pp. 120–1 and n. 92, p. 521.

12 A.L. Rowse, *Raleigh and the Throckmortons* (London: Macmillan, 1962), p. 87. For the lease of Alderminster to Shakespeare's executor, Thomas Russell, see p. 276.

13 Edwyn Sandys, *Europae Speculum* (London: 1599), quoted in Simpson, op. cit. (note 1), pp. 108–9.

14 Alison Shell, *Catholicism, Controversy and the English Literary Imagination, 1558–1660* (Cambridge: Cambridge University Press, 1999), p. 173.

15 Ibid., p. 174.

16 Quoted in Simpson, op. cit. (note 1), p. 109.

17 See R.J.W. Evans, *Rudolf II and His World* (London: Thames and Hudson, 1997), pp. 100–15.

18 Ibid., p. 132; Simpson, op. cit. (note 1), p. 93.

19 Ibid., p. 88.

20 Alan Stewart, *Philip Sidney: A Double Life* (London: Chatto and Windus, 2000), p. 165.

21 Philip Sidney, *The Works of Philip Sidney*, ed. A. Feuillerat (Cambridge: Cambridge University Press, 1923), vol. 3, pp. 109–14.

22 Quoted in Simpson, op. cit. (note 1), p. 115.

23 Stewart, op. cit. (note 20), p. 177. The theory of Sidney's secret Catholic sympathies has been canvassed in Katherine Duncan-Jones, *Sir Philip Sidney* (London: Jonathan Cape, 1991), pp. 124–7; and 'Sir Philip Sidney's Debt to Edmund Campion', in T. McCoog (ed.), *The Reckoned Expense: Edmund Campion and the Early English Jesuits* (Wood-

bridge: Boydell and Brewer, 1996), pp. 82–105. See also R.A. Rebholz, *Life of Fulke Greville* (Oxford: Clarendon Press, 1971), pp. 24ff; and Blair Worden, *The Sound of Virtue* (New Haven: Yale University Press, 1996), pp. 32–7 and 95–6. Stewart's scepticism receives support, however, from John Bossy in *Under the Molehill: An Elizabethan Spy Story* (New Haven: Yale University Press, 2001), p. 71.

24 Quoted ibid., p. 123.

25 David Scott Kastan, *Shakespeare After Theory* (London: Routledge, 2001), p. 210.

26 A.D. Wright, 'The Borromean Ideal and the Spanish Church', in Headley and Tomaro, op. cit. (note 3), p. 190.

27 Robert Southwell, 'Life of Edward Throckmorton', quoted in Christopher Devlin, *The Life of Robert Southwell: Poet and Martyr* (London: Longmans and Green, 1956), p. 21.

28 Simpson, op. cit. (note 1), pp. 58–9 and 153; Stephen Greenblatt, *Hamlet in Purgatory* (Princeton: Princetone University Press, 2001), p. 50.

29 Quoted Simpson, op. cit. (note 3), p. 153.

30 Jean Howard (ed.), *'The Two Gentlemen of Verona': The Norton Shakespeare* (New York: Norton, 1997), p. 126.

31 Robert Greene, quoted in Samuel Shoenbaum, *Shakespeare's Lives* (Oxford: Clarendon Press, 1970), p. 50: 'There is an upstart crow beautified with our feathers'. In *The Phoenix and the Turtle*, the 'treble-dated crow' who creates 'sable gender ... With the breath thou giv'st and tak'st' (17–19), looks very like a Jesuit who sends his seminarians to the deaths with which he then inspires their successors.

32 T.S. Eliot, 'The Love Song of J. Alfred Prufrock', *The Complete Poems and Plays of T.S. Eliot* (London: Faber and Faber, 1969), p. 16; Tom Stoppard, *Rosencrantz and Guildenstern Are Dead* (London: Faber and Faber, 1967), Act I, p. 27.

33 Celeste Turner, *Anthony Mundy: An Elizabethan Man of Letters* (Berkeley: University of California Press, 1928), p. 54.

34 Giorgio Melchiori, 'In Fair Verona: *Commedia Erudita* into Romantic Comedy', in Marrapodi et al., op. cit. (note 8), pp. 100–11.

35 Devlin, op. cit. (note 27), p. 328.

36 Quoted Turner, op. cit. (note 33), pp. 18–19.

37 Anthony Munday, *Discovery of Edmund Campion* (London: 1582), quoted Turner, ibid., pp. 11 and 13.

38 Anthony Munday, *The English Roman Life* (London: 1582), repr. ed. G.B. Harrison (London: Bodley Head, 1922), pp. 88–90; quoted ibid., p. 19.

39 Donna Hamilton, 'Anthony Munday and the Catholics', unpublished paper, 'Northern Literary Renaissance' Conference, Hoghton Tower, May 1998. Hamilton elaborates this defence in 'Anthony Munday and *The Merchant of Venice*', *Shakespeare Survey: 52* (Cambridge: Cambridge University Press, 2000), pp. 89–99.

40 Tracey Hill, 'Eggs and Oysters: Anthony Munday's Counterfeit Truths', unpublished paper, 'In Shakespeare's Shadow' Conference, University of Hertfordshire, November 1997.

41 William Allen, *A Brief History of the Glorious Martyrdom of Twelve Reverend Priests*, ed. J.H. Pollen (London: Burns and Oates, 1908), p. 63; Francis Meres, *Palladis Tamia* (London: 1598), quoted in Turner, op. cit. (note 33), p. 120.

42 Charles Nicholl, *The Reckoning: The Murder of Christopher Marlowe* (London: Picador, 1992), p. 174.

43 All quotations from Anthony Munday, *Fedele and Fortunio*, ed. Richard Hosley (New York: Garland, 1981).

44 William Slights, *Ben Jonson and the Art of Secrecy* (Toronto: Toronto University Press, 1994), pp. 21, 26 and 98.

45 Anat Feinberg, 'Observation and Theatricality in Webster's *The Duchess of Malfi*', *Theatre Research International*, 6 (1980), pp. 36–7.

46 Thomas Nashe, 'An Almond for a Parrot', in Ronald Mckerrow (ed.), *The Works of Thomas Nashe* (4 vols, Oxford: Basil Blackwell, 1966), vol. 3, p. 374.

47 Ben Jonson, *The Case Is Altered*; quoted in Turner, op. cit. (note 33), p. 122.
48 Anon., *A Caveat to the Reader touching A.M. his discovery* (London: 1582), quoted ibid., p. 39.
49 Simpson, op. cit. (note 1), pp. 439–40.
50 Antony Munday, *A Second and Third Blast of Retreat from Plays and Theatres* (London: Henry Denham, 1580), ed Arthur Freeman (New York: Garland, 1973), pp. v, vii, 89, 110–11 and 115; Munday, op. cit. 1582 (note 38); Turner, op. cit. (note 33), p. 41.
51 Munday, op. cit., 1580 (note 37), pp. 126–8.
52 *A Caveat* quoted by Turner, op. cit. (note 33), p. 39; cf. Stephen Gosson, *Plays Confuted in Five Actions* (London: 1582), p. 1: 'Having once already written against the stage, which no man that ever wrote plays did, but one, who hath changed his copy and turned himself like the dog to his vomit to plays again … it is needful for me to write again'; Ephesians, 5:13.
53 Munday, op. cit. 1580 (note 37), pp. 95–6.
54 Jean Howard, 'Renaissance Anti-Theatricality and the Politics of Gender and Rank in *Much Ado About Nothing*', in Jean Howard and Marion O'Connor (eds), *Shakespeare Reproduced: The Text in History and Ideology* (London: Methuen, 1987), pp. 166–8.
55 Martin Jay, *Downcast Eyes: The Denigration of Vision in Twentieth-Century French Thought* (Berkeley: University of California Press, 1994), pp. 87–9.
56 Anthony Munday, *Fedele and Fortunio*, ed. Richard Hosley (New York: Garland, 1981), Prologue, p. 113. All quotations from this edition.
57 John Archer, *Sovereignty and Intelligence: Spying and Court Culture in the English Renaissance* (Stanford: Stanford University Press, 1993), pp. 64–6.
58 Turner, op. cit. (note 33), pp. 67–8.
59 For evidence that Falstaff is intended as a caricature of a hypcritical Puritan, 'fully in keeping with the tenor of late-sixteenth-century anti-Puritan literature, especially the anti-Marprelate tracts and the burlesque stage performances of the Marprelate controversy' see Kristen Poole, 'Facing Puritanism: Falstaff, Martin Marprelate and the Grotesque Puritan', in Ronald Knowles (ed.), *After Bakhtin: Shakespeare and Carnival* (Basingstoke: Macmillan, 1998), pp. 97–122.
60 Slights, op. cit. (note 44), pp. 21 and 26.
61 Anthony Munday, 'Beauty sat bathing', quoted in Turner, op. cit. (note 33), p. 65.
62 Frank Kermode, *The Genesis of Secrecy: On the Interpretation of Narrative* (Cambridge, Mass.: Harvard University Press, 1979), pp. 1–2.
63 Thomas Nashe, *The Terrors of the Night* (London: 1594), in *Selected Works*, ed. Stanley Wells (London: Arnold, 1964), vol. 1, p. 175. For a commentary on the theme of 'night' in Elizabethan drama see Jean-Marie Maguin, 'The Rise and Fall of the King of Darkness', in Jean-Marie Maguin and Michele Willems (eds), *'What Would France with Us?': French Essays on Shakespeare and His Contemporaries* (Newark: University of Delaware Press, 1995), pp. 247–9.
64 Richard Hosley in Munday, op. cit. (note 56), p. 18.
65 Munday, op. cit., 1582 (note 38), p. 41.
66 Ibid., p. 66.
67 *Zelauto, the Fountain of Fame, Erected in an Orchard of Amorous Adventures, containing a Delicate Disputation gallantly discoursed by Two Noble Gentlemen of Italy* (London: 1580): see Turner, op. cit. (note 21), pp. 33–4.
68 Quoted, Turner, op. cit. (note 33), p. 189.
69 Simpson, op. cit. (note 1), pp. 322–3.
70 Munday, op. cit. 1582 (note 38), p. 66.
71 *Records of the English Province of the Society of Jesus* (London: Manresa Press, 1875), 2nd, 3rd and 4th series, p. 159.
72 Hallam, quoted in Simpson, op. cit. (note 1), p. 440.
73 See I.A. Shapiro, 'Shakespeare and Mundy', *Shakespeare Survey: 14* (Cambridge: Cambridge University Press, 1961), pp. 25–34.

74 John Carney Meagher (ed.), *The Huntingdon Plays: A Critical Edition on 'The Downfall' and 'The Death of Robert, Earl of Huntingdon'* (New York: Garland, 1980), pp. 26 and 523.

75 See Frank Lestringant (ed.), *Le Théâtre des Crautés de Richard Vestegan, 1587* (Paris: Editions Chandeigne, 1995).

76 *Much Ado About Nothing*, New Variorum edition, ed. Horace Howard Furness (New York: Dover, 1964), p. 29.

77 Thomas Pound, 'Jesus: A challenge unto Fox the martyrmonger with a comfort to all afflicted Catholics', quoted in Henry Foley (ed.), *Records of the English Province of the Society of Jesus: III* (London: Burns and Oates, 1878), pp. 623–4.

78 Elizabeth Hanson, *Discovering the Subject in Renaissance England* (Cambridge; Cambridge University Press, 1998), pp. pp. 25–6.

79 William Cecil, *A Declaration of the Favourable Dealing of Her Majesty's Commissioners* (London: 1583), p. 48; Thomas Smith, *De Republica Anglorum*, ed. Mary Dewar (Cambridge: Cambridge University Press, 1982), p. 117; Edward Coke, *The Third Part of the Institutes of the Laws of England* (London: 1797), pp. 34–5: quoted ibid., pp. 28 and 32.

80 Ibid., p. 31; Robert Southwell, *An Epistle of Comfort to the Reverend Priests* (Saint-Omer: 1616), p. 387, quoted ibid., p. 33.

81 Jonathan Bate, plenary lecture, Fifth World Shakespeare Congress, Valencia, 2001.

82 John Lynch, *Spain Under the Habsburgs* (2 vols, Oxford: Blackwell, 1964) vol. 1, p. 228; see also pp. 286–7 and 304–5.

83 Marina Warner, *From the Beast to the Blonde: On Fairy Tales and Their Tellers* (London: Chatto and Windus, 1994), pp. 243–4; and see also *No Go the Bogeyman: Scaring, Lulling and Making Mock* (London: Chatto and Windus, 1998), pp. 31–5.

84 Katherine Eisaman Maus, *Inwardness and Theater in the English Renaissance* (Chicago: Chicago University Press, 1995), pp. 83–4.

85 Stephen Greenblatt (ed.), *'Much Ado About Nothing': The Norton Shakespeare* (New York: Norton, 1997), p. 1384.

86 Ibid.

87 See P.M. Handover, *The Second Cecil: The Rise to Power, 1563–1604, of Sir Robert Cecil, Later First Earl of Salisbury* (London: Eyre and Spottiswoode, 1959), pp. 188–9; and *Arbella Stuart: Royal Lady of Hardwick and Cousin of King James* (London: Eyre and Spottiswoode, 1957), pp. 125–8. Cecil's interest in the Infanta is discussed in L. Hicks, 'Sir Robert Cecil, Father Parsons, and the Succession', *Archivum Historicum Societatis Jesu*, 25 (1955), pp. 20 ff.

88 Quoted Simpson, op. cit. (note 1), p. 455.

89 Repr. in Turner, op. cit. (note 33), pp. 189–90; Simpson, op. cit. (note 1), p. 457.

90 Bertrand Evans, *Shakespeare's Comedies* (Oxford: Clarendon Press, 1960), p. 85.

91 Slights, op. cit. (note 44), p. 28.

92 Howard, op. cit. (note 54), p. 177.

93 Terry Eagleton, *William Shakespeare* (Oxford: Basil Blackwell, 1986), p. 74.

94 Howard, op. cit. (note 54), p. 175.

95 John Bossy, *Under the Molehill: An Elizabethan Spy Story* (New Haven: Yale University Press, 2001), p. 5.

96 Simpson, op. cit. (note 1), p. 428.

97 Jack Zipes, *The Oxford Companion to Fairy Tales* (Oxford: Oxford University Press, 2000), p. 56.

98 Lynch, op. cit. (note 82), vol. 1, p. 100. The Duchy was excluded from the terms of Philip's later marriages, so that none of his other wives became Duchess of Milan.

99 See Roland Mushat Frye, 'The Roman Catholic Censorship of Shakespeare, 1641–1651', in *Shakespeare and Christian Doctrine* (Princeton: Princeton University Press, 1963), pp. 275–93.

100 Gary Taylor, 'Forms of Opposition: Shakespeare and Middleton', *English Literary*

Renaissance, 24:2 (1994), pp. 303–4.

101 Fernand Braudel, *The Mediterranean and the Mediterranean World in the Age of Philip II*, rev. ed., trans Sian Reynolds (London: Harper Collins, 1992), pp. 584 and 593.

102 Roland Mousnier, *The Assassination of Henry IV*, trans. Joan Spencer (London: Faber and Faber, 1973), pp. 135–7.

103 Evans, op. cit. (note 90), p. 17.

104 Katherine Eisaman Maus, 'Horns of Dilemma: Jealousy, Gender, and Spectatorship in English Renissance Drama', *ELH*, 54:1 (1987), pp. 561–83, esp. pp. 564 and 570.

105 As reported in William Allen, *A True, Sincere and Modest Defence of English Catholics* (Rheims, 1583), ed. Robert M. Kingdon (Ithaca: Cornell University Press, 1965), p. 72.

106 Elizabeth I quoted by Francis Bacon in *Certain Observations Made Upon a Libel Published this Present Year, 1592*, in James Spedding (ed.), *Letters and Life of Francis Bacon*, vol. 1 (London: Longmans, Green and Co., 1890), p. 178.

4

No news but the old news

Shakespeare and the tragedy of Arden

There's no news ... but the old news: that is, the old Duke is banished ...
(*As You Like It*, 1.1.86–90)

IN the autumn of 1599 Shakespeare's father, John, applied to Garter King of Arms for permission to combine his arms with those of his wife's family, the Ardens. The draft, which survives in the College of Arms, records how the heralds had first planned to authorise the Shakespeares to divide their device with that of the main branch of the Warwickshire Ardens, whose seat was at Park Hall at Curdworth in the Forest of Arden, but then changed their minds, scratched out the blue-and-gold check band of the Park Hall branch, and substituted the red martlet and three gold crosses used by cadet branches of the family. This hesitation has always been interpreted as a rebuff to the Shakespeares, who are assumed to have snobbishly claimed a closer kinship with the Park Hall Ardens than they could prove, and then to have reacted to the award of the less illustrious coat by deciding not to impale their arms at all.[1] In fact, both forms of the Arden arms derived from the Beauchamp Earls of Warwick, and the questions this aborted application begs have less to do with the Shakespeares' social climbing than the circumstances that might have prompted them to claim such a spectacular connection in 1599, and then to have let their petition lapse with the death of John in September 1601. For what is extraordinary about their move to affiliate with the Ardens is not the arrivism of the Shakespeares but their temerity in aligning themselves at this moment with one of the most notorious Catholic families in all of England, and the risk they thereby ran of incriminating themselves by association with one of the most flagrant acts of Elizabethan treason. Shakespeare's claim to the Arden arms can stand, in this sense, for the larger mystery of his relationship to his historical situation and, in particular, to Catholic resistance, a question that has been suspended since 1601, like his maternal inheritance, under official erasure.

Biographers guess that Shakespeare's relationship with the Warwickshire Ardens was through his great-grandfather, Thomas, who may have been a younger son of Walter of Park Hall, who died in 1502. When the heralds erased the Arden arms on the draft certificate it could have been, therefore, that they were not so much calling the dramatist's origins in question as holding the disgraced and impoverished Ardens themselves in limbo. For in 1599 the Park Hall Ardens had lost their right to bear arms under act of attainder, their estate was forfeit to the Crown and their family seat was occupied by an avid monopolist, Sir Edward Darcy, one of Walsingham's agents who had won this prize sixteen years earlier as an attaché to William the Silent, in the days leading up to the Protestant hero's assassination. Ministers may, indeed, have intended this grant as poetic justice, because the reason for the confiscation was alleged Arden involvement in the international chain of Catholic conspiracies which would fell not only the Dutch leader but two French kings, and menace even the Queen of England. For as is well known, but hardly ever considered by Shakespeare's biographers, on 25 October 1583 John Somerville, the twenty-three-year-old heir of Edstone, five miles north of Stratford, who was married to Margaret Arden, the daughter of Edward Arden of Park Hall, had set out for London with the intention of shooting the Queen with a hidden pistol. Somerville's property was held until his twenty-fourth year by a trust of six local landowners well known to Shakespeare;[2] but though the dramatist's proximity to this sensational episode of religious terrorism has for long hovered on the margins of Shakespeare studies, none of the numerous biographies published in the last ten years so much as mentions it, evidently taking their cue from the tradition that the assassin acted alone and was 'clearly mad', with what Samuel Schoenbaum calls 'a fever in his brain'.[3] They take their lead, that is to say, from the disingenuous report of the affair in the archives of the Spanish embassy in Paris, which was almost certainly written with the intention of misleading English intelligence by minimising the importance of both the gunman and his collaborators:

> A gentleman named Somerville, being out of his mind, said in the presence of many others that it was necessary the queen of England should be killed, as she was the bane of the Catholic Church. The other gentlemen paid no attention to what he said, as they saw he was not in his right senses, but he continued in the same way of thinking and went towards London, saying openly that he was going there to kill the Queen. He was arrested on the road by a judge, who sent him to London. In prison he accused several persons, amongst others his father-in-law, and a priest, his confessor. Some of these persons are already in prison, and they are seeking others on the charge of high treason for not having revealed to the Council the words of the madman.[4]

The Somerville Plot remains one of the most under-researched episodes of Shakespeare's lifetime, and it is because it has been so little analysed that, despite the implausibility of so many witnesses remaining indifferent, this protest of innocence has always been taken at face value. For whether or not the minute was deliberately designed to be leaked, its duplicity is revealed by a simultaneous relay from Paris of reassurance to Philip II from 'our English friends' that none of the arrests was 'caused by real suspicion on the part of the Queen of the plan they have in hand'. To which the King's envoy added, 'God grant they may be right ... I urged them to have any suspicion lulled, so that she might sleep soundly. They tell me they have taken steps with this object, which I hope is true. The lady is so suspicious that there was always danger in the matter being in so many hands.'[5] This letter was dated 22 December, and by then the steps taken to limit damage to 'the plan in hand' probably included the liquidation of Somerville himself, who was found strangled in his Newgate cell, just two hours after arriving there, on the night before his execution: silenced by his co-conspirators, according to Walsingham's informants, 'to avoid a greater evil' of a scaffold speech.[6] For what is overlooked by the unlikely theory that a madman simply 'set out alone, blabbed *en route*, and arrived at the Tower instead of the palace', is just how much assistance he might have expected.[7] In fact, the Queen's sworn killer was seized by Oxford officers at an inn north of the town near Aynho, in what James McConica has called 'the heartland' of Catholic resistance, with its 'invisible networks of support' sustained by powerful families such as the Stonors; and if he did rave to his hosts, as the Merton magistrate recorded, 'that he intended to shoot her with his dag, and hoped to see her head set on a pole, for that she was a serpent and a viper', then that may have been because he saw them as accomplices.[8] One other neglected piece of evidence suggests such expectations. At Crawley, in far-off Sussex, there were concerted plans to receive Somerville in some hideaway of the Earl of Northumberland, the most illustrious of those the Spanish counted as 'our English friends'.[9]

Rumours of John Somerville's escape route betrayed a more complex plot than even he may have realised. For far from being aimless, his itinerary would have connected some of the strongholds of recusant England, and by the time of the trial, on 16 December, Northumberland was himself under house arrest. As Dennis Flynn has detailed, support from Henry Percy, Earl of Northumberland, who was 'committed to reconciliation with the religion for which his father and brother died', was crucial to Catholic resistance in the 1580s, as 'it was his retainers and relations who opened and closed doors in Sussex, London and the north, where (it was still said) people knew no prince but a Percy'.[10] Northumberland's estates, from Tynemouth to Petworth, offered a string of safe houses for passage between England and France, but it was this network that began to unravel with Somerville's arrest. Ministers soon discovered, for instance, that from Crawley the assassin had been expected in the Sussex village of Washington, close to Petworth, where a recusant, Nicholas Wolf, was waiting to ferry him down the Arun to a boat anchored off the port of Littlehampton.[11] This was the exit, across the Channel from Arundel, bastion of the Catholic Howards, hurriedly taken after Somerville's detention by the most exposed of the conspirators, beginning with their Paris link-man, Lord Paget. And that Somerville was being manipulated by these plotters is suggested by the letter Paget wrote to the Queen of Scots immediately after the young man's supposed suicide, assuring her of 'the great sorrow' he had 'to see the house of Arden ruinated, and my dear friend murdered, which God's enemies and his said … he did himself'.[12] But what Somerville may not himself have known when he rode southwards is that the estuary of the Arun had just been surveyed as a planned beachhead by Paget's exiled brother, Charles, on behalf of the Duke of Guise, and that on 16 September, in a wood outside Petworth, the local Catholic gentry had been briefed on the 'great enterprise' the assassination was timed to ignite.[13] For the past six months Walsingham had patiently eavesdropped on these preparations to invade England and impose a Catholic regime, and Somerville's arrest was his cue to pounce on the ring-leaders: Lord Henry Howard and the Warwickshire landowner who would give his name to the entire imbroglio, Francis Throckmorton.

When he came to file his report on the so-called Throckmorton Conspiracy, *A Chain of Treasons*, the chief interrogator, Thomas Norton, concluded that it had been destroyed by its divided aims, since, though the Duke of Guise had prepared the troops, 'there wanted two things: money and a convenient party in England to join the foreign force'.[14] That somebody gave the assassin away at the very start of the complicated arrangements is symptomatic of this confusion, which was ultimately caused by the reluctance of Spain to finance Guise's dynastic ambition to instal his cousin Mary Stuart over a united Britain. For while the Spanish Ambassador to London, Bernardino Mendoza, was plotting to take Elizabeth hostage and convert her to Catholicism, in Paris Guise had been intriguing with the papal nuncio, Cardinal Gallio, to have her murdered, on the grounds that she was now an irreconcilable Protestant. Until very recently, Catholic historians have been loth to admit their Church's involvement in any such acts of terrorism against Queen Elizabeth, but in 1996 John Bossy reluctantly concluded, in a landmark essay entitled 'The Heart of Robert Persons', that 'there can be no reasonable doubt' that, in defiance of his own General, Aquaviva, the English Jesuit leader had been instrumental in persuading Pope Gregory XIII that 'Elizabeth's life was the only obstacle to the success of the enterprise, and that Guise ought therefore to be given permission to arrange her assassination'.[15] The key conference took place in Paris in August 1583, attended by William Allen, brother-in-law of Throckmorton and President of the English College at Rheims, and it agreed the Sussex landing, and then despatched Parsons to Rome for a death sentence on Elizabeth in the form of a fresh excommunication. So, though the Spanish had signed up only for a missionary crusade, Guise persisted with his own agenda, and, when government agents raided Throckmorton's house at St Paul's Wharf on 4 November, they caught him not only red-handed with Paget's harbour charts for Sussex but actually writing a letter in code to Mary Stuart. Thus, the Exeter informant who put it on record that Somerville's attempt was 'a mischievous practice intended for the Queen of Scots' concocted between Jesuits at the court of her son and 'popish rogues' in the Midlands, may have been near to the truth when he insisted that it was these illustrious friends who saw to it that 'Somerville was hanged to avoid mischief'.[16] As Paget was reassured on 20 December, the day after the squire had been silenced, the suppporters of Mary Stuart knew how to keep their secrets:

> F.V. to Charles Paget at Rouen: Informed him that his mother's house in Fleet Street had been searched, and also in Staffordshire and at the Charter House; also Lady Walgrave's house and the money and plate taken by the Sheriff. Somerville, Arden and his wife, and Hall have been arraigned and condemned. The Earls of Northumberland and Arundel confined to their houses. Thomas Throckmorton to be arraigned tomorrow. He had often been racked and confessed nothing.[17]

Though the Queen of Scots would haughtily deny her own 'participation en toutes ces dernières brouilleries', and swear, 'sur le salvation de mon âme', that she had had contact with neither 'Sommerfeld ny Arden',[18] it was in fact her cousin's plans for her that accounted for the sudden importance of Throckmorton and his Warwickshire neighbours. A nephew of Elizabeth's Paris ambassador, Sir Nicholas, who had already tripped up once over his entanglement with the Scottish Queen, Throckmorton had acted as the courier between France and Mary's prison at Sheffield Castle since early 1583, and it was this activity that scrambled the high politics of the 'great enterprise' with the resistance war of the Midlands gentry. In her survey of Warwickshire society, Ann Hughes has attributed the persistence of recusancy in the county to the fact that its Catholicism was 'a "seigneurial" religion: most recusants amongst the minor gentry were clients or "servants" of the elite group and in villages dominated by magnates like the Throckmortons and Sheldons recusancy flourished in all ranks of society'.[19] Catholicism in the Shakespearean Midlands was a hierarchic and deferential movement, practically mandatory for client families. And its cohesiveness was epitomised by the *curriculum vitae* of Hugh Hall, the priest maintained by Sir John Throckmorton, the conspirator's father, who had previously 'resided fourteen years' with Lord Edward Windsor, Francis's cousin, after time 'at Mr Ralph Sheldon's house' and with William Sheldon, his neighbours. Hall also said Mass for Sir Thomas Cornwallis, who headed Burghley's list of recusants, was said to have built his fortune 'by selling Calais' to France, and conspired with the Earl of Southampton in plans for a French invasion; and for Sir John Talbot of Grafton, a relation of the Earl of Shrewsbury, who was Mary's gaoler. Operating as a gardener, expert in tunnelling, he had smuggled 'naughty books concealed in reams of paper with trees and plants' in consignments from Jesuits in Rouen; and then worked for the Catholic sympathiser, Sir Christopher Hatton, on his estate in Lincolnshire, where he may, however, have been 'turned' by Leicester.[20] He had run, in other words, between many of Guise's English contacts, and so it was dangerous knowledge that he took with him when he left the Throckmortons in 1583, to live with the Ardens at Park Hall.

When Somerville was stopped, he gave his name as Holland, and this pseudonym may have been inspired by one of the 'books of seditious and insidious character' the priest brought to Park Hall. This was a tribute to Juan Jaureguy, a young fundamentalist who in 1582 shot William of Orange with a hidden pistol, and though unsuccessful in killing him, proved the fatal attraction of both the handgun and of a new Catholic theory, twisted out of Calvinism: that the assassin of a tyrant could be 'absolved in advance of the deed, if he did not do it for gain but glory of God and zeal'.[21] Burghley, for one, was sure that it was his incitement by 'vile seditious books' which left this 'furious young man of Warwickshire' vulnerable to the 'enticements of certain traitorous persons, his allies and kinsmen'; and the Crown would make much of another recent work in his pocket, the Jesuit *Prayers and Meditations* of Luis de Granada, translated by Richard Hopkins, enjoining Catholics 'to suffer all calamity, affliction, persecution, imprisonment and torment of the world', rather than submit to Protestant rule.[22] This incendiary volume had been prised from an inmate of the Marshalsea by Somerville's uncle, Edward Grant, whose manor at Norbrook, near Snitterfield, had been listed as a recusant retreat as early as 1564. There his sister Elizabeth was supposed to have found it hidden, and spirited it away for him to study; as a result of which he confided in another relative, Sir John Conway of Arrow, his conviction that 'he must die for the commonwealth'. Conway had just been the object of a murder plot himself, at the hands of the Puritan Grevilles; but, when later imprisoned, he would protest his allegiance with his own *Prayers and Meditations*, 'disposed in form and alphabet of Her Majesty's Name', which was a rewriting of Granada to provide 'Comfortable Consolations (drawn out of the Latin) to Afflicted Minds'.[23] But Somerville's 'afflicted mind' can only have been inflamed when he turned for counsel to Sir Henry Goodere, the crypto-Catholic M.P. for Coventry, who silently pointed to an ornate set of 'buttons of gold he wore on his doublet and cap'. These, Sir Henry hinted, had been given him, for his 'service and suffering', by the Queen of Scots, when he had been imprisoned in the Tower for carrying her mail. This was a sinister interview, as Goodere may have turned his information immediately over to Burghley, to whose 'great favour' he later admitted he owed his sudden rehabilitation at this time.[24] But beset by inflammatory books and heraldic buttons, it must have been hard for the impressionable young squire of Edstone not to imagine he had been picked out by the great to sit on fortune's cap.

In his recent reappraisal of the Throckmorton affair, *Under the Molehill: An Elizabethan Spy Story*, Bossy continues to sideline the Somerville Plot, for the reason (which he expressed to Shakespeareans at their 1999 Stratford conference on 'Catholic Warwickshire') that 'your man knew nobody'. Given the historian's own findings on the machinations of the Jesuits and Guise, this seems both a misreading and a missed opportunity.[25] For what emerged when Arden was arrested at the London house of the Earl of Southampton, no less, and the family was tortured in the Tower was a case of the type of collective mentality studied by Roland Mousnier in his classic account of Jesuit tyrannicide in Renaissance France, *The Assassination of Henry IV*: a complex form of mass hysteria in which 'many people expected the sovereign to be assassinated. Some feared it, some longed for it passionately. Some actively worked for it. And the mere fact that people feared the prince's death and thought it so possible prompted further attempts on his life. In such situations, fear creates its object.'[26] Thus, just as François Ravaillac, the French assassin, was gripped by an obsession to murder the King tacitly shared by those who told him 'to go home, follow a wholesome diet, tell his rosary, and say his prayers', the Queen's self-appointed nemesis was said to be so excited on the evening of 24 October 'that his wife had to fetch her relatives to see him in his bedroom. To them he disclosed his plan, but they advised him to lay aside his fancies and go to sleep.' Next night in the Northamptonshire inn, it was said that 'his room again became filled with startled auditors of his frenzied exclamations that he was going to London to shoot the Queen'.[27] These statements are clearly disingenuous. As Mousnier remarks, the paradox in such a fevered atmosphere is of a figure dismissed as 'a neurotic who goes without sleep in order to walk and meditate, and lives in his imagination', by witnesses who themselves 'shared his views and had reached the same conclusion that the assassination of the King was highly desirable, or who had been tempted to assassinate him themselves', and who, had he been successful, would have 'voiced their approval of the deed and perpetrator'. Subtle and well-connected confidants such as Goodere – who had actually devised Mary Stuart's supposedly unbreakable cipher – did not need to express their opinion of the act of tyrannicide in words. In Mousnier's terms, Somerville was living in a mental world like that of the Islamic *intafada*: of virtual assassins, 'possible murderers and potential Ravaillacs'.[28]

When Jaureguy blew away the jaw of William of Orange, the Prince survived, but, as Somerville's pseudonym suggests, the assailant created a scenario to be imitated by marksmen throughout Europe. Mousnier dates the cult of assassination precisely to the instant in the early 1580s when Protestantism seemed ascendant, and 'There was a rapid reversal by Catholic and Protestant polemicists: as Protestants began stressing the inviolability of rulers, Catholics dilated on the sovereignty of the people'. And of all the ideologues who preached death to tyrants, none was more militant than the ultramontanist cadre about the Duke of Guise who would form the Catholic League. It was their *fatwa* on Protestant rulers which inflamed Balthazar Gerard, the young firebrand who eventually finished William off on 10 July 1584, by aiming three poisoned bullets at his heart; as they inspired the stabbing of Henry III by the Dominican monk, Jacques Clément, in 1589. As Mousnier relates, Henry IV suffered over twenty frenzied attacks on his life by would-be Leaguer jackals between his 1585 excommunication and his knifing by Ravaillac in 1610, the most serious of which were those made by a Flemish Dominican, Ridicauwe, in 1593; a Jesuit student, Jean Chastel, in 1594; a Carthusian, Pierre Ouin, in 1598; and an English Capuchin, Francis Langlet, in 1599. That Henry's actual murder then produced an epidemic of copycat regicides – including a boy of twelve, condemned to death for boasting he would kill the nine-year-old Louis XIII – only confirms, for Mousnier, the interaction of these deeds with the religious doctrine that demanded they be done, and that reached 'potential Ravaillacs' through sermons, pamphlets and 'directors of conscience, whose power was no less for being exercised in secret'.[29] And so, in the year of the 'great enterprise', Guise had no need to solicit gunmen for his conspiracy to kill the Queen. Like George Gifford, who volunteered in April, or William Parry in December, they presented themselves as free agents, freely choosing their subjection. A student (with Throckmorton and the martyr Alexander Briant) at Hart Hall, when Oxford was known as an 'academy of saints', John Somerville needed no prompting from his 'ghostly father' in the garden at Park Hall. In the autumn of 1583 this Warwickshire tyrannicide was at the exact point where theory found practice and discourse met disaster. The Jesuit reports exposed what Bossy terms this 'state of euphoria', even as they denied its political motivation:

> Ten gentlemen of the county of Warwick were recently seized and thrown into the Tower. Of these, the two Throckmortons and a man called Arden were most cruelly racked, and at the same time, a priest named Hall. The cause is their devotion to the Apostolic See. Some reason, however, is invented, namely that they should too much favour the Queen of Scots, and had a hand in some revolutionary purpose. Whatever it be, I hear that many have good hope of England being brought back to the faith within a short time ... Our brethren are so animated by these dangers that it is difficult to hold them back.[30]

Immediately he was questioned in Oxford gaol, Somerville declared 'That he hath heard his father-in-law say the Queen would not suffer the Catholic religion and doth execute all good Catholics'. And later, in the Tower, he divulged that 'the idea of murdering the Queen struck him after what his wife had said at Park Hall in the presence of Edward Arden and his brother that touched very greatly on her honour'.[31] The insinuation was to Elizabeth's sexual relations with Robert Dudley Earl of Leicester, the Protestant overlord of Warwickshire, whose enmity had cost Edward Arden his office as High Sheriff of the county. And its specificity was keyed to the bitter politics of Shakespearean Warwickshire, divided on religious lines between reformers – Dudleys, Lucys, Grevilles and Combes – and conservatives – Ardens, Catesbys, Cloptons, Somervilles and Throckmortons. This was a district, historians have shown, where 'religious factionalism caused Puritans and Catholics to take exceptionally hostile positions to one another', which were more diehard than in any other part of England.[32] It was a region where the new Counter-Reformation fundamentalism was easily grafted on to the grievances of a *fronde* of impoverished squires such as Thomas Trussell of Billesley, whose library (which conceals a priest-hole behind its panelling) is supposed to have been a room where Shakespeare studied.[33] No wonder, then, that when Edward Arden was hanged at Tyburn, and his property seized by the Crown, his widow and dependents were taken in by the Throckmortons at Coughton, where they were still lodging in 1593, when the pursuivants rearrested 'Mistress Arden, wife of the traitor, and her servants', for possessing 'superstitious things and furniture for mass', as well as for 'harbouring a seminary priest in some secret place'.[34] Her son Robert was imprisoned once again for recusancy in 1596; while her nephew, John Grant, became notorious for the contempt with which he obstructed searchers when they raided Norbrook hunting for hidden priests. In 1598 this cousin of the Ardens made a match which connected them to an even more sensational terrorist conspiracy than the one for which they had already suffered so much, when he married Dorothy, the sister of Thomas and Robert Winter, and a cousin of Robert Catesby and Francis Tresham. Even as the Shakespeares were appealing to be publicly allied with the disgraced family, the knot was being tied by them which would seal the Gunpowder Plot.

Considering how crucial the theme of 'killing the king' would become in his plays, it is astonishing biographers make so little of Shakespeare's familiarity with the Counter-Reformation culture that produced the Jesuit tyrannicide cult, and even less of his closeness to the Somerville Plot. One of the few Shakespeareans ever to have considered the possible impact of his relatives' suicidal terrorism on the dramatist was the Victorian scholar Richard Simpson, whose researches on Edmund Campion gave him privileged insight into the Stratford papist undergound, where the martyr was hidden during his mission to England in 1580, when John Shakespeare himself signed up to the conspiratorial *Spiritual Testament* of Catholic faith, so it appears, brought by the Jesuits from the Counter-Reformation ideologue Carlo Borromeo in Milan.[35] This was no mere vow of conscience but, in the atmosphere of the Wars of Religion, the equivalent of joining the Taliban. In his biography of Campion, Simpson was able to situate the swearing of this pledge, in fact, as one of the initiation rites practised by the Jesuits to cement an English sodality of vigilantes, in direct imitation of the French Catholic League.[36] So he found it significant that Somerville had been escorted on his fatal ride towards London by one of Edward Arden's young pages, who later testified how he seemed so 'tormented of mind' that he deserted him before he was shopped to magistrates by the suspicious publican at Aynho.[37] This page, Simpson inferred, was possibly the nineteen-year-old Shakespeare himself, whom, he speculated, the gunman made his secretary in the weeks when he paced the Park Hall library, book in hand, torn 'between fear and resolution', and so became 'the original of Hamlet'.[38] Such a theory was far-fetched and did the critic harm; but it did highlight what must have been a traumatic crisis for Shakespeare's neighbourhood, when Arden's Protestant usurper as Sheriff, Sir Thomas Lucy, with 'Griffin the Preacher', the Clerk of the Privy Council, Thomas Wilkes, and officers from London ransacked the homes of suspected terrorists hunting for incriminating evidence. What the investigators had to report, however, was that, as if by plan, Somerville's relatives 'alleged that since Midsummer he had been affected with a frantic humour grown of jealousy conceived of his wife', and that unless Rackmaster Norton extracted more hard evidence from his torture of the prisoners, it would be impossible to make further arrests:

> Unless you can make Somerville, Arden, Hall the priest, Somerville's wife, and his sister, speak directly to those things which you desire to have discovered, it will not be possible for us to find out more than is found already; for the Papists in this county do generally work upon the advantage of clearing their houses of all show of suspicion, and therefore, unless you can charge them with matter from the mouths of your prisoners, look not to wring any thing from them by finding matter of suspicion in their houses.[39]

'Like Hamlet', Simpson thought, the suicide attacker had 'concealed his determination to kill the prince under the mask of an alienated mind', and at the torturing hour, when the Ardens were being racked in the Tower, their friends and relations saved their necks with the fiction that it was through sexual jealousy of his own (rather than sexual disgust with the Queen) that he had fallen 'Into the madness wherein he now raves / And all we mourn for' (*Hamlet*, 2.2.150). So there was a deep complicity, the critic inferred, between Shakespeare's creative imagination and his community's dire necessity to 'throw dust in the eyes of the watchful Puritans',[40] and the Somerville disaster taught the dramatist a lesson he never forgot, in the perils (suggested by the terrorist's very name) of standing 'too much i'th' sun' (1.2.67) of a public account. Thus, with the searchers' efforts to 'pluck out the heart' of the townsmen's allegiance (3.3.336), and their own panic to ensure that it was not possible to 'wring any thing' from them, this Stratford tragedy could be seen as the template for all of Shakespearean drama, in which, over and again, the scene was set by the sovereign's despotic allegiance test – to find out 'Which of you shall we say doth love us most' – and the subject's obstinate refusal to 'heave heart' into mouth (*King Lear*, 1.1.49; 89). So, between despotism and desperation, public acclaim and private anguish, or what was displayed and what could never be disclosed, the catastrophic events of 1583 plunged the young Shakespeare into the secrecy that would make his work so enigmatic, Simpson concluded, and motivate his stage. Shakespeare had been described as the son of a butcher in John Aubrey's seventeenth-century anecdote, who 'When he killed a calf would do it in high style, and make a speech', the critic recalled; but was not this legend an allegory of the dramatist's own mediated relationship to religious terrorism, and of an art which displaced the burning question of the day – 'Whether to suffer the slings and arrows' of outrageous oppression (like some medieval martyr), or take arms, 'And, by opposing, end them' (*Hamlet*, 3.1.59–61) (like the modern regicide) – by ritualising the 'killing' on stage?[41] Hence, as Edward Arden was disembowelled and hanged at Tyburn, and his son-in-law silenced, Shakespeare played the fool when the investigators called, according to the Victorian critic, and, in the greatest crisis of his young life, learned how to act in order to survive.

The Somerville episode was so dramatic that it was interpreted by Simpson as the crucial turning-point of the dramatist's life; and he even wondered whether Aubrey's story that 'there was another butcher's son in the town ... held not inferior to him for natural wit, that died young', might not refer to the assassin.[42] Whatever the likelihood of such a twin, this phantom did vividly illustrate Simpson's theme: that there was a historic choice in the writer's development between resistance and collaboration; and that his plays derived tension from this counterpoint between the road to London and the never-taken path to Rome his father may have urged. For as the first to realise that John Shakespeare's claim to be absent from church out of fear of 'process of debt' was a 'common excuse of recusants', and that 'mortgage of the greater part of his property' was 'the recognised means of evading the iniquitous robberies of the penal laws', Simpson grasped how much he risked when he was twice 'called to account for recusancy to Sir Thomas Lucy'.[43] He also perceived that the vicious conflicts which split Stratford – such as the 1607 enclosure riots; the 1601 corn dispute, in which Shakespeare's friend Richard Quiney was murdered by Greville hit-men; and the legendary poaching from Lucy, when the poet was said to have been whipped out of town – were all manifestations of sectarian hate.[44] 'Deer-poaching was no mere lark', Simpson noted, 'but an act of retributive justice or revenge';[45] and the deer in question made them targets for just such a slaughter. For their park, research suggests, was Fulbrook, near Warwick, entrusted to the Ardens after its owner, Sir Francis Englefield, had sailed to France, in protest at the coronation of a heretic Queen.[46] In the Ardennes Englefield became a rabid agitator for an Armada; so Lucy had royal warrant when he seized Fulbrook from the Ardens, acting on a certificate of 'the death of Francis Englefield overseas' (in fact, he had over twenty years to live). After the Arden executions, a deer-poaching raid on this lost domain would have had the colour, then, of a symbolic invasion. So, though trivialised by biographers, Shakespeare's participation in this religious riot looks ominous in the light of Catholic resistance. Touchstone may express the player's hind-sight, when the clown regrets, 'now am I in Arden, the more fool I' (*As You Like It*, 2.4.12); for the season of the deer-poaching was also when, we think, Shakespeare's father hid his Testament of Catholic faith in their attic, panicked by Lucy's investigation. And it might be that Shakespeare's elusiveness dates from this crisis, when, rather than take up 'arms against a sea of troubles'

(*Hamlet*, 3.1.61), like their suicidal cousins, his family learned to conceal their loyalties in that dark and secret place that made cowards of them all.

'There's no news ... but the old news: that is, the old Duke is banished ... and three or four loving lords have put themselves into voluntary exile with him, whose lands and revenues enrich the new Duke; therefore he gives them good leave to wander' (*As You Like It*, 1.1.86–90): all the elements of Shakespeare's essential dramatic scenario were presented to him in the stark outlines of the Arden tragedy. But so too was the existential choice which, in his biography of Donne, John Carey has described as a 'communal agony', of whether to side with 'sanctified and holy traitors' (2.3.13) such as Campion, or 'live, / And pray, and sing, and tell old tales ... In a walled prison' (*Lear*, 5.3.11–18) of Anglican conformity. Thus, for Simpson, and again for recent biographers, the tension of his plot-lines came from the dramatist's own historical situation, when, like Donne in Carey's account, this 'kinsman of martyrs committed mortal sin against the Faith, as he 'betrayed his father's spirit' and defected from Catholicism, yet, by this very act of desertion, created an 'apostate art' out of 'self-doubt, divided loyalty, sundering of ties, spiritual estrangement, and loss of trust'. 'Though he forsook the Roman Church', Carey remarks, Donne 'never escaped its grasp ... his Catholic upbringing marked him indelibly'; but he also reminds us that (far from being sensationalised or novelistic, as objectors imagine)[47] this was, in fact, the plight of an entire generation of Elizabethans who confronted what the poet and martyr Robert Southwell called 'the dreadful moment' of collaborationist choice, 'whereupon dependeth a whole eternity'.[48] Speculating that John Shakespeare was one of those 'Catholics who had great difficulty bringing up their children to follow their religion', Simpson dated the dramatist's own defection to the instant he fled 'to the dissipations of London', where 'a strict and troublesome religion, involving persecution and hardship, was scarcely likely to be professed by fast young men'. Seeking 'safety from continual change of residence', Shakespeare spent his adulthood, according to the Victorian critic, in the constant effort to live down his bloody fundamentalist affiliations, escaping the holy war for which he had been primed in the refuge of a profession which was a standing mockery of martyrdom:

> Luckily for himself, he was but a poor despised player, to whom as much licence on matters of state was allowed as to Motley himself; and still more, who was necessary to the amusement of the persons who might have hanged him if he had been a more important personage.[49]

'An you should do it too terribly you would fright the Duchess ... and that were enough to hang us all': the actors' tactic, rehearsed in *A Midsummer Night's Dream*, to 'leave the killing out' so as not to offend the court 'ladies' (2.1.61; 3.1.12), provided the dramatist with his own survival strategy, according to Simpson's account of a career in which 'his "motley" saved him, because he was necessary to the Queen's amusement'.[50] We do not know whether Shakespeare was personally present, in fact, to see Arden hanged, or witnessed the martyrdom in December 1581 of Campion himself, though Simpson argued that 'we cannot suppose that he was less moved than the rest of the London crowds at the harrowing barbarities practised at Tyburn'.[51] The dramatist would have doubtless heard, in any case, reports like the one relayed by Allen to Rome, how 'Somerville was induced to make his accusation by a new and unheard-of kind of torture: they put on his feet shoes three inches too short, then they place his feet in an iron cauldron and apply fire to them. By this burning hot shoe his feet are further constricted, causing extraordinary pain. Finally, on the thoroughly roasted shoes they pour oil, which makes the fiery torment unbearable'.[52] But, as Graham Greene complained, his decision to 'leave out the killing' means there is 'one whole area of the Elizabethan scene that we miss' on Shakespeare's stage, which seems so 'removed from the routine of the torture chamber'. Francis Bacon, the novelist observed, had been one of the lawyers sitting quietly in attendance when Catholics were racked, 'and given orders for the torture'. But 'for a moment one would like to imagine oneself a follower of the Baconian heresy', Greene confessed, 'and to believe that it was William Shakespeare who faced [the martyrs] on their examination in the Tower'.[53]

Like Queen Elizabeth herself, who was 'extremely loath to be known to her subjects, to foreign princes, and to Christendom at large as a torturer',[54] Shakespeare has been accused of drawing a veil over the culture of violence in which he thrived. Thus, from the absence of the martyrs, objected Greene, 'one might have guessed there was a vast vacuum where the Faith had been: the noise of the pilgrimages has been stilled: ... one might say that the Christians are silent in the grey world of Lear's blasted heath. An old Rome has taken the place of the Christian Rome', where characters speak like stoics or 'pay lip service to Venus' as the code for Elizabeth. Greene had evidently not noticed how the Quarto spelling meant that Gloucester was tortured and blinded to extract an answer to the question 'Wherefore to Douer?' or Douai (Lear, 3.7.52). But the same disgust at Shakespeare's effacement of contemporary violence was expressed by the cultural materialist critic Francis Barker, who theorised that it was, in fact, the dramatist's essential project to occlude the barbarity of Tyburn and the Tower, by 'locating safely "out there" the violence which he codes as barbarism but which may in fact belong dangerously "in here" ... making violence into a spectacle of the exotic ... in another time, in another place, among other people'.[55] Yet, as Simpson contended, what is most striking about the dramatist's muteness on the Elizabethan despotism and its resisters is how it goaded his Protestant rivals, such as Henry Chettle, into deploring his refusal 'to dissemble, flatter and lie' to praise a tyrant he may have despised.[56] Shakespeare's canniness was not, therefore, a modern invention, but had always been the subject of disappointment, scandal and resentment, as from the first his critics voiced dismay with what he wrote, in contrast to their hopes of what he might. The institution of Shakespeare criticism originated precisely from this disillusionment, Simpson thought, and the reproach of his very earliest readers, such as the Jesuit Southwell, that by 'leaving out the killing' on the scaffold and the rack, this 'smooth and ambiguous' young writer had failed to live up to their expectations of becoming the great religious poet of his age.

Richard Simpson's researches into Shakespeare's Catholic Warwicksire established, with a wealth of archival detail, the inescapable horizon for a historicist reading of the plays, which only a criticism sunk in what Michel Foucault termed the 'historically well-determined little pedagogy' of 'the death of the author' continues to reject.[57] Yet the rediscovery of his Catholic terrorist affiliations means not only that critics have more cause for confidence about where, geographically and ideologically, Shakespeare was coming from in the 1580s. It also means that they have begun to grasp more of where he was going, in contrast to the itinerary that might have been expected. As Gary Taylor summarises it, all the evidence suggests that 'for much of his life Shakespeare was a church papist', or occasional conformist to the state religion; that 'once he began dividing his life between Stratford and London, he might have become a recusant', absenting from the Church of England; but that 'like a majority of English Catholics, he had no appetite for martyrdom'.[58] The question for modern biographers has therefore become, how far down the Roman road taken by Somerville and his relations did Shakespeare go before he diverged from the calvary of the martyrs? How much of the dark and seditious narrative of Elizabethan Catholicism, of which Shakespeare did *not* speak, can be projected, that is to say, into the bright, spectacular spaces of which he did? And this question is imperative, because, as Stephen Greenblatt remarks, if there is now 'a clear implication' to be drawn from the archives, that 'the playwright was probably brought up in a Roman Catholic household in a time of official suspicion and persecution of recusancy'; and if, in 1580, John Shakespeare's pledge of loyalty to Campion's Catholic League was seriously sworn, when he buried his father, twenty-one years later, an apostate who had himself con-formed would surely have been 'haunted by the spirit of his Catholic father', reproaching him from the grave.[59]

'Did his kinsfolk help him afterwards with their Masses, prayers, and alms?' Simpson wondered, when he described how John Shakespeare had very likely been buried without any monument because of his inflexible recusancy, in contrast to the temporising that secured his son an honoured tomb.[60] If there are, Jonathan Bate declares, 'good reasons to suppose the *Spiritual Testament* is authentic', upon Simpson's question now hangs not just 'irresistible biograph-ical speculation' but crucial issues about 'the whole range of Shakespeare's plays'. Since we know enough about John Shakespeare to support 'the inference that he died a Catholic', as Bate asserts, and that 'as a faithful Catholic he would believe that he would do penance in Purgatory until he could gain remission through the prayers of those he left on earth', the dramatist's relationship to this Catholic 'cult of the dead' suddenly becomes central to our interpretation of Shakespeare's stage.[61] It does so because, as Greenblatt explains, at moments like the close of *A Midsummer Night's Dream*, when the Fairies return to bless the house; or when Edgar quotes Jesuit exorcists in *King Lear*, the plays are 'haunted' by the ghosts of their Catholic past, 'by rituals and beliefs that have been *emptied out*' or abandoned, 'leaving only vivid empty ceremonies' behind.[62] Thus, it is as if Simpson's question itself returns to haunt the critics of a secular age; and Greenblatt has recently made Shakespeare's own haunting by his recusant father the focus of a commentary on *Hamlet*, where he elaborates his thesis that the Elizabethan playhouse stole its props and rituals from the Church, but now in the context of old Hamlet's claim to be in a Catholic Purgatory, like that envisioned by Borromeo: 'I am thy father's spirit, / Doomed for a certain term to walk the night, / And for the day confined to fast in fires / Till the foul crimes done in my days of nature / Are burnt and purged away' (*Hamlet*, 1.5.9–13). The Ghost's cry from the grave – 'Adieu, adieu, remember me' (91) – becomes so significant, in this interpretation, because Shakespeare's entire drama is indicted by Greenblatt as a case of *bad faith*: a perversion of papistry into poetry, spirits into actors, and, as Prospero puns (in the last lines of the last play), prayers into praise (*Tempest*, Ep, 16–20). Solemnly sworn, as he may have been, to witness his father's Catholic pledge, Shakespeare's dramatic career was nothing but a faithless betrayal, if the oath had any meaning, of the cause he had promised to remember and uphold.[63]

'How long will a man lie i'th'earth ere he rot?' (*Hamlet*, 5.1.151): Hamlet's encounter with the putrid skull of the father-figure he once kissed was scripted, the Arden editor points out, on the basis of a chapter Shakespeare also quoted in one of his earliest plays, about 'How filthy and loathsome the body is after it is dead: And the burying of it in the grave', from the *Prayers and Meditations* of Granada.[64] If Freudians are right, therefore, to connect *Hamlet* with the death of the 'tanner' (154), John Shakespeare, it seems that this graveyard abreacts the ghosts of more than one of the son's Catholic forefathers. For in *3 Henry VI* it is the dying Earl of Warwick who cites Granada, lamenting his 'glory smeared in dust and blood', and grieving that 'My parks, my walks, my manors that I had, / Even now forsake me, and of all my lands / Is nothing left me but my body's length. / Why, what is pomp, rule, reign, but earth and dust?' (5.2.23–7). Warwick dies with a kiss for the 'sweet soul of Montague', in a clear tribute to Viscount Montague, the papist stalwart and grandfather of Shakespeare's patron, Southampton, who, as the text reports, had just 'breathed his last' when the play was staged (32–48). So, it is tempting to read the citation of the book the Ardens learned by heart as a similar reference to Catholic resistance, and to those talks between an assassin and a labourer who spoke by 'equivocation' (*Hamlet*, 5.1.127) as he dug the garden at Park Hall. Warwick's speech begs such decipherment, since it features an allegorical forest which contains a lofty cedar tree standing beside an ancient oak, a sovereign eagle blown far south by winter wind and a heraldic lion slumbering in the undergrowth. In the 1590s these were the recognised symbols of papist pastoralism, and, like the sheltering cedar in Montague's own *Entertainment at Cowdray*, the Warwickshire tree seems to epitomise the seigneurialism of an Adamic nobility before the Fall:[65]

> Whose arms gave shelter to the princely eagle,
> Under whose shade the ramping lion slept,
> Whose top-branch over-peered Jove's spreading tree
> And kept low shrubs from winter's powerful wind.
> (*3 Henry VI*, 5.2.11–14)

The lion, the shrubs and the oak: Shakespeare would elaborate the same Edenic allegory in *As You Like It*, where, though there is a gap in the forest where the cedar stood, the lionesss 'couching, head on ground, with catlike watch', for the 'green and gilded snake' to wake the wretch lying beneath an 'old oak, whose boughs were mossed with age / And high top bald with dry antiquity', looks very like a symbol of Elizabeth, hungrily waiting for the Jesuit 'guild' to sting Catholics out of their torpor beneath a senile and unprotecting Rome: 'For 'tis / The royal disposition of that beast / To prey on nothing that doth seem as dead.' In the comedy, Orlando fancifully fights the lioness to rescue Arden, while the guilty snake 'unlinked itself, / And with indented glides did slip away / Into a bush' (4.3.103–17). But in the first version the poisonous propaganda of the Catholic League is entwined with Warwick's fall, and the news comes too late that 'The Queen from France hath brought a puissant power even now' (*3 Henry VI*, 5.2.31). 'Thus yields the cedar', the old lord sighs, 'to the axe's edge' (11); and the image of execution, together with his name, makes it reasonably certain that this is a portrait of Edward Arden on the scaffold, viewing with eyes that had been 'piercing as the midday sun / To search the secret treasons of the world', the betrayal which brought him and his son-in-law to a treason verdict and 'death's black veil' (16–18). If so, then the 'princely eagle' which has lost its Warwickshire perch would be the 'Queen from France', Mary Stuart; and those 'low shrubs' exposed by the crash of the branching tree, when Arden failed to 'over-peer' the machinations of the Pope, would be his poor relations, such as the Shakespeares themselves. We can draw these inferences because Warwick's death is immediately preceded by what reads like a résumé of the treacheries and confusions which led to the Somerville debacle, when the Lancastrians are betrayed and then ambushed by the House of York:

> WARWICK: Say, Somerville – what says my loving son?
>   And, by thy guess, how nigh is Clarence now?
> SOMERVILLE: At Southam I did leave him with his forces,
>   And do expect him here some two hours hence.
> (*A march afar off*)

WARWICK: Then Clarence is at hand – I hear his drum.
SOMERVILLE: It is not so, my lord. Here Southam lies.
                   The drum your honour hears marcheth from Warwick.
WARWICK: Who should that be? Belike, unlooked-for friends.
SOMERVILLE: They are at hand, and you shall quickly know.
                   (*Flourish. Enter King Edward and Richard Duke of Gloucester
                   with soldiers*)

                                                                   (*3 Henry VI*, 5.1.7–15)

Editors have searched for a historical Somerville contemporary with the episode staged in this exchange, which ostensibly occurs in 1471 on the walls of Coventry, where Warwick and the Mayor await reinforcements on the eve of the Battle of Barnet. Yet they are unable to suggest any convincing candidate, or to explain why Shakespeare names Somerville at all, when two previous scouts, who report that Oxford is marching from Dunsmore while Montague is still at Daventry, are designated only as First and Second Messenger.[66] Warwick's question to Somerville – 'what says my loving son?' – again makes it plain, however, that this is an allusion to the Ardens, that the father this 'son' calls 'your honour' is the ex-High-Sheriff, and that the interlude honours the kinsmen all but named when the Earl affirms, 'In Warwickshire I have true-hearted friends, / Not mutinous in peace, yet bold in war' (4.9.9–10). So, it is the geographical specificity that raises the incident out of the Wars of Roses and places it, like the Induction of *The Taming of the Shrew*, in the dramatist's own time. But if this is the case, then this reconstruction of events might be one of the best reports we have on Somerville's fatal ride and provide a map of his betrayal. For the most important piece of evidence added by the dramatisation is, of course, that, far from being a solitary lunatic, the horseman was a player in a much more extensive conspiracy, involving a coalition of Catholic peers, and timed to coincide with a landing by 'those powers that the Queen / Hath raised in Gallia' (5.3.7–8). The play confirms, then, everything we can deduce about the assassin's backers from diplomatic papers; and a later diversion puts the Midland plot into just such a perspective, when Queen Margaret shrugs at the loss of the English 'holding-anchor' of 'our poor barque', using a standard figure for the Roman Church to assign affairs to 'the skilful pilot's charge' (5.4.1–20), which is to say, the Pope. Her obliviousness to Warwick's death may signify Mary Stuart's callousness towards her pawns; but treachery occurs closer to home, in this testimony, after Somerville departs Southam, the town where the squire of Edstone would join the road south to Aynho. Warwick's uncertainty about where 'Southam lies' becomes telling, therefore, in this scenario, because the manor there belonged to Job Throckmorton, the Puritan M.P. and cousin of the plotter, Francis.[67] Whoever rode ahead from Southam on 25 October 1583 to alert the authorities in Oxford, by harping on the treachery of the place the text could hardly point a more accusing finger at this black sheep of the Throckmortons, as the Judas of his family, the likeliest informer, and a model for 'false, fleeting, perjured Clarence' (*Richard III*, 1.4.55) himself:

WARWICK:	And lo, where George of Clarence sweeps along,
	Of force enough to bid his brother battle;
	With whom an upright zeal to right prevails
	More than the nature of a brother's love.
CLARENCE:	Clarence, Clarence, for Lancaster!
KING EDWARD:	*Et tu Brute* – wilt thou stab Caesar too?
	A parley, sirra, to George of Clarence.
WARWICK:	Come, Clarence, come – thou wilt if Warwick call.
CLARENCE:	Father of Warwick, know you what this means?
	He takes his red rose out of his hat and throws it at Warwick.
	Look – here I throw my infamy at thee!
	I will not ruinate my father's house ...

(3 Henry VI, 5,1,76–86)

On 13 January 1584 Walsingham 'received from Job Throckmorton his list of certain papists in Warwickshire he suggests should be examined, especially of Rowington'. Those then arrested 'touching Edward Arden' came from both sides of the informer's family, and included Shakespeare's friend John Robinson.[68] If the zealot from Southam was indeed the traitor in his father's house, then the 'upright' words attributed to him on stage had a bitter point. For when Shakespeare came to Bankside in the 1580s, he would see the heads of Arden and Somerville impaled on London Bridge. The reprieve of the priest, Hall, like the snake of the allegory, can only have aggravated the shame of these relics with which the writer would claim to share blood. And at the moment when John Shakespeare applied to resuscitate the outlawed arms, Arden's daughters were petitioning for a pittance from 'the revenue assured their mother, come, by reason of her offence, into Her Majesty's hand'.[69] What can have impelled the Shakespeares to declare an affinity with such a cause? An answer is suggested by the bravado of their other neighbours – Catesbys, Winters and Treshams – who by 1599 were already aligning with the Earl of Essex. In his essay on the Essex Revolt, Mervyn James notes the number of Catholics in its inner circle, among them 'the Treshams and the ultramontane crusader Robert Catesby'. The reason for their sabre-rattling was the hope Essex gave of toleration, and in the last days of the Tudor century this prospect was focused on negotiations with King James.[70] Nor was their optimism misplaced, for among of the first acts of James in England was to award a pension to the heir of Edward Arden, and a knighthood to the brother of John Somerville, in honour of their service to his mother, the Queen of Scots. Sir William Somerville would climb to be Sheriff of Warwickshire, and, it is said, a drinking companion, 'who lived with him in habits of intimacy', of the master of New Place.[71] For the son of John Shakespeare, the recusant, would also rise in the new dispensation, 'beyond the imagination of his neighbours ... to an unspeakable estate' (*Winter's Tale*, 4.2.34–5) The poet learned to trust the fence-sitting of a Stanley more than the heroics of a Percy; but his father's championship of the Ardens – retracted on the fall of Essex – must have confirmed him in the patience he made a mainspring of his plots: the faith that, in the words of Southwell, 'Times go by turns':

> Not always fall of leaf, nor ever spring,
> No endless night, yet not eternal day;
> The saddest birds a season find to sing,
> The roughest storm a calm may soon allay;
> Thus with succeeding turns God tempereth all,
> That man may hope to rise, yet fear to fall.[72]

'Hitherto we have washed our hands, as it were, in milk; henceforward, however, we shall steep not only our hands, but our arms, in the brightest and best blood that is in the hearts of the papists': whether or not this terrifying threat was actually 'spoken openly and with great anger by the Queen of England herself', on hearing of Somerville's confession, as William Allen reported, the image of butchery darkly illustrated the sensation felt by Shakespeare's friends and relations, that, however much times went by turns, the 1583 events marked a catastrophe in the situation of English Catholics, and their fear that 'there is imminent the greatest and most bitter persecution we have had'.[73] And an intriguing story told by Robert Parsons concerning Somerville's arrest suggests that those who knew about his ride understood exactly what they had at stake, and may have tried to call him back. For what alerted the informers, the Jesuit claimed, was a noisy fracas on the Oxford road, when the young squire 'happened to thrash a certain butcher, for the reason that he would not lend him some money'. Somerville had reacted to this rejection like 'a raging lunatic', the story went, and, when questioned by magistrates about the assault, 'he answered in the maddest way that he had done it because he imagined this butcher to be the Queen'. For the Father, this 'very mad speech' certified that the assailant was indeed 'a madman … incensed on account of Arden's daughter, whom he had treated very badly'.[74] But it may be that there was method in the madness. For though we can never, of course, identify the mystery 'butcher', who may or may not have been the same boy as the Arden page, it is easy enough to conjecture a scenario in which the assassin's associate, charged with his baggage, took fright at Southam crossroads, and tried to save their lives by withholding the money he had been entrusted. For the 'madman' this sudden obstruction was tantamount to siding with the Queen. But the 'butcher' sensed that the real foolishness would be to give what had been asked. 'When he killed a calf, he would do it in high style and make a speech': whoever he was, and whatever his part in the tragedy of Arden, this Warwickshire 'butcher' was evidently one of those who had foreseen the difference, in Elizabeth's England, between playing the fool and 'the bleeding business' (*Julius*, 3.1.168) soon to come.

NOTES

1 Samuel Schoenbaum, *Shakespeare: A Documentary Life* (Oxford: Oxford University Press, 1975), pp. 166–73.
2 They were Thomas Blount, George Bromley, Sir Fulke Greville, Sir Thomas Lucy, Ralph Sheldon and William Sheldon. For Somerville's numerous family and business links with Shakespeare, see Christopher Whitfield, 'Some of Shakespeare's Contemporaries in the Middle Temple', *Notes and Queries*, December 1966, pp. 443–8.
3 Samuel Schoenbaum, *Shakespeare's Lives* (Oxford: Clarendon Press, 1970), p. 640. For Edward Darcy and events leading up to the assassination of William the Silent see *Calendar of State Papers (CSP) Foreign: 1583*, pp. 80, 84–6 and 89.
4 *CSP Spanish: 1580–86* (henceforth *CSPS*), p. 512. The Jesuit protest of innocence is taken to an extreme by Leo Hicks, S.J., who argues in *An Elizabethan Problem: Some Aspects of the Careers of Two Exile-Adventuers* (London: Burns and Oates, 1964), that the government fabricated not only the case against Arden and Somerville but the entire Throckmorton Plot: see pp. 39 and 50–3. Cf. William Dugdale, *The Antiquities of Warwickshire* (London: 1656), vol. 2, p. 830: 'John Somerville, Esq., who in 1583, being a hot-spirited Gentleman and about 23 years of age, but a Roman Catholic by profession, is said to have been so far transported with zeal for the restoring of that religion, by the instigation of one Hall, a priest, that he resolved to kill the Queen, and to that purpose made a journey to London, and upon his apprehension confessed his intent: but being arraigned, condemned and committed to Newgate, within three days after he was found strangled in his lodging. How far guilty of this, God knows; for with what a high hand things were then borne through the power of Robert Dudley, Earl of Leicester is not unknown to most men: which Earl had a particular spleen against Mr Arden of Park Hall, father-in-law of this gentleman, as by sundry aged persons of credit I have often heard'. See also *Victoria County History: Warwickshire*, vols 3, p. 92, and 4, p. 45.
5 *CSPS*, pp. 511–12.
6 *Calendar of State Papers Domestic: 1581–90* (henceforth *CSPD*), p. 161: 'Secret advertisements of priests and papists in England', despatch from Exeter, February 1584.
7 J.E. Neale, *Queen Elizabeth* (London: Jonathan Cape, 1934), p. 264.
8 James McConica, 'The Catholic Experience in Tudor Oxford', in Thomas McCoog (ed.), *The Reckoned Expense: Edmund Campion and the Early English Jesuits* (Woodbridge: Boydell Press, 1996), p. 53; *CSPD*, p. 126: 'Examination of diverse persons taken before John Doyley of Merton touching certain speeches against the Queen's Majesty supposed to have been spoken by John Somerville'.
9 Ibid., pp. 131, 132 and 135: 26 November: 'Report of conversations with Peter Snell, servant of Mr Walter Covert, tracing the participation of one Nicholas Wolf of Washington in Sussex in the late pretended mischief of of Somerfield against Her Majesty'; 28 November: 'Evidence against Nicholas Wolf touching dangerous words against the Queen. Examination of Mary Wolf as to certain books found in the house'; 6 December: 'Examination of Peter Snell of Crawley and Edward Wolf of Washington in Sussex touching Nicholas Wolf's designs against Her Majesty'.
10 Dennis Flynn, '"Out of Step": Notes on Jasper Heywood', in McCoog, op. cit. (note 8), p. 185.
11 *CSPD*, pp. 131, 135, 277 and 285.
12 Lord Paget to Mary Queen of Scots, quoted in Richard Simpson, 'What was the Religion of Shakespeare? Part I' *The Rambler*, 9 (1858), p. 186.
13 *Dictionary of National Biography* (henceforth *DNB*).
14 Quoted in Michael Graves, *Thomas Norton: The Parliament Man* (Oxford: Blackwell, 1994), p. 266.
15 John Bossy, 'The Heart of Robert Persons', in McCoog, op. cit. (note 8), p. 150.
16 *CSPD*, p. 295: Undated: 'Further secret intelligence from one at Exeter'.
17 Ibid., p. 138: 20 December.

18 *Historic Manuscripts Commission: Salisbury (Cecil) Papers*, vol. 13, pp. 247–8.

19 Ann Hughes, *Politics, Society and Civil War in Warwickshire, 1620–1660* (Cambridge: Cambridge University Press, 1987), p. 63.

20 *CSPD*, p. 142; *DNB*; Dwight Peck (ed.), *Leicester's Commonwealth: The Copy of a Letter Written by a Master of Art of Cambridge, 1584* (Athens: Ohio University Press, 1985), pp. 173 and 219, n. 261; William Herle (government spy) to Lord Burghley, 23 November 1583, repr. in John Bossy, *Giordano Bruno and the Embassy Affair* (New Haven: Yale University Press, 1991), p. 208.

21 *CSPD*, p. 135. For 'Somerfield *alias* Holland' see also Charlotte Carmichael Stopes, *Shakespeare's Warwickshire Contemporaries* (rev. ed., Stratford-upon-Avon: Shakespeare Head, 1907), pp. 75–6.

22 Ibid., pp. 76 and 81.

23 *DNB*: Conway's book is entitled, *Prayers and Meditations, gathered out of the Sacred Letters and Virtuous Writers, disposed in Form of the Alphabet of the Queen, her Most Excellent Majesty's Name; whereunto are added Comfortable Consolations (drawn out of the Latin) to afflicted minds.*

24 Stopes, op. cit. (note 21), p. 75 and 78–9; *CSPD*, pp. 124 and 129; Philip Hasler, *The Elizabethan House of* Commons (London: HMSO, 1986), p. 203; Bernard Newdigate, *Michael Drayton and His Circle* (Oxford: Shakespeare Head Press, 1961), pp. 27–31; *DNB*.

25 John Bossy, *Under the Molehill: An Elizabethan Spy Story* (New Haven: Yale University Press, 2001), pp. 78, 87 and 108; and op. cit. (note 20), p. 207. The 1999 conference on 'Shakespeare's Catholic Warwickshire' took place at the Old Grammar School, Stratford-upon-Avon, under the auspices of the Centre for Renaissance Studies of the University of Warwick.

26 Robert Mousnier, *The Assassination of Henry IV: The Tyrannicide Problem and the Consolidation of the French Absolute Monarchy in the Early Seventeenth Century*, trans. Joan Spencer (London: Faber and Faber, 1973), pp. 48–9.

27 Quoted in Stopes, op. cit. (note 21), pp. 78–9.

28 Mousnier, op. cit. (note 26), pp. 34–5, 38 and 48.

29 Ibid., pp. 97 and 104–5.

30 Bossy, op. cit. (note 25), p. 78. P. Renold (ed.), *Letters of William Allen and Richard Barret, 1572–1598* (London: Catholic Record Society, 1967), pp. 59–60: Richard Barret to Alphonso Agazzari, Rheims, 28 December 1583.

31 Stopes, op. cit. (note 21), p. 93.

32 Roger Manning, *Village Revolts: Social Protest and Popular Disturbances in England, 1509–1640* (Oxford: Clarendon Press, 1988), p. 237.

33 For John Trussel, historian, poet and publisher of the martyr Robert Southwell, see Clara Longworth de Chambrun, *Shakespeare: A Portrait Restored* (London: Hollis and Carter, 1957), pp. 25–6.

34 *CSPD*, p. 35.

35 See Richard Wilson, 'Shakespeare and the Jesuits', *Times Literary Supplement*, 19 December 1997, pp. 11–13.

36 Richard Simpson, *Edmund Campion: A Biography* (London: John Hodges, 1896), pp. 205 and 222–3.

37 *CSPD*, p. 126.

38 Simpson, op. cit. (note 12), pp. 183–5.

39 *CSPD*, p. 129.

40 Richard Simpson, 'What was the Religion of Shakespeare? Part III', *The Rambler*, 9 (1858), p. 303.

41 Simpson, op. cit. (note 12), p. 187.

42 Ibid.

43 Simpson, ibid., pp. 176–8; op. cit. (note 40), p. 303.

44 Simpson, 'What was the Religion of Shakespeare? Part II', *The Rambler*, 9 (1858), p. 248; op. cit. (note 12), pp. 170–4; op. cit. (note 40), p. 319.

45 Simpson, op. cit. (note 12), p. 172; Manning, op. cit. (note 32), pp. 90–1 and 238–9.

46 The most detailed account is in Peter Razell, *William Shakespeare: The Anatomy of an Enigma* (London: Caliban Books, 1990), pp. 85–137. For the colourful story of Sir Francis Englefield see Albert J . Loomie, *The Spanish Elizabethans: English Exiles at the Court of Philip II* (London: Burns and Oates, 1963), pp. 14–51.

47 See, for instance, recent sniping in David Ellis, 'Biography and Shakespeare: An Outsider's View', *The Cambridge Quarterly*, 29:4 (2000), p. 301; and Michael Davies, 'The Canonisation of the Catholic Shakespeare', *Cahiers Elisabethains*, 58 (2000), pp. 31–47.

48 John Carey, *John Donne: Life, Mind and Art* (London: Faber and Faber, 1981), pp. 25, 27, 36 and 59.

49 Simpson, op. cit. (note 40), p. 303; (note 44), pp. 235–7.

50 Simpson, op. cit. (note 40), p. 307.

51 Simpson, op. cit. (note 44), p. 237.

52 Renold, op. cit. (note 30), p. 76: William Allen to Alphonso Agazzari, Paris, 6 March 1584.

53 Graham Greene, Introduction, *John Gerard: The Autobiography of an Elizabethan*, ed. and trans. Philip Caraman (London: Longmans, 1951), pp. x–xi.

54 Bossy, op. cit. (note 25), p. 87.

55 Francis Barker, *The Culture of Violence: Essays on Tragedy and History* (Manchester: Manchester University Press, 1993), p. 191.

56 Simpson, op. cit. (note 40), p. 307, quoting Henry Chettle, *England's Mourning Garments* (London: 1603).

57 Michel Foucault, 'My Body, This Paper, This Fire', trans. Geoffrey Bennington, in *Michel Foucault: The Essential Works: Aesthetics* (Harmondsworth: Allen Lane, 1998), p. 416.

58 Gary Taylor, 'Forms of Opposition: Shakespeare and Middleton', *English Literary Renaissance*, 24:2 (1994), p. 298.

59 Stephen Greenblatt, *Hamlet in Purgatory* (Princeton: Princeton University Press, 2001), p. 249.

60 Simpson, op. cit. (note 44), p. 248.

61 Jonathan Bate, 'No Other Purgatory but a Play', *The Sunday Telegraph*, 8 April 2001.

62 Stephen Greenblatt, *Shakespearean Negotiations* (Oxford: Clarendon Press, 1990), pp. 10–11, 112–13 and 119.

63 Greenblatt, op. cit. (note 59), pp. 248–61.

64 Harold Jenkins (ed.), *Hamlet* (London: Methuen, 1982), pp. 150–1.

65 For the fraught Catholic pastoralism of Montague's entertainment see Curtis Breight, 'Caressing the Great: Viscount Montague's Entertainment of Elizabeth at Cowdray in 1591', *Sussex Archaeological Collections*, 127 (1989), pp. 154–63.

66 See, for instance, Michael Hattaway (ed.), *The Third Part of Henry VI* (Cambridge: Cambridge University Press), p. 6.

67 *Victoria County History: Warwickshire*, vol. 6, p. 222.

68 *CSPD*, pp. 152 and 158.

69 Stopes, op. cit. (note 21), pp. 104–5.

70 Mervyn James, *Society, Politics and Culture: Studies in Early Modern England* (Cambridge: Cambridge University Press, 1986), pp. 426–7 and 435–6.

71 Letter of Sir James Bland-Burgess to James Boswell, June 1818, quoted in Whitfield, op. cit. (note 2), pp. 447–8. It was Sir William Somerville who supposedly commissioned the so-called Hilliard portrait of Shakespeare.

72 'Time Goes by Turns', in James H. McDonald and Nancy Pollard Brown (eds), *The Poems of Robert Southwell, S.J.* (Oxford: Clarendon Pres, 1967), p. 69.

73 Renold, op. cit. (note 30), pp. 60 and 75: Richard Barret to Alphonso Agazzari, Rheims, 28 December 1583; William Allen to Agazzari, Paris, 6 March 1584.

74 Leo Hicks (ed.), *Letters and Memorials of Father Robert Parsons, S.J.* (London: Catholic Record Society, 1942), p. 192: Robert Parsons to Claudio Aquaviva, Paris, 12 June 1584.

5

A bloody question

The politics of *Venus and Adonis*

Venus and Adonis was Shakespeare's most instantaneous success, with sixteen editions printed before 1640, yet the earliest recorded commentary on the poem was one of bitter disappointment, and since it came from a writer Ben Jonson rated so highly he said 'he would have been content to destroy many of his poems' to have written just one of his,[1] the criticism must have stung. For in the days before his arrest in June 1592, the Jesuit poet Robert Southwell responded to one of the manuscripts of *Venus and Adonis* which circulated, we know, in recusant households, with a poem of his own in identical stanzas, entitled *Saint Peter's Complaint*, which he prefaced with a dedication rejecting Shakespeare's image of poetry as a passive distillation of experience and deploring the waste of his artistic gifts:

> This makes my mourning Muse resolve in tears,
> This themes my heavy pen to plain in prose:
> Christ's thorn is sharp, no head his garland wears,
> Still finest wits are 'stilling Venus' rose,
> In paynim toys the sweetest veins are spent,
> To Christian works few have their talents lent.[2]

Southwell's dismissal of *Venus and Adonis* as a 'pagan toy' has been ignored by almost all Shakespeareans, and this may be because the implications are so sensational. For not only is this the first critical reaction to Shakespeare's work, it is also the clearest indication of how the 'finest wit' and 'sweetest vein' of his generation had been expected to produce 'Christian works' that 'lent his talent' to the Catholic cause. At the end of his career Shakespeare would be publicly exposed with the Jesuit leader Robert Parsons by the Puritan historian John Speed, as 'this papist and his poet, of like conscience for lies, the one ever feigning, the other ever falsifying the truth';[3] and Southwell's belief that the young writer would have been better employed weaving a martyr's crown of thorns for himself than distilling a lover's rose confirms that the Society of Jesus did indeed look to him as one of its brightest potential stars. As Gary

Taylor has observed, 'It is a short step from Parsons and Southwell to Shakes-peare'; but just how short a step was revealed only in the 1616 edition of the priest's poem published by the Jesuit press in Belgium, where the text was capped by a prose-letter 'To my worthy good cousin, Master W.S'., signed 'Your loving cousin, R.S.'.[4] For William Shakespeare was actually a distant relative of Robert Southwell through his mother, Mary Arden, and the martyr's secret handshake pulled him firmly within the family circle of aristocratic Elizabethan Catholicism, where, as Antonia Fraser writes, 'everyone was related to everyone else'.[5] And if, as Southwell claimed in the letter, it had been 'Master W.S'. himself who 'importuned' the publication of *Peter's Plaint*, 'and therefore must bear part of the penance when it shall please sharp censures to impose it',[6] the Jesuit poem can be read both as a guide to the politics of *Venus and Adonis*, and a pass into the dangerous company for which the 'first heir' of Shakespeare's invention was composed. Above all, as a criticism from within the zealot Howard household, where Southwell had been chaplain, it offers a mark of Shakespeare's early disengagement from Catholic extremism. For, punning on Shakespeare's name at the end of the verse dedication, his cousin left no doubt that if he aimed his shaft to some Catholic end this 'sweetest' Ovidian poet would have been a worthy peer:

> License my single pen to seek a peer;
> You heavenly sparks of wit show native light,
> Cloud not with misty loves your orient clear;
> Sweet flights you shoot, learn once to level right.
> Favour my wish, well-wishing works no ill;
> I move the suit, the grant rests in your will.

The 'grant' who waits on Will's word in this coded message may be a shared kinsman, John Grant, whose house near Stratford was a contact-point for the terrorist cell behind the 1583 plot to shoot the Queen, named after yet another Arden relative, John Somerville. Later, with his brothers-in-law, Thomas and Robert Winter, Grant would destroy himself in the Gunpowder Plot; but, whether or not he was their go-between, Southwell's punning overture to 'seek a peer' in Shakespeare evokes the ardour with which the poet's 'pagan toy' would have been received when it was published in 1593. And *Peter's Plaint* confirms the hopes with which *Venus and Adonis* was scanned by its first textual community, when it opens by comparing the exile of a seminarian upon a sea of tears – with 'Torment thy haven, shipwreck thy best reward' – to the plain-sailing of 'Ambitious heads … plung'd in Folly's tide', who 'Fill volumes with your forged goddess' praise', or 'Devote … fabling wits to lovers' lays' (stanzas 1, 6). What follows is a scalding sermon on betrayal, in which the poet's choice of profane over sacred verse – 'Writing in works lessons of ill advice; / The doing-tale that eye in practise reads' (40) – is equated with St Peter's denial of Christ. As Nancy Pollard Brown notes, Southwell revised his account of Peter's desertion several times, with the effect of heightening the role of the 'damsel' who, in the Gospels, 'kept the door' of the court where Jesus was on trial, and said 'unto Peter, Art thou not also one of this man's disciples? [And] He saith, I am not' (*John*, 18: 16–17). Thus, in the final version, it is the seductiveness with which this woman poses her question that compels Peter to drop his sword, and the misogyny of his railing then leaves no doubt that what is implied is a parallel, as Brown observes, 'between her questions and the actions of the Queen, whose demands for an Oath of Supremacy and show of allegiance tempted Catholics to deny their loyalty to Rome'.[7] More specifically, if the porteress figures Queen Elizabeth, Southwell seems to interpret *Venus and Adonis* as an example of the craven capitulation to the Crown that followed the introduction of the notorious 'Bloody Question' in 1588, when all English Catholics were confronted with a deadly test: 'If the Pope were to send over an army ... whose side would you be on: the Pope's or the Queen's?'[8] For in *Peter's Plaint* those 'words ... delivered from a woman's tongue' (49) are likewise a trap to catch an entire generation of the soldiers of Christ:

> O port'ress of the door of my disgrace,
> Whose tongue unlock'd the truth of vowed mind;
> Whose words from coward's heart did courage chase,
> And let in deathful fears my soul to blind;
> O had thou been the port'ress of my tomb,
> When thou wert port'ress to that cursed room!
>
> (stanza 36)

'And the servants and officers stood there', in the words of the Gospel, 'who had made a fire of coals, for it was cold; and they warmed themselves: and Peter stood with them and warmed himself' (*John*, 18: 18). Southwell's exclamation that he 'rather had congeal'd to ice, / Than bought my warmth at such a damning price!' (43) condenses, in his favourite imagery of fire and snow, contempt for all those Catholic intellectuals who answered the 'Bloody Question' by defecting to 'so ill a Court' (39). In fact, Burghley had expressly drafted the Question, according to a memorandum, so as to split militants from such deserters, who could then be neutralised 'by a process of guile and attrition: by inciting their tenants against them ... taking their children hostage under colour of education ... or stripping them of armour so that twenty thousand will be helpless before one thousand Protestants';[9] and the letter to 'Master W.S'. is heavy with disappointment that his cousin was one who had warmed himself at court. The reproof may date from late in the priest's imprisonment, as it misquotes Theseus's line, in *A Midsummer Night's Dream*, that the lunatic, lover and poet 'Are of imagination all compact' (5.1.8), which it refutes with the 'authority of God, Who delivering many parts of Scripture in verse, and willing us to exercise devotion in hymns and spiritual sonnets, warranteth the art good, and the use allowable'. Against the Duke's idea of art for art's sake, therefore, Southwell insists that poetry 'hath been used by men

of greatest piety in matters of most devotion', and that the morality of literature has been attested by Christ, who, by staging His Last Supper and Passion
as a 'pageant', gave to dramatists 'a method to imitate … and … a pattern to
know the true use of this measured style'. The inference is unavoidable that,
like St Peter, the author of the *Dream* and *Venus and Adonis* has 'quailed at
words … delivered from a woman's tongue', and, by trivialising politics, sold
himself, in 'fear of woman's breath', for 'Hire of a hireling mind' (49, 53, 34):

> Poets, by abusing their talent, and making the follies and feignings of love the
> customary subject of their base endeavours, have so discredited this faculty
> that a poet, a lover, and a liar are by many reckoned but three words of one
> signification … [For] the devil, as he affecteth deity and seeketh to have all
> complements of divine honour applied to his service, so hath he among the rest
> possessed most poets with his idle fancies. For in lieu of solemn and devout
> matter, to which in duty they owe their abilities, they now busy themselves in
> expressing such passions as only serve for testimonies to what unworthy
> affections they have wedded their wills.[10]

Written more in sorrow than anger, Southwell's appeal to his literary
kinsman ends with the wish that his own 'few ditties' will inspire the 'skilfuller
wit', who does not fear 'Of mirth to make a trade', to 'begin some finer piece,
wherein it may be shown how well verse and virtue suit together … add you
the tunes, and let the Mean, I pray you, be still a part in all your music'. In 1914
John Trotman proposed that the British Museum manuscript of *Peter's Plaint*,
10422, used as a copy-text by early editors, is in fact in Shakespeare's hand, and
that his personal engagement with the poem is witnessed by the signature
'W.S'. appended at the end. This startling claim has never been properly
examined, though Christopher Devlin inferred that 'pricked by Southwell's
example', Shakespeare did indeed 'try his hand at tapping a loftier, more
metaphysical vein' than *Venus and Adonis*, and devised *The Rape of Lucrece* as
the 'graver labour' he had pledged in the dedication to his earlier poem.[11] Yet
the question this raises is why Shakespeare's 'unpolished lines' should have
provoked such a sad rebuke from England's leading Catholic poet, and why an
unashamedly erotic text should have been construed as such a *political* betrayal
by the recusant community. The answer lies, of course, in the similarity of
Southwell's temptress and Shakespeare's Venus, who both sweeten their
coercion with what the Jesuit calls 'These Syrens' sugared tunes' (52), and offer
'A thousand honey secrets' if their men disarm (*Venus*: 15). Read with the
hindsight of the poem it prompted, *Venus and Adonis* is Ovid moralised, as
Shakespeare's Queen herself says, with painful relevance to its occasion:
'Applying this to that, and so to so, / For love can comment upon every woe'
(713). This was the type of Aesopian allegory that Southwell himself trusted
'the better sort' of reader would not confuse with 'idle fancy … For in fables are
often figured moral truths, covertly uttered to a common good, which without
mask would not find so free a passage.' The priest excused the 'inconvenience'

of such fables, he wrote, 'if the drift of their discourse levelled at any virtuous mark';[12] but what evidently shocked him in his cousin's work was that it so missed the mark of papist virtue. For compared to *Peter's Plaint*, *Venus and Adonis* presents the worst possible prospectus for martyrdom:

> The picture of an angry chafing boar,
> Under whose sharp fangs on his back doth lie
> An image like thyself, all stain'd with gore;
>   Whose blood upon the fresh flowers being shed,
>   Doth make them droop with grief and hang their head.
>
> (662–6)

'This looks like the last stage before the expected end', Southwell had exulted, when the government introduced its Bloody Question, 'and it puts us, as some fear and others hope, very close to martyrdom'.[13] The poems that he then wrote, between 1588 and 1592, with their imagery of 'hunting, falconry, trapping birds, fishing and coursing', but, above all, their euphoria 'in shedding blood: / The whips, the thorns, the nails, the spear, and rod', created a discourse of sacrifice for a generation of Catholics living in expectation of imminent massacre. And it was in the context of this fatalistic cult of the Christian hero as a 'young flower' who, 'with flowers in flower ... may ... hang on a tree',[14] that Shakespeare's fable of the purple flower springing from a boy's blood would have been immediately interpreted. For what this iconography clarifies, with a sharpness lost to modern readers, is that, at its core, *Venus and Adonis* is a critique of martyrdom. The poet-priest's disenchantment with his lay-brother becomes explicable, therefore, once the poem is reinserted into the masochistic semiotics of Catholic martyrology, where the slaughter of the chase affirms – as it does in Southwell's lyrics – that the massacre of innocents will not be in vain: 'The merlin cannot ever soar on high, / Nor the greedy greyhound still pursue the chase; / The tender lark will find a time to fly, / And fearful hare to run a quiet race.'[15] The Jesuit had adopted this hunting metaphor, according to his editors, whilst hiding at Baddesley Clinton in the Warwickshire Forest of Arden;[16] and it was in such Catholic houses, with their hidden chambers and secret passageways, that Venus's enticement of Adonis to escape his death by turning against 'the timorous flying hare' (674) would indeed have been moralised – as the Queen expects – for its contemporary relevance: as the invitation made to Elizabeth's Catholic subjects, to save their skins by betraying their 'earth-delving' (687) co-religionists to the 'hot scent-snuffing hounds' (692) of the pursuivants and priest-finders:

> 'And when thou hast on foot the purblind hare,
> Mark the poor wretch, to overshoot his troubles,
> How he outruns the wind, and with what care
> He cranks and crosses with a thousand doubles;
>   The many musits through which he goes
>   Are like a labyrinth to amaze his foes ...

'Then shalt thou see the dew-bedabbled wretch
Turn, and return, indenting with the way.
Each envious briar his weary legs do scratch,
Each shadow makes him stop, each murmur stay:
    For misery is trodden on by many,
    And being low, never reliev'd of any.
                        (679–84; 703–8)

Itself constructed like one of those secret 'musits' or priest-holes through which outlawed Catholics evaded capture, *Venus and Adonis* conceals politics beneath erotics; yet behind the false façade of a pornographic narrative the text discloses its topicality as nothing less than a 'Bloody Question' of loyalty or betrayal, when the boy is warned that Cynthia will 'obscure her silver shine' from him until his own mother-goddess, 'nature', is 'condemn'd of treason'. In her study of the multi-faceted 'Gloriana', Frances Yates explains how Cynthia, the moon, was a name for Elizabeth in her militant Protestant guise, as 'The virgin of imperial reform who withstood the claims of the Papacy by shedding beams of pure religion'; whereas the Queen could be cynically aligned with Venus, or even the Virgin Mary, in her kinder mask as 'a nursing mother' to her erstwhile Catholics. Yet what Yates also notes is that Shakespeare's treatment of this ambivalent iconography – in episodes such as the one in *Titus Andronicus* where the sign of Virgo is shot to pieces with arrows – was 'so surprising and unconventional … so remote from the stock-in-trade of a court poet', as to 'leave an eternal question-mark against his name'.[17] It belongs, that is to say, to the oppositional symbolism that has also been analysed by Philippa Berry, who demonstrates how 'by comparing Elizabeth with the dark phase of the moon, the phase associated with Cynthia or Diana', texts such as Shakespeare's 'uncover the "other" side of the queen's courtly cult', and challenge her worshippers by predicting her eclipse, or implicating her with 'the lunar deity who was most difficult to idealize – Hecate, goddess of witchcraft, death, and the underworld'.[18] Certainly, the overcast moon of his poem is quite unlike the 'Queen and huntress, chaste and fair', idealised in court festivities,[19] being 'cloudy and forlorn', and the authoress of 'the tyranny / Of mad mischances and much misery: / As burning feavers, agues pale and faint, / Life-poisoning pestilence and frenzies wood, / The marrow-eating sickness whose attaint / Disorder breeds by heating of the blood'. With 'Surfeits, imposthumes, grief and damned despair' her malign effects, this jealous despot plots 'nature's death' because Adonis is 'so fair' (725–44); and the insinuation seems obvious, as it is in *A Midsummer Night's Dream*, that while her people remain with 'no hymn or carol blest', the writer will not be deceived by moonshine into love for this Queen of the Night:

Therefore the moon, the governess of floods,
Pale in her anger, washes all the air,
That rheumatic diseases do abound.

> And thorough this distemperature we see
> The seasons alter ...
>
> (*Dream*, 2.1.102–7)

Shakespeare's misogynistic caricature, in *Venus and Adonis*, of a suspicious, vindictive and self-pitying moon, who provokes rebellion when she 'attaints' for treason those suffering 'The marrow-eating sickness' of despair, prefigures the 'cold', 'fruitless', 'wandering', 'wat'ry' planet of the *Dream* (1.1.73; 2.1.156–162; 4.1.98), whose decrepitude prompts such impatience in the land: 'But O, methinks, how slow / This old moon wanes! She lingers my desires, / Like to a step-dame or a dowager / Long withering-out a young man's revenue' (1.1.3–6). The wicked crone of the comedy, who spies through windows pretending a 'maiden meditation, fancy free' (2.1.164), shows how far Aesopian satire could go 'to disfigure ... the person of Moonshine' (3.1.56) on the public stage; though Falstaff may also be flaunting the ruin of Catholic families such as the Percys when he begs Hal to consider that 'we that take purses by the moon' to be 'men of good government, being governed, as the sea is, by our noble and chaste mistress the moon, under whose government we steal' (*1 Henry 4*, 1.2.13–19). But the oppositional politics of the poem are already blatant when Adonis is assured that 'one minute's fight' with Cynthia will 'bring his beauty under; / Both favour, savour, hue and qualities, / Whereat th'impartial gazer late did wonder' (746–8). This is a chilling prophecy, which connects the text to 'The place of death and sorry execution / Behind the ditches' of Holywell that is the terminus of *The Comedy of Errors* (5.1.121). In that optimistic scenario an Abbess emerges from her convent, as if to rescue the [Sy]recusant 'merchant'from hanging, disembowelling and quartering; but in the poem the tender mercies of the Queen seem equally pitiless, as Venus 'murders' resistance 'with a kiss', like a ravenous eagle tearing 'with her beak on feathers, flesh and bone, / Shaking her wings, devouring all in haste, / Till either gorge be stuff'd or prey be gone' (55–8). A Jove with Ganymede, this 'vulture' kills the 'yielding prey' she claims to love: 'Her lips are conquerors', as 'With blindfold fury she begins to forage' (547–55). As Katherine Maus points out, much of the irony of this poem arises from the discovery that when Venus 'locks her lily fingers' (228) to take Adonis prisoner 'in a jail of snow' (362) 'she turns out to have a grip of steel'.[20] So, if this is allegory, its desperation seems close to that of the *Humble Supplication* Southwell wrote in December 1591, begging his 'most merciful and best beloved Princess' to own up to the executions, tortures and extortions inflicted on the Catholics in her care:

> We presume that your Majesty never heareth the truth of our persecutions, your lenity and tenderness being known to be so professed an enemy to these cruelties that you would never permit their continuance, if they were expressed to your Highness as they are practised upon us. Yet, since we can bring the ruin of our houses ... the poverty of our estates, and the weeping

eyes of our desolate families for witnesses of the truth of these complaints, let us not be so far exiled out of all compassion, as besides all other evils, to have it confirmed under your Majesty's hand, *that we suffer no punishments for Religion* – suffering in proof all punishments for nothing else.[21]

As the Protestant Archbishop declares in *Henry VIII*, Elizabeth would always alternate 'Peace, plenty, love' and 'truth' with 'terror' to ensure her foes would 'shake like a field of beaten corn' (5.4.47); and it is in the light of her ministers' hypocritical denial of persecution, and disingenuous claim that 'Our gaolers are guilty of felony … if they torment any prisoner committed to their custody',[22] that the irony of Shakespeare's portrait of the 'Queen of Love' (252) can best be read. For if the whorishness of the 'love-sick Queen' (175) towards her helpless victim analogises Elizabeth's exploitation of loyal papists, the police state she mobilises against her suspected enemies is also starkly recognisable. As Venus herself admits, 'where love reigns, disturbing jealousy / Doth call himself affection's sentinel', and surveillance depends on the 'sour informer', 'bate-breeding spy', 'carry-tale' and 'dissentious' *agent provocateur*, who 'Gives false alarms, suggesteth mutiny, / And in a peaceful hour doth cry, "Kill, kill!"' (649–60). This is the paranoid system operated by the psycho-pathic priest-hunter Richard Topcliffe, which involved planting in all Catholic 'houses and chambers, traitors, spies, intelligencers, and promoters that take watch for all their ways, words, and writings';[23] and which gave him, as the poem records, a sinister hold on Elizabeth: 'For who hath she to spend the night withal, / But … parasites, / Like shrill-tongu'd tapsters answering every call … She says, "'Tis so," they answer all, "'Tis so," / And would say after her, if she said "No."' (847–52). This 'time-honoured fiction of evil counsellors' here reproduces the *politique* deconstruction of the regime in the 1584 pamphlet, *Leicester's Commonwealth*;[24] In fact, Shakespeare's anatomy of the court – where the Queen berates her security chief, Death, as a 'Grim-grinning ghost … ugly, meagre, lean' (931–3), and then 'adds honours to his hateful name … Tells him of trophies, statues, tombs' (994, 1113) – accurately reports the duplicity of this reign of terror, which Elizabeth was liable to disown (as she did the death warrant of Mary Stuart) by setting one faction against another: '"'Tis not my fault, the boar provok'd my tongue: / Be wreak'd on him, invisible commander"' (1003). In 1592 this is surely the limit of comment on a monarch whose 'sick heart commands her [eyes] to watch' with such suspicion (584); though it does provide the possibility of a startlingly negative picture of the 'ageless' Eliza:

> Were I ill-favour'd, foul, or wrinkled old,
> Ill-nurtur'd, crooked, churlish, harsh of voice,
> O'erworn, despised, rheumatic and cold,
> Thick-sighted, barren, lean, and lacking juice,
>   Then mightst thou pause, for then I were not for thee;
>   But having no defects, why dost abhor me?

> Thou canst not see one wrinkle in my brow ...
> My beauty as the spring doth yearly grow ...
> (133–41)

Romantic critics have sentimentalised Shakespeare's relations with his monarch, but the sceptical portrait that emerges from *Venus and Adonis* in fact corresponds to the irreverence of the circle in which it was composed, typified by Swithin Wells, tutor to the Earl of Southampton, when he praised the papal Bull excommunicating Elizabeth with the jest to his hangman, 'Better a roaring bull than a diseased cow'.[25] Shakespeare may not quite have shared William Allen's view of Anne Boleyn's 'incestuous bastard' as a 'depraved, accursed, excommunicate heretic', as Peter Milward maintains;[26] but their dedication 'To the Right Honourable Henry Wriothesley' places his poems firmly at the heart of recusant England. Wriothesley's papist sympathies have always been downplayed by Shakespeareans, but by 1592 the nineteen-year-old Earl had replaced Philip Howard, the imprisoned Earl of Arundel, as the great hope of Catholic resistance. He inherited his religion from his father, who had solved the problem whether 'subjects of this land may, with safe conscience, obey the Queen as our Righteous Princess', by deciding that 'it were better to lose all he had', and paid with his life, dying suddenly in suspicious circumstances soon after aiding the Jesuit Edmund Campion. At the age of eight, Southampton was then taken away from his mother and put into Burghley's custody to be educated as one of the minister's score of aristocratic wards. But as Lawrence Stone writes, 'he was already so well indoctrinated' that he not only refused to attend Anglican services but kept his religious loyalties so dark that they 'remained uncertain until about 1605', when he at last conformed.[27] Southampton's mother was a Montague, moreover, and in her widowhood sustained the Montague tradition of quietist piety by keeping sanctuaries for priests at Battle Abbey, Cowdray Park in Sussex and Southampton House in Holborn. So, though it was often raided for massing books and missionaries, the Wriothesley's London home survived as a bastion of court Catholicism, and a counterweight to Cecil House, where the Earl was held hostage. As he approached maturity, therefore, this son of 'the most illustrious and leading Catholic in England', became the prize in a three-way struggle between the coercion of the regime, the temporising of the Montagues and the activism of the missionary movement which John Bossy has characterised as a 'revolution of the clerks'.[28] This was a contest that reached a crisis when Burghley commanded Southampton to marry his own granddaughter. Instead, the boy pleaded for time and conferred with a priest. Years later, Topcliffe discovered that the Earl's spiritual adviser at this turning-point had been a cousin: young 'Father Robert' – the Jesuit, Southwell.[29]

'The young Earl of Southampton refusing the Lady de Vere', reported the Jesuit Henry Garnet in 1594, 'payeth £5,000 of present payment'.[30] The minute is important as a record not only of the colossal cost of thwarting the

Lord Treasurer but of the interest invested by Rome in Wriothesley's resistance. This was, perhaps, what the poet meant by inscribing *Venus and Adonis* to 'so noble a godfather', and commending the Earl 'to your heart's content, which I wish may always answer your own wish, and the world's hopeful expectation'. As critics long ago noted, Shakespeare's poem is the only version of the Adonis story in which the boy resists the goddess and, in diverging so radically from the sources, it may have 'functioned as a form of advice literature which enabled Southampton to avoid complicity' with his guardian.[31] Thus, G.P.V. Akrigg has argued that in *Venus and Adonis* Shakespeare is 'discreetly excusing his lordship's aversion to marriage … knowing how Southampton had begged old Burghley for more time before taking a bride'. Akrigg sees the poem as a reply, therefore, to the first work dedicated to the teenage patron: *Narcissus*, written in 1591 by John Clapham, a clerk in Burghley's office.[32] But the trouble with this reading, as recent editors point out, is that *Narcissus* is hardly an argument for marriage, since it consists of a diatribe against Cupid that shifts into an attack on self-love. Nor is the grisly fate of Shakespeare's Adonis a compelling advertisement for bachelorhood. Read alongside Southwell's poem, however, the three texts do form a sequence, in which Peter glories in the martyrdom that annihilates Adonis and Narcissus. As a group, then, they suggest that the young Earl may have contemplated a choice far more subversive than misogamy, when he talked with 'Father Robert' in the chapel of the Montagues. Venus spells it out, when she says that worse than infanticide, suicide or civil war is the calling to the monasticism of the Roman Church:

> Therefore despite of fruitless chastity,
> Love-lacking vestals and self-loving nuns,
> That on the earth would breed a scarcity
> And barren dearth of daughters and of sons,
>   Be prodigal; the lamp that burns by night
>   Dries up his oil to lend the world his light.
>   (751–6)

In Clapham's poem, *Narcissus*, 'nurtured with the warm milk of Error', joins the young men who throng, 'as massed crows seek dead bodies', to the temple of Cupid, enthroned in the clouds. Struck in the heart with an arrow, the boy says: 'I am yours … I will be Love's slave,' and bends his knee. Then Love addresses him from the throne: '"As you are to others, be always loveable to yourself. Thus your opinion of yourself will allure you until you are caught by a shadow and perish." So saying, Love plucks a branch steeped in the water of Lethe and sprinkling it over his brow, says, "Henceforth, Narcissus, you will not know yourself".'[33] With its black 'massed crows' and incense clouds, this seems such a transparent skit on the genuflecting Jesuits at St Peter's that the surprise is that it has never been decoded; but it does offer an intriguing new perspective on the lesson that 'Narcissus so himself forsook, / And died to kiss his shadow in the brook' (161–2), not only as it appears in *Venus and Adonis* but also in the Sonnets on the 'Sin of self-love' (Sonnet 62). Clapham's erotic satire is a perfect instance, in fact, of the way in which the Elizabethan association of popery and sodomy complicates our understanding of both sexual and religious identity in the Shakespearean period. It had been Southwell, after all, who perfected what Louis Martz calls the 'sacred parody' of sexual love, by arguing that 'If on thy beauty God enamoured be, / Base is thy love of any less than he';[34] and when Burghley's secretary scorned such sublimation, he may have been cued by the fervent homoeroticism in which the Jesuit moved. Famous himself, in his black satin, as 'The beauteous English youth', Southwell taught that God made a seminarian handsome so that 'who so viewed his person might desire like comeliness of soul'; but when he was escorted round Cambridge by a 'bevy of aristocratic youths' (which may have included Southampton) the 'boy priest' was asking for his self-fashioning to be mis-construed. As Robert Ellrodt remarks, in this militant Counter-Reformation culture, care of the self quickly hardened into egotism as 'self-centredness became self-display'.[35] Shakespeare may be closer to the Protestant clerk, therefore, than to the Catholic cleric, when he has Venus castigate self-love:

> Is thine own heart to thine own face affected?
> Can thy right hand seize love upon thy left?
> Then woo thyself, be of thyself rejected;
> Steal thine own freedom, and complain on theft.
>
> (157–60)

'To grow unto himself was his desire' (1180): Adonis's epitaph acquires a tragic urgency if it refers to the martyr complex that has been described by Alison Shell in her revelatory survey of the English Catholic literary imagination, and if the techniques of self-invigilation that propelled Catholic youths to internalise the 'martyrological ideal' inspire his plea: '"Before I know myself, seek not to know me"' (525).[36] Then, this doomed youth would no longer figure merely selfish adolescence but the self-immolation of an entire generation of Catholic émigrés, lost to the Queen as 'a bright star shooteth from the sky', and mourned by the England they abandoned: 'as one on shore / Gazing upon a late embarked friend, / Till the wild waves will have him seen no more, / Whose ridges with the meeting clouds contend' (815–20). Shell's research now makes it difficult to read these lines without seeing them as a variant of the theme of 'weeping England' which elided Queen and country in the Catholic poetry of exile of the period.[37] And in 1592 this was exactly the exile beckoning Southampton, as he weighed the 'Bloody Question' and the order to dismount his 'imperious' steed (261–5). For when Venus woos Adonis to disarm, she raises, in the issue of decommissioning, one of the most contentious measures facing Catholic Englishmen. The 1585 Privy Council Order for Catholics to be dispossessed of weapons and armour was, in fact, such an affront, in a society where, as Sir Thomas Tresham protested, 'to go armed was the badge' of gentility, that its main purpose was again to divide the extremist from the moderate – like Mars, according to Venus – who made a token offer of some antique lance, 'battered shield' or crest (103–4).[38] Thus, while Southampton's grandfather, Lord Montague, went through the dutiful motions of disarming in the *Entertainment at Cowdray* he staged for the Queen in 1591,[39] his brother-in-law, Thomas Arundell, actually enlisted in the imperial army of Rudolf II. And in a recent article, John Clause has argued that the petition scenes in *Titus*, when the Emperor hangs the clown sent by Andronicus with a humble 'supplication' (4.3.109; 4.4.45), allude to the futile appeal for Catholic toleration organised by the Montagues in 1585, which likewise ended in the instant arrest of the messenger, Richard Shelley, who was left to rot, a tragic fool, in gaol.[40] On a knife-edge, therefore, between treason and betrayal, Southampton was uniquely placed to grasp how for his generation 'the question' was indeed (as Hamlet says) whether 'to suffer / The slings and arrows of outrageous fortune, / Or to take arms against a sea of troubles / And by opposing end them' (*Hamlet*, 3.1.57). So, when he read *Venus and Adonis*, Shakespeare's patron can have had no doubt about the political implications of the boy's decision, when he spurns the Queen's embrace, 'And homeward through the dark laund runs apace' (813).

If the Earl's surname was pronounced 'Rosely', as local historians insist, his journey home would have carried this 'Rose-cheek'd Adonis' (3) to an equally evocative place, since Boarhunt is the name of the wooded region between his mansion at Titchfield and the sea. Here Southampton would have returned to the hunting country that was the last hideaway of Catholicism in southern England, and to a chain of safe-houses which ran from Titchfield along the Channel coast. And here he would have been welcomed back into 'a tightly-knit clan of recusant families who provided Catholic leadership in Sussex and Hampshire', and 'preserved their faith in face of persecution by quasi-feudal marital alliances and economic interdependence'.[41] All his father's executors were from this papist ring; his 'earthly mother' was determined (as the poem hints) to restore him to its 'light' (863); and, like Adonis, he was keenly 'expected of his friends' (718). The text almost begs us to identify the group, when the boy excuses his absence from the Queen: 'He tells her no, tomorrow he intends / To hunt the boar with certain of his friends' (587–8). And if these hunting friends are those said in the Dedication to have such 'hopeful expectation', it is tempting to guess their identity, as they might have been the poem's first reading community. 'Certain friends' of Southampton, then, meant the Montague, Copley, Shelley and Gage families, who formed 'a particularly strategic link between the continental seminaries and London', by operating 'a communication network that smuggled priests from south-coast ports' to the capital.[42] When Topcliffe cracked this system, he discovered the route led up to Southampton House via Cowdray, with the missionaries disguised as commercial travellers, but that its orchestrator was imprisoned in the Marshalsea. He was Southampton's uncle, Thomas Pound, whose mansion in the woods near Boarhunt was a vital entry-point from France. For a haven of Catholic relief, where young clerics came and went disguised as merchants of the Queen, this house also carried a suggestive name, as it was called Belmont.

'Come ho! And wake Diana with a hymn': the sacred music that rouses Belmont, while its owner 'doth stray about / By holy crosses where she kneels and prays', is sung expressly to dissociate the household from all 'treasons, stratagems, and spoils' against a Protestant Queen (*Merchant*, 5.1.30–1; 66; 85); but under the mantle of Southampton's mother and grandmother the Montague houses in Sussex and beside the Globe in Southwark sustained, even after the death of the old Lord in 1592, a freedom of worship 'not seen in all England besides', and astonished visitors by the size of their chapels and the boldness with which Mass was celebrated 'every week with singing and musical instruments'. Lady Montague, it was said, kept so many priests at Battle Abbey that it was known as 'Little Rome'.[43] Likewise, the master of Belmont continued to work in prison as 'a great maintainer of priests',[44] and funded the Sodality of young gentry formed in 1580 to imitate the French Catholic League which may have recruited the teenage Shakespeare. Moreover, it was he who converted to the priesthood the London schoolteacher Thomas Cottam, who was the brother of John Cottam: the Master of Stratford Grammar School and a protégé of Shakespeare's first Lancashire benefactors. In fact, Thomas Pound might be considered the guardian angel of the young poet's world, since he not only connected Midland recusancy to the southern network through his Southwark base but exercised that restraint over this 'race of youthful and unhandled colts' which Shakespeare attributes to the benign influence of Belmont (*Merchant*, 5.1.72). By always drawing 'a careful distinction between what they considered to be legitimate means of preserving their faith and what could be construed as treason',[45] Pound and the Montagues saved their kinsmen from annihilation; but moving between them, smuggled into some hunting party, slipped Father Robert, preaching, by contrast, the politics of refusal coded in his poems: that the Queen of Love is a 'tyrant cruel' and 'Lewd Love is Loss' compared to 'True love in Heav'n'.[46] It cannot be chance, therefore, that, when Adonis finally rejects Venus, he does so in what sounds exactly like a parody of the homely similes of Southwell:

> 'Call it not love, for love to heaven is fled,
> Since sweating lust on earth usurp'd his name;
> Under whose simple semblance she hath fed
> Upon fresh beauty, blotting it with blame;
> > Which the hot tyrant stains and soon bereaves,
> > As caterpillars do the tender leaves.
>
> 'Love comforteth like sunshine after rain,
> But lust's effect is tempest after sun;
> Love's gentle spring doth always fresh remain,

> Lust's winter comes ere summer half be done;
> Love surfeits not, lust like a glutton dies;
> Love is all truth, lust full of forged lies.
>
> (793–804)

'Hunting he lov'd, but love he laughed to scorn' (4): from its opening lines, the politics of *Venus and Adonis* are expressed in the oppositional terms of the recusant culture that promoted the poet from the heartland of the Old Religion, in Warwickshire, to feudal Lancashire, and then to the clan around the Earl of Southampton, in the other bulwark of Catholic resistance. It was Ted Hughes who noticed that Shakespeare's first poem is, in fact, a version of Catholicism's founding myth, 'of the Mother Goddess and her dying son'. Hughes saw the Bard as 'the shaman of Old Catholicism', who wrote, 'from a secret and passionate (even fanatic) cell of illicit religious loyalty', a lament over 'the threatened extermination of the Catholic tribe'; but he then deciphered the text as a nightmare in which the Puritan Adonis spurns 'the Catholic Church, personified ... by the Great Goddess of Love'.[47] In other words, Hughes overlooked the historic irony that a Protestant Queen had usurped the role of the Virgin Mary, even as her Catholic sons adopted the Counter-Reformation's puritanical clothes. Shakespeare carried this irony over from *Narcissus*, however (where Venus is expressly identified as the Virgin Queen who rules 'the Fortunate Island' in the West),[48] and made it the reason for his dire alteration when, for the first time ever, Love is refused. *Venus and Adonis* is thus more topical than even Hughes supposed, because it presents the 'Bloody Question' confronting Shakespeare's generation as a catastrophic ultimatum not from some 'Goddess of Complete Being' but from a Queen of Hell. As the text declares, the game of resistance Catholic opponents of Elizabeth were now playing was 'no gentle chase, / But the blunt boar, rough bear, or lion proud' (883–4), where the 'king of beasts' was the heraldic emblem of the monarch, no less; the 'bear' who dined off gentlemen (*Winter's Tale*, 3.3.97), Leicester; and the 'hunted boar', with 'frothy mouth ... bepainted all with red' (901), the minister responsible for the savagery at Tyburn. For if Adonis and his friends do make up a group portrait of the knot of Catholic nobles in league against the Protestant state, there can be no doubt that the creature who is their nemesis is the punning picture of the Queen's own thing of darkness: in reality, the arch-priest-hunter and grand inquisitor, whom Southwell said was like a 'storm in the air, that all fear and shun, but none loves',[49] who would drag them all down to earth, and whose 'boorish' name was as much an omen as the Earl's: *Burghley* himself:

> But this foul, grim, and urchin-snouted boar
> Whose downward eye still looketh for a grave,
> Ne'er saw the beauteous livery that he wore
> Witness the entertainment that he gave ...
>
> 'Tis true, 'tis true, thus was Adonis slain:
> He ran upon the boar with his sharp spear,

> Who did not whet his teeth at him again,
> But by a kiss thought to persuade him there;
> And nuzzling in his flank, the loving swine
> Sheath'd unaware the tusk in his soft groin.
>
> (1105–16)

'His courage, nobility, gentleness, and the beauty of his face and form, so won the hearts of all', recalled Father Garnet of Southwell's execution, 'that even the mob gave their verdict that this was the properest man that ever came to Tyburn for hanging'. The 'beautiful English youth' had gone to the gallows protesting that 'I never intended, God Almighty knows, to commit any treason to the Queen'; but in *Venus and Adonis* his cousin had predicted how, if he refused her embrace, Burghley would still be content to 'nuzzle in his flank' to mutilate and castrate him, 'Like to a mortal butcher, bent to kill' (618).[50] Shakespeare, writes Clause, saw Catholic martyrs as 'victims in a war in which one side found the shedding of blood expedient, and the other found it a heroic sacrifice', and 'he seems to have felt their attitude towards the spilling of blood was either too enthusiastic or too casual'.[51] Certainly, the dramatist knew enough about the erotics of martyrdom to foretell how, like Campion, a 'boy priest' would be amorously 'entertained' by the 'swine' who tortured and killed him; and sure enough, the hangman 'took him down with great reverence and carried him in his own arms, assisted by his companions, to the place where he was to be quartered ... [And] when he was being disembowelled, his heart leapt into the hands of the executioner. All who stood around spoke of him with respect and there was none to cry "Traitor" according to custom.'[52] There was even a coda to confirm the poem's final perverted *pietà*, when Elizabeth was visited by one of the witnesses. He was a friend of Southampton, Lord Mountjoy, who had asked Southwell on his last night 'whether it was true that he had come to detach subjects from obedience to the Queen. To [which] the Father replied that his intention had never been anything but the good of their souls.' Next day, Mountjoy stepped forward to prevent the hangman from cutting the rope before the victim had died; and now he had come to the Queen, he explained, to prove to her that the young priest had been innocent of politics:

> When the Queen had heard him, she replied that they had all deceived her with calumnies telling her that the Father had come to raise sedition; and she showed signs of grief for his death, especially when she saw the book he had composed in the English tongue on different topics, pious and devout ... a book designed to teach Poets how to safeguard their talent and employ it as befitted.[53]

'She bows her head, the new-sprung flower to smell, / Comparing it to her Adonis' breath, / And says within her bosom it shall dwell' (1171–3): if Elizabeth wept over Southwell's book, it must have been a performance of those crocodile tears which she had shed already for so many other 'bright stars', such as Campion. Like Venus, however, she was also careful to 'crop the stalk' (1175) of martyrdom, by burning all remains, so as to deprive Catholics of those 'handkerchiefs dipped in blood' or 'pieces of bone and hair' for which they begged.[54] So, when she read the dead poet's criticism of *Venus and Adonis*, was she sincerely persuaded that it proved Southwell an innocent? And was this why Shakespeare had 'importuned' his cousin to publish it? If so, the Queen may have had a shrewder insight than the Jesuit into the real oppositional politics of Shakespeare's poem. For there, the young Earl had been confronted not with a glorification of martyrdom but with a cautionary tale of its futility in the sadistic arms of a 'hard-favour'd tyrant' (931) and a state 'most deceiving when it seems most just' (1156). Though Southwell conceded that he went to death like one of 'God Almighty's fools',[55] the playwright, it appears, understood better than the priest the 'Bloody Question' of loyalty and treason. Quick to celebrate his patron's later escape from execution, and the death of the old 'tyrant' herself when 'the mortal moon her eclipse endured' (Sonnet 107); he clearly had no illusions either that his 'loving cousin' and the other martyrs were anything but what he called them, after history had turned the traitors into heroes: 'fools of time, / Which die for goodness, who have lived for crime' (Sonnet 124). Shakespeare may not have shared the seigneurial quietism which prayed that it could wear out 'packs and sects of great ones / That ebb and flow by th'moon' (*King Lear*, 5.3.17–19), and that took English Catholicism, in John Bossy's phrase, 'from inertia to inertia in three generations';[56] but his representations of martyrdom confirm that neither was he provoked into the 'thralled discontent' that captured so many of those he claimed, in Sonnet 124, as of 'our fashion' in religion. Instead, he summoned up the ghosts of the Elizabethan martyrs to witness what his cousin once denied: that his loyalism was deeper than 'policy', and that, far from trivialising politics, it stood 'all alone' and 'hugely politic'.

NOTES

1　Cited in James H. McDonald, *The Poems and Prose Writings of Robert Southwell, S.J., a Bibliographical Study* (Oxford: Clarendon Press, 1937), p. 134. See also Richard Dutton, *Ben Jonson: Authority: Criticism* (London: Macmillan, 1996), p. 134. The poem so admired by Jonson was 'The Burning Babe'.

2　Robert Southwell, *Saint Peter's Complaint and Saint Mary Magdalen's Funeral Tears* (Saint-Omer: Society of Jesus, 1616), A4.

3　John Speed, *The History of Great Britain* (London: 1611), p. 237; in John Munro (ed.), *The Shakespeare Allusion Book* (London: Chatto and Windus, 1909), vol. 1, p. 224.

4　Gary Taylor, 'Forms of Opposition: Shakespeare and Middleton', *English Literary Renaissance*, 24 (1994), pp. 283–314, esp. p. 306; Southwell, op. cit. (note 2), A2.

5　Antonia Fraser, *Treason and Faith in 1605: The Gunpowder Plot* (London: Weidenfeld and Nicolson, 1995), p. 35.

6　Southwell, op. cit. (note 2), A2.

7　James H. McDonald and Nancy Pollard Brown (eds), *The Poems of Robert Southwell, S.J.* (Oxford: Clarendon Press, 1967), p. lxxxix.

8 Christopher Devlin, *The Life of Robert Southwell, Poet and Martyr* (London: Longmans, 1956), p. 166.

9 Quoted ibid., pp. 330–1.

10 Southwell, op. cit. (note 2), A2.

11 John William Trotman, *The Triumphs over Death by the Ven. Robert Southwell, S.J.* (London: Manresa Press, 1914), pp. 130–6; Devlin, op. cit. (note 8), p. 273.

12 Quoted ibid., pp. 268–9.

13 Quoted ibid., p. 167.

14 Nancy Pollard Brown, 'Robert Southwell: The Mission of the Written Word', in Thomas M. Mcoog (ed.), *The Reckoned Expense: Edmund Campion and the Early English Jesuits* (Woodbridge: Boydell Press, 1996), p. 198; Southwell, 'Christ's Return out of Egypt', in McDonald and Brown, op. cit. (note 7), p. 10.

15 Southwell, 'Scorn not the least', ibid., p. 69.

16 John Gerard, *The Autobiography of an Elizabethan*, trans. and ed. Philip Caraman (London: Longmans, 1951), pp. 15 and 218; Devlin, op. cit. (note 8), pp. 208–9.

17 Frances A. Yates, *Astraea: The Imperial Theme in the Sixteenth Century* (Harmondsworth: Penguin, 1977), pp. 75–80.

18 Philippa Berry, *Of Chastity and Power: Elizabethan Literature and the Unmarried Queen* (London: Routledge, 1989), pp. 143–4.

19 Ben Jonson, 'Hymn to Diana', from *Cynthia's Revels*, ed. George Burke Johnston (London: Routledge, 1954), p. 261.

20 Katherine Maus, 'Introduction to *Venus and Adonis*', in Stephen Greenblatt et al., *The Norton Shakespeare* (New York: Norton, 1997), p. 603.

21 Quoted Devlin, op. cit. (note 8), p. 252.

22 William Harrison, *Description of England* (London: 1587), quoted ibid., p. 212.

23 William Allen, *Admonition to the Nobility and People of England* (Douai: 1588), quoted in Lacey Baldwin Smith, *Treason in Tudor England* (London: Jonathan Cape, 1986), pp. 159–60.

24 John Bossy, 'The Character of Elizabethan Catholicism', *Past and Present*, 21 (1962), pp. 39–59, esp. p. 43; Dwight Peck (ed.), *Leicester's Commonwealth: The Copy of a Letter Written by a Master of Art of Cambridge (1584) and Related Documents* (Athens: Ohio University Press, 1985).

25 Quoted Devlin, op.cit. (note 8), pp. 238–9.

26 Peter Milward, *Shakespeare's Religious Background* (Chicago: Loyola University Press, 1973), p. 191.

27 G.P.V. Akrigg, *Shakespeare and the Earl of Southampton* (London: Hamish Hamilton, 1968), pp. 9–10; Lawrence Stone, *The Crisis of the Aristocracy, 1558–1641* (Oxford: Clarendon Press, 1965), pp. 739–40.

28 Letter of Thomas Stephens (page to Thomas Pounde), Stonyhurst MSS, *Collectio Cardwelli*, f. 16; quoted Devlin, op. cit. (note 8), p. 14; Bossy, op. cit. (note 24), p. 46.

29 Ibid., p. 219. Southwell's family connection with Southampton – he was twice a cousin by marriage – meant that Shakespeare was also distantly related to the Earl.

30 A.L. Rowse, *Shakespeare's Southampton* (London: Macmillan, 1965), p. 103.

31 Patrick M. Murphy, 'Wriothesley's Resistance: Wardship Practices and Ovidian Narrative in Shakespeare's *Venus and Adonis*', in Phlip Kohn (ed.), *'Venus and Adonis': Critical Essays* (New York: Garland, 1997), pp. 323–40, esp. pp. 323–4.

32 Akrigg, op. cit. (note 27), pp. 194–5. See also Charles Martindale and Colin Burrow, 'Clapham's *Narcissus*: A Pre-text for Shakespeare's *Venus and Adonis?*', *English Literary Renaissance*, 22 (1992), pp. 147–75.

33 Ibid., pp. 159–63.

34 Louis Martz, *The Poetry of Meditation* (New Haven: Yale University Press, 1962), p. 186; Southwell, 'At Home in Heaven', in McDonald and Brown, op. cit. (note 7), p. 56.

35 Southwell, unpublished manuscript quoted ibid., p. xxii; Devlin, op. cit. (note 8), pp. 26 and 185–6; Robert Ellrodt, 'The Search for Identity: Montaigne to Donne', *Confluences*

9 (Paris: Centre de Recherches sur les Origines de la Modernité, 1995), p. 12.

36 Alison Shell, *Catholicism,Controversy and the English Literary Imagination* (Cambridge: Cambridge University Press, 1999), p. 226.

37 Ibid., pp. 184–5.

38 See B.W. Quintrell, 'The Practice and Problems of Recusant Disarming, 1585–1641', *Recusant History*, 17 (1985), pp. 208–22.

39 See Curtus Charles Breight, 'Caressing the Great: Viscount Montague's Entertainment of Elizabeth at Cowdray, 1591', *Sussex Archaeological Collections*, 127 (1989), pp. 147–66.

40 John Clause, 'Politics, Heresy and Martyrdom in Shakespeare's Sonnet 124 and *Titus Andronicus*', in James Schiffer (ed.), *Shakespeare's Sonnets: Critical Essays* (New York: Garland, 1999), pp. 219–40.

41 Roger B. Manning, *Religion and Society in Elizabethan Sussex* (Leicester: Leicester University Press, 1969), p. 156.

42 Ibid. See also Devlin, op. cit. (note 8), pp. 127–8 and 217–18.

43 Manning, op. cit. (note 41), pp. 159–60; A.C. Southern (ed.), *An Elizabethan Recusant House: Comprising 'The Life of Lady Magdalen Viscountess Montague, 1538–1608'* (London: Sands, 1954), pp. 42–3.

44 Government informer quoted in Thomas Graves Law, *Jesuits and Scholars in the Reign of Elizabeth* (London: David Nutt, 1889), p. 137.

45 Manning, op. cit. (note 41), p. 161.

46 Southwell, 'Love's Servile Lot' and 'Lewd Love is Loss', in McDonald and Brown, op. cit. (note 7), pp. 60–3.

47 Ted Hughes, *Shakespeare and the Goddess of Complete Being* (London: Faber and Faber, 1992), pp. 12, 57, 86, 90 and passim.

48 Martindale and Burrow, op. cit. (note 32), pp. 159 and 173.

49 Southwell, 'An Humble Supplication', quoted in Peter Holmes, *Resistance and Compromise: The Political Thought of the English Catholics* (Cambridge: Cambridge University Press, 1982), p. 172.

50 Southwell quoted in Devlin, op. cit. (note 8), pp. 320–1.

51 Clause, op. cit. (note 40), p. 237.

52 Quoted Arthur Marotti, 'Southwell's Remains: Catholicism and Anti-Catholicism in Early Modern England', in Cedric Brown and Arthur Marotti (eds.), *Texts and Cultural Change in Early Modern England* (Basingstoke: Macmillan, 1997), p. 52.

53 Quoted Devlin, op. cit. (note 8), pp. 317–18.

54 Ibid., p. 324.

55 Quoted Milward, op. cit. (note 26), p. 60.

56 Bossy, op. cit. (note 24), p. 57.

6

Love in idleness

The stripping of the altars in
A Midsummer Night's Dream

'Fᴇᴛᴄʜ me that flower; the herb I show'd thee once. / The juice of it, on sleeping eyelids laid, / Will make or man or woman madly dote / Upon the next live creature that it sees': Oberon's command to Puck to harvest him a sprig of the 'little western flower' that 'maidens call … "love in idleness"' keys the entire plot of *A Midsummer Night's Dream* to a version of pastoralism which – as William Empson remarked of the 'Lilies that fester' in Sonnet 94 – is 'profoundly ambivalent' in oscillating between 'the power of beauty and political power … the power to hurt or the determination not to hurt – cruelty or mercy'.[1] The flower named for inconsequence turns out, when 'the liquor of it' is applied to the eyes of its victim, to be so far from mere idleness that 'The next thing then she waking looks upon / (Be it lion, bear, wolf, or bull, / On meddling monkey, or on busy ape) / She shall pursue it with the soul of love'. And when Oberon botanises that this pansy, 'Before milk-white', is 'now purple with love's wound' (2.1.166–82), its metamorphosis crystallises not only the theme of transformation but the danger of a world where 'everything seems double' (4.1.189), and, as Anne Barton says, those with power to bless 'have also power to destroy'.[2] Known also as 'hearts-ease', the herb *viola tricolar* was prescribed for those 'rheumatic diseases' said in the play to derive from 'the moon, the governess of floods' (2.1.103–5); so it is telling that Oberon should deploy against his queen, 'Ill-met by moonlight' (60), a remedy credited by herbalists with most efficacy in counteracting lunar influence. For what emerges from this interlude of the planet and the plant is that the wild pansy has been changed, in its 'western' habitat, from a symbol of unstained innocence to one of resistance to 'the imperial votress' whose powers had been so identified with the 'watery beams' of the moon in the idolatry of poets such as Sir Walter Raleigh (162–3).[3] Wounded incidentally by Elizabeth's enemy, this bloom belongs, it seems, to the same order of symbolic violence as 'The forward violet' whose 'purple pride' is destined to be 'eaten up to death' in Sonnet 99; or that lurid 'purple flower sprung up' to memorialize the blood of the martyred Adonis (*Venus*, 1167):

That very time I saw (but thou couldst not)
Flying between the cold moon and the earth,
Cupid all arm'd: a certain aim he took
At a fair vestal, throned in the west,
And loos'd his love-shaft smartly from his bow
As it should pierce a hundred thousand hearts.
But I might see young Cupid's fiery shaft
Quench'd in the chaste beams of the watery moon;
And the imperial votress passed on,
In maiden meditation, fancy-free.
Yet mark'd I where the bolt of Cupid fell:
It fell upon a little western flower,
Before milk-white, now purple with love's wound:
And maidens call it 'love in idleness'.

(2.1.155–68)

Ever since William Warburton conjectured that, when Oberon recalls how Cupid's assault on the Virgin Queen was timed to music by 'a mermaid on a dolphin's back' the allusion is to Mary Queen of Scots, critics have decoded this mythological perspective as a political allegory. And though the Arden editor thinks 'Elizabeth was far too sensitive for a dramatist to refer with safety to Mary and those who with her connivance in treason plunged to destruction',[4] the memory of how 'certain stars shot madly from their spheres / To hear the sea-maid's music' (150–4) does seem to echo the lament for the Catholic traitor as 'a bright star' shot from the sky detectable in *Venus and Adonis* (815). Certainly, it is the events of 1586–88 – when the Scottish Queen was carried to disaster on the back of a Dauphin as pretext for invasion – that best match Oberon's scenario, with its pincer attack on a western empress. Moreover, the image of how 'Cupid all arm'd' took 'a certain aim … And loos'd his love-shaft smartly from his bow / As it should pierce a hundred thousand hearts', seems too specific not to point to the hundred thousand papists expected to rise up in support of the 'Enterprise of England'. The inset has been connected to the 1591 Elvetham Entertainment, when Elizabeth was amused by a masque in which another 'sea-maid' was exploited by her 'old supposed love', Sylvanus, in his scheme to sail 'from the South / To spoil these blessed fields of Albion'; and, as Philippa Berry notes, that water-pageant had been a celebration of victory over the Armada.[5] So, when the 'arm'd' god misfires his 'fiery shaft' on to the flower, 'love's wound' could well signify the stigmata of England's recusant community, penalised for acquiescing in a deluded international conspiracy. As such, the mixed blessing of 'love-in-idleness' would distill the madness of a fanatic devotion – like that of the Athenian lovers. And this interpretation gains resonance from the fact that in the Tudor cultural revolution 'idleness' was the punning code used by Protestant reformers to condemn Catholic idolatry, and the emptiness – in the words of the 1538 Injunction – of all 'men's fantasies besides Scripture': 'as in wandering to pilgrimages, offering of money, candles or tapers to images or relics, or kissing or licking the same, saying over a number of beads, not understood or minded on, and such-like superstition'.[6]

A Midsummer Night's Dream ends with Puck's plea that we think its 'weak and idle theme, / No more yielding than a dream' (5.1.417); but Stephen Greenblatt remarks how its final moments depend on a belief that there is after all 'something of great constancy' (26) about 'love in idleness', for 'when the fairies "consecrate" the marriage beds with field-dew they are, in a mode at once natural and magical, enacting (and appropriating to the stage) the Catholic practice of anointing the marriage bed with holy water'.[7] Thus, a popish ritual that earlier led those annointed to 'dote in idolatry' (1.1.109) is literally rehabilitated, as Oberon now orders the sprinkling of 'all the couples' (397) in the house. Greenblatt sees this nuptial blessing as an instance of the process of transmigration from church to theatre in Elizabethan England, whereby 'a sacred sign is emptied' by being 'deemed suitable for the stage', and he infers that to Anglicans it would confirm that, just as theatre worked by 'evacuation of divine presence from religious mystery, leaving only vivid, empty cere-monies', so Catholicism was nothing but 'the Pope's playhouse'.[8] Yet, far from such abandonment, this benediction seems designed to reinvest validity in ritual. As Eamon Duffy relates, even before the Reformation objections were raised against those who followed Oberon, 'insomuch that against tempests of thunder and lightning many run to the church for holy water to cast about their houses to drive away evil spirits and devils'; and the 1549 Act of Uni-formity expressly prohibited the asperging of holy water on the congregation at Mass. So whether or not liquid is sprinkled on the audience (as the text might imply) from an aspergillum, this ending returns the play to a pre-Reformation liturgy that had been explicitly concerned, Duffy shows, 'with the objective power of holy words, gestures, and things over the Devil', and in which hallowed water had 'effectual power to cast out demons and drive away disease', power 'not only over people, but over inanimate objects, so that "whatever in the houses or places of the faithful shall be sprinkled with it, may be freed from all pollution, and delivered from harm"'.[9] For a culture that had even prescribed the drinking of font water (so Duffy records) for the cure of haemorrhoids,[10] would have had no qualms about the efficacy of Oberon's 'dew':

> So shall all the couples three
> Ever true in loving be,
> And the blots of nature's hand
> Shall not in their issue stand.
> Never mole, harelip, nor scar,
> Nor mark prodigious, such as are
> Despised in nativity,
> Shall upon their children be.
>
> (5.1.397–404)

Oberon's relegitimation of the asperging ceremony restores the dukedom of the play to a late-medieval Christianity in which, as Duffy details, holy water was supplied to the laity for protection of every household, whether it was 'sprinkled in the hearth to fend off evil', given sick animals to drink or splashed, as here, 'in the marriage-bed to promote fertility'.[11] Moreover, this final blessing not only revives one of the rituals that most offended reformers, but does so with a solemnity to wash away all previous reservations about a religion that had seemed like 'remembrance of an idle gaud' – or amulet – according to Demetrius, doted on in childhood (4.1.166). It ignores, that is to say, the hostility of Puritans towards the holy water carriers who still went the rounds of country parishes in Shakespeare's childhood; and their scorn of those who denied the evidence that 'not so much as a chicken is nowadays cured of the pip by holy water', as Jeremy Taylor mocked, but continued to 'throw it upon children's cradles and sick cows' horns'.[12] To Greenblatt, this conclusion partakes of the same playful prevarication as Sir Philip Sidney's *Defence of Poetry*, when it teases that 'for the poet, he nothing affirms, and therefore never lieth';[13] and it is true, as Keith Thomas confirms, that the status of holy water was seen by some theologians as a question of belief, with 'nothing improper about such actions, provided they were performed out of genuine Christian faith … The Devil, it was agreed, was allergic to holy water, so wherever his influence was suspected it was an appropriate remedy.'[14] But the blessing at the end of this play seems less equivocal than Shakespeare's representation of other rites of exorcism, such as the scenes with Edgar in *King Lear*. There, Greenblatt contends, the text is 'haunted by a sense of rituals and beliefs that are no longer efficacious, that have been *emptied out*', and we are always reassured that the difference between exorcism and theatre is that the latter elicits 'complicity rather than belief'.[15] Whereas, what is demanded by this and Shakespeare's later comedies is precisely, as Greenblatt admits, that we *do* awake our faith:

> The close … requires the audience to will imaginatively a miraculous turn of events, often against the evidence of our senses, as when the audience persuades itself that two actors playing Sebastian and Viola in *Twelfth Night* really *do* look identical, in spite of ocular proof to the contrary.[16]

Shakespeare's miracle plays depend, Greenblatt proposes, on our willing suspension of disbelief in the punning *doubleness* of fact and fiction that is incarnated in the actor's own body, whether it is as an identical twin, as an androgyne, or – in the clinching instance which enables us 'to experience the wonder of her resurrection' – of Hermione as 'an unbreathing statue'.[17] In this society that attacks theatre as idolatry, the fictive idol turns out, Shakespeare reveals, to be something more (or less) than factually idle. As Judith Konenfeld argues (in a book that, moreover, attempts to situate Shakespeare within a *Protestant* tradition) among the areas in which historicism 'may not be historicist enough' is in writing 'as if the suspicion of Catholic "magic" and "theater" were equivalent to an admission that the signs were merely empty, and as such comparable to "representations"', without realising that for Shakespeare's generation 'the absence of a material presence of the sacred is not tantamount to the absence of the holy altogether', or for ever.[18] For it is, in fact, a pattern of reconsecration that recurs throughout the early Shakespeare, where characters repeat the lesson of Lucentio, a 'young scholar long studying at Rheims' (*Shrew*, 2.1.80), who states that 'while I stood idly looking on, / I found the effect of love in idleness' (1.1.148). For while it is 'the superstitious idle-headed eld' (*Merry Wives*, 4.4.34) who credit tales like that of Herne the Hunter, it is the young who recover in these plays what Julia calls the 'sense in idolatry', when apparently 'senseless form' is 'worshipped, kissed, loved, and adored!' (*Two Gents*, 4.4.195–7). Here, for every Venus iconoclastically inveighing against an Adonis as a 'well-painted-idol, image dull and dead' (*Venus*, 212), there is a pious Juliet primed to call a Romeo 'the god of my idolatry' (*Romeo*, 2.2.114). Rather than 'wear out youth in shapeless idleness' (*Two Gents*, 1.1.8), the route of these Elizabethan lovers is set by Valentine's escape to the Counter-Reformation citadel of Milan, with its Borromean doctrine that 'the idol you worship so' is a 'heavenly saint' and 'earthly paragon' (2.4.142–4). Silvia may protest she is 'loath to be your idol ... To worship shadows and adore false shapes' (4.2.125–7); Berowne scorn the 'Pure, pure idolatry' which 'makes flesh a deity' (*Love's*, 4.3.71) and Antonio moan 'How vile an idol proves this god!' after he 'did devotion' to his 'image' of Sebastian (*Twelfth*, 3.4.353–6), but the end of their journey is always to meet one of 'Pygmalion's images, newly made' (*Measure*, 3.2.43), and so justify Helena's vow to let 'idolatrous fantasy sanctify his relics' (*All's*, 1.1.96). In fact, the path to Rome can be projected in these plays from the very name of Romeo – the wanderer – and his pilgrimage with Juliet:

> ROMEO: If I profane with my unworthiest hand
>   This holy shrine, the gentle sin is this.
>   My lips, two blushing pilgrims, ready stand
>   To smooth that rough touch with a tender kiss.
> JULIET: Good pilgrim, you do wrong your hand too much,
>   Which mannerly devotion shows in this.
>   For saints have hands that pilgrims' hands do touch,
>   And palm to palm is holy palmers' kiss.
> ROMEO: Have not saints lips, and holy palmers too?
> JULIET: Ay, pilgrim, lips that they must use in prayer.
> ROMEO: O, then, dear saint, let lips do what hands do!
>   They pray: grant thou, lest faith turn to despair.
> JULIET: Saints do not move, though grant for prayers' sake.
> ROMEO: Then move not while my prayer's effect I take.
>
> (*Romeo*, 1.5.93–106)

When the monastery at Boxley in Kent was ransacked in 1538, its most sacred image was discovered to have been an automaton, which tricked the faithful by means of a 'hundred wires to make the image goggle with the eyes', John Foxe reported, 'to nod with the head; to hang the lip; and shake the jaws; according to the value of the gift which was offered'.[19] This mechanical icon was paraded and burned as the Bishop of London preached a sermon against idolatory, but was still being cited in 1623 as 'the famous Kentish idol' who 'moved her eyes and hands by those secret gimmers which now every puppet-play can imitate'.[20] Idolatry was always liable to be collapsed into the idleness of theatre, 'just as Catholic clerical garments – the copes, albs, amices and stoles that were the glories of the medieval church – were sold to the players', and an actor taking the part of a bishop 'could have worn the actual robes of the character he was representing'.[21] What is notable, therefore, about Shakespeare's idolatrous dramaturgy is that it pulls in the opposite direction, away from idleness, towards the moment when 'You do awake your faith', and Paulina proves she can 'make the statue move indeed, descend / And take you by the hand' (Winter's Tale, 5.3.95; 88), and so restore a world of wonder-working icons, where statues of the Madonna are no longer 'like to take dust' – as Sir Toby reports the neglect of 'Mistress Mall's picture' (Twelfth, 1.3.120). Such imagery is often interpreted as merely conventional, but, in her survey of the Virgin Mary and Elizabeth I, Helen Hackett has noticed a 'reduced anxiety about mentioning the Virgin and saints' in the 1590s, and concludes that, far from 'satirizing "idolatrous" practices and hymns to the Virgin, emptying their terms of spiritual significance in an act of secularisation or verbal iconoclasm', this resurgence of Catholic metaphor can be keyed to a new regret for the old devotional rites, when 'long enough had passed for these terms to have nostalgic appeal for an older generation and novelty value for the young'.[22] Thus, recent research reinforces the intuition of an earlier biographer like Edgar Fripp, that in these plots 'Shakespeare's imagination wandered' into the past 'before the savage destruction of monasteries and burning of martyrs, when Englishmen and women were of one Church, and godly "fathers" heard confession, sang requiem, and offered prayers for others' sins, or penance for their own, in lonely cells and forest retreats'.[23] As Arthur Marotti concludes, far from desacralising this Catholic inheritance, the Stratford dramatist 'rescued from an older culture, and from the "old religion", those very modes of perception and belief that were under attack':

> Shakespeare composed both tragedies and tragicomedies that contain non-satiric expressions of the very experiences of the miraculous and wondrous that Protestant polemicists and rationalists were debunking as part of the old religion's supposed superstition and trickery. Thus, in one sense, Shakespeare might have been trying to salvage for a post-Catholic English culture some of those emotionally powerful features of medieval Catholicism that broadened the range of religious experience and perception, preserving a sense of the mysteriousness of both the natural and supernatural worlds ... Shakespeare did not wish to separate himself absolutely from the older ways of perceiving the mysterious, the miraculous, and the wondrous.[24]

Shakespeare's festive characters live in a mental world of shrines and holy days that dates from before the Reformation, habitually swearing 'by Saint Anne' (*Shrew*, 1.1.250); 'by Saint Anne and ginger' (*Twelfth*, 2.3.117); by 'Saint Dennis' (*Love's*, 5.2.87); 'by Saint George' (*Shrew*, 2.1.236); by Saint James the Great as both 'Jaques' (*All's Well*, 3.4.4) and 'Jamy' (*Shrew*, 3.2.82); and 'by Saint Jeronimy' (*Shrew, Ind*, 1.9); or insulting someone as a 'Bartholomew boar-pig' (*2 Henry 4*, 221). This practice is remarkable given that from the middle of the sixteenth century the tide of official action was flowing so strongly against any invocation of the saints, 'the lights before their images were extinguished by 1538, their shrines despoiled, and images banned. The clergy were encouraged to omit invocations to the saints from the litany, and they discouraged saints for specific favours.'[25] Even when not taught by an 'old religious uncle' (*As You Like It*, 3.2.332); or converted by an 'old religious man' (5.4.157), however, Shakespearean characters like to wear relics of 'Saint George's half-cheek in a brooch' (*Love's*, 5.2.613); bless one another with, 'Saint Nicholas be thy speed!' (*Two Gents*, 3.1.292); refer their affairs to 'the old priest of Saint Luke's church' (*Shrew*, 4.4.85); hurry 'presently to Saint Luke's' (*Measure*, 3.1.274); attend 'the votarists of Saint Clare' (1.4.5); meet 'At Saint Gregory's Well' (*Two Gents*, 4.2.81); listen for 'the bells of Saint Bennet' (*Twelfth*, 5.1.39); and go on 'pilgrimage to Saint Jaques le grand' (*All's Well*, 4.3.48). In fact, Shakespeare refers to specific saints some hundred and fifty times, and his calendar includes the figures of Alban, Charity, Clement, Colme, Crispin, David, Edmund, Francis, Gregory, Helen, 'mother of great Constantine' (*1 Henry 6*, 1.2.142), Joan, Katherine, Lambert, Lucy, Magnus, Martin, Patrick, Philip, Stephen and Valentine, as well as John, Mary Magdelen, Michael, Peter and Paul. The omission of august London patrons such as Barnabas, Lawrence, Mark, Matthew or Thomas only underlines the populist and provincial allegiance of Shakespeare's list, which reflects what Duffy characterises as the 'neighbourliness and homeliness' of hagiolatry in late medieval England, where 'the saints who gazed down from screens and tabernacles were … country people themselves, like Saint James the Great, with his sensible shoes'.[26] Such was the devotional choice which tied the dramatist to an unofficial cult needing no sanction, as Thomas More said, but 'the hearts of the whole congregation',[27] and what it demonstrated was the dramatist's immersion in the deep symbolic structures of what the *Annales*-school historians termed the 'long duration', at a time when, as François Laroque observes in his *Annales*-style account of *Shakespeare's Festive World*:

> despite the official abolition of the cult of saints … the old calendar of feast days was still central to the life of the nation … its series of days consecrated to saints still played a role of major importance in Elizabethan England. It constituted a veritable matrix of time.[28]

Shakespeare's choice of saints is an indication of what recent historians emphasise as the deep continuity of popular Catholicism in Elizabethan England,

and evidence that in their rural heartlands 'the culture of Catholics was barely influenced by the Reformation'. In the words of Christopher Haigh, there 'Catholicism still meant masses and rites of passage, Latin prayers learned by rote, protective magic and village pipers, plays and pilgrimages. Catholics used charms, relics and holy water after the Reformation as before, and miracles at Holywell and exorcisms in Lancashire became even more common.'[29] But the list may also epitomise the persistence with which the rites and symbols of medieval Catholicism were deliberately perpetuated in defiance of the iconoclasts. It suggests something of the sly recalcitrance with which 'monuments of idolatry had yet to be dismantled in Lancashire in the 1570s'; officers found 'images, relics and the entire paraphernalia of "vain popish trish-trash" in Coventry' as late as 1584; and even in London in 1601 there were inquiries into persons who had secreted church ornaments, 'which it is to be conjectured they do keep for a day, as they call it'.[30] It is in the context of this recently rediscovered Catholic survivalism that the dramatist's popish stage-props can now, perhaps, best be explained. For in his study of Elizabethan iconoclasm, *The Reformation of the Images*, John Phillips has stressed how the 'old ways died slowly' because 'hiding places were innumerable', and 'sometimes, when the rood was removed, parishioners sketched in a cross with chalk or paint', while 'many of the works of the old religion were hidden against the day when it was hoped the tide would turn again'.[31] In particular, Shakespeare's 'weak and idle theme' that, as Timon's says, 'I am no idle votarist' (*Timon*, 4.3.27), can be compared directly to a tactic he may have learned at Stratford itself, which was to conceal the trappings of Catholic worship beneath a nominal conformity, by overpainting the offending icon with a superficial coat of soluble distemper: 'slubbered over with a whitewash that in a house may be undone, standing like a Dianae's shrine for a future hope and daily comfort of old popish beldames and young perking papists'.[32]

On 10 January 1564 John Shakespeare, Chamberlain of Stratford, recorded the sum of three shillings 'paid for defacing images in the chapel'.[33] He did so in compliance with orders of 1547 which had been updated in 1559 to prohibit 'abused images, tables, pictures and paintings' and specifically 'monuments of feigned miracles, pilgrimages and idolatry'.[34] The images in Stratford's Gild Chapel of the Holy Cross that had so offended were murals of favourite scenes of medieval iconography, such as the murder of St Thomas Becket, the dream of St Helena and the Day of Judgement. And so, as part of a thorough Protestantising that required removing the stone altar, dismantling the rood loft, inserting pews and erecting a screen between the nave and chancel, Shakespeare's father supervised the defacement of these idols, by ordering them to be painted over. To sceptics such as Samuel Schoenbaum, determined to maintain 'a secular agnosticism' over 'the faith in which William Shakespeare was reared', this collaboration in 'the rape of the chapel' has always been a compelling circumstance 'to stir misgivings in the non-sectarian biographer'.[35] But, in an authoritative essay of 1994, the foremost historian of Elizabethan religion, Patrick Collinson, has argued that, on the contrary, 'the fact that the great doom painting was whitewashed over rather than destroyed suggests the kind of crypto-Catholic conduct of which Puritans complained'. That John Shakespeare, who first took office under Mary, was a municipal officer when the Gild Chapel was Protestantised, or when its popish copes and vestments were later sold, 'proves nothing', Collinson insists; but what does align him with the strategy of survivalism is that the murals, protected until 1560 by the Catholic Clopton family, and for three more years by a temporising Corporation, were at last secreted with sufficient care to remain intact until rediscovered in 1804.[36] By concealing, rather than obliterating, the popish idols of Stratford, and so preserving them for a future age, 'against the day', like some 'Dianae's shrine', the father had thereby set an 'idol theme' of loss and restoration to a son whose works would indeed include, in *Pericles*, a crypto-Catholic chapel disguised as a temple of Diana:

> DIANA: My temple stands in Ephesus. Hie thee hither
> And do upon mine altar sacrifice.
> There, when my maiden priests are met together,
> Before the people all,
> Reveal how thou at sea didst lose thy wife.
> To mourn thy crosses, with thy daughter's, call,
> And give them repetition to the life.
>
> (*Pericles*, 22.224–31)

'They say miracles are past, and we have our philosophical persons to make modern and familiar, things supernatural and causeless' (*All's Well*, 2.3.1): Shakespeare – who began with iconoclasm on the imposture of Simpcox, the supposedly 'blind man at Saint Alban's shrine' (*2 Henry VI*, 2.1.63) – developed a theatre out of the ambiguity between science and religion, until, in a work such as *Pericles*, he and his recusant collaborator, George Wilkins, could end by vindicating the entire Catholic universe of chantries, bells, midwives with holy girdles, and pilgrimages to statues of virgin saints. No wonder this play was toured through Yorkshire in 1609 by recusant actors, and became a set text of the Jesuit school at Saint-Omer,[37] for it leaves no doubt, as its hero says, 'who to thank, / Besides the gods, for this great miracle' (5.3.57). And even in his most direct disclaimer of 'love in idolness', Sonnet 105, the poet's denial – 'Let not my love be called idolatry' – complements Stratford's whitewashing, being a secret prayer to the Holy Trinity, whispered as lip-service to the 'Homily against Idolatry'. Here the very text of the Homily, that 'images in temples be none other than idols, unto which idolatry hath been, is, and ever will be committed', is referred to the *Gloria Patri* – 'As it was in the beginning, is now, and ever will be' – until, as John Kerrigan states, it is impossible to tell whether Shakespeare is worshipping the Homily or the Trinity.[38] This is a poet, then, who denies idolatry, on the idolatrous grounds that he is devoted 'To one, of one, still such, and ever so' – or 'God the Father, Son and Holy Ghost'. So, when he opened his Globe theatre with the Protestant injunction to 'idle creatures' to 'get you home' and 'disrobe the images' (*Julius*, 1.1.1; 64), there can be no question that some of his audience would have heard the pun, and stayed in the playhouse, on the understanding that their own love of idleness was synonymous with papistry. 'Prelatical trash' is what Puritans called Shakespeare's *Works*, such as crypto-Catholic 'clergymen spend their canonical hours on'.[39] But the secret papist Ben Jonson must have known exactly what he meant, and chose his words carefully, when he demurred, and said that he 'loved the man', and honoured his memory very precisely 'on this side idolatry'.[40]

NOTES

1 William Empson, *Some Versions of Pastoral* (Revised, Harmondsworth: Penguin, 1966), pp. 79–82.
2 Anne Barton, Introduction to the Riverside edition (Boston: Houghton Mifflin, 1974), p. 218.
3 Elizabeth's nickname for Raleigh was 'Water', so there may be a slight on his *The Ocean to Cynthia* in the image of 'the watery moon'.
4 Harold Brooks, *The Arden Shakespeare: 'A Midsummer Night's Dream'* (London: Methen, 1979), p. lxvii.
5 Philippa Berry, *Of Chastity and Power* (London: Routledge, 1989), pp. 108–9.
6 Eamon Duffy, *The Strpping of the Altars: Traditional Religion in England, 1400–1580* (New Haven: Yale University Press, 1992), p. 407.
7 Stephen Greenblatt, *Shakespearean Negotiations* (Oxford: Clarendon Press, 1990), pp. 10–11.
8 Ibid., pp. 112–13.
9 Duffy, op. cit. (note 6), pp. 281–2, 437–8, 465–6.
10 Ibid., p. 439.
11 Ibid., pp. 281–2.
12 Quoted in Keith Thomas, *Religion and the Decline of Magic* (Harmondsworth: Penguin, 1973, p. 33.
13 Greenblatt, op. cit. (note 7), p. 116.
14 Thomas, op. cit. (note 12), p. 32.
15 Greenblatt, op. cit. (note 7), p. 119.
16 Ibid., p. 124.
17 Ibid.; and for the concept of 'doubleness' see also pp. 78, 92 and 158.
18 Judith Kronenfeld, *'King Lear' and the Naked Truth: Rethinking the Language of Religion and Resistance* (Durham: Duke University Press, 1998), p. 232.
19 John Foxe, *The Acts and Monuments of the Church*, ed. M.H. Seymour (London: 1563), p. 582.
20 Joseph Hall, *The Works of Bishop Joseph Hall*, ed. P. Wynter (Oxford: Oxford University Press, 1863), p. 284.
21 Greenblatt, op. cit. (note 7), p. 112.
22 Helen Hackett, *Virgin Mother, Maiden Queen: Elizabeth I and the Cult of the Virgin Mary* (New York: St Martin's Press, 1995), pp. 150–3, 199–201 and 161.
23 Edgar Fripp, *Master Richard Quyny* (Oxford: Oxford University Press, 1924), pp. 76–7.
24 Arthur Marotti, 'Shakespeare and Catholicism', in Richard Dutton, Alison Findlay and Richard Wilson (eds), *Theatre and Religion: Lancastrian Shakespeare* (Manchester: Manchester University Press, 2003), p. 337.

25 Duffy, op. cit. (note 6), pp. 511–12.
26 Ibid., p. 161.
27 Ibid., p. 165.
28 François Laroque, *Shakespeare's Festive World: Elizabethan Seasonal Entertainment and the Professional Stage*, trans. Janet Lloyd (Cambridge: Cambridge University Press, 1991), p. 15.
29 Christopher Haigh, 'The Continuity of Catholicism in the English Reformation', *Past and Present*, 93 (1981), p. 68.
30 Alexandra Walsham, *Church Papists: Catholicism, Conformity and Confessional in Early Modern England* (Woodbridge: Boydell and Brewer, 1993), pp. 15–16.
31 John Phillips, *The Reformation of the Images: Destruction of Art in England, 1535–1660* (Berkeley: University of California Press, 1973), pp. 133–4.
32 Quoted ibid., p. 134.
33 John Henry de Groot, *The Shakespeares and 'The Old Faith'* (New York: King's Crown Press, 1946), p. 16.
34 Phillips, op. cit. (note 31), p. 114.
35 Samuel Schoenbaum, *William Shakespeare: A Documentary Life* (Oxford: Oxford University Press, 1975), p. 46; *William Shakespeare: A Compact Documentary Life* (Oxford: Oxford University Press, 1977), pp. 53–4.
36 Patrick Collinson, 'William Shakespeare's Religious Inheritance and Environment', in *Elizabethan Essays* (London: The Hambledon Press, 1994), p. 250.
37 Willem Schrickx, '*Pericles* in a Book-List of 1619 from the English Jesuit Mission and Some of the Play's Special Problems', *Shakespeare Survey*, 29 (1976), pp. 21–32.
38 William Shakespeare, *The Sonnets and A Lover's Complaint* (Harmondsworth: Penguin, 1986), p. 310.
39 *Mercurius Britannicus*, 2 September 1644; quoted in Ernest Sirluck, 'Shakespeare and Jonson among the Pamphleteers of the First Civil War', *Modern Philology*, 53 (1955), p. 94.
40 Ben Jonson, '*Timber: Or Discoveries*', ed. R.S. Walker (Syracuse: Columbia University Press, 1953), vol. 2, pp. 665–6.

7

Dyed in mummy

Othello and the mulberries

BARDOLATRY, so the crypto-Catholic Ben Jonson was quick to point out, was only ever just 'this side idolatry';[1] and as Cultural Materialists protest, celebration of Shakespeare has long been 'an attentuated form of relic-worship', centred on prostration before 'vatic, totemic images'.[2] Not surprisingly, therefore, from the time when his tomb at Stratford first began to acquire aura as a tourist site, critical debate has revolved around the problem of the author's relationship to canonicity,[3] and the question posed by Stephen Greenblatt, of 'what happens when a piece of cloth', such as Cardinal Wolsey's hat, 'is passed from church to playhouse', and 'a consecrated object is reclassified, transferred from a sacred to profane setting, deemed suitable for the stage?'[4] For as Graham Holderness observes, it can be no accident that 'in the garden of New Place, the house where Shakespeare lived in retirement, the mulberry tree reputed to have been planted by the Bard's own hand' had acquired, by the early eighteenth century, sufficient sanctity to become the object of a devotional cult. Nor that in 1756 the Reverend Francis Gastrell, the Anglican clergyman who bought the property, claimed to be so exasperated by 'the frequent importunities' of the Shakespeare-worshippers, 'and so annoyed with the hoary and ancient growth obstructing the sunlight and engendering rising damp', that in an act of truly radical criticism or 'Gothic barbarity', he had the mulberry chopped down, 'whereupon it began, like the wood of the true cross, to increase and multiply into innumerable relics'.[5] To Samuel Schoenbaum, the enterprise of Thomas Sharpe – the watchmaker who, knowing 'the value of sacred objects', bought the felled tree and 'over forty years carved from it more curios and useful articles than one would expect a single mulberry capable of yielding' – epitomises the Shakespeare industry, since, as he dryly concludes, 'in such circumstances, a miracle is not surprising'.[6] And Sharpe's advertisement, swearing 'upon the four Evangelists, in presence of Almighty God', that all his 'snuff-boxes, goblets, punch-ladles, toothpicks and tobacco-pipes' were fabricated from 'the very Mulberry-tree which was planted by the immortal Bard', did require as much of a leap of faith as medieval Canterbury or modern Stratford.[7] So, whether or not the Reverend Gastrell signalled that 'Anglican clergy set the seal on the fact he was no child of theirs', when he cut down the poet's mulberry, as the Catholic critic Richard Simpson inferred,[8] from the earliest days it was recognised that the roots of his plays were entangled with popish religion, and that the canonisation of Shakespeare had somehow supplanted the Christian cult of relics:

> Honey-tongu'd Shakespeare, when I saw thy issue
> I swore Apollo got them and none other.
> Their rosy-tainted features cloth'd in tissue,
> Some heaven-born goddess said to be their mother:
> Rose-cheek'd Adonis with his amber tresses;
> Fair fire-hot Venus charming him to love her;
> Chaste Lucrece, virgin-like her dresses;
> Proud lust-stung Tarquin seeking still to prove her;
> Romeo, Richard; more whose names I know not.
> Their sugared tongues and power-attractive beauty
> Say they are Saints, although like Saints they show not,
> For thousands vow to them subjective duty:
>   They burn in love: thy children, Shakespeare, heat them.
>   Go, woo thy Muse, more nymphish brood beget them.[9]

Shakespeare wrote at a time when there could be no more pilgrimages, when the cult of saints survived only in 'the interior exile spaces of Tudor culture, in the secret underground of a now-illegal Catholicism', and when holy relics were subject to desacralisation, decaying like those snot-stained rags that had once been Becket's hairshirt, which John Colet 'touched with disgust and shrank from kissing'.[10] Yet the very first critical comment on his plays, from the Lancashire writer John Weever in 1599, pointedly praises the playwright for 'begetting' a new generation of 'saints', whose votaries 'burn in love', rather than sectarian hate. Weever later recorded the fan-worship of *Julius Caesar*; and his analysis of the emerging Shakespeare cult is a prediction of the Greenblatt thesis: that in these plays theatre took over from religion, substituting for the audiences who 'vow to them subjective duty', secular saints for spiritual martyrs. Shakespeare's creations are true icons for a post-Reformation society, according to Weever, even if, in slipping from Rome to Romeo, their maker defected, it is implied, from one idolatory to another. So, if his poems are 'said' to carry the look of the Virgin – 'Some heaven-born goddess' – with their red quartos reminiscent of Roman missals, his plays will live precisely because in them Shakespeare chose the 'heat' of the playhouse over the flames of the scaffold stoked by the 'fire hot' Queen. Weever's sonnet *'Ad Gulielmum Shakespeare'* is confirmation that Shakespeare criticism hinged from the start on the question of religious affiliation, as it purports to be an affidavit, affirmed on the new Bible, the book of the Bard, vouching the plays' exemption from Catholic influence: 'I swore Apollo got them and none other.' Yet Weever's mock-testimony to the defendant's devotion to the god of art, 'and none other', contradicts itself by making the plays so canonical that evidence of their apostasy can be sworn upon them. Thus, this deposition, pledged by a protégé of the Catholic aristocracy, itself turns out to be proof of just how much Shakespeare still needed to be defended, in mid-career, from suspicions of Catholic sympathies. With such witnesses, it comes as no surprise that the first recorded purchaser of the Folio, when it was published in 1623, was the ardent collector of martyrs' relics and Spanish ambassador, Count Gondomar; nor that as early as 1651 there were calls to make the grave of this 'true priest elect' – 'boldly blasphemed' by 'those that seem to preach, but prate' – the object of an annual pilgrimage on the lines of the former devotions at Holywell and Walsingham:

> Where thy honoured bones do lie
> Thither every year will I
> Slowly tread and sadly mourn.[11]

Shakespeare's canonicity was seen from earliest days, it seems, in terms of a 'popish' pilgrimage, and the more Puritans 'prated' of the plays as 'prelatical trash',[12] the more others, such as the young Milton, praised them as substitutes for the 'hallow'd relics' in cathedrals, or visualised the dramatist's own 'honour'd bones' transcending 'The labour of an age in piled stones', by becoming enshrined, like the forbidden faith, in 'each heart … And so sepulchr'd, in such pomp … That kings, for such a tomb should wish to die'. The *Works* would replace the relics of saints such as Edward the Confessor, according to this theory, and the act of taking their 'Delphic lines' to heart would amount to a form of encrypted resistance to those desecrators by whom they were yet 'unvalued'. For as the twenty-four-year-old Milton affirmed: 'What needs my Shakespeare' to be buried 'Under a star-ypointing pyramid' of an alabaster shrine, like those ruined in the Reformation, when 'thou, our fancy of itself bereaving, / Dost make us marble' ourselves?'[13] And Leonard Digges actually imagined the author of the First Folio risen to 'live eternally' on account of his *Works*, when 'that stone is rent' and 'Time dissolves thy Stratford Monument'.[14] Thus, at a time when reformers were adamant that 'There is no analogy between Preachers and Players, Sermons and Players, Theatres and Churches',[15] the idea that critics have rediscovered, that there was indeed a correlation between pilgrimages to shrines and processions to playhouses, had a special attraction for those with a vested interest in supporting the stage as a continuation of suppressed religion by other means, and for those consoling themselves that, in an age of iconoclasm, 'Not marble, nor the gilded monuments / Of princes shall outlive this powerful rhyme' (Sonnet, 111). The consciousness that, as Louis Montrose argues, experience of plays might provide an alternative to 'the ritual practices and popular religious festivities of late medieval Catholic culture' had a special appeal, that is to say, for those who most needed 'a substitute for the metaphysical aid of the medieval church', because they could not find one in the ceremonies of the Protestant state.[16] More specifically, the very notion of a displacement of relics by scripts, or the corpse of an author by the corpus of a work, was bound up, according to Arthur Marotti, with the Catholic discovery, 'after relics came under attack, from the late 1530s, when the shrine of Becket was destroyed and the saint's bones scattered', that the object of their worship could become a text, as it already was for Protestants.[17] In this hermeneutic, Shakespearean drama could become not merely the signifier of evacuated religion, 'emptied out', in Greenblatt's phrase, of its original meaning, like the stains round a voided tomb,[18] but a *real presence* that, for those able, like the popish young Milton, to understand its 'Delphic lines', filled the space formerly occupied by the now vanished remains of the English saints:

> Relics were, of course, one of the strong markers of difference between Catholicism and Protestantism. In one of the first proclamations of her reign, Queen Elizabeth ordered her clergy, 'to the intent that all superstition crept into men's hearts may vanish … [to] take away, utterly extinct and destroy all shrines, covering of shrines, tables, candlesticks, rolls of wax, pictures, paintings, and all other monuments of feigned miracles, pilgrimages, walls, glasses, or windows within their churches and houses'. To this day, the centre of the English Church, Canterbury Cathedral, is marked by an absence, the space formerly occupied by the relics and shrine of Thomas a Becket. [Thus] the association of an author's body with his body of work was more than a witty turn of phrase. It was historically grounded in the cultural conflicts and discourses of early modern England [when] the reverence for relics began to migrate into print culture, where the remains of a person were verbal.[19]

By installing the Shakespeare canon in the space vacated by relics of canonised saints, therefore, readers like Milton and Weever were not simply attributing Romanist tendencies to the plays. They were locating them just 'this side idolatry', in Jonson's careful phrase, in the key theological division over the sacramentals of holy bread and water, transubstantiation of wine into blood, and cult of the dead. For these early worshippers of Shakespeare, it was if his canonisation was a guarantee of the survival of Catholic ceremonial, which required only the minimum concession to the Protestant doctrine of faith. Such a position would be that of the Laudian Church. And it may not be coincidence that the moment when the dramatist achieved establishment status – among those new King's Men appointed to attend James I as Grooms of the Chamber in the coronation procession on 4 March 1604 – was also the time of the genesis of the Shakespearean play which stages the downfall of one who lacks that modicum of faith, unless 'his eyes had seen the proof' in a 'magic' piece of cloth (*Othello*, 1.1.28; 3.4.367). *The Tragedy Othello the Moor of Venice*, which was acted for the court at Whitehall on 1 November, All Saints' Day, 1604, was the first of two dramas, along with *The Tempest* in 1611. which seem crafted to reflect upon the Hallowmas themes of martyrdom and mourning, and the fact that the Gospel of the day is the Beatitudes, with the King's personal motto,

'Blessed are the peacemakers', and prayers for those 'that suffer persecution'.[20] In *The Tempest* the exiled Prospero turns away from the popish 'trumpery' he has kept hidden in his house, and accepts that 'The rarer action is / In virtue than in vengeance' for oppressions past (4.1.186; 5.1.27–8). But in *Othello* the freed slave continues to sanctify the 'antique token' (5.2.223) inherited from his ancestors, and makes this 'handkerchief / Which [he] so loved' (5.2.50–1) into a fetish with which to persecute the innocent and 'rack' himself (340). So, there are manifest connections in these two plays with the rituals of Hallowmas, which traditionally included the processional display of relics of the saints. But the fact that in each one Shakespeare situated himself so emphatically on 'this side idolatry' also relates them to the context of Jacobean religious politics, and to hopes for Catholic emancipation which, at the time of *Othello*, had never been more contingent on the readiness of the persecuted to relinquish their worship of those bloodstained remainders of their hungry ghosts. For a year later, the same feast would be the trigger for the fundamentalists' Gunpowder Plot.

The summer of *Othello* was a season of unique opportunity for English Catholics. The king suspended recusancy fines, and in August an embassy from Spain arrived at Somerset House, Queen's Anne's palace, which had been vacated for negotiations. Crowds lined the Thames, as courtiers, disguised with carnival masks, applauded the Spaniards from gondolas. After decades of war between England and Spain, James's ambition to be *Rex Pacificus*, the peace-maker of Europe, promised not only a solution to the continent's sectarian divisions but, by implication, toleration for English Catholics. Yet fireworks were followed by the game of poker that has been frozen for ever in the different kind of relic retained by the chief English negotiator, Robert Cecil, the group portrait of the conference attributed to John de Critz. In this painting, old enemies confront each other without exchanging eyes, gazing into air rather than revealing thoughts about the treaty they have signed, which sits on the table before the ever-patient Cecil. In fact, their accord opened Europe to English goods, as *quid pro quo* for the peace Spain needed, but produced not a word about religious freedom, which Cecil staked against 'the central English claim, to trade in the East and West Indies'.[21] No wonder the minister's colleagues look dissatisfied. For his team includes two Catholic fellow-travellers, or 'schismatics', Richard Sackville and Charles Blount, and the most conspicuous of all the court Catholics, Henry Howard, Earl of Northampton. The Earl, invaluable to the regime as 'a Catholic willing to serve any government cause',[22] has a card literally up his sleeve, however, in this picture, which is a paper he half conceals; while, opposite, the Spanish ambassador, Juan de Tassis, has not quite withdrawn the offer crushed into his hand. Each engages the viewer as if tempting speculation about business unresolved. What this might have entailed was signalled at the ensuing banquet, when the head of the Spanish delegation, the Duke of Frias, presented the king and queen with goblets packed with pearls, from which he had toasted their healths.[23] Though 'to some, including the Pope, it was abhorrent, the question of *buying* liberty of conscience' was indeed the subject of the memorandum drafted by Tassis, calculating just how much treasure of the Indies would suffice to purchase a decree.[24] So, Howard (who had accepted jewels worth 6000 *felipes* and a pension of 3000 for life) seems to signify through his tantalising gesture with the document that might, or might not, be an edict of toleration, that the consequence for his co-religionist of clinging to relics of the past would truly be the loss of a jewel of great price:[25]

> Then must you speak
> Of one that loved not wisely but too well,
> Of one not easily jealous but, being wrought,
> Perplexed in the extreme; of one whose hand,
> Like the base Indian, threw a pearl away
> Richer than all his tribe.
>
> *(Othello*, 5.2.352–57)

The inconclusive Treaty of London was signed on 19 August 1604, and from 9 to 27 August the King's Men were paid two shillings a day to wait on the Spanish. We do not know whether they acted at the palace on the Strand, but Park Honan thinks 'this unrewarding time' produced in *Othello* a work self-conscious about the value of an acting troupe.[26] Yet someone paid Shakespeare, we could infer, more than all his tribe, as the occasion of his tragedy was a moment when the sacramental question he stages – of 'ocular proof' as opposed to 'an essence that's not seen' (3.3.365; 4.1.16) – had never been more loaded or more 'base'. For the 'pearl of great price' had been the Biblical metaphor adopted by the Jesuit Edmund Campion, in his disguise as a jeweller, for martyrdom.[27] In this text, however, the spirit of the treaty seems to dictate that the symbol of the Catholic martyr has been perverted into a sacrifice squandered through loving 'not wisely but too well'. So, like the boy 'stol'n from an Indian king' as a royal ward in *A Midsummer Night's Dream* (2.1.22), the 'base Indian' of Othello's suicide speech enacts the self-inflicted punishment of those who persist 'Indian-like', as Helena calls her idolatry, 'Religious in … error' (*All's Well*, 1.3.188–9). Protestants habitually denigrated Catholics for being 'as ignorant of the true god as the Indians of Virginia' in their worship of relics;[28] and the flash of the image in *Othello* caps a series of strikes at the folly of those 'As ignorant as dirt' (5.2.171) which seems so one-sided an 'attack on Catholic misunderstandings of the sacraments' that it has been tempting to read the play as 'protestant propaganda', on a par with Samuel Harsnett's lumping of papists with 'the silly Indian nation, that falls down and performs divine adoration to a rag of red cloth'.[29] But this is to forget how the metaphor of the pearl must have worked two ways for a Whitehall audience: as a signifier, like pearls stolen from enslaved Indians and paid to Catholic courtiers, of religious freedom, and a token of the sacrifice of the martyrs now to be pawned by their own 'tribe'. If Shakespeare had taken the offer of toleration brokered by the Earl of the painting without hesitation, he would indeed have written to 'make his audience into more committed Protestants'.[30] But, in fact, he was living in a society which could adore a Roman rag as well as despise an Indian pearl, and so he wrote a tragedy about someone 'Perplexed in the extreme'.

'Sweet are the uses of adversity / Which, like the toad, ugly and venomous, / Wears yet a precious jewel in his head' (As You Like It, 2.1.12–13): Shakespeare had been close enough to the negative dialectics of Catholic martyrdom to reproduce the masochistic pride of those who embraced their persecutor to achieve a 'pearl of great price', and wore 'Th'impression of keen whips … as rubies' (Measure, 2.4.101). It had been recusants who called martyrs 'merchants', moreover, and the dramatist who used this commercial code in his plays about the escape of a Syracusan merchant and a merchant of Venice from the law based Othello on the self-inflated pitch of such a merchant of death. Thus, at a time when 'the toad' – the hunchback Cecil – was taking the economic discourse so literally that he was offering to give up the 'precious jewel' of Catholic persecution for the 'rich pearl' of Indian trade, the protagonist of this All Saint's play is given a poetry which makes 'the uses of adversity' seem usuriously sweet. Critics have long noticed that while 'Iago, characteristically, speaks of actual money', Othello talks always of the 'added value' of love's 'wealth'.[31] So, Othello affirms his love expressly as a rejection of the Somerset House proposals to barter the love of 'heaven' for the globe, when he says of Desdemona that 'Had she been true, / If heaven would make me such another world / Of one entire and perfect chrysolite / I'd not have sold her for it' (Othello, 5.2.150–3). In 1604 this was no mere figure of speech, as the treaty stalled on the precise point that Philip III's world empire dated from the fifteenth-century papal Bull dividing the globe between Portugal and Spain, so that the claim to free trade was also an attack on the Pope's deposing power, the very dogma for which the Tudor martyrs had paid the great price. As a Catholic, Northampton would know just what he was selling, therefore, when he argued at the conference that traders owed more to the 'Indians themselves, they paying to those Indians custom for their freight', than to any Pope.[32] Tribe for tribe, in this exchange of faith for jewels, or freedom of religion for free trade, the pearl thrown away by the 'base Indian' had become specifically the price of a soul. For Brabanzio, who may caricature the Puritan parliamentary bloc opposed to détente, his daughter is therefore a 'jewel' his 'soul' would hoard (1.3.194). But at the other extreme, her husband is equally persuaded by Iago that her value is non-negotiable, as 'Good name in man and woman … Is the immediate jewel of their souls. / Who steals my purse steals trash … But he that filches from me my good name / Robs me of that which not enriches him / And makes me poor indeed' (3.3.160–6). Not surprisingly, therefore Othello grandiloquently talks up his faith in implacably absolutist terms that would have been music to Spanish ears, as an affirmation of *pontifical* supremacy over rights of passage on the road to the Indies of even the Turks in their own Black Sea. Disclaiming papal power for natural law, Catholic patriots led by North-ampton had maintained that it 'did not rest in the liberty of any potentate under heaven to limit or stint' the ocean.[33] But in *Othello* the very name of the supreme pontiff runs literally beneath the surface to suggest the reverse:

> Like to the Pontic Sea,
> Whose icy current and compulsive course
> Ne'er knows retiring ebb, but keeps due on
> To the Propontic and the Hellespont,
> Even so my bloody thoughts with violent pace
> Shall ne'er look back, ne'er ebb to humble love,
> Till that a capable and wide revenge
> Swallow them up.
> [*He kneels*[
> Now, by yon marble heaven,
> In the due reverence of a sacred vow
> I here engage my words.
>
> (3.3.456–65)

The religious 'quarrels and heart burnings between England and Spain cannot easily be reconciled', advised Northampton's aide, Sir Robert Cotton, 'without traffic to the Indies'. But when the Earl pushed for 'this vent to the Indies', and extolled the 'great senate' of the Venetians for conceding that the Pope had no power to grant a monopoly of the waves, the deliberations came to an abrupt halt.[34] And so hopes for Catholic toleration foundered, at the time of Shakespeare's play, on the 'icy and compulsive' veto from that 'pontic' source which Othello likewise seems to invoke, when he kneels to his 'marble heaven' and swears 'blood, blood, blood!' (454). The 'soft phrase of peace' (1.3.82) had been spoken at Somerset House to bless an unholy league, 'Against all rules of nature' (101), like the marriage in the play, in the eyes of its opponents, and a 'Christian Union' of the kind upheld by those 'potent, grave, and reverend signors' of Venice (76), who had allowed the Signory, so James's envoy, Sir Henry Wotton reported in 1603, to slip 'almost into a neutrality of religion'.[35] For when it passed a law in June 1604 outlawing seditious priests, 'the Venetian state' (5.2.410) became the ideal for grandees like Northampton, who looked to the 'temperance and moderation' of an oligarchy that defied the Pope, whilst remaining Catholic, as a model for the *via media* espoused by James.[36] In *Volpone* Jonson satirised this 'politic' Republic as a moral limbo; but Shakespeare had done his best, with *The Merchant of Venice*, to envision such 'Vene-tianism', where the mercy of the Catholic mansion redeems the mercenariness of the Protestant market. A Venetian solution depended, however, on Catholic compromise with Protestant commerce; and, as Marc Shell remarks, the marriage in Belmont seems 'a stop-gap measure', shadowed by 'suggestions of a tragedy to come', in which the 'tension between purse and person' will force the old order to a reckoning.[37] Thus, by 1604, it was easier to dramatise the submission of Puritan fundamentalism (as Shakespeare did, in *Measure for Measure*, to mark the earlier Hampton Court Conference on Calvinism chaired by the king) than it was to envisage the surrender of its tribal customs by the Romanist extreme. For as Othello insists, when his wife obfuscates the whereabouts of the handkerchief which is the symbol of his loyalty to his tribe, 'To lose't, or give't away were such perdition / As nothing else could match' (3.4.65–6). And so Shakespeare registered that while 'the vast majority of English Catholics longed to worship without compromising their allegiance', to the Counter-Reformation men who led them, 'the idea of such a compromise was unthinkable'.[38] In the autumn of 1604, however, the tragedy was that even these sectarian warriors could admit, as Othello does, that while they might be damned to hell for entering into it, the alternative to 'the curse of marriage' (3.3.272) must be a return to the mayhem of the century of massacres:

> Excellent wench! Perdition catch my soul
> But I do love thee, and when I love thee not,
> Chaos is come again.
> (3.3.91–3)

Performed during a religious crisis, before an audience vigilant to possible allegory, *Othello* looks back to the era of sectarian wars, when Catholic resistance would have incited the reprisals relished by Graziano, who reflects that, had the old man been alive, his daughter's death would have made Brabanzio 'do a desperate turn, / Yea, curse his better angel from his side, / And fall to reprobance' (214–16). In the morality play of Jacobean politics, however, the 'good angel' of Christian love personified by Desdemona was no longer threatened by diehard Puritanism, but by 'the blacker devil' (5.2.140) of papist revanchism Othello claims to detect, when he plays the Roman game called *mora* and reads the future in her palm: 'this hand of yours requires / A sequester from liberty; fasting, and prayer, / Much castigation, exercise devout, / For here's a young and sweating devil here / That commonly rebels'. Even this veteran, it seems, would like to indulge King James's project, realised in 1611, to ensure that while 'hearts of old gave hands ... our new heraldry is hands, not hearts' (3.4.37–45), as he alludes to the badge of a red hand, signifying a baronet, added to arms of Catholic gentry who renounced the violence commemorated in their relics, by subsidising Ulster Protestants. But though a 'devout and politically disengaged Catholicism' of the kind imagined by Othello had been valorised through the nun Isabella of *Measure for Measure*,[39] in this tragedy there is no escape from the activism of the 'young devil' whose name identifies him with Catholic zealotry, and the pilgrim route to the shrine of Santiago, St James of Compostela. In fact, worship of Iago had a particular history for Londoners, as the hand of this saint had been one of those donated by 'hearts of old' when it was enshrined at Reading Abbey, which had been the scene of a passionate cult in its own right.[40] That 'saints have hands that pilgrims' hands do touch' (*Romeo*, 1.5.96), because so many were preserved,[41] was a macabre consideration for Shakespeare, who lent Helena the 'zealous fervour' of 'Saint Jaques' pilgrim' (*All's Well*, 3.4.4–11), and may have had in mind the 'aye-remaining lamps ... Lying with simple shells' at Compostela for the tomb of Thaisa (*Pericles*, 11.61–3). In *Othello*, moreover, editors note, Iago is affiliated with the most morbid aspect of St James, as defender of Christendom and the slayer of the Moors.[42] And it was the cult of the Basque idol as Santiago Matamoros which also inspired his near-namesake and fanatical countryman: the maimed soldier, street-fighter, and Jesuit founder, Inigo de Loyola.[43]

In the season of *Othello*, as the Jesuits were expelled from Venice, the Moors were conspiring against the King of Spain.[44] This unholy affinity seems to define Iago, who from his first words, swearing on Christ's blood (1.1.4), is marked as a Marlovian deicide, whose 'dire yell / As when, by night and negligence, the fire / Is spied in populous cities' (75–7) affiliates him with Catholic Leaguers, like the Guise, who similarly 'rings the bell' (2.3.144) for the devil's tocsin in *Massacre at Paris*. In that play paranoia over a politicised priesthood focuses on the assassination of Henry III by a Dominican. But what thrilled Marlowe, by his account, was the Baroque theatricality of a Church that produced the carnivalesque spectacle of the St Barthomomew's Day Massacre, where 'the service of god is performed with more ceremonies, as elevation of the mass, organs, singing men, shaven crowns, etc.' than in any Protestant rite.[45] This is also the aesthetic of Iago, who 'pushes theatricality to such an absurd extreme' in orchestrating Othello's violence, while remaining so detached,[46] that he is seen by Michael Bristol as an exemplar of the 'knowledgeable misrecognition' practised by Jesuits who improvised upon the rituals of late medieval piety, such as exorcism, with a superior sense of their own chicanery.[47] In his essay on this Jesuit inauthenticity, 'Shakespeare and the Exorcists', Greenblatt side-steps the question whether the missionaries *themselves* saw through 'the holy water, smouldering brimstone, and sacred relics', as their detractors alleged, with contempt for the dupes of their 'cunning manipulation of popular superstititions' and 'deliberate arousal of anxiety'. So he overlooks the extent to which the 'drastic swerve' from literal to metaphorical belief he ascribes to Shakespeare was already a demystifying part of Jesuit thinking, and may have been what perturbed the dramatist.[48] For from the first days of the Society, the 'Black Robes' were willing to validate the Holy House of Loreto, or 'a column on which Christ was scourged', and even to sanctify Indian totems, but only for what they took to be papal purposes. Thus, while their 'Rules for Thinking with the Church' stipulated that 'We should show esteem for relics of the saints by venerating them', they did so 'in their own "way", as a statement against Protestants'. They directed 'the devotion of the people towards relics "to the confusion of the heretics"'. In short, 'they made pragmatic use of them as occasion suggested. They made them into symbols of loyalty.'[49] So, Iago is never more the Jesuitical medicine man than when he appropriates tribal customs, and catalogues Othello's superstitions among those drugs and jewels, like the trade in pearls and 'poppy', that the Jesuits controlled:

> I will in Cassio's lodging lose this napkin,
> And let him find it. Trifles light as air
> Are to the jealous confirmations strong
> As proofs of holy writ. This may do something.
> The Moor already changes with the poison.
> Dangerous conceits are in their natures poisons,
> Which at the first are scarce found to distaste,
> But, with a little act upon the blood,
> Burn like the mines of sulphur.
>
> (3.3.325–333)

For Othello, stories about 'the cannibals that each other eat, / The Anthropophagi, and men whose heads / Do grow beneath their shoulders', are a 'witchcraft' he uses to seduce his hearers, but against which he differentiates his own beliefs. So, Desdemona, who calls them 'passing strange' (1.3.142–68), finds nothing strange in the idea that 'there's some wonder in the handkerchief' (3.4.97). But for Iago, the recording of 'dangerous conceits' is part of the 'Machiavellian anthropology' which makes any belief system appear 'an idle and most false imposition' (2.3.251), and all religions performative. Greenblatt contends that the colonists who first tested this hypothesis about 'the function of illusion in the establishment of religion' recoiled from 'the suggestion that religions should be ranked according to their demonstrated ability to control their adherents', but he underestimates the Jesuits.[50] For unlike the Spaniards who 'could not entertain the odd relation between cannibalism and the Eucharist', and broke 'the Idols to pieces' wherever they encountered them,[51] the Jesuits in Paraguay in the 1540s were struck by the logic of the cannibals who ate only the strong in order to 'acquire valour, dipped their hands in the prisoner's blood while they were being instructed as warriors, and assumed a new name when the dead man's flesh was served up in the form of fritters'.[52] In Ethiopia in the 1600s Jesuits consecrated yeasted bread and grape juice instead of wine and wafers for communion;[53] and in India they were already being rebuked by other orders for adopting 'paganism and Saracenism', by allowing converts to 'lay food on graves, which the Fathers distributed', or to 'touch graves in cemeteries' for cures. In Lahore, the priests even preached in mosques, 'so long as they did not speak against Muhammed', and permitted their congregations to persist with non-Christian ceremonies at home.[54] But Jesuits went native most spectacularly in the pantomimes they staged in cities such as Goa at Christmas, where 'extraordinary devotion by Muslims and Hindus' would be excited by the 'artificial birds that sang, apes that spouted water, figures of Magi that wept tears', fireworks, guns and 'immense din from the playing of drums and tom-toms'.[55] When their critics scoffed that such circuses restricted converts to 'the base Indian', the Fathers replied with Iago's words, that 'base men being in love have then a nobility in their natures more than is native in them' (2.1.212).[56] Jesuits were happy to employ shamanism, such as sending the sick texts of the Lord's Prayer to tie around their necks, provided they won souls.[57] The result, however (as Shakespeare had shown with his Dr Pinch), was that they acquired the reputation for juggling the sacraments to which Cassio's nausea alludes, when he retches that 'Every inordinate cup is unblessed, and the ingredient is a devil' (2.3.285); and that Iago confirms by swearing 'By the mass' (351), and joking that the Eucharist will never make the hot blood of Desdemona 'blessed', for 'The wine she drinks is made from grapes' (2.1.243). By playing Devil's advocate, the 'prattling, juggling Jesuits' invited their own demonisation as a 'Divinity of hell' (2.3.324), and that of their charlatanism as 'a Devil theatre' or 'the Pope's playhouse':[58]

> When devils will the blackest sins put on,
> They do suggest at first with heavenly shows,
> As I do now.
>
> (2.3.325–7)

'Some wine, ho!': Iago's bacchanalia, as he intoxicates his 'flock of drunkards' to the profane liturgy, 'let me the cannikin clink' (52–60), can be seen as a parodic representation of the Eucharist in Jesuit colonies, a devilish 'Mass-game' or Black Mass.[59] Likewise, his brag to Roderigo, that 'If sanctimony and a frail vow betwixt an erring barbarian and a super-subtle Venetian be not too hard for my wits and all the tribe of hell, thou shalt enjoy her' (1.3.346–8), reiterates a scandalous Jesuit expedient, which was to rule that, where a plurality of wives was tribal custom, 'the concept of "first wife" was meaningless', and if 'a decision based on European law would make progress impossible', a blind eye should be turned to 'barbarian' bigamy.[60] So, Othello's tormentor bases his plot on the Jesuit reasoning that 'These Moors are changeable in their wills', and 'She must change for youth' (339–42). If this is 'Villainy in a black cassock',[61] Shakespeare's characterisation highlights the Jesuit penchant for exploiting the flesh, typified by John Gerard when he converted the young playboy Sir Oliver Manners over a game of cards.[62] It was the standard Jesuit tactic, laid down by George Gilbert in 1583, to seize on psychological weakness in a waverer, 'as for instance, if he should see him in a fit of melacholy or desolation of soul, under the pretext of consoling him'. Thus, evening was best for conversion, when 'the earth has been clothed in darkness, the image of death'.[63] And Iago, who puts himself in the confessor's collusive role when he divulges that 'In Venice they do let God see the pranks / They dare not show their husbands; their best conscience / Is not to leav't undone, but keep't unknown' (3.3.206–8); and even mimics the Jesuit pledge to serve 'body and soul' when he kneels and swears by 'ever-burning lights above' to 'give up / The execution of his wit, hands, heart / To wronged Othello's service' (3.4.468–70); methodically follows the *Spiritual Exercises* of Loyola in his instruction of his convert to subvert his vows to Desdemona. From the outset the Moor draws 'a prayer of earnest heart' from Desdemona by imaging his life in the key term of Loyola's own *Autobiography* and the Jesuit tradition, as a 'pilgrimage' (1.3.151–2). So, it is no accident that this play can be read as an anticipation of the Althusserian theory that the subject of ideology is 'free to choose subjection', as the Jesuit technique of self-examination Iago teaches Othello has long been considered the prototype of ideological interpellation.[64] And it consists, Iago's textbook catechisation shows, in inducing the subject to visualise images of that enslavement, so that, as Loyola dictates, the 'retreatant' appears to be 'left to his own abilities'.[65] Or, as Althusser puts it, ideology's 'echo-effect' is such that its subject 'works by himself':

IAGO:	Did Michael Cassio, when you wooed my lady,
	Know of your love?
OTHELLO:	He did, from first to last. Why dost thou ask?
IAGO:	But for a satisfaction of my thought,
	No further harm.
OTHELLO:	Why of thy thought, Iago?
IAGO:	I did think he had been acquainted with her.
OTHELLO:	O yes, and went between us very oft.
IAGO:	Indeed?
OTHELLO:	Indeed? Ay, indeed. Discern'st thou aught in that?
	Is he not honest?
IAGO:	Honest, my lord?
OTHELLO:	Honest? Ay, honest.
IAGO:	My lord, for all I know.
OTHELLO:	What dost thou think?
IAGO:	Think, my lord?
OTHELLO:	'Think, my lord?' By heaven, thou echo'st me
	As if there were some monster in thy thought
	Too hideous to be shown!

(3.3.96–112)

'Imagine hell, the width, and depth, and length of it':[66] the Loyolan *Exercises*, which armed the Jesuits with a revolutionary technology of 'imagining', are so well internalised by Othello that he is soon in the dialectical grip of 'the green-eyed monster which doth mock / The meat it feeds on' (170–1), but which Emilia, like a good pupil of Iago's, warns his wife is 'a monster / Begot upon itself, born on itself'. Desdemona is not so sure, and prays, 'Heaven keep the monster from Othello's mind' (3.4.156–8). For as Robert Watson explains, there are many features of the Moor's thralldom to Iago which recapitulate the legend of the evil Jesuit, including homoeroticism, but it is the voluntarist emphasis on the free choice of one who has 'shut up in [the] brain / Some horrible conceit' (3.3.118–19), which links their relations most firmly to the

Catholic doctrine of salvation by works. Thus, though Othello and Iago are often seen as opposing representatives of 'shame' and 'guilt' cultures, the exhibitionism of the one and eqivocation of the other are two sides of the Jesuit coin, since the instructor, who stabs Roderigo 'under guise of a protective embrace', damns his converts 'by promoting their self-love'.[67] The ensign's own grudge at lack of 'election', and certainty that 'I know my price', can be related to the same Romanist resistance to the Protestant doctrine, assumed by Cassio, that 'there be souls must be saved, and there be souls must not' (1.1.11–35; 2.3.89). For Loyola's readers thought was itself an active 'exercise' in salvation. So Iago is being strictly Jesuitical when he replies to Othello's craving to 'know thy thoughts', that there is no access to the soul beyond its works: 'You cannot, if my heart were in your hand; / Nor you shalt not whilst 'tis in my custody' (3.3.166–8). The reference is to the gruesome ceremony at Tyburn, where hagiographers liked to believe that the beating heart ripped by the executioner out of the body of a martyr 'seemed to leap of its own accord', as was said of Robert Southwell, 'to join the faithful'.[68] No wonder, then, that Othello tells Iago that 'Thou has set me on the rack' (340) with his proselytising; nor that when he is himself condemned to 'The time, the place, the torture' which he is assured 'will ope your lips', the 'hellish villain' faces his 'torments' like the Spartan boy who let the stolen fox gnaw at his entrails rather than confess: 'Demand me nothing. What you know, you know. / From this time forth I never will speak word' (5.2.309–12; 372–9). For this self-elected martyr, who claims that 'Heaven is my judge', the truth will only be disclosed, as he predicted, at the instant of 'The execution of his ... heart' (3.4.469), when the organ is indeed torn out of his ribcage by the hangman to be spiked on ceremonial display:

> For when my outward action doth demonstrate
> The native act and figure of my heart
> In compliment extern, 'tis not long after
> But I will wear my heart upon my sleeve
> For daws to peck at. I am not what I am.
>
> (1.1.61–5)

'For when he was cut up and his bowels cast unto the fire, and his heart pulled out and showed to the people with the words that are ever used in such cases, "Behold the heart of a traitor!" there was not heard any applause'.[69] It is within the conventions of Jesuit martyrdom that Shakespeare places Iago's self-glorifying defiance. By 1604 these were so familiar that the real question posed by 'the silence of Iago' is why the author should have chosen to villify the Jesuit as the villain of the story of a broken union. For to see this as evidence that 'the play endorses an unsympathetic response to Catholics enduring persecution ... eliding that persecution with the punishment of the villainous Iago',[70] is to align Shakespeare with the Anglican orthodoxy represented (as in the other Venetian drama) by the graceless Graziano. It is also to assume that hostility to Jesuits is identical to anti-Catholicism; a fallacy that, Gary Taylor observes, 'governs biographies of Shakespeare', but which forgets that 'Catholicism cannot be equated with recusancy'.[71] The notion of *Othello* as 'Protestant propaganda' is simply not sufficiently acute. But in fact the text is keyed very closely to the revulsion from Roman tribalism as an apocalyptic mischief expressed by the Catholic loyalists with most to gain from the Spanish negotiations. Its scapegoating of Iago mirrors, in particular, the *Petition Apologetical* drafted in July 1604 by the Midland magnate Thomas Tresham, as the record of a meeting of recusants and ministers at Hampton Court, in which Catholic gentry offered to expel the Jesuits in return for toleration, and ensure that priests swore allegiance 'before they shall be admitted to our houses, otherwise they shall not have relief of us'.[72] The background to this sell-out was the Appellant Controversy of 1598–1602, when accommodating secular priests appealed to the Pope against Jesuit domination; and, more generally, the social disdain, reflected in Cassio's 'show of courtesy' (2.1.102) towards Iago as an obsequious upstart, felt by the gentry for such 'clerks', which John Bossy describes as a poisonous component of anti-Jesuit phobia among the Catholic upper class. From the point of view of Appellant gentlemen such as Tresham, *Othello* would be completely recognisable as a reminder of the dire need 'to get rid of the Jesuits'.[73] Written, however, in the 'heady months' between 'the high-water of Catholic hopes', when the Catholic elite was 'ecstatic that concessions were not far off', and the cruel discovery that these 'soaring expectations' were betrayed,[74] Shakespeare's play begins and ends not with marriage but with the excess of Iago's execution, and a picture from the Catholic 'theatre of cruelties': of the 'bruis'd heart' (1.3.218) torn from the body of the condemned, for jackdaws to devour.[75]

'He lies to th' heart: / She was too fond of her most filthy bargain' (5.2.163): if *Othello* does register the disgust of the Catholic gentry with the Jesuit cult of violence in the aftermath of the abortive toleration talks of 1604, then its characterisation of Iago as a 'demi-devil' (307) is matched by the trust invested in Desdemona as an idealisation of the good faith of those who entertained the possibility of such a 'filthy bargain'. And if this allegory holds, it also suggests a suspension of disbelief by the author in the sincerity of King James's plans for 'Christian Union'. Historians help to put this shift of responsibility on to the Jesuit bogeyman into context, when they explain that for the Catholic patriot the situation was so 'perplexed' (350) because 'in his eyes, the political establishment that was persecuting the church had validity, and he had a strong sense of obligation to that establishment'. Thus, 'he wanted to satisfy both authorities', even as each made it impossible to do so. But 'the Jesuits provided a solution to the dilemma. The image of the Jesuits that the Appellants set forth was just close enough to truth to make it plausible, and the image, horrifying as it was, helped in keeping the Appellants' world comprehensible' when talks broke down. *Othello* therefore corresponds exactly with the mindset of Shakespeare's own 'tribe', whose 'tirade against the Jesuits' was that it was 'this powerful, cunning conspiracy of men devoted to nothing but the power of their order' which was 'responsible for the war between England and the church'. So, though they may, as Bossy contends, have been 'wildly overoptimistic in their hopes' for the 'perfect marriage' in 1604, the loyalists' 'hysteria about the Jesuits is understandable, for it made the world they lived in bearable by providing an explanation for what had gone horribly wrong'. According to this analysis, in other words, the demonisation of Iago is a contribution to the manoeuvre whereby those of what Shakespeare called 'our fashion' struggled to avoid 'the blow of thralled discontent' during 'th'inviting time' of militancy (Sonnet 124) that followed the breakdown of discussions, by 'killing the messenger' who had told them that their hopes were all in vain.[76] But the fact that *Othello* ends with Desdemona's uncle enforcing a renewed persecution implies deep foreboding about the future, in these months when the king likewise reimposed recusancy fines, and in the houses of Shakespeare's Midland neighbours the Jesuit Henry Garnet prayed for the 'Catholic Cause' with the irreconcilables who were planning the ultimate excess of their Gunpowder Plot:[77]

> Graziano, keep the house
> And seize upon the fortunes of the Moor,
> For they succeed on you. To you, Lord Governor,
> Remains the censure of this hellish villain.
> The time, the place, the torture. O, enforce it!
> Myself will straight abroad, and to the state
> This heavy act with heavy heart relate.
>
> (5.2.3765–81)

'It was a handkerchief, an antique token / My father gave my mother' Othello insists, that caused his downfall; and if this 'recognizance and pledge of love' is invested in this play 'with a solemn earnestness – / More than indeed belonged to such a trifle' (223–35), then that is because it is so saturated with the supplementary meaning of its tribal provenance. In an essay on 'The Phoenix and the Turtle' and the Sonnets as meditations on the hermeneutics of sacrifice, Richard McCoy has described Shakespeare's perspective on such relics as 'cool and aloof' or 'profoundly *politique*', yet awed by 'the terrible logic of martyrdom', that death is the truest test of faith. For 'the dust and bones of martyrs and implements of their torture and death' are signs that Shakespeare could recognise, according to McCoy, 'of a spiritual victory over physical dismemberment and destruction … They are the antithesis of a *momento mori*', having been rescued from the grave and encased in splendour, and it is the lasting capacity of these objects 'to stimulate emotion that is the source of their power'.[78] But as *Othello* shows, that emotional supplement could itself be seen as a 'knowledgeable misrecognition' and form of excess. Thus, although we cannot know what will become of Iago's remains when they are impaled on the city gates (and doubt whether anyone will salvage his heart from those carrion birds), shades of his counterpart, Father Garnet, will appear eighteen months later, in *Macbeth*, when the ghost of the hanged Jesuit enters, in the mind of the Porter, carrying its own entrails and 'napkins enough' (2.3.5), to claim responsibility for King Duncan's death. The scene is a satanic burlesque of the mania after the priest's execution, when 'Garnet's straw' (an ear of corn supposedly imprinted with his face), napkins stained with his blood, and the silk hose he wore to the scaffold, were 'esteemed of more than their weight in gold' by Romanist zealots. 'Set upon a pole' on London Bridge, Garnet's parboiled head became the object of adoration for 'citizens flocking thither in their hundreds', until it was 'turned upwards' for the crows.[79] So, though Malcolm will have Macbeth's head 'upon a pole' (5.10.26; SD: 5.11.19), its tribal status is as incalculable as that of Garnet's remains, which Shakespeare imagines desecrated by a drunken clown. The only certainty about relics, the plays suggest, is that so long as they exist their semiotic remainder will be *too much*, like that of the hands and heads hacked off by the self-mutilating Romans in *Titus Andronicus* (3.1); or of the napkins, nails and body parts used by Jesuits in exorcisms to induce demoniacs to 'frame themselves, jump and fit unto the priests' humours, to mop, mow, jest, rave, roar, commend and discommend, upon fitting occasions',[80] in foaming convulsions of the kind suffered by Othello, when in an abreaction (or premonition) of the scaffold, Iago instructs him in the 'shadowing passion' of the handkerchief:

> Handkerchief – confessions – handkerchief. To confess and be hanged for his labour. First to be hanged and then to confess! I tremble at it. Nature would not invest herself in such shadowing passion without some instruction. It is not words that shakes me thus! Pish! Noses, ears, and lips! Is't possible? Confess? Handkerchief? O devil!
> [*He falls down in a trance*[
>
> (*Othello*, 4.1.36–41)

'To confess and be hanged': 'It comes o'er my memory', says Othello of the effect of the spotted handkerchief, 'As doth the raven o'er the infectious house, / Boding to all!' (20–2). And although we never learn how his father is supposed to have acquired it before he gave it to his mother, it may be as a result of Jesuitical 'instruction' that he contradicts himself when he also claims the 'handkerchief / Did an Egyptian to my mother give'. (3.4.53–5). For what his 'napkin ... light as air' (3.3.325–6) accumulates by this *Romany* association is the symbolic weight of those 'tictures, stains [and] relics' which, as Caesar's killers learn, noble 'Romans' 'press' to retrieve from scenes of martyrdom (*Julius*, 2.2.89). Othello's epileptic revolt against his vows is cued, that is to say, by a recollection which must also have come over the memory of the audience, of how 'Romans' 'go and kiss' a martyr's body, 'And dip their napkins in his sacred blood' (3.2.129). As Gary Wills remarks, Shakespeare's stage handkerchiefs inevitably carry such 'Romany' connotations, as 'handkerchiefs were associated with the emptying of all a man's blood in the savage castrating, disembowelling, and quartering of hanged bodies of traitors', when because 'there could be no containment' of the bloodbath, pious Catholics felt compelled 'to dip handkerchiefs and other bits of cloth' in the precious fluid to salvage every drop. Thus, whether or not he witnessed the execution of Jesuits such as Campion, 'the picture of people trying to sop up blood for relics with handkerchiefs, or any cloth at hand', was clearly 'napkins enough' for this dramatist, which explains why these 'trifles' are made to carry an 'earnestness' in his work that would have been suspect to Protestants.[81] For what Shakespeare stages is also what appals historians, namely the effluvium of excess meaning from items that look 'embarrassingly domestic', or even, 'from a *politique* angle, tragically absurd'.[82] But that this supplement is so surplus to requirement, from such an angle, becomes the motor of the plot, as in episodes like the Forum scene, Jesuitical demagogues wring 'gracious drops' from pathetic objects such as 'Caesar's vesture wounded' (*Julius*, 3.2.188–90). However close he came to those Jesuit exorcists, who trained in a Roman college where 'paintings of the torture chamber and scaffold adorned each room', and at the time of *Julius Caesar* installed the toga of Loyola at the centre of their cult,[83] Shakespeare's is a drama continuously alive to the fatal 'Romany' propensity to sacralise tribal hatred by projecting 'confirmations strong / As holy writ' on to the tissue of 'Trifles light as air' (*Othello*, 3.3.326–8), or 'a twist of rotten silk' (*Coriolanus*, 5.6.98):

> That handkerchief
> Did an Egyptian to my mother give.
> She was a charmer, and could almost read
> The thoughts of people. She told her, while she kept it
> 'Twould make her amiable, and subdue my father
> Entirely to her love; but if she lost it,
> Or made a gift of it, my father's eye
> Should hold her loathed ...
>
> (*Othello*, 3.4.53–60)

When Orlando sends Rosalind the 'bloody napkin' used to stanch his arm after 'The lioness had torn some flesh away, / Which all this while had bled', the questions posed are those that prompt critics of the later play, of 'why, and where / This handkerchief was stained' (*As You Like It*, 4.3.92–6; 145–7). Rosalind faints at 'this napkin / Dyed in his blood', and though we are told that 'Many swoon when they do look on blood', Celia's instinct that 'There is more in it' (153–8) seems apt for a collapse that has the same importance as the unconsciousness into which Othello falls at the thought of his 'handkerchief / Spotted with strawberries' (3.3.439). For given the royal status of that lioness, Orlando's sanguinary keepsake carries an imprint of martyrdom redundant in a comedy, like debris from the Histories. In *3 Henry VI*, for instance, Margaret's savagery is eternalised in the napkin 'stained with the blood ... from the bosom' of the child Rutland, who, his father swears, 'cannibals / Would not have stained with blood'. But when she gives him this 'napkin steeped in harmless blood', York makes it his comforter in death: 'See, ruthless Queen ... This cloth thou dipped'st in blood of my sweet boy, / And I with tears do wash the blood away' (1.4.80–2; 157–9; 2.1.61–2). Much later, the talisman is still treasured by the Yorkists to incite revenge: 'present to her, as sometimes Margaret / Did to thy father, steeped in Rutland's blood, / A handkerchief which, say to her, did drain / The purple sap from her sweet brother's body' (*Richard III*, 4.4.260–3). The Marian excess of such 'incensing relics' (*All's Well*, 5.3.25) is explicit in *Love's Labour's Lost*, with the 'dish-clout of Jaquenetta's' Don Armado 'wears next to his heart' as a penance 'enjoined him in Rome' (5.2.696–7). But what intrigues feminists is how these 'bloody napkins' are all stigmatised as female in this way, coded by the incontinence that soils them with the superflux that gushes as a 'crimson river of warm blood' (*Titus*, 2.4.22) in the despised supplement of menstruation. Thus, Caesar's corpse, 'spouting blood in many pipes / In which so many smiling Romans bathed' (*Julius*, 2.2.85–6); or Duncan's, pouring 'so much blood' that 'all great Neptune's ocean' will never wash the 'damned spot' (*Macbeth*, 2.2.58; 5.1.30–4), can be attributed to Calpurnia or Lady Macbeth, for what is at stake in this haemorrhaging, Gail Paster remarks, is 'anxiety that in bleeding the male body resembles the body of a woman'.[84] In the case of *Othello*, Valerie Wayne connects this misogyny specifically to the Tridentine Catholic fear of married sexual excess.[85] So, it is to the point that in a play which features the unfolding of a handkerchief as the signifier of loving 'too well', and which stages the exorbitance of those who fail to fold away the surplus of 'napkins enough', the very names of the protagonist toy with this embarrassing superfluity, as that of one who 'Sees and knows more, much more than ... unfolds' (3.3.248), but by cutting his own throat, imagines that he can finally put a 'bloody period' (5.2.366) to the swallowing *maw* of *Venus*:

> EMILIA: O thou dull Moor, that handkerchief thou speak'st of
> I found by fortune and did give my husband,
> For often, with a solemn earnestness -
> More than indeed belonged to such a trifle -
> He begged of me to steal't.
>
> (5.2.232–6)

The Renaissance handkerchief has been interpreted as an artefact which both 'helped to produce the patriarchal ideology that figured women as "leaky"' and complicated this by transferring "leakiness" to men.[86] Thus, with one of Shakespeare's 'bloody napkins' there is always 'more in it' to exude signification. So, Othello's stigma as 'the Moor' writes him into an indelible and ceaseless tide of unclean interpretation. And in a riposte to Thomas Rymer's sarcasm that *Othello* is 'a warning to all wives, that they look well to their linen', Dympna Callaghan counters that the injunction was of deep significance to a culture that reified sexual control in the 'ocular proof' of wedding sheets, and for which Desdemona's napkin would 'constitute a miniature of the nuptial linen, bearing as berries the bloodstains of marital defloration'. This heirloom belongs, that is to say, within the trousseau of uncanny fabrics 'produced, preserved, and accumulated over generations' by female labour, which besides 'bed hangings, cushions, towels, and table cloths', included textiles that were inscriptions of the blood 'irreducibly attached to feminity': such as Veronica's Veil, the cloth with which the woman cured by Jesus of a flux of blood had wiped his face on the way to Calvary, which became the object of a hysterical cult at St Peter's in Rome. With that relic, the attribution of male violence to female contamination was inscribed in the bloodstained impress of Christ's face.[87] And in *Othello* the same gendering of sectarian excess as matriarchal in origin is effected with the unstoppable semiotic bleeding that flows from the word 'Moor', and that marks drama's most egregious stage property with connotations that, to original audiences, might have suggested how there was literally 'more in it', in the bloody imprint of the name of Catholic England's prime hero, memorialised by his female heirs as a pretext for continued resistance: Thomas More, no less. For the idea that Jacobeans would hear in the 'Moorish' subtitle and 'murmuring' wordplay of *Othello* an allusion to the man whose name meant 'increase', and an analogy paralleling the 'morosity' of the 'dull Moor' with the 'moronic' politics of the 'tribe of More', is confirmed by Thomas Docherty's analysis of the poetry of More's actual descendant, John Donne, where we are reminded that More's name became an iconic incitement for Catholic ultras, as a result of the torrent of hagiography that issued, from the day of his execution, with Erasmus's *Praise of Folly* (punning on Greek and Latin, *morias/morus*, for dullard/fool), and with the martyr's oxymoron, as he bound his eyes with the handkerchief preserved by his daughters, that God would judge whether he was 'a foolish wiseman or a wise fool' for 'demurring' at the King's divorce:

> It has been rightly stressed that Donne was descended from the family of Thomas More ... Might it be also be apposite to suggest that Donne is writing a concealed 'praise of More', and, by the slightest of anagrammatical shifts which is startlingly appropriate to the name of More, a praise of *Rome*, or of Roman Catholicism? ... The ghost of More, as it were, echoes in many 'more-more-ings' or murmurings, alerting critics to the 'impurities' that reveal residual Roman Catholicism in Donne's verse ... But in so far as Donne owes a great debt to the name 'More' and all its close analogies with 'Rome', it becomes clear that Donne's covert praises of Rome through the name of More, at a time when he was an Anglican preacher ... produces a 'more', an excess, which threatens to undo the confessor, [and] approaches the condition of *morias*, of folly.[88]

Donne's uncle, Ellis Heywood, commemorated their ancestor in a drama that played up the polymorphic possibilities of the family name, *Il Moro*, the title of which implied what one of its characters says, that the phrase *memento mori* would 'put me in mind not of death, but of you, Mr More'.[89] But for the

plenteous seed of Christ' and 'the fruitful liquor' to win England to the Church.[94] So, it is significant that in the tragedy the mortal relic which is Desdemona's 'first remembrance of the Moor' (3.3.295) is expressly connected with the More tree, having been woven from silk and therefore produced by worms that fed off the mulberry, which explains why Othello claims that 'The worms were hallowed that did breed the silk'. No wonder he maintains that 'There is magic in the web of it' (3.4.67–71), nor that Emilia and Cassio both immediately want to have 'the work ta'en out' (3.3.300; 3.4.174), a task Bianca spurns (4.1.145–50). The text is ambiguous about whether this means the *moresca* embroidery will be copied, or removed according to the Anglican demand that Catholics ceased 'to dye garments in blood'.[95] But the strawberry pattern with which it was 'spotted' (3.3.440) is again explictly associated, as Othello rages, with martyrs' 'blood, blood, blood!' (354), by being 'dyed in mummy, which the skilful / Conserved of maidens' hearts' (3.4.72–3). To Bianca, and feminists who see only hymeneal connotations,[96] these blood-spots imply 'some minx's token' (4.1.147). But since strawberries were classed as types of 'morel' (a word, according to the *OED*, given to 'any dark-complexioned fruit'), the morello stains are equally suggestive, in contrast to what Cassio calls 'vile guesses', of the murrain harvest sown, as he says, from 'the devil's teeth' (179): a term directed at the Jesuit 'hydra', and the Society's vaunt that while 'dead men bite not', a martyr 'bites with his friends' teeth'.[97] Even Othello admits the fatal cloth was 'sewed' by 'a sibyl' in a trance of 'prophetic fury' (3.4.68–70); and it is this history of crazed Marianism which ties the relic to the celebration of the real More, sacrificed to Venus for decrying the dirty wedding-sheets of the 'minx' Boleyn, which centred on his blood-spotted blindfold and hairshirt, venerated by generations of Mores after being salvaged by the kinswomen who dressed his corpse, and entrusted for safe-keeping to the Canonesses of Louvain.[98] For as he was himself 'the great champion of the cult of the saints and doctrine of Purgatory',[99] preservation of More mementoes became a furious act of symbolic wall-building in the century after his execution, through a mortuary cult which, in the absence of an actual body and a tomb, reconfigured the whole of English Catholicism as, in effect, a morgue:

> The killers employed by Henry VIII were not so foolish as to leave Thomas More's body lying in a church. More was beheaded on Tower Hill and his body was buried in the Tower. More's daughter and foster-daughter bore away his bloodstained shirt ... But with no tomb or shrine there could be no pilgrimages, no public ceremonies. The cult of More developed instead in the privacy of the recusant family. Deprived of a body, a public site, a shrine, the cult centred instead around substitute bodies, metaphors for the body, or even metaphors themselves .... In this standoff between prohibition and subterfuge, the economy of sacred death was transformed. The realm of icon worship was driven into the interior space of private devotion, enveloped by a new public world of iconoclasm.[100]

The hallowed relic of Thomas More's winding-sheet had been bought, hagiographers marvelled, from a linen shop beside the Tower.[101] Editors who find that in *Othello* 'domestic affairs get in the way of official duties' in fact define the English Reformation, which turned on opposing treatments of laundry, like bridal sheets and holy shrouds, and the demeaning of the name of More.[102] 'Is this the noble Moor whom our full senate / Call all-in-all suffici-ent?' (4.1.261–2): the harping on this name 'more fair than black' (2.3.289) makes it hard not to see similarities between the blackening of 'his Moorship' (1.1.33), as one who has 'done the state some service' (5.2.348), and that of the Tudor statesman whose name came to be 'begrim'd and black' as itself (3.3.392) through the politics of treason. As Parker observes, 'evocations of blackness' and 'blackest sins' (2.3.325) connect the smearing of Othello as the 'lascivious Moor' (1.1.127), or 'lusty Moor' (2.1.283), with 'mulberry's emblematic stain-ing', while 'the white evoked in "fair" Des*demon* (or Bianca) is blackened as the play proceeds'.[103] But 'the black man' (as Erasmus called 'the noble More') had, in fact, himself revelled in his 'Indian' negritude, when he claimed descent from the very Moor of Venice, the Black Doge, Cristofero Moro – whose arms were spotted with mulberries – on whom Shakespeare based this plot.[104] So, in the 'echo-chamber' of *Othello*, Parker argues, the 'sick amor' dirge of the 'maid called Barbary', who 'died singing it', hanged, 'her head all at one side', when 'he she loved proved mad' (4.3.25–30), cues an infernal chain of associations with Mauretania, Moors, skulls and death, as the plot carries Desdemona, en-thralled to a black *amor*, into the moraine of night.[105] Above More's empty tomb, in Chelsea church, pilgrims must likewise face the dark humour of his crest: the head of a blackamoor impaled.[106] This death's-head is a reminder that More's tribe devoutly pickled his actual head in spices, after they rescued it from London Bridge.[107] But the question raised by Shakespeare's rewriting of their story as a drama bound for Hades is why he chose, at the instant of a moratorium, to give a grim reposte to communion with the skull of 'the King's jester', in the objection that to address the dust of such a 'whoreson mad fellow ... 'Twere to consider too curiously' (*Hamlet*, 5.1.162–90). The answer is that there had never been a moment when their addiction to the morphine of mourning would cost the 'tribe of More' so much; nor when 'the will to see things as they are not', which T.S. Eliot noted in Othello's self-pity,[108] would be so dependent on more preservatives; like the *myrrh* in which his putrifying head was mummified, and that, trickling from those sightless sockets, must have provided Shakespeare with a final pun, in the ghastly *morbidezza* of the Moor as:

> one whose subdued eyes
> Albeit unused to the melting mood,
> Drops tears as fast as the Arabian trees
> Their medicinable gum.
>
> (5.2.357–60)

'Dyed in mummy', the black tar, rich in myrrh, that 'the skilful /
Conserved' (3.4.72–3) from embalmed bodies, Othello's handkerchief comes,
with his sob-story, to signify the morosity of the 'tribe of More', and morbid-
ity of their cult of death. There is another painting, a counterpart to the record
of the Spanish treaty, which corresponds perfectly to the suicidal woe of
Shakespeare's Moor, and helps locate this lachrymosity within the 'uneasy but
sincere conflict of loyalties' afflicting 'the great majority of Catholics' on the
eve of the Gunpowder Plot.[109] This is the group portrait of five generations of
the Mores commissioned in 1593 by Thomas More II, as an elaboration of the
picture of the Chancellor and his family painted by Holbein. In this lugubrious
icon, Catherine Belsey observes, the intimacy of Holbein's sitters, 'unaware
they are being watched', is succeeded by the self-dramatising zeal of 'the
threatened descendants of a Catholic martyr', who react to persecution by staring
defiantly at the viewer, as if humanism gives way to 'a declaration of unbroken
allegiance' to Rome.[110] In Rowland Lockey's picture, the survivors of the clan
are gaunt with grief, and brandish Catholic missals or medals of the hero, in an
act of ancestor-worship that 'explicitly constitutes the community of faithful as
the More family', and can be viewed only as the signal of Counter-Reformation
fervour and political resistance.[111] Here then, in the necrophilia of fanatics, was
the reaction to peace-making by King James. And it may be that, as Greenblatt
writes, 'Shakespeare, with his recusant background, education by teachers
linked to Campion and Lancashire recusants, felt covert loyalty' to such
sectarianism;[112] in the same way that More's kinsman, Donne, who also imaged
'the Church's grisly bric-a-brac' as necromancy, felt the family ties of one
whose uncles each 'possessed a half of More's miraculous tooth'.[113] This might
be why Shakespeare planted a mulberry, and why legend has it that his own
heart was buried under a mulberry, in his ancestral grounds at Wroxall Abbey,
where Jane and Isabel Shakespeare had been among the last nuns.[114] But, just as
Donne's texts can be said to undo *More Rome*,[115] so *Othello* has to be read as a
deconstruction of the Romish 'cause' (5.2.1) which identifies the tribe of faith
by the amassing of *ever more* remains. What happens when a piece of cloth,
such as a saint's relic, is passed from church to playhouse, Shakespeare
therefore shows, is not so much that it is desacralised, as that its violence is
'taken out'. No wonder, however, that the critics accuse Othello of self-pity,
since it is possible to see here an alibi for the entire Catholic community, in the
feminisation of the cult of relics as witchcraft and the demonisation of their
purveyor as 'a devil in Jesuit habit'.[116] For all the excuses that make Macbeth so
self-justifying a character were latent in this play of 1604, a year before the
Gunpowder Plot would for ever blacken the 'tribe of More' with its Roman
name of 'fool, fool, fool!' (5.2.333).

NOTES

1 Ben Jonson, *Timber, Or Discoveries*, ed. R.S. Walker (Syracuse: Columbia University Press, 1953), vol. 2, pp. 665–6.

2 Graham Holderness, 'Bardolatry: or, The Cultural Materialist's Guide to Stratford-upon-Avon', in Graham Holderness (ed.), *The Shakespeare Myth* (Manchester: Manchester University Press, 1988), p. 3.

3 See, for example the Thersites-like diatribe against recent research on the dramatist's recusant associations by Michael Davies, 'The Canonisation of the Catholic Shakespeare', *Cahiers Elisabethains*, 58 (2000), pp. 31–47, which never discloses the bad faith that is, in fact, revealed in the notes to contributors, where it is stated that the author's 'research interests currently focus on the relationship between Calvinism and English literature, particularly in the drama of William Shakespeare'.

4 Stephen Greenblatt, *Shakespearean Negotiations: The Circulation of Social Energy in Renaissance England* (Oxford: Clarendon Press, 1990), p. 113.

5 Holderness, op. cit. (note 2), p. 3.

6 Samuel Schoenbaum, *Shakespeare's Lives* (Oxford: Clarendon Press, 1970), p. 159.

7 Quoted in F.E. Halliday, *The Cult of Shakespeare* (London: Duckworth, 1957), p. 64. The Stratford mulberry is discussed, though without noticing its Elizabethan Catholic symbolism, in Peter Davihazi, *The Romantic Cult of Shakespeare: Literary Reception in Anthropological Perception* (Basingstoke: Macmillan, 1998), pp. 38–40, 78–9 and passim.

8 Richard Simpson, 'What Was the Religion of Shakespeare?' *The Rambler*, 9:53 (1858), p. 319.

9 John Weever, 'Ad Gulielmum Shakespeare', *Epigrams* (London: 1599), 4th Week, 22; repr. in Ernst Honigmann, *John Weever: A Biography of a Literary Associate of Shakespeare and Jonson, together with a Photographic Facsimile of Weever's 'Epigrams'* (Manchester: Manchester University Press, 1987), p. 109.

10 Clark Hulse, 'Dead Man's Treasure: The Cult of Thomas More', in David Lee Miller, Sharon O'Dair and Harold Weber (eds), *The Production of English Renaissance Culture* (Ithaca: Cornell University Press, 1994), pp. 204 and 208.

11 Samuel Shepherd, 'In Memory of our Famous Shakespeare', *Epigrams Theological, Philosophical and Romantic* (London: 1651), Bk 6: 17, pp. 150–4. For Gondomar's collection of relics of the English martyrs, now partly at Downside Abbey, see Dom Bede Camm, *Forgotten Shrines: An Account of Some Old Catholic Halls and Families in England and of Relics and Memorials of the English Martyrs* (London: Macdonald and Evans, 1910), pp. 357 and 367.

12 *Mercurius Britannicus*, 2 September 1644: see Ernest Sirluck, 'Shakespeare and Jonson among the Pamphleteers of the First Civil War: Some Unreported Seventeenth-Century Allusions', *Modern Phililogy*, 53 (1955), p. 94.

13 John Milton, 'An Epitaph on the Admirable Dramatic Poet, W. Shakespeare', prefixed to the Second Folio of the *Works* (London: 1632).

14 Leonard Digges, 'To the Memory of the Deceased Author, Master William Shakespeare', prefixed to the First Folio of *Shakespeare's Works* (London: 1623).

15 William Prynne, *Histrio-Mastix* (London: 1633), ed. Arthur Freeman (New York: Garland, 1974), p. 934.

16 Louis Montrose, *The Purpose of Playing: Shakespeare and the Cultural Politics of the Elizabethan Theatre* (Chicago: University of Chicago Press, 1996), pp. 30–1.

17 Arthur Marotti, 'Southwell's Remains: Catholicism and Anti-Catholicism in Early Modern England', in Cedric Brown and Arthur Marotti (eds), *Texts and Cultural Change in Early Modern England* (Basingstoke: Macmillan, 1997), p. 53.

18 Greenblatt, op. cit. (note 4), p. 126.

19 Marotti, op. cit. (note 17), pp. 52–3.

20 Matthew, 5:1; see R. Chris Hassel, *Renaissance Drama and the English Church Year* (Lincoln: University of Nebraska Press, 1979), pp. 167–70. It follows that the interpretation

of this essay is incompatible with Ernst Honigmann's dating of the play to 1601/2: see his Appendix to the Arden 3 edition (London: Nelson, 1999), pp. 344–50.

21 Linda Levy Peck, *Northampton: Patronage and Policy at the Court of James I* (London: George Allen and Unwin, 1982), p. 106.

22 Ibid., p. 105. Cf. Alan Haynes's description of Northampton, in *The Gunpowder Plot: Faith in Rebellion* (Stroud: Sutton, 1994), as 'a perfect specimen of cultivated aristocratic villainy': p. 32.

23 G.P.V. Akrigg, *Jacobean Pageant: The Court of King James I* (London: Hamish Hamilton, 1062), p. 62.

24 Antonia Fraser, *The Gunpowder Plot: Terror and Faith in 1605* (London: Weidenfeld and Nicolson, 1996), pp. 78–9.

25 Mark Nicholls, *Investigating Gunpowder Plot* (Manchester: Manchester University Press, 1991), p. 149.

26 Park Honan, *Shakespeare: A Life* (Oxford: Oxford University Press, 1998), p. 312.

27 Matthew, 23:45–6; Richard Simpson, *Edmund Campion* (London: John Hodges, 1896), p. 172 and passim. For recent influential readings of the play in terms of the evidential problem of 'ocular proof' see Joel Altman, '"Preposterous Conclusions": Eros, *Energeia*, and the Composition of *Othello*', *Representations*, 18 (1987), pp. 129–57; Katharine Eisaman Maus, *Inwardness and Theater in the English Renaissance* (Chicago: Chicago University Press, 1995), pp. 104–27; and Patricia Parker, 'Dilation and Deletion in *Othello*', in *Shakespeare and the Question of Theory* (London: Methuen, 1985), pp. 54–74.

28 Sir Benjamin Rudyerd in the House of Commons, 1628; see J.E.C. Hill, 'The Puritans and the "Dark Corners" of the Land', *Transactions of the Royal Historical Society*, 5th series, 13 (1963), pp. 96–7.

29 Robert Watson, '*Othello* as Protestant Propaganda', in Claire McEachern and Debora Shuger (eds), *Religion and Culture in Renaissance England* (Cambridge: Cambridge University Press, 1997), pp. 234–57; Samuel Harsnett, *Declaration of Egregious Popish Impostures* (London: 1603), sigs A2v–A3r, quoted ibid., p. 247.

30 Watson, op. cit. (note 29), p. 237.

31 Kenneth Muir (ed.), *Othello: New Penguin Shakespeare* (Harmondsworth: Penguin, 1968), p. 43.

32 Report of the Somerset House negotiations by Sir Thomas Edmondes, BL Add. Mss 14033, quoted in Peck, op. cit. (note 21), pp. 107–8.

33 Quoted in Linda Levy Peck, 'The Mentality of a Jacobean Grandee', in Linda Levy Peck (ed.), *The Mental World of the Jacobean Court* (Cambridge: Cambridge University Press, 1991), p. 109.

34 BL Cotton Mss Vespasian CXIII, ff. 47–52, quoted in Peck, op. cit. (note 21), pp. 108–9.

35 Henry Wotton, *Life and Letters*, ed. Logan Pearsal Smith (2 vols, Oxford: Clarendon Press, 1907), vol. 1, p. 318. For James's plans for a 'Christian Union' see Fraser, op. cit. (note 24), pp. 88–9; and William McElwee, *The Wisest Fool in Christendom: The Reign of James I and VI* (London: Faber and Faber, 1958), pp. 127–44.

36 Jonathan Goldberg, *James I and the Politics of Literature: Jonson, Shakespeare, Donne, and their Contemporaries* (Stanford: Stanford University Press, 1983), pp. 74–80. For 'Venetianism' as a variety of Anglicanism see Roland Mousnier, *The Assassination of Henry IV: The Tyrannicide Problem and the Consolidation of French Absolute Monarchy in the Early Seventeenth Century*, trans. Joan Spencer (London: Faber and Faber, 1973), pp. 176–83.

37 Marc Shell, *Money, Language, and Thought: Literary and Philosophical Economies from the Medieval to the Modern Era* (Baltimore: Johns Hopkins University Press, 1993), pp. 82–3.

38 McElwee, op. cit. (note 35), p. 142.

39 Peter Thomson, *Shakespeare's Professional Career* (Cambridge: Cambridge University Press, 1992), p. 169.

40 David Farmer, *The Oxford Dictionary of Saints* (Oxford: Oxford University Press, 1987), p. 222.

41 Among the Elizabethan martyrs whose hands are still preserved are Margaret Clitheroe, Ambrose Barlow and Francis Ingleby. In the seventeenth century the 'Holy Hand' of Edmund Arrowsmith became the focus of a major Lancashire cult: see Camm, op. cit. (note 11), pp. 369 and 187–201.

42 See, in particular, Barbara Everett, 'Spanish *Othello*: the Making of Shakespeare's Moor', *Shakespeare Survey*, 35 (Cambridge: Cambridge University Press, 1982), p. 103; François Laroque, *Shakespeare's Festive World* (Cambridge: Cambridge University Press, 1991), p. 291; and Watson, op. cit. (note 29), p. 237.

43 For Loyola's Iago-like career and his brawl at the Venice carnival see David Mitchell, *The Jesuits: A History* (London: Macdonald, 1980), pp. 22–9.

44 Mousnier, op. cit. (note 36), p. 125.

45 Christopher Marlowe, *The Massacre at Paris*, 5.5.58; in J.B. Steane (ed.), *Christopher Marlowe: The Complete Plays* (Harmondsworth: Penguin, 1969); Richard Baines (1593) quoted in Frederick Boas, *Christopher Marlowe: A Biographical and Critical Study* (Oxford: Oxford University Press, 1940), p. 251.

46 Judd Hubert, *Metatheater: The Example of Shakespeare* (Lincoln: Nebraska University Press, 1991), p. 78. Hubert's is one of the surprisingly few discussions of the play's self-referentiality: Anne Barton, in *Shakespeare and the Idea of the Play* (Harmondsworth: Penguin, 1967); Meredith Ann Skura, in *Shakespeare the Actor and the Purposes of Playing* (Chicago: Chicago University Press, 1993); Alvin Kernan, in *Shakespeare, the King's Playwright: Theater in the Stuart Court, 1603–1613* (New Haven: Yale University Press, 1995); and Louis Montrose, in *The Purpose of Playing: Shakespeare and the Cultural Politics of the Elizabethan Theatre* (Chicago: Chicago University Press, 1996), all ignore *Othello*.

47 Michael Bristol, 'Charivari and the Comedy of Abjection in *Othello*', in Linda Woodbridge and Edward Berry (eds), *True Rites and Maimed Rites: Ritual and Anti-Ritual in Shakespeare and His Age* (Urbana: University of Illinois Press, 1992), pp. 75–97, esp. pp. 80–1.

48 Greenblatt, op. cit. (note 4), pp. 100 and 126.

49 John O'Malley, *The First Jesuits* (Cambridge, Mass.: Harvard University Press, 1993), pp. 266–72.

50 Greenblatt, op. cit. (note 4), pp. 33, 36 and 39.

51 Stephen Greenblatt, *Marvellous Possessions: The Wonder of the New World* (Chicago: Chicago University Press, 1991), pp. 136–7; Hernando Cortez quoted ibid. p. 137.

52 Luis Muratori, *A Relation of the Missions of Paraguay* (London: 1759), quoted in Philip Caraman, *The Lost Paradise: An Account of the Jesuits in Paraguay, 1607–1768* (London: Sidgwick and Jackson, 1975), pp. 23–4. See also Thomas Campbell, S.J., *The Jesuits, 1534–1921: A History of the Society of Jesus from its Foundation to the Present Time* (London: Encyclopaedia Press, 1921), p. 87: 'They were cannibals of an advanced type, and no food delighted them more than human flesh. To make matters worse, the white settlers encouraged them in their horrible practices, probably in the hope that they would eat each other up'.

53 Philip Caraman, *The Lost Empire: The Story of the Jesuits in Ethiopia, 1555–1634* (London: Sidgwick and Jackson, 1985), pp. 68–9.

54 Edward MacLagan, *The Jesuits and the Great Mogul* (London: Burns, Oates and Washbourne, 1932), pp. 275 and 293; Derek Massarella, *A World Elsewhere: Europe's Encounter with Japan in the Sixteenth and Seventeenth Centuries* (New Haven: Yale University Press, 1990), p. 44. See also Dauril Alden, *The Making of an Enterprise: The Society of Jesus in Portugal, Its Empire, and Beyond, 1540–1750* (Stanford: Stanford University Press, 1996), p. 286, for the Jesuit use of litters, which they were forbidden.

55 MacLagan, op. cit. (note 54), pp. 291–2.

56 Ibid., pp. 274–5. The 'base Indian' jibe recurs in criticisms of Jesuit conversion: e.g., the

Venetian traveller Vechiete, writing from Agra in 1604: 'vero e che della gente basa'. Father Xavier, reporting from Lahore in 1606, admits that converts were from the lower clases: 'gente comu e baixa', while 'Father Botelho, fifty years later, found them to be mostly servants, or else embroiderers, and the like'.

57 O'Malley, op. cit. (note 49), p. 268.
58 Gauvin Bailey, 'Jesuit Catechism and the Arts in Mughal India', in John O'Malley, Gauvin Bailey, Steven Harris and Frank Kennedy (eds), *The Jesuits: Cultures, Sciences, and the Arts, 1540–1773* (Toronto: Toronto University Press, 1999), p. 391; Samuel Harsnett, *A Discovery of Egregious Popish Impostures* (London: 1603), quoted in Greenblatt, op. cit. (note 4), p. 113. For the ideological construction of Catholicism as an anti-religion see Peter Lake, 'Anti-popery: The Structure of a Prejudice', in Richard Cust and Anne Hughes (eds), *Conflict in Early Stuart England: Studies in Religion and Politics, 1603–1649* (London: Longman, 1989), pp. 72–106.
59 John Rainolds claimed that Catholic priests 'have transformed the celebrating of the Sacrament of the Lord's Supper into a Mass-game': quoted in Jonas Barish, *The Antitheatrical Prejudice* (Berkeley: University of California Press, 1981), p. 163.
60 Caraman, op. cit. (note 52), pp. 41–2. Later the expedient that 'priests should act on their own opinion' in the matter was formalised, after an appeal 'on behalf of Paraguay in the West Indies', by Pope Urban VIII.
61 Daniel Stempel, 'The Silence of Iago', *Publications of the Modern Language Association (PMLA)*, 84 (1969), p. 253.
62 John Gerard, *The Autobiography of an Elizabethan*, trans. Philip Caraman (London: Longmans, 1951), p. 185.
63 Quoted in Michael Questier, *Conversion, Politics and Religion in England, 1580–1625* (Cambridge: Cambridge University Press, 1996), p. 183.
64 For Loyola's dramatisation of his story as a 'pilgrimage', and the image of the pilgrim in Jesuit tradition, see O'Malley, op. cit. (note 49), pp. 270–1; Louis Althusser, 'Ideology and Ideological State Apparatuses', in *Lenin and Philosophy and Other Essays* trans. B. Brewster (London: Verso, 1971), pp. 142–5; Michel Foucault, 'Governmentality', in *Michel Foucault: The Essential Works: 3: Power*, trans. Robert Hurley et al. (London: Allen Lane, 2001), pp. 201–22.
65 Ignatius Loyola, 'Exercise 18', quoted in Antonio de Nicolas, *Powers of Imagining: A Philosophical Hermeneutic of Imagining Through the Collected Works of Ignatius de Loyola* (New York: New York University Press, 1986), p. 41.
66 Loyola, 'Exercise 65', quoted ibid., p. 42.
67 Watson, op. cit. (note 29), pp. 239–40.
68 Henry Garnet to Claudio Aquaviva, 7 March 1595, quoted in Christopher Devlin, *The Life of Robert Southwell, Poet and Martyr* (London: Longmans, 1956), p. 324. Similarly, it was the Catholic doctrine of works which was supposedly validated when the seminary priest Arthur Bryant, 'himself dismembered, his heart and entrails burned, to the great admiration of some, being layed upon the block, his belly downward, lifted up his whole body then remaining from the ground': William Allen, *A Brief History of the Glorious Martyrdom of Twelve Reverend Priests* (Douai: 1582); quoted in Marotti, op. cit. (note 17), pp. 42 and 59, n.16.
69 John Gerard, *A Narrative of the Gunpowder Plot*, describing the execution of Father Garnet on 3 May 1606 at St Paul's, quoted in Philip Caraman, *Henry Garnet, 1555–1606* (London: Longmans, 1964), p. 439
70 Watson, op. cit. (note 29), p. 239.
71 Gary Taylor, 'Forms of Opposition: Shakespeare and Middleton', *English Literary Renaissance (ELR)*, 24 (1994), pp. 297–8.
72 Anon. (but attributed to Thomas Tresham), *A Petition Apologetical presented to the King's most excellent Majesty by the lay Catholics of England in July last* (Douai: 1604), quoted in John Bossy, *The English Catholic Community, 1570–1850* (London: Darton, Longman and Todd, 1975), p. 38.

73 Ibid., p. 39.

74 Sandeep Kaushik, 'Resistance, Loyalty and Recusant Politics: Sir Thomas Tresham and the Elizabethan State', *Midland History*, 21 (1996), p. 62.

75 Richard Verstegan's *Theatrum Crudelitatum haereticorum nostri temporis* (Antwerp: 1587) included (p. 83), among many illustrations of atrocities committed on Catholics, the picture of heads and body parts displayed on pikes over the gates to the City of London; a scene familiar, in any case, to all Elizabethan Londoners.

76 Arnold Pritchard, *Catholic Loyalism in Elizabethan England* (London: Scolar Press, 1979), pp. 190–1.

77 Nicholls, op. cit. (note 25), p. 64.

78 Richard McCoy, 'Love's Martyrs: Shakespeare's "Phoenix and the Turtle" and the sacrificial sonnets', in McEachern and Shuger, op. cit. (note 29), pp. 198 and 203–4.

79 Simpson, op. cit. (note 27), p. 247; Caraman, op. cit. (note 69), pp. 439 and 443–7.

80 Harsnett, op. cit. (note 29), p. 38; quoted in Greenblatt, op. cit. (note 4), p. 107.

81 Gary Wills, *Witches and Jesuits: Shakespeare's 'Macbeth'* (New York: Oxford University Press, 1995), pp. 99–100, where Wills points out that Harsnett ridiculed the Catholic collection of 'sops for blood'.

82 Dympna Callaghan, *Woman and Gender in Renaissance Tragedy* (Hemel Hempstead: Harvester Wheatsheaf, 1989), p. 35; McCoy, op. cit. (note 78), p. 198.

83 Claire Cross, 'An Elizabethan Martyrologist and His Martyr: John Mush and Margaret Clitheroe', in Diana Wood (ed.), *Martyrs and Martyrologies: Papers read at the 1992 and 1993 Meetings of the Ecclesiastical History Society* (Oxford: Blackwell, 1993), p. 276; Jeffrey Chipps Smith, 'The Art of Salvation in Bavaria', in O'Malley et al., op. cit. (note 58), p. 588.

84 Gail Kern Paster, '"In the spirit of men there is no blood": Blood as Trope of Gender in *Julius Caesar*', in Richard Wilson (ed.), *'Julius Caesar': New Casebook* (Basingstoke: Palgrave, 2002), p. 153; and 'Leaky Vessels: The Incontinent Women of City Comedy', in *The Body Embarrassed: Drama and the Disciplines of Shame in Early Modern England* (Ithaca: Cornell University Press, 1993), p. 25.

85 Valerie Wayne, 'Historical Differences: Misogyny in *Othello*', in Valerie Wayne (ed.), *The Matter of Difference: Materialist Criticism of Shakespeare* (Hemel Hempstead: Harvester, 1991), pp. 166–7.

86 Will Fisher, 'Handkerchiefs and Early Modern Ideologies of Gender', *Shakespeare Studies*, 28 (2000), pp. 199–207, esp. pp. 201–3. See also Diana O'Hara, 'The Language of Tokens and the Making of Marriage', *Rural History* (1992), pp. 1–40; and Stephanie Dickey, 'Women Holding Handkerchiefs in Seventeenth-Century Dutch Portraits', *Beeld en zeefbeeld in de Nederlandse kuns, 1550–1750* [*Image and Self-Image in Netherlandish Art, 1550–1750*]: *Kunsthistorich Jarrboek*, 46, ed. Reindert Falkenburg, Jan de Jong, Herman Roodenburg and Fritz Scholten (Zwolle: Waanders Uitgevers, 1995), pp. 336–40.

87 Dympna Callaghan, 'Looking Well to Linens: Women and Cultural Production in *Othello* and Shakespeare's England', in Jean Howard and Scott Shershow (eds), *Marxist Shakespeares* (London: Routledge, 2001), p. 57. For the cult of 'Veronica's Veil' see Farmer, op. cit. (note 40), p. 422; and E. Kuryluk, *Veronica and Her Cloth: History, Symbolism and Structure of a Love Image* (Oxford: Blackwell, 1991).

88 Thomas Docherty, *John Donne, Undone* (London: Methuen, 1986), pp. 198–9, 235 and 239. For More's handkerchief see Richard Marius, *Thomas More* (London: Weidenfeld, 1993), p. 514; and for the play on the 'wise fool' or 'fool of Christ' of 1 Corinthians 1 and 2, see ibid., p. 88, and Walter Kaiser, *Praisers of Folly: Erasmus, Rabelais, Shakespeare* (London: Gollancz, 1964), pp. 27–34. And for 'murmuring' as the Tudor code for political and religious dissent see also Simon Shepherd, *Marlowe and the Politics of Elizabethan Theatre* (Brighton: Harvester, 1986), pp. 31–3.

89 Ellis Heywood, *Il Moro*, ed. R.L. Deakins, trans. G.P. Marc'hadour (Cambridge, Mass.: Harvard University Press, 1972), p. 62. See also Dennis Rhodes, '*Il Moro*: An Italian

View of Sir Thomas More', in Edward Chaney and Peter Mack, *England and the Continental Renaissance: Essays in Honour of J.B. Trapp* (Woodbridge: Boydell, 1990), pp. 67–72.

90 Patricia Parker, 'What's in a Name: and More', *Sederi*, 11 (Universidad de Huelva: 2002), pp. 101–49, esp. p. 117.

91 Ibid., p. 145; James Joyce, *Ulysses* (Harmondsworth: Penguin, 1990), pp. 212–16.

92 Simpson, op. cit. (note 27), p. 104.

93 Robert Southwell, quoted in Peter Milward, *Shakespeare's Religious Background* (Chicago: Loyola University Press, 1973), p. 60: 'We, like God almighty's fools (as some scornfully call us), lay our shoulders under every load.'

94 John Mush and an anonymous tribute to Campion, quoted in Cross, op. cit. (note 83), p. 277.

95 Richard Hooker, *Complete Works* (3 vols, London: Dent, 1948), vol. 3, p. 527.

96 See, for instance, Lynda Boose, 'Othello's Handkerchief: The Recognizance and Pledge of Love', *English Literary Renaissance* (ELR), 5 (1975), pp. 360–75.

97 Quoted Simpson, op. cit. (note 27), p. 462.

98 The shirt was subsequently transported by the Canonesses to Newton Abbot, where it remains; see Camm, op. cit. (note 11), pp. 349–50, 364, 372 and 377.

99 Eamon Duffy, *The Stripping of the Altars: Traditional Religion in England, 1400–1580* (New Haven: Yale University Press, 1992), p. 381. For an account of More and the cult of the dead see also Stephen Greenblatt, *Hamlet in Purgatory* (Princeton: Princeton University Press, 2001), pp. 134–50.

100 Hulse, op. cit. (note 10), pp. 190–225, esp. pp. 208 and 224–5.

101 E.E. Reynolds, *The Field Is Won: The Life and Death of Saint Thomas More* (London: Burns and Oates, 1968), pp. 379–80.

102 Honigmann, op. cit. (note 20), p. 73, n. 2.

103 Parker, op. cit. (note 90), pp. 133–4.

104 Ibid., p. 107; Domenico Regi, *Vita di Tommasso Moro* (Venice: 1675), quoted in G.P. Marc'hadour, 'A Name for All Seasons', in R.S. Sylvester and G.P. Marc'hadour (eds), *Essential Articles for the Study of Thomas More* (Hamden, Conn.: Anchor Books, 1977), p. 545. See also *Moreana*, 47–8 (1975), pp. 4 and 72.

105 Parker, op. cit. (note 90), pp. 133–5.

106 *Notes and Queries*, 4th series, 4 (1869), p. 61; Frank and Majie Padberg, *Moreana: Material for the Study of Saint Thomas More* (Los Angeles: Loyola University Press, 1964), pp. 246–7.

107 For the migrations of More's head see Hulse, op. cit. (note 10), pp. 223–5.

108 T.S. Eliot, 'Shakespeare and the Stoicism of Seneca', *Selected Essays* (London: Faber and Faber, 1953), pp. 130–1.

109 Catherine Hibbard, 'Early Stuart Catholicism: Revisions and Re-Revisions', *Journal of Modern History*, 52 (1980), p. 21.

110 Catherine Belsey, 'Disrupting Sexual Difference: Meaning and Gender in the Comedies', in John Drakakis (ed.), *Alternative Shakespeares* (London: Methuen, 1985), p. 171.

111 Hulse, op. cit. (note 10), p. 213. For Catholic missals as an instrument of Counter-Reformation militancy see Roger Chartier, *A History of Private Life: III: The Passions of the Renaissance* (Cambridge, Mass.: Harvard University Press, 1989), pp. 74–5.

112 Greenblatt, op. cit. (note 99), p. 254.

113 John Carey, *John Donne: Life, Mind and Art* (London: Faber and Faber, 1981), pp. 44–5.

114 I am grateful to Michael Wood for information about this Warwickshire oral tradition.

115 Docherty, op. cit. (note 88), pp. 191–3, 202–3 and 235.

116 Etienne Pasquier, *The Jesuits' Catechism* (London: 1602), sig. A2r, quoted in Watson, op. cit. (note 29), p. 237.

8

The pilot's thumb

Macbeth and the martyrs

'WHEN shall we three meet again? / In thunder, lightning, or in rain?' Editors point out that the satanic verses which open *Macbeth* make this non-naturalistic prologue unique in all Shakespearean drama, and that the 'drumming insistence' of their four-beat rhythm produces a musical effect which is irresistibly conspiratorial, 'hovering between a ritual and a threat'.[1] Like the first bars of Beethoven's Fifth Symphony, this diabolical tattoo fixes Shakespeare's witch scenes (unlike those added to the play by Middleton) as uncannily compelling, because so urgently repetitive. As the Porter later says, 'Here's a knocking indeed' (2.3.1) that raps like fate. For Terry Eagleton this repetitiveness is a signifier of the 'sisterly community' in which the Witches exist, revolving around 'dance, the moon, pre-vision', and a co-operation that is the sororial opposite of Macbeth's male egomania.[2] And, by reciprocating in rhyme, the Weird Sisters do seem to accumulate a collective purpose that may, in fact, be Shakespeare's decisive contribution to the witch repertoire. For what is most striking about the riddle that both convokes and disperses 'we three' at the beginning of *Macbeth* is that this was the first time in an English drama when witches had ever been represented as congregating in a group. Though they have associations with those 'Sisters Three' or 'Furies fell' who shear the thread of life in *A Midsummer Night's Dream* (5.1.274; 323), the source for this demonic trio was Holinshed's *Chronicles*, where Macbeth and Banquo encounter the three baleful women by chance. But it was in the opening of Shakespeare's play that the idea was introduced on to the London stage of witches convening deliberately for their own malign purposes, and with it a new paradigm of witchcraft as conspiracy centred on rituals of the witches' sabbath. *Macbeth* dates from August 1606, when it was staged at court for a visit of the King of Denmark.[3] All leaders of the English judiciary would have been in attendance at this state occasion, and this is significant, because just six years later the fantasy of a convention of 'the most dangerous, wicked and damnable witches in the country' would first appear in English law – at the trials of the witches of Lancashire.[4] There is a conceptual affinity, therefore, between these two key manifestations of the Jacobean witch craze, and this might be more than a sheer coincidence. For *Macbeth* is, of course, a tragedy darkly aware of its own prophetic status:

> The Weird Sisters, hand in hand,
> Posters by the sea and land,
> Thus do go, about, about,
> Thrice to thine, and thrice to mine,
> And thrice again, to make up nine.
> Peace, the charm's wound up.
>
> (1.3.32–7)

Like Shakespeare's Weird Sisters, the Lancashire witches, it was alleged, had come together at 'a special meeting', and 'according to solemn appointment, solemnized this great festival day ... with great cheer, merry company, and much conference'.[5] Never before had it been alleged in England that witches gathered for ritual meetings, according to a recent study of the case by Jonathan Lumby;[6] yet it was precisely by weaving 'Thrice to thine, and thrice to mine' in trifold collusion that Macbeth's witches generated a compound malevolence that far exceeded the powers conjured by Shakespeare's earlier solitary sorceresses, Joan of Arc and Margaret of Gloucester. According to the New Historicist critics, Shakespearean theatre 'shapes the fantasies by which it is shaped, begets that by which it is begotten'; and, if this is so, then 'the charm wound up' in these hypnotic verses was powerful enough to inaugurate an entire genre of witch dramas by writers such as Dekker, Marston and Jonson.[7] What has never been discussed, though, is how unprecedented Shakespeare's convocation of 'weird women' (3.1.2) was to his London audience, and how his representation of a satanic confederacy may have influenced the contemporary criminalisation of witchcraft as a political conspiracy. For though, as James Sharpe confirms in his recent survey of English witchcraft, *Instruments of Darkness*, terror that a coven of witches might go 'hand in hand' in combination together was the essential incentive in mobilising all seventeenth-century witch-hunts, allegations of such a conspiratorial assembly were alien to English law before the acting of Shakespeare's tragedy. In fact, it was precisely the *absence* of a concept of conspiracy, Sharpe argues, that separated Elizabethan witch beliefs from those of contemporary Europe, for not only is there 'absolutely no evidence that early modern English witches ever were organised' in collectives, 'there is very little trace in English records of the blasphemous orgiastic sabbath found in continental trial records'. Sharpe's research supports the view, therefore, that 'little or nothing of the black mass is to be traced' in early modern England, and that 'English witches showed no sign of co-operation'; so, wherever he does uncover accusations of collaboration or belief in communities of witches – as at Windsor in 1579, or with the three Throckmorton sisters of 1599 – he concludes that these were 'little more than suspicions of *ad hoc* co-operation and certainly nothing by way of organised rituals'.[8] Editors who question the authenticity of the opening of *Macbeth*, on the ground that these witches have no function other than to meet to say they will meet again, underestimate, therefore, the malefic potential they acquire, simply, as the First Witch boasts, by assembling in such an unholy trinity together. For by sealing their triple alliance, Macbeth's 'secret, black, and midnight hags' (4.1.63) became the first witches in English culture to pervert the words of the Book of Common Prayer: that prayers will be heard and requests granted 'When two or three are gathered together'.[9]

Summoned by Grey Malkin at the climactic moment of Christ's denial, when 'Thrice the brinded cat hath mewed' (4.1.1), Macbeth's interceptors display by their league – 'thrice … And thrice again, to make up nine' – how they multiply their powers so exponentially. And, as the American journalist Gary Wills observes, 'No one in Shakespeare's time would have been in doubt' about 'what brought all three together on this battlefield', when it offered such rich pickings of 'the most vital ingredients of witches' work: dead body parts'.[10] In fact, it was not until the Lancaster trials that English law incorporated the French idea that the aim of witches was to exhume dead bodies, 'carry them to their synagogue and college, and offer them to the Prince of Devils'.[11] Then, it was claimed, one set of accused smuggled human teeth dug from corpses to their meeting-place at Malkin Tower in Pendle Forest, while the other disinterred a dead baby from Salmesbury churchyard, stewed it in a casserole, ate the flesh, 'and with the fat that came from the bones' anointed themselves, so as to copulate with Satan.[12] These were standard fantasies in continental demonology, but historians are at a loss to explain why they were imported into Lancashire;[13] so it cannot be chance that *Macbeth* had given credibility to just such a phantasmagoria, with the irruption on to stage of a coven whose entire conclave is founded on scavenging ingredients for the cauldron from gallows, graveyards and shipwrecks. Whether 'Liver of blaspheming Jew … Nose of Turk … Tartar's lips … grease that's sweaten / From the murderer's gibbet', or 'Finger of birth-strangled babe / Ditch-delivered by a drab' (4.1.26–36) what gives these *objets trouvés*, culled from corpses of condemned religious and sexual heretics, sensationalism is their human origin (in contrast to the banal animal extracts, such as 'juice of toad' or 'oil of adder' (55), dreamed up by Middleton). The 1604 Witchcraft Act had specifically decreed death for those who 'take up any dead man, woman, or child out of his, her, or their grave, or any other place where the dead body resteth – or the skin, bone, or any other part of any dead person – to be employed or used in any manner of witchcraft, sorcery, charm, or enchantment';[14] but it was not until Shakespeare's tragedy was performed for the courtiers and lawyers at Hampton Court that the full repertoire of the black mass was witnessed in England, complete with the pact, infanticide, cannibalism and necromancy that would all soon be projected on to the accused of Lancashire.

'Double, double' (4.1.20): Macbeth's Sisters were the first stage characters to confront the Jacobean authorities with the nightmare of a witches' sworn combination that had haunted European elites since printing of the persecutorial *Malleus Maleficarum* by the Dominicans in 1486. But whereas, as Stuart Clark notes in his account of 'The Idea of Witchcraft in Early Modern Europe', *Thinking With Demons*, continental demonologists were obsessed with the powers raised through rituals of *inversion* (a fixation reflected by Jonson in his 1609 *Masque of Queens*, where the devilish anti-masquers 'do all things contrary'), nothing suggests these Weird Women derive pleasure from things 'That befall preposterously' (*Dream*, 3.2.121). Their unprecedented 'double trouble' is generated by the *duplication*, rather than reversal, of liturgical ceremonies, for they seem, in contrast to French or Italian satanists who were reported to 'say the Mass upside-down',[15] to accumulate their horrific morsels with something like a popish adoration. And the fact that they collaborate to collect and preserve such gallows carrion does link their necrophilia to Protestant suspicions, like those in Samuel Harsnett's *Declaration of Egregious Popish Impostures*, that likened the abuse of dead bodies in witchcraft to the worship of body parts by Catholic congregations. Editors have fretted over Shakespeare's cue for his Witches' brew, but his itemisation of 'poisoned entrails' or 'ounces of a red-haired wench' (4.1.5; 58) resembles nothing so much as those nauseated inventories compiled by Tudor commissioners of the contents of monastic reliquaries, which rather than containing 'hair of the Blessed Virgin ... parings of St. Edmund's nails', or 'the finger of St. Stephen', as claimed, they denigrated as compacted of 'stinking boots, mucky combs, rotten girdles, filthy rags, and gobbets of wood under the names of parcels of the holy cross'.[16] 'I think you have heard of St Blaise's heart at Malvern, and St Algar's bones', sneered Latimer, 'how long they deluded people' into reverencing at 'their solemn and nocturnal bacchanals ... pigs' bones instead of saints' relics';[17] and in *Macbeth* the recipe to make 'a hell-broth boil and bubble' (4.1.19) seems to tap the same discourse of reformist disgust. More specifically, Shakespeare's staging of a witches' sabbath looks like a demonisation of the torchlit vigils at which papist women embalmed the debris of martyrs in Stuart London, on behalf of collectors such as the Habsburg Ambassador, Count Egmont, whose catalogue avidly listed the macabre fruits of their 'diligence and devotion' as a provocation to revenge:

> Of the venerable William Ward, his heart, drawn from the fire wherein it had laid, and the handkerchief he had in his hand when he died... Of Father Bartholemew Roe, a thumb, a piece of burnt lung, a kidney burned to a cinder, and a towel dipped in his blood; of Mr Arnold Green, a thumb, a piece of burnt liver, and the apron of his torturer. Of the venerable John Morgan ... pieces of burnt flesh, three pieces of his *praecordia*, some hair, four towels dipped in his blood, the straw on which he was disembowelled, some papers greased with his fat. Of the venerable Paul ... a toe, three small bones, a piece of windpipe, some

burnt flesh, four napkins dipped in his blood. Of the venerable Francis Bell, a right-hand quarter of his body, six pieces of flesh and fat, three napkins dipped into his melted fat, with remains of flesh, two fingers, and his *thyrotheca*. Of the venerable Thomas Holland, a bone, some pieces of skin, a nail, a little box of fat, the shirt in which he suffered … Of Mr Duckett, the right hand, a piece of his neck, one vertebra and a half. Of Father Corby, a tooth, a few napkins stained with his blood, two handkerchiefs that he used at his martyrdom, his girdle and his hat, some remains of burnt viscera. Of the venerable Henry Morse, his liver pulled out of the fire, a handkerchief stained with his blood, ashes of his burnt intestines, the rope wherewith he was hanged …[18]

'Fire burn and cauldron bubble': if their mummy, tooth, stomach, gullet, liver, gall, nose, lips, blood and entrails (22–37) do align Shakespeare's midnight hags with the 'pious Catholics' who 'came back to the gallows' after the executions of the English martyrs, 'and scraped up the ashes where the bowels had been burnt', to 'search for some lump of flesh all parched and singed by the embers',[19] then it is no wonder their spells are so strong. For ever since the regime had obliterated each remnant after the beheading of Mary Queen of Scots, salvage of these grisly remains had become an act of collective resistance, as 'Catholics vied in taking away handkerchiefs dipped in dismembered bodies, or bloodstained straw from the ground; while some snatched intestines thrown in the cauldron'.[20] Arthur Marotti speculates that this fetishism was prompted by the rediscovery of the Roman catacombs in 1578; but the Catholic ideologue Robert Bellarmine put it into sectarian context, when he wrote that 'There is nothing [Protestants] shudder at more than veneration of relics', and the Tridentine church took his lead by enjoining relic-worship expressly to inspire a new crusade.[21] It was reviving, that is to say, the medieval cultic procession of relics for political purposes, and from Mexico to Manila its missions paraded the rags and bones of martyrs as signs of suicidal militancy.[22] As Sharpe comments, the question of how the witch panic related to 'concerns of the upper echelons of the Church of England' over this ecstatic cult is therefore moot;[23] but what is certain is that, by the time of *Macbeth*, English witch specialists regularly asserted that the miracles attributed to relics were 'mere Satanical wonders', and that, just as witches were supposed to raise demons from the organs of the dead, so the Jesuits 'do cog and coin devils, spirits, and *souls departed this life*', in exorcisms.[24] We know one such scandalised outburst by Harsnett caught Shakespeare's attention, because he quoted it extensively in *King Lear*. Its fascination for him was that it retailed the grotesque uses put in 1586 by his townsman (and possible cousin) Robert Debdale, when exorcising the young Williams sisters of Denham in Buckinghamshire, to relics of priests he may also have known: Alexander Briant, Edmund Campion and the brother of the Stratford schoolmaster Thomas Cottam. And when his three Witches stirred fingers and noses into their boiling cauldron, it would have been difficult for a Jacobean audience not to think of such 'home-bread relics' as 'the thumbs, bones, and joints' of these 'three champions sent for fire-work in England', who in Harsnett's scathing report, had been 'executed at Tyburn, canonised at Rome, and sainted by the devils':

> We never read in all the miracle book that the devil trembled at the name of our blessed Saviour; but Bryant's bone being applied and St. Cottam being called upon, the devil answered in a trembling, quivering voice, 'Thou shalt not have thy prayer.' And he was scarcely to be understood, the poor devil chattered his teeth so sore. What then should I tell you of Campion's thumb put into Fid's mouth, Bryant's bone pinched hard to Sarah's bare leg, as hard as a priest could hold it, the great old rusty nail crammed into Fid's mouth amongst an handful of other choking relics, what wonders they wrought with these poor she-devils: how these made them to vomit, screech and quack like geese that had swallowed down a gag?[25]

'Here I have a pilot's thumb, / Wrack'd as homeward he did come' (1.3.28): like the martyrs' bones used at Denham, in Shakespeare's text the Witches' trophies are what Harsnett calls 'fresh green new relics, that were not antiquated or out of date'; but the one that cements their conspiracy when the First Witch puts it on show, since it instantly cues Macbeth's drum, seems to be nothing less than a relic of 'The pilot of the Galilean lake', and keeper of the keys of heaven,[26] St Peter: or rather, the hallowed thumb of his representative and the Pied Piper of his mission, notoriously *racked* in the Tower of London to confess treason, on returning in 1580 from Prague: that of Campion himself. If 'thumb' rhymes with 'drum' in *Macbeth*, then that is because this grisly remainder was both a physical cause and effect of sectarian war in Shakespeare's England. By far the most celebrated relic of the Catholic martyrs, it had been hacked from one of the quarters of Campion's body in the mêlée at Tyburn, when the crowd rushed to dip handkerchiefs in his blood, in an incident to which Shakespeare may be alluding when Caesar's killers learn how 'great men press / For tinctures, stains, relics and cognizance' at scenes of martyrdom, as the Romans 'dip their napkins in his sacred blood' (*Julius Caesar*, 2.2.89; 3.2.135). According to the Jesuit Robert Parsons, 'the loss was quickly discovered, but the thief could never be found', and since the hangman 'reluctantly refused twenty pounds for another joint', the digit became the sole piece of the martyr preserved.[27] Later, it was divided, and the two halves were enshrined in Rome and Roehampton; but its immediate fate was to become the member that, as Harsnett exclaimed, was 'applied to such a diabolical service as the devil himself without such a relic could never have accomplished', when the exorcists inserted it in 'the most secret part' of the girl Sarah Williams, to confound 'the devil that did reside in that place' while she menstruated.[28] So, it may be that the obscene glee with which Macbeth's Witches flaunt the 'pilot's thumb' reflects the lengths to which the authorities went to prevent papists acquiring any further relics after the mass hysteria at Campion's execution, when, as the author of *A Yorkshire Recusant's Relation* grieved, 'they used singular diligence that no part of blood, or flesh, or garment, or anything belonging to the martyr be unburnt or escape their hands', and even 'the apparel the murderers take and disperse, the pins, points, buttons, and all, lest Catholics get them and use them for relics'.[29] But the lurid pornographic reputation of the thumb also suggests that in *Macbeth* the prop was introduced at the opening of the play as a symbol of religious fanaticism, affiliating the Witches immediately with what Harsnett condemned as 'the most impious and unnatural villainy' in the Denham exorcisms, and placing the entire action under the sign of this 'devil's dildo':

> Good God, what do we here? Or is it but a dream? St. Campion or sainting devil help us out with this, for I am at a stand. Relics to that place? It is able to possess a man with fury to cry out, *Earth gape and hell swallow* such devil-saints, such devil-relics, such devil-priests and all. Was it ever heard that any heathen durst ever abuse the vilest thing consecrated to their idol-devils in such execrable manner? Holy saints, holy relics, holy priests, holy devil that made them and moved them to this! It was no marvel they made so fast with the devil to Saint their Champions, Campion and his crew from hell, and to deify and hellify their relics, since they were to be applied to such a diabolical purpose.[30]

Devil's dildo, or sacred relic: if the stump paraded by Macbeth's Witches like a god in their cultic procession was indeed a fragment of the martyr's relic, there could be no more apt instrument to initiate a drama about assassination. For the reason why Campion's thumb had acquired veridical importance is that the priest made it his witness at his trial, when 'with his hands folden in linen cloth', he demonstrated such feebleness 'he was neither able to pluck off his own mitten, nor lift a cup to his mouth', as proof that, after the rack, he could never have signed a confession of treason.[31] According to Parsons, Thomas Norton, the Rackmaster and author of *Gorboduc*, liked to jest how he had pulled one priest a 'foot longer than God made him' before he confessed;[32] but though Campion was tortured until his nails were torn out, he swore he 'never declared any secrets', and would not, 'come rack, come rope'.[33] His silence ensured he never saw 'paper, ink, and pen', rejoiced one poem, for he won glory with 'every wrench'.[34] Yet Campion did crack under 'the intolerable torment',[35] and so the thumb that signed the paper, and from which he was strung, became a symbol of his slipperiness on the 'Bloody Question' of conspiracy; as Shakespeare recalled in an earlier parodic inquisition, where Feste, dressed as 'Sir Topas the curate', which may be a disguise for the Jesuit Henry Garnet, and pretending to be 'parson' Parsons, taunts Malvolio with the tale of how 'the old Hermit of Prague, that never saw pen and ink, very wittily said to a niece of King Gorboduc, "That is, that is."' (*Twelfth*, 4.2.1–13). This caricature of the Rackmaster as a 'Goneril, with a white beard' reminds us how much in Shakespeare's rewriting of *Gorboduc*, 'He hates him / That would on the rack of this tough world / Stretch him out longer' (*Lear*, 4.6.95; 5.3.313–15), and implies that the Witches who severed the Hermit's thumb could be identified with prosecutors as well as priests. Hagiographers always did insist that horror attached not to the victims, 'but the brutes who presided over their butchery', with blood splashing the judges or bowels staining the hangmen;[36] but, in *Macbeth*, the effect of flaunting Campion's thumb at a witches' sabbath must have been to taint all who found a meaning in martyrdom, whether of treason or truth. Indeed, Elizabeth Hanson relates how, during his ordeal, Campion withdrew into 'a kind of conceptual pun' of deniability, that thwarted his interrogators and still baffles historians.[37] So, when Macbeth's temptresses enter brandishing what looks to be the relic of this 'pilot' of the Jesuit invasion, the bloody baton – which would travel from Tyburn to Tiber *via* the devils of Denham, and on which detractors and idolators would look with fanaticism – generates similar anxiety. This gory fetish associates the Witches directly with the 'prattling, juggling, Jesuits' whose theatricality made them into the 'divine sorcerers' of the exorcisms, but whose equivocation and fireworks also made them, to Protestant eyes, a suicide squad of crazed assassins.[38]

Stephen Greenblatt remarks that when they first meet the Witches, 'So wither'd and so wild in their attire' that they 'look not like th'inhabitants o'th'earth', Banquo and Macbeth are plunged into a perceptual quandary, and that the latter sets the scene for the epistemological 'queasiness' of the plot when he admits, 'You should be women, / And yet your beards forbid me to interpret / That you are so' (1.3.38–44). For Greenblatt, 'What is happening here is that Shakespeare is staging the ontological dilemmas that in the deeply contradictory situation of the time haunted all attempts to determine the status of witchcraft';[39] but there is a more acute context for this enigma, and this is made explicit in the contemporary witch play by Dekker, *The Whore of Babylon*, where it is Campeius – or Campion – and his Jesuits who are ordered to 'unsex' themselves (1.6,39) to slip undetected into England: 'Have change of hairs, of eye-brows ... Be shaven and be old women, take all shapes / To escape taking.'[40] As often with this writer, Dekker's text reads like an X-ray of Shakespeare's intentions, and, with Marston's *Sophonisba* and Barnabe Barnes's *The Devil's Charter*, also dating from 1606, confirms that what happens when Macbeth confronts these bearded ladies is part of a concerted campaign, equating Jesuits with witches, and their equivocation with the treachery of 'juggling fiends' (5.10,19). Such was the theme of a sermon delivered at court by Lancelot Andrewes two days before *Macbeth*, which condemned the missionaries as creatures with 'a man's face, women's hair, but lion's teeth';[41] and editors have noticed how Shakespeare's play contributes to the manoeuvre, as it slides from martyrs to devils, with the entry into the Porter's scene of the ghost of the executed Garnet, alias 'Farmer', himself, carrying his own relics in Limbo. Limbo was the name given 'Death Row' by priest-hunters; and in this interlude the Charon-like keeper of Hell-gate mocks the hanged man as 'an equivocator... who committed treason enough for God's sake, yet could not equivocate to heaven' (2.3.9), as courtiers joked Garnet would 'equivocate to the gallows, but be hanged without equivocation'.[42] The scene is a dark judgement, then, on the holy war inspired by the 'pilot's thumb'; though, when Garnet's head was impaled on London Bridge, its uncorrupted flesh was seen as a proof of his innocence.[43] But in *Macbeth*, a play which opens by defiling Campion's remains wastes no tears on those who dipped 'napkins' in Garnet's corpse, or the 'English tailor' who stole a miraculous husk of blood-stained corn 'out of a French hose' worn to the scaffold by the priest:

> PORTER: Knock, knock, knock. Who's there i'th'name of Beelzebub? Here's a farmer, that hang'd himself on th'expectation of plenty, come in time – have napkins enough about you. Here you'll sweat for it. (2.3.3–6)

Henry Garnet was executed on 3 May 1606 for alleged involvement in the Gunpowder Plot, and the Porter's gallows humour has therefore been read as a gesture towards *Macbeth*'s historical occasion. But the question this topicality begs is why its author should collude with the Puritan discourse that made Catholicism equivalent to witchcraft, drafting an entire drama around the fact that just as 'Catholics sought relics from the scaffold', so 'witches took body parts from the gallows'.[44] What prompted this transfer of guilt from the Gunpowder assassins to Macbeth's Witches, and why were the Weird Sisters presented, like Garnet's Jesuits, as an organised political conspiracy? Why, indeed, did Shakespeare write a tragedy about witches at all, when he might have written one expressly (like Jonson's *Catiline*) on 'Roman' nobles? For while it comes as no surprise that this 'royal play' of 1606 speaks of the traumatic events of 1605, the mystery is why *Macbeth* itself *equivocates* about Macbeth's crime, by invoking the 'black legend' of international Jesuit terrorism? The answer lies, of course, in the author's own compromising proximity to the Gunpowder conspirators. For, as Antonia Fraser reminds us in her study of the Plot, the epicentre of the Gunpowder treason was Shakespeare's world, since 'the great arc of Plotters' houses that spread across the Midlands' converged around Stratford-upon-Avon: on the homes of Robert Catesby, at Lapworth Park, and the dramatist's own relative, John Grant, at Norbrook. It was at Lapworth in 1580 that Shakespeare's father probably received a copy of the Catholic Testament of Faith brought by Campion from Milan; and at Norbrook in 1583 that his kinsmen Edward Arden and John Somerville planned their suicidal mission to shoot the Queen. Both here and at the Mermaid Tavern, where Catesby conferred, the Plot was laid, as Fraser says, in 'Shakespeare country'.[45] So, as Leslie Hotson concluded, 'when we consider he had known Catesby and Grant from childhood; that Francis Tresham and the Winters were connected by marriage with his daughter ... and that his friend Jonson dined with Catesby and Winter just a few days before the explosion' was due, it is 'far from impossible' that *Macbeth* was provoked by Shakespeare's inside knowledge of the Plot, and that its anti-hero was inspired by Catesby: 'this daring, able and magnetic gentleman, who turned fanatic king-killer and bloody butcher, and like Macbeth died fighting'.[46] Rumours of 'a huge conspiracy among local Catholics' had, in fact, been rife in Stratford for a year before the event;[47] so, it is closeness to the plans that may explain the dramatist's need to formulate, with a near-anagram of the surname, the same extenuation as the excuse offered by Catesby's neighbours and kin: that this 'valiant cousin [and] worthy gentleman' (1.2.24) was nothing but 'an idiot, full of sound and fury' (5.5.26), betrayed by the Jesuitical 'equivocation of the fiend' (5.5.41):

> oftentimes, to win us to our harm,
> The instruments of darkness tell us truths,
> Win us with honest trifles to betray's
> In deepest consequence.
>
> (1.3.121–4)

'Shakespeare makes us pity Macbeth', it is said, when 'meeting with the Witches', this 'brave and loyal soldier is seduced by their equivocation'; and critics have registered how, by empathising with his villain, the dramatist creates a disconcertingly evasive tragedy, in which a traitor whose face 'is as a book' (1.5.62), and so 'does not deceive anyone for very long', is himself 'undone by treason's amphibolic tongue'.[48] Such exculpation extends, they point out, to the imagery of the play itself, which is dominated by an opposition between hand and heart, figuring Macbeth's inability to make the 'firstlings of [his] heart … The firstlings of [his] hand' (4.2.163). The effect of this exoneration is to objectify the protagonist's hand, as if 'the murderous hand detaches itself from the murderer', when Macbeth bids 'the eye wink at the hand' (1.4.52); his 'hangman's hands' bear 'filthy witness' to his deed (2.2.25; 45); his hands return to 'pluck out' his eye; 'all great Neptune's ocean' will not wash 'blood / Clean' from his hand (57–60); and lastly, he feels 'His secret murders sticking on his hands' (5.2.17).[49] Macbeth's weirdly dissociated hand becomes, in other words, a metonym for the deniability his own acts, and, as such, an eerie correlative of the rush, in the wake of the Plot, to displace guilt from English Catholics on to the Jesuits, whose mission had been fired by that peripatetic relic of Campion's thumb. It is the symbolic equivalent of the arm's-length strategy adopted by court Catholics such as the Howard family, three of whose members sat on the Bench at Garnet's trial; or by tame clerics such as the Archpriest George Blackwell, who urged the laity to take the Oath of Allegiance, imposed in 1606 deliberately to prise 'his Majesty's subjects that adhere in their hearts to the popish religion' away from 'the devilish counsel of Jesuits'.[50] In its anathematising of the Jesuits as Witches, *Macbeth* conforms, in fact, to the tactics of the English Benedictines, who 'hedged their bets' over the Oath because the rival Jesuits opposed it, with the result that their leader, Thomas Preston, was lodged at public expense, and had the freedom 'to go out to the theatre with priests who shared his views'.[51] This tragedy famed for the feverishness of its punning, condenses, that is to say, 'The panic-stricken dismay of leading Catholic activists when the Oath was formulated',[52] but, above all, the shifty opportunism of Catesby's co-religionists, frantic to deflect the blame for his conspiracy on to fanatical zealots, with their 'supernatural' and supranational 'soliciting' (1.3.129).

'Noble she is, but if she have ... conversed with such / As, like to pitch, defile ... I banish her my bed' (2 *Henry VI*, 2.1.204–7): once before, at the start of his career, Shakespeare articulated the panic of Catholic blame-calling, and against a similar backdrop of Lancashire sectarianism, when he had Eleanor, Duchess of Gloucester, disowned by her husband, the Lord Protector, for staging 'exorcisms' with a conjuror and two priests, Hume and Southwell. In 1592, when 2 *Henry VI* was written, the latter's name could only have pointed to the dramatist's own kinsman, the Jesuit Robert Southwell, who had been arrested by Topcliffe on 25 June, and racked about treasonable negotiations over the succession with Ferdinando Lord Strange, the patron of Shakespeare's troupe. Strange's claim to the throne came through his mother, Margaret Clifford, who had been 'banished the bed' of her husband, the Earl of Derby, since being put under house arrest in 1580 for consulting 'wizards and cunning men' to 'discover by means of witchcraft whether the Queen would live long', and if she should entertain 'ambitious hope' for her son.[53] Strange and his father defused the crisis by rigging a pretend purge on Catholics in their Lancashire fiefdom, and during August safe-houses, such as Crosby Hall and Salmesbury, were stripped on their orders of 'seditious books and Mass furniture'. Some eight hundred duly appeared in court at Lancaster, but, with a mere dozen fined, no one was deceived, and 'a few weeks later fresh complaints came from London' that the Stanleys were shielding recusants.[54] Shakespeare's history can be read, therefore, as a smokescreen for his Lancastrian patrons, and a dress-rehearsal for *Macbeth*, in the way that it shifts the blame for Catholic treason on to the Jesuit exorcist and the female demoniac, presenting metropolitan audiences with a ready scapegoat in the divorced Countess, whose representative is likewise indicted for 'Dealing with witches and with conjurors ... Demanding of King Henry's life and death' (2.1.171–4). The dramatist must have had pressing reasons for his symbolic betrayal of Southwell, whose namesake is condemned to 'be strangled on the gallows' (2.3.8) three years before the priest's actual execution. But this displacement trick ensured that 'all the keys of Lancashire' continued to 'hang at the Earl of Derby's old girdle'.[55] And Shakespeare shares the joke, by sending the witch back to 'Live in your country ... in banishment', with the Earl's own ancestor, 'Sir John Stanley, in the Isle of Man' (2.3.12–13). From Catholics to Jesuits to Lancashire witches was an effective slippage for Strange's Men to make, and their star-writer would remember the tactic and use it again at a time of even greater exposure.

Gunpowder Plot would always be called 'the Jesuit treason', opined Sir Edward Coke, the Attorney General, in which 'Garnet ... as *author*, was more to blame than all the *actors*';[56] but what was striking about popular culture is how it failed to follow this line, burning instead the Catholic gentry, in the effigy of Guy Fawkes. As Richard Hardin observes, the unofficial reaction to the Plot focused unmercifully on the knot of provincial aristocrats, and was 'much closer to the story told by modern historians than to the mythic version' (followed by Milton), which villified 'Satan, in friar's disguise'. In *Traitorous Percies and Catesbies*, for instance, the schoolboy poet Edward Hawes abused Catesby and Thomas Percy as 'Atheists' driven by 'Envy and hope of gain'; while 'the most influential of all the early poems', Francis Herring's *Pietas Pontificia*, had Fawkes take the rap as the eternal terrorist bogeyman. By 1610, Hardin shows, the 'Guy' of 5 November was well on the way to becoming a perennial 'focus of the culture's hatreds and fears', in a story 'propelling into history a ready scapegoat for collective failure' in the guise of the Catholic cavalier. In the 'demon-haunted atmosphere' of post-Plot politics the hunt for the villain fixed on Fawkes as the archetypal 'enemy-within', who looked like any English nobleman, 'with an English family, education, and tongue', yet with a 'foxy' foreign name.[57] Much of this class hatred, which lingers on modern Guy Fawkes Night, flared up in the Midland Rising of 1607, when it was Catholic landlords, notably the Catesbys and Treshams, who were targeted by the rioters;[58] but what was absent from all such popular anti-popery was what makes *Macbeth* problematic: namely, the offloading of culpability on to a transvestite clerical foe. That the execution of priests was restarted, therefore, in 1607, could owe something to the seriousness with which Shakespeare took Coke's theatre metaphor, and depicted the aristocratic assassin as but 'a poor player / That struts and frets his hour upon the stage' (5.5.23) under the wicked direction of the Jesuits' thumb. As John Bossy contends, the attitude to the missionaries of their patriarchal hosts was always one of latent hostility, since gentry like the Northamptonshire magnate Sir Thomas Tresham could never concede 'clerical pretensions' to leadership. Thus, though he was prosecuted for harbouring Campion, Tresham could still greet the accession of James I by offering to expel the Jesuits in return for Catholic emancipation. To such grandees, 'The idea that priests might be counselling them to abandon allegiance was fantastic';[59] but when in 1605 Tresham's heir, Francis, incriminated Garnet to save his own neck, the tragedy written by their Midland neighbour betrayed the bad faith of the entire cabal of Ardens, Throckmortons and Catesbys, as it had its conspirator likewise blame the 'filthy hags' (4.1.131) for leading him astray:

> And be these juggling fiends no more believed,
> That palter with us in a double sense,
> That keep the word of promise to our ear
> And break it to our hope.
>
> (5.10.19–22)

Whether or not Macbeth's recrimination against 'these juggling fiends' expresses the sense of betrayal felt by recusants at the Jesuit failure to sustain the 'Enterprise of England', from the day Campion came to Stratford, the

Catholic *fronde* to which Shakespeare was tied was far more deeply steeped in terrorism, concludes a recent study of the Treshams, than its protestations of 'mouth-honour' (5.3.28) would ever suggest.[60] But it was their ability to 'lie like truth' (5.5.40), and evade the consequences of this collusion, even when 'old Sir Fulke Greville raised the militia against the papists' in the aftermath of the Gunpowder Plot,[61] that made a text such as *Macbeth* their blueprint for escape. Meanwhile, the poet's *politique* aloofness from martyrdom was deployed in his most Montaigne-like meditation, Sonnet 124, which taxes 'our fashion' as too quick to be drawn into 'thralled discontent', and contrasts premature 'fools of time, / Which die for goodness, who have lived for crime', with the faith that outlasts 'the child of state ... fortune's bastard ... that heretic' (Elizabeth), because it stands 'all alone' and 'hugely politic'. And here the Montaigne metaphor of a secluded tower, 'builded far from accident', was revealing, for it was indeed as a quietist sect in seigneurial retreat that Jacobean Catholics would learn to survive in the decades after 1605.[62] To do so, however, they had first to repeat the symbolic substitution effected in Shakespeare's play, and shift responsibility for treason on to a demonised extreme. So it cannot be chance that the testing-ground for *Macbeth* should have been in the only region visited by Campion's crusade to share with Warwickshire a similar religious community, under 'a cohesive, much inter-married Catholic group', whose domination of the county ensured that 'recusancy flourished in all ranks'.[63] For in 1580 it was to Lancashire that the missionaries rode from Stratford, and at Hoghton Tower that the 'pilot' of the mission pitched his headquarters, during a fervent six months when the household may have included the boy Shakespeare. From Hoghton, Campion made recruiting-drives through adjoining estates, staying with the Allens at Rossall, Heskeths at Rufford, Listers at Westby, Sherburns at Stoneyhurst, Southworths at Salmesbury, Tempests at Bracewell, Towneleys at Towneley Hall and Worthingtons at Standish.[64] This itinerary would yield a rich harvest, for aside from the Allens, who had already produced Cardinal William Allen, and the Heskeths, who would soon be lured into a calamitous plot, the Hoghton, Lister, Sherburn, Southworth, Tempest, Towneley and Worthington families would all send sons to Douai and receive them back as priests. Yet a generation later, it was the same network, Lumby relates, that was the core of a different mania, when as a fall-out of the Gunpowder conspiracy, the Hoghtons and Towneleys mimicked Shakespearean drama, to dissociate from terrorist attacks by projecting on to their Catholic neighbours the satanic nightmare of *Macbeth*.[65]

The myth of the witches' sabbath, insists Robert Muchembled, is 'simply and solely a figment created by the elite classes of Europe', who 'revived stereotypes that had no popular basis in order to demonstrate the existence of a huge satanic plot ... Their imaginary sabbath was a copy of the Mass, a dark, morbid parody of the original.'[66] If this analysis holds, then *Macbeth* may be its classic instance. For in this play Shakespeare tapped into the force-field of early

modern persecution, located by historians on the interface between rival confessional extremes. A Catholic gentry divided against itself, and a magistracy
primed to reawaken the Inquisition fear of some demonic sect, were all the
elements required to ignite a conflagration. For 'where those who promoted
conformity met resistance, there dissidents would be created. Scape-goated and
marginalised, they were charged with the same crimes as the deviants of the
middle ages. It was said that they boiled babies and met in unspeakable
sabbaths.'[67] Lumby's summing-up of the 1612 witch-hunt suggests that one
answer to the riddle in *Macbeth* is that, while Shakespeare's coven may have
been modelled on secret Masses in Midland mansions, when the 'hellish and
devilish band of witches'[68] did 'meet again' it would be on Good Friday at
Malkin Tower in Pendle. There may have been, Lumby infers, some Catholic
ritual behind this Good Friday feast of so-called witches, but what is telling is
how their accusers belonged to families that hosted Campion, and now stood
guilty by association. None more so than that of Thomas Lister, whose allegations instigated the Lancastrian pogrom. A great-nephew of Alexander Hoghton,
who died in gaol for aiding the 1580 mission, as well as of Allen, Lister counted
two Jesuits among kin: John Lister, who suffered years of imprisonment; and
Thomas Lister, a neurotic hothead Garnet 'kept at his side', until he put them
all in danger by refusing to obey. Convinced he was deranged, Garnet sent
Lister home to Lancashire in 1602, hoping 'visits to his family will make him
completely healthy'.[69] In fact, it is easy to see in Lister's disloyalty to superiors
the blame-calling which would divide the English Catholics and lead, in the
after-shock of the Plot, to the accusations of witchcraft that fell first upon a
group that had never disowned its priests: the family of John Nutter, hanged in
1584, and Robert Nutter, martyred in 1600 at Lancaster, and the one member
of Garnet's inner cell whose hanging and dismemberment had actually taken
place in the locality.[70]

'The County of Lancashire may now be said to abound as much in Witches',
declared the Clerk of the Court, Thomas Potts, in his 'Discovery' of the 1612
trials, 'as Seminaries, Jesuits, and Papists'. With this parallel in mind, it was
logical he should dedicate the book to Thomas Knyvet, Lord Escrick, the
'discoverer' of Guy Fawkes in the cellars of Westminster, and allege that the
Malkin meeting was another powder conspiracy, 'to blow up the Castle' at
Lancaster.[71] Paranoia over 'dire combustion, and confus'd events, / New hatch'd
to th'woeful time' (2.3.57), followed *Macbeth* in mixing witches with Jesuits
and gunpowder; and the trail of suspicion led inevitably to Lancashire, where
the 1605 plotters had been racing before they blew themselves up, and to the
tightly knit Lancastrian gentry from which they had hoped for aid. No wonder,
then, that, beside Lister, fomentors of the Lancashire persecution included
recusants such as Robert Holden, who may have sparked the inquiry at Salmesbury Hall to smoke out its Jesuit chaplain, Christopher Southworth; and Sir
Thomas Gerard, brother of the 'most wanted' priest in England, John Gerard,

who in fact escaped to France on the day that Garnet died. As historians point out, a magistrate such as Sir Thomas, 'with a suspect family to live down', needed to look zealous, and since 'he could hardly attack his own Catholic relations', it was by searching for witches that he could prove himself both 'loyal and religious'.[72] With his brother-in-law, Sir Richard Hoghton, Gerard had displayed tangible loyalty in 1611, when the two crypto-Catholics each paid £1000 to be the very first of the baronets created to fund Protestants in Ulster. But it was by witch-hunting that these suspected fifth-columnists were relegitimated, when their *épuration* signalled what Shakespeare staged with his Scottish play: that in the far North 'the time' was now 'free' (5.9.21) from treason. Macbeth's impaled head may be the ghoulish symbol of this disassociation, a debasement of all those papist relics that had haunted the dramatist, ever since he had been traumatised at sixteen by his proximity to Campion at Hoghton. And though Lancashire Catholicism would long remain a cult of saints' heads in secret shrines, Shakespeare might well have intimidated the Hoghton circle with his boiling cauldron of religious violence. For whether or not Gerard and Hoghton were present, beside the judges, when *Macbeth* was first performed, 'The works of Mr Shakespeare' stood, we know, in Sir Richard's library.[73] And as the poet John Weever reported, when he placed the dramatist with them in his Lancastrian *Epigrams*, alongside the actor Edward Alleyn, whose mother was a Towneley, 'honey-tongued Shakespeare' – who was once, perhaps, among the Jesuit recruits who received 'entertainment and great maintenance' in their houses[74] – had created with his plays new 'saints' to whom these converts could safely transfer their 'subjective duty'.[75]

On 15 August 1617 James I was welcomed to Hoghton with a masque, in which 'the Landlord of this ancient Tower, / Thrice fortunate to see this happy hour', offered the King a 'trembling heart', which had been 'set on fire' by the royal visit to this 'heart of all the shire'. 'This Knight is thine, he is thy Ward', proclaimed a 'Household God', in punning allusion to the fact that Sir Richard had been adopted as a royal ward and forcibly educated in the state religion; yet the baronet had indeed proved the difference of his heart from those ripped out of papist martyrs, by his part in the 1612 show-trials of his neighbours. Three times, the 'burning heart' recalled, Lancashire gentry had flirted with rebellion, in 1569, 1580 and 1605; but now James reacted to their homage by 'knighting' Sir Richard's sirloin of beef, and declaring, with his Book of Sports, a coded edict of Catholic toleration. In the North, as in the Midlands, the lesson of *Macbeth* was learned, and an elite stained with blood was rehabilitated when, in the words of the masque, it put the King before its faith: 'seeing that thy Majesty we see / Greater than Country Gods, more good than we'.[76] The 'guilt of religious schism' felt by this clan was a prime cause, historians believe, of the Lancashire witch craze;[77] but, if so, Shakespeare's tragedy had taught these Hoghtons that the way to clear themselves was to demonise outsiders in their midst. As Greenblatt admits, this play 'may not be reducible to its consequences', but by imagining witches as a 'monstrous threat to civilisation … it cannot escape having a direct effect on lives'.[78] James summoned the surviving 'Lancashire witches' to Hoghton, where, to avoid the evil eye, the King observed the old women from behind a screen. But Shakespeare apparently had no doubt that 'the horrid deed' of Gunpowder treason had been blown back into the eyes of its perpetrators by Christ: 'like a naked new-born babe, / Striding the blast' (1.7.21). The reference may be to the playwright's kinsman, the Plotter Grant, blinded by his own explosives; but the verdict falls on all who followed Campion, as the retort is to a famous poem by the martyred Southwell, whose 'babe all burning bright / Did in the air appear' like an incendiary device.[79] To the end, then, Shakespeare associated martyrdom with conspiracy; and in *The Tempest* even draped Caliban's plot in the 'trumpery' left hanging by 'Mistress Line'. Anne Line was the Jesuits' aged landlady, hanged for hiding priests; but when these plotters garb themselves in the 'trash' from her 'line', she is roped into their crime, and the 'saintly widow' becomes a witch, as assassins reduce to a 'frippery', or rag-and-bone shop (4.1.186; 222–4), the spectacle of 'the noble and heroic Mistress Line suspended upon the gallows', where Father Garnet had 'cut the sleeve from her gown, dipped it in blood, and obtained one of her stockings' to be ripped to pieces for relics: 'For she used to have bandages on her legs, and thus her stockings were very large, but her legs were as thin as the rope on which she was hanged.'[80]

NOTES

1 G.K. Hunter (ed.), New Penguin edition (Harmondsworth: Penguin, 1967), pp. 42–3. See also Nicholas Brooke's similar comments in the Oxford edition (Oxford University Press, 1990), p. 1.

2 Terry Eagleton, *William Shakespeare* (Oxford: Blackwell, 1986), pp. 2–4.

3 For the state visit as the occasion of the first performance see the Arden edition of the play, ed. Kenneth Muir (London: Methuen, 1951), p. xxiv; Alvin Kernan, *Shakespeare, The King's Playwright: Theater in the Stuart Court, 1603–1613* (New Haven: Yale University Press, 1995), pp. 71–7; and Henry Paul, *The Royal Play of 'Macbeth'* (New York: Macmillan, 1950).

4 Thomas Potts, *The Trial of the Lancashire Witches, 1612*, ed. G.B. Harrison (London: Peter Davis, 1929; repr. 1971), p. 27.

5 Ibid.

6 Jonathan Lumby, *The Lancashire Witch Craze: Jennet Preston and the Lancashire Witches* (Preston: Carnegie Publishing, 1995), p. 57.

7 Louis Montrose, '*A Midsummer Night's Dream* and the Shaping Fantasies of Elizabethan Culture', in Richard Wilson and Richard Dutton (eds), *New Historicism and Renaissance Drama* (Harlow: Longman, 1992), p. 130. John Marston's *Sophonisba*, Thomas Dekker's *The Whore of Babylon*, and Barnabe Barnes's *The Devil's Charter* all date from late in 1606; Ben Jonson's *Masque of Queens* from 1609.

8 James Sharpe, *Instruments of Darkness: Witchcraft in England, 1550–1750* (Harmondsworth: Penguin, 1997), p. 76; C. L'Estrange Ewen, *Witchcraft and Demonianism: A Concise Account Derived from Sworn Depositions and Confessions Obtained in the Courts of England and Wales* (London: Heath Cranton, 1933), p. 57; G.R. Quaife, *Godly Zeal and Furious Rage: The Witch in Early Modern Europe* (London: Croom Helm,

1987), p. 59.

9 Prayer of St Chrysostom.

10 Gary Wills, *Witches and Jesuits: Shakespeare's 'Macbeth'* (Oxford: Oxford University Press, 1995), p. 38.

11 Sebastian Michaelis, *Pneumalogie* (Avignon: 1587), trans. E.A. Ashwin; quoted in Lumby, op. cit. (note 6), p. 39.

12 Ibid., pp. 42 and 139–40.

13 Sharpe, op. cit. (note 8), p. 99.

14 I James I, c. 12 (1604), quoted in Barbara Rosen (ed.), *Witchcraft in England: 1558–1618* (Amherst: University of Massachusetts Press, 1991), p. 57.

15 Stuart Clark, *Thinking with Demons: The Idea of Witchcraft in Early Modern Europe* (Oxford: Clarendon Press, 1997), p. 15.

16 Quoted Eamon Duffy, *The Stripping of the Altars: Traditional Religion in England, 1400–1580* (Yale: Yale University Press, 1992), pp. 164, 384 and 414–15.

17 Ibid. p. 390.

18 Quoted Dom Bede Camm, *Forgotten Shrines: An Account of Some Old Catholic Halls and Families in England and of Relics and Memorials of the English Martyrs* (London: Maacdonald and Evans, 1910), p. 361.

19 Quoted ibid., p. 362.

20 Richard Simpson (ed.), *The Rambler*, 8 (new series, 1857), p. 114.

21 Arthur Marotti, 'Southwell's Remains: Catholicism and Anti-Catholicism in Early Modern England', in Cedric Brown and Arhur Marotti (eds), *Texts and Cultural Change in Early Modern England* (London: Macmillan, 1997), p. 63, n. 47; Robert Bellarmine, *De controversiis christianae fidei* (Ingolstadt: 1601), vol. 2, p. 826, quoted in Simon Ditchfield, 'Martyrs on the Move: Relics as Vindicators of Local Diversity in the Tridentine Church', in Diana Wood (ed.), *Martyrs and Martyrologies* (Oxford: Blackwell, 1993), p. 283.

22 For the popular cultic procession of relics see, in particular, Michael Goodich, *Violence and Miracle in the Fourteenth Century: Private Grief and Public Salvation* (Chicago: Chicago University Press, 1995), pp. 14–21, 36–7, 110–23 and 153–5; and for the Tridentine revival of the tradition see John O'Malley, Gauvin Bailey, Steven Harris and Frank Kennedy (eds), *The Jesuits: Cultures, Sciences, and the Arts, 1540–1773* (Toronto: University of Toronto Press, 1999), pp. 262, 391, 588, 662 and 682: among objects discussed are blood samples taken by surgeons (Quebec), mechanical birds (Akbar), bones (Manila), wax effigies (Mexico City) and the toga of Ignatius Loyola (Cologne). For a politicised English cult see Claire Cross, 'An Elizabethan Martyrologist and His Martyr: John Mush and Margaret Clitherow', in Wood, op. cit. (note 21), pp. 271–94.

23 Sharpe, op. cit. (note 8), p. 209.

24 William Perkins, *A Discourse of the Damned Art of Witchcraft*, 'Epistle Dedicatory' (London: 1610), quoted in Clark, op. cit. (note 15), p. 533; Samuel Harsnett, *A Declaration of Egregious Popish Impostures* (London: 1603), repr. in Frank Brownlow, *Shakespeare, Harsnett, and the Devils of Denham* (Newark: University of Delaware Press, 1993), p. 294.

25 Quoted ibid., pp. 294–5.

26 John Milton, 'Lycidas', l. 109, in *Milton's 'Lycidas': The Tradition and the Poem*, ed. C.A. Patrides (Missouri: University of Missouri Press, 1983), p. 8: the allusion is to Matthew 16:19, 'but is by some readers said to be to Christ, and by others to a composite portrait' of the 'mitred' (l. 112) – i.e. Roman – priest.

27 Quoted in Richard Simpson, *Edmund Campion* (London: John Hodges, 1896), p. 455. For the later history of the relic see Dom Bede Camm, *Forgotten Shrines: Relics and Memorials of the English Martyrs* (London: Macdonald and Evans, 1910), pp. 363 and 377–8.

28 In Brownlow, op. cit. (note 24), p. 297.

29 In John Morris (ed.), *The Troubles of Our Catholic Forefathers* (3 vols, London: Burns and Oates, 1877), vol. 3. pp. 98–9.

30 In Brownlow, op. cit. (note 24), p. 297.

31 Robert Parsons, *A Defence of the Censure given upon Two Books of William Charke and Meredith Hanmer, which they wrote against Mr Edmund Campion* (Rouen: 1582), p. 8; quoted in Michael Grieves, *Thomas Norton: Parliament Man* (Oxford: Blackwell, 1994), p. 273.

32 Robert Parsons, *An Epistle of the Persecution of Catholics in England* (Douai: 1582), quoted ibid., p. 272.

33 Quoted Elizabeth Hanson, *Discovering the Subject in Renaissance England* (Cambridge: Cambridge University Press, 1998), p. 48.

34 Evelyn Waugh, *Edmund Campion* (London: Longmans and Green, 1935), p. 216; 'Verses made by a Catholic in praise of Campion that was executed at Tyburn for Treason', *The New Oxford Book of Sixteenth Century Verse*, ed. Emrys Jones (Oxford: Oxford University Press, 1991), pp. 332–7, ll. 1 and 148: the poem is now generally attributed to Henry Walpole.

35 Quoted Hanson, op. cit. (note 33), p. 51.

36 Richard Simpson, quoted in Camm, op. cit. (note 27), p. 361.

37 Hanson, op. cit. (note 33), pp. 48 and 53. For the debate about the degree of Jesuit complicity in assassination plots against Elizabeth see, in particular, John Bossy, 'The Heart of Robert Parsons', in Thomas McCoog (ed.), *The Reckoned Expense: Edmund Campion and the Early English Jesuits* (Woodbridge: Boydell Press, 1996), pp. 141–58.

38 Dominique Deslandres, 'The French Jesuits' Missionary World', and Gauvin Bailey, 'Jesuit Catechism and the Arts', in O'Malley et al., op. cit. (note 22), pp. 262 and 391; Thomas Middleton, *A Game at Chess*, 3.1.330; cited in Robert Watson, '*Othello* as Protestant Propaganda', in Claire McEachern and Debora Shuger (eds), *Religion and Culture in Renaissance England* (Cambridge: Cambridge University Press, 1997), p. 247.

39 Stephen Greenblatt, 'Shakespeare Bewitched', in *New Historical Literary Study* (Princeton: Princeton University Press, 1992), pp. 108–35.

40 Thomas Dekker, 'The Whore of Babylon', in Fredson Bowers (ed.), *The Dramatic Works of Thomas Dekker*, 4 vols (Cambridge: Cambridge University Press, 1953–61), vol. 2: 3.1.162–4.

41 Quoted Kernan, op. cit. (note 3), p. 75.

42 Henry Foley (ed.), *Records of the English Province of the Society of Jesus* (6 vols; London: Burns and Oates, 1877), vol. 1, p. 364; Sir Dudley Carleton reported in *Calendar of State Papers: Domestic, 1603–10*, p. 315.

43 Philip Caraman, *Henry Garnet and the Gunpowder Plot* (London: Longmans, 1964), pp. 442–3.

44 Wills, op. cit. (note 10), p. 102.

45 Antonia Fraser, *The Gunpowder Plot: Terror and Faith in 1605* (London: Weidenfeld and Nicolson, 1996), pp. 114–15. For the Stratford nucleus of the Plot see also David Mosler, 'Warwickshire Catholics in the Civil War', *Recusant History*, 15 (1979–81), p 259; R.G. Abrahams, *The Gunpowder Plot in Warwickshire* (Birmingham Archaeological Society: unpublished typescript, 1951), Birmingham Reference Library; E.A. Barnard, *A Seventeenth Century Country Gentleman: Sir Francis Throckmorton* (Cambridge: Cambridge University Press, 1948), p. 2; and Alice Fairfax-Lucy, *Charlecote and the Lucys* (London: Jonathan Cape, 1958), pp. 117–18.

46 Leslie Hotson, *I, William Shakespeare* (London: Jonathan Cape, 1937), pp. 197–8.

47 Sandeep Kaushik, 'Resistance, Loyalty and Recusant Politics: Sir Thomas Tresham and the Elizabethan State', *Midland History*, 21 (1996), pp. 48–9.

48 Frank Huntley, '*Macbeth* and the Background of Jesuitical Equivocation', *PMLA*, 79 (1964), p. 397; Camille Wells Slights, *The Casuistical Tradition in Shakespeare, Donne, Herbert, and Milton* (Princeton: Princeton University Press, 1981), p. 109; and Steven Mullaney, *The Place of the Stage: License, Play, and Power in Renaissance England* (Chicago: Chicago University Press, 1988), p. 128. For the debate on Shakespeare and Jesuit theory see also G.I. Duthie, 'Antithesis in *Macbeth*', *Shakespeare Survey*, 19

(1966), pp. 25–33; David Kaula, 'Hamlet and the Sparing Discovery', Shakespeare Survey, 24 (1971), pp. 71–7; Steven Mullaney, 'Lying Like Truth: Riddle, Representation and Treason in Renaissance England', ELH, 47 (1980), pp. 320–47; and William Scott, 'Macbeth's – And Our – Self-Equivocations', Shakespeare Quarterly, 37 (1986), pp. 160–74.

49 Lawrence Danson, Tragic Alphabet: Shakespeare's Drama of Language (New Haven: Yale University Press, 1974), p. 129. See also Muir, op. cit. (note 3), p. xxiii; G. Wilson Knight, The Imperial Theme (London: Methuen, 1951), p. 153; and Stephen Greenblatt, Hamlet in Purgatory (Princeton: Princeton University Press, 2001), p. 188: 'a rhetorical effect produced again and again in Macbeth, an expression of psychic and social dissociation'.

50 Statutes of the Realm, 3 Jac. I, c. 4 (1606): 'An Act for the discovering and repressing of popish recusants', quoted Marvin Havran, The Catholics in Caroline England (Stanford: Stanford University Press, 1962), p. 13.

51 Quoted Maurus Lunn, 'English Benedictines and the Oath of Allegiance, 1606–1647', Recusant History, 10 (1969), p. 151.

52 Michael Questier, Conversion, Politics and Religion in England, 1580–1625 (Cambrige: Cambridge University Press, 1996), pp. 106–7. For analysis of Catholic reaction to the Plot and the Oath of Allegiance see also John LaRocca, '"Who Can't Pray With Me, Can't Love Me": Toleration and the Early Jacobean Recusancy Policy', Journal of British Studies, 23:2 (1984), pp. 22–36, esp. pp. 31–5; and Alexandra Walsham, Church Papists: Catholicism, Conformity and Confessional Polemic in Early Modern England (Woobridge: Boydell and Brewer, 1993), pp. 84–5.

53 J.J. Bagley, The Earls of Derby, 1485–1985 (London: Sidgwick and Jackson, 1985), p. 55; Barry Coward, The Stanleys, Lords Stanley and Earls of Derby, 1385–1672 (Manchester: Manchester University Press, 1983), p. 144.

54 Bagley, op. cit. (note 53), p. 62.

55 Ibid., p. 56.

56 Quoted Caraman, op. cit. (note 43), pp. 397–8.

57 Richard Hardin, 'The Early Poetry of the Gunpowder Plot: Myth in the Making', English Literary Renaissance, 22:1 (1992), pp. 62–79, esp. pp. 62–3.

58 Roger Manning, Village Revolts: Social Protests and Popular Disturbances in England, 1509–1640 (Oxford: Oxford University Press, 1988), pp. 237–8.

59 John Bossy, The English Catholic Community, 1570–1850 (London: Darton, Longman and Todd, 1975), p. 37.

60 Kaushik, op. cit. (note 47), pp. 37–72.

61 Anne Hughes, 'Warwickshire on the Eve of the Civil War', Midland History, 7 (1982), p. 51.

62 For Sonnet 124 as a critique of the Jesuit martyrs see Richard McCoy, 'Love's Martyrs: Shakespeare's "Phoenix and the Turtle" and the Sacrificial Sonnets', in McEachern and Shuger, op. cit. (note 38), pp. 196–9.

63 Ibid. See also Anne Hughes, 'Religion and Society in Stratford-upon-Avon, 1619–1638', Midland History, 19 (1994), pp. 58–9; Politics, Society and Civil War in Warwickshire, 1620–1660 (Cambridge: Cambridge University Press, 1991), pp. 61–4; and J.M. Martin, 'A Warwickshire Market Town in Adversity: Stratford-upon-Avon in the Sixteenth and Seventeenth Centuries', Midland History, 7 (1982), pp. 26–41.

64 Simpson, op. cit. (note 27), pp. 265–6.

65 For the Catholic context of the Lancashire trials see Lumby, op. cit. (note 6), esp. pp. 119–33.

66 Robert Muchembled, 'Satanic Myths and Cultural Reality', in Bengt Ankarloo and Gustav Heningsen (eds), Early Modern European Witchcraft: Centres and Peripheries (Oxford: Clarendon Press, 1990), pp. 139–40.

67 Lumby, op. cit. (note 6), p. 141.

68 Potts, op. cit. (note 4), p. 81.

69   Quoted Caraman, op. cit. (note 43), pp. 205 and 296. For Thomas Lister's erratic career, see also pp. 91–2, 102, 115, 223–5, 233–4, 247 and 296.

70   Ibid., p. 271. For the careers of John, Robert and Ellis Nutter see Godfrey Anstruther, *The Seminary Priests: A Dictionary of Secular Clergy of England and Wales, 1558–1603* (Durham: Ushaw College, 1964), pp. 258–60.

71   Potts, op. cit. (note 4), p. 153; 'The Arraignment and Trial of Jennet Preston', in Lumby, op. cit. (note 6), p. 169.

72   Rachel Hasted, *The Pendle Witch-Trial, 1612* (Preston: Lancashire County Council, 1987), p. 42.

73   Catalogue of the Cartmel Collection, University of Lancaster.

74   Potts, op. cit. (note 4), p. 84.

75   John Weever, 'Ad Gulielmum Shakespeare', repr. in Ernst Honigmann, *Shakespeare: The 'Lost Years'* (Manchester: Manchester University Press, 1985), pp. 53–4. For the possibility that Shakespeare travelled to Hoghton in the company of Edmund Campion, as a potential Jesuit recruit see Richard Wilson, 'Shakespeare and the Jesuits', *Times Literary Supplement*, 19 December 1997, pp. 11–13.

76   'A Speech made to King James at his coming to Hoghton Tower', in John Nichols, *The Progresses … of James the First* (London: Royal Society of Antiquaries, 1828), pp. 398–9; see also George Miller, *Hoghton Tower* (Preston: Guardian Press, 1948), pp. 83–7.

77   Lumby, op. cit. (note 6), pp. 129–33.

78   Greenblatt, op. cit. (note 39), pp. 114 and 128.

79   'The Burning Babe', in Robert Southwell, *The Poems of Robert Southwell, S.J.*, ed. James McDonald and Nancy Pollard Brown (Oxford: Clarendon Press, 1967), p. 15.

80   Quoted Caraman, op. cit. (note 43), p. 281; Foley, op. cit. (note 42), pp. 414–16 and 497. Martyred in 1601, 'Mistress' Anne Line was canonised in 1970.

9

Voyage to Tunis

New history and the old world
of *The Tempest*

O N 'Hallowmass Night' – 1 November – 1611, according to the Revels
Accounts, 'was presented at Whitehall before the King's Majesty, a play
called *The Tempest*',[1] and, if this was Shakespeare's comedy, the spectators
would have been impressed by the aptness, for All Saints' Day, of a drama of
repentance and forgiveness. From Halloween to All Souls' Day, on 2 November,
the festival of the dead had been retained by the Church of England; yet even
the ambassadors and 'court Catholics' in that first-night audience must also
have been startled by the theological tenor of the play's epilogue, which ends
with what seems to be a heartfelt repetition of the Catholic commemoration of
'the souls of the Faithful Departed, for whose release from purgatory prayers
are at this time offered and masses performed'.[2] For when Prospero begged
them to grant an 'indulgence', they would have heard not just a breach of the
Anglican Thirty-Nine Articles, which condemned the 'Romish Doctrine
concerning purgatory and pardons' as 'a fond thing vainly invented, and
grounded upon no warranty of Scripture',[3] but the most positive affirmation
ever made on an English Renaissance stage of the Catholic belief in the power
of intercessory prayer to the Saints and Virgin: 'Which pierces so that it
assaults / Mercy itself and frees all faults' (Epi, 17–18). This is a play, we
discover, that turns on 'her help, of whose soft grace' and 'sovereign aid'
Prospero rests content (5.1.143). So, as recent commentators have grasped, its
last lines are at once 'a courtly plea to retire from the stage', and 'a religious
plea for prayers, with Shakespeare addressing his audience: "as you English
Protestants would be pardoned for your crimes, let me, as a Catholic, be set free
from temporal punishment and purgatorial confinement by an indulgence"'.[4]
In punning on prayers as 'Praise in departing' (3.3.39), *The Tempest* thus closes
with a clear petition to its Whitehall audience, on the day of the Saints, for an
act of religious toleration. No wonder, then, that this was the moment when
the Puritan hack John Speed attempted to expose the 'petulant poet' as a
'malicious papist', bracketing Shakespeare with the Jesuit Robert Parsons, as by

implication, a fellow-travellor of Catholic treason and an abettor of the Gunpowder Plot.[5] For whether or not this unmasking actually compelled his withdrawal from London, as some have speculated,[6] the last words of his final unaided play do seem to be Shakespeare's own declaration of Catholic faith and appeal for religious reconciliation:

> Now I want
> Spirits to enforce, art to enchant;
> And my ending is despair
> Unless I be relieved by prayer,
> Which pierces so that it assaults
> Mercy itself and frees all faults.
> As you from crimes would pardoned be,
> Let your indulgence set me free.

The recovery of Roman Catholic hopes of emancipation embedded in its plea for 'the help of your good hands' (Epi, 10), has reminded critics of the plausibility of what they long ago discounted as a 'totally spurious' identification of Prospero's story with the dramatist's.[7] Although this comedy has been Americanised on campuses as a tragedy of colonialism in the New World, its imagery of prayer and indulgence connects it to New Place and a retirement in Stratford. These colonial and religious interpretations seem, in fact, to straddle the play's two hemispheres, and it may be that the New Historicist success in relocating *The Tempest* in Virginia has transported it too far from Virgil, and the Old World of Aeneas where its action is set, between Tunis and Naples. For it is now axiomatic that, as Frank Kermode stated in the Arden edition, Shakespeare had America 'in mind' when he wrote his 'Virginian masque', based Ariel's songs on Algonquian dances and intended Caliban 'to be a representative Indian, and Prospero a planter'. Yet this certainty about the American context of *The Tempest* is matched by agnosticism over its European pretext, which seems, Kermode presumed, to have been 'a wedding in 1611 of which we know nothing'. Ever since 1809, when Malone noted analogies with the Jacobean Virginia Company pamphlets, the Americanisation of *The Tempest* has been accompanied by obliviousness towards its festive occasion, typified by Kermode's belief that 'there is no need to imagine such a wedding'. So, though Stephen Orgel's Oxford edition ventured an affinity with King James's dynastic plans, no attempt has been made to explain how these might relate to the Shakespearean *realpolitik* that necessity makes 'strange bedfellows' (2.2.38), or motivate a plot which carries its actors irresistibly *away* from the 'still vex'd Bermoothes' (1.2.129), and towards 'quiet days, fair issue, and long life' in a pastoral English landscape, through the spectacular effects of a firestorm in the Mediterranean, off the Barbary coast of Africa.[8]

'It will be difficult to denote with precision the role played in the age of Philip II by the ill-defined sea between Africa and Sicily, with its deep waters full of fish, its reefs of coral and sponges, and its many islands, often uninhabited because they are so small': Braudel's words in his great history of the Mediterranean suggest a location both mysterious and concrete enough for the setting of *The Tempest*.[9] In fact, Braudel's *Mediterranean* is a reminder that the topography which American critics elide was charged with significance for Shakespeare's audience; and that this intersection of the east–west shipping lane from the Levant to the Atlantic with the north–south axis from Africa to Italy defines Prospero's plea for clemency, and the 'direful spectacle of the wreck' (1.2.26) with which he engineers his revenge, in terms for which the region was infamous: as piracy. In this location, Prospero is that 'gentleman of fortune', a king of the pirates: 'The only fear and terror of the cruel pirates of Argier, / That damned train, the scum of Africa.'[10] Critics efface this elementary fact of maritime law, yet it confirms their insight that Prospero's magic occupies the metaphoric space of gunpowder in the symbolic logic of the play, and it suggests a paradigm for religious and cultural toleration, when he pleads, kneeling beside his own victims, for mercy from the London spectators. For when Ariel 'boarded the King's ship' and 'flamed … the topmast, / The yards and bowsprit' with 'fire and cracks of sulphurous roaring' (1.2.196–200), the most obvious discursive context of this brigandage was not American propaganda but the death sentence decreed by James I for 'carrying munition to Algiers and Tunis', and on pirates who 'commit most foul outrages, murders, spoils and depradations within the Mediterranean, to the great offence of our friends and extreme loss of our merchants'. It was a topical context, moreover, that may explain some of the complexity of *The Tempest*, for, as Braudel writes, the villains of these decrees, issued to protect international shipping from the Barbary corsairs, were English:

> By the end of the sixteenth century the English were everywhere in the Mediterranean, in Moslem or Christian countries … They had two strings to their bow, Islam and Christendom, and fell back on a third – piracy. The English had been pirates from the very beginning and of the worst kind … Their cannons were not merely used to force a passage through the Straits … They were fired indiscriminately at anything considered worth taking – Turkish, French, or Italian, it was all the same to the English.[11]

With the hulk of the burned vessel hidden in harbour, 'The mariners all under hatches stowed' (1.2.230), and the royal passengers held to ransom, the wreck on which Prospero rebuilds his fortune corresponds closely to the marine disasters which set bells tolling in the financial markets in the period of *The Tempest*, when 'insurance rates tell the whole story', as Braudel comments, and in Venice soared to 20 per cent in 1611 and 25 per cent in 1612. Indeed, in the view of historian Alberto Tenenti, it was the irruption of English piracy that precipitated the decline of the Republic, which he dates from about the year 1610 and the sack of galleons such as the 1500-ton *Reniera e Soderina*: abandoned with a cargo valued at £100,000, after its sails had been set on fire with shot, in a blaze, like Ariel's, 'designed to terrify, which succeeded excellently', in the words of the maritime inquest. The commander of that pyrotechnic raid was Jack Ward, who according to John Smith, the Virginia planter, typified the war veterans for whom James I had no use, and who 'turned pirates; some because they became slighted by those that had wealth; some for that they could not get their due; some that had lived bravely and would not abase themselves to poverty; others for revenge'. It was Ward who reputedly introduced gunpowder to Tunis, where he had 'turned Turk', travellers reported, and built a palace, 'with fifteen circumcised English renegades' for servants. Braudel estimates that over three thousand Venetian ships were captured by such buccaneers between 1592 and 1609; but the ethical confusion of such crimes, he believes, was as disturbing as the cost to the insurers. For, as pirate superseded privateer, 'it was not only in Algiers that men hunted each other, sold or tortured their enemies, and became familiar with the miseries and horror of the "concentration camp" world: it was all over the Mediterranean'. So, though it was reckoned that some 466 English ships were hijacked and their crews enslaved in the Berber states between 1609 and 1616, the irony was that they fell victim to a system commanded not by terrorist 'barbarians' – but by Christians such as Prospero.[12]

Power at its most barbaric is everywhere in Braudel's *Mediterranean*, and not limited, as the so-called Barbary Legend would have it, to Islam. 'What kind of history have we been taught', he asks in the acid style of his protégé, Foucault, 'that these acts, familiar to seamen of all nationalities, should seem so astonishing?'[13] It is a question that helps to situate those successive deeds of enslavement and liberation which propel the plot of *The Tempest*, from the moment when Sycorax employs techniques perfected in Algiers to 'confine' Ariel 'By help of her more potent ministers … Into a cloven pine' (1.2.274–9). For, like Marlowe in *The Jew of Malta* and *Dido Queen of Carthage*, Shakespeare highlights what political correctness occludes, that to sail to the Ottomon regencies of Algiers, Tripoli and Tunis was to traffic in an entire economy driven by the *corso* (or lottery) of the slave market, and run, as Stephen Clissold has detailed in *The Barbary Slaves*, for the lucrative turnover of capture and ransom. Prospero's exacting negotiations to free Ariel, Caliban, Ferdinand, his aristocratic hostages, and finally the crewmen, belong precisely to this calibrated business of redemption, which confounded Eurocentrism by revolving not on the enslavement of Africans (who were in fact employed as 'more potent ministers' or guards) but on the bondage of Europeans, captured both on the high seas and in slaving raids on Naples, Provence or the Canaries, and even, in 1627, on Iceland. Thus, in 1631, 237 peasants, including women and children, seized from Baltimore in Ireland, were auctioned in Algiers; and the redemptionist priest Pierre Dan estimated that at the time of *The Tempest* over a million Europeans, ranging from Portuguese to Russians, had tasted slavery, in a white slave population of twenty-five thousand at Algiers and seven thousand at Tunis. Speaking pidgin, this huge mass of captives was packed into labour camps, according to the imprisoned Father Gracian in 1593, 'like silk worms waiting to be hatched', under the eye of pashas who often took Christian wives.[14] Such was the cycle, then, into which Shakespeare's Neapolitans traded 'the King's fair daughter Claribel', to be one of the wives of the Bey of Tunis, and out of which came Caliban, bastard son of Sycorax, a 'blue-eyed' Algerine slave-owner (2.1.70; 1.2.269). So, as Prospero prepares to ' manacle' the neck and feet of his prize hostage, Prince Ferdinand (462), the chain forms a link in that grim nexus which bound captive and captor together across the Mediterranean, as when:

> A redemptionist father returned to Leghorn [Livorno] from a mission to Tunis just as a shipload of captured Moslems was brought in. They were Tunisians, and amongst them the Christian ex-slaves recognised some who had been their own masters. Some of the ex-captives jeered over this sudden turn of fortune. But others were filled with fear at the sight of their old masters. They could not believe that they were free. These victims had lost their chains, but still bore the brand of slavery: 'Your turn today, mine, perhaps, tomorrow.'[15]

'It was mine art, / When I arrived and heard thee, that made gape / The pine and let thee out': though he threatens to 'peg' Ariel in oak fetters until he 'hast howled away twelve winters' (1.2.291–3), Prospero's intervention in the Mediterranean slave economy is evidently far less that of a colonist than that of a redemptor. The ambiguity of this role can be glimpsed from the story of one of the most famous hostages, Miguel de Cervantes, captured by corsairs in 1575 on a voyage, like that of Shakespeare's courtiers, from Naples. Enslaved in Algiers for five years, Cervantes plotted four mass escapes before being ransomed by redemptionists, but was compromised by his sexual liaisons with a Moorish woman and his master, Hassan Pasha, an Islamicised Venetian pirate. These experiences inspired both the 'carefully shaded picture of relationships between Christians and infidels' in his play *Life in Algiers* and the sympathetic portrait of the typical renegade in *Don Quixote* as 'morally a good man, who treated his captives with much humanity'.[16] It is not necessary to imagine, as Spanish critics do, an actual meeting between the novelist and dramatist (who died on the same day) to see how this Cervantine empathy with 'the drama of the tens of thousands lost in the clash of civilizations' might inspire Shakespeare's referral of his own hopes for religious freedom back to the redemptionists of 'Argier' (261), and events following the ironic banishment of the false priestess Sycorax from the metropolis of slavery. In 1609 Cervantes would join a redemptionist confraternity of ex-slaves; but in England the instant legacy of this liberated prisoner was a new genre of pirate plays inspired by his example, with titles such as *A Christian Turn'd Turk*, invoking not the barbarity of Islam but the reversibility of slaves and masters. For when the Spanish writer ended his comedy with a chorus of ransomed captives praying for pardon, he broke 'the conventions of a Manichean universe that would oppose good and bad', according to a recent biographer, by staging his own belief in 'the ambiguity of the exchanges transacted between Chistendom and Islam'.[17] This was a relativism unprecedented in Renaissance theatre, so it may not be chance that Shakespeare's next commission should be to adapt a story from *Don Quixote* – *Cardenio* – at the behest of the Catholic Howard faction. For it was a truly Cervantine identification with the cultural and religious Other which would be crucial to Prospero's traffic with the Barbary slaves and slavers:

> Two of these fellows you
> Must know and own. This thing of darkness I
> Acknowledge mine.
>
> (5.1.275–7)

Though it was the American navy which helped put an end to white slavery, after the Algerians overreached themselves, in the 1800s, with raids on Boston shipping, post-colonial critics forget that for three centuries it was the *escape* from Islam and the seraglio that formed the shaping narrative of orientalism. And in England this originated, through popularisation of the exploits of Catholic travellers such as the Shirley brothers, as a myth of enfranchisement that spoke to hopes of religious emancipation. It may be telling, therefore, that in *The Tempest* there is no release from the underworld for its Persephone-figure, Claribel. As Dominique Mannoni commented in a momentous study of the psychology of colonialism, *Prospero and Caliban*, 'The colonial situation is portrayed in *The Tempest* more clearly than in *Robinson Crusoe*', as one of interdependence between the colonised and coloniser.[18] So, if Mannoni's work is not much quoted by New Historicists, that may be because it depicts slave and slave-trader as mutually incarcerating. Yet reoriented towards its actual Mediterranean context, and away from an American agenda, the cries of Prospero's captives for 'Freedom, highday!' and 'release from my bands' (2.2.181; 5.1.327), seem more keyed to the early modern discourse of redemption, with its Catholic missions and Jewish brokers, than to the later, anachronistic discourse of plantation colonialism. Certainly, its final spectacle of sailors freed with 'roaring, shrieking, howling, jingling chains' (233), has its nearest analogue in those carnivalesque processions of ransomed hostages that danced through European cities in the age of the white slave trade, in France as late as 1785. And it is in this quest for escape and repatriation that Shakespeare's comedy departs most from the Virginia pamphlets, with their commitment to a westward domination. Here, as even New Historicism concedes, 'Prospero's Mediterranean isle steadfastly resists the colonial analogy', since his prisoners 'had been travelling east; had been trying to go home, and do go home in the end'.[19] They do so, moreover, in exchange for the pardon of their captor, whose own liberty and restoration is thereby made conditional on their emancipation. In July 1611 James I did indeed grant English Mediterranean pirates a pardon on condition they released their victims and returned hijacked ships as 'bravely rigged as when [they] first put out to sea' (224). That one of them, Peter Easton, chose to remain 'a king himself', and was promptly made a marquis by the Duke of Savoy, says a lot about the dynastic chess-board of Shakespeare's Mediterranean. But that Prospero does realise the wishful-thinking fantasy of a contemporary ballad about the glorious homecoming of Jack Ward also suggests how much was now at stake in London:

> Strike up, ye lusty gallants, with music loud and drum,
> For we have descry'd a rover upon the sea is come ...
> For he hath sent unto our king, the sixth of January,
> Desiring that he might come back in, with all his company;
> 'And if you king will let me come, till I may tale hath told,
> I will bestow for ransom full thirty ton of gold.
> Go tell the King of England, go tell him this from me,
> If he reign king of all the land, I will reign king at sea.'[20]

'Thy dukedom I resign, and do entreat / Thou pardon me my wrongs' (5.1.118–19): the ironic reversal of king and outlaw on which *The Tempest* ends can be keyed precisely to the transformation of English policy during the period of its rehearsal, when the promise of a free pardon was repeated with increasing urgency as an essential component of the diplomacy surrounding the Shakespearean occasion. For it was not coincidence that the specific problem of Mediterranean piracy had been staged earlier in London, when the young Prince Henry was saluted as Prince of Wales by the Lord Mayor in a sea pageant that climaxed, on 6 June 1610, with pyrotechnics designed to represent a merciless military solution. Antony Munday's text, *London's Love to Prince Henry*, shipped a 'worthy fleet of citizens' on to the Thames to enact a water-fight in which 'A Turkish Pirate, prowling the Seas to find a booty', raked a flotilla of unarmed merchant vessels with 'shot upon shot very fiercely', until 'two men of war made in to help', and 'after a long and well fought skirmish', in which 'divers men were hurled over into the Sea ... proved too strong for the Pirate', whose flagship was finally blown up with 'a whole batttery of rare and admirable fireworks'.[21] Preceded by allegorical tableaux in which the 'deformed sea-shapes' of a dolphin and whale were changed into Amphion and the nymph Corinea, to bring greetings from Wales and Cornwall, this bellicose display was sponsored by the mercantile Protestant lobby around Prince Henry, to publicise the need for armed convoys to protect English shipping from the 'spoil and rapine' of the Mediterranean freebooters; so it was all the more pointed that when Shakespeare set his scene with an act of gunpowder piracy on the same high seas, it was as an overture to a comedy of marine salvage. *The Tempest* has been connected with Munday's romance *Primaleon*, featuring escape from another Enclosed Isle;[22] but Shakespeare's revision of the belliger-ent Lord Mayor's show suggests a still more urgent dialogue between the court playwright and the priest-hunting City propagandist. And the topicality of Prospero's benign metamorphosis of imperialist firepower is only amplified by new research which suggests that the very costumes worn by Richard Burbage and John Rice of the King's Men, in their roles as Amphion and Corinea, were recycled for Ariel and Caliban.[23] Shakespeare was generating a comedy of sea-changes, it appears, out of some very 'fishlike' yet 'marketable' material (2.2.26; 5.1.266).

A Renaissance prince, 'for the liberal arts / Without a parallel', who forfeits the title of 'prime duke' to his rapacious family through absorption in 'secret studies'; is hurried into exile accompanied only by a young girl; plots revenge with his books and 'brave utensils'; arms a roving strikeforce to hijack 'the King's ship'; confronts his hostages in ducal robes to demand his restoration; but agrees to break his 'staff' and retire to his library in return for his property and reprieve (1.2.71–7, 110, 224; 5.1.310): Prospero's story has been banalised as an American colonial prospectus, but belongs just as much to the orientalism of the Arabian Nights. In fact, it is the circumstances of its first recorded performance that offer the best clue to its narrative of persecution and pardon, though the occasion has been ignored in favour of a later date in 1613, when the comedy was restaged to mark the wedding of Princess Elizabeth to the Elector Palatine. No one has ever considered the implications of what may have been its original context: one of feverish negotiations over the proposed marriage of the Protestant prodigy, Prince Henry, to Caterina, the daughter of the Catholic Grand Duke Ferdinand of Tuscany. Yet Prospero's plot to regain his dukedom does coincide with the Tuscan motives for this ecumenical match, which were to restore the independence of Milan, whose usurping Duke was actually Philip III, and to blockade Naples, the other Italian city under Spanish occupation. In 1610 Henri IV of France had been about to liberate Milan by arms when he was assassinated; and it was to sustain his anti-Spanish league thar his Stuart namesake now acquiesced in a Medici alliance. In August 1611 portraits were exchanged; in September the bride won freedom of worship in consideration of a dowry of 600,000 crowns; on 21 October the Medici envoy gloated how the English Catholics were rejoicing that 'the prince now turns to Tuscany for a bride'; and a week later *The Tempest* was performed.[24] It cannot be chance, therefore, that the hopes of Catholic toleration depended at that moment on a pardon offered to an exiled English duke whose story was precisely that of Prospero's.

'He was a person of great learning and parts', recorded the Warwickshire antiquarian, William Dugdale, 'of stature tall and comely, strong, valiant, and famous at the art of tilting, singularly skilled in all Mathematical Learning, but chiefly in Architecture and Navigation, a rare Chemist and of great knowledge in Physic'. To Antony Wood he was the 'most complete gentleman, an exact seaman, good navigator, and excellent architect'; but Horace Walpole ironised that 'considering how enterprising and dangerous a minister he might have been, and what talents were called forth by his misfortunes, it would seem to have been happy both for this duke and his country that he was unjustly deprived of the honours to which his birth gave him pretensions'.[25] Don

Roberto Dudleo, as he styled himself, Duca di Northumbria, was the son of Elizabeth's great favourite, the Earl of Leicester, by Douglas Howard, the sister of the Earl of Nottingham, and grandson of the Northumberland who lost his head and dukedom for installing his daughter-in-law, Lady Jane Grey, as Queen. His claim to the lost dukedom was formally recognised by the Holy Roman Emperor in 1620, as much for 'his knowledge and rare ingenious inventions', it was said, as his blood; but when he burst into Tuscany in 1607 he announced himself to the Grand Duke with the title. He was first in a position to 'require' his dukedom – as Prospero does (132) – in 1611, because it was he who was then charged with the critical task of securing the papal indulgence for a Medici to marry the heretic Protestant Prince. Through the offices of a 'good old lord' (5), Sir Thomas Challoner, Prince Henry's Chamberlain, who had tutored them both and was 'the chief foundation of the match', Dudley thus found his zenith dependent on 'a most auspicious star', which he could either court or let his fortunes 'ever after droop' (1.2.181–4).[26] Editors have long inferred some link between *The Tempest* and Prince Henry, eulogised in stellar imagery by poets such as Drayton for his naval and colonial ambitions; but it is Dudley's role in these interdenominational plans that suggests how fraught and tortuous a commission this performance may have been. For what made this pretend duke suddenly so indispensable to hopes of religious reconciliation was his prominence not only as England's most illustrious Catholic exile but as the most enterprising of all the Mediterranean pirates.

'We granted you leave to travel', King James thundered, 'in the hope that you might thereby prove of service to our State. We now understand that you bear yourself inordinately, attempting many things prejudicial to our Crown, which we cannot suffer to endure'. Dudley had caused a sensation in 1605 by abandoning his wife and eloping to France with a teenage maid of the Queen – Elizabeth Southwell, a niece of the Jesuit martyr – in fury at failure to prove his legitimacy in a manic Star Chamber trial. From Lyons, where Elizabeth 'gave out she hath a purpose to put herself into some religious house', and 'They were both reconciled to the Church and went lovingly to Mass together every morning', the couple sailed to Pisa in a small boat, with just two servants and £80, it was reported (though Dudley had transferred £40,000 into his Italian account). In Tuscany, however, Ferdinand instantly made the émigré overseer of the Medici shipyards, on the strength of his expertise as a 'nephew of three Grand Admirals of England', and the brother-in-law of Hakluyt, the explorer, and Cavendish, the circumnavigator.[27] The first warship built to his design, the *John the Baptist*, was launched in March 1608, in time to ambush the Turkish treasure fleet, and 'with but little help', he boasted, 'capture 9 vessels, 700 prisoners, and jewels valued at two million ducats'. At Dudley's instigation the Grand Duke then began to 'entice English mariners and shipwrights into his service', Sir Henry Wotton relayed, buy 'ordinance from English ships and take English pirates under his protection', until his 'fleet consisted principally of English sailors'. One of these 'sailors corrupted from religion and allegiance' was the corsair, Ward, whom James condemned in January 1609, as it became clear that Dudley, declared a rebel to his face by the English envoy, planned to rig a blockade between Tunis and Livorno, which he had fortified.[28] This private war of revenge would eventually lead the renegade to secure a total papal embargo on English trade, 'by reason of the unjust occupation and confiscation of his Dukedom'; but its targets were obvious from 1608, when he equipped an expedition to the Caribbean, manned with English prisoners and 'commanded to those parts by order of the Grand Duke Ferdinand, his lord'.[29] They were his Rich and Sidney cousins, the Protestant rivals who had stolen his birthright by contesting his legitimacy, and, as projectors of the Bermuda and Virginia Companies, were changing America into something 'rich and strange' (1.2.402) for England.[30]

In Dudley's six-volume treatise published in 1646 as the *Arcano del Mare*, pride of place goes to the maps the 'Duke' had engraved; and of these, the one that prompts most pride is the chart of Trinidad drawn for the 1608 expedition, by means of which, 'and instructions in the author's own hand, the Captain went and returned prosperously, and although he had never been to the West Indies before, yet he achieved his voyage without loss'. Dedicated to Ferdinand, and decorated with seamonsters and a cartouche framing the Medici arms and Dudley's title above a tribe of natives, this Mannerist map provides a perfect analogue of the overdetermined text of *The Tempest*, with its inscription of English and Italian politics on to a New World geography and people: 'who were of those Caribs who eat human flesh', a note advised, 'six of whom were presented to their Highnesses in Florence', though but 'one survived, who afterwards served for some years the Cardinal Medici, and learned to speak the Italian tongue passably well'.[31] Like the designs for cannon which Dudley smuggled him, the chart illustrates those 'secret studies' which drew Henry to the 'Duke' despite their religious differences, and on the basis of which which the exile himself 'entertained no small hopes of returning to England by means of the Prince's favour', so Dudley Carleton attested, 'to be employed in some special charge about the King's navy'.[32] And it suggests a new source for Shakespeare's passage to America via Tunis, being projected from Dudley's own expedition of 1594, when he had himself explored the Orinoco Delta a few weeks before Raleigh, and even named an island of his own (depicted in the centre), Dudleana. In 1600 he summarised this adventure for the *Voyages* of his brother-in-law Richard Hakluyt; but the secret log kept for Robert Cecil by an officer, Abram Kendal, was never published, presumably because its depressing realism would have upstaged Raleigh's optimistic self-promotion. It records, for instance, how, having claimed Trinidad for the Queen, the fleet suffered a violent tempest off 'the Bermudes: a climate so far differing from the nature of all others, that we might think ourselves happiest when furthest from it'. One of his few biographers, James Pope-Hennessy, wonders what impact

Dudley's voyage had on writers, such as his cousin, the Countess of Pembroke at Wilton, where he stayed after his return.[33] In fact, Leicester's son would earn most immediate fame fighting at Cadiz in the *Nonpareil*; but what resonates with *The Tempest* is his ordeal off 'the still vex'd Bermoothes' (229), in a boat named after the Dudley emblem, the *Ragged Staff*:

> For often before we have had dangerous gusts ... but these were ever ordinary and their dangers still extraordinary, their dreadful flashing of lightning, the horrible claps of thunder, the monstrous raging of the swelling seas forced up into the air by the outrageous winds, all together conspiring in a moment our destruction and breathing out, as it were, in one breath the very blast of our confusion, so that, this being of all seafaring men delivered of a verity, hell is no hell in comparison to these Bermudes. But at last when we expected nothing less than the splitting of sails, breaking of shrouds, spending of masts, spring-ing of planks – in a word, the dreadful devouring of us all by some sea-swallowing whirlpool – we were most miraculously delivered ... Thus as men prepared for God, always leading our lives as if we should die hourly, we passed on forward of our course towards the islands of the Flowers [Azores] with a most forseeable wind, sailing between the Bermudes and these islands with an incredible swiftness.[34]

Editors have tracked the origin of the tornado in *The Tempest* to William Strachey's *True Report of the Wreck*, reporting the salvage of the 1609 Virginia convoy off Bermuda, which the dramatist is presumed to have read in manuscript; but, as Kenneth Muir objects, 'There is hardly a shipwreck in fiction' that does not itemise exactly the same catalogue of wind and wreckage.[35] The Virginia pamphlets, which declare themselves tragi-comedy, read like an invitation to guaranteed financial disaster. By comparison, Dudley's logbook may be a corrective to Raleigh's Eldorado, but what characterises it is its Eliza-bethan faith in a happy ending, imaged in the metaphor of the 'never-surfeited sea' belching survivors (3.3.55). The log of his expedition may have confirmed the news that his discoveries were 'still vex'd' by hurricanes that were 'ever ordinary and their dangers still extraordinary', but it was surely the contrast between the Jacobean fiasco and its Elizabethan precursor that recommended Dudley, therefore, as a Prospero to London investors. It was he, after all, who had recently promoted the Levant trade by persuading Ferdinand to declare Livorno a free port, 'exceedingly open to all points of the compass', in the words of another famous Catholic explorer, Robert Shirley.[36] And if this Promethean inventor had tamed the elements, it was because, like Prospero, he had conjured his fire-power from an Isle of Devils, as Bermuda was called, where he had outfaced what the log describes as 'a substance resembling a fiery dragon, which fell into our sails and upon deck, passing from place to place, ready to set all on fire'. As he plotted revenge on his family by piloting a royal wedding, the banished 'Duke' must indeed have seemed uncannily blessed by 'this warning messenger, which vanished without any harm done unto our ships or our company', which was 'not so strange as true'. Strachey's report on

St Elmo's Fire for the Virginia Company, on which the characterisation of Ariel may draw, in fact echoes the older text, though without its belief that the fire 'foretelleth some great thing to come'. Since Cecil was a key promoter of the Medici marriage, however, it seems as likely that Shakespeare had access to both manuscripts, and followed Dudley, now at a climacteric in his war against his usurpers, in greeting the aerial message as propitious:[37]

> At this hour
> Lies at my mercy all mine enemies.
> Shortly shall all my labours end, and thou
> Shalt have the air at freedom.
>   (4.1.263–66)

Prospero's promise of liberty to Ariel has always seemed to underwrite what Stephen Greenblatt calls the 'magic of art', which 'resides in the freedom of the imagination' from the discourses of power. Thus, Ariel's capacity 'to fly, / To swim, to dive into the fire, to ride / On the curl'd clouds' (1.2.190–2), figures for Greenblatt the plenitude of the aesthetic space, which so transcends all 'coercion, discipline, and pardon', that 'it doesn't matter whether the story "really" happened'.[38] But what if, as Dudley's logbook hints, the fiery demon of devil's island was indeed an avatar of gunpowder, and Prospero identifiable as that very 'prince of power' (55) who had done most, according to the Tuscan envoy, to release English crewmen and firepower into the Mediterranean from Barbary and Bermuda?[39] The episode that follows the tempest in the log begs just such a question about the relation of dramatic text to context, when it records how Dudley inspired his gunners during a battle in the Atlantic by staging a scene from *The Spanish Tragedy* on the burning deck, and how, after reciting 'those verses of old Hieronymo', he rewarded his page with a rifle, to replace one that 'by charging and recharging, brake about his ears', and a wounded sailor with the 'promise of an alms room in his hospital at Warwick'.[40] What Greenblatt calls the 'unresolvable doubleness' of Prospero's isle, as a site of both art and empire, was evidently the very element of this pretender, whose hope of pardon from King James was based partly on his close friendship with Galileo, and readiness to divulge 'the discoveries revealed in his telescope'.[41] Like Shakespeare's magus, this heir apparent could both reach for airy nothing in the stars, in Greenblatt's terms, and at the same moment manipulate wretches who clung to 'barren ground, long heath, brown furze' (1.1.66), or a bed in Warwick's Hospital. So, whether or not his seafaring did inspire *The Tempest*, Roberto's grand scheme to reclaim his title does suggest how much of the play's vision of plenitude, of 'barns and garners never empty' (4.1.111), might have been prompted, as Greenblatt senses, by the 'want, craving, and absence' of real estate and of actual material possession.[42]

Diplomatic correspondence from the time of *The Tempest* is punctuated by signals in which the disgraced 'Duke' promises London that in return for restoration of his title and a pardon he will 'deliver all' to the Royal Navy in both the Caribbean and the Mediterranean: 'calm seas, auspicious gales, / And sail so expeditious that shall catch / Your royal fleet far off' (5.1.313–16). Thus, he pledges that 'Though unknown to him, he rejoices in zeal for the King's service, and wishes to be an instrument of good for his country'. Like Shakespeare's wizard, Roberto riddles that 'Though the matter, by its great importance, may seem strange and difficult' to his correspondents, it is vital 'to the security of England. He has had long study and practice and can perform what he offers.' He makes these overtures, he protests, 'out of pure loyalty, having received too many discourtesies from his friends and kindred, the greatest persons in the kingdom, to desire his return'; but he will, as earnest, 'gladly make of use to his country' his own invention of a new type of battleship, 'of such extraordinary force and swiftness that no three of the King's ships could stand against it'.[43] What most concerns ministers, however, is Dudley's part in incidents such as the one reported on 11 July 1611, when 'Certain merchants of London', *en route* between Tunis and Naples, 'are taken off Sicily by English pirates', who now have '40 ships and 2,000 men at their place of rendezvous in Barbary' ready to help him enforce the blockade.[44] For, as the English agents suspected and historians confirm, from Africa the 'English pirates headed for [Livorno] with their plunder and sold it', and 'goods arrived there in abundance' once Dudley had organised the gigantic clearing-houses 'for such booty which emerged by 1610'. Thus, in October 1614, 'two English pirate ships presented the Grand Duke with a gift of slaves' in return for berthing no fewer than nine galleons laden with spoils. According to Tenenti, it was this clearing system, devised and orchestrated by Dudley, which first transformed Mediterranean piracy into a multinational business; so prospects would have looked alarming when in 5 October 1611 the Privy Council minuted that 'The pirates refuse pardon and are gone to Florence there to be commanded by Sir Robert Dudley'.[45] What London required most urgently from this papist sorcerer, evidently, was exactly the reassurance about its vanished crews and cargoes that Prospero gives Miranda:

> Have comfort.
> The direful spectacle of the wreck, which touched
> The very virtue of compassion in thee,
> I have with such provision of mine art
> So safely ordered that there is no soul,
> No, not so much perdition as an hair
> Betid to any creature in the vessel
> Which thou heard'st cry, which thou saw'st sink.
> (1.2.25–32)

Editors have long concluded, as does Anne Barton, that any connection between the plot of *The Tempest*, with 'its emphasis upon the sea, upon loss and recovery, travel, chastity, parents and children', and the performance 'at Court on Hallowmass 1611 is likely to remain a mystery';[46] yet at least one member of the audience that night had been primed to decipher the topicality of this bizarre combination of marine and sexual politics. He was the Venetian ambassador, who reported on 19 July that with 'the goods plundered from English vessels sold at [Livorno] … many see the only remedy in the marriage of the Tuscan woman to the Prince of Wales'.[47] Venetian despatches in fact offer a sardonic commentary on the cynicism of Shakespeare's audience, as they reveal that while the prospect of this Catholic match was 'generally loathed' in England, the marriage and pardon were urged as necessities by the 'merchants who have been plundered', and specifically by leaders of the Levant Company.[48] They literally *reorient* the play, therefore, within a struggle that has been analysed by Robert Brenner: the contest between an emergent American lobby, led by Puritan adventurers such as Robert Rich and Robert Sidney, and the East India establishment, chaired by grandees such as Dudley's uncles, the Catholic Earls of Nottingham and Northampton. Thus, though the King 'said he would never pardon' Dudley or his pirates, the despatches reported that 'the avarice of Northampton', and 'interests of some great minister [Cecil]', combined to 'place obstacles in his way'.[49] And they confirm that it was Dudley, in concert with his Howard relations, who first prompted the marriage, 'by means of letters to the Prince's Chamberlain (Challoner)', expressly 'to remove difficulty about the pirates, and grant them a port where they can bring goods without taxation, which would cause [Livorno] to flourish'. So, if this exiled 'Duke' was one model for Prospero, he lived up to the name, since, as Queen Anne let slip, 'the quantity of gold passing into the hands of private individuals' in London 'amounted to a million pounds' in bribes. No wonder that the Prince 'lent his authority to this scheme, and wished to see the mariners of his kingdom augmented by those seeking refuge' at Livorno; nor that the King himself 'now condoned past crimes and turned his attention to sharing the piratical loot'. As spies counted the numbers of trees felled for Dudley's ships and pirates he converted to Rome, the only mystery in the autumn of 1611 was whether this Midas would accept a pardon or be tempted after all 'to enter the service of the King of Spain', since, as the Venetian envoy wrote in August:

> The interested parties have begged a pardon, but as the pirates have already made great plunder, there is a doubt whether they will accept the conditions under which it has been obtained. If they do not, seeing that there a number of very rich ships making now for London, which cannot escape the ambuscades, this market will receive a very severe shock, and nor will the royal ships which they may send out be sufficient, for they cannot be in every place at once.[50]

'Now does my project gather to a head. / My charms crack not, my spirits obey, and time / Goes upright in his carriage' (5.1.1–3): if timing is the essence of Prospero's plot, that may be because so many returns were contingent, at the hour of *The Tempest*, on the marriage it heralded; not least for the Howards, whose sponsorship, through the Lord Chamberlain, the Earl of Suffolk, may have been instrumental in its composition. As early as 1607 the Grand Duke had signalled to Northampton how he had allowed Dudley to settle in Tuscany, 'in the religion he has so far observed … the more willingly for his relationship to you, and extended him the affection I have for you'. So from the day of his arrival in Italy the fate of the exile was keyed to Howard fortunes, as Ferdinand had implied when he told the Earl that, 'As he regards you as a father, I would ask you to treat him as your son and keep him in the good graces of the king'.[51] The fact that Dudley was the actual son of Leicester, the Howards' old enemy, could only have recommended him for such adoption, and Northampton was eager to administer his estates. This papist heir of a Puritan hero personified Howard's own strategy of religious conciliation; while his reputation as a Florentine magus had particular resonance for a statesman who liked to surround himself with icons of sybils and hermits, or present himself at court dressed as the arch-magician and wise man, Merlin. Secret knowledge was irresistible to Northampton, Linda Levy Peck has shown, 'whether in the form of astrology, of Jesuitical doctrines, or of the *arcana imperii*'; so it is no wonder that at the time of *The Tempest* Dudley should have been told by Challoner that it was only 'through my Lord Northampton's especial care (as I may term it)', that he had 'received the life' of his inheritance, which through 'debts and other intricacies was ready to perish'. Northampton had contrived the return of numerous Catholic exiles in the 1600s; but, if this émigré was his favoured beneficiary, that was because Dudley's repatriation would have been a triumph for the Howards.[52] Roberto's homecoming would have clinched a story that had become the defining narrative, Alison Shell argues, for homesick Catholics in the age of Shakespeare.[53] So it must have seemed like poetic justice for Northampton to divert a portion of the bonanza that poured from Florence through the hands of his business manager, Lionel Cranfield, into the funding of a play which staged that very romance.

At the end of his career, recorded John Ward, Vicar of Stratford, in 1661, Shakespeare 'had an allowance so large' that 'he spent at the rate of £1000 a year, as I have heard';[54] and it may have been at the time of *The Tempest*, and the fantastic sums accompanying its original performance, that stories of the dramatist's colossal wealth began to do the rounds. Certainly, it would be odd if some of the Tuscan booty distributed by the Howard faction to smooth the wedding preparations did not go to reward those charged with managing the entertainment. In any event, it should have been a highly receptive audience that heard Prospero's appeal to be neither sentenced to exile nor 'sent to Naples' to stand trial (5.1.323). For though a royal navy squadron would have to be despatched to the Mediterranean to rescue the fifteen hundred English sailors enslaved there in 1620, at the instant of *The Tempest* Roberto's power was so comparable to Prospero's that he could indeed offer to Prince Henry's mediator, Edward Cecil, to trade their lives. And in the marriage negotiations, where the entreaties of his Catholic uncles, and even a secret letter from the Queen professing Roman Catholicism, failed to move the Pope, the most famous English convert, suspected of complicity in the Gunpowder Plot, might yet secure the essential indulgence. Three weeks after Shakespeare's play was acted, at any rate, having had his crime mitigated from treason to contempt, Dudley signed a contract with Henry drafted to expedite his pardon: the sale for a song of the mansion he had forfeited when 'proclaimed a rebel', to house the newly weds. This deal saved the property from his grasping cousins; but in a memorandum the 'Duke' set it on record that 'no motive induced him to pass so rich a castle at so low a price, except to give satisfaction for contempt ... as Prince Henry was so confident the King would pardon the contempt, he sent to make a pardon ready for the King to grant it'.[55] We can guess that Shakespeare had wind of this contract when he ended his play with Prospero's hope of an 'indulgence' to set him free, for the castle in question, where bride and groom were indeed intended to spend 'Hourly joys' amid 'bosky acres' (4.1.81; 108), was none other than Kenilworth: Leicester's 'gorgeous palace' (152) in Warwickshire.

'Our revels now are ended' (148): if the banishment of Don Roberto did influence *The Tempest*, it was apt that a voyage to Trinidad via Tunis should come full circle at Kenilworth, where young Shakespeare is supposed to have 'heard a mermaid on a dolphin's back', and to have seen the badge of bear and ragged staff worn by Leicester's players. But though the heir to Kenilworth rose to be Chamberlain to the Medici, and to devise some of their most brilliant masques, he never justified Drayton's hopes, in a 1593 dedication, to be the patron of English drama. Nor did he ever flaunt in England the finery he designed for himself as Grand Master of his own Caesarean Order.[56] A year after *The Tempest* was performed, he was still awaiting pardon when he wrote to remind the Prince how he had sold 'Kenilworth for a small matter, only reserving to myself the Constableship of the Castle, so I may have some command there whenever I happen to be in England'. With this letter went a tome arguing that 'Whoever is patron of the sea commands the land', but, before they arrived, Henry suddenly died, and with him the mercy for which the Don had bargained to break his ducal staff and abjure his rough piratic powers. Long ago he had lost Essex House and Warwick Castle to his cousins; but his failure to win the papal indulgence for the 'sun-rising' on which he 'fastened all his hopes' cost him the last of his 'cloud-capped towers' (152). Thus, amid 'the lamentations of many gentlemen now at Florence who were the Prince's servants', and the desolation of the English envoy, who 'had all his mirth marred', when he 'appeared like a comet, in crimson velvet and gold', and 'expected as much feasting and entertainment' as among the pirates of Naples, the player-duke returned to the slave trade to 'outride his sorrow';[57] while his cousins pillaged the New World to buy the earldoms he claimed of Warwick and Leicester. Such is the narrative of empire and bondage that New Historicism projects from *The Tempest*; but, restored to its Old World archives, Shakespeare's gunpowder plot also pleads for liberty and pardon. So, while Americans may be right to transpose the play to Virginia, Europeans can respond that had Milan been liberated, and Prospero retired to his library in Warwickshire, one of the many titles restored 'in one voyage' (5.1.208) would have been Dudley's lost Lordship of the Manor of Stratford-upon-Avon.

'In this worthy enterprise of bringing two hemispheres into one world', trumpeted the publisher of Dudley's *Arcano del Mare*, 'if one man is more eminent than others, it this Duke of Northumberland, who, to make himself master of marine science, tore himself away from the great House where he had princely birth, and sacrificed full forty years in unveiling the mighty secrets of the sea'.[58] 'No source has been discovered for the plot of *The Tempest*', Muir regrets;[59] but it seems improbable that Shakespeare was unaware of the role played by this global impresario in the actual circumstances of the play's commission, or the story of his life, which must certainly have taken the ears of Statford 'strangely' (313). For like Prospero, Don Roberto had grown a stranger to his Midland estate long before his expulsion, by 'being transported / And rapt in secret studies' (1.2.76–7), such as the planning of the 1597 Islands Voyage, which sailed west with 'A Commendation by Her Majesty to the Great Emperor of China', Hakluyt stated, 'principally at the charge of the Honourable Sir Robert Dudley'. And, like Shakespeare's dethroned magician, the discoverer of Dudleana had literally found his dukedom 'in a poor isle' (5.1.212), after being thrust from his palace by a treacherous family conspiracy: 'through forcible entry', the Sheriff of Warwickshire deposed, 'by servants of the Countess of Leicester on the Castle of Kenilworth, then in the sole and quiet possession of Mr. Robert Dudley'. 'Hurried aboard' the *Nonpareil* in 'dead of darkness' (1.2.130; 144), with his young companion disguised as a pageboy, Roberto had indeed been supplied by his old tutor, Challoner, with volumes he prized 'above his dukedom' (168), and that today line the Florentine Natural History Museum, beside his astrolabe and apparatus 'to find the ebb and flow of tides'. So, whether or not Prospero's magic does allude to those black arts with which the Warwickshire seadog 'set roaring war' in the sky between Tunis and Naples, it seems unlikely that the circle which he draws to compass 'the ebbing Neptune' (5.1.35–44) was imagined in total ignorance of the work for which Dudley was hailed in his own day as 'the world's wonder': the study of 'scientific or spiral navigation by Great Circles' he wrote at Kenilworth in 1599.[60]

'By far the greatest English chart-maker of all time', Dudley had completed four volumes of his magnum opus in English by 1611, yet critics of *The Tempest* have forgotten this magus who spanned its two worlds;[61] 'probably suggested' the unpopular royal marriage it legitimated to engineer his own personal revenge;[62] set slaves logging to build the fleet that terrorised the seas where it takes place; and may even have cued its comic subplot of Trinculo and Stephano through his manipulation of the rivalry between the two redeptionist orders of freed slaves: the Trinitarians and Knights of San Stephano.[63] Yet it is his claim to the Manor of Stratford, one of the 'diverse fair lordships' he looked to inherit from the Earl of Warwick, that raises the most intriguing implications for *The Tempest*.[64] For had Prince Henry carried his bride to Kenilworth, Stratford's usurping Lord, the Puritan Edward Greville, would have been displaced by this 'convenor of the knot of bastard Catholics' who had made Florence such a hotbed of conversion. Such were the hopes conveyed to Rome by an unnamed 'English visitor', who assured the Inquest on the marriage that, while 'English Catholicism is almost extinct, the English will follow the Crown into Jewry, if need be'. So persuasive was this argument that the inquiry minuted that 'the Pope may sanction the match', if 'the coming of the Princess will ease the sufferings of English Catholics', and advised that a union of the Stuart and Medici was as likely to issue happily as the Bourbon–Valois wedding that sparked the St Bartholomew's Day Massacre! This was precisely the fear in London, where 'it was said that if a Tuscan woman comes she will cause as much damage as one did in France';[65] so, whether or not the secret emissary was Dudley, these quips do illuminate the religious subtext of Shakespeare's comedy, which, as Orgel perceives, has more to do with James's ecumenical plans than the actual Protestant wedding the play was later staged to mark. Editors who think Prospero's masque irrelevant to 1611, 'when no marriage or betrothal was celebrated', have therefore allowed their New World to eclipse the Old, for it cannot be chance that the nuptials which Shakespeare's exorcism did precede on All Saints' Day were to be contingent on the homecoming of a persecuted Catholic lord to Stratford. Nor that, through all his years of exile, Dudley's staunchest allies were two other cousins, William and Philip Herbert: that 'most Noble and Incomparable pair of Brethren', the dedicatees of the First Folio, where the first text printed was *The Tempest*.[66]

'Amongst the famous rank of our sea-searching men', boasted Drayton in 1622, Warwickshire could claim 'Sir Robert Dudley, by sea that sought to rise', and 'Hoist sails with happy winds to th'Isles of Trinidado'.[67] As Hugh Trevor-Roper exclaimed, it seems extraordinary that this transatlantic voyager, who was 'the most important Englishman in Italy', should be 'so forgotten, in Tuscany as in England'. It seems equally surprising that this 'Italianized duke' from Stratford, who stood at the very centre of its world of 'shipwrights, cartographers, and pilots', is never associated with *The Tempest*, even though the expedition to which it may allude foundered on a shore where, 'twelve year since' (1.2.53), Dudley had 'landed / To be the lord on't' (5.1.161).[68] Critics who connect *The Tempest* only with Virginia have overlooked the fact that its plot concerns *two* contrasting expeditions; but the reason for their oversight was already implicit when Drayton insinuated that those 'happy winds' which swept a Midlander to Trinidad would never waft him home again to Stratford. James I sealed the papers on which Dudley had staked his legitimacy to appease the American faction of his cousins, who by 1612 were in hock to the Duke of Savoy, a rival for the Stuart match.[69] And, after Henry's death, his bid to ingratiate himself with yet another treatise, exhorting the King to 'bridle the impertinence of parliaments' by martial law and gunboats, consigned him to oblivion as a despotic Machiavel.[70] Though he survived to see Charles I approve his title, by the time he died in 1649 he was remembered chiefly as patentee of 'The Earl of Warwick's Powder': a panacea prescribed by Shakespeare's son-in-law, John Hall. Yet this anti-Duke, whose crimes chained Warwickshire and Italy to Barbary and Bermuda, may explain some of the paradoxes of Prospero, such as his tantalising but unfulfilled promise to 'resolve you, / Which to you shall seem probable, of every these happened accidents' (5.1.248–50). For if his relatives did sponsor *The Tempest*, that may have been because it was North-ampton who 'was one of the few judges who decided that the evidence by which he claimed legitimacy should not be suppressed'.[71] Above all, this pirate's plea for pardon reprieves *The Tempest* from the tragedy of colonialism, prompting us to share with our 'good hands' (5.1.329) in the benefits of a voyage bound 'home for Naples' (1.2.235), where the meaning of all 'the particular accidents gone by' will be revealed 'in the morn' (5.1.306–7) of All Souls':

> It was customary on this day for persons dressed in black to walk the streets ringing a bell and calling on inhabitants to remember souls suffering in purgatory, and join in prayer for their liberation. At Naples, it used to be a custom to throw open charnel houses, where crowds thronged to visit the bodies of their friends, the skeletons of which were dressed up in robes in niches along the walls. A custom also prevailed of providing in every house on All Souls' Eve a banquet for the souls in purgatory, who were supposed to revisit and make merry. Every one quitted the habitation, and returned in the morning to find the whole feast consumed, it being deemed unlucky if a morsel remained. The thieves who made a harvest of this pious custom took care to avert any evil omen by carrying off whatever they were unable to consume.[72]

'Now 'tis true / I must be here confined by you, / Or sent to Naples' (321–3): the epilogue of *The Tempest* is unique for its appeal to the audience to free the actor not from the fiction but from the reality in which they are detained. No other Shakespearean work ends in this surprising way with a prayer for 'release' from the 'bands' of an imprisoned present into the imaginary future of the play (27). As Barton remarks, the freedom Prospero craves is 'not from the stage, but from the island. He wishes to return to his dukedom, not simply to the tiring-house. The play may be done, but the epilogue perpetuates the illusion, and with great deference, involves the audience.'[73] It may be that this plea for a willing suspension of disbelief in liberation is keyed to the fragile optimism of its original occasion. The entreaty to exchange confinement on 'this bare stage' for the latitude of 'my Milan' can be heard, in this sense, as the author's own petition for that liberty of conscience which might have followed 'the nuptial of these our dear-beloved' (308–11): the Protestant Prince and Catholic Infanta. Shakespeare asks for the 'indulgence' to practise his faith in exchange for that other – papal – indulgence on which this marriage, and so much else, would depend. And, if this is so, his call for 'help of your good hands' (327) must also mean that the audience is begged to pray for his soul with its own gesture of emancipation. An appeal for 'gentle breath' (329) of collective prayer was a defining request, historians confirm, of the Catholic testator, whose instructions for such aid, 'when I lie in the point of death, labouring towards the everlasting life', were inspired by faith 'that 'The best remembrance was that in which the whole community participated'.[74] So, Prospero's epilogue, written at a time when, because of an expected marriage, 'prospects for the English Catholic community seemed brighter than they had for several generations',[75] can truly stand as Shakespeare's testament. For by entreating our praise, it identifies the writer himself with the hopes of all those former captives begging alms whose 'chains and shackles hung in churches' as reminders of the powers of redemption.[76] And no one better personified those hopes than 'Duke' Roberto Dudley: pirate, redemptor, and renegade Lord of Stratford-upon-Avon.

NOTES

1 E.K. Chambers, *William Shakespeare: A Study of Facts and Problems*, 2 vols (Oxford: Oxford University Press, 1936), vol. 2, p. 342.

2 R. Chambers, *The Book of Days: A Miscellany of Popular Antiquities*, 2 vols (London: W. and R. Chambers, 1869), vol. 2, p. 538.

3 E.J.A. Bicknell, *A Theological Introduction to the Thirty-Nine Articles of the Church of England*, 2nd edition (London: Longmans, 1925), p. 347.

4 David N. Beauregard, 'New Light on Shakespeare's Catholicism: Prospero's Epilogue in *The Tempest*', *Renascence*, 49:3 (Spring 1997), pp. 159–74, esp. p. 171.

5 John Munro (ed.), *The Shakespeare Allusion Book*, 2 vols (London: Chatto and Windus, 1909), vol. 1, pp. 224–5.

6 Ian Wilson, *Shakespeare: The Evidence* (London: Headline, 1993).

7 Peter Hulme, *Colonial Encounters: Europe and the Native Caribbean, 1492–1797* (London: Routledge, 1986), p. 115.

8 William Shakespeare, *The Tempest*, ed. Frank Kermode (London: Methuen, 1954), pp. xxiii and xxxiii–iv; and *The Tempest*, ed. Stephen Orgel (Oxford: Oxford University Press, 1987), p. 31; Edmund Malone, *An Account of The Incidents from which the Title and Part of the Story of Shakespeare's 'Tempest' Were Derived* (London: 1809).

9 Fernand Braudel, *The Mediterranean and the Mediterranean World in the Age of Philip II*, trans. Sian Reynolds, 2 vols (London: Collins, 1972), vol. 1, p. 116.

10 Christopher Marlowe, *Tamburlaine the Great, Part One*, ed. James W. Harper (London: Black, 1971), 3.3.55–6.

11 *Stuart Royal Proclamations*, ed. J.F. Larkin and P.L. Hughes, 2 vols (Oxford: Oxford University Press, 1973), vol. 1, pp. 146 and 574; see also pp. 53–6, 98–1 and 203–6. Braudel, op. cit. (note 9), pp. 629 and 635.

12 *Stuart Royal Proclamations*, vol. 2, pp. 880–7; Alberto Tenenti, *Piracy and the Decline of Venice, 1580–1615* (London: Routledge, 1967), pp. 77 and 86; John Smith, *True Travels and Adventures of Captain John Smith* (London: 1630), quoted in Christopher Lloyd, *English Corsairs on the Barbary Coast* (London: Collins, 1981), p. 72; William Lithgow, *The Total Discourse of the Rare Adventures of William Lithgow* (London: 1632), quoted in Lloyd, p. 53.

13 Braudel, op. cit. (note 9), p. 867.

14 Braudel, ibid., p. 869; Stephen Clissold, *The Barbary Slaves* (New York: Barnes and Noble, 1992), pp. 48–55 and 102–30, esp. p. 53 and 55. The most important account of

the Mediterranean slave economies remains Godfrey Fisher, *Barbary Legend: War, Trade and Piracy in North Africa, 1415–1830* (Oxford: Clarendon Press, 1957).

15 Clissold, op. cit. (note 14), p. 52.

16 Jean Canavaggio, *Cervantes*, trans. J.R. Jones (New York: Norton, 1990), p. 273; Ellen G. Friedman, *Spanish Captives in North Africa in the Early Modern Age* (Madison: University of Wisconsin Press, 1983), p. 73.

17 Canavaggio, op. cit. (note 16), pp. 91, 123, 222 and 273. Robert Osborne's 1612 play *A Christian Turn'd Turk* was based on the exploits of Jack Ward in Tunis.

18 Dominique O. Mannoni, *Prospero and Caliban: The Psychology of Colonialism*, trans. Pamela Powesland (New York: Praeger, 1956), p. 105.

19 Jeffrey Knapp, *An Empire Nowhere: England, America, and Literature from 'Utopia' to 'The Tempest'* (Berkeley: University of California Press, 1992), p. 221.

20 'The Famous Sea Fight Between Captain Ward and the Rainbow', anon.; quoted in C. Firth, *Naval Songs and Ballads* (London: Navy Records Society, 1908), p. 30. The offer of a pardon was repeated frequently during the months preceding and following the first performance of *The Tempest*: see *Calendar of State Papers Domestic, James I* (London: Longman, 1858), vol. 9, 17 July 1611; 7 February 1612; and 26 November 1612. Hereafter abbreviated *CSPD*. For Peter Easton see Lloyd, op. cit. (note 12), p. 66.

21 David M. Bergeron (ed.), *Pageants and Entertainments of Anthony Munday* (New York: Garland, 1985), pp. 43–4.

22 See Gary Schmidgall, '*The Tempest* and *Primaleon*: A New Source', *Shakespeare Quarterly*, 36 (1986), pp. 423–39.

23 Michael Baird Saenger, 'The Costumes of Caliban and Ariel Qua Sea-Nymph', *Notes and Queries*, 42 (1995), pp. 334–6.

24 For a detailed account of this sequence of events see Roy Strong, 'England and Italy: The Marriage of Henry Prince of Wales', in Richard Ollard and Pamela Tudor-Craig (eds), *For Veronica Wedgwood: Studies in Seventeenth Century History* (London: Collins, 1986), pp. 59–88. The relationship of *The Tempest* to the Hallowmass themes of persecution and pardon is discussed in R. Chris Hassel, *Renaissance Drama and the English Church Year* (Lincoln: University of Nebraska Press, 1979), pp. 167–70.

25 William Dugdale, *The Antiquities of Warwickshire* (London: John Osborn, 1730), p. 252; Antony Wood, *Athenae Oxonienses*, 3 vols (London: 1813), vol. 3, p. 260; Horace Walpole, *Catalogue of Royal and Noble Authors*, 6 vols (London: 1806), vol. 5, p. 339.

26 The patent of the Emperor Ferdinand II recognising Dudley as legitimate heir of his grandfather is reproduced in John Temple Leader, *The Life of Robert Dudley, Earl of Warwick and Duke of Northumberland* (Florence: Barbera, 1895), pp. 197–201. For Dudley's letter of introduction to the Grand Duke of Tuscany, dating from early in 1606, where he claimed 'la Duchee de Northumberland, la Comtee de Warwick et celle de Leicester' see Leader, p. 182. For his role in the Medici marriage negotiations see Leader, p. 65; Strong, op. cit. (note 24), p. 71; and *Henry Prince of Wales and England's Lost Renaissance* (London: Thames and Hudson, 1986), pp. 80–81. For Challoner as the 'chief foundation' of the Medici marriage, 'to whom promises have not been wanting if he should dispose the Prince to the match', see Thomas Birch, *The Life of Henry Prince of Wales* (London: 1760), p. 216; and *Calendar of State Papers Venetian* (London: Longman, 1905), vol. 12, p. 329: 16 April 1612 (hereafter abbreviated to *CSPV*).

27 Maurice Lee (ed.), *Dudley Carleton to John Chamberlain, 1603–1624* (New Brunswick: Rutgers University Press, 1972), p. 74. See also Arthur Gould Lee, *The Son of Leicester: The Story of Robert Dudley, Titular Earl of Warwick, Earl of Leicester, and Duke of Northumberland* (London: Gollancz, 1964), pp. 123–5 and 129. For the Howard navy connection see Robert Dudley, *Direttorio Marittimo*, unpub. ms, quoted in George F. Warner (ed.), *The Voyage of Robert Dudley to the West Indies, 1594–1595* (London: Hakluyt Society, 1899), p. xii. The first of Dudley's three wives was Margaret Cavendish, a sister of the circumnavigator, Thomas. When the latter died at sea in 1592, his ships, the *Leicester* and *Roebuck*, were inherited by Dudley for his Trinidad expedition.

Dudley's connection with the American colonists was further cemented by the marriage of Margaret's sister, Douglas, to Richard Hakluyt (*Voyage of Dudley*, pp. x–xi).

28 See Gigliola Pagano De Divitiis, *English Merchants in Seventeenth-Century Italy* (Cambridge: Cambridge University Press, 1990), pp. 48–9. Launched in March 1608, the *San Giovanni Battista* had been the 'ship made at Leghorn by the Earl of Warwick' to be 'more perfect than any', whose design had been sent in 1607 to Sir Thomas Challoner in London: Warner, op. cit. (note 27), p. 55. Wotton quoted in Lee, op. cit. (note 27), p. 136; Lloyd, op. cit. (note 12), pp. 48–53 and 85; Tenenti, op. cit. (note 12), p. 85; Larkin and Hughes, op. cit. (note 11), pp. 203–6. Tuscan attacks on English shipping date from Dudley's arrival in 1607. On 29 January 1609 Venetian despatches reported 'great resentment' in London against the Grand Duke, a proposal to prohibit Florentine imports in retaliation for Dudley's blockade, and a threat to expel the Tuscan ambassador (*CSPV*, vol. 11, p. 224). For details of Dudley's Tuscan naval projects see P.F. Kirby, 'Roberto Dudley e le navi granducali', and M. Pinna, 'Sulle carte nautiche prodotte a Livorno nei secoli XVI e XVII', in *Atti del convegno 'Gli Inglesi a Livorno e all'Isola d'Elba'* (Livorno: 1980) , pp. 35–40 and 139–45; and G. Guarnieri, *Livorno medicea* (Livorno: 1970), pp. 50ff.

29 Roberto Dudleo, *Arcano del Mare*, 6 vols (Florence: Francesco Onofri, 1646–7), vol. 3, pp. 47–8, rep. in Warner, op. cit. (note 27), pp. 93–7. For Dudley's promotion of the Florentine expedition see Joyce Lorimer (ed.), *English and American Settlement on the River Amazon, 1550–1646* (London: Hakluyt Society, 1986), pp. 29–34. And for his private trade war see A. Lee, op. cit. (note 27), pp. 192–4. The 'letters of marque' issued by the Curia Apostolica authorising him to recover eight million ducats in compensation for the loss of his dukedom by impounding all English vessels 'wherever they may be found', are reproduced in Leader, op. cit. (note 26), pp. 203–4.

30 For the American investments of Robert Sidney, Viscount Lisle, afterwards Earl of Leicester, see 'The Names of the Adventurers for Virginia' (1620), in Philip L. Barbour (ed.), *The Complete Works of Captain John Smith*, 3 vols (Chapel Hill: University of North Carolina Press, 1992), vol. 2, p. 278. For the American interests of the Rich clan, especially Sir Robert Rich, later Earl of Warwick, see Vernon A. Ives (ed.), *The Rich Papers: Letters from Bermuda, 1615–1646* (Toronto: University of Toronto Press, 1984).

31 Quoted in Warner, op. cit. (note 27), p. 95.

32 M. Lee, op. cit. (note 27), pp. 135–6.

33 'The Voyage of Sir Robert Dudley to the Isle of Trinidad', in *Principal Navigations*, ed. Richard Hakluyt (London: 1600; repr. Hakluyt Society, 1903–5), vol. 10, pp. 203–12; 'Robert Dudley's Voyage to the West Indies, Narrated by Abram Kendal, Master', in Warner, op. cit. (note 27), pp. 52–3; James Pope-Hennessy, *West Indian Summer* (London: Batsford, 1943), p. 32.

34 Warner, op. cit. (note 27), pp. 53–7.

35 Kenneth Muir, *The Sources of Shakespeare's Plays* (London: Methuen, 1977), p. 278.

36 Quoted in Lloyd, op. cit. (note 12), p. 77. For the importance of Livorno under Dudley's control see Braudel, op. cit. (note 9), pp. 878–9.

37 Warner, op. cit. (note 27), p. 56. For Cecil as the 'Right Honourable' to whom the log of Dudley's voyage is addressed, see Warner, p. 54; as chief promoter of the Medici match, Strong, op. cit. (note 24), p. 71; and as 'General Cecil', in Venetian despatches, 'the person entrusted with the negotiations', *CSPV*, vol. 12: p. 329. For the evil reputation of Bermuda see Jean Kennedy, *Isle of Devils: Bermuda and the Somers Island Company, 1609–1685* (London: Collins, 1971).

38 Stephen Greenblatt, *Shakespearean Negotiations: The Circulation of Social Energy in Renaissance England* (Oxford: Clarendon Press, 1990), pp. 159 and 163.

39 A. Lee, op. cit. (note 27), p. 131.

40 Warner, op. cit. (note 27), pp. 61–2.

41 Greenblatt, op. cit. (note 38), p. 158. For Dudley's friendship with Galileo, which dated from 1609, see A. Lee, op. cit. (note 27), p. 163.

42 Greenblatt, op. cit. (note 38), p. 160.

43 *CSPD*, 9: pp. 222, 233 and 245.

44 Ibid., p. 55.

45 Ibid., p. 79; Tenenti, op. cit. (note 12), p. 85.

46 *The Tempest*, ed. Anne Barton (Harmondsworth: Penguin, 1968), pp. 23–4.

47 *CSPV*, vol. 12: p. 396.

48 *CSPV*, vol. 12: pp. 42 and 283.

49 Robert Brenner, *Merchants and Revolution: Commercial Change, Political Conflict, and London's Overseas Trade, 1550–1653* (Cambridge; Cambridge University Press, 1993); *CSPV*, vol. 11, pp. 311–12.

50 *CSPV*, vol. 11: pp. 301, 309, 311–12, 430 and 435; vol. 12: pp. 42, 44, 67, 170, 192, 274, 283, 300, 327–9 and 388–9. For Dudley's activities at Livorno and the hostile reactions in London see also vol. 11: p. 224, and vol. 12: pp. 53, 101, 121, 138, 140, 178, 289 and 393.

51 Historic Manuscripts Commission, *Salisbury Manuscripts*, vol. 19, p. 63: 17 March 1607.

52 Linda Levy Peck, 'The Mentality of a Jacobean Grandee', in Linda Peck Levy (ed.) *The Mental World of the Jacobean Court* (Cambridge: Cambridge University Press, 1993), p. 167; *Northampton: Patronage and Policy at the Court of James I* (London: George Allen and Unwin, 1982), pp. 55–6.

53 Alison Shell, *Catholicism, Controversy and the English Literary Imagination, 1558–1660* (Cambridge: Cambridge University Press, 1999), pp. 194–5.

54 Samuel Schoenbaum, *William Shakespeare: A Documentary Life* (Oxford: Clarendon Press, 1975), p. 155: the figure of £1000 would be equivalent to over £500,000 in modern terms.

55 Sir Edward was the nephew of Robert Cecil; for his role as intermediary with Dudley see Strong, op. cit. (note 24), pp. 46–7 and 80–1; for the letter from the Catholic Earls see p. 81; and for Queen Anne's letter to Pope Paul V, signed 'humilissima et diligentissima figliuola et serva', in the State Archives, Florence (Miscellanea Medicea 293, inserto 29, no. 2), ibid., p. 70. For Dudley's memorandum on the sale of his property in exchange for a royal pardon see A. Lee, op. cit. (note 27), p. 149; and for his suspected involvement in the Gunpowder Plot, see *CSPD*, vol. 8: p. 317.

56 *A Midsummer Night's Dream*, 2.1.150. For Dudley's – later Leicester's – Men and the 'princely pleasures' at Kenilworth in 1575 see Schoenbaum, op. cit. (note 54), p. 89; Michael Drayton, *The Shepherd's Garland* (London: Thomas Woodstock, 1593): 'To the Noble and Valorous Gentleman, Master Robert Dudley: Enriched with all Virtues of the Mind and Worthy of all Honourable Desert', in *The Works of Michael Drayton*, ed. J.W. Hebel, 5 vols (Oxford: Clarendon Press, 1961), vol. 1, p. 46. See also A. Lee, op. cit. (note 27), p. 55. For Dudley's costume as Grand Master of his Caesarean Order see Leader, op. cit. (note 26), pp. 102–5.

57 A. Lee, op. cit. (note 27), pp. 156–7; Dudley Carleton to John Chamberlain, 14 December 1612, in M. Lee, op. cit. (note 27), pp. 135–6. Within weeks of *The Tempest* being acted it was being said that 'the pardon offfered the pirates comes too late' to stop them 'going over to Florence' (*CSPD*, vol. 9: pp. 60, 109 and 115).

58 Roberto Dudleo, *Arcano del Mare*, ed. Jacopo Lucini (2nd. ed., Venice: 1661), quoted in A. Lee, op. cit. (note 27), p. 228.

59 Muir, op. cit. (note 35), p. 278.

60 A. Lee, op. cit. (note 27), pp. 50–1, 90–1; Leader, op. cit. (note 26), pp. 39–40.

61 Edward Lynham, *British Maps and Map Makers* (London: Nelson, 1904), p. 24; quoted in A. Lee, op. cit. (note 27), p. 229.

62 Leader, op. cit. (note 26), p. 65.

63 For the rivalry of the two redemptionist orders of San Stephano and the Holy Trinity, see Clissold, op. cit. (note 14), pp. 12–14, 108–10, 117–18 and 122–5.

64 A. Lee, op. cit. (note 27), p. 192; Edmund K. Chambers, *Sources for a Biography of Shakespeare* (Oxford: Clarendon Press, 1946), p. 10.

65 Sir Henry Wotton to Cecil, quoted in A. Lee, op. cit. (note 27), p. 128; James D. Mackie, *Negotiations Between King James VI and I and Ferdinand I, Grand Duke of Tuscany* (St Andrews: Humphrey Milford, 1927), pp. 93 and 98; *CSPV*, vol. 12: p. 396.

66 Orgel, op. cit. (note 8), p. 31; Kermode, op. cit. (note 8), p. xxiii; Schoenbaum, op. cit. (note 54), p. 258. For Dudley's reliance on the Herbert brothers see A. Lee, op. cit. (note 27), pp. 92, 168, 176 and 199. Philip's son, Lord Charles Herbert, died on a visit to Dudley in Florence in 1635 (Lee, pp. 208–9).

67 Michael Drayton, *The Second Part of Poly-Olbion* (London: Augustine Mathews, 1622), vol. 14: pp. 372–3, in Hebel, op. cit. (note 56), p. 406.

68 Hugh Trevor-Roper, 'The Anti-Dukes of Northumberland', *Journal of Anglo-Italian Studies*, 2 (1992), pp. 50–70, esp. pp. 61, 64 and 68.

69 In 1612–13 Robert Rich organised expeditions to both the West and East Indies under commission from the Duke of Savoy: see Ives, op. cit. (note 30), p. 391.

70 Robert Dudley, *A Proposition for His Majesty's Service to Bridle the Impertinences of Parliaments*, quoted in A. Lee, op. cit. (note 27), pp. 169–72. Possession of copies of this *Proposition* severely compromised Sir Robert Cotton in 1630 and the Earl of Strafford in 1642 (pp. 197–8).

71 Linda Levy Peck, *Northampton: Patronage and Policy at the Court of James I* (London: George Allen and Unwin, 1982), p. 229, n. 63.

72 R. Chambers, *The Book of Days: A Miscellenany of Popular Antiquities*, 2 vols (Edinburgh: W. and R. Chambers, 1869), vol. 2, p. 538.

73 Barton, op. cit. (note 46), p. 51.

74 Eamon Duffy, *The Stripping of the Altars: Traditional Religion in England, 1400–1580* (New Haven: Yale University Press, 1992), pp. 329 and 347.

75 Michael Mullett, *Catholics in Britain and Ireland* (London: Macmillan, 1998), p. 25.

76 Friedman, op. cit. (note 16), p. 166.

10

Unseasonable laughter

The context of *Cardenio*

Escorted by one hundred and forty 'poor men in gowns', who filed behind 'the chief mourner, Prince Charles', the coffin emerged from St James's Palace at ten in the morning to 'a fearful ourcry among the people', and was wheeled to Westminster Abbey on a spectacular hearse flanked by six horses amidst an 'ocean of tears'. But though the cortège took four hours to assemble, and was a mile long, with two thousand mourners in black, what struck onlookers was the 'universal silence' that descended on the crowd, whose 'utter desolation' was 'as if they felt they own ruin in that loss'. 'I confess never to have seen such a sight of mortification', recorded one official, 'nor so just a sorrow so well expressed as in all the spectators whose streaming eyes made known how inwardly their hearts did bleed'. The funeral of James I's eldest son, Henry, Prince of Wales, on 7 December 1612, was the occasion of an unprecedented display of grief on the streets of London, and was followed by a deluge of printed souvenirs perpetuating the misery of 'Great Britain's mourning garment'; 'Tears shed by his country or His Highness' dear loss'; 'England's sorrow for the death of this most virtuous and peerless Prince'; 'Great Britain all in Black for its incomparable loss'; 'The Muses Tears for the Loss of Hope … Together with Time's Sobs'; and even 'His Three Sisters' Tears shed at the Funeral of Henry, Prince of Wales'. Campion, Chapman, Donne, Drummond, Heywood, Taylor, Tourneur, Webster and Wither all contributed to the myth that 'there were few', in the words of the funeral sermon, 'who mourned not bitterly and shed abundant tears'. But in fact one refusal to grieve in public provoked such resentment that 'the cry of "Poison!" was raised'. The king, who 'loathed the sight of mourning', remained at Kensington, where his chief concern was said to be that 'the wind blew through the walls' so much 'he could not lie warm in his bed'.[1]

While thousands queued at the Abbey to pay respects to a macabre waxwork of the prince, 'decked with robes, collar, crown and golden rod, as he went when he was alive', which was to lie in state inside the hearse until the end of year, courtiers who had expected a 'black Christmas' were caught by surprise. Though Queen Anne was said to have 'wept alone in her room', and publicists put it about that James repeatedly 'burst out crying, "Henry is dead"', the King's instant reaction was that his daughter Elizabeth's wedding to Prince Frederick of the Rhine must proceed as planned. Court mourning should have prevented the ceremony until June, but the date was confirmed as 14 February, St Valentine's Day; and in the meantime, John Chamberlain reported, 'they are very busy preparing plays and exercises', so that 'our Christmas can come to an end without the least show of any alteration in Court or town'. So, 'Christmas was kept as usual at Whitehall', and the climax of the forced festivities went ahead on 27 December, with a formal betrothal in the Banqueting House, 'in the presence of the King sitting in state'. There the dark side of this 'strangest winter that was ever seen' was symbolized by the groom's black velvet cloak, while 'to make an even mixture of joy and mourning', the bride trailed twenty yards of black satin behind a plume of white feathers. The couple had earlier prayed before the effigy of the dead prince, but now their tension found embarrassing release, when the Secretary of State read the service in such comic French that the two sixteen-year-olds collapsed into fits of 'unseasonable laughter', followed by many of the court. That night the King was also 'noticed to be extremely cheerful', as he enjoyed one of the 'fourteen several plays' performed at Whitehall by the King's Men in these weeks when Prince Henry's hearse stood beside his grave in the silence of the church.[2]

Throughout the Christmas celebrations of 1612 the catafalque of the Prince of Wales remained at Westminster alongside the sumptuous new tomb of his grandmother, Mary Queen of Scots, in which her body had been rein-terred only a month before: 'The Tapers placed in the Cathedral smoking like an Offertory'. To David Bergeron, this mortuary chapel, where smoke formed 'a smouldering sacrifice for James's conscience', seems a perfect setting of a Shakespearean late play. For 'the royal family resembled a paradigm of tragi-comedy' during this winter when 'Two great hopes were lost: one by death, the other by a marriage which separated parents from child'. Likewise, the motive for persisting with the entertainments, he infers, was 'the desire to transmute the tragedy of Henry's death into a romantic comedy, to create a fiction to displace difficult reality'. At this 'turning point for the Stuarts', when 'un-certainty clouded the kingdom', the tragi-comic form answered the need expressed also in Donne's 'Epithalamium' for Elizabeth, to heal the rift left by the disaster.[3] Alvin Kernan agrees with this analysis, and proposes *Much Ado About Nothing*, 'with its war between the sexes and multiple marriages', as 'the most obvious' choice of all the works staged between the funeral and the wedding.[4] No commentator has considered the topicality of the only play attri-buted to the leading playwrights, Shakespeare and Fletcher, specifically com-missioned for the King's Men to present that fatal Christmas, and which might even have been a new variation of the old Elizabethan comedy to fit the tragic

Jacobean circumstances. Yet from what we know about it, it was *Cardenio* which seems more than any other play listed in the season's repertoire to have straddled the mixed emotions of festivities concluded almost literally over a prince's dead body.

Though confidently dated to the second half of 1612, as the first of three known Shakespearean collaborations with Fletcher, no attempt has been made to contextualise *Cardenio* in relation to its sensational Jacobean occasion. The reason is that a historicist reading of this 'lost' tragi-comedy has been obstructed by the debate over its text, which survives only in the transcription published by Lewis Theobald in 1728, as 'revised and adapted' from a work 'Written originally by W. Shakespeare', under the perilous title of *Double Falsehood; or the Distressed Lovers*. The legend of how Theobald acquired no fewer than *three* manuscripts of the play, the best in the hand of a Restoration prompter, John Downes; who inherited it from the actor Thomas Betterton; who received it from an illegitimate daughter of Shakespeare; and of how this copy was 'treasured up' in the library of the Covent Garden Theatre that burned down in 1808, has always seemed fanciful; but recent criticism has swung decisively towards Stephen Kukowski's verdict that 'the evidence makes it clear that the play cannot be a forgery'; that 'if not a forgery, then the case for it being a relic of *Cardenio* is very strong'; and that 'from the various stages of revision ... Theobald did manage to salvage a few scraps of a Shakespearean original'. As Jonathan Bate likewise affirms, in *Double Falsehood* 'one hears a faint cry of a play by Shakespeare and Fletcher trapped below layers of rewriting'. That stifled cry suggests the presence of at least the story-line of the 'lost' late play; but, whatever value is attached to its language and style, it is ironically because so much of it sounds like Fletcher that readers are now increasingly convinced that some of the surviving text can be attributed to Shakespeare:

> It has verbal similarities to a number of Shakespearean plays ... which were frequently staged in Theobald's time. This suggests that it could be a good imitation. But then most of acts four and five are in a style highly reminiscent of the tragicomic romances pioneered by Fletcher ... If Theobald was fabricating a Shakespeare play, why on earth did he write the second half in the style of Fletcher?[5]

Double Falsehood is full of Shakespearean and Fletcherian echoes that have led critics, Clifford Leech states, to near-unanimity that 'Theobald made use of a Jacobean original' which 'owed something to *All's Well That Ends Well*, *The Winter's Tale* and *Cymbeline*'. But the real justification for the leap of faith in Theobald's text is that this has slowly come to appear more plausible than even he could have hoped in the light of facts of which he was certainly oblivious. Crucially, his firm denial of Fletcher's involvement was made at a time when '*nobody knew Shakespeare collaborated*'; for, as Bate points out, had he been aware of joint authorship of *Henry VIII* and *The Two Noble Kinsmen*, 'he would have been able to argue that marks of Fletcher's hand are proof of authenticity'.[6] Nor did he know that in 1653 the Stationers' Register had entered a '*History of Cardenio* by Mr Fletcher and Mr Shakespeare'; and that in 1613 the King's Men had been paid for twice performing *Cardenna* or *Cardenio*, a drama presumably based on the tale of Cardenio in *Don Quixote*. Moreover, Theobald made nothing of this source, which he correctly connected with Thomas Shelton's 1612 version, the first English translation of Cervantes. Yet, as John Freehafer notes, some of the Shakespearean echoes in the published work are, in fact, so closely related to Shelton, and 'so out of place in *Double Falsehood*, that they can scarcely be anything but relics of a Jacobean play'.[7] And Michael Wood has recently claimed that a song newly attributed to Shakespeare's regular collaborator, the King's lutenist, Robert Johnson, 'Woods, rocks, and mountains' (BL Add A 11608 / Bodleian Don.c.57), is, in fact, one cut by Theobald from Act Four; and that the words of this lyric are so tightly keyed to the language of the corresponding lines in Shelton as to make it virtually certain that the 1728 publication was indeed 'based on a genuine text of the lost play'.[8] The sheer accumulation of evidence is now such, then, that Bate summarises the current consensus when he recommends the existing text for qualified admission to the Shakespearean canon:

> The chances of Theobald having fabricated a Shakespeare play, unintentionally written half of it in the style of Fletcher, and used for its source the very book Shakespeare and Fletcher used for a play of whose existence he was ignorant are infinitesimal. The inference has to be that Theobald's play is indeed a version of *Cardenio*, which Shakespeare and Fletcher must have written while Shelton's translation was new and popular.[9]

Like *Much Ado*, which was also twice acted at Christmas in 1612, the story of Cardenio is a variant of the 'broken nuptial' genre described by Carol Neely as designed to incite both male fantasy and female sympathy, by first giving women 'power to resist or alter courtship', and then taking it away when they resume the dance into marriage.[10] Such a plot might have seemed apt for a betrothal that resulted from the rejection of a parade of rival suitors, and that placed the Princess Royal in the liminality of one who walked ahead of all these men, but only until she married. As David Lindley says, 'It is unimaginable that Elizabeth would have rejected Frederick';[11] yet what is extraordinary about *Cardenio* as a wedding entertainment is that its happy ending depends not on the heroine's submission to filial duty but on her unswerving resistance to an arranged alliance. In this play the action turns on Leonora's resolve to 'disappoint these nuptials', and 'fall a bleeding sacrifice' by stabbing herself at the altar, rather than acquiescing in the match with Prince Henriquez into which she is coerced by her father. This is also the point of the most important divergence from *Don Quixote*, where, just when she is expected to 'take out the poniard to stab herself', the bride answers the priest 'with a dismayed and languishing voice, "I will"'.[12] For in the tragi-comedy Leonora not only arms herself, but arranges for her lover, Julio, to hide behind the arras from which he leaps between bride and groom before they exchange vows. Just how exceptional this violent interruption is in Shakespeare Anne Jennalie Cook shows, by reminding us that though the plays 'provide few women whose marriages do not require the approval of some masculine figure', only Juliet and Capulet fail to reach the 'multilateral consent' that was the social norm.[13] And, as Leonora protests to her father, his own marriage provides the model of such a conventional romantic solution:

> I conjure you,
> By all the tender interests of Nature,
> By the chaste love 'twixt you and my dear mother
> (O, holy Heav'n, that she were living now!)
> Forgive and pity me. O, Sir, remember
> I've heard my mother say a thousand times,
> Her father would have forced her virgin choice,
> But when the conflict was 'twixt love and duty,
> Which should be first obey'd, my mother quickly
> Paid up her vows to love and married you.
> You thought this well, and she was praised for this;
> For this her name was honour'd; disobedience
> Was ne'er imputed to her. Her firm love
> Conquer'd whate'er oppos'd it, and she prosper'd
> Long time your wife. My case is now the same;
> You are the father which you then condemn'd;
> I, what my mother was; but not so happy.
>
> (2.3.104–20)

Don Bernard's reply, that 'you have old stories enough to undo you … go thy ways, and … get ready within these two days to be married to a husband you don't deserve … or by my dead father's soul, you are no acquaintance of mine', affiliates him with Capulet as the most mercenary of Shakespearean fathers. And his aside that 'The girl says right: her mother chose me purely to spite that surly old blockhead, my father-in-law', reveals why he thinks his daughter needs no 'precedent' in Elizabethan stories. For, as Leonora complains, in her mother's day 'the choice were not so hard', but the marriage market has since drastically curtailed the freedom of daughters: 'Interest, that rules the world, has made at last / A merchandise of hearts, and virgins now / Choose where they're bid, and wed without esteem' (140–53). This is an exchange, then, which confirms Lindley's claim that, if the arranged match is a problem for modern audiences, 'it was problematic also in the seventeenth century'; and that, situates the play within the 'deeply embedded contradictions' of a moment when 'Even the King "fell to inveighing against the marriage of young couples before they became acquainted"'. By caricaturing patriarchy, *Cardenio* seems, in fact, to be aligned with George Wilkins's 1607 play *The Miseries of Enforced Marriage*, which, as Lindley points out, is an otherwise extreme exposé of 'the rights of parents to overrule children's affections'.[14] But in that play, as in *All's Well*, the victim of the arranged match is a bridegroom; and the question posed by *Cardenio* is how this drama of a reluctant bride could possibly have been thought appropriate to the wedding of a Stuart princess. The answer may lie in the patronage of its source, which Shelton dedicated to Theophilus, Lord Howard de Walden, the son of Thomas Howard, Earl of Suffolk and Lord Chamberlain. As Antonia Fraser writes, the Suffolks wallowed in a 'sweetly corrupt world' of bribes, where 'the promise of pensions – paid secretly by Spain – became a weapon in maintaining a pro-Spanish party at court', and in which, 'thanks to their amazing peculations', they could easily afford to buy literary promotion for their favourite cause of *liberty of conscience* of all kinds:

> Outstanding for her avarice was the beautiful, wilful Countess of Suffolk. Her husband, a son of the executed Duke of Norfolk, had been given his Suffolk title as part of James' rehabilitation of the Howard family he loved, and it was as a leading courtier that he intended to shine – a courtier and a rich man … At the beginning of James' reign, the Countess of Suffolk had indicated Catholic sympathies and pro-Spanish feelings to an emissary from the Archdukes: she had emphasised the prime importance of pensions and gifts in the delicate matter of establishing liberty of conscience … [And] by the time the Constable of Castile arrived … Catherine Suffolk had thoroughly infiltrated herself into the process by which Spanish money was to be paid over for English influence at court. She received at the least twenty thousand pounds, possibly more, as well as certain wonderful jewels.[15]

A Jacobean taste for Cervantes was lubricated, evidently, by sponsorship from the friends of Madrid; and in the spring of 1612, when Shelton's publisher, Edward Blount, presented a copy of his translation to their 'very good lord, the Lord of Walden', in the hope that he would 'lend it a favourable countenance, to animate the parent thereof to produce some worthier subject',[16] the Howard family was at its most beneficent. The Lord Treasurer, Lord Salisbury, died on 24 May, and until his own death in 1614 the serpentine Henry Howard, Earl of Northampton, would dominate the Privy Council. An English version of *Don Quixote*, published by a stationer who specialised in continental bestsellers, and himself translated works of Spanish *realpolitik*, slotted neatly into the pro-Spanish and crypto-Catholic culture of the Howard faction. As Linda Levy Peck has detailed, both the *éminence grise*, Northampton, code-named *El Cid*, and his nephew Suffolk, patronised Counter-Reformation art, as well as Catholic charities.[17] The overtly Castilian aesthetic of these grandees might therefore explain why the new work performed for their first Christmas in power was the sole Shakespearean drama set in Spain, and one of the few Jacobean plays with sympathetic Spanish characters. One of the others, tellingly, was, of course, *Much Ado*, with its Aragonese Prince and Spanish troops. Howard patronage of *Cardenio* could have dated from the support they earlier gave for a match between Princess Elizabeth and King Philip. But, if the members of their faction did read *Don Quixote*, it was more likely their own domestic concerns which led to the earmarking of the story of the unwilling bride and her secret lover, and which ensured that in the staged adaptation the marriage vows were never spoken. For it would have been very difficult for the Whitehall audience of the new play not to recognise in this torrid melodrama the case of Frances Howard, sister of Theophilus, whose arranged marriage to the Earl of Essex and intrigue with the royal favourite, Robert Carr, Viscount Rochester, were about to feature in the most lurid of all Jacobean scandals. Indeed, Frances's lawyers were already drafting grounds for annulment when the court heard Leonora rehearse her identical plea for the priority of lovers' oaths over legal enforcement:

> How may I be obedient and wife too?
> Of my obedience, Sir, I cannot strip me;
> Nor can I then be wife: Grace against Grace!
> Ungracious, if I not obey a father;
> Most perjur'd if I do. Yet, lord, consider
> Or e'er too late, or e'er that knot be tied,
> Which may with violence damnable be broken,
> No other way disserv'd. Yet consider,
> You wed my body, not my heart, my lord;
> No part of my affection. Sounds it well
> That Julio's love is Lord Henriquez' wife;
> Have you an ear for this harsh sound?
>   (3.2.96–107)

'This comes of forcing women where they hate', Don Bernard admits, when the wedding he has engineered explodes, 'It was my own sin and I am rewarded' (3.3.84). If Frances Howard's father did sponsor *Cardenio*, then this change of heart would seem to reflect what Lindley sees as 'signs of guilt among those who surrounded her for having married her off so young', and the volte-face her father and great-uncle managed during these months when the deaths of Salisbury and Henry, and her liaison with Carr, offered such a 'tremendous opportunity' to her clan. The play thus tends to confirm his thesis, in *The Trials of Frances Howard*, that, contrary to rumour, the affair took the Howards by surprise, and that divorce proceedings opened while they still despised the upstart Carr. Certainly, Leonora's courage reinforces Lindley's image of Frances as 'braver and more heroic' than her critics allowed, while her characterisation as without 'fervour / Which youth and love kindle', seems designed to protect the real lovers from slander. In this romance the heroine is one whose 'affection / Is such … as will break untouch'd / Die frosty, e'er it can be touch'd' (1.2.64–71), and her suitor an innocent bemused to be the centre of attention. In fact, it is with Julio's vacuousness that the text nods most towards the gossips. For when his father demands to know 'How comes the Duke to take such notice of my son?' the youth answers that it is through being 'commended for my seat, or mocked': a risqué joke about the episode when Carr first attracted James by breaking his leg falling off his horse, and so proved, as Thomas Howard laughed, that 'if any mischance be to be wished, 'tis breaking a leg in the King's presence, for this fellow owes all his favour to that bout; I think he hath better reason to speak well of his own horse than the King's roan jennet'.[18] So, like Carr, the Cardenio-character here must solve a problem which was undreamed of in Cervantes, though it was crucial at the Stuart court: 'Which is better, to serve a mistress or a duke?' (1–28). One function of this play is clearly to reconcile this affective choice:

> Duke, I obey thy summons, be its tenour
> Whate'er it will. If war, I come thy soldier;
> Or if to waste my silken hours at court,
> The slave of fashion, I with willing soul
> Embrace the lazy banishment for life …
> Tomorrow, love, so runs the Duke's command;
> Stinting our farewell-kisses, cutting off
> The forms of parting and the interchange
> Of thousand precious vows with haste too rude.
>
> (123–52)

In *Shakespeare's Romances and the Royal Family*, Bergeron has argued that 'events in the life of the Stuarts helped to shape the action of these plays', by prompting radical revision of sources.[19] If so, it is significant that, while in *Don Quixote* Henriquez ensures his plan to marry Leonora remains 'unknown to his father' by keeping Cardenio 'out of his presence',[20] the first change made in the play is to put Julio in the pay of Duke Angelo as 'An honest spy' on the Prince (1.1.46). The effect is not only to place the lovers under an omniscient benefactor but to establish the monarch in opposition to his son. Critics have questioned the relevance of this familiar Shakespearean situation, which, as Freehafer observes, is 'introduced with evident loss of context and is scarcely referred to again'.[21] Yet nothing ties *Cardenio* more to its historical moment than the suspicion with which the Duke views Henriquez's activities, beginning with his scheme to take youths such as Julio 'riding in France'. For since Julio, like Carr, 'can no more but gallop a hackney' before crossing the Channel, this French interlude, which has no parallel in Cervantes, seems a transparent satire on the chivalric pretensions of the actual Henry. As Roy Strong relates, the Prince's military ambitions were focused on a monumental riding school, built at St James's Palace in 1609 to 'train youths of the Prince's circle in the new art' of *dressage*. Its Master, Saint-Antoine, had been riding trainer to Henry IV; and, sure enough, *Cardenio* opens with Henriquez in Paris, 'buying coursers' and raising calvary with the Duke's gold. It was 'because they did not desire to exalt him too high', the Venetian envoy relayed, that Henry was forbidden to ride in state;[22] but a century later Theobald can hardly have been aware of this contentiousness when he published a text that begins with a prince pursuing the same equestrian mania in France, and a father voicing identical fears to a favourite son about the secret agenda of the heir:

> Worthy the man,
> Who, with my dukedom, heirs my better glories ...
> Like a fair glass of retrospection, thou
> Reflect'st the virtues of my early youth,
> Making my old blood mend its pace with transport;
> While fond Henriquez, thy irregular brother,
> Sets the large credit of his name at stake,
> A truant to my wishes and his birth.
> His taints of wildness hurt our nicer honour,
> And call for swift reclaim ...
> But I, by fears weighing his unweigh'd course,
> Interpret for the future from the past,
> And strange misgivings, why he hath of late,
> By importunity and strained petition,
> Wrested our leave of absence from the court,
> Awake suspicion.
>
> (1.1.8–31)

It is the French locale of Henriquez's Hal-like truancy that cements this play into a Jacobean context. For, according to biographers, it was Henry's hero-worship of his French namesake, who cultivated him and his circle, which most infuriated his father. And if *Cardenio* did open with a ruler spying on his son, to discover whether he 'Will, by vantage of his cooler wisdom ... redeem the hot escapes of youth' (22), its scenario could hardly come closer to English politics in 1612, when the Prince was 'cut off from communication with the King; St James's Palace became an "opposition" to Whitehall; and Henry found himself in total isolation from the government'. In particular, Angelo's favouritism towards his preferred son, Roderick, echoes reports that James was not 'pleased to see the Prince so beloved of the people', and was 'growing jealous' enough to warn that 'if he did not attend more earnestly' to orders, 'the crown would be left to his brother'. So, the 'unwonted strain' (1) in this court parallels what Strong calls 'the cold war atmosphere' of a London where factions polarised around hopes pinned by the pro-French on Henry as Protestant champion, and by the pro-Spanish on Carr as a Catholic sympathiser. And it is the antagonism between these camps which seems to fuel the enmity between Julio and Henriquez. So violent was Henry's loathing of his father's favourite that, when one of his guards 'offered to kill him, the Prince [said], if there were cause, he would do it'; adding that 'if ever he were King, he would not leave one of that family [the Howards] to piss against the wall'. No wonder, then, that in this Spanish comedy a Francophile prince is so demonised, for by late 1612 the real Henry was lined up not only with his old playmate, the jilted Essex, but with Carr's own ex-boyfriend, Sir Thomas Overbury, in a 'deadly quarrel' with the lovers.[23] And it was, perhaps, this final personal betrayal that inflamed the grievance of the 'injur'd Julio' (2.3.65):

Is there a treachery like this in baseness
Recorded anywhere? It is the deepest:
None but itself can be its parallel.
And from a friend professed! Friendship?
Why, 'tis a word ever maim'd. In human nature
It was a thing the noblest; and 'mong beasts
It stood not in mean place. Things of fierce nature
Hold amity and concordance. Such a villany
A writer could not put down in his scene,
Without taxation of his auditory,
For fiction most enormous.

(3.1.16–26)

'No killing, Julio' (46): Leonora's reversal of Hero's command to 'Kill Claudio' (*Much Ado*, 4.1.288) reveals the collective anxiety about the murderous vortex which swirled around Frances Howard in these days when her family prepared to duel with the husband they reviled as 'My Lord the gelding'. 'If my Lord would draw sword in defence of a good prick it were worth his pains ... but never such a poor pudding', Northampton taunted; and the gibe would seem to support those who see the homophobic violence of the case as a displacement of that 'fiction most enormous' which 'A writer could not put down in his scene' without taxing his audience, but which *Cardenio* insinuates: namely, the homoerotic desire of all the men involved, from Carr, Overbury and Northampton to Essex, Henry and, of course, the King, and the open secret that the handsome favourite was 'the central figure in five erotic triangles, four of them in part homosexual'.[24] It may be no coincidence, therefore, that the heroine of this play says that she must think love 'a cordial' even 'When I see poison in't' (4.1.42), because within a year of its performance Overbury was to die of suspected poisoning by his former friend, and even the death of the Prince was to be attributed to Carr. The King blocked the duel with Essex by imprisoning Frances's brother for 'daring to speak of drawing swords, especially at court, in favour of these foul things'.[25] Yet the love that dared not speak at court all but does so on stage, when the villain who seems to be a composite of Carr's accusers is accused of sodomy himself, on the evidence of a letter to 'A young he-bawd' he has 'bobb'd'. This 'minion' is, in reality, Henriquez's disguised mistress, Violante; but an astonishing scene that has no literary source (and cannot, surely, be by Theobald) comes close to flaunting what Carr must have preserved as his ultimate deterrent: the scandalous 'letter in his casket' compromising the King (5.2.160–230). The crucial motive for the murder, according to court gossip, was that the victim 'knew more state secrets than did the Privy council', since 'packets were sent, sometimes opened by my Lord [Carr], sometimes unbroken, unto Overbury, who perused them, copied them, registered them, made table-talk of them, as he thought good'.[26] In the event, however, the 'letter in Somerset's casket found by my Lord Coke' was never produced in open court, though 'James never forgave Coke for having uncovered such sensitive material, and this was the reason for [the attorney's] subsequent disgrace.[27] Evidently, this was what was meant at the trial, when it was alleged that the fallen favourite had plotted to destroy the entire Stuart dynasty, and something of the danger he posed to his interrogators may indeed therefore be threatened when Julio bursts in like some 'boist'rous sworder' upon the royal wedding:

> Ungen'rous Lord! The circumstance of things
> Should stop the tongue of question. You have wronged me
> Wronged me so basely, in so dear a point,
> As stains the cheek of honour with a blush;
> Cancels the bonds of service; bids allegiance
> Throw to the wind all high respects of birth,
> Title, and eminence; and in their stead
> Fills up the panting heart with just defiance.
> If you have sense of shame, or justice, Lord,
> Forgo this bad intent; or with your sword
> Answer me like a man, and I shall thank you.
>
> (3.2.131–41)

Prince Henry, it was reported, had 'utterly disliked' Carr: 'forbears his company, and falls flatly at odds with him, not once giving him any countenance or vouchsafing him his company'.[28] In his 1653 history of the reign, Arthur Wilson records moreover how the relationship between the heir and the favourite was one of bitter emotional jealousy: 'For the Prince, being a high-born spirit, and meeting a young competitor in his father's affections, that was a mushroom yesterday, thought the venom would grow too near him, and therefore gave no countenance, but opposition to it.'[29] So, it is the incipient violence of *Cardenio*, in the hindsight of the Overbury affair, which suggests that the prime movers of the 1612 celebrations were those with least cause to mourn the Prince: the Lord Chamberlain and the Howards. Thus, the picture emerges of Shakespeare at the end of his career in the orbit of England's last great Catholic family, and writing his romances as a legitimation of the Howard programme of religious reconciliation. Some time in late summer, we might therefore speculate, the first three acts of this tragi-comedy were sent from Shakespeare to be completed by Fletcher, for their urgency is signalled with a drumming providentialism that is typical of the late plays. Leonora has fainted at the altar; Julio has fled the city 'raging mad'; Violante, discarded by Henriquez, has walked into the wilderness; and the fathers are left to 'bid the bell knoll' for death: 'Now I am like an aged oak, alone, / Left all for tempests.' But in returning to the theme of 'maimed rites' the author of *Much Ado* has this time been certain to preserve the lovers' faith, and what may be his last lines are ringing cues for the revelations of Fletcherian romance: 'You've equal losses; urge no further anger. / Heav'n, pleas'd now at your love, may bring again, / And, no doubt, will, your children to your comforts' (3.3.72–111). If *The*

Tempest can be keyed to James's project, in the autumn of 1611, to orchestrate a religious peace by tying his son to some 'strange bedfellow' from Italy, then the play which followed remains as hopeful of détente and co-existence. Its Catholic Car/denio may 'solicit every saint in heaven / To lend me vengeance' on Henri/quez (4.1.120), but Shakespeare's fathers shake hands and agree to let 'quest for our lost friends' make 'brothers of us, whom our cross fates / Could never join. What we have been, forget; / What we intend to be, believe and nourish … Time may bring forth a wonder' (3.3.120–41). A final Shakespear-ean couplet strews fatherly advice on the future King and Queen of Bohemia which seems, by implication, more appropriate to the future Lord and Lady Rochester:

> This is my only counsel:
>   … Let not rewards nor hopes
> Be cast into the scale to turn thy faith.
> Be honest but for virtue's sake, that's all;
> He that has such a treasure cannot fall.
>   (3.3.172–6)

Shakespeare's Spanish offering for a German wedding appears to set the scene not only for a policy of religious toleration but also for a dissolution of the marriage that was the greatest obstacle to the ascendancy of his patrons. Pursuing their factional priorities, Nottingham and Suffolk had succeeded with this play, it seems, in diverting the nuptials of 'the Phoenix of the earth, / The bird of paradise' (4.1.50), into something like a technical deposition for their own impending divorce case. Richard Dutton has documented their vigilance in censoring hostile dramatisations of both their family's sexual and religious practices;[30] and *Cardenio* suggests that they were as active in the commission-ing of favourable propaganda. For by disrupting Henriquez's marriage plans, rather than holding his peace, the English Cardenio defends his lover from any possible taint of adultery. Frances Howard's annulment would hinge on her claims of just such a non-consummation; but in the theatre the heroine's virginity can be preserved only at the cost of depriving the hero of provocation for his defining madness. The absence of this indispensable motive is never filled, as Fletcher takes the story up once again where Cervantes started, with love-lorn lads and cross-dressed lasses surprising the shepherds in arcadia. Now the collaborator's signature salacity is all that is needed to strip them of their rustic garb and restore them to their reunited parents. But Echo has barely sounded in the baroque mountain scenes when these pastorals are truly broken. Suddenly, the text confides, 'a vacant hearse pass'd by / From rites new perform'd' (4.1.247). Just as the finishing touches were being put to the wedding programme by the officers of the Lord Chamberlain, the Prince of Wales had died.

Commentators on *Cardenio* are baffled by the incongruity of the funeral hearse which is announced in Act 4 and carried on stage for the denouement. In

Cervantes the villain had 'entered the Abbey' where the bride hid after 'he found the gates open', and abducted her by force.[31] But in the Jacobean version Henriquez and his brother hire the 'opportune' hearse and pretend to 'transport a body / As 'twere a funeral: and coming late by, / Crave a night's leave to rest i'th'convent' (241–4). The episode takes place off-stage, but when Leonora appears she has been 'snatch'd from that seat of contemplation', and is told that for love Henriquez has steeled himself 'To feign a corpse', and sleep in the 'hearse one night within the hallow'd walls'. This mysterious catafalque has indeed brought a 'black Christmas' to the bride, who is now 'veil'd' and escorted by 'Attendants as mourners' (5.1.1–14); but a night in the Abbey has also transformed the Prince, who is ready to beg for pardon. 'Do you bring joy or grief my lord?' asks old Camillo, when Roderick leads on the wanderers, presumed dead, in a cortège that 'Follows the hearse with all due rights of mourning' (5.2.36). The question is soon answered, when they unveil themselves to their parents; but the 'even mixture of joy and mourning' persists, emphasised by the 'vacant hearse' that stands throughout the reconciliation. Critics have scoured Cervantes in vain for the origin of this tableau. To Kenneth Muir, its symbolism is 'not properly developed, and there seems little point in reintroducing the hearse' for the finale; and Harold Metz conjectures that 'the hearse was an invention of one of the writers … or perhaps a bit of folklore folded' into the action.[32] In fact, there is no feature of *Cardenio* that links the play more concretely to its occasion, for at Whitehall in 1612 the empty bier could only have reminded the audience of the opportunities that attended that other cenotaph in the Abbey:

> A great stately hearse, built quandrangle-wise with six pillars, showing three to the view on each side four square, canopy-like, rising small on the top, trimmed and set thick within with diverse scutcheons, small flags and pennants of His Highness' and several arms of the Union chained … with his motto, *Fax mentis honestae Gloria*, and that of the funeral hearse, *Jurat ire per altum*.[33]

'His glory … fitted him for heaven': if Theobald's text is faithful to *Cardenio*, then its emotions do seem to register the ambivalence of those who organised the funeral towards this 'flower of his country and admiration of the world'. In Strong's opinion, 'To the King, terrible as it may seem, the death of the Prince was to come as a relief';[34] and the tragi-comedy catches this callousness in its last scenes, which, having first consigned Henriquez to a coffin, and then resurrected him to accusations that he has 'abused men, women and children' (192), crowns his rivals with the Duke's approval: 'E'en as you are, we'll join your hands together. / A providence above rules all' (302). Critics liken this scapegoating to the disgrace of Bertram, but the cruelty is closer to the triumphalism with which, after Henry's death, Carr and his in-laws manoeuvred for Overbury's removal: first to Russia, and, when he evaded that posting, to the Tower. Sir Thomas had been confident that, knowing what he did, Carr 'would not dare to leave him' for 'that base woman'; but the disappearance of the Prince left him isolated, and by June 1613 the Howards could relax that 'Not a man enquires after him, nor doth the Lord Carr miss him'. The prisoner could utter all the 'undecent and unmannerly speeches' he liked about his prosecutors, but they would not save him.[35] Likewise, in the play, the eclipse of Henriquez and his faction is hailed as a judicial *fait accompli*: 'When lovers swear true faith, the list'ning angels / Stand on the golden battlements of heaven / And waft their vows to the eternal throne' (298). Thus, the panel of elders assembled in *Cardenio* anticipates the 1613 nullity commission, in ruling that 'Lovers have things of moment … More than a Prince or dreaming statesmen know: / Such ceremonies wait on Cupid's throne' (1.2.153). It was the triumph of this tragi-comedy, it must have seemed, to raise loves like Carr's above the laws of 'a Prince or dreaming statesmen'.

'Make thy fair appeal / To the good Duke', *Cardenio* assures the court, 'and doubt not but thy tears / Shall be repaid with interest from his justice' (5.1.93). If this play was a fanfare for Carr's alliance with the Howards, then that may explain its instant suppression, for this is a text that knows how much such 'gaudy days' (3.2.35) depend upon the goodwill of an Angelo. It was one of the paradoxes of James's infatuations, however, that he was 'free from jealousy when his favourites acquired wives';[36] and Fletcher and Shakespeare optimistically reproduce this quirk with the Duke's generosity to Julio. Parents, he orates, are 'Heav'n's Lieutenants: / Made fathers … but to steer / The wanton freight of youth thro' storms and dangers' (5.2.84–8); so at the close he speeds the divorcees on their travels, hoping the 'griev'd lovers' in the audience, 'that your story read, / With true love's wanderings may like yours succeed' (329). It is to be presumed that two, at least, of those 'griev'd lovers' took heart from this annulment. The late plays insistently remind us that 'A man may weep upon his wedding day' (*Henry VIII*, Pro, 32); and if Hermione's statue was added to *The Winter's Tale* in 1613, as Bergeron has argued, to signify a welcome end to the court's winter of mourning, then it may be no surprise that in *Cardenio* an 'opportune' hearse was the centre of such 'unseasonable laughter'.[37] Yet for all the dancing on the graves of their enemies, the sponsors of 'this business so discordant' (3.2.43) should also have been warned of their own impending nemesis. The premonition comes when the Duke first sets eyes on the page 'bobb'd' by Henriquez, and enthuses, 'What's thy name boy? A pretty child. Where wast thou born? What are thy friends? How camest thou hither? How to leave thy father?' In the play, this rustic Florio, born 'On t'other side the mountain', is a girl (5.2.160–8); but his living counterpart had no such disadvantage. Even as Carr enjoyed the pastoral fiction, the real Florio was being groomed for his irresistible appearance. He came from Leicester-shire, his friends were Prince Henry's mourners, his family had been paid to dress him for the court and his name was George Villiers: very soon, great Duke of Buckingham.

NOTES

1 Isaac Wake to Lady Dudley Carleton, 19 December 1612, quoted in Roy Strong, *Henry, Prince of Wales and England's Lost Renaissance* (London: Thames and Hudson, 1986), p. 7; John Nicholls, *The Progresses, Processions, and Magnificent Festivities of King James the First* (4 vols, London: Society of Antiquaries, 1828), vol. 2, pp. 502 and 504–7.

2 Ibid., pp. 503 and 513–14; Strong, op. cit. (note 1), p. 220; Carola Oman, *Elizabeth of Bohemia* (London: Hodder and Stoughton, 1938), pp. 66–7.

3 David Bergeron, *Shakespeare's Romances and the Royal Family* (Lawrence: Kansas University Press, 1985), p. 160; and *Royal Family, Royal Lovers: King James of England and Scotland* (Columbia: University of Missouri Press, 1991), pp. 74 and 114–16.

4 Alvin Kernan, *Shakespeare: The King's Playwright: Theater in the Stuart Court, 1603–1613* (New Haven: Yale University Press, 1995), p. 156.

5 Stephen Kukowski, 'The Hand of John Fletcher in *Double Falsehood*', *Shakespeare Survey: 43* (Cambridge: Cambridge University Press, 1991), pp. 81–9, esp. p. 89; Jonathan Bate, *The Genius of Shakespeare* (London: Picador, 1997), pp. 78–81. See also Harold Metz, *Sources of Four Plays Ascribed to Shakespeare* (Columbia: Missouri University Press, 1989), pp. 259–83; Kenneth Muir, *Shakespeare as Collaborator* (London: Methuen, 1960), pp. 148–60; Richard Proudfoot, '*Henry VIII, The Two Noble Kinsmen,* and the Apocryphal Plays', in Stanley Wells (ed.), *Shakespeare: Select Bibliographical Guides* (Oxford: Oxford University Press, 1973), p. 293; John Freehafer, '*Cardenio,* by Shakespeare and Fletcher', *PMLA,* 84 (1969), pp. 501–13.

6 Clifford Leech, *The John Fletcher Plays* (London: Chatto and Windus, 1962), pp. 150–3; Bate, op. cit. (note 5), p. 79.

7 Freehafer, op. cit. (note 5), p. 507.

8 Michael Wood, 'A Sound from Heaven: Lost Music from *Cardenio*', unpub. manuscript; private correspondence with the author, February 2003; and *In Search of Shakespeare* (London: BBC, 2003), p. 315.

9 Bate, op. cit. (note 5), p. 80.

10 Carol Thomas Neely, *Broken Nuptials in Shakespeare's Plays* (Chicago: University of Chicago Press, 1993), p. 53.

11 David Lindley, *The Trials of Frances Howard: Fact and Fiction at the Court of King James* (London: Routledge, 1993), p. 39.

12 *Cardenio,* 3.2.65–74: all quotations of the play are from Kenneth Muir (ed.), *Double Falsehood or the Distressed Lovers* (London: Cornmarket, 1970), a reproduction of Theobald's 1728 text from the copy in Birmingham Reference Library: S359.1728; Metz, op. cit. (note 5), pp. 317–18.

13 Ann Jennalie Cook, *Making a Match: Courtship in Shakespeare and his Society* (Princeton: Princeton University Press, 1991), pp. 89–91. See also Martin Ingram, *Church Courts, Sex and Marriage in England, 1570–1640* (Cambridge: Cambridge University Press, 1987), p. 136.

14 Lindley, op. cit. (note 11), p. 41.

15 Antonia Fraser, *The Gunpowder Plot: Terror an Faith in 1605* (London: Weidenfeld and Nicolson, 1996), pp. 79–80.

16 Thomas Shelton, *The History of Don Quixote of the Mancha translated from the Spanish of Miguel de Cervantes,* ed. James Fitzmaurice-Kelly (4 vols, London: David Nutt, 1896), vol. 1, pp. 3–4.

17 Linda Peck Levy, 'The Mentality of a Jacobean Grandee', in Linda Peck Levy (ed.), *The Mental World of the Jacobean Court* (Cambridge: Cambridge University Press, 1991), pp. 148–68; and *Northampton: Patronage and Policy at the Court of James I* (London: George Allen and Unwin, 1982), pp. 70–2. Lindley, op. cit. (note 11), p. 85.

18 Quoted in David Bergeron, *King James and Letters of Homoerotic Desire* (Iowa City: Iowa University Press, 1999), p. 65.

19 Bergeron 1985, op. cit. (note 3), p. 160.
20 Metz, op. cit. (note 5), p. 314.
21 Freehafer, op. cit. (note 5), p. 505.
22 Strong, op. cit. (note 1), pp. 60–3.
23 Ibid., pp. 14–15 and 56–7; Lindley, op. cit. (note 11), p. 119.
24 Ibid., p. 125; William McClung and Rodney Simard, 'Donne's Somerset Epithalamium and the Erotics of Criticism', *Huntington Library Quarterly*, 50 (1987), p. 95.
25 Anne Somerset, *Unnatural Murder: Poison at the Court of King James* (London: Weidenfeld and Nicolson, 1997), pp. 162–3 and 354.
26 William Sanderson quoted Bergeron, op. cit. (note 18), p. 73.
27 Sir Simon d'Ewes quoted Somerset, op. cit. (note 25), p. 61.
28 Michael Sparke quoted Bergeron, op. cit. (note 18), p. 71.
29 Arthur Wilson, *The History of Great Britain, Being the Life and Reign of King James the First* (London: 1653), p. 55, quoted ibid.
30 Richard Dutton, *Mastering the Revels: The Regulation and Censorship of English Renaissance Drama* (London: Macmillan, 1991), pp. 198–201.
31 Metz, op. cit. (note 5), p. 360.
32 Ibid., p. 288; Muir, op. cit. (note 12), p. 2.
33 Nicholls, op. cit. (note 1), vol 2, p. 501.
34 Strong, op. cit. (note 1), pp. 15 and 225.
35 Somerset, op. cit. (note 25), pp. 125–6, 130 and 132.
36 Ibid., p. 123.
37 Bergeron 1985, op. cit. (note 3), p. 160.

11

The statue of our queen

Shakespeare's open secret

A T the end of *The Winter's Tale* Paulina marches Leontes on an exhausting tour of her art gallery, which seems like a reprise of the penance he has paid at the tomb of his wife and son ever since he promised, sixteen years before, that 'Once a day I'll visit / The chapel where they lie, / And tears shed there shall be my recreation' (3.2.236). The chapel in which Queen Hermione and Mamillius are buried side by side, with 'The causes of their death' engraved to Leontes's 'shame perpetual', is thought to have been inspired by the royal one at Westminster Abbey, where between 1605 and 1612 artists toiled on twin marble effigies of King James's pretended parent, Queen Elizabeth, and actual mother, Mary Stuart.[1] Here the inheritor of two rival kingdoms had tried to reconcile the irreconcilable, by laying the final English monarch alongside the tragic Scottish Queen, whose execution she ordered, yet by elevating the one he called his 'dearest mother' on to 'a grander scale, as if to indicate the superiority of the mother to the predecessor, of the victim to the vanquisher'.[2] Like Leontes, James I and VI 'performed / A saint-like sorrow' at the grave of the Queen he had helped to kill, by 'remember[ing] / Her and her virtues' (5.1.1–7) in a spectacular Renaissance icon that depoliticised Mary as a saint herself: 'with her hands raised in prayer … the marble in its incandescent whiteness seemingly illuminated from within; the whole body, not merely the head, emanating an aura of sanctity'. As art historians have noted, with this 'masterly readjustment' of history the sculptors imaged the Queen of Scots not as the duplicitous, volatile, sexually promiscuous political intriguer of Protestant accusation but 'as a nun-like lady of purity and sanctity; helpless victim of forces beyond her control', and a sacrifice to slander and suspicion, whose very name associated her with the Virgin.[3] If editors are correct, therefore, Shakespeare may well have taken heart from the Marian iconography of this monument to a royal Catholic martyr, when he had his King and court kneel, with similar genuflection, before the shrine of their murdered queen of tears, in one of the most incense-laden scenes in all of Jacobean drama:

LEONTES: O royal piece!
             There's magic in thy majesty, which has
             My evils conjured to remembrance, and
             From thy admiring daughter took the spirits,
             Standing like stone with thee.
PERDITA: And give me leave,
             And do not say 'tis superstition, that
             I kneel and then implore her blessing. Lady,
             Dear queen, that ended when I but began,
             Give me that hand of yours to kiss.

                                         (5.3.38–46)

As soon as Queen Elizabeth died, English Catholics rejoiced that her picture was 'hidden everywhere, and Mary Stuart's shown instead with declaration that she suffered for no cause other than her religion';[4] so when it was at last unveiled, the tomb of the martyred mother-Queen was viewed as a triumphant affirmation of the return of her supporters to the centre of Jacobean politics, and the chapel where it stood became a kind of waiting-room for the so-called court Catholics who schemed for England's reconversion. As their leader, Henry Howard, Earl of Northampton, reported, Britain's madonna was buried there 'with honour, as dead rose-leaves are preserved, whence the liquor that makes the kingdom sweet hath been distilled'.[5] Northampton was so fervently devoted to the cult of Mary that he surrounded himself with her portraits, one of which 'hung in his bed-chamber opposite a depiction of the Passion of Christ'; while, as a recent feminist biographer remarks, the ardour of continental martyrology was brazen in Jacobean engravings of the dead Queen, which enshrined her as a true daughter of the Roman Church, complete with crucifix, missal and weeping worshippers, though deliberately aged, as if 'fraught with the burden of grief and passing time'.[6] So, when Shakespeare's Perdita kneels for blessing to the statue of her 'Lady' – likewise 'wrinkled' by its 'carver's excellence, / Which lets go by some sixteen years and makes her / As she lived' (28–32) – it seems unlikely that audiences would not connect this exact passage of time with the sixteen years separating the execution of Mary from her son's succession; nor that they would have been unconscious of the popish idolatory that was being infiltrated into the inner sanctum of the Stuart court. David Bergeron has speculated, indeed, that the statue scene was precisely added to *The Winter's Tale* to honour the Queen's entombment in the Abbey, where perpetual candles burned to assuage King James's guilt.[7] Certainly, when Simon Forman saw the play at the Globe in 1611 he made no mention of Hermione's resurrection, and it may be that all public performances of the play ended with the reunion of Leontes and his heir. If so, it would be in keeping with Shakespeare's evasiveness that, even in the version acted for the private playhouse, the statue scene was shifted from the chapel where the penitent King had prayed, and Paulina was scripted instead to conduct the characters on the detour through her gallery that ends with Leontes's exasperation:

> O Paulina
> We honour you with trouble; but we came
> To see the statue of our Queen. Your gallery
> Have we passed through, not without much content
> In many singularities, but we saw not
> That which we came to look upon,
> The statue of her mother.
>
> (5.3.8–14)

'I thought she had some great matter there at hand', comments a courtier after he learns how Paulina secretly commissioned the Queen's statue, 'for she hath privately twice or thrice a day ever since the death of Hermione visited that removed house' (5.3.10; 5.2.94). If this finale was inserted at the Blackfriars theatre in 1613, then when 'the kings and princes' (156) leave the imaginary environs of the Anglican cathedral for Paulina's clandestine retreat, to kneel there in the very last scene Shakespeare may have written, they do so to vindicate his tactics of survival. For from the moment when Aemilia steps from the Abbey in *The Comedy of Errors*, where she fulfils 'A charitable duty' of her order by administering 'wholesome syrups, drugs, and holy prayers' to distressed travellers (5.3.104–7), the ultimate resort of Shakespearean romance is always in some curtained recess of the stage, with 'a lady richly left' (*Merchant*, 1.1.161); princess playing 'housewife' in a cave (*Cymbeline*, 4.2.44); or 'nun' of Diana's temple (*Pericles*, 14.11). So, like Mariana pining at St Luke's (*Measure*, 3.1.265); Hero hiding in a chapel of the 'goddess of the night' (*Much Ado*, 5.3.12); or Helena pretending to travel to the shrine of St James at Compostella (*All's Well*, 3.4.4–7), the pious widow who has attended to the statue of her 'Lady' in *The Winter's Tale* 'twice or thrice a day' (5.3.44) has retreated to the latest of all those moated granges and secluded hermitages on which power in these plays attends. Like that 'widow aunt' whose mansion is a last resort, 'remote seven leagues' from Athens, in *A Midsummer Night's Dream* (1.1.159), Paulina has resorted to one of the isolated female places, unseen by patriarchal power, and impenetrable even to the eyes of the theatre audience, for which they exist only as a rumour, on which the principle of hope in Shakespeare therefore depends. In *Measure for Measure*, for instance, even the Duke's marriage offer to Isabella is contingent on her 'vocation' to 'the votarists of Saint Clare' (1.4.4). It is not necessary to identify the Isabella and Joan Shakespeare who were among the last prioresses of Wroxall Abbey, near Stratford, as his aunts,[8] to see how the remains of convents might have constituted for the dramatist such a rich imaginative resource. But what is striking about all these women's alcoves, removed houses and safe havens is how they function in the plays not as escapist otherworld locations but as the type of emplacement – secreted *within* society, rather than projected on to some other world, and therefore a kind of open secret – which Foucault terms a *heterotopia*, the purpose of which, unlike that of a utopia – is to suspend reality, by placing events under the sign of an indefinite erasure:

All these emplacements have the curious property of being connected to all the other emplacements, but in such a way that they suspend, neutralize, or reverse the set of relations that are designated, reflected, or represented by them ... Utopias have no real space ... [but] these heterotopias are real places, actual places, places that are designed into the very institutions of society, in which all the other emplacements within the culture are represented, contested and reversed ... The mirror is a utopia after all, since it is a placeless place. In the mirror I see myself where I am not ... But it is also a heterotopia in that the mirror really exists, and has a return effect on the place I occupy ... These different spaces are a kind of contestation, both mythical and real, of the space in which we live ... they are sacred or forbidden spaces, reserved for individuals who are in a state of crisis with respect to the society and the milieu in which they live.[9]

Foucault describes such 'virtual spaces', which function in emergencies as the reverse of the actual space of society, as 'crisis heterotopias', in which 'Adolescents, menstruating women, women in labour, or the aged' are sequestered, but has noted how these 'privileged or sacred or forbidden places reserved for individuals in a state of crisis with respect to society ... have all but disappeared' under modernity, so that their vestiges seem today 'fundamentally and essentially unreal'. Likewise, recent studies of Jacobean drama confirm how rare such sanctioned havens are in a theatre that is dedicated not to concealment, intimacy or evasion, but to the 'discovery space for scenes of stunning revelation'. In this spectacular medium, where 'a disappearing act is seldom perfect', as 'someone always seems to be watching', it is the spy or informant who ultimately commands the action.[10] So, beside this panoptic theatre of surveillance, exposure and revelation, Shakespeare remains determinedly anti-modern, in that the multi-perspectivism of his dramaturgy is at last referred not to the empire of the gaze but to the claustral interiority of a suspect woman, or the sororial enclave of a confined nun. It cannot be chance, therefore, that the most extended Shakespearean testing of the conventual solution should date precisely from the instant in 1604 of the founding of the order of English nuns at Saint-Omer, and that in *Measure for Measure* the novice Isabella and nun Francesca are carefully assigned to 'the sisterhood' of this new mission, as 'votarists of Saint Clare' (1.4.5). Shakespeare's daughters were both unmarried, aged twenty-one and nineteen, at this moment, when 'the prioress' (11), Mary Ward, was recruiting the first wave of English 'Poor Clares' to 'enable women to aid in the conversion of England'. From the outset, the issue which worried the mainly gentry parents was the danger of social contact to which their daughters would be exposed in such an active mission. So, by attaching Isabella to these 'female Franciscans', and then subjecting her to attempted rape, the writer was projecting a nightmare scenario out of the question she raises about 'farther privileges' when she professes the cloister: 'not as desiring more, / But rather wishing a more strict restraint / Upon the sisterhood' (1–5). In fact, Isabella's quest for seclusion proves impossible in face of the trials imposed by the Puritan Angelo, and the play seems to authorise the 'mixed kind of life' and social activism espoused by Ward in the lay Institute of the Blessed Virgin Mary she later founded. It does so, however, without Isabella ever quite renouncing the conventual ideal, an ideal so compelling that even the rake Lucio is obliged to pay it lip-service:[11]

> I hold you are a thing enskied and sainted
> By your renouncement, an immortal spirit,
> And to be talked with in sincerity
> As with a saint.
>
> (*Measure*, 1.4.33–6)

The importance assigned to female self-immurement and women of 'renouncement' in Shakespeare's works is one of the structural features that connects them most obviously with recusant culture and tactics of Catholic survival. No other English Renaissance writer accords anything near the respect given by this dramatist to those who 'endure the livery of a nun, / For aye to be in shady cloister mewed', and who even a serial rapist such as Theseus can honour as 'Thrice blessed', to 'master so their blood / To undergo such maiden pilgrimage' (*Dream*, 1.1.70–5). In Shakespeare, it is Hector's awe at the 'high strains / Of divination' in his 'mad sister' Cassandra that overrules Troilus's contempt for 'This foolish, dreaming superstitious girl' (*Troilus*, 2.2.112; 5.3.82). Likewise, Helena's 'sainted vow' to 'barefoot plod' as 'Saint Jacques' pilgrim' makes her an 'angel' sent to redeem her husband, according to his mother (*All's Well*, 3.5.4–25). And *The Lover's Complaint* is a poem wholly given over to shock at a young courtier's ploy to 'pervert a reconciled maid' and seduce 'a nun, / A sister sanctified of holiest note', who vowed 'To spend her living in eternal love' (232–8; 329). Hamlet's order to Ophelia, to 'Get thee to a nunnery' (*Hamlet*, 3.1.122) is a defilement which is purged, over an entire play, by Mariana's purification of the brothel and prayers beside the 'maiden priests' of 'Diana's altar' (*Pericles*, 5.1.226; 5.3.17). Likewise, in *Measure for Measure* Angelo is finally judged beside the symbolically virginal 'consecrated fount / A league below the city' (4.3.89–90). So, considering how intensely Protestant writing negated conventual life, what is striking about Shakespeare's work is the allowance it makes for the 'concave womb' of the 'sistering vale' as a refuge from patriarchal power, even if, as in the 'plainful story' of the 'fickle maid', 'Storming her world with sorrow's wind and rain' (*Complaint*, 1–7), or in Isabella's silence at the Duke's marriage proposal, the ultimate status of this 'different space' remains in doubt. Feminist critics who maintain that Shakespeare shared the Puritan contempt for single life,[12] overlook what makes his representation of women's space different, therefore, from that of his contemporaries, which is the 'return effect' in his texts between society and the convent, and the fact that, if the values of the cloister are tested in them by the world, the world is also tested by the cloister. They ignore, that is to say, what is emphasised by recent historians,[13] and repeatedly envisaged by Shakespeare, which is that in early modern societies enclosure and self-confinement were still the route to female empowerment:

> While a hostile Protestant literature referred to families deciding to imprison their daughters in convents to save the expense of marrying them, the nuns themselves wrote of choosing a monastic life as a means of finding spiritual satisfaction. Alexia Gray was 'in the height of transitory glory for youth and bravery,' enjoying balls and masques, when she had a 'dream or vision' which prompted more serious thoughts. God called her 'whilst she was actually dancing' and she professed as a nun in 1631. Lucy Knatchbull struggled in her vocation ... but during her novitiate, 'she saw with the eyes of her soul a most Glorious and Supernatural Star,' which vision of the greatness of God so comforted her soul that she found that she 'could pray, read, sing, sweep, wash dishes, or whatsoever else with pleasure' ... Personal austerity attracted many nuns: 'Her delight was to debar herself of all Delights'. Some found their chief comfort in the sacraments, others were remarkable for charity. Nuns were also praised for their insatiable zeal for the conversion of England ... but it should be remembered that they were exercising choices about their preferred modes of spirituality. Gertrude More, who died of smallpox in 1633, had used her sisterhood to emancipate herself from the need of any priest at her deathbed. She had attained such spirituality 'that she could confidently go out of this life without speaking to any man.'[14]

'When you have vowed you must not speak with men / But in the presence of the prioress': a generation of feminists gripped by the 'repressive hypothesis' interpreted the self-enclosure of Shakespeare's women as forms of contain ment, without weighing the possibility that Francesca's instruction to Isabella, that 'if you speak, you must not show your face, / Or if you show you face, you must not speak' (*Measure*, 1.4.10–13), might constitute a means of resistance.[15] Within a contemplative tradition silence is not always consent, however, and in Shakespeare it is often golden. Thus, Olivia's retreat from society, 'mewing herself up in her chantry to mourn out her youth and beauty for her dead brother', might be a kind of folly, as Juliet Dusinberre objects, but chiefly in the eyes of males like the Duke, with reasons to break her seclusion. Dusinberre quotes the parasitic Sir Toby to argue that by hiding her face from the world this heiress is 'like to take dust, like Mistress Mall's picture', as a mock-Madonna, in Feste's image, or 'veiled Mary' (*Twelfth*, 1.3.107; 1.5.37–61). But this critic's distaste for Catholicism, and for the bereaved as 'an ordinary Mistress Mall playing at Madonna and taking dust behind her veil', has trouble with the fact that this 'mouse of virtue' (1.5.54) herself decides when to 'draw the curtain' from her face 'and show you the picture' (204–5). Dusinberre's determination to root Shakespeare in Puritanism does less than justice, in other words, to the dialectic in *Twelfth Night* between Carnival and Lent, Catholic and Protestant, or secrecy and disclosure, and she ignores the irony that the stock Reformation critique of virginity is given, in *All's Well That Ends Well*, to the rogue Parolles.[16] Within the economy of these plays, however, Paulina's piety, Helena's pilgrimage, Olivia's mourning or Portia's exploitation of her father's will are classic evasive manoeuvres. And they align these widows and daughters not with Puritanism, but with 'Catholic matriarchalism': the power exercised by women of recusant households, which was to keep the faith as an open secret, at a time when, because men faced harsher penalties, male conformity was a regular façade for female resistance. That was why 'around 1600, a lot of conformist gentlemen had Catholic wives' who decided their children's religion.[17] So, the gender politics of Shakespearean theatre seem keyed to the irony that 'a woman's inferior legal and public identity afforded her a superior devotional status, a fuller membership of the Catholic Church'.[18] For the self-immurement of the Catholic community made it, 'in effect, a matriarchy'.[19]

On 5 May 1606 Shakespeare's daughter Susanna was listed among the twenty-two Stratford residents flouting legislation introduced after the Gunpowder Plot to force 'persons popishly affected' to receive Anglican communion at least once a year. She was then one of seven who risked increasing the fine of up to £60 by ignoring a summons to appear in court, though before her case could be heard again it was 'dismissed', perhaps as a result of family influence.[20] This episode (which came to light only in 1964) is evidence that the Shakespeare household might itself have been one of those maintaining an 'internal recusant regime', and that Susanna may have acted as just the type of female resistant about whom 'much dispute' was then taking place in Parliament.[21] That she must have conformed some time before her marriage to the Protestant John Hall, in June 1607, therefore looks very like submission to the coercion which accompanied the imposition of the new Oath of Allegiance, which required suspected Catholics to declare James their ruler, and swear 'the Pope neither of himself, nor by authority of the Church of Rome, hath any power or authority to depose the King'.[22] The aim of this oath, the King joked, was simply to separate 'the sheep and the goats in my own pasture', or 'good Papists and bad',[23] but its trick was to 'seek out the secret recesses of the heart', the Shakespeares' own local bishop admitted, 'and put a doubtful matter beyond all doubt'.[24] So, it seems significant that this was also the moment of *Pericles*, the play cited by recusant actors in Yorkshire and taught by the Jesuits, which opens with another trial to quiz those who hope to appease a king, the love-test posed by Antiochus 'To keep [his daughter] still, and men in awe, / That whoso asked her for his wife, / His riddle told not, lost his life' (1.36–8). The starkest of Shakespeare's plays, *Pericles* is also the most didactic in countering tyranny with legitimate resistance on lines of Catholic ideas of popular sovereignty, since 'As jewels lose their glory if neglected, / So princes their renown, if not respected' (6.12–13). And Phoebe Jensen has pointed out that resistance is here an attack on James's own philosophy of patriarchalism, which places Marina in a recusant position, as a daughter whose part is to defy her social superiors with a rationale for insubordination: 'Let not authority, which teaches you / To govern others, be the means to make you / Misgovern much yourself' (19.91–3).[25] A role-model for pious virgins, this 'votress' of Diana (15.4) is given a *curriculum vitae*, in fact, that makes her an exemplar of the prospectus which might once have been open to Shakespeare's daughter, if placed among those 'sisters' at Saint-Omer:

> She sings like one immortal, and she dances
> As goddess-like to her admired lays.
> Deep clerks she dumbs, and with her nee'le composes
> Nature's own shape, of bud, bird, branch, or berry,
> That e'en her art sisters the natural roses.
> Her inkle, silk, twin with the rubied cherry;
> That pupils lacks she none of noble race,
> Who pour their bounty on her, and her gain
> She gives the cursed Bawd.
>
> (*Pericles*, 20.3–11)

'Come, ho, and wake Diana with a hymn. / With sweetest touches pierce your mistress' ear, / And draw her home with music' (*Merchant*, 5.1.65–7): the call from Belmont is a reminder that Shakespeare's stage is organised according to a medieval concept of space, as an ensemble of positions, in Foucault's terms, composed out of alternating *places*: 'sacred and profane places, protected places', in opposition to 'places that are open and defenceless'. What interested the theorist, however, in 'this interconnection of places', was the fact that the system had a history, whereby localised places were superseded by global space, as 'from the seventeenth century, extension supplanted localization'.[26] Few schemata are more useful for analysis of Shakespearean drama, in which desacralisation of space does proceed, in play after play, as an assault on the *topoi* of the 'green world':[27] places like those 'Bare ruined choirs where late the sweet birds sang' (Sonnet 73). These are relics of monasticism, but also sites of rebirth, and therefore analogous, in sexual terms, to the 'consecrated wall' of virginity (*Rape*, 723), which is likewise menaced by hypocritical Puritan despoilers, such as Angelo, Falstaff, Malvolio or Tarquin. For while the 'green world' may be eroding in his plays, Linda Woodbridge is surely right to think that Shakespeare's space is never completely desacralised, and that, even as 'magic is starting to bleach out of the landscape', his stage is still haunted by guardians of 'a ghostly organic society'.[28] It might be possible to trace the origin of English Gothic, with its dark woods and silent convents, to this Shakespearean dereliction, like 'Ovid among the Goths' (*As You Like It*, 3.3.6), amid the ransacked ruins of medieval Catholicism. For, as Peter Milward insists, it cannot be chance that nostalgia for the 'well-noted face / Of plain old form' (*John*, 4.2.21), 'constant service of the antique world' (*As You Like It*, 2.3.58), 'better days' (2.7.119), 'old custom' (2.1.2), and 'old fashions', by those who refuse 'To change true rules for odd inventions' (*Shrew*, 3.1.78–9), is projected so often on to the 'holy edifice of stone' (*Merchant*, 1.1.30) pre-dating the

Reformation.[29] But what the summons to Belmont, and its association with virginity, suggests is that in Shakespeare's imaginative geography the 'sweet birds' are 'still choiring' behind walls, and 'Within the house', where the 'mistress is at hand', the 'young-eyed' continue to bring their 'music forth into the air' (5.1.51):

> Look how the floor of heaven
> Is thick inlaid with patens of bright gold.
> There's not the smallest orb which thou behold'st
> But in his motion like an angel sings,
> Still choiring to the young-eyed cherubims.
>
> (*Merchant*, 5.1.57–61)

Shakespeare's bipolar theatre, with its alternation between Venice and Belmont, court and country, or marketplace and mansion, turns out to be highly historically specific, when its spatial dialectic is contextualised in relation to the social geography of Elizabethan recusancy. For, as John Bossy reiterates, if 'the Catholic community owed its existence to gentlewomen's dissatisfaction at the Reformation settlement', there is also no question that the Catholicism of this 'matriarchal era' was essentially a religion of the nobility and gentry, based on the control by women of the seigneurial household: 'its buildings, lands, and the villages it dominated'. The reason for this seigneurialism, as Lorenzo's picture of Portia's household implies, is that the Catholic community remained 'less concerned with dramas of conscience than with a set of ingrained observances that gave meaning to the cycle of the week and seasons of the year, to birth, marriage and death'.[30] Hence, 'so long as the mark of Catholicism was adherence to the cycle of fast and feast', it depended on the self-immurement of the great house, and the devotion of those who either worked in it or, in the words of one later report, 'remain round the old mansion, for the conveniency of prayers, and because they hope to receive favour from their former masters'.[31] Belmont, with its 'lady richly left', who has been, she says, 'the lord / Of this fair mansion, master of my servants, / Queen of myself' (1.1.161; 3.2.167–9), and who is accustomed to 'stray about / By holy crosses, where she kneels and prays' for hours, accompanied by 'None but a holy hermit and her maid' (5.1.30–4), seems to be the epitome of the matriarchal Catholicism described by Bossy. Portia's sponsorship of a singing-master, choir and 'temples' with plate of 'bright gold', are evidently what 'makes her seat of Belmont Colchis' strand' (1.1.170–1), and a safe haven for those drawn by 'That light we see is burning' in her hall, which 'throws his beams' like 'a good deed in a naughty world'. 'When the moon shone we did not see the candle', Nerissa recalls; and those eucharistic 'patens' imply that this is, indeed, an altar-lamp, formerly eclipsed by Elizabeth, but now, with the return to the house of Christ the 'king', the signal that 'the greater glory' doth 'dim the less' (5.1.88–94).

'Heterotopias always presuppose a system of opening and closing which isolates them and makes them penetrable at the same time', observes Foucault:

'There are heterotopias that look like openings, but conceal curious exclusions. Everybody can enter these heterotopian emplacements, but actually this is only an illusion: one believes one is going inside and, by the very fact of entering, one is excluded.'[32] In Shakespeare's heterotopic theatre, therefore, the inner sanctum associated with virginity belongs to the enigmatic *locus* of the inner stage that Robert Weimann differentiates from the openness of the down-stage *platea*.[33] There the tiring-house brackets the boundary of the stage in exactly the ambiguity in which Catholicism is shrouded by his evasive terminology. This is a space that perfectly fits the 'Don't ask; don't tell', status of belief in 'a world of open secrets, where hypocrisy is a fundamental constituent of being'.[34] There is an affinity, in other words, between Shakespeare's doubtful confessional position and his preference for private places over public spaces. This means that Portia's 'temple' (2.1.43) remains screened behind its classical decoration in *The Merchant of Venice*, as an open secret, without ever closing the door on the public inclusiveness towards which its owner aspires, when she apologises that 'If to do were as easy as to know what were good to do, chapels had been churches' (1.2.11). Thus, to see through the Elizabethan 'moon shine', which the lovers identify with a history of violence and betrayal (5.1.1–24), to perceive the truth and goodness of that 'little candle' burning in the oratory (89), is itself an initiation ritual, for both the actors and the audience. One can only enter this type of heterotopia, as Foucault says, 'with a certain permission and after a certain number of gestures have been performed'.[35] Such is the liminality of religious experience in play after play by Shakespeare, where social inclusion is contingent on an act of worship which the characters will celebrate afterwards, when they proceed inside, 'And to the chapel presently' (*Much Ado*, 5.4.71). But in this case, Portia's welcome must have had more urgent resonance, as Belmont was not only a pun on the surname of the dramatist's patrons, the Montagues, but the actual name of one of their seats in Hampshire, famous as a Mass centre. So, Shakespeare reverses the malaise of the House of Mont*ague* with his *Bel*mont. And if this play was staged, as is possible, under the aegis of the Earl of Southampton, at one of the great houses of his pious grandmother, Lady Magdalen Montague – Montague House, on the site of the former priory of St Mary Overy beside London Bridge, and Battle Abbey and Cowdray in Sussex – a journey from the mercenary Rialto to a merciful Belmont would have prepared the audience with an idea of just what to imagine in that chantry in the country, with its inlaid floor, altar-plate, swinging censers and 'concord of sweet sounds' (*Merchant*, 5.1.83):

> She built a chapel in her house (which in such a persecution was to be admired) and there placed a very fair altar of stone, whereto she made an ascent with steps and enclosed it with rails, and, to have everything conformable, she built a choir for singers and set up a pulpit for the priests, which perhaps is not to be seen in all England besides. Here almost every week was a sermon made, and on solemn feasts the sacrifice of the Mass was celebrated with singing and with musical instruments, and sometimes also with deacon and subdeacon. And

such was the concourse and resort of Catholics, that sometimes there were 120 together, and 60 communicants at a time had the benefit of the Blessed Sacrament. And such was the number of Catholics resident in her house and the multitude and note of such as repaired thither, that even the heretics, to the eternal glory of Lady Magdalen, give it the title of *Little Rome*.[36]

'The man that hath no music in him ... Is fit for treasons, stratagems, and spoils': the Matins sung at Belmont are scrupulously curtained to separate the loyalism of Shakespeare's worshippers, whose coltish rebelliousness has now been tamed, from the politics of traitors whose affections are 'dark as Erebus. Let no such man be trusted' (82–7). The specificity of Lorenzo's warning against one who is 'dull as night', like the Moroccan Prince misliked for his complexion (2.1.1), seems to point, through the 'Moorish' pun that would be developed in *Othello*, at the most dangerous of all those 'strangers suspected to be priests' as they filtered through 'Little Rome': Father Thomas More, 'direct heir of that famous Sir Thomas More', who came to live at Battle in 1592 from Madrid, on a mission to intrigue for Spain.[37] In fact, he was lodging with kin, Lord Montague's sister having married Thomas Roper, the grandson of the martyr. And historians are sure the Montagues were vital to 'the underground system that channelled priests coming from overseas to other parts of England'.[38] This did not stop them receiving Elizabeth at Cowdray in 1591 with a masque by John Lyly protesting that it was 'such a disguised world, that one can scarce know a Pilgrim from a Priest', yet defying the 'goddess of the hunt' to punish them: 'Strike one, strike all, for none at all can fly, / They gaze you in the face although they die'.[39] Their 'hymn' to 'Diana' may have woken her to the distinction between these loyalists and those 'fit for spoils', but it was a daring song to sing on 'an estate whose owners specialized in the treasonous activity of protecting, transporting and disguising priests'.[40] Commentators therefore describe the Cowdray Entertainment as a plea that 'as long as a nobleman was loyal, his household should be exempt' from law. The 'line between what was God's and what was the Queen's' was tested by the guest, however, when she arrived on Saturday, after imposing herself on other members of the More clan, to prevent Mass next day in the room she was never to be allowed to see.[41] But like their neighbours, the Shelleys, who kept the vents from a subterranean chapel hidden by shrubs,[42] the Montagues were adept at braving any who pried (such as the Spaniard of the play) 'to th'interior', instead of accepting that they had nothing to hide: as 'the martlet / Builds in the weather on the outward wall' (2.9.27–8). They could identify with the Portia who excuses her casket charade as a necessity in 'these naughty times' that 'Put bars between owners and their rights', and guides Bassanio to trust the truth of 'paleness', because it 'rather threaten'st than doth promise aught' (3.2.18–19; 105–6). Such was the message of their masque, which insisted that their 'wall is rampired with true hearts'.[43] And the dramatist, who may also have written *Romeo and Juliet* and *A Midsummer Night's Dream* for this family,[44] made the mortal name of their executed ancestor 'a good moral' in play after play,[45] by staging both the tragic need for that 'sweet and lovely wall' which divided the Montagues from their enemies, and the comic possibility of a happy end, when the actor could finally pronounce that 'The wall is down that parted their fathers' (*Dream*, 5.1.120; 174; 337).

'We must have a wall in the great chamber; for Pyramus and Thisbe, says the story, did talk through the chink of a wall' (3.1.53–5): Shakespeare's punning self-referentiality over the mural politics of seigneurial Catholicism implies that he understood the functional relation between the survival tactics of those descendants of More who needed to partition their faith behind fake mortar, and the Aesopian poetics of his own stage. And Belmont, where you must look *up* to see a heavenly *floor*, epitomises the inverted logic of both Catholic resistance and Shakespearean theatre, which each move to what Alexander Pope termed the 'Godly Garret', or space of secret meaning, concealed behind a trick perspective, 'as false / As stairs of sand' (*Merchant*, 3.2.83).[46] It could be that the attic of the Henley Street house where Shakespeare's father hid his Testament of Faith functioned as such a chapel, in which Mass would be said by one of the numerous priests listed during the 1590s as serving 'gentlemen known to be ill-affected in religion in Warwickshire'.[47] But, in any case, the country around Stratford offered some of the most successful examples of clandestine Mass centres constructed anywhere in England, such as the oratory in the rafters at Compton Wynyates, that pre-dated the Queen's visit in 1572; the chapel in the garret at Clopton House, enclosed by masonry cut to look like exterior walls; or the rooftop cell above the gatehouse at Coughton, which the Throckmortons sealed so well it was discovered, complete with a Spanish-leather altar, only in 1858.[48] Bossy has proposed that this architecture of concealment itself imposed a mentality of deferral on the recusant community over the decades of seigneurial retreat, when the celebration of Mass 'followed a well-marked itinerary around the house, from the halls and "fair large chambers" where the congregations of the Elizabethan pioneers assembled … up to the less vulnerable attics, where many of the first-generation of chaplain-missioners sat "like sparrows upon the house-top" and most of the earliest Mass-chambers were fitted up', then down to the first floor about 1700, and so back to the ground in the middle of the eighteenth century.[49] But if the historical experience of English Catholics was defined, as Bossy contends, by the spatial logistics of their self-exclusion 'in a wall'd prison' (*Lear*, 5.3.18), it is equally suggestive how Shakespeare always yearns for a time to 'draw the curtain' (*Merchant*, 2.9.1) on his open secret, when the excluded are included, the concealed is revealed, and 'Wall away doth go' (*Dream*, 5.1.203):

> Who would be thence, that has the benefit of access?
> Every wink of an eye some new grace will be born.
> Our absence makes us unthrifty to our knowledge.
> Let's along.
>
> (*The Winter's Tale*, 5.2.98–101)

Editors explain Paulina's name as an allusion to St Paul, and to the Pauline faith in 'things not seen, the primacy of the spirit over the letter';[50] and if this is so, then it may be no coincidence that *The Winter's Tale* is perhaps the first of Shakespeare's plays to be written or revised specifically for the Burbages' enclosed Blackfriars Playhouse, in the monastic quarter on the opposite bank of the Thames to the Globe amphitheatre, in the shadow of St Paul's. There, according to theatre historians, the dramatist could experiment with the illusion of darkness reported by Thomas Dekker as a special effect of private play-houses, where 'the windows are clapped down, as if some nocturnal or dismal tragedy were to be acted'; or with the contrast between a brilliant auditorium, lit by candelabra, and an inner stage area kept, as Paulina maintains the statue, 'Lonely, apart' (5.3.18), within the 'dark backward and abysm' (*Tempest*, 1.2.50) of hangings and screens. And there too he could employ a complex system of trap-doors beneath the stage that was a prized feature of this theatre inserted into the upper floor of a pre-existing building, through which supernatural figures could be made to vanish, with the warning, like that of Time in the play, not to search for truth, but 'let Time's news / Be known when 'tis brought forth' (4.1.26).[51] Paulina's stipulation, as she stands before the statue, that 'It is required / You do awake your faith' (5.3.95), may therefore rely on the sense of the imponderable that was produced mechanically on this stage, like that when Antigonus disappears with the famous stage direction, 'Exit pursued by a bear' (3.3.57). Shakespeare's characters are forever dropping into the cellarage, lurking behind the arras or climbing into the trunks, as William Slights says,[52] but this mystery theatre was equipped to literalise 'The undiscovered country' beyond the curtain, (*Hamlet*, 3.1.79), and affirm his belief that 'what's to come is still unsure' (*Twelfth*, 2.3.50). With a mistress like Paulina to control the entrances and exits, the Blackfriars Playhouse was therefore fulfilling the historic function of this 'little Rome' or foreign corner of the Square Mile, which was as the gateway to London's recusant underground.

The statue scene was added to *The Winter's Tale*, it is suggested, when it was acted at Blackfriars in the spring of 1613, and on 10 March of that year Shakespeare himself bought the upper floor of the Gatehouse straddling the entrance into the walled precinct of the former priory of the Dominicans who had given the place its name. This purchase has always baffled scholars, as it consisted of a complicated transaction in which title went to the playwright and three trustees, who leased the property back to the vendor for a giveaway rent, with the effect that Shakespeare's wife was denied any rights of ownership. Since all of his other investments had been made in the interests of his family, and the price of this nominal one was over twice what he had paid for his Stratford mansion, researchers have investigated the history of the building Shakespeare bought in Blackfriars, and what they have discovered is that, as well as leading to the playhouse, the Gatehouse was a command-post for London Catholics. Here, for instance, the dramatist's immediate neighbours were Robert Dormer and his family, one of the most revanchist recusant families, connected not only to the Montagues but through the marriage of Robert's aunt to Philip II's envoy, the Count of Feria, to the leaders of the émigré cabal in Madrid.[53] The building had been redeveloped by the Marian Bishop of Ely, Thomas Thirlby, who died there in disgrace in 1570; and as early as 1586 had been listed as a maze of hiding-places and escape routes, having 'sundry back-doors and byways, and many secret vaults and corners'. 'It hath been searched for papists', reported one agent, 'but no good done for want of knowledge of the back-doors and byways and dark corners'.[54] Even the priest-hunter Richard Topcliffe, was frustrated by its 'many places of secret convey-ance' leading to 'secret passages towards the water'; and the reason was, of course, that the Gatehouse stood upon the maze of crypts and tunnels, some dating from prehistoric times, which underlay the medieval Priory.[55] These passageways led down to the quayside as well as into the cellars of connecting houses, and the importance of the Gatehouse was that it was there that the porters locked the gate each night to seal the entire 'liberty' from the City, making good the claim to 'freedom from arrest within the precinct', and exemp-tion from official searches, 'except with the inhabitants' cooperation'. For what attracted entrepreneurs such as the Burbages to 'the Friars', and made it the favourite quarter of 'courtiers, preachers, artists, actors and audiences, gold-smiths and printers, bookbinders and booksellers', were the privileges which also drew the politically exotic to live there, such as Ludovic Stuart, Duke of Lennox, the King's French nephew, and Arbella, his erratic cousin.[56] Even today, the Bishop of Ely's other City enclave, Ely Place, later the Spanish embassy, remains a Catholic island nominally in Cambridgeshire. So, with the rivers Fleet and Thames on two sides, and ramparts on the other, the Blackfriars triangle was a state-within-a-state, and possession of its Gatehouse guaranteed that it would remain a sanctuary of religious freedom, complete with the monks' own water supply:

> It is chronicled that the whole [district] was undermined with secret passages, stairs and vaults, some of which, through long and lazy windings, com-municated with other parts of the monastery. Below the foundations a large vault had been constructed with a broad, deep spring in the centre, in which clear bubbling spring spirted in voluminous quantity the water supply needful for its builders and for subsequent dwellers.[57]

No sooner had he purchased his Blackfriars property than Shakespeare leased it again, and in his will it was itemised as occupied by one John Robin-son, who, since he was also one of the witnesses to the document, has been raised by the most recent research into 'the highly interesting status of being the only individual from Shakespeare's London world to have been with him at his deathbed'.[58] And it is the career of this presumably close associate that offers a key to Shakespeare's intentions in assuming legal ownership of such a notorious centre of Catholic resistance. For Robinson was steward of the

Master of the Queen's Wardrobe, Sir John Fortescue (whose office opposite the Gatehouse was linked to it by a 'bridge of sighs'), and manager, therefore, of one of the most active Catholic families in England. It had been during the tenancy of Sir John's nephew in the 1580s, in fact, that the Gatehouse had become a linchpin in the network of safe houses that ran from the Fortescue and Montague estates in Sussex to London refuges, like that kept on Bankside by the actor Richard Tarlton.[59] Earlier tenants included relations of Campion and Mary Bannister, the sister of the poet Southwell; and it was there that Katherine Carus, a kinswoman of the Lancashire Hoghtons, and the widow of a defiantly recusant judge, had died 'in all her pride and popery'.[60] In 1591 the priests Anthony Tyrrell and John Ballard had filled the house with 'stuff we brought from Rome'.[61] But shortly it was reported that 'Fennell the priest doth come very much to Mr John Fortescue's house', and in 1598 the property was searched by the pursuivants.[62] By 1602 the family had to prosecute an Oxford don for alleging that 'Sir John Fortescue made way for Papistry'; and they came very close to disaster in 1605, when the Gunpowder Plotters actually planned to make the Gatehouse their bolthole, and Father Gerard had hidden there, 'disguised in a false beard and hair', before escaping to Flanders.[63] As late as 1610, it was said in Naples that the house Shakespeare would soon buy was a base for Jesuits plotting to 'send the King an embroidered doublet and hose, which are poisoned and will be death to the wearer'.[64] But as the precinct included the residence of the French Ambassador, all such comings and goings were masked by diplomatic immunity. The Fortescues sent their daughters to be nuns at Saint-Omer, where Robinson himself seems to have acted as a recruiting agent, from where he was reported to welcome priests, and to which he sent his own son Edward, who in 1613 presented himself in Rome. It may be this Fortescue connection which explains why *Pericles* became the only non-religious text on the Saint-Omer curriculum.[65] For Shakespeare's Blackfriars was a house of many doors, apparently, some of which led up into the Playhouse, others into the Embassy chapel, and a few into the secret chambers of Jesuit sedition.

In the autumn of 1651 Charles II was on the run following the royalist disaster at the Battle of Worcester, when he made his way to Racton, the Sussex home of the Fortescues. There he hid in the critical days before his boat was ready to carry him to France, concealed in one of the chain of hiding-places the Fortescues had constructed across southern England in the days of his grandfather.[66] Thus the Stuarts would eventually come to be realigned with the Catholicism for which Mary Queen of Scots had died; but in the meantime it was the cunning of aristocratic families such as Fortescues which ensured that religion remained quite literally compartmentalised from power. It did so thanks to work they commissioned in houses such as Faulkbourne Hall in Essex, the home of Edward Fortescue, where Jesuits from London were hidden in some of the priest-holes devised by the maestro of this neglected form of

Counter-Reformation architecture, the friar known as 'Little John', Nicholas Owen. Active between 1588 and 1606, when he was arrested and tortured to death, Owen could be called the Shakespeare of the hiding-place because of his genius for multi-dimensional illusionism and the visual pun. For what made his artistry truly Baroque, according to historians, is that, while conventional priest-holes had been 'designed in straight lines and two dimensions', his were 'by a man who could think in three dimensions and in curves'.[67] Typically, this involved a confusing Escher-like construction around a staircase, where different levels could be exploited by the insertion of a cavity between floors or within the panelling, for Owen's hallmark was that he never extended an existing building, but always hollowed spaces out of timber or burrowed into masonry, 'in consequence of his liking for sites away from outside walls, where the structure of a house could remain unaltered, and nothing would project from it'.[68] The favourite site for such insertion, Robert Cecil warned his priest-hunters, would be in the roof, where 'if there be any double loft, some two or three feet one above another … it must of necessity be looked into, for these be ordinary places of hovering'.[69] But the exact location of such contrivances was something that, as Father Garnet recorded, Owen took with him, in spite of torture, to his grave:

> His chief employment was in making of secret places to hide priests and Church stuff from the fury of searches; in which kind he was so skilful both to devise and frame the places in the best manner … that I verily think he was the immediate occasion of saving the lives of many hundreds of persons, and of the estates that had been forfeited if the priests had been taken in their houses; of which some escaped not once but many times, in several searches that have come to the same house, and sometimes five or six priests together at the same time. One reason that made him so much desired by Catholics of account … was a tried care he had of secrecy … But, above all, that which did most commend him in the sight of God was that … [after his arrest] he might have made it almost an impossible thing for priests to escape, whom he might have taken like partridges in a net, knowing all their secret places which himself had made, and like conveyances in most of the chief Catholics' houses in England, and the means and the manner how all such places were to be found.[70]

It is because 'her dead likeness … Excels whatever yet you looked upon, / Or hand of man hath done', explains Paulina, when Leontes begs to see Hermione's image, that she has been so careful to 'keep it / Lonely, apart' (5.3.15–18). A moment later, when she draws the curtain, she orders the company to 'Quit … the chapel, or resolve you / For more amazement' (84); and Stephen Orgel notes that the very fact that she claims 'to have kept the statue not in her gallery but in a chapel makes the religious associations explicit'.[71] As Stephen Greenblatt observes, Shakespearean theatre thrives upon such metaphorical exchange between art, power and religion, yet 'equally depends upon a deliberate distancing or distortion that precedes the disclosure of likeness'. For when Protestants characterized the Catholic mass as 'a kind of theater, their attack conjured up a theater in which (1) the playhouse disguised itself as a holy place; (2) the audience thought of itself as a community of believers; (3) the perform-ance not only refused to concede it was an illusion but claimed to be the highest truth; (4) the actors actually believed in the roles they played; and (5) the spec-tacle demanded of the audience not a few pennies but a lifelong commitment'. At moments like that in *Henry VIII* when the text seems to call attention to the fact that 'the copes, albs, amices and stoles' that were the glories of the medieval church had been sold to the players, and that Cardinal Wolsey's hat was now worn by his impersonator, Shakespeare deliberately punctured the 'wooden walls' dividing the sacred and profane, Greenblatt concludes, and his theatre acquired its 'social energy' from the *frisson* that 'the most solemn formulas of church and state could find their way onto the stage'.[72] Shakespear-ean theatre was analogous to the recusant Mass chamber or priest-hole, accord-ing to this analysis, in the evasiveness with which Catholic practices were insinuated into the performance, yet dissimulated behind false partitions that separated the fiction from the fact. In the age of priest-hunters and persecution, this was a highly dangerous manoeuvre, that could, perhaps, be undertaken only in the open secrecy of a precinct such as Blackfriars. The last heretic was burned in London in 1612; and Paulina, who holds that 'It is an heretic that makes the fire, / Not she which burns in't (2.3.114), is as skilful as a Jesuit in concealing her 'Church stuff' from the eyes of disbelievers:

> If you can behold it,
> I'll make the statue move indeed, descend
> And take you by the hand – but then you'll think,
> Which I protest against, I am assisted
> By wicked powers ...
> It is required
> You do awake your faith. Then all stand still –
> Or those that think it is unlawful business
> I am about, let them depart ...
> Music; awake her – strike!

> (5.3.85–98)

In a brilliant critique of this moment, Julia Lupton has interpreted Herm-ione's return from stone and sequestration as a post-Reformation allegory, symbolising the persistence of Marian iconography through an age of Protestant iconoclasm, and 'Christianizing the Sicily of broken laws and deadly idolatry into the Sicily of redeeming faith and resurrected art'.[73] Starting from James Siemon's reading of Leontes's 'deadly art' of jealousy as a perversion of 'image making' into idolatry,[74] Lupton argues that 'the play's coding of Paulina's chapel as a reliquary' of Catholicism opposes iconoclasm to hagiography, and the reformist contempt for 'pilgrimages unto dead saints and images' against 'the fascination of the saint and the statue' that Paulina activates, when she defies the tyrant, in 'a shorthand catalogue' of martyrology, to torture her with 'wheels.. racks ... fires ... flaying ... boiling ... In leads or oils' (3.2.174–5). By this light, it is the 'remainders' of the saints which are 'collected in Paulina's gallery, a setting loaded with the signs of ... Catholic forms of worship', and which, for all its owner's disavowals, 'remains tainted by signs of Catholicism, sounded in Shakespeare's references to "sects" and "proselytes" [5.1.107–8], to Hermione's "sainted spirit" [57]; and to the "chapel" that houses the statue [5.3.86], an image graven by an artist with "Rome" in his name'. There, Lupton confirms, 'Hermione as statue has become a kind of Madonna who bestows her gifts on those who pray in her Roman chapel', whilst Perdita's words to her 'resemble a prayer to the Virgin, that other "Lady, dear queen," and mother whose iconography was outlawed under Protestantism'. Thus, 'the generalized "Christianity"' evoked by the setting is strongly 'coded as Catholic'. Yet the point of the statue scene, according to this commentary, is that it 'stages the visual conditions of Catholic image worship, but only as cancelled, with equal emphasis on both the act of staging and the fact of cancellation'. For though 'the idolatrous ambience' of Catholicism 'serves to heighten the sense of mystery and magic, when this supernaturalism is finally naturalized ... the play's rationalizing deflation ... definitively undercuts the Catholic iconography the scene so powerfully evokes'. *The Winter's Tale* is therefore a play about the *afterlife* of the saints, in Lupton's view, and what it shows is that the 'remains' of Catholicism can be recuperated into art. For 'the play does not dissipate' the energy of the Roman Church, 'so much as transport it onto itself' by transforming religion into art:[75]

> *The Winter's Tale* smashes the Catholic idols in order to extract their fascinating power ... to draw new wine from old skins ... for an art and drama that establishes itself as the afterlife of the saints ... [The play] takes up the fragments of the idols as fragments, stones of Rome whose vestigial ... redeployments animate Shakespearean drama.[76]

Like much New Historicism, Lupton's take on the statue scene is a characteristically American attempt to save Shakespeare from the Church of his origins and salvage his theatre for secular modernity. But the problem with the argument that *The Winter's Tale* demystifies 'the worship of relics' is that this depends on Orgel's editorial assumption that 'Hermione was alive all along', and that 'the statue reveals itself as human'.[77] Unfortunately, for a humanist criticism, there is nothing in the text that definitively supports this naturalistic interpretation, any more than there is for Father Milward's contrasting belief that the ending is 'an apparent miracle by which "dear life redeems" [5.3.103] Hermione' from actual death.[78] Both Christian and secularising readings underestimate the systematic ambiguity of Shakespeare's staging of the Pygmalion legend, though the fact that they are equally convinced of their explanations is itself a testimony to the illusionism with which the play equivocates about whether or not it is true that, as Antigonus attests as an article of faith, 'Hermione hath suffered death' (3.3.41). They overlook, that is to say, the historical context of this denouement, which, if added for the Blackfriars theatre, would have constituted a perfect paradigm of the circumspection of court Catholics in the house, in its simultaneous religiosity and dissociation from those 'peevish papists' who, as out-and-out Protestants, such as John Marston, jeered, 'crouch and kneel / To some dull idol with their offering, / As if a senseless carved stone could feel / The ardour of [their] bootless chatter'.[79] Shakespeare had assigned such Protestant polemic to the tyrannical Queen in *Venus and Adonis*, who rails against the 'cold and senseless stone, / Well-painted idol, image dull and dead, / Statue contenting but the eye alone, / Thing like a man, but of no woman bred!' (211–16). But in *The Winter's Tale* evasiveness as to whether Hermione is dead or alive turns the final tableau into a model for what Bossy has called 'Catholic royalism for royal Catholicism': the ecumenical inclusiveness of those, like the Howards, who finessed doctrinal differences in the hope of a religious reunion, and in the *politique* assurance that 'the majority of Catholics and Protestants, who do not know what all the arguments are about, will fall in behind'. Such a 'gentlemen's agreement to differ' about the doctrines of 'a political and social order [in which] the functions of the clergy become largely ceremonial', seems to be precisely what Shakespeare expects of his audience in this dramatisation of the resurrection, as they 'fall in behind' a performance which avoids putting art before religion, as much as it refuses to put religion before art.[80] Not knowing 'what all the arguments are about', at the end of the play, Shakespeare's audience is ready, one might say, for the future Church of England; while by his strategic equivocation between life and death – with actors who are said to weep tears of blood, like statues of the Madonna Vulnerata which was the icon of exiled English Catholics[81] – the dramatist himself disavows the pride of Pygmalion for the humility of the juggler of Notre Dame:

> One of the prettiest touches of all … was when at the relation of the Queen's death, with the manner of it bravely confessed and lamented by the King, how attentiveness wounded his daughter till from one sign of dolour to another she did, with an 'Alas', I would fain say, bleed tears, for I am sure my heart wept blood. Who was most marble there changed colour. (5.2.74–81)

The curtain is drawn back, and a place that seemed an art gallery turns out to be a chapel, the sculpture an effigy, like the illusionistic effigies of royalty at Westminster, 'as a monument, thus in a chapel lying' (*Cymbeline*, 2.2.32). The two courtiers earlier stated that 'the Queen's picture' (*Winter's Tale*, 5.2.167) was 'a piece many years in doing and now newly performed by that rare Italian master Julio Romano' (93), and it may be that the image now revealed is supposed to be like the altarpiece of the Virgin that the Mannerist artist completed for Santa Maria dell'Anima in Rome. It is certainly Romano's purported workmanship which raises this instant of connoisseurship into the heady atmosphere of the Counter-Reformation, and gives this Roman detour its climax. For 'as emblematized by his name' (which reverses the tragedy of

Romeo and Juliet) the Giulio Romano Shakespeare read about in Vasari's *Lives* was 'a pointedly Roman artist', a painter of the stones of Rome, 'and servant of the Roman Church, the Catholic patron of classical rebirth'.[82] So, here a Jacobean audience must indeed have come close to thinking itself a congregation of believers. Yet at the least objection, Shakespeare's popish altar might be transformed back into an art-show. Blackfriars residents (who consisted of numerous Catholic recusants, among them Jonson) would have understood the precautions that kept this chapel such a liminal emplacement. It was the freedom enjoyed within the precinct that explained why it became the residence of so many 'rare Italian' and Flemish artists, who would include Gentileschi, Mytens, Steenwijck, Van der Doort and Van Dyck.[83] So, when the Parliament Chamber of the Priory was sectioned in the 1570s, the one half that became the Playhouse was divided from the other, which was then quietly converted, under the patronage of the French embassy, into the most fashionable Mass centre in London. Thus, when they climbed the grand staircase at Blackfriars, Shakespeare's audience would truly face the choice between art and religion. What they could not know, however, was that power also had its space there, and that, some time around the Gunpowder Plot, that other 'rare master', 'Little John' had been at work beneath the floor of the chapel, carving a hiding-chamber for the Jesuit conspirators. For years, assisted by benefactors such as Shakespeare, the Blackfriars congregation swelled, until one day in 1623 the wall which separated an open secret from its inner truth did literally come crashing down, with catastrophic consequences. What happened then would be seen by many as a divine judgement on the politics of English Catholics, but might also be interpreted as symbolic of the dangers of Shakespearean evasion. For on the afternoon of Sunday 26 October the Jesuit Father Drury was at the fervent climax of his sermon to the packed congregation, Protestants as well as papists, scholars and others, when Owen's clever carpentry gave out, and 'The floor whereon that assembly stood or sat, not falling by degrees, but at one instant', suddenly collapsed:

> by the breaking asunder of a main beam of that floor, which, together with the joists and planking adjoined, with the people thereon, rushed down with such violence that the weight and fall thereof broke in sunder another far stronger beam of the chamber directly underneath; and so both ruined floors, with the people crushed under or between them, fell upon the floor of the French Ambassador's withdrawing chamber, which was supported underneath by archwork of stone, and so became the boundary of that confused and doleful heap ... At the opening whereof, what a chaos! What fearful objects! What lamentable representations! ... Of those whom it pleased God to call out of this world, the number is estimated to be between ninety and one hundred.[84]

When excavated in 1923, the foundations of Shakespeare's Blackfriars property were indeed revealed as indestructible vaults which affirmed his debt to medieval Catholicism. But the disaster that occurred next door, so soon after he sponsored the recusant community, was also a tragic verdict on the perils of the strategy his plays project, and which had seemed so safe when the Queen of Scots was rehabilitated, of the discreet insertion into English life of a depoliticised Catholicism, segregated from treason. That, at least, is how Protestant preachers interpreted the catastrophe, arguing, like the chaplain to the Archbishop of Canterbury, that 'a topical inference' might be drawn for Catholics 'from the fall of both floors' of the 'Massing room' and secret annex, 'namely, that both Doctrine and Sacrifice were weakly supported'.[85] As Alexandra Walsham comments, 'the collapse of a house swarming with Catholics and their sympathizers' was an invitation to crow about 'the symbolic overthrow' of King James's policy of *de facto* toleration, especially as the incident occurred hot on the debacle of his final effort to marry his heir to a Habsburg Infanta.[86] Catholics might convince themselves that the disaster had been caused by Calvinists, who had 'secretly drawn out the pins or sawed half of the supporting timber' of the building;[87] but it was easy for both sides to see the 'Doleful Evensong', as it came to be called, as the price of religious freedom. In *The Winter's Tale* 'the meeting of the two kings' had promised just such an act of liberation, with its assembly of 'gentlemen born', 'ballad-makers', 'franklins' and 'boors' (5.2.22; 36; 114). Shakespeare may thus have been honouring the cultural inclusiveness that was the glory of his London enclave, where on the day of the great sermon, Lady Webb, sister to Francis Tresham, the Gunpowder plotter; Lady Blackstone's daughter; Thomas Brisket of Montague Close; Master Frowell, a Warwickshire gentlemen; and Johannes Brabant, a Flemish painter, were all pressed fatally together in the upper chamber, along with the likes of 'a Pewterer in Fancy Street', 'Clarentia, a maid'; 'one Barbaret'; and 'Davie, an Irishman'.[88] But even as the dramatist was creating a space for the open secret of religious toleration, underneath his trap-doors the 'fellow in the cellarage' was still busily tunnelling, and the 'old mole' of Jesuit conspiracy, that 'Canst work I'th'earth so fast', was proving a 'worthy pioneer' (*Hamlet*, 1.5.159–70), by undermining the entire precarious structure of co-existence and accommodation.

NOTES

1 See Stephen Orgel (ed.), *The Winter's Tale*, in the Oxford Shakespeare (Oxford: Oxford University Press, 1996), p. 56.

2 Cecil Papers (Marquess of Salisbury, Hatfield House), vol. 121, fol. 1; A.P. Stanley, *Historical Memorials of Westminster Abbey* (London, 1869), pp. 179–80.

3 David Howarth, *Images of Rule: Art and Politics in the English Renaissance, 1485–1649* (Macmillan, Basingstoke, 1997), p. 169.

4 *Calendar of State Papers Domestic*, vol. X, pp. 9–10.

5 10 October 1612, *Calendar of State Papers Domestic*, vol. IX, p. 90.

6 Jayne Elizabeth Lewis, *Mary Queen of Scots: Romance and Nation* (London, Routledge, 1998), pp. 66–7.

7 David Bergeron, *Shakespeare's Romances and the Royal Family* (Lawrence: Kansas University Press, 1985), p. 160.

8   John Henry de Groot, *The Shakespeares and the 'Old Faith'* (New York: King's Crown Press, 1946), pp. 103–4.

9   Michel Foucault, 'Different Spaces', in *Michel Foucault: The Essential Works 2: Aesthetics*, ed. James Faubion (London, Allen Lane, 1998), pp. 178–9.

10 William Slights, *Ben Jonson and the Art of Secrecy*, p. 21.

11 The Poor Clares had been banned from England in 1540, re-established at Gravelines in 1575, and then transferred to the convent at Saint-Omer: see May Winefride Sturman, 'Gravelines and the English Poor Clares', *London Recusant*, 7 (1977), pp. 1–8. See also A.C.F. Beales, *Education Under Penalty: English Catholic Education from the Reformation to the Fall of James II* (London: Athlone Press, 1963), pp. 203–4; Patricia Crawford, *Women and Religion in England, 1500–1720* (London: Routledge, 1992), p. 85; and the indispensable essay by Marie Rowlands, 'Recusant Women, 1540–1640', in Mary Prior (ed.), *Women in English Society, 1500–1800* (London: Routledge, 1985), pp. 168–74, esp. p. 169.

12 See, in particular, the account of 'Shakespeare's modernity in his treatment of women' in Juliet Dusinberre, *Shakespeare and the Nature of Women*, 2nd edition (Basingstoke: Macmillan, 1996), pp. 5–7 and 30–51.

13 See, for example, Mary Laven, *Virgins of Venice: Enclosed Lives and Broken Vows in the Renaissance Convent* (London: Viking, 2002).

14 Crawford, op. cit. (note 11), pp. 83–5.

15 For the fallacy of the 'repressive hypothesis' see Michel Foucault, *History of Sexuality: Volume One: An Introduction*, trans. Robert Hurley (Harmondsworth: Penguin, 1980).

16 Dusinberre, op. cit. (note 13), pp. 45 and 47–8.

17 John Bossy, *The English Catholic Community, 1570–1850* (London: Darton, Longman and Todd, 1975), p. 155.

18 Alexandra Walsham, *Church Papists: Catholicism, Conformity and Confessional Polemic in Early Modern England* (Woodbridge: Boydell, 1993), pp. 78–80.

19 Bossy, op. cit. (note 18), p. 153.

20 Hugh Hanley, 'Shakespeare's Family in Stratford Records', *Times Literary Supplement*, 21 May 1964, p. 441: the records are in the Act Books of Kent County Records Office, via the Sackville papers.

21 Walsham, op. cit. (note 19), p. 80; *House of Commons Journals*, I, p. 454, 1 February 1606.

22 G.W. Prothero (ed.), *Select Statutes and Other Constitutional Documents Illustrative of the Reigns of Elizabeth and James I* (Oxford: Clarendon Press, 1913), p. 259.

23 James I, *Political Works of James I*, ed. C.H. McIlwain (New York: Russell and Russell, 1918), p. 97.

24 William Barlow, *An Answer to a Catholic Englishman* (London: 1609), p. 17.

25 Phoebe Jensen, 'Papists and *Pericles*', unpublished paper, 'Lancastrian Shakespeare' Conference, University of Lancaster, July 1999.

26 Foucault, op. cit. (note 10), p. 176. For the distinction between 'place' and 'space' see also Louis Marin, *Utopiques: Jeux d'espaces* (Paris: Minuit, 1973), English trans., *Utopics: The Semiological Play of Textual Spaces*, trans. Robert Vollrath (Atlantic Highlands, N.J.: Humanities Press, 1990).

27 Northrop Frye, *Anatomy of Criticism* (Princeton: Princeton University Press, 1957), p. 182; John Holloway, *The Story of the Night* (London: Routledge and Kegan Paul, 1961), p. 66. For the recent re-engagement with the power of place see J. Hillis Miller, *Topographies* (Stanford: Stanford University Press, 1995); Edward W. Soja, *Post-modern Geographies: The Reassertion of Space in Critical Social Thought* (London: Verso, 1989); and Cynthia Wall, *The Literary and Cultural Spaces of Restoration London* (Cambridge: Cambridge University Press, 1998). For *topoi* as linguistic places see Marion Trousdale, *Shakespeare and the Rhetoricians* (Chapel Hill, N.C.: North Carolina University Press, 1982).

28 Linda Woodbridge, *The Scythe of Saturn: Shakespeare and Magical Thinking* (Urbana, Ill.: University of Illinois Press, 1994), pp. 163, 192–3 and 199.

29 Peter Milward, *Shakespeare's Religious Background* (Chicago: Loyala University Press, 1973), pp. 78, 176 and 180–1. For the antecedents of the Gothic in lamentation over the destruction of the monasteries see Margaret Ashton, 'English Ruins and English History: The Dissolution and the Sense of the Past', *Journal of the Warburg and Courtauld Institutes*, 36 (1973), pp. 232–55.

30 John Bossy, 'The Character of Elizabethan Catholicism', *Past and Present*, 21 (1962), p. 39; op. cit. (note 18), p. 158.

31 Ibid., pp. 168 and 173; Joseph Berington, *The State and Behaviour of English Catholics* (Birmingham: 1780), p. 115.

32 Foucault, op. cit. (note 10), p. 183.

33 Robert Weimann, *Shakespeare and the Popular Tradition in the Theater: Studies in the Social Dimension of Dramatic Form and Function* (Baltimore: Johns Hopkins University Press, 1978), pp. 208–15.

34 Clark Hulse, 'Dead Man's Treasure: The Cult of Thomas More', in David Lee Miller, Sharon O'Dair and Harold Weber (eds), *The Production of English Renaissance Culture* (Ithaca: Cornell University Press, 1994), pp. 224–5; cf. Jonathan Goldberg's analysis of Renaissance homosexuality as an 'open secret' in 'Colin to Hobbinol: Spenser's *Familiar Letters*', *South Atlantic Quarterly*, 88 (1989), pp. 107–26.

35 Foucault, op. cit. (note 10), p. 183.

36 A.C. Southern (ed.), *An Elizabethan Recusant House: The Life of the Lady Magdalen Viscountess Montague, 1538–1608: Translated from the Latin of Dr. Richard Smith by Cuthbert Fursden, O.S.B. in the Year 1627* (London: Sands, 1954), p. 43.

37 Ibid., pp. 42–3 and 80–1; Joseph Gillow, *Biographical Dictionary of English Catholics* (London: Burns and Oates, 1887–); *Catholic Record Society*, 37 (1940), p. 66.

38 Roger Manning, *Religion and Society in Elizabethan Sussex* (Leicester: Leicester University Press, 1969), pp. 156–63.

39 The Entertainment at Cowdray (transcribed. from BL C.33.d.ll and BL C.142.dd.23) in Curtis Breight, 'Caressing the Great: Viscount Montague's Entertainment of Elizabeth at Cowdray, 1591', *Sussex Archaeological Collections*, 127 (1989), pp. 147–66, esp. p. 161.

40 Ibid., p. 154.

41 Manning, op. cit. (note 39); Michael Leslie, '"Something Nasty in the Wilderness": Entertaining Queen Elizabeth on Her Progresses', in John Pitcher (ed.), *Medieval and Renaissance Drama in England: 10* (Madison: Faileigh Dickinson University Press, 1998), pp. 63–9.

42 *Calendar of State Papers Domestic, 1582–90*, p. 248.

43 'The Pilgrim's Speech', Breight, op. cit. (note 40), p. 161.

44 G.P. Akrigg, *Shakespeare and the Earl of Southampton* (London: Hamish Hamilton, 1968), pp. 222–3; M.C. Bradbrook, *Shakespeare: The Poet in his World* (London: Weidenfeld and Nicolson, 1978), pp. 98–101.

45 See Patricia Parker, 'What's in a Name: and More', *Sederi: XI* (Huelva: Universidad de Huelva, 2002), pp. 101–49, esp. pp. 138–41.

46 Alexander Pope, 'Epistle to Miss Blount, On her leaving the Town after the Coronation', quoted in Michael Hodgetts, 'The Godly Garret, 1560–1660', in Marie Rowlands (ed.), *English Catholics of Parish and Town, 1558–1778* (London: Catholic Record Society, 1999), p. 36.

47 *Worcester Recusants*, 30 (1980), pp. 8–27; 5 (1965), pp. 18–31: quoted ibid., pp. 49–50.

48 Ibid., pp. 39–42; Michael Hodgetts, 'A Topographical Index of Hiding Places', *Recusant History*, 16 (1982), pp. 193–6.

49 Bossy, op. cit. (note 18), p. 127.

50 Orgel, op. cit. (note 2), pp. 59–60.

51 Irwin Smith, *Shakespeare's Blackfriars Playhouse: Its History and its Design* (New York: New York University Press, 1964), pp. 301–3, 349–50 and 358–65; Dekker, *The Seven Deadly Sins of London*, quoted ibid., p. 302.

52 Slights, op. cit. (note 11), p. 21.

53 E.K. Chambers, *William Shakespeare: A Study of Facts and Problems* (2 vols, Oxford: Clarendon Press, 1930), vol. 2, pp. 159–64. Lady Jane Dormer, the Countess of Feria, was a leader of the 'court-in-exile' of Mary and a close friend of the Warwickshire émigré Sir Francis Englefield: see Albert Loomie, *The Spanish Elizabethans: English Exiles at the Court of Philip II* (London: Burns and Oates, 1963), pp. 94–127. It had been for the double marriage of Robert Dormer's father and aunt Mary to Anthony Browne, later Viscount Montague, and Elizabeth Browne, in October 1572 that George Gascoigne wrote the 'Masque of the Montagues and Capulets' which is one of the sources of *Romeo and Juliet*: see C.T. Prouty, *George Gascoigne: Elizabethan Courtier, Soldier, and Poet* (New York: Benjamin Blom, 1966), pp. 57–8 and 172–7.

54 T.Wright (ed.), *Queen Elizabeth and Her Times: A Series of Original Letters* (2 vols, London, 1838), vol. 2, p. 249.

55 J. Morris, *Troubles of our Catholic Forefathers Related by Themselves* (3 vols, London, Burns and Oates, 1972), vol. 1, p. 141.

56 Brian Burch, 'The Parish of St. Anne's Blackfriars, London, to 1665', in *Guildhall Miscellany*, III, 1 (1969), p. 12; P.M. Handover, *Arbella Stuart, Royal Lady of Hardwick and Cousin to King James, 1575–1615* (London: Eyre and Spottiswoode, 1957), pp. 238–41.

57 Beatrice Marshall, *Blackfriars, or the Monks of Old* (London: Longman, 1864), p. 157.

58 Ian Wilson, *Shakespeare: The Evidence* (London: Headline, 1993), p. 396.

59 Wright, op. cit. (note 55), p. 250. In 1585 Tarlton's house was reported 'sundry times searched', without success, 'for the fore-doors are no sooner knocked at but any within may pass out at the back'. John Fortescue, the nephew of Master of the Wardrobe, was married to Ellen Henslowe, daughter of the head keeper of the Earls of Southampton, and a probable relation of the developer of the Montague estate on Bankside, Philip Henslowe.

60 Recorder Fleetwood to Burghley, in Morris, op. cit. (note 56), p. 67. For Edward and Mary Bannister, who also lived at Iddsworth, on the Southampton Hampshire estate, see Christopher Devlin, *The Life of Robert Southwell, Poet and Martyr* (London: Longmans, 1956), pp. 13 and 217.

61 Morris, op. cit. (note 56), vol. 2, p. 372.

62 Henry Foley (ed.), *Records of the English Province of the Society of Jesus* (London: Burns and Oates, 1877), vol. 1, p. 380.

63 Ibid., p. 18; Wilson, op. cit. (note 59), p. 375.

64 Morris, op. cit. (note 56), p. 144.

65 Willem Schrickx, '*Pericles* in a Book-List of 1619 from the English Jesuit Mission and Some of the Play's Special Problems', *Shakespeare Survey*, 29 (Cambridge: Cambridge University Press, 1976), pp. 21–32.

66 Michael Hodgetts, *Secret Hiding-Places* (Dublin: Veritas, 1989), pp. 214–15.

67 Ibid., pp. 58–9.

68 Michael Hodgetts, 'Elizabethan Priest-Holes: I: Dating and Chronology', *Recusant History*, 11 (1972), p. 290.

69 Quoted ibid., p. 291.

70 Quoted ibid., pp. 284–5.

71 Orgel, op. cit. (note 2), p. 59.

72 Stephen Greenblatt, *Shakespearean Negotiations: The Circulation of Social Energy in Renaissance England* (Oxford: Clarendon Press, 1990), pp. 10–11, 14–15, 19 and 112.

73 Julia Reinhard Lupton, *Afterlives of the Saints: Hagiography, Typology and Renaissance Literature* (Stanford: Stanford University Press, 1996), p. 210.

74 James Siemon, *Shakespearean Iconoclasm* (Berkeley: University of California Press, 1985), pp. 289–92.

75 Lupton, op. cit. (note 74), pp. 177, 182, 206–7, 210–14 and 216.

76 Ibid., pp. 217–18.

77 Ibid., pp. 182 and 217.

78 Peter Milward, *Shakespeare's Religious Background* (Chicago: Loyola University Press, 1973), p. 171.

79 John Marston, 'Metamorphosis of Pygmalion's Image', in Arnold Davenport (ed.), *The Poems of John Marston* (Liverpool: Liverpool University Press, 1961), cited in Siemon, op. cit. (note 75), p. 35.

80 John Bossy, 'The Character of Elizabethan Catholicism', *Past and Present*, 21 (1962), p. 55.

81 See Alison Shell, *Catholicism, Controversy and the English Literary Imagination, 1558–1660* (Cambridge: Cambridge University Press, 1999), pp. 201–7.

82 Lupton, op. cit. (note 74), p. 212.

83 See Christopher Brown, *Van Dyck* (Oxford: Oxford University Press, 1982), pp. 215–16; Mary Edmond, 'Limners and Picture Makers', *Walpole Society*, 47 (1980), pp. 64–5; Susan Foister, 'Foreigners at Court: Holbein, Van Dyck and the Painter-Stainers Company', in David Howarth (ed.), *Art and Patronage in the Caroline Courts* (Cambridge: Cambridge University Press, 1993), pp. 32–50; and Oliver Millar, 'Van Dyck in London', in Susan Barnes and Arthur Wheelock (eds), *Anthony Van Dyck* (Washington, D.C.: National Gallery of Art, 1990), pp. 53–8.

84 William Gouge, *The Extent of God's Providence ... on Occasion of the Downfall of the Papists in a Chamber at the Blackfriars* (London, 1631), quoted in Burch, op. cit. (note 57), p. 20; Thomas Gee, 'The Doleful Evensong', in Philip Caraman (ed.), *The Years of Siege: Catholic Life From James I to Cromwell* (London: Longmans, 1966), pp. 30–4. See also Thomas Agius, 'Memorable Sites of London: Hunsdon House: Massing House', *Society of Jesus: Letters and Notices*, 7 (1937), pp. 292–303.

85 Thomas Goad, quoted in Alexandra Walsham, *Providence in Early Modern England* (Oxford: Oxford University Press, 1999), p. 268.

86 Ibid, pp. 267–8.

87 Quoted ibid., pp. 270–1.

88 'A Catalogue of the names of such persons as were slain by the fall of the room wherein they were in the Blackfriars, at Master Drury's sermon, the 26th of October 1623. Taken by information of the Coroner's jury', in Henry Foley (ed.), *Records of the English Province of the Society of Jesus: I* (London: Burns and Oates, 1877), pp. 85–6.

12

A Winter's tale

King Lear in the Pennines

I N the autumn of 1605, a few weeks before the Gunpowder Plot, the conspirators took their families on a pilgrimage to St Winifred's Well in Flintshire,
in a gesture that has been described by Antonia Fraser as 'an elegy for the old
Catholic England'.[1] The shrine had been a site of healing and devotion for
centuries, and their prosecutors would allege that the thirty pilgrims rode from
the house of John Grant at Norbrook, near Stratford-on-Avon, with an aim of
dedicating themselves there to terrorism, in their fanatical belief that 'the
disease requires so sharp a remedy'.[2] Certainly, when the pilgrimage split up,
after saying Mass and bathing in the holy spring, the three Winter brothers
charged with procuring arms made straight for a war council in Yorkshire, held
from 12 to 15 September at Gowthwaite Hall in Nidderdale, the remote Pennine
home of their uncle, Sir John Yorke. There, according to informers, the Winters
were joined by more Catholic kinsmen, led by another uncle, Sir William
Ingleby, and the Jesuit John Gerard, and Robert Winter was heard to declare
that 'We are even now upon the point of blowing up the Parliament House. We
want but a little money'. With rifles and ammunition stockpiled, Gowthwaite
was the hub of a Yorkshire Catholic network which had recruited half the
plotters, including Guy Fawkes, so it is no surprise that deep 'gloom fell on the
household' when the Plot was discovered on 5 November, and the authorities
ordered 'a secret search' of the building, certain that, if Robert Winter fled north,
he would 'resort to his mother's kindred about Ripon, where he has plentiful
alliance, most of them papists'.[3] What is startling is that, after escaping the
scaffold, the Yorkes were so unrepentant that four years later their house was
the focus of another Star Chamber trial, when they were reported for hosting a
different kind of conspiracy: this time of actors, who at Candlemas in 1610 were
said to have staged there 'a seditious interlude' to an uproarious crowd of a
hundred locals. The audience that night included Robert Winter's five children,
now 'rooted in Popery' with their Yorkshire cousins, and, it was rumoured,
Father Gerard, who had just slipped back into England.[4] And the revels were so

rousing that 'the popish people affirmed to their neighbours that if they had seen the play as it was played at Gowthwaite, they would never care for going to church'. Accounts differed as to what was actually staged over Candlemas in Nidderdale, but Shakespeareans are fascinated by the incident, because the clown, William Harrison, testified that, in addition to the interlude and a morality called *Saint Christopher*, one of the plays offered during the festivities, and 'commonly acted' by his troupe 'at other gentlemen's houses' in Yorkshire, was '*Pericles, Prince of Tyre*, and the other was *King Lear*'.[5]

The Gowthwaite trial offers critics an intriguing perspective on the question of how his Catholic contemporaries read Shakespeare. Thus, 'it is difficult to escape the conclusion', comments Stephen Greenblatt, 'that someone in Stuart Yorkshire believed that *King Lear* was not hostile, was strangely sympathetic even, to the situation of persecuted Catholics'.[6] But whether or not the play was thought a fitting seasonal entertainment for the orphaned Winter children, the entire episode, with its secret rides and sacred shrines, typifies the tantalisingly circumstantial threads connecting William Shakespeare with Catholic resistance in the north of England. Grilled by the Star Chamber attorneys at Ripon, for instance, it was the boy who would have played Cordelia, Thomas Pant, who turned king's evidence and offered lawyers and critics the most detailed description of the circumstances in which *King Lear* was alleged to have been toured in the Dales. The actors were a band from the seaside parish of Egton, near Whitby, 'the largest and most notorious recusant community' in the North, reckoned in 1599 to be a 'bishopric of papists', under protection of their young squire, Richard Cholmley, and the management of a firm of recusant shoemakers named Simpson.[7] So, young Master Pant was being disingenuous when he protested that, after joining the group in 1607 to train as a shoemaker, he was disappointed to waste three years instead 'wandering the country playing in interludes', because Robert and Christopher Simpson had been listed as 'common players' as early as 1595,[8] and had been sponsored by the Cholmleys from the beginning as Catholic standard-bearers in the fierce sectarian strife which polarised the region. In fact, the Cholmley Players can be seen as a perfect instance of the way Catholic customs and terrorist politics fused in Shakespeare's Counter-Reformation. For Egton was famous for its traditional Christmas game, in which youths known as Plough Stots, ribboned like oxen, stamped out a dance to flyting derision by fools called Toms, while their 'Pegs' in women's clothes begged money for the feast. The play then ended with the symbolic violence of a sword-dance.[9] But classic studies of folk festivals by C.L. Barber, Emannuel Le Roy Ladurie and Natalie Zemon Davis have reminded us how the Wars of Religion added a real aggression to the 'rites of violence' across Western Europe during the 1580s and 1590s, and the Egton mumming may likewise have been radicalised under the sponsorship of the Cholmleys.[10] Because what was notable about this family was how they opened their mansion at Whitby as 'a receptacle to seminary priests coming from beyond the seas', with the result that the North Sea harbour became a key entry-point for Jesuits arriving from France, Milan and Rome. And there these priests had themselves been taught to stage plays as part of their curriculum, one of which – the single secular work catalogued in 1619 among the religious texts for their school at Saint-Omer – was *Pericles*.[11]

Theatre historians downplay the Catholic politics of the Cholmleys, yet the family controlled a priest-running operation across northern England, the centre of which was a secluded farm they built over the ruins of the former Grosmont Priory in Egton, where 'the vaults led down to the cliff on which the house stood, and so enabled men to get away in boats on the river that ran at the foot'.[12] By 1590 Grosmont was 'the place where they are especially directed when they come over from Rheims', a headquarters for a system that ran to the Simpsons' home at Hunt House on the edge of the moors. So, it is the possibility that Cholmley's Men 'had been coached by priests who had been brought up to the performance of plays' that might explain how their organisation and repertoire came to be so ambitious.[13] Their patron himself took the woman's part in a play while at Trinity College, Cambridge. But what Shakespeareans have never appreciated is that the Simpsons' expertise was such that Christopher's son grew up to be 'the most important musician of his time' in England.[14] And it is because of the eminence of this composer and musicologist, also called Christopher, that we are able to piece together so much of the background of these Yorkshire actors. Since they regularly included boys as young as seven, Christopher Simpson junior, who was born about 1602, would have been just old enough to take part in the Gowthwaite revels, alongside his cousin Nicholas Postgate, for example, who was listed among the actors in 1616, then aged thirteen, and who later became a venerated priest and preacher, martyred at York in 1679.[15] They were both tutored by an uncle, William Postgate, of whom it was reported in 1604 that he 'teacheth the children' of the Cholmley household, where other Catholic youths were employed 'as pages or singing boys'.[16] Such tuition, in a house where priests regularly arrived from the continent, might account for one great mystery in Simpson's career, which is how 'the acknowledged master of English viol music' acquired the technique of extempore playing with combined viols that became his speciality, but that originated in 'the strumming of Spanish guitarists'.[17] Recently, it has even been claimed that like Postgate, who left Whitby in 1621 to enrol in the college at Douai, Simpson himself became a Jesuit, and spent twenty years, from 1619, in Saint-Omer and Rome.[18] If so, it would confirm the lines of communication connecting the Yorkshire players with Counter-Reformation culture and the intense world of the continental Baroque.

Purcell considered Christopher Simpson's treatise, *The Principles of Practical Music*, 'the most ingenious book I ever met with upon this subject',[19] and the same sophistication seems to have characterised his father's acting team. For when they arrived at Gowthwaite on 2 February 1610, the troupe numbered no fewer than fifteen, with Pant and another boy, Robert Lownde, apprenticed for female roles. And it was the professionalism of this company which most impressed the scholar Charles Sisson, who first publicised the story in an essay of 1942 which traced their touring route through a chain of Catholic house-holds between the Pennines and the North Sea. With a repertoire of four plays, as well as dances and interludes; a stock of costumes and props for characters such as angels, devils, priests and kings; and a range of musical and lighting effects that climaxed with fireworks; 'even if they were shoemakers' or spoke with northern accents, the Simpsons were sufficiently equipped, skilled and versatile, Sisson believed, to quash for ever the idea of provincial acting groups as 'rude mechanicals'. These north-country players were, in effect, he argued, 'serious rivals to a travelling London company', and their staging of 'the very plays a London company could offer as its latest and best' explains why metro-politan actors were 'loath to part with their plays to publishers, and might put every obstacle in the way of printing even old plays', seeing that they 'went on tours themselves, and that these were an important factor in their economics'. For, as Sisson pointed out, *King Lear* was first printed only in 1608, and *Pericles* in 1609; and the possibility that these could be acted so soon after publication by a large company, capable of producing storm effects or fireworks, as well as celestial music, suggested to him that production values in the Dales were more those of 'The Mousetrap' than 'Pyramus and Thisbe'.[20] The northern gentry had access to professional theatre at York, where even the Protestant overlords, Lord Sheffield and the Earl of Huntingdon, retained players while installed as Lord President. So (though it has been almost totally ignored by authorities on touring),[21] Sisson inferred that the company which rolled its wagons across the Yorkshire moors must have been one of the most competent of the eighty-odd troupes known to have operated in the livery of minor aristocrats between 1558 and 1642; which, if true, means that the Gowthwaite revels provide us with a unique glimpse into the non-metropolitan Jacobean theatre world:

> Shakespeare himself gives in *Hamlet* a picture of the arrival of Cholmley's Men at Gowthwaite ... They were received in the court-yard by Roger Haber-geon, Sir John Yorke's bailiff, and some of the leading actors were taken into the Hall where Sir John himself met them and discussed their repertory with them. Sir John decided for the play of *Saint Christopher*. The performance took place the same evening in the Hall, into which were crowded some hundred people. The bailiff supervised entries at the Hall door. Some sixty persons were kept out, and one girl, damaged in the crush at the door, was consoled by Sir John with a gift of money. The performance took place on an improvised stage, with properties and stage effects. It appears that young John Yorke, Sir John's nephew and heir, then eleven years of age, may have taken some part in the performance.[22]

According to Sisson, the participation of the young Yorke heir in the entertainment at Gowthwaite was a relic of customs of Catholic theatricality stretching back to Thomas More, who as a boy 'often stepped in among the players, when the wandering actors put on plays at Christmastide'.[23] And the choice of plays listed by the Simpsons does imply a streak of self-dramatisation in the household. For one of the alternatives was a topical show about the most flamboyant of all Catholic émigrés: *The Travels of the Three Shirley Brothers* by John Day, William Rowley and, significantly, George Wilkins, the recusant co-author of *Pericles*.[24] Perhaps, like the Duke of Athens presented by the actors with *Three Muses*, Sir John rejected *Three Brothers* because it simply seemed too 'keen and critical' (*Dream*, 5.1.54), for, of all the plays proposed, it was this tragi-comedy that alluded most overtly to the schemes of English Catholics, and thus suggests the hopes which might still have been nurtured in Shakespeare's recusant audience. First staged in 1607 by Queen Anne's Men to the crypto-Catholic coterie of the Curtain Theatre, its heroes were cadets of the Catholic Montague clan which included Shakespeare's own patron, the Earl of Southampton, who had achieved notoriety for episodes like one highlighted, when Sir Anthony Shirley is welcomed by the Pope, whom he salutes as 'the Father of our Mother Church, / The stair of men's salutations, and the Key / That binds or looseth our transgressions'.[25] For at a time when Protestants were forging treaties with the Turks against the Habsburg states, the Shirleys were infamous for their efforts to outflank this alliance by tying Persia to Rome. So, a central scene of *Three Brothers* has Thomas racked by 'the Great Turk' to break his 'Roman spirit'; while, to drive home the analogy with Tudor tyranny, Shakespeare's clown Will Kemp ridicules a play entitled *England's Joy* for its naive celebration of Queen Elizabeth. The English joy to which the Shirleys aspire, we soon learn, will instead be to build 'a Church / To sacrifice thy prayers unto that name / To whom all names should kneel': a church, that is to say, such as the 'grave Father' Robert encounters in Iran, where the missionary has travelled 'to advance the glory of our God'. In 1622 Robert Shirley would be painted by Van Dyck in the spectacular robes and turban of his office as the Persian ambassador to Pope Gregory XV. And the play ends on a similarly ecumenical theme, when this brother persuades the Shah to promulgate religious freedom and license a Catholic seminary in Tehran. Since 'your Mr' (as James I is irreverently styled) has been beholding to Muslims throughout the action, the implication cannot have been lost on a Jacobean audience that, in terms of religious toleration, the Church of England had everything to learn from the spiritual generosity of Islam:

> ROBERT: I would entreat I might erect a Church
> Wherein all Christians that do hither come
> May peaceably hear their own Religion.
> SOPHY: 'Tis granted, erect a stately Temple.
> It shall take its name from thee: Great Shirley's Church.
> Finish thy suit. Whate'er it be.
> ROBERT: You are too prodigal, I too presuming.

> Yet, since yourself doth thus authorise me,
> I will not hide my heart. Your further leave:
> I would by your permission raise a house
> Where Christian children from their cradles
> Should know no other education,
> Manners, language, nor Religion,
> Than what by Christians is deliver'd them.
> SOPHY: We'll ask no other counsel to confirm that grant,
> 'Tis obtain'd.[26]

At a time when an Ottoman alliance against Spain was a favourite Puritan plan, the Shirley brothers made Persia a screen for Catholicism, this play shows, with their schemes to unite Persia and England in a new Crusade.[27] This is doubtless what Lear means when he tells the disguised Kent that he dislikes his clothes: 'You will say they are Persian; but let them be changed' (Lear, 3.6.73). For, as Anthony Parr notes, the authors of Three Brothers 'do not merely avoid anti-Papal propaganda: they actively counter it ... by enlisting the Pope in a larger Christian cause'.[28] The Catholic project to 'combine / The blood of malice in a league' against the Turks was also a theme of Shakespeare's Histories (John, 5.3.37–8). But it is the audacity of such a policy which might explain one of the mitigating pleas offered at the trial, when the actors repeatedly claimed to work from printed texts. Thus, Richard Simpson swore 'the book by which he and the other persons did act Saint Christopher was a printed book, and they only acted the same according to the contents, and not otherwise'. Harrison likewise described King Lear and Pericles as their 'usual plays and such as were acted in Common and public places and stages and played publicly and printed in the books'.[29] Commentators view this testimony as proof of collusion between witnesses to distract from the interlude that gave offence. But the subject of The Three Brothers suggests a stronger motive. For the implication of the insistence on printed authority was that the actors had sanction for from those officials who licensed publications on the orders of the Lord Chamberlain, Thomas Howard, Earl of Suffolk. And this is significant, because the religious politics of Three Brothers correspond exactly with those of Suffolk and his uncle, Henry Earl of Northampton, in the years after the Gunpowder Plot, when England's leading Catholic dynasty clung to the project exemplified by the Shah in the play: of religious toleration by royal decree. This was the regalian solution the Howards were, in fact, subsidised to promote by Spain; and which Northampton almost achieved in 1604, in an episode when 'some of the Lords kneeled down to the King for a toleration in religion'.[30] If it was acted in the Dales over the winter of 1609/10, The Three Brothers must therefore have spoken to Catholic hopes for some version of Henri IV's Edict of Nantes, which would secure the freedom James I appeared to promise in hints, such as his reproof to Cecil, that he would 'never allow the blood of any man to be shed for the diversity of opinions in religion'.[31] And by insinuating that their texts were licensed by the Howards, the Simpson Players were referring the prosecution to the authors of this policy of toleration, who were the crypto-Catholic courtiers and judges sitting in the Star Chamber itself.

It is the actors' reference to the Lord Chamberlain that hints why the record of the trial is tangled with action taken by the Howards to scotch rumours of their bias to protect Ingleby, who was their relative, from prosecution for the Gunpowder conspiracy. And it also explains why the instigators of the suit were two leaders of the local Puritan faction: Sir Posthumus Hoby, a nephew of Lord Burghley, and his ally, Sir Stephen Proctor. When Proctor infiltrated a spy named Stubbs, the Puritan preacher of Pateley Bridge, to inform on the revels, this was, in fact, a manoeuvre in the power struggle at the heart of Jacobean government, between the Cecils and Howards. That contest had become a furious beating of jurisdictional bounds from the day in 1596 when Hoby married Margaret Sidney, a rich heiress of the manor of Hackness in Egton, for the deliberate purpose of intruding Cecil influence into 'the north parts of this realm'.[32] 'A troublesome, vexatious neighbour', in the words of Richard Cholmley, 'who having married a widow, the inherior of all Hackness lordship, a full purse, no children (and as it was thought not able to get any), delighted to spend money and time in suits',[33] Thomas Posthumus Hoby had also acquired the same spinal curvature and dwarfism as his cousin Robert Cecil, and was ridiculed by his hard-riding neighbours as a 'little knight that useth to draw up his breeches with a shoeing horn', 'a spindle-shanked ape', 'a scurvy urchin', and 'the busiest saucy little Jack in all the country who would have an oar in everybody's boat'. Yorkshire folk sneered that this clerk 'came over the water with his coach and three horses, scant worth sixpence'; and the resentment he provoked as a carpet-bagger boiled over when he was humiliated in the county parliamentary election in 1597.[34] His reaction to this rebuff was then to antagonise the powerful Eure family by elbowing his way into their Scarborough seat, and to wage religious war on the Cholmley tenants, over eighty of whom he now forced, as Justice of Peace, to take Anglican communion, 'which they had not done for three years'.[35] Inevitably, the interloper clashed with Richard Cholmley in court, when the latter 'would not suffer this Hoby to carry matters upon the Bench according to his humour, which he loved to have satisfied, whether right or wrong'. There ensued a string of Star Chamber cases, in which Hoby 'endeavoured to overthrow all the Royalties and Liberties belonging to the manor of Whitby', by alleging that Cholmley was protecting recusants at the petty sessions.[36] Customary society responded to this litigation, as it always did in Shakespearean England, by resorting to the time-honoured folk justice of the 'horn-beasts' (*As You Like It*, 3.3.41), and a version of their game that was primly recorded by Hoby's wife:

> After I was ready I spake with Mr Eure, who was so drunk that I soon made an end of that I had no reason to stay for; and after … I had prayed I went about the house and walked with Mr Hoby. After, I prayed, and so I dined and bestowed the afternoon in going about and taking order for the entertaining

strangers, and so went to private prayer and examination. After, I went to supper, then, having talked with Mr Hoby about the abuse offered by Mr Eure and his Company, I went to private prayer and so to bed.[37]

The pursed-lipped regime of prayers and practicality itemised in the celebrated diary of Lady Margaret Hoby registers the cultural divide separating the lady of the manor from the Egton horn-dance, when Richard Cholmley, William Eure and thirty 'ruffianly servingmen and boys all weaponed with swords, rapiers and daggers', swooped on Hackness Hall late on 27 August 1600, intent on exacting a ritual revenge for her husband's intrusions. Stonily self-possessed in face of festive mockery, Lady Hoby simply refused in her account to recognise the symbolic rules of the game. Whereas Sir Posthumus was sufficiently constrained by what he called 'the partial customs of these frozen parts' to admit the rowdies when they demanded lodging, and to acquiesce while they 'played cards and dice most of the night, swapped dirty stories, drank the house dry', and then, when he 'set the household to pray ... and his family began to sing a psalm, made an extraordinary noise with their feet', or 'stood at a window and laughed all the time of prayers'. As a crowning insult, young Eure next morning threatened to rape Lady Hoby in her chamber, and then led his gang out of the house, smashing windows as they went, amid ribaldry about setting antlers from the hall on the cuckold's head.[38] Eure later deposed that Sir Posthumus gave them 'cold welcome' and 'scurvy messages', before he 'shut himself in the study, being unwilling to be spoken with, but watching there, to take advantage if I should use any unseemly speeches'.[39] Certainly, Hoby lost no time making a complaint of riot in the Council of the North, and, since the Vice-President there was Lord Eure himself, in Star Chamber. The case, which ended two years later in an annual fine of £100 levied on the Eures in perpetuity, is well known to Shakespeareans as the possible source for the stand-off in *Twelfth Night* between Malvolio and 'Sir Toby and his fox-hunting companions', who likewise swear to drink healths as long as 'there is drink in Illyria' (1.3.33).[40] What has not been considered however, is the place of this *charivari* in the pattern of social conflict which culminated, a decade later, in Hoby's pursuit of the Cholmley Players, and the way in which Shakespeare seems to have been quoted then as a pretext for Catholic resistance, comparable to this earlier appeal to custom. For what is striking about the Hackness affray is how far even 'Sir Hoby', the Cecil placeman and prudish Puritan, was inhibited by the model of hospitality on which Lear also calls, when he descends, with his 'insolent retinue' (*King Lear*, 1.4.196), on the homes of his daughters:

> So heavily did the protocols of the model weigh on this Puritan (who could hardly have accepted this version of the model) that Hoby admitted the party and entertained the whole to the letter. In fact, the Puritan approached the Star Chamber, complaining that hospitality was a strict code that *his guests* had violated. As a context for the household confrontation between Goneril, Regan

and Lear, the case is startling. So powerful were the protocols of hospitality that Eure's household could count on using them as a weapon against a house-holder whose religious beliefs denied a like interpretation. So powerful were the protocols that Hoby and his wife endured countless abuses rather than forgo the cultural model.[41]

When Cholmley's players claimed to have 'acted and played' *King Lear* and *Pericles*, it may not have been lost on them that both plays pose the problem for traditional society of households, such as that of the King of Antioch, 'more concerned with entrapment than with entertainment'.[42] So, if they purported to be lovers of Shakespeare, then that could have been because they saw an affinity between their own position, as defenders of customary culture, and that of the dramatist. For at the same time as the Hoby family was waging cultural war in Yorkshire it also opened another front in London, against the impresario James Burbage and Shakespeare's company, the Chamberlain's Men, with a petition organised by Sir Posthumus's formidable mother, Lady Russell, opposing plans to open a playhouse in Blackfriars.[43] Since Chomley was such a keen theatregoer, who around the time of *Twelfth Night* fought a duel over an altercation during a play at Blackfriars,[44] it seems likely that he kept his own players up-to-date on this conflict, which was still raging twenty years later, when Sir Posthumus collected a second petition to close Burbage's theatre. And the possibility that the comedy was written in the thick of this controversy has been strengthened by a recent study of its micro-history by Anthony Arlidge, which details how Shakespeare's play was performed at Middle Temple with funds from a set of lawyers affiliated to the Earl of Essex, in mockery of the designs of the Cecils and the Hobys, who were members of Gray's Inn.[45] Such research reveals how minutely Shakespeare's Illyria maps the religious politics of Elizabethan London. Thus, Lady Russell objected to a playhouse on the grounds that 'drums and trumpets' would disturb church sermons; so it may not be chance that, when Malvolio prohibits 'cakes and ale', Feste jokes of upholding them 'by Saint Anne' (2.3.105), the Blackfriars chapel, next to the playhouse, that the Hobys had made a Puritan headquarters; and begs alms by 'the bells of Saint Bennet' (5.1.35), the nearby resort of crypto-Catholics and the popish College of Heralds.[46] And Malvolio's boast that 'the Lady of the Strachey married the Yeoman of the Wardrobe' (2.5.34) is also keyed, it appears, to Blackfriars, and Hoby's wedding there with the lady of the Sidneys, in a ceremony absurdly devoid of entertainment bar 'a sermon and a dinner'.[47] But the most material link between Shakespeare's Inns of Court entertainment and the power struggle in Yorkshire is that *Twelfth Night* was produced under the auspices, Arlidge reveals, of the Treasurer of the Middle Temple, Sir John Shirley: head of the swashbuckling family of Essexian Catholics who were as much heroes to the Cholmley Players as to the London actors they bankrolled (*via* an agent happily named Pay), out of the 'pension of thousands to be paid from the Sophy' (3.1.156), for their secret service to the

Pope:[48] 'he pays you as surely as your feet hits the ground they step on. They say he has been a fencer to the Sophy' (*Twelfth Night*, 3.4.246–8).

'My Lady's a Cathayan, we are politicians, Malvolio's a Peg-o-Ramsey' (2.3.68): Sir Toby's gloss on revels in Illyria relates them pointedly to the 'rough music' of the Yorkshire and north-eastern Sword Plays, performed, like the Egton game, on Plough Monday, the first Monday after Twelfth Night.[49] Folklorists have recorded how the demand for 'largesse' with which these games climaxed tipped over into hostility if money was denied, and 'the ground in front of the house was roughly ploughed up by way of punishment for the owner's want of generosity'.[50] So, in Shakespeare's play, the sword-dance between mock-duellists veers into victimisation of the 'Peg' (Malvolio) when 'My Lady' (Olivia) acts like a 'Chinese' in curbing hospitality. As Toby says, these 'merry men' are 'politicians' now that their 'caterwauling' is provoked (65–9). And politics likewise entered the Christmas play in Yorkshire in 1602, when the Simpsons inserted a scandalous jig about 'Michael and Frances' in a show toured through the Dales, which goaded an ally of Hoby's, Michael Steel of Skelton, over his seduction of his maid. As in *Twelfth Night*, the 'old and antic' folksongs, supposedly chanted by the Pennine 'knitters', lost their medieval 'innocence' (2.4.3–45) when updated to satirise the faction of 'spindle-shanked Hoby', whose very name made him a right 'hobby-horse', or fall-guy.[51] For there is no question that this jeering topicality was abetted by Cholmley, and that 'the Simpsons introduced controversial Catholic elements into interludes' in reaction to Hoby's pursuit of his papist neighbour after his exposure in Essex's aborted putsch.[52] As 'the most prominent Yorkshire Essexian',[53] Cholmley's defence had been that he had been 'there by chance' when Essex stormed the City on 8 February 1601, and that, at the age of twenty-one, he was 'a man of no power'. But this plea had been expressly contradicted by Hoby, who took it upon himself to inform Cecil that the young desperado had resources 'to raise 500 men, if they should show themselves as traitorous as they do already show themselves disobedient to Her Majesty's laws'. Sir Posthumus advised his cousin to investigate Grosmont Abbey, 'a place famous for priests', where his 'confining neighbours' had prepared an invasion. And he reiterated that the Cholmley lands 'lieth in the most dangerous parts of Yorkshire for hollow hearts, for popery. The most part thereof lieth along the sea coast, very apt to entertain bad intelligenced strangers'. Finally, Hoby ticked off Cholmley's motives for joining the Plot as insolvency, 'love to the Earl' and his 'backward-ness in religion'.[54] The result of this ruthless denunciation was that Cholmley was imprisoned, alongside ringleaders such as Southampton, and fined £3000. He had, of course, been up to his neck in the rebellion, and likely attended the rally at the performance of *Richard II* the night before.[55] But Hoby's cynical intervention would poison Yorkshire politics for decades to come.

'Sometimes he is a kind of puritan … O, if I thought that I'd beat him like a dog' (2.3.125): in his study of the Cholmley Players, Yorkshire archivist G.W.

Boddy suggests that it was because Hoby recognised himself in these lines that he invested 'such extraordinary zeal and energy in tracking down and arresting the progress of Simpson's company', and in suppressing what he called 'their ridiculous plays'.[56] If the Justice did read *Twelfth Night* in this way, and the coast of Illyria as papist Whitby, it would follow that, like his enemies, he identified Shakespeare as a Catholic fellow-traveller, and would resent their touting of *King Lear* as an insufferable affront. The actors may have meant to rub his face in his humiliation by claiming to be performing the latest provocations from his own Blackfriars backyard. Such partisan interpretations would, of course, have grossly oversimplified Shakespeare's comedy, which in fact puts sectarian factions on a par, first by making the 'papist' Sir Toby the near-namesake of the real Puritan, and then by having his niece disown him, in a sermon that might have issued from Lady Hoby, and exactly suits the Cholmley we know from his Blackfriars fracas, as a north-country 'Rudesby' and 'Ungracious wretch, / Fit for the mountains and the barbarous caves, / Where manners ne'er were preached' (4.1.43–5). But a strong misreading on these lines would itself be significant, as it would confirm how even in life Shakespeare was bracketed, as he was by Hoby's co-religionists in the Civil War, as an enemy to 'Moses and the Prophets', and among writers such as Jonson, 'detested by Puritans for their crypto-Catholicism'.[57] Hoby and his adversaries are sure to have picked up on the black humour of Malvolio's 'exorcism' by Feste in the voice of 'Master Parson' – the Jesuit Parsons – with its allusion to the famous poem saluting 'the old hermit of Prague' – Edmund Campion – entitled 'Paper, pen and ink' (4.2.10; 75), since the martyr had actually stayed with the Cholmleys in Whitby. So, both sides may have looked to Shakespeare as their precedent for the rattling of sectarian violence in the wooden sabres of the sword-dance:

> Like to the old Vice …
> Who with dagger of lath
> In his rage and his wrath
>   Cries 'Aha' to the devil,
> Like a mad lad,
> 'Pare thy nails, dad,
>   Adieu, goodman devil.'
> (*Twelfth*, 4.2.111–22)

It was, of course, Hoby's Puritan friends who literally pulled the nails from the racked Jesuits. But Feste's turning of tables on Malvolio, as being like the Vice of a Christmas farce, plays on the similarity between exorcisms and mumming which would be noted by the future Archishop of York, Samuel Harsnett, who sneered that the Jesuits had learned their chicanery from 'the old Church plays, when the nimble vice would skip nimbly like Jack-an-Apes onto the devil's neck, and ride the devil a course, and belabour him with his wooden dagger, till he made him roar, whereat the people would laugh to see the devil so Vice-haunted'.[58] The same parallel was drawn by John Gee, the Blackfriars preacher, paid by Hoby, of St Anne's, who ironised that the Jesuits were such fine actors 'they should set up a company by themselves'.[59] Thus, the tight intertextuality of these quips suggests that in tormenting Malvolio Shakespeare may well have been rubbing salt into Sir Posthumus's wounds for the mockery he received on stage at Christmas-time in the North. If so, Feste's taunt confirms how the Yorkshire players were already known, in 1602, for attempting, 'under clerical influence, to graft contemporary polemic on to customary forms'.[60] And that was certainly what they did when they performed, eight years on, before the survivors of the Gunpowder conspiracy at Gowthwaite Hall. For the crime for which they were prosecuted then was for seditious libel, not in acting plays 'printed in the books', but in inserting into the morality of the patron saint of voyagers an extra scene, like Feste's jibe, based on the Christmas duel between 'the old Vice' and the Devil, in which the role of the Vice was assigned to an Anglican vicar, who, after being worsted in debate by a 'popish priest', was condemned to hell amid 'flashes of fire', as 'he that played the Devil did carry the English minister away', helped by 'one or two devils and a fool'. The pretext for this skit was the ferryman-saint's customary rout of Satan with a crucifix, which the players acted, even in Protestant houses, with 'a great yellow-coloured cross'. But by capping the tradition at Gowthwaite with a mime of the clergyman pulled down, 'like a mad lad', by the 'goodman devil', the Simpsons were literally telling the Puritan Hoby to go to hell 'In his rage and his wrath'. No wonder that Proctor relayed that the audience 'greatly laughed and rejoiced a long time' at the Protestant's fall. Nor that other witnesses smiled that 'when the person that played the devil's part took the English minister on his back and carried him away there were great rejoicings', as 'the people went after making a merriment and sport at it'.[61] Five years after the Gunpowder catastrophe, the 'flashes of fire' which consumed their enemy still expressed the fantasy nurtured by these Catholics, at the very site of their armoury, of a violent deliverance.

Sir John Yorke and his wife, brothers and cousin were finally found guilty, on 6 July 1614, of libel in 'bringing of religion on stage', after charges of collusion with their Winter relations in the Gunpowder terrorism had been dropped. They were fined over £4000, and the severity of the punishment demonstrates how much the government was persuaded in the end by Hoby's accusations of seditious intent. But if the *Saint Christopher* burlesque was viewed, in this way, as a last fling of the Gunpowder conspiracy, the question this raises is, of course, what a play like *King Lear* might have meant to these irreconcilables who quoted it, and who included not only those, like the Inglebys and Winters, devastated by the failure of their plots on behalf of Mary Queen of Scots, the Earl of Essex and Catesby, but their children, like the young Postgate and Simpson, or the boy Christopher Yorke who played one of the devils and grew up to be a Carthusian monk, who lived to lead their community into the long night of persecution. What message did Shakespeare's drama carry to this household in the Dales, which, far from being a rustic outpost, turns out to have been the epicentre of papist revolt?[62] As John Murphy writes in a book on the case, the question is crucial, as 'the single most important source of the language of Shakespeare's play is Harsnett's *Popish Impostures*, a savage attack on an English Catholic world such as we find in the Yorkshire Ridings in 1610'. For this critic, *King Lear* is concerned with those 'who in disguise / Followed [their] enemy king' (5.3.218–19), 'the nobles and gentry whose tragical plots … all culminating in the Gunpowder Treason, had driven English Catholic life into darkness and devils', and whose 'fury, madness, and idiocy' are vented in Lear's cry: 'Then, kill, kill, kill, kill, kill, kill!' (4.6.181).[63] But, in a later article, Murphy adds that, if this were the whole story, it would not explain why the terrorists appear to have found *King Lear* sympathetic to their cause, and he infers that they looked to the play because they knew it had been applauded at Whitehall as a favourable representation of court Catholics, such as the Howards, who, though they sat in Star Chamber, were as implicated in plots as themselves. Shakespeare's tragedy gave something more by way of encouragement to the religious renegades of 1610, it seems, than it does to modern readers.[64] And it is possible that there is a clue to what this may have been in the fact that the 1623 Folio cuts any mention of the prospects on which the 1608 Quarto turned, and on which papist polemics such as *Leicester's Commonwealth* also hinged: the impeachment of 'Bessy' – or Elizabeth – and her Anglican 'boat' as a 'leaky vessel' by those Catholics to whom 'she dare not come over', and to whom 'she must not speak' (3.6.23–4); and the dour persistence of those, like the servants who watch the blinding of Gloucester by Cornwall and Regan, determined to resist:

SECOND SERVANT: I'll never care what wickedness I do
If this man come to good.
THIRD SERVANT: If she live long
And in the end meet the old course of death,
Women will all turn monsters.
SECOND SERVANT: Let's follow the old Earl and get the bedlam
To lead him where he would. His roguish madness
Allows itself to anything.
THIRD SERVANT: Go thou. I'll fetch some flax and whites of eggs
To apply to his bleeding face. Now heaven help him!
(3.7.103–11)

In *King Lear* 'No port is free', and, rather than look for respite from across the waves, like the Histories, the play seems to present the predicament of a captive community, confined by penal laws to the desperate remedies of an inner exile, such as Edgar's disguise: 'Whiles I may scape, / I will preserve myself' (2.3.3–6). Now the resolution of the Elizabethan *émigré*, to 'shape his old course in a country new' (1.1.188), gives way to the stoic resignation of the

Jacobean quietist, to 'sing like birds i'th'cage', and so 'wear out, / In a wall'd prison, packs and sects of great ones / That ebb and flow by th'moon' (5.3.8–19). This 'religion of inaction' has been disparaged by John Bossy as a 'gentleman's theology' of 'social convenience' which replaced the Jesuits' 'alarm spiritual' with the contemplative 'inertia' of a revived Benedictine order.[65] But, as Frank Brownlow observes, Lear's lines are, in fact, a recitation of Southwell's *Epistle of Comfort* enjoining Catholics to imitate the birds 'that in the cage sing sweetlier and oftener than abroad', and to exchange roles with their gaolers by becoming 'god's spies' (17), 'as his angels behold us'. For Southwell, the stone cage is the Roman arena, where Christians suffer in 'glorious combat' as 'Christ looketh on'. So, Shakespeare's quotation of this world-as-stage *topos* is the sign of his 'cool and cunning authority', Brownlow concludes, 'in face of his times'.[66] The fact that the stoic words of the Jesuit martyr who may have been the author's cousin are cut off by Edmund's command to 'Take them away' (19), only confirms how much 'this great stage of fools' (4.6.177) is like the moonlit Colosseum, where 'packs and sects' of persecutors come and go, and 'As flies to wanton boys are we to the gods; / They kill us for their sport' (4.1.37–8). Southwell warned that it was 'senseless' for such Roman 'comedians' to be 'always poring at every cranny to see whether they may escape', and he had gone to the scaffold rejoicing 'to play out the last act' as one of 'God almighty's fools'.[67] So, it was in the savage spirit of this circus of cruelty, where martyrs are 'the fools of time' (Sonnet 124), that in his revision of *King Lear* Shakespeare took away from his Catholic admirers not only hope of revolt from below, with the omission of the servants who dress the sockets of Gloucester's eyes, but the last glimpse of any possible escape. For as editors notice, of the three hundred lines cut from the Folio, 157 are from the scenes involving Cordelia's invasion, where the excision of a third of the Quarto text ensures that every reference to a world beyond Dover is blanked out. This means that there is no mention in 1623 of the rumours that Edgar 'is with the Earl of Kent / In Germany' (4.7.91–2), nor any tribute to those exiles who followed the 'enemy king' (5.3.219). But, most significantly, the entire scene is struck in which the failure to reinstate the old regime is shifted onto the French:

KENT: Why the King of France is so suddenly gone back know you the
               reason?
GENTLEMAN: Something he left imperfect in the state
               Which, since his coming forth, is thought of; which
               Imports to the kingdom so much fear and danger
               That his personal return was most required
               And necessary.
KENT: Who hath he left behind him general?
GENTLEMAN: The Marechal of France, Monsieu la Far.

(4.3.1–8)

The defection from Cordelia's side, in the Quarto, of her husband, France, looks very like the desertion of Mary Stuart, who was also Queen of France, by her Lorraine in-laws, and may reflect the disillusion felt by the 1605 plotters over foreign help, when the flock of exiled Catholic 'wildgeese' failed to fly home, and even 'the financial support formerly guaranteed to English Catholics remained a promise unperformed'.[68] Gary Taylor is wrong, therefore, to discount censorship of the invasion scenes on the grounds that 'James I had little to worry about on that score'; for if Lear's party can be aligned, as Murphy and Brownlow argue, with Catholic peers, their lunacy is similarly to count on rescue from France. They repeat the folly, for instance, of the Earl of Northumberland, who in 1605 gave support to Catesby's plan to blow up King and Parliament in the mad belief that French troops would land in Kent, and 'backed by the 300 English cavalry expected to join once news of the invasion spread, strike out from Dover to hold London at their mercy'.[69] In the Quarto even Albany seems to share the confusion of such Catholics on hearing of the Plot, when he says he cannot be 'valiant' in defence of the realm, because although 'It touches us as France invades our land', the enemy has a 'most just and heavy cause' (5.1.22–7). The Duke's confession of divided loyalty is so contorted that some suspect textual corruption. But his words in fact betray the lingering faith of Jacobean Catholics in the fantasy of the 'Enterprise of England'. Thus, it is very telling that Albany's hesitation is erased from the Folio, along with every regret in the English party that 'friend hath lost friend' on the other side (5.3.56). In the Quarto, Goneril had expressly called Albany a 'moral fool' for such fence-sitting (4.2.59), punning on the dilemma of Thomas More's fellow-Catholics. So, while Taylor thinks it 'most implausible that this business at Dover' was cut for political reasons, Greg may have been near the truth when he inferred that 'Shakespeare found himself in a patriotic dilemma' over a landing by an émigré armada under French command, exactly like the coup planned by his Catholic friends.[70] For, if this was self-censorship, retraction would have been made imperative by the Yorkshire scandal, especially if 'Dover' did point, as the Quarto prints it, to 'Douer' – or Douai. So, though Gloucester's torturers repeat the question 'Wherefore to Douai?' (3.7.50) with which the Rackmaster had tormented prisoners, the revisionist ended all possible ambiguity about the futility of hoping for some solution beyond the 'chalky bourn' of Dover Cliff (4.5.57). In fact, the gaps in the Folio simply confirm the void symbolised by the cruel deceit of Gloucester's 'fall', namely the emptiness of any thought of aid or approbation from Peter's 'anchoring bark' (4.6.18), that ship supposed to bring the rich gift of the martyrs into Dover Bay:

> There is a cliff, whose high and bending head
> Looks fearfully in the confined deep.
> Bring me to the very brim of it,
> And I'll repair the misery thou dost bear
> With something rich about me. From that place
> I shall no leading need.
>
> (4.2.73–8)

'See me safe up, and for my coming down, let me shift for myself': from Gloucester's quotation of More on the scaffold; and Lear's reminiscence of his quip to the executioner, 'This' a good block' (4.6.177); to the King's entry dressed in the 'idle weeds' of Campion's 'sustaining corn' (4.4.5–6), and his final declaration that 'my poor fool is hanged' (5.3.304), the text of *King Lear* is crossed by memories of the 'side-piercing sight' (4.6.85) of the 'great stage' of Catholic martyrdom.[71] Lear himself says he cannot get these 'crosses' out of his eyes (5.3.277); and the allusions to St Lucy's eyeballs (3.7.57), St Catherine's 'wheel of fire' or St Juliana's boiling in 'molten lead' (4.7.47–8), are truly from the book of horrors lovingly compiled by Catholic martyrologists, such as Richard Verstegan, in the pious belief that 'He hates him much / That would upon the rack of this tough world / Stretch him out longer' (5.3.312–14). Yet what Catholic critics have, perhaps, not grasped is the implication of the 1623 revision, which is to subtract from the Quarto the remotest possibility of an audience for these histrionics, whether in heaven or in Rome. As William Elton remarked, the theatre of suffering in even the conflated *King Lear* represents 'the death of an illusion' in the extinction of belief in any spectator, and its absurdist theology is that of the *Deus Absconditus*, who no longer watches the play.[72] But the effect of the Folio abbreviation is to seal the text from any conceivable misunderstanding about the concern of God, working of providence, influence of the planets, power of the Pope, decision of the King of France, or effect of the Armada over the cruelties suffered on stage, and to ram home the helplessness of Lear's cry: 'No rescue? What, a prisoner? I am even / The natural fool of fortune' (4.6.184–5). The Catholic critic Richard Simpson thought that in the Histories 'the dramatist seems to say to the malcontents of his day – "Whatever you think about the justice of your cause or crimes of your opponents, whatever outrages you have to endure, whatever the merits of the losers or demerits of the winners, beware of foreign intervention"'.[73] But, with the disabused *King Lear*, it seems, what Shakespeare told these 'fools of time' was to despair of looking for even feeling from a world elsewhere. Instead, the Folio merely adds to Lear's lines his last delusion to 'Look there, look there!' on the lips of the hanged Cordelia (5.3.309). Thus, a play which had problematised the longing to 'see better' (1.1.158), and discounted 'spies and speculations' (3.1.24), closes with the intelligencer's deception of taking 'upon's the mystery of things, / As if we were God's spies' (5.3.16–17), and the paranoid language of the government informer confirms that, when there is nobody to watch over us, there is truly nothing to be seen.

Shakespeare's extinction of the light on the French coast from the horizon of *King Lear* suggests that some time after 1608 he became alert to the potential for the original text to be misconstrued as gesturing towards unfinished business with 'the hot-blooded France' (2.4.207), and a further violent 'arbitrement' (4.7.95). It seems likely, therefore, that this self-suppression was the result of the publicity of the Gowthwaite trial, since, whether or not the

Cholmley Players did tour the play, as they claimed, across their chain of Catholic houses, or merely familiarised themselves with the so-called 'Pied Bull' Quarto as the cover for their unreconstructed militancy, it would have been deeply compromising that they looked to this 'book' for legitimation. For they cited *King Lear* as if it were indeed what the Fool promises with his song of 'the wind and the rain' (3.2.73): the sequel to *Twelfth Night*. In that comedy, and in the context of the Essex Revolt, the dramatist came closer than anywhere in his work to authorising the festive violence of a putsch. But by systematically expunging from the tragedy the last glimmer of belief that there might come from France 'a power / Into this scattered kingdom' – and even crediting the invasion, in new lines for Kent, to 'snuffs and packings of the Dukes' (3.1.20–34) – Shakespeare dissociated, at the close of his life, from the rump of the Essex faction, and disowned the diehard politics of the papist exiles with which he had been affiliated for so long. The metatheatricality of *King Lear*, as a play without an audience, thus becomes significant not only as a reflection of Shakespeare's religious doubt but also as an image of his alienation from the Catholic patrons of his youth. As Lear defies the storm to 'Rumble thy bellyful! Spit, fire! Spout, rain!' (3.2.13), this is a drama, we see, about broken patronage relations, in which the fury of the 'great gods' (49) comes to symbolise the insane destructiveness of the writer's own father-figures, his papist mentors and minders. The cut *King Lear* is, certainly, a work about the ruin of Catholic England. But it is also the story of Shakespeare's disillusion with his aristocratic sponsors, his wrenching alienation from the passion of the martyrs, Campion's mission, Jesuit gunpowder and games at Gowthwaite Hall. 'Here I stand, your slave', says the player-king to his pontifical overlords, 'But yet I call you servile ministers' (18–20). This tragedy of separation is truly a play about absent spectators, a drama of one who has lost his faith in being heard or understood.

'You sulphurous and thought-executing fires, / Vaunt-couriers to oak-cleaving thunder-bolts, / Singe my white head!': if the 'all-shaking thunder' which is finally rendered, Elton claims, 'amoral and incomprehensible' in *King Lear* once belonged, as the symbolism implies, to the same sign-system of bulls, excommunications, armadas and assassinations as the thunder of 'holy gods' which resolves *Pericles* (5.1.185); the thunder with which Jupiter 'batters all rebelling coasts' in *Cymbeline* (5.5.190); the 'ear-deaf'ning voice o'th'oracle / Kin to Jove's thunder' in *The Winter's Tale* (3.1.9); or 'the thunder, / That deep and dreadful organ-pipe' which pontificates in *The Tempest* (3.3.98–9); then the expurgation of *King Lear* to reinforce the sensation of universal emptiness can be read only as a statement, at the end of his career, of Shakespeare's disavowal of all such declarations from Rome.[74] To conclude as much is not to fall into the trap of 'the burning question of the moment ... "Was he a Roman Catholic?"'[75] But still less is it to reduce the plays to the cliché that in them 'Shakespeare was paying tribute to the triumph of the Stuart monarchy over its popish enemies'.[76] What the self-censorship of *King Lear* demonstrates instead is how much the dynamic of these works arose out of conflict between the 'more or less "catholic" readings and glosses' given them 'within the privileged space of the theatre'[77] and the author's own dialectical drive, for once explicit, to resist these resistant interpretations, literally to 'play them down'. Shakespeare's quietness about religion does not make him into some 'orthodox Protestant', insists Jeffrey Knapp; nor, since in Elizabethan England 'opposition to sectarianism was itself sectarian', does reluctance to preach Christian doctrine appear 'a mark of secularism, as most scholars claim'. Rather, the dramatist's confessional secrecy seems a sign of his fears 'regarding the potential divisiveness of his religious beliefs'.[78] And there is one other example of Shakespearean censorship which supports this inference. For in the 1640s the second Folio was a set text at the English Jesuit College in Valladolid, a fact which exemplifies the extent of Shakespeare's Catholic reading community. But times had now moved on, the Jesuits had renounced tyrannicide, and so the rector, Father William Sankey – who underlined in *Macbeth* Malcolm's cry that 'our country sinks beneath the yoke, / It weeps, it bleeds' (4.3.40) – erased each reference in *King John* to the papal power to depose and 'batter all rebelling coasts'.[79] Long misunderstood as proof of Shakespeare's offensiveness to Rome, what this Jesuit censorship therefore completed was the neutralisation begun with the redaction of the original *King Lear*: the repudiation of the suicidal politics of martyrdom, and the defusing of a text which now appeared more Catholic than the Pope.

'Winter's not gone yet if the wild geese fly that way' (2.4.45): the cryptic observation of the Fool, inserted into the Folio among other 'images of revolt and flying off' (256), when the king vows 'By Jupiter' (191) to be reinstalled, confirms that Shakespeare understood well enough the migration instincts of those 'wild geese' who still gathered in northern fastnesses, years after the Gunpowder Plot, in hope of their promised spring, his own kin, the orphaned Catesbys, Grants and Winters. Simply to list the death-toll in Shakespeare's circle is to grasp how attuned he must have been to their mournful call to martyrdom, starting, as research now suggests it did, with Edmund Campion and the missionaries, Thomas Cottam, brother of the Stratford schoolmaster, Robert Debdale, neighbour of Anne Hathaway, William Hartley, friend of the teacher, Simon Hunt, and his 'cousin', Robert Southwell; then cutting off his Arden, Somerville and Throckmorton cousins; before scything through his patronage circles, with the assassination, execution or judicial murder of the Heskeths and Hoghtons; Henry Wriothesley, second Earl of Southampton, and his brother-in-law Anthony Browne, heirs to the Montagues; Ferdinando Stanley, Earl of Derby; and at last the Earl of Essex; before stopping just short of his most important patron, the 'Adonis' of the Sonnets, the third Earl of Southampton himself. The stabbing of his closest friend, Richard Quiney, by hitmen of the Puritan Grevilles looks, in such a roll call, to be part of a sinister pattern. As the descendant of the proto-martyr Thomas More, Donne liked to claim to have been 'ever kept awake in meditation of Martyrdom, by being derived from such a stock and race as, I believe, no family hath endured more in their persons and fortunes, for obeying the teachers of Roman doctrine';[80] which led John Carey to open his study of the poet with the assertion that, when he deserted the faith of his fathers, 'he chose hell ... and there are still Catholics who believe that in doing so he damned himself'.[81] But the book of Shakespeare's dead suggests that a similar verdict could be levelled at him, as a writer primed in the English Catholic cause. Read against such a blacklist, Shakespeare's theatre becomes truly deafening in its silence, its reticence a critique of martyrdom and its despair a resistance to the resistance in which its author had been raised. Politic Shakespeare reduced *King Lear*, it might be said, to complete his separation from the Jesuits: his retreat into an impregnable fortress of selfhood, which had been the thrust of his entire life. Thus, if the first thing to remember about Shakespeare is that he was born among the martyrs, the last is that he believed these motley 'Weeds among weeds, or flowers with flowers gathered', had enough treason to betray themselves: 'To witness which I call the fools of time, / Which die for goodness, who have lived for crime' (Sonnet 124).

'The weight of this sad time we must obey; / Speak what we feel, not what we ought to say' (5.3.322–3): the last lines of *King Lear* – transferred in the Folio from the time-serving Albany to the resistant Edgar – gain irony if this tragedy of a generation was indeed doctored in obedience to the weight that pressed on its first performances. Then, deletion of the trial of 'Queen Bess'; omission of satire on her 'head-lugged bear' Leicester (3.1.12–13; 4.2.43); and removal of allusions to her reign as one of 'death, dearth' and division (1.2.133), do look like a disowning of that 'poor fool' Campion and his disciples, who lived as traitors to be hanged as saints (5.3.304). Likewise, retraction of the Harsnett jibes (4.1.57–63), and of Edgar's plan to equivocate (3.6.95–108), confirms how, far from aesthetic tinkering, this redaction was the climax to a lifetime of political retreat. Taylor dates the new *Lear* precisely to the period of the Gowthwaite scandal, and a revival at Blackfriars theatre after it reopened in the winter of 1610.[82] The King's Men acquired the playhouse in the precinct only when the Children of the Revels were expelled on royal orders, for 'offending in matters of France' by traducing Henri IV in Chapman's *Byron*.[83] So, with Hoby in the wings, the politic poet had cause to befog the world beyond Dover Cliff. But, in the event, the Folio retrenchment was an epitome of his art: a 'fierce abridgement' (*Cymbeline*, 5.6.383) which produced, as Taylor attests, a drama more 'emotionally and intellectually' satisfying, by speaking *not* was what was felt but only what 'ought' to be said. Thus, the author's 'anticipation of censorship' combined with the modern belief that less is more to canonise the most secret text.[84] Throughout his career Shakespeare staged the silence of those enjoined to speak but inhibited by a love 'more ponderous' than their tongues (1.1.76). His art 'made tongue-tied by authority' (Sonnet 66), he assumed the dumbness of a Brutus, to the extent of making the 'antic disposition' (*Hamlet*, 1.5.173) of the wise fool the subject of his most elliptic play. So, when he offended by guying the Protestant saint, he gagged, protesting that 'Oldcastle died a martyr, and this is not the man' (*2 Henry IV*, Epi, 27). And when in *Henry V* he blurted advance knowledge of Essex's plot, his blunder was expunged from the Quarto (5, Pro, 30). 'Our bending author' mangled truth (Epi, 2) to gain applause, and wiped the oaths from the Folio *Othello*. Some things were too big for fooling: 'She that's a maid now, and laughs at my departure, / Shall not be a maid long, unless things be cut shorter' (*King Lear*, 1.5.43–4). It was apt, then, that he should bow out with the self-erasure of one who, for all his facility, knew well enough when 'it was necessary he should be stopped',[85] and when to 'Love and be silent' (1.1.60).

NOTES

1 Antonia Fraser, *The Gunpowder Plot: Terror and Faith in 1605* (London: Weidenfeld and Nicolson, 1996), p. 135.

2 Robert Catesby, quoted in Hugh Ross Williams, *The Gunpowder Plot* (London: Faber and Faber, 1951), p. 109.

3 Christopher Howard, *Sir John Yorke of Nidderdale, 1565–1634* (London: Sheed and Ward, 1939), pp. 38–9; Historic Manuscripts Commission, *Cecil Papers*, 17, pp. 503–4.

4 Godfrey Anstruther, *Vaux of Harrowden: A Recusant Family* (Newport, Monmouth: R.M. Johns, 1953), pp. 390–1.

5 Ibid., p. 25; Public Record Office, Stac 8 19/10, f. 14 and 30. The Gowthwaite Hall incident was first brought to the notice of Shakespeareans by E.K. Chambers in *The Elizabethan Stage*, 4 vols (Oxford: Clarendon Press, 1923), vol. 1, pp. 304–5, and discussed by Clifford Leech in his 1935 University of London doctoral dissertation, 'Private and Amateur Theatricals (excluding the Academic Stage) from 1580 to 1660'; and by C. J. Sisson in 'Shakespeare's Quartos as Prompt Copies, with Some Account of Cholmeley's Players and a New Shakespeare Allusion', *Review of English Studies*, 18 (April 1942), pp. 129–43. By far the most detailed account is by G.W. Boddy in 'Players of Interludes in North Yorkshire in the Early Seventeenth Century', *North Yorkshire County Record Office Journal*, 3 (April 1976), pp. 95–130; and the most extended discussion of the Shakespearean implications is by John Murphy in *Darkness and Devils: Exorcism and 'King Lear'* (Athens: Ohio University Press, 1984), pp. 93–118. See also J.C.H. Aveling, *Northern Catholics: The Catholic Recusants of the North Riding of Yorkhire, 1558–1790* (London: Chapman and Hall, 1966), pp. 288–91; Adam Fox, 'Religious Satire in English Towns', in Patrick Collinson and John Craig (eds), *The Reformation in English Towns, 1500–1640* (London: Macmillan, 1998), pp. 221–40; W.J. Sheils, 'Catholics in a Rural Community', *Northern History*, 34 (1998), pp. 116–17; and Tessa Watt, *Cheap Print and Popular Piety in Early Modern England* (Cambridge: Cambridge University Press, 1991), pp. 30–1.

6 Stephen Greenblatt, *Shakespearean Negotiations: The Circulation of Social Energy in Renaissance England* (Oxford: Clarendon Press, 1988), p. 122.

7 W.J. Sheils, 'Household, Age and Gender among Jacobean Yorkshire Recusants', in Marie Rowlands (ed.), *English Catholics of Parish and Town, 1558–1778* (London: Catholic Record Society and Wolverhampton University, 1999), p. 142.

8 Boddy, op. cit. (note 5), p. 103.

9 Ibid., pp. 116–17.

10 C.L. Barber, 'License and Lese Majesty in Lincolnshire', in *Shakespeare's Festive*

Comedy: A Study of Dramatic Form and its Relation to Social Custom (Princeton: Princeton University Press, 1959), pp. 36–57; Emmanuel Le Roy Ladurie, *Carnival at Romans: A People's Uprising at Romans, 1579–1580* (Harmondsworth: Penguin, 1981), passim; Natalie Zemon Davis, *Society and Culture in Early Modern France* (Stanford: Stanford University Press, 1975), pp. 97–123. See also Clifford Geertz, 'Ritual and Social Change', in *The Interpretation of Cultures* (New York: Basic Books, 1973), pp. 142–69.

11 G.W. Boddy, 'Catholic Missioners at Grosmont Priory', *North Yorkshire County Record Office Journal*, 4 (December 1976), pp. 76–77; Willem Schrickx, '*Pericles* in a Book-List of 1619 from the English Jesuit Mission and Some of the Play's Special Problems', *Shakespeare Survey*, 29 (1976), pp. 21–32; Aveling, op. cit. (note 5), p. 290.

12 Aveling, op. cit. (note 5), p. 161.

13 Ibid., p. 290; Michael Hodgetts, 'A Topographical Index of Hiding Places', *Recusant History*, 16 (1982), p. 201. Grosmont was searched by priest-hunters on the night of 29–30 June 1599, when an elaborate hiding-place was discovered behind false timber.

14 *Grove's Dictionary of Music and Musicians* (London: Macmillan, 1980), vol. 17, p. 139.

15 The date of Christopher Simpson's birth, usually given as 1605, has been revised as a result of the research by Margaret Urquhart in 'Was Christopher Simpson a Jesuit?' *Chelys*, 21 (1992), pp. 3–26, esp. p. 5. Besides the thirteen–year-old Postgate, the 1616 company included Christopher's brother Robert, then aged seven: Boddy, op. cit. (note 5), p. 110.

16 Ibid., p. 6; Boddy, op. cit. (note 11), p. 117.

17 Percy Young, *A History of British Music* (London: Ernest Benn, 1967), p. 219; John Caldwell, *The Oxford History of English Music*, 3 vols (Oxford: Clarendon Press, 1991), vol. 1, p. 544.

18 Urquhart, op. cit. (note 15).

19 Quoted Young, op. cit. (note 17), p. 220.

20 Charles J. Sisson, 'Shakespeare Quartos as Prompt-Copies: with Some Account of the Cholmeley Players and a New Shakespeare Allusion', *Review of English Studies*, vol. 18:70 (April 1942), pp. 129–43.

21 There is no mention of them at all, for example, by Andrew Gurr in his otherwise exhaustive recent survey, *The Shakespearean Playing Companies* (Oxford: Clarendon Press, 1996).

22 Sisson, op. cit. (note 20), p. 137.

23 Ibid.; Richard Marius, *Thomas More* (London: Weidenfeld, 1993), p. 22.

24 For Wilkins as Shakespeare's Catholic collaborator see Schrickx, op. cit. (note 11); Roger Prior, 'The Life of George Wilkins', *Shakespeare Survey*, 25 (1972), pp. 137–52; and 'George Wilkins and the Young Heir', *Shakespeare Survey*, 29 (1976), pp. 33–9.

25 John Day, *The Works of John Day*, ed. A.H. Bullen and Robin Jeffs (London: Holland Press, 1963), p. 352.

26 Ibid. pp. 370–1; 395; 396–7; 402–3.

27 See R.J.W. Evans, *Rudolf II and His World* (London: Thames and Hudson, 1997), pp. 77–9.

28 Anthony Parr (ed.), *Three Renaissance Travel Plays* (Manchester: Manchester University Press, 1995), p. 10.

29 PRO, op. cit. (note 5), f. 29 and 30.

30 Linda Levy Peck, *Northampton: Patronage and Policy at the Court of James I* (London: George Allen and Unwin, 1982), pp. 70–1, 80–3; N.E. McLure (ed.), *The Letters of John Chamberlain*, 2 vols (Philadelphia: American Philosophical Society, 1939), vol. 1, p. 396.

31 John Bruce (ed.), *Correspondence of James VI with Robert Cecil and Others in England* (London: Camden Society, 1861), p. 36.

32 Lady Elizabeth Russell, mother of Sir Thomas Hoby, quoted in Dorothy Meads, *Diary of Lady Margaret Hoby*, 1599–1605 (London: Routledge, 1930), p. 32.

33 Hugh Cholmley, *Memoirs of Sir Hugh Cholmley* (London: 1787), p. 14.

34 J.E. Neale, *The Elizabethan House of Commons* (London: Jonathan Cape, 1949), pp. 90–1.

35 Anthony Arlidge, *Shakespeare and the Prince of Love: The Feast of Misrule in the Middle Temple* (London: Giles de la Mare, 2000), pp. 106–7.

36 Boddy, op. cit. (note 5), p. 97; Meads, op. cit. (note 32), p. 33.

37 Joanna Moody (ed.), *The Private Life of an Elizabethan Lady: The Diary of Lady Margaret Hoby, 1599–1605* (Stroud: Sutton Publishing, 1998), p. 108.

38 Lawrence Stone, *The Crisis of the Aristocracy, 1558–1641* (Oxford: Clarendon Press, 1965), p. 567; Sir Thomas Hoby to the Privy Council, *Historic Manuscripts Commission: Salisbury Papers*, 10, pp. 302–4.

39 Ibid., 11, pp. 11–12.

40 Violet Wilson, 'Shakespeare and a Yorkshire Quarrel', *North American Review*, 219 (1924), pp. 653–61.

41 Daryl Palmer, *Hospitable Performances: Dramatic Genre and Cultural Practices in Early Modern England* (West Lafayette, Ind.: Purdue University Press, 1992), pp. 181–2.

42 Ibid., p. 182.

43 Irwin Smith, *Shakespeare's Blackfriars Playhouse: Its History and Its Design* (New York: New York University Press, 1964), pp. 172–3 and 480–1. See also Brian Burch, 'The Parish of St Anne's Blackfriars', *The Guildhall Miscellany*, 3:1 (1969), pp. 18–19.

44 Boddy, op. cit. (note 5), p. 96. In his 'Memoirs', Cholmley's son, Sir Hugh, dates the incident to about his father's twenty-third year, which would mean that it took place in 1602, but the details suggest the tensions around the time of the Essex Revolt.

45 Arlidge, op. cit. (note 35), passim.

46 Smith, op. cit. (note 43), p. 480: 'The same playhouse is so near the church [St Anne's, rebuilt in 1597] that the noise of the drums and trumpets will greatly disturb both the ministers and parishioners in time of divine service and sermons'.

47 Posthumus Hoby to Anthony Bacon, quoted in Meads, op. cit. (note 32), p. 32.

48 Arlidge, op. cit. (note 35), pp. 55–9.

49 For the violence of the Plough Day sword-dance see in particular François Laroque, *Shakespeare's Festive World: Elizabethan Seasonal Entertainment and the Professional Stage* (Cambridge: Cambridge University Press), pp. 93–6; and Robert Weimann, *Shakespeare and the Popular Tradition in the Theatre: Studies in the Social Dimension of Dramatic Form and Function* (Baltimore: Johns Hopkins University Press, 1978), pp. 15–17, 30–1, 43–5, 54 and 170.

50 Christina Hole, *A Dictionary of British Folk Customs* (London: Hutchinson, 1976), p. 238.

51 Boddy, op. cit. (note 5), pp. 98–103.

52 Ibid., p. 118.

53 Mervyn James, 'At a Crossroads of the Political Culture: The Essex Revolt, 1601', in *Society, Politics and Culture: Studies in Early Modern England* (Cambridge: Cambridge University Press, 1986), p. 426, n. 38.

54 Quoted Meads, op. cit. (note 32), p. 34.

55 Boddy, op. cit. (note 5), p. 96.

56 Ibid., pp. 98 and 107.

57 Thomas Trescot, *The Zealous Magistrate* (London: 1642), quoted in Jeffrey Knapp, *Shakespeare's Tribe: Church, Nation, and Theater in Renaissance England* (Chicago: Chicago University Press, 2002), p. vii; Gary Taylor, 'Forms of Opposition: Shakespeare and Middleton', *English Literary Renaissance (ELR)*, 24 (1994), p. 295.

58 Samuel Harsnett, *A Declaration of Egregious Popish Impostures* (London: 1603), pp. 114–15.

59 John Gee, *New Shreds of the Old Snare* (London: 1624); quoted in Greenblatt, op. cit. (note 6), p. 190, n. 36.

60 Sheils, op. cit. (note 5), p. 117.

61 Quoted Boddy, op. cit. (note 5), pp. 105–6.

62 For the political importance of the Ingleby–Yorke–Winter family network see K.M.

Longley, 'David Ingleby, the "Fox" that Got Away', *Northern Catholic History*, 34 (1993), pp. 18–35.

63 Murphy, op. cit. (note 5), p. 116.

64 John Murphy, 'Sheep-Like Goats and Goat-Like Sheep: Did Shakespeare Divide *Lear's Kingdom?*', *Papers of the Bibliographical Society of America*, 81 (1987), pp. 53–63.

65 John Bossy, 'The Character of Elizabethan Catholicism', *Past and Present*, 21 (1962), pp. 56–7. For Catholic neo-Stoicism see J.H.M. Salmon, 'Seneca and Tacitus in Jacobean England', in Linda Levy Peck, *The Mental World of the Jacobean Court* (Cambridge: Cambridge University Press, 1991), pp. 184–6.

66 Frank Brownlow, *Shakespeare, Harsnett, and the Devils of Denham* (Newark: Delaware University Press, 1993), pp. 129–31; Robert Southwell, 'Imprisonment in a good cause', in *An Epistle of Comfort* (London: 1587), chap. 8.

67 Christopher Devlin, *The Life of Robert Southwell, Poet and Martyr* (London: Longmans, Green and Co, 1956), p. 321; Peter Milward, *Shakespeare's Religious Background* (Chicago: Loyola University Press, 1973), p. 60.

68 Mark Nicholls, *Investigating Gunpowder Plot* (Manchester: Manchester University Press, 1991), p. 41; and for hopes placed in Henry IV of France see also p. 69.

69 Gary Taylor, 'Monopolies, Show Trials, Disaster, and Invasion: *King Lear* and Censorship', in Gary Taylor and Michael Warren (eds), *The Division of the Kingdom: Shakespeare's Two Versions of 'King Lear'* (Oxford: Clarendon Press, 1983), p. 80; Nicholls, op. cit. (note 68), p. 7; and see A.H. Dodd, 'Spanish Treason, the Gunpowder Plot, and the Catholic Refugees', *English Historical Review*, 53 (1938), pp. 627–50.

70 Taylor, op. cit. (note 69), p. 80; W.W. Greg, 'Time, Place, and Politics in *King Lear*', in *Collected Papers of Sir Walter Greg*, ed. J.C. Maxwell (Oxford: Oxford University Press, 1966), p. 333. See also Madeleine Doran, *The Text of 'King Lear'* (Stanford: Stanford University Press, 1931), pp. 73–6.

71 Thomas More, quoted in Richard Marius, *Thomas More* (London: Weidenfeld and Nicolson, 1993), p. 513.

72 William Elton, *'King Lear' and the Gods* (San Marino: Huntington Library, 1968), p. 238 and passim.

73 Richard Simpson, 'The Politics of Shakespeare's Historical Plays', *New Shakespere Society's Transactions*, 1874, p. 406.

74 Elton, op. cit. (note 72), pp. 197–219.

75 Dympna Callaghan, 'Shakespeare and Religion', *Textual Practice*, 15 (2001), p. 1.

76 Peter Lake and Michael Questier, *The Antichrist's Lewd Hat: Protestants, Papists and Players in Post-Reformation England* (Princeton: Princeton University Press, 2002), p. 388.

77 Ibid. pp. 391–2.

78 Knapp, op. cit. (note 57), p. 51.

79 A.C.F. Beales, *Education Under Penalty: English Catholic Education from the Reformation to the Fall of James II* (London: Athlone Press, 1963), pp. 150–1; Roland Mushat Frye, *Shakespeare and Christian Doctrine* (Princeton: Princeton University Press, 1963), pp. 275–93.

80 John Donne, *Pseudo-Martyr*, ed. Anthony Raspa (Montreal: McGill-Queen's University Press, 1993), 'An Advertisement to the Reader', p. 1.

81 John Carey, *John Donne: Life, Mind and Art* (London: Faber and Faber, 1981), p. 25.

82 Gary Taylor, *'King Lear*: The Date and Authorship of the Folio Version', in Taylor and Warren, op. cit. (note 69), p. 428.

83 Smith, op. cit. (note 43), pp. 193–8.

84 Taylor, op. cit. (note 69), p. 100.

85 Ben Jonson, *Timber: or, Discoveries Made upon Men and Matter*, in *Works* (London: 1641), pp. 97–8; quoted in Samuel Schoenbaum, *William Shakespeare: A Compact Documentary Life* (Oxford: Oxford University Press, 1977), p. 259.

Epilogue

Our bending author

'HE WAS not of an age, but for all time': Ben Jonson's homage 'To the memory of my beloved, the Author, Mr William Shakespeare', has been so successful in creating the myth of the Bard as a timeless genius that we forget how calculated Shakespeare's silence on his times must have seemed to contemporaries, and how much it might have been resented. The modern aesthetic that values art to the extent that it defies its time, and originates without commission, was so alien to Renaissance culture, however, that we may suspect Jonson of special pleading when he insisted that Shakespeare's work was never dictated by the headlines of 'the years'.[1] And this suspicion is confirmed by the fact that in the one year of his life when he might have been expected to comment on events it was precisely Shakespeare's silence which provoked hostile complaints. For in 1603, when, according to Thomas Dekker's eulogistic almanac of 'The Wonderful Year', the grieving poets of England 'rained showers of tears' over the body of Queen Elizabeth,[2] Shakespeare's refusal to mourn became conspicuous as the result of a concerted campaign to out his allegiance and blow his religious cover. Thus, within a month of the Queen's passing the anonymous author of 'A Mournful Ditty entitled England's Loss' was challenging 'You poets all, brave Shakespeare, Jonson, Greene,' to 'Bestow your time to write for England's Queen'.[3] The fact that Robert Greene had, in fact, himself died cursing Shakespeare as an 'upstart' Jesuitical 'crow' ten years before, looked here less like ignorance, as someone pointed out, than a ghoulish rhyme to shame two crypto-Catholic slackers by conjuring 'help of spirits in their sleeping graves, / As he that called to Shakespeare, Jonson, Greene, / To write of their dead noble Queen'.[4] So, the Protestant hack Henry Chettle must have known exactly what he was doing when he sneered that Will's saccharine sweetness was the reason why 'Melicert', as he now dubbed him, was so conspicuous by his absence, in the spring of 1603, from those writers grieving for their dead Queen:

Nor doth the silver-tongued *Melicert*
Drop from his honeyed muse one sable tear
To mourn her death that graced his desert
And to his lays opened her royal ear.
    Shepherd, remember our *Elizabeth*,
    And sing her rape done by that *Tarquin*, Death.[5]

'He was not of an age': yet the attacks on Shakespeare for failing to mourn Elizabeth suggest how his aesthetic pose of obliviousness towards current affairs must have exasperated his detractors. 'Supremely ill-judged', is how Peter Thomson rates Chettle's comparison of the Queen's death to Lucrece's rape, in *Shakespeare's Professional Career*.[6] But as the jibe at his 'sable', or *Moorish*, tears insists, the poet's contemporaries may have had their suspicions about his true mourning, and read a work like *The Rape of Lucrece*, which ends with an oath 'To rouse our Roman gods' [1831], as a lament for the persecution of the Catholic 'Tribe of More'. Yet that poem had arisen precisely after criticism of the author of *Venus and Adonis* from his 'cousin', the Jesuit Robert Southwell, as one of those who might 'have their talents lent' to 'Christian works', if they had not sold out to the tyrant Queen.[7] So, what seems to have defined Shakespeare's relation to his times was, in fact, his refusal to bow to blackmail or coercion to speak for either the regime or its resisters in the great drama of conscience that was acted out in England from the day in 1580 when Edmund Campion arrived on his fool's crusade. All the evidence now points to the conclusion that the dramatist was born into a Catholic elite up to its neck in plots against Elizabeth on behalf of Mary Queen of Scots, in a suicidal Counter-Reformation milieu where whether 'to take arms' against persecution was, as Hamlet asserts, 'the question' of the age [*Hamlet*, 3.1.58–61]. Historians such as John Bossy have forced us to recognise, more clearly than ever before, that Shakespeare's recurring dramatic scenario articulated the predicament of this Catholic *fronde* of 'victims of the state, enthusiasts and malcontents, vindictive exiles, conspirators and potential assassins'.[8] Such was the violent revanchist backdrop to the Shakespearean stage. But the theme of this book has been that the genius of Shakespeare was to create *a drama out of silence*, by resisting this resistance and thereby avoiding the 'Bloody Question' of loyalty and faith. Shakespeare will always give interrogators the slip, in this interpretation. Yet the dangers of such a dramaturgy argue, in turn, for the idea of the author as a conscious artist, who wrote and revised his texts for readers in country houses as much as the audiences on Bankside.[9] For when his 'ancestor spirits', as Stephen Greenblatt terms Shakespeare's Catholic father-figures,[10] implored him to 'swear' to 'remember' and avenge their wrongs, like the 'old mole' in the 'cellarage' [*Hamlet*, 1.5.91; 153–64], this son of the martyrs staged instead a disavowal of that Jesuitical 'devil in the vault'. Thus, Shakespeare made a drama out of his refusal of a terror which, as historian Emmanuel Le Roy observes, we recognise all too well; when, from 1580 on, across Europe the repressed did indeed return:

... It resurrected fundamentalism triumphant in its most archaic and fanatical forms. Zealous monks and preachers formed the basis of the organization, [but] it was a true apparatus in the modern sense ... pre-revolutionary, manipulative, even totalitarian. We have just witnessed events of the same type, where a vast popular movement is directed by the *mullahs*. Perhaps in the light of these very recent events we can better understand how reactionary Catholicism and the revolutionary spirit formed their odd alliance.[11]

'When we came forth, we looked so like ghosts that the fellow that found us ran away for fear', wrote Father Henry Garnet after he and Edward Old-courne were hauled out of their priest-hole, near Stratford, in the hue and cry after the Gunpowder Plot.[12] Garnet was to be butchered in front of St Paul's, a hundred yards from where his fellow Jesuit John Gerard was hidden in the cellars of the Blackfriars Gatehouse, which would serve as the Catholic haven in London until it was bought, in 1613, by Shakespeare himself.[13] In *Secret Shakespeare* I have interpreted the playwright's proximity to this 'worthy pioneer' of Jesuit treason [1.5.165] as a source of both the conflicted power of Shakespearean drama and of its strategic opacity, the evasive slipperiness which the Prince of Denmark demonstrates when his reaction to such spectres underground is to force his companions into silence: '*Hic et ubique*? Then we'll shift our ground. – / Come hither, gentlemen, / And lay your hands upon my sword. / Never to speak of this that you have heard, / Swear by my sword' [158–62]. And this is a reading that gains credibility from new discoveries about the author's patronage network, which place him among those 'court Catholics' whose 'native hue of resolution' was indeed 'sicklied o'er with the pale cast of thought', when they defected from the 'great enterprise' of the Essex Revolt [3.1.86–8].[14] Shakespeare's complex loyalism matches, that is to say, that of the grouping in which research locates him at the time of *Hamlet*: in the train of the Earl of Worcester, who switched sides at the last moment in 1601, from being Essex's ally to joining his prosecutors, and so earned Elizabeth's gratitude as one who had 'reconciled what she believed impossible, a stiff papist to a good subject'.[15] Thus, the picture that emerges of his trajectory is the reverse of the myth of a 'Shakespeare in love' with Protestant empire, who feared regime-change and accommodated himself to James only as a *fait accompli*. From the private *Titus Andronicus* presented on New Year's Eve 1595 in the house of the Stuart fixer Sir John Harington,[16] to the Christmas *Love's Labour's Lost* staged for Anne of Denmark by the Earl of Southampton in 1604,[17] his writings can be aligned instead with the *politique* faction which formed around Ferdinando, Lord Strange; took its philosophy of toleration from Florio's Montaigne in the library of the Montagues; split over the Essex rebellion; and at last regrouped behind the Howard project of religious detente. In Warwickshire, Lancashire and London, Shakespeare moved, it appears, from one crypto-Catholic patronage network to the next at increasingly elevated levels. But it comes as no surprise that Leeds Barroll finds him, at the end, in the entourage of Queen Anne, whose confessional dance of veils, which began when she 'very quietly' rejected the Anglican rites at her own coronation and so side-stepped the question of faith,[18] accords perfectly with his own theatrics of mystery, errors, deniability, supposes, and doubt:

> The question is more nuanced than simply, 'Was Queen Anna a Catholic?' Whether [or not] 'she *died* a Catholic', Anna puzzles, if we are to think of her as doctrinaire. For if Anna was a Catholic, her religious affiliation does not appear to have done the Catholic nobles any great good … A remark of 1618, included in a report to the Doge, is an appropriate summary: 'Some consider her a Catholic because she would never go to the English church, but really her religion is not known.'[19]

'He lays a heavy curse upon anyone who shall remove his bones. He died a papist':[20] Richard Davies's report implies that Shakespeare affirmed with his last breath what his father swore to the Jesuits to uphold, the Catholic doctrine of intercession for souls of the dead, and the belief that 'my ending is despair, / Unless I be relieved by prayer, / Which pierces so, that it assaults / Mercy itself, and frees all faults' [*Tempest*, Epi., 15–18]. Yet Davies also implies that proof of this affirmation is subject to the interdiction on the writer's tomb in Stratford's Holy Trinity Church, blessing 'the man that spares these stones' but cursing him 'that moves my bones'.[21] This paradox of a secret both open and concealed tempts us to guess that what lies in the grave beside the body of the Bard, 'full seventeen foot deep', according to one account,[22] is in fact his own copy of the Borromeo Testament of faith brought by Campion from Milan, with its vow made 'in presence of the Blessed Virgin Mary, my Angel Guardian, and all the Celestial Court', to carry 'the same continually about me, that it may finally be buried with me after my death'.[23] We might infer this. But the fact that we could not prove it, unless we broke the taboo and desecrated the tomb, is the ultimate guarantee of Shakespeare's secrecy and so sets the seal upon his work, which likewise depends for cultural power on remaining forever questionable, its motive buried 'certain fathoms in the earth', and its book of inspiration drowned, 'deeper than did ever plummet sound' [5.1.55–6]. Secret Shakespeare may have been a covert Romanist, Church papist, Catholic loyalist, premature Laudian, or as Jeffrey Knapp proposes, simply a 'good fellow' whose 'tribe' consisted of his theatrical companions, and whose lay brotherhood was his audience at the Globe.[24] The only certainty about the religious joker who laughed that 'Though honesty be no Puritan, yet it will do no hurt; it will wear the surplice of humility over the black gown of a big heart' [*All's Well*, 1.3.82-4], is that whatever cloth he did wear nearest to his heart, 'he must have struck alert contemporaries', in Eamon Duffy's words, 'as a most unsatisfactory Protestant'.[25] So, it is hardly necessary to fantasise that the shirt he was buried in was the black robe of a Jesuit, or the garb of a Franciscan,[26] to perceive that the curse on tomb-robbers inscribed in his epitaph is a malediction against all who would intrude 'the question' of allegiance to 'pluck out the heart' [*Hamlet*, 3.2.336] of his beliefs. In his writings he had reiterated that 'Not marble nor the gilded monuments / Of princes shall outlive this powerful rhyme' [Sonnet 55]. So, his own monument marks, for as long as it remains unopened, a determination to 'lead us from hence' – as Leontes begs to be led from the tear-stained graveside [*Winter's Tale*, 5.3.156] – and to be abstracted from the scene of mourning into art:

> My love looks fresh, and death to me subscribes,
> Since spite of him I'll live in this poor rhyme
> While he insults o'er dull and speechless tribes,
> And thou in this shalt find thy monument
> When tyrants' crests and tombs of brass are spent.   [*Sonnet 107*]

'My tongue is weary; when my legs are too, I will bid you good night, and so kneel down before you – but, indeed, to pray for the Queen' [2 *Henry IV*, Epi., 28–30]: like Campion praying for Elizabeth the instant before his execution, at the end of his day this player will not deny the 'mortal moon' [Sonnet 107] his prayers. But aside from such perfunctory lip-service to Tudor 'tyrants' crests and tombs', 'Our bending author', as he styled himself on one of the apologetic occasions, in the Epilogue of *Henry V*, when he ate his own words, systematically cancelled his historicity, and bowed for our secular 'Praise in departing' [*Tempest*, 3.3.39] as much as for sectarian prayers. Thus, by resolving to 'leave the killing out, when all is done' [*Dream*, 3.1.13], and making so light of the sufferings of the Elizabethan martyrs, rather than heeding ancestral voices from the tomb, Shakespeare became perhaps the greatest exemplar of Freud's theory in 'Mourning and Melancholia', that the work of bereavement is only achieved when the secrets of the past are encrypted, and the ego articulates its loss in language, creating a verbal substitute for the lost object, which is thereby finally interred. If the latest research is correct to interpret 'The Phoenix and the Turtle' as a funeral elegy, set to music by William Byrd, for the Catholic martyr Anne Line and her Jesuit charges, after they were hanged in the wake of the Essex disaster, then the player may well have had reason to admit, as he seems to do in Sonnet 74, that 'My life hath in this [L]ine some interest,' and to fear a day 'when that fell arrest / Without all bail shall carry me away' to a different scaffold, with 'The coward conquest of a wretch's knife'.[27] Secret Shakespeare, who lived in terror of Tyburn, if these investigations are believed, from the instant missionaries first arrived in his home town, had cause to immure the relics of the martyrs in their urn through an encryptment that has indeed proved virtually impenetrable. As Leo Bersani and Ulysses Dutoit observe in *Caravaggio's Secrets*, with such Counter-Reformation encodings it is as if we are invited to decrypt precisely what has been constructed to remain buried and entombed.[28] So, 'Our bending author' takes his bow at the end to be freed from the weight of his own times, 'As you from crimes would pardoned be' [*Tempest*, Epi., 19], having written his play in order to have no face. We duly release him, with our applause, from the ghosts that claim him, and absolve him of the secrets of the crypt. But 'how he terrifies me', as Rilke commented of the author of *The Tempest*, this man who is freed from history at last:

> The way he draws
> the wire into his head, and hangs himself
> beside the other puppets, and henceforth
> begs mercy of the play![29]

NOTES

1 E.K. Chambers, *William Shakespeare* (2 vols., Oxford: Clarendon Press, 1930), vol. 2, pp. 207-9.
2 Thomas Dekker, 'The Wonderful Year 1603', in *Non-Dramatic Works of Thomas Dekker*, ed. Alexander Grosart (London: Longmans, 1884), p. 88.
3 Chambers, op. cit. (note 1), p. 213.
4 Ibid., p. 214.
5 From 'England's Mourning Garment', ibid., p. 189.
6 Peter Thomson, *Shakespeare's Professional Career* (Cambridge: Cambridge University Press), p. 148.
7 Robert Southwell, *Saint Peter's Complaint and Saint Mary Magdalen's Funeral Tears* (St.-Omer: Society of Jesus, 1616), A4.
8 John Bossy, *Under the Molehill: An Elizabethan Spy Story* (New Haven: Yale University Press, 2001), p. 9.
9 See Lukas Erne, *Shakespeare as Literary Dramatist* (Cambridge: Cambridge University Press, 2003).
10 Stephen Greenblatt, *Hamlet in Purgatory* (Princeton: Princeton University Press, 2001), p. 198.
11 Emmanuel Le Roy Ladurie, *Carnival at Romans: A People's Uprising at Romans, 1579–1580*, trans. Mary Feeney (Harmondsworth: Penguin, 1981), xv–xvi.
12 Henry Garnet to Anne Vaux, March 4 1606, quoted in Philip Caraman, *Henry Garnet, 1555-1606, and the Gunpowder Plot* (London: Longmans, 1964), pp. 339–40.
13 E.K. Chambers, op. cit. (note 1), p. 168.
14 Stanley Wells, 'By the placing of his words: Shakespeare's first close critic', *Times Literary Supplement*, September 26 2003, 14–15. Wells discusses *The Model of Poesy*, a previously unknown manuscript by William Scott, in which this official of the Ordnance Office, on the edge of the Essex Revolt, writes a detailed critique of *Richard II* and *The Rape of Lucrece*.
15 Quoted in Roy Strong, *The Cult of Elizabeth: Elizabethan Portraiture and Pageantry* (London: Thames and Hudson, 1977), p. 27. See also John Finnis and Patrick Martin, 'Another turn for the Turtle: Shakespeare's intercession for Love's Martyr,' *Times Literary Supplement*, April 18 2003, 12–14.
16 See Gustav Ungerer, 'An Unrecorded Elizabethan Performance of *Titus Andronicus*', *Shakespeare Survey*, 14 (1961), 102–9.
17 See Leeds Barroll, *Politics, Plague, and Shakespeare's Theater* (Ithaca: Cornell University Press, 1991), pp. 126-7.
18 *Calendar of State Papers Venetian*, vol. 10, p. 81.
19 Leeds Barroll, *Anna of Denmark, Queen of England: A Cultural Biography* (Philadelphia: University of Pennsylvania Press, 2001), pp. 162–6 and 172. For Shakespeare in the circle of Queen Anne, see also pp. 55-6.
20 Richard Davies quoted in Chambers, op. cit. (note 1), vol. 2, p. 257.
21 Repr., Samuel Schoenbaum, *William Shakespeare: A Documentary Life* (Oxford: Clarendon Press, 1975), p. 253.

22 William Hall 1694, repr., ibid., p. 251.

23 Repr., ibid., pp. 44-5.

24 Jeffrey Knapp, *Shakespeare's Tribe: Church, Nation, and Theater in Renaissance England* (Chicago: Chicago University Press, 2002), pp. 53 and 169.

25 Eamon Duffy, 'Bare Ruined Choirs: Remembering Catholicism in Shakespeare's England,' in Richard Dutton, Alison Findlay and Richard Wilson (eds.), *Theatre and Religion: Lancastrian Shakespeare* (Manchester: Manchester University Press, 2003), p. 56.

26 *Franciscan Annals*, August 1898, quoted in Samuel Schoenbaum, *Shakespeare's Lives* (Oxford: Clarendon Press, 1970), p. 460.

27 See Finnis and Martin, op. cit. (note 15), and letters from Claire Asquith and Gerard Kilroy, *Times Literary Supplement*, May 2 2003, 17.

28 Leo Bersani and Ulysse Dutoit, *Caravaggio's Secrets* (Cambridge, Mass.: MIT Press, 1998), p. 2 and *passim*.

29 Rainer Maria Rilke, 'The Spirit Ariel', in *Rilke: Selected Poems*, trans. J.B. Leishman (Harmondsworth: Penguin, 1964), p. 74.

Bibliography

Abrahams, R.G., 'The Gunpowder Plot in Warwickshire,' (unpub. typescript, Birmingham Archaeological Society, 1951), Birmingham Reference Library

Agius, Thomas, 'Memorable Sites of London: Hunsdon House: Massing House,' *Letters and Notices of the Society of Jesus*, 7 (1937)

Akrigg, G.P.V., *Shakespeare and the Earl of Southampton* (London: Hamish Hamilton, 1968)

Alden, Daniel, *The Making of an Enterprise: The Society of Jesus in Portugal, Its Empire, and Beyond, 1540–1750* (Stanford: Stanford University Press, 1996)

Allen, William, *A Treatise Made in Defence of the Lawful Power of Priests to Remit Sins* (Louvain, 1567)

—— *An Admonition to the Nobility and People of England* (Douai: 1588)

—— *A True Sincere and Modest Defence of English Catholics*, ed. Robert Kingdon (Ithaca: Cornell University Press, 1965)

—— *An Apology and True Declaration of the Institution and Endeavours of the Two English Colleges* (London: Scolar Press, 1971)

—— *A Brief History of the Glorious Martyrdom of Twelve Reverend Priests*, ed. J.H. Pollen (London: Burns and Oates, 1908)

Altman, Joel, 'Preposterous Conclusions: Eros, *Enargeia*, and the Composition of *Othello*,' *Representations*, 18 (1987)

Anstruther, Godfrey, *Vaux of Harrowden: A Recusant Family* (Newport: R.M. Johns, 1953)

—— *The Seminary Priests: A dictionary of the secular clergy of England and Wales: I: Elizabethan, 1558–1603* (Durham: Ushaw College, 1964)

Archer, John, *Sovereignty and Intelligence: Spying and Court Culture in the English Renaissance* (Stanford: Stanford University Press, 1993)

Arlidge, Anthony, *Shakespeare and the Prince of Love: The Feast of Misrule in the Middle Temple* (London: Giles de la Mare, 2000)

Asquith, Claire, 'A Phoenix for Palm Sunday: Was Shakespeare's Poem a requiem for Catholic martyrs?' *Times Literary Supplement*, April 13 2001

Aubrey, John, *Brief Lives*, ed. Oliver Lawson Dick (Harmondsworth: Penguin, 1962)

Aveling, J.C.H., *Northern Catholics: The Catholic Recusants of the North Riding of Yorkshire, 1558–1790* (London: Chapman and Hall, 1966)

Bacon, Francis, *The Works of Francis Bacon*, ed. James Spedding (14 vols., London: Macmillan, 1857–1874)

Bagley, J.J., *The Earls of Derby, 1485–1985* (London: Sidgwick and Jackson, 1985)

Baker, Oliver, *Shakespeare's Warwickshire and the Unknown Years* (London: Simpkin Marshall, 1937)

Baldwin, T.W., *William Shakspere's Small Latine and Lesse Greek* (2 vols., Urbana: Illinois University Press, 1944)

Barber, C.L., *Shakespeare's Festive Comedy: A Study of Dramatic Form and its Relation to Social Custom* (Princeton: Princeton University Press, 1959)

Barish, Jonas, *The Anti-Theatrical Prejudice* (Berkeley: University of California Press, 1981)

Barker, Francis, *The Tremulous Private Body: Essays on Subjection* (London: Routledge, 1984)

—— *The Culture of Violence: Essays on tragedy and history* (Manchester: Manchester University Press, 1993)

Barlow, William, *An Answer to an English Catholic Gentleman* (London: 1609)

Barnard, E.A., *A Seventeenth-Century Country Gentleman: Sir Francis Throckmorton* (Cambridge: Cambridge University Press, 1948)

Barroll, Leeds, *Politics, Plague, and Shakespeare's Theater* (Ithaca: Cornell University Press, 1991)

—— *Anna of Denmark, Queen of England: A Cultural Biography* (Philadelphia: University of Pennsylvania Press, 2001)

Barton, Anne, *Shakespeare and the Idea of the Play* (Harmondsworth: Penguin, 1967)
'London Comedy and the Ethos of the City,' *London Journal*, 4 (1978)

Basset, Bernard, *The English Jesuits: From Campion to Martindale* (London: Burns and Oates, 1967)

Bate, Jonathan, 'Lucius: the Severely Flawed Redeemer of *Titus Andronicus*: A Reply,' *Connotations*, 63 (1997)

—— *The Genius of Shakespeare* (London: Picador, 1997)

—— 'No Other Purgatory but a Play,' *The Sunday Telegraph*, April 8 2001

Beales, C.P., *Education Under Penality: English Catholic Education from the Reformation to The Fall of James II, 1547–1689* (London: Athlone Press, 1963)

Bearman, Robert, 'Was William Shakespeare William Shakeshafte?' *Shakespeare Quarterly* 53 (2002)

Beauregard, David N., 'New Light on Shakespeare's Catholicism: Prospero's Epilogue in *The Tempest*,' *Renascence*, 49 (1997)

Beckingsale, B.W., *Burghley: Tudor Statesman* (London: Macmillan, 1967)

Belsey, Catherine, *The Subject of Tragedy: Identity and Difference in Renaissance Drama* (London: Methuen, 1985)

—— 'Disrupting Sexual Difference,' in John Drakakis (ed.), *Alternative Shakespeares* (London: Methuen, 1985)

Bennett, J.H.E. (ed.), *The Rolls of the Freemen of the City of Chester* (Chester: Corporation of Chester, 1906)

Bergeron, David M., *Shakespeare's Romances and the Royal Family* (Lawrence: Kansas University Press, 1985)

—— *Royal Family, Royal Lovers: King James of England and Scotland* (Columbia: University of Missouri Press, 1991)

—— *King James and Letters of Homoerotic Desire* (Iowa City: University of Iowa Press, 1999)

Berington, Joseph, *The State and Behaviour of English Catholics* (Birmingham: 1780)

Berry, Philippa, *Of Chastity and Power: Elizabethan Literature and the Unmarried Queen* (London: Routledge, 1989)

Bersani, Leo, and Ulysse Dutoit, *Caravaggio's Secrets* (Cambridge, Mass.: MIT Press, 1998)

Bicknell, E.J.A., *A Theological Introduction to the Thirty-Nine Articles of the Church of England* (London: Longmans, 1925)

Bindoff, S.T., and Joel Hurtsfield and C.H. Williams (eds), *Elizabethan Government and Society* (London: Athlone Press, 1961)

Birch, Thomas, *The Life of Henry Prince of Wales* (London: 1760)

Black, John, *The Reign of Elizabeth, 1558–1603* (Oxford: Clarendon Press, 1959)

Bloom, Harold, *Shakespeare: The Invention of the Human* (London: Fourth Estate, 1999)

Blundell, F.O., *Old Catholic Lancashire* (2 vols., London: Burns, Oates and Washbourne, 1925)

Boddy, G.W., 'Players of Interludes in North Yorkshire in the Early Seventeenth Century,' *North Yorkshire County Record Office Journal*, 3 (1976)

—— 'Catholic Missioners at Grosmont Priory,' *North Yorkshire County Record Office Journal*, 4 (1976)

Boose, Lynda, 'Othello's Handkerchief: The Recognizance and Pledge of Love,' *English Literary Renaissance (ELR)*, 5 (1975)

Bossy, John, 'The Character of Elizabethan Catholicism,' *Past and Present*, 21 (1962)

—— 'Rome and the Elizabethan Catholics: A Question of Geography,' *The Historical Journal*, 7 (1964)

—— 'The Social History of Confession in the Age of the Reformation,' *Transactions of the Royal Historical Society*, 5th series, 25 (1975)

—— *The English Catholic Community* (London: Darton, Longman and Todd, 1975)

—— 'The Continuity of English Catholicism,' *Past and Present*, 93 (1981)

—— *Giordano Bruno and the Embassy Affair* (New Haven: Yale University Press, 1991)

—— 'The Heart of Robert Parsons,' in Thomas McCoog (ed.), *The Reckoned Expense: Edmund Campion and the Early English Jesuits* (Woodbridge: Boydell and Brewer, 1996)

—— *Under the Molehill: An Elizabethan Spy Story* (New Haven: Yale University Press, 2001)

Bourdieu, Pierre, *Homo Academicus*, trans. Peter Collier (Cambridge: Polity Press, 1988)

Bowden, Henry, *The Religion of Shakespeare, Chiefly from the Writings of the late Mr Richard Simpson* (London: John Hodges, 1899)

Bradbrook, Muriel, *Shakespeare: The Poet in his World* (London: Weidenfeld and Nicolson, 1978)

Braudel, Fernand, *The Mediterranean and the Mediterranean World in the Age of Philip II*, Trans. Sian Reynolds (2 vols., London: Collins, 1972)

Breight, Curtis, 'Caressing the Great: Viscount Montague's Entertainment for Elizabeth at Cowdray in 1591,' *Sussex Archaeological Collections*, 127 (1989)

Brennan, Elizabeth, 'Papists and Patriotism in England,' *Recusant History*, 19 (1988)

Brenner, Robert, *Merchants and Revolution: Commercial Change, Political Conflict, and London's Overseas Trade, 1550–1653* (Cambridge: Cambridge University Press, 1993)

Brown, Christopher, *Van Dyck* (Oxford: Oxford University Press, 1982)

Brown, Meg Lota, 'The Politics of Conscience in Reformation England,' *Renaissance and Reformation*, 26 (1991)

Brownlow, 'John Shakespeare's Recusancy: New Light on an Old Document,' *Shakespeare Quarterly*, 40 (1989)

—— *Shakespeare, Harsnet, and the Devils of Denham* (Newark: University of Delaware Press, 1993)

Bruce, John (ed.), *The Correspondence of James VI with Robert Cecil and others in England* (London: Camden Society, 1861)

Burch, Brian, 'The Parish of St. Anne's Blackfriars, London, to 1665,' *Guildhall Miscellany*, 3 (1969)

Callaghan, Dympna, *Woman and Gender in Renaissance Tragedy* (Hemel Hempstead: Harvester, 1989)

—— 'Looking well to linens: women and cultural production in *Othello* and Shakespeare's England,' in Jean Howard and Scott Shershow (eds), *Marxist Shakespeares* (London: Routledge, 2001)

—— 'Shakespeare and Religion,' *Textual Practice*, 15 (2001)

Camm, Bede, *Forgotten Shrines: An Account of Some Old Catholic Halls and Families in England and of Relics and Memorials of the English Martyrs* (London: Macdonald and Evans, 1910)

Campbell, Thomas, *The Jesuits: A History of the Society of Jesus from its Foundations to the Present Time* (London: Encyclopaedia Press, 1921)

Canavaggio, John, *Cervantes*, trans. J.R. Jones (New York: Norton, 1990)

Caraman, Philip, *Henry Garnet: 1555–1606, and the Gunpowder Plot* (London: Longmans, 1964)
—— *The Years of Siege: Catholic Life from James I to Cromwell* (London: Longmans, 1966)
—— *The Lost Paradise: An Account of the Jesuits in Paraguay, 1607–1768* (London: Sidgwick and Jackson, 1975)
—— *The Lost Empire: The Story of the Jesuits in Ethiopia, 1555–1634* (London: Sidgwick and Jackson, 1985)
Carey, John, *John Donne: Life, Mind and Art* (London: Faber and Faber, 1981)
Cecil, William, *A Declaration of the Favourable Dealing of Her Majesty's Commissioners* (London: 1583)
Chambers, E.K., *The Elizabethan Stage* (4 vols., Oxford: Oxford University Press, 1923)
—— *William Shakespeare: A Study of Facts and Problems* (2 vols., Oxford: Oxford University Press, 1936)
—— *Shakespearean Gleanings* (Oxford: Oxford University Press, 1944)
—— *Sources for a Biography of Shakespeare* (Oxford: Oxford University Press, 1946)
Chambers, R., *A Book of Days: A Miscellany of Popular Antiquities* (2 vols., London: Chambers, 1869)
Chambrun, Clara Longworth de, *Shakespeare: A Portrait Restored* (London: Hollis and Carter, 1957)
Chartier, Roger, *Passions of the Renaissance: A History of Private Life III*, trans. Arthur Goldhammer (Cambridge, Mass.: Harvard University Press, 1989)
Cheyney, Edward, *A History of England from the Defeat of the Armada to the Death of Elizabeth* (London: Longmans, 1914)
Cholmley, Hugh, *The Memoirs of Hugh Cholmley* (London: 1787)
Clancy, Thomas H., 'English Catholics and the Papal Deposing Power, 1570–1640,' 3 parts, *Recusant History*, 7 (1963)
—— *Papist Pamphleteers: The Allen-Parsons Party and the Political Thought of Counter-Reformation England, 1572–1615* (Chicago: Loyola University Press, 1964)
—— *English Catholic Books, 1641–1700: A Bibliography* (rev. ed., Aldershot: Scolar, 1996)
Clark, Stuart, *Thinking with Demons: The Idea of Witchcraft in Early Modern Europe* (Oxford: Clarendon Press, 1997)
Clissold, Stephen, *The Barbary Slaves* (New York: Barnes and Noble, 1992)
Clopper, Lawrence (ed.), *Records of Early English Drama: Chester* (Toronto: Toronto University Press, 1979)
Cohen, Walter, *Drama of a Nation: Public Theater in Renaissance England and Spain* (Ithaca: Cornell University Press, 1985)
Coke, Edward, *The Third Part of the Institutes of the Laws of England* (London: 1797)
Collinson, Patrick, 'William Shakespeare's Religious Inheritance and Environment,' in *Elizabethan Essays* (London: Hambledon Press, 1994)
—— (ed.), with John Craig, *The Reformation in English Towns* (Basingstoke: Macmillan, 1998)
Cook, Ann Jennalie, *Making a Match: Courtship in Shakespeare and his Society* (Princeton: Princeton University Press, 1991)
Corthell, Ronald, 'The Secrecy of Man: Recusant Discourse and the Elizabethan Subject,' *English Literary Renaissance*, 19 (1989)
Coward, Barry, *The Stanleys, Lords Stanley and Earls of Derby, 1385–1672* (Manchester: Manchester University Press, 1983)
Crawford, Patricia, *Women and Religion in England, 1500–1720* (London: Routledge, 1992)
Cressy, David, 'Binding the Nation: Bonds of Association, 1584 and 1696,' in *Tudor Rule and Revolution*, ed. Dellroyd Guth and John McKenna (Cambridge: Cambridge University Press, 1982)
Crewe, Jonathan, *Hidden Designs: The Critical Profession and Renaissance Literature* (London: Methuen, 1986)
Crockett, David, *The Play of Paradox: Stage and Sermon in Renaissance England* (Philadelphia: Pennsylvania University Press, 1995)

Cross, Claire, 'An Elizabethan Martyrologist and his Martyr: John Mush and Margaret Clitheroe,' in Diana Wood (ed.), *Martyrs and Martyrologies: Papers read at the 1992 and 1993 meetings of the Ecclesiastical History Society* (Oxford: Blackwell, 1993)

Cust, Richard, and Ann Hughes (eds), *Conflict in Early Stuart England: Studies in Religion and Politics, 1603–1649* (London: Longman, 1989)

Danson, Lawrence, *Tragic Alphabet: Shakespeare's Drama of Language* (New Haven: Yale University Press, 1974)

Davies, Michael, 'On This Side Idolatry: The canonisation of the Catholic Shakespeare', *Cahiers Elisabethains*, 58 (2000)

Davihazi, Peter, *The Romantic Cult of Shakespeare: Literary Reception in Anthropological Perception* (Basingstoke: Macmillan, 1998)

Davis, Natalie Zemon, *Society and Culture in Early Modern France* (Stanford: Stanford University Press, 1975)

Day, John, *The Works of John Day*, ed. A.H. Bullen and Robin Jeffs (London: Holland Press, 1963)

Dekker, Thomas, *Non-Dramatic Works of Thomas Dekker*, ed. Alexander Grosart (London: Longmans, 1884)

Devitiis, Gigliola Pagano De, *English Merchants in Sixteenth Century Italy* (Cambridge: Cambridge University Press, 1990)

Devlin, Christopher, *The Life of Robert Southwell, Poet and Martyr* (London: Longmans and Greeen, 1956)

—— *Hamlet's Divinity and Other Essays* (London: Rupert Hart-Davis, 1963)

Dickens, A.G., *The English Reformation* (London: Batsford, 1964)

Dickey, Stephanie, 'Women Holding Handkerchiefs in Seventeenth-Century Dutch Portraits,' *Beeld en zeefbeeld in de Nederlandse kuns, 1550–1750 (Image and Self-Image in Dutch Art, 1550–1750), Kunsthistorich Jarrboek*, 46 (Zwolle: Waanders Uitgevers, 1995)

Diehl, Huston, *Staging Reform, Reforming the Stage: Protestantism and Popular Theater in Early Modern England* (Ithaca: Cornell University Press, 1997)

Ditchfield, Simon, 'Martyrs on the Move: Relics as vindicators of local diversity in the Tridentine Church,' in Diana Wood (ed.), *Martyrs and Martyrologies* (Oxford: Blackwell, 1993)

Dobson, Michael, and Nicola Watson, *England's Elizabeth* (Oxford: Oxford University Press, 2002)

Docherty, Thomas, *John Donne Undone* (London: Methuen, 1986)

Dodd, A.H., 'Spanish Treason, the Gunpowder Plot, and the Catholic Refugees,' *English Historical Review*, 53 (1938)

Dollimore, Jonathan, *Radical Tragedy: Religion, Ideology and Power in the Drama of Shakespeare and His Contemporaries* (Hemel Hempstead: Wheatsheaf, 1984)

Donne, John, *Pseudo-Martyr*, ed. Anthony Raspa (Montreal: McGill-Queen's University, 1993)

Doran, Madeleine, *The Text of 'King Lear'* (Stanford: Stanford University Press, 1931)

Drayton, Michael, *The Works of Michael Drayton*, ed. J.W. Hebel (5 vols., Oxford: Clarendon Press, 1961)

Duffy, Eamon, *The Stripping of the Altars: Traditional Religion in England, 1400–1580* (New Haven: Yale University Press, 1992)

—— 'Bare Ruined Choirs: Remembering Catholicism in Shakespeare's England,' in Richard Dutton, Alison Findlay and Richard Wilson (eds), *Theatre and Religion: Lancastrian Shakespeare* (Manchester: Manchester University Press, 2003)

Dugdale, William, *Antiquities of Warwickshire* (London: 1656)

Duncan-Jones, Katherine, *Sir Philip Sidney: Courtier Poet* (London: Hamish Hamilton, 1991)

Dures, Alan, *English Catholicism, 1558–1642: Continuity and Change* (Harlow: Longman, 1983)

Dusinberre, Juliet, *Shakespeare and the Nature of Women* (rev. ed., Basingstoke: Macmillan, 1996)

Duthie, G.I., 'Antithesis in *Macbeth*,' *Shakespeare Survey*, 24 (1971)

Dutton, Richard, *William Shakespeare: A Literary Life* (London: Macmillan, 1989)

—— *Mastering the Revels: The Regulation and Censorship of English Renaissance Drama* (London: Macmillan, 1991)

Eagleton, Terry, *William Shakespeare* (Oxford: Basil Blackwell, 1986)

Earne, Lukas, *Shakespeare as Literary Dramatist* (Cambridge: Cambridge University Press, 2003)

Eccles, Mark, *Shakespeare in Warwickshire* (Madison: University of Wisconsin Press, 1963)

Edmond, Mary, 'Limners and Picture Makers,' *Walpole Society*, 47 (1980)

Ellis, David, 'Biography and Shakespeare: An Outsider's View', *Cambridge Quarterly*, 29:4 (2000)

Ellrodt, Robert, 'Self-Consciousness in Montaigne and Shakespeare,' *Shakespeare Survey*, 28 (1975)

—— 'The Search for Identity: Montaigne to Donne,' *Confluences: 9* (Paris: Centre de Recherches sur les Origines de la modernite, 1995)

Elton, William, *'King Lear' and the Gods* (San Marino: Huntingdon Library, 1968)

Enos, Carol, 'Catholic Exiles and *As You Like It*: Or, What if You Don't Like It at All?' in Richard Dutton, Alison Findlay and Richard Wilson (eds), *Theatre and Religion: Lancastrian Shakespeare* (Manchester: Manchester University Press, 2003)

Evans, Bertrand, *Shakespeare's Comedies* (Oxford: Clarendon Press, 1960)

Evans, Ifor, and Heather Lawrence, *Christopher Saxton: Elizabethan Map-Maker* (Wakefield: Wakefield Historical Publications, 1979)

Evans, N.E., and D.L. Thomas, 'John Shakespeare in the Exchequer,' *Shakespeare Quarterly*, 15 (1984)

Evans, R.J.W., *Rudolf II and his world* (London: Thames and Hudson, 1997)

Everett, Barbara, 'Spanish *Othello*: the Making of Shakespeare's Moor,' *Shakespeare Survey*, 35 (1982)

Ewen, C. L'Estrange, *Witchcraft and Demonianism: A Concise Account Derived from Sworn Depositions and Confessions* (London: Kegan Paul, 1933)

Fairfax-Lucy, Alice, *Charlecote and the Lucys* (London: Jonathan Cape, 1958)

Farmer, David, *The Oxford Dictionary of Saints* (Oxford: Oxford University Press, 1987)

Farrall, L.M. (ed.), *Parish Register of the Holy and Undivided Trinity in the City of Chester, 1532–1837* (Chester: G.R. Griffith, 1914)

Fea, Alan, *Rooms of Mystery and Romance* (London: Hutchinson, 1931)

Feinberg, Anat, 'Observation and Theatricality in Webster's *The Duchess of Malfi*,' *Theatre Research Journal*, 6 (1980)

Finnis, John, and Patrick Martin, 'Another turn for the Turtle: Shakespeare's intercession for Love's Martyr,' *Times Literary Supplement*, April 18 2003

Fisher, Godfrey, *Barbary Legend: War, Trade and Piracy in North Africa, 1415–1830* (Oxford: Clarendon Press, 1957)

Fisher, Will, 'Handkerchiefs and Early Modern Ideologies of Gender,' *Shakespeare Studies*, 28 (2000)

Foister, Susan, 'Foreigners at Court: Holbein, Van Dyck and the Painter-Stainers Company,' in David Howarth (ed.), *Art and Patronage in the Caroline Courts* (Cambridge: Cambridge University Press, 1999)

Foley, Henry (ed.), *Records of the English Province of the Society of Jesus* (9 vols., London: Burns and Oates, 1878)

Forster, Anne C., 'The Oath Tendered,' *Recusant History*, 14 (1978)

Foucault, Michel, *Discipline and Punish: The Birth of the Prison*, trans. Alan Sheridan (Harmondsworth: Penguin, 1977)

—— *History of Sexuality: I: An Introduction*, trans. Robert Hurley (Harmondsworth: Penguin, 1980)

Fraser, Antonia, *The Gunpowder Plot: Terror and Faith in 1605* (London: Weidenfeld and Nicolson, 1996)

Freehafer, John, Cardenio, by Shakespeare and Fletcher,' *Publications of the Modern Language Association (PMLA)*, 84 (1969)

Friedman, Ellen, *Spanish Captives in North Africa in the Early Modern Age* (Madison: University of Wisconsin Press, 1983)

Fripp, Edgar, *Master Richard Quyny* (Oxford: Oxford University Press, 1924)

—— *Shakespeare's Haunts Near Stratford* (Oxford: Oxford University Press, 1929)

—— *Shakespeare: Man and Artist* (Oxford: Oxford University Press, 1938)

Frye, Roland Mushat, *Shakespeare and Christian Doctrine* (Princeton: Princeton University Press, 1963)

Fumerton, Patricia, *Cultural Aesthetics: Renaissance Literature and the Practice of Social Ornament* (Chicago: Chicago University Press, 1991)

Garnett, Henry, *Portrait of Guy Fawkes: An Experiment in Biography* (London: Robert Hale, 1962)

George, David, *Records of Early English Drama: Lancashire* (Toronto: Toronto University Press, 1991)

Gerard, John, *John Gerard: The Autobiography of an Elizabethan*, trans. Philip Caraman (London: Longmans, 1951)

Gifford, George, *A Dialogue Between a Papist and a Protestant, applied to the capacity of the unlearned* (London: 1582)

Gillow, Joseph, *Biographical Dictionary of English Catholics* (6 vols., London: Burns and Oates, 1887–90)

—— *The Haydock Papers: A Glimpse into English Catholic Life* (London: Burns and Oates, 1888)

—— *Lord Burghley's Map of Lancashire in 1590* (London: Arden Press and Catholic Records Society, 1907)

Girouard, Mark, *Life in the English Country House* (New Haven: Yale University Press, 1978)

Goldberg, Jonathan, *James I and the Politics of Literature* (Baltimore: Johns Hopkins University Press, 1983)

—— 'Colin to Hobbinol: Spenser's *Familiar Letters*,' *South Atlantic Quarterly*, 88 (1989)

—— *Writing Matters* (Stanford: Stanford University Press, 1990)

Goldmann, Lucien, *The Hidden God: A Study of the Tragic Vision in the "Pensees" of Pascal and the Tragedies of Racine*, trans. Philip Thody (London: Routledge, 1964)

Goodich, Michael, *Violence and Miracle in the Fourteenth Century: Private grief and public salvation* (Chicago: Chicago University Press, 1995)

Graves, Michael, *Thomas Norton: The Parliament Man* (Oxford: Basil Blackwell, 1994)

Greenblatt, Stephen, *Renaissance Self-Fashioning: From More to Shakespeare* (Chicago: Chicago University Press, 1980)

—— *Shakespearean Negotiations: The Circulation of Social Energy in Renaissance England* (Oxford: Clarendon Press, 1988)

—— *Learning to Curse: Essays in Early Modern Culture* (London: Routledge, 1990)

—— *Marvellous Possessions: The Wonder of the New World* (Chicago: Chicago University Press, 1991)

—— 'Shakespeare Bewitched,' *New Historical Literary Study*, ed. Stephen Greenblatt (Princeton: Princeton University Press, 1992)

—— *Hamlet in Purgatory* (Princeton: Princeton University Press, 2001)

Greg, Walter, 'Time, Place, and Politics in *King Lear*,' in *Collected Papers of Sir Walter Greg*, ed. J.C. Maxwell (Oxford: Oxford University Press, 1966)

Groot, John Henry de, *The Shakespeare's and 'The Old Faith'* (New York: Crown Press, 1946)

Hackett, Helen, *Virgin Mother, Maiden Queen: Elizabeth I and the Cult of the Virgin Mary* (New York: St. Martin's Press, 1995)

Haigh, Christopher, *Reformation and Resistance in Tudor Lancashire* (Cambridge: Cambridge University Press, 1975)

—— 'The Fall of a Church or the Rise of a Sect? Post-Reformation Catholicism in England,' *Historical Journal*, 21 (1978)

—— 'From Monopoly to Minority: Catholicism in Early Modern England,' *Transactions of the Royal Historical Society*, 5th series, 31 (1981)

Hakluyt, Richard, *Principal Navigations* (12 vols., London: Hakluyt Society, 1903–05)

Halliday, F.E., *The Cult of Shakespeare* (London: Duckworth, 1957)

Hallie, Philip, *The Scar of Montaigne: An Essay in Personal Philosophy* (Middleton, Conn.: Wesleyan University Press, 1966)

Hamilton, Donna, *Shakespeare and the Politics of Protestant England* (Lexington: University of Kentucky Press, 1992)

—— 'Anthony Munday and *The Merchant of Venice*,' *Shakespeare Survey*, 52 (2000)

Handover, P.M., *Arbella Stuart: Royal Lady of Hardwick and Cousin of King James* (London: Eyre and Spottiswoode, 1957)

—— *The Second Cecil: The Rise to Power, 1563–1604, of Sir Robert Cecil, later First Earl of Salisbury* (London: Eyre and Spottiswoode, 1959)

Hanley, Hugh, 'Shakespeare's Family in Stratford Records,' *Times Literary Supplement*, 21 May 1964

Hanson, Elizabeth, *Discovering the Subject in Renaissance England* (Cambridge: Cambridge University Press, 1998)

Hardin, Richard, 'The Early Poetry of the Gunpowder Plot: Myth in the Making,' *English Literary Renaissance (ELR)*, 22 (1992)

Harington, John, *A Tract on the Succession to the Crown*, ed. Clement Markham (London: J.B. Nichols, 1880)

Harrison, G.B., The Life and Death of Robert Devereux, Earl of Essex (London: Cassell, 1937)

Harsnet, *A Declaration of Egregious Popish Impostures to withdraw the Hearts of Her Majesty's Subjects from their Allegiance* (London: 1603)

Hassel, Chris R., *Renaissance Drama and the English Church Year* (Lincoln: Nebraska University Press, 1979)

Hasted, Rachel, *The Pendle Witch-Trial, 1612* (Preston: Lancashire County Council, 1987)

Havran, Martin J., *The Catholics in Caroline England* (Stanford: Stanford University Press, 1962)

Haynes, Alan, *The Gunpowder Plot: Faith in Rebellion* (Stroud: Sutton, 1994)

Hazard, Mary, *Elizabethan Silent Language* (Lincoln: University of Nebraska Press, 2000)

Headley, John M, and John B. Tomaro (eds), *San Carlo Borromeo: Catholic Reform and Ecclesiastical Politics in the Second Half of the Sixteenth Century* (Washington: Folger, 1988)

Heywood, Jasper, *Il Moro*, trans. G.P. Marc'hadour, ed. R.L. Deakins (Cambridge, Mass.: Harvard University Press, 1972)

Hibbard, Catherine, 'Early Stuart Catholicism: Revisions and Re-Revisions,' *Journal of Modern History*, 52 (1980)

Hicks, Leo, 'Sir Robert Cecil, Father Parsons, and the Succession,' *Archivum Historicum Societatis Jesu*, 25 (1955)

—— *An Elizabethan Problem: Some Aspects of the Careers of Two Exile-Adventurers* (London: Burns and Oates, 1964)

—— (ed.), *Letters and Memorials of Father Robert Parsons, S.J.* (London: Catholic Records Society, 1942)

Hill, J.E.C., 'The Puritans and the "Dark Corners of the Land",' *Transactions of the Royal Historical Society*, 5th series, 13 (1963)

Hoby, Margaret, *The Diary of Lady Margaret Hoby, 1599–1605*, ed. Dorothy Meads (London: Routledge, 1930)

Hodgetts, Michael, 'Elizabethan Priest-Holes: Dating and Chronology,' *Recusant History*, 11 (1972)

—— 'Elizabethan Priest-Holes: Harvington,' *Recusant History*, 14 (1978)

—— 'A Topographical Index of Hiding Places,' *Recusant History*, 16 (1982)

—— 'The Godly Garret,' in Marie Rowlands (ed.), *English Catholics of Parish and Town, 1558–1778* (London: Catholic Record Society, 1999)

Holden, Anthony, *William Shakespeare: His Life and Work* (London: Little, Brown, 1999)

Holderness, Graham, *The Shakespeare Myth* (Manchester: Manchester University Press, 1988)

Holloway, John, *The Story of the Night: Studies in Shakespeare's Major Tragedies* (London: Routledge and Kegan Paul, 1961)

Holmes, Peter, *Resistance and Compromise: The Political Thought of the Elizabethan Catholics* (Cambridge: Cambridge University Press, 1982)

Honan, Park, *Shakespeare: A Life* (Oxford: Oxford University Press, 1998)

Honigmann, Ernst, *Shakespeare: the 'lost years'* (Manchester: Manchester University Press, 1998)

—— *John Weever: A biography of a literary associate of Shakespeare with a facsimile of Weever's 'Epigrams'* (Manchester: Manchester University Press, 1987)

Hook, Judith, *The Baroque Age in England* (London: Thames and Hudson, 1976)

Hooker, Richard, *The Complete Works of Richard Hooker* (3 vols., London: Dent, 1948)

Hotson, Leslie, *I, William Shakespeare* (London: Jonathan Cape, 1937)

Howard, Christopher, *Sir John Yorke of Nidderdale, 1565–1634* (London: Sheed and Ward, 1939)

Howard, Jean, 'Renaissance anti-theatricality and the politics of gender and rank in *Much Ado About Nothing*,' in Jean Howard and Marion O'Connor (eds), *Shakespeare Reproduced: The Text in History and Ideology* (London: Methuen, 1987)

Howarth, David, *Images of Rule: Art and Politics in the English Renaissance, 1485–1649* (Basingstoke: Macmillan, 1997)

Hubert, Judd, *Metatheater: The Example of Shakespeare* (Lincoln: Nebraska University Press, 1991)

Hughes, Ann, *Politics, Society and Civil War in Warwickshire, 1620–1660* (Cambridge: Cambridge University Press, 1987)

—— 'Religion and Society in Stratford-upon-Avon, 1619–1638,' *Midland History*, 19 (1994)

Hughes, Ted, *Shakespeare and the Goddess of Complete Being* (London: Faber and Faber, 1992)

Hulme, Peter, *Colonial Encounters: Europe and the Native Caribbean, 1492–1797* (London: Routledge, 1986)

Hulse, Clark, 'Dead Man's Treasure: The Cult of Thomas More,' in David Lee Miller, Sharon O'Dair and Harold Weaver (eds), *The Production of English Renaissance Culture* (Ithaca: Cornell University Press, 1994)

Huntley, Frank, '*Macbeth* and the Background of Jesuit Equivocation,' *Publications of the Modern Language Association (PMLA)*, 79 (1964)

Ives, Vernon A., *The Rich Papers: Letters from Bermuda, 1615–1646* (Toronto: Toronto University Press, 1984)

James I, *Political Works of James I*, ed. C.H. McIlwain (New York: Russell and Russell, 1918)

James, Mervyn, *Society, Politics and Culture: Studies in Early Modern England* (Cambridge: Cambridge University Press, 1986)

Janelle, Pierre, *Robert Southwell the Writer* (London: Sheed and Ward, 1935)

Jones, David Martin, *Conscience and Allegiance in Seventeenth-Century England: The Political Significance of Oaths and Engagements* (Rochester, N.Y.: University of Rochester Press, 1999)

Jonson, Ben, *Ben Jonson*, ed. C.H. Herford and Percy and Evelyn Simpson (11 vols., Oxford: Oxford University Press, 1925–52)

Kaiser, Walter, *Praisers of Folly: Erasmus, Rabelais, Shakespeare* (London: Gollancz, 1964)

Kastan, David Scott, *Shakespeare After Theory* (London: Routledge, 2001)

Kaushak, Sandeep, 'Resistance, Loyalty and Recusant Politics: Sir Thomas Tresham and the Elizabethan State,' *Midland History*, 21 (1996)

Keen, Alan, and Roger Lubbock, *The Annotator* (London: Putnam, 1954)

Kendall, Alan, *Robert Dudley, Earl of Leicester* (London: Cassell, 1980)

Kermode, Frank, *The Genesis of Secrecy: On the Interpretation of Narrative* (Cambridge, Mass.: Harvard University Press, 1979)

Kernan, Alvin, *Shakespeare, the King's Playwright: Theater in the Stuart Court, 1603–1613* (New Haven: Yale University Press, 1995)

Kerrigan, John, 'Secrecy and Gossip in *Twelfth Night*,' *Histoire et Secret à la Renaissance*, ed. Francois Laroque (Paris: Presses de la Nouvelle Sorbonne, 1997)

Kerrigan, William, *Shakespeare's Promises* (Baltimore: Johns Hopkins University Press, 1999)

King, John, *English Reformation Literature* (Princeton: Princeton University Press, 1982)

Klause, John, 'Politics, Heresy, and Martyrdom in Sonnet 124 and *Titus Andronicus*,' in *Shakespeare's Sonnets: Critical Essays*, ed. James Schiffer (New York: Garland, 1999)

Knapp, Jeffrey, *An Empire Nowhere: England, America, and Literature from 'Utopia' to 'The Tempest'* (Berkeley: University of California Press, 1992)

—— *Shakespeare's Tribe: Church, Nation, and Theater in Renaissance England* (Chicago: Chicago University Press, 2002)

Knecht, R.J., *The French Wars of Religion* (Harlow: Longman, 1996)

Knowles, Ronald (ed.), *After Bakhtin: Shakespeare and Carnival* (Basingstoke: Macmillan, 1998)

Kronenfeld, Judith, *'King Lear' and the Naked Truth: Rethinking the Language of Religion and Resistance* (Durham: Duke University Press, 1998)

Kukowski, Stephen, 'The Hand of John Fletcher in *Double Falsehood*,' *Shakespeare Survey*, 43 (1991)

Kuryluk, *Veronica and Her Cloth: History, Symbolism and Structure of a Love Image* (Oxford: Blackwell, 1991)

Ladurie, Emmanuel Le Roy, *Carnival at Romans: A people's Uprising at Romans, 1579 1580*, trans. Mary Feeney (Harmondsworth: Penguin, 1981)

Lake, Peter, and Michael Questier, 'Agency, Appropriation and Rhetoric under the Gallows: Puritans, Romanists and the State in Early Modern England,' *Past and Present*, 153 (1996)

—— *The Antichrist's Lewd Hat: Protestants, Papists and Players in Post-Reformation England* (Princeton: Princeton University Press, 2002)

Larkin, J.F., and P.L. Hughes (eds), *Stuart Royal Proclamations* (Oxford: Oxford University Press, 1973)

Larocca, John, J., '"Who Can't Pray With Me, Can't Love Me": Toleration and the Early Jacobean Recusant Policy,' *Journal of British Studies*, 23 (1984)

Laroque, Francois, *Shakespeare's Festive World: Elizabethan Seasonal Entertainment and The Professional Stage*, trans. Janet Lloyd (Cambridge: Cambridge University Press, 1991

Laven, Mary, *Virgins of Venice: Enclosed Lives and Broken Vows in the Renaissance Convent* (London: Viking, 2002)

Law, Thomas Graves, *Jesuits and Scholars in the Reign of Elizabeth* (London: David Nutt, 1889)

Leader, John Temple, *The Life of Robert Dudley, Earl of Warwick and Duke of Northumberland* (Florence: Barbera, 1895)

Lee, Arthur Gould, *The Son of Leicester: The Story of Robert Dudley, Titular Earl of Warwick, Earl of Leicester, and Duke of Northumberland* (London: Gollancz, 1964)

Lee, Maurice (ed.), *Dudley Carleton to John Chamberlain, 1603–1624* (New Brunswick: Rutgers University Press, 1972)

Leech, Clifford, 'Private and Amateur Theatricals (excluding the Academic Stage) from 1580 to 1660' (unpublished thesis: University of London, 1935)

—— *The John Fletcher Plays* (London: Chatto and Windus, 1962)

Leslie, Michael, 'Something Nasty in the Wilderness: Entertaining Queen Elizabeth on Her Progresses,' in John Pitcher (ed.), *Medieval and Renaissance Drama in England: 10* (Madison: Fairleigh Dickinson University Press, 1998)

Lestringant, Frank (ed.), *Le Theatre des Crautés de Richard Vestegan, 1587* (Paris: Editions Chandeigne, 1995)

Levi, Peter, *The Life and Times of William Shakespeare* (London: Macmillan, 1988)

Lewis, Jayne Elizabeth, *Mary Queen of Scots: Romance and Nation* (London: Routledge, 1998)

Lindley, David, *The Trials of Frances Howard: Fact and Fiction at the Court of King James* (London: Routledge, 1993)

Lloyd, Christopher, *English Corsairs on the Barbary Coast* (London: Collins, 1981)

Longley, K.M., 'David Ingleby, The "Fox" That Got Away,' *Northern Catholic History*, 34 (1993)

Loomie, Albert J., *The Spanish Elizabethans: English Exiles at the Court of Philip II* (London: Burns and Oates, 1963)

Lumby, J.H. (ed.), *De Hoghton Deeds and Papers* (Manchester: Lancashire and Cheshire Records Society, 1936)

Lumby, Jonathan, *The Lancashire Witch Craze: Jennet Preston and the Lancashire Witches* (Preston: Carnegie, 1995)

Lunn, Maurus, 'English Benedictines and the Oath of Allegiance, 1606–1647,' *Recusant History*, 10 (1969)

Lupton, Julia Reinhard, *Afterlives of the Saints: Hagiography, Typology and Renaissance Literature* (Stanford: Stanford University Press, 1996)

Lynch, John, *Spain Under the Habsburgs* (2 vols., Oxford: Basil Blackwell, 1964)

MacClagan, Edward, *The Jesuits and the Great Mogul* (London: Burns, Oates and Washbourne, 1932)

Mackie, James, *Negotiations Between King James VI and I and Ferdinand I, Grand Duke of Tuscany* (St. Andrews: Humphrey Milford, 1927)

Maguin, Jean-Marie, 'The Rise and Fall of the King of Darkness,' in Jean-Marie Maguin and Michelle Williams (eds), *'What would France with us?': French Essays on Shakespeare and His Contemporaries* (Newark: University of Delaware Press, 1995)

Manning, Roger, *Village Revolts: Social Protest and Popular Disturbance in England, 1509–1640* (Oxford: Clarendon Press, 1988)

Manning, Roger B., 'Anthony Browne, 1st Viscount Montague: The Influence in County Politics of an Elizabethan Catholic Nobleman,' *Sussex Archaeological Collections*, 106 (1968)

—— *Religion and Society in Elizabethan Sussex* (Leicester: Leicester University Press, 1969)

Mannoni, Dominique, *Prospero and Caliban: The Psychology of Colonialism*, tran. Pamela Powesland (New York: Praeger, 1956)

Marc'hadour, G.P. 'A Name for All Seasons,' in R.S. Sylvester and G.P. Marc'hadour (eds), *Essential Articles for the Study of Thomas More* (Hamden, Conn.: Anchor, 1977)

Marin, Louis, *Utopics: The Semiological Play of Textual Spaces*, trans. Robert Vollrath (Atlantic Highlands: Humanities Press, 1990)

Marius, Richard, *Thomas More* (London: Weidenfeld and Nicolson, 1993)

Marotti, Arthur, 'Southwell's Remains: Catholicism and Anti-Catholicism in Early Modern England,' in Cedric Brown and Arthur Marotti (eds), *Texts and Cultural Change in Early Modern England* (Basingstoke: Macmillan, 1997)

—— 'Shakespeare and Catholicism,' in Richard Dutton, Alison Findlay and Richard Wilson (eds), *Theatre and Religion: Lancastrian Shakespeare* (Manchester: Manchester University Press, 2003)

Marshall, Beatrice, *Blackfriars, or the Monks of Old* (London: Longmans, 1864)

Martin, A. Lynn, *The Jesuit Mind: The Mentality of an Elite in Early Modern France* (Ithaca: Cornell University Press, 1988)

Martin, J.M., 'A Warwickshire Market Town in Adversity: Stratford-upon-Avon in the Sixteenth and Seventeenth Century,' *Midland History*, 7 (1982)

Martindale, Charles, and Colin Burrow, 'Clapham's *Narcissus*: A Pre-Text for Shakespeare's *Venus and Adonis*?' *English Literary Renaissance*, 22 (Spring 1992)

Martz, Louis, *The Poetry of Meditation* (New Haven: Yale University Press, 1962)

Massarella, Derek, *A World Elsewhere: Europe's Encounter with Japan in the Sixteenth and Seventeenth Centuries* (New Haven: Yale University Press, 1990)

Mathew, David, *Catholicism in England: The Portrait of a Minority: Its Culture and Tradition* (London: Eyre and Spottiswoode, 1955)

Maus, Katharine Eisaman, 'Horns of Dilemma: Jealousy, Gender, and Spectatorship in English Renaissance Drama,' *English Literary History (ELH)*, 54 (1981)

—— 'Proof and Consequence: Inwardness and its Exposure in the English Renaissance,' *Representations*, 34 (1991)

—— *Inwardness and Theater in the English Renaissance* (Chicago: Chicago University Press, 1995)

McCann, Timothy, 'The Parliamentary Speech of Viscount Montague Against the Act of Supremacy, 1559,' *Sussex Archaeological Collections*, 108 (1970)

McCoog (ed.), *The Reckoned Expense: Edmund Campion and the Early English Jesuits* (Woodbridge: Boydell and Brewer, 1996)

McDonald, James H., *The Poems and Prose Writings of Robert Southwell, S.J., A Bibliographical Study* (Oxford: Clarendon Press, 1937)

McEachern, Claire, and Debora Shuger, *Religion and Culture in Renaissance England* (Cambridge: Cambridge University Press, 1997)

McElwee, William, *The Wisest Fool in Christendom: The Reign of James VI and I* (London: Faber and Faber, 1958)

McGrath, Patrick, 'Elizabethan Catholicism: a Reconsideration,' *Journal of Ecclesiastical History*, 35 (1984)

—— 'The Bloody Question Reconsidered,' *Recusant History*, 20 (1991)

Melchiori, Giorgio, 'In Fair Verona: *commedia erudite* into romantic comedy,' in Michelle Marrapodi, A.J. Hoenslaars, Marcello Cappuzzo and L. Falzon Santucci (eds), *Shakespeare's Italy: Functions of Italian Locations in Renaissance Drama* (Manchester: Manchester University Press, 1997)

Metz, Harold, *Sources of Four Plays Ascribed to Shakespeare* (Columbia: Missouri University Press, 1989)

Meyer, Arnold Oscar, *England and the Catholic Church under Queen Elizabeth*, trans. J.R. McKee (London: Routledge and Kegan Paul, 1967)

Millar, Oliver, 'Van Dyck in London,' in Susan Barnes and Arthur Wheelock (eds), *Anthony Van Dyck* (Washington, D.C.: National Gallery of Art, 1990)

Miller, D.A., *The Novel and the Police* (Berkeley: University of California Press, 1990)

Miller, George, *Hoghton Tower* (Preston: Guardian Press, 1948)

Milward, Peter, *Shakespeare's Religious Background* (London: Sidgwick and Jackson, 1973)

Miola, Robert, 'Jesuit Drama in Early Modern England,' in Richard Dutton, Alison Findlay and Richard Wilson (eds), *Theatre and Religion: Lancastrian Shakespeare* (Manchester: Manchester University Press, 2003)

Mitchell, David, *The Jesuits: A History* (London: Macdonald, 1980)

Montaigne, Michel de, *The Complete Essays of Michel de Montaigne*, trans. M.A. Screech (London: Allen Lane, 1991)

Montrose, Louis, '*A Midsummer Night's Dream* and the Shaping Fantasies of Elizabethan Culture,' in Richard Wilson and Richard Dutton (eds), *New Historicism and Renaissance Drama* (Harlow: Longman, 1992)

—— *The Purpose of Playing: Shakespeare and the Cultural Politics of the Elizabethan Theatre* (Chicago: Chicago University Press, 1996)

Moody, Joanna (ed.), *The Private Life of an Elizabethan Lady: The Diary of Lady Margaret Hoby, 1599–1605* (Stroud: Sutton, 1998)

Morley, Adrian, *The Catholic Subjects of Elizabeth I* (London: Allen and Unwin, 1978)

Morris, John, *The Troubles of Our Catholic Forefathers* (3 vols., London: Burns and Oates, 1877)

Morris, Rupert, *Chester in the Plantagenet and Tudor Reigns* (Chester: Private pub., 1887)

Mosler, David, 'Warwickshire Catholics in the Civil War,' *Recusant History*, 15 (1981)

Mousnier, Roland, *The Assassination of Henry IV: The Tyrannicide Problem and the Consolidation of the French Absolute Monarchy in the Early Seventeenth Century*, trans. Joan Spencer (London: Faber and Faber, 1973)

Muchembled, Robert, 'Satanic Myth and Cultural Reality,' in Bengt Ankarloo and Gustav Heningsen (eds), *Early Modern European Witchcraft: Centres and Peripheries* (Oxford: Clarendon Press, 1990)

Mullaney, Stephen, 'Lying Like Truth: Riddle, Representation and Treason in Renaissance England,' *English Literary History (ELH)*, 47 (1980)

—— *The Place of the Stage: License, Play, and Power in Renaissance England* (Chicago: Chicago University Press, 1988)

Mullett, Michael, *The Catholics in Britain and Ireland* (London: Macmillan, 1998)

Munday, Anthony, *A Second and Third Blast of Retreat from Plays and Theatres* (London: 1580)

—— *Zelauto, the Fountain of Fame, Erected in an Orchard of Amorous Adventures ... Discoursed by Two Noble Gentlemen of Italy* (London: 1580)

—— *Discovery of Edmund Campion* (London: 1582)

—— *The English Roman Life*, ed. G.B. Harrison (London: Bodley Head, 1922)

—— *Fidele and Fortunio*, ed. Richard Hosley (New York: Garland, 1981)

—— *The Huntingdon Plays: A Critical Edition of 'The Downfall' and 'The Death of Robert, Earl of Huntingdon'*, ed. John Meagher (New York: Garland, 1980)

—— *Pageants and Entertainments of Anthony Munday*, ed. David Bergeron (New York: Garland, 1985)

Munro, John, *The Shakespeare Allusion Book* (2 vols., London: Chatto and Windus, 1909)

Murphy, John, *Darkness and Devils: Exorcism and 'King Lear'* (Athens: Ohio University Press, 1984)

—— 'Sheep-Like Goats and Goat-Like Sheep: Did Shakespeare Divide *Lear's* Kingdom?' *Papers of the Bibliographical Society of America*, 81 (1987)

Murphy, Patrick M., 'Wriothesley's Resistance: Wardship Practices and Ovidian Narrative in Shakespeare's *Venus and Adonis*,' in Philip Kohn (ed.), *'Venus and Adonis': Critical Essays* (New York: Garland, 1997)

Nashe, Thomas, *The Works of Thomas Nashe*, ed. Ronald McKerrow (4 vols., Oxford: Basil Blackwell, 1966)

Neale, John, *Queen Elizabeth* (London: Jonathan Cape, 1934)

—— *The Elizabethan House of Commons* (London: Jonathan Cape, 1949)

Neely, Carol, *Broken Nuptials in Shakespeare's Plays* (Chicago: Chicago University Press, 1993)

Newdigate, Bernard, *Michael Drayton and His Circle* (Oxford: Shakespeare Head, 1961)

Nicholas, Antonio de, *Powers of Imagining: A Philosophical Hermeneutic of Imagining Through the Collected Works of Ignatius de Loyola* (New York: New York University Press, 1986)

Nicholl, Charles, *A Cup of News: The Life of Thomas Nashe* (London: Routledge and Kegan Paul, 1984)

—— *The Reckoning: The Murder of Christopher Marlowe* (London: Picador, 1992)

Nicholls, Mark, *Investigating Gunpowder Plot* (Manchester: Manchester University Press, 1991)

Nichols, John, *The Progresses, Processions, and Magnificent Festivities of King James the First* (4 vols., London: Royal Society of Antiquaries, 1828)

O'Malley, John, and Gauvin Bailey, Steven Harris and Frank Kennedy (eds), *The Jesuits: Cultures, Sciences, and the Arts, 1540–1773* (Toronto: Toronto University Press, 1999)

Oman, Caroline, *Elizabeth of Bohemia* (London: Hodder and Stoughton, 1938)

Padberg, Frank and Majie, *Moreana: Material for the Study of Saint Thomas More* (Los Angeles: Loyola University Press, 1964)

Palmer, Daryl, *Hospitable Performances: Dramatic Genre and Cultural Practices in Early Modern England* (West Lafayette: Purdue University Press, 1992)

Parker, Patricia, '*Othello* and *Hamlet*: Dilation, Spying, and the "Secret Place" of Woman,' *Representations*, 44 (1993)

—— *Shakespeare From the Margins: Language, Culture, Context* (Chicago: Chicago University Press, 1996)

—— 'What's in a Name: and More,' *Sederi XI: Revista de la Sociedad Espanola de Estudios Renascentistas Ingleses* (Huelva: Universidad de Huelva, 2002)

—— (ed.), *Shakespeare and the Question of Theory* (London: Methuen, 1985)

Parr, Anthony (ed.), *Three Renaissance Travel Plays* (Manchester: Manchester University Press, 1995)

Parsons, Robert, *A Defence of the Censure given upon Two Books by William Charke and Meredith Hamner* (Rouen: 1582)

—— *An Epistle of the Persecution of Catholics in England* (Douai: 1582)

Paster, Gail Kern, *The Idea of the City in the Age of Shakespeare* (Athens: University of Georgia Press, 1985)

—— *The Body Embarrassed: Drama and the Disciplines of Shame in Early Modern England* (Ithaca: Cornell University Press, 1993)

—— '"In the spirit if men there is no blood": Blood as trope of Gender in *Julius Caesar*,' in Richard Wilson (ed.), *'Julius Caesar': New Casebook* (Basingstoke: Palgrave, 2002)

Patterson, Annabel, *Shakespeare and the Popular Voice* (Oxford: Basil Blackwell, 1989)

—— 'Re-Opening the Green Cabinet: Clement Marot and Edmund Spenser,' *English Literary Renaissance*, 16 (1986)

Peck, Dwight (ed.), *Leicester's Commonwealth: The Copy of a Letter Written by a Master of Art of Cambridge* (Athens: Ohio University Press, 1985)

Peck, Linda Levy, *Northampton: Patronage and Policy at the Court of James I* (London: George Allen and Unwin, 1982)

—— (ed.), *The Mental World of the Jacobean Court* (Cambridge: Cambridge University Press, 1991)

Petti, Anthony (ed.), *Recusant Documents from the Ellesmere Manuscripts* (London: Catholic Record Society, 1968)

Pfister, Manfred, 'Shakespeare and Italy, or, the law of diminishing returns,' in Michelle Marrapodi, A.J. Hoenslaars, Marcello Cappuzzo and L. Falzon Santucci (eds), *Shakespeare's Italy: Functions of Italian Locations in Renaissance Drama* (Manchester: Manchester University Press, 1997)

Phillips, James, *Images of a Queen: Mary Stuart in Sixteenth-Century Literature* (Berkeley: University of California Press, 1964)

Phillips, John, *The Reformation of the Images: Destruction of Art in England, 1535–1660* (Berkeley: University of California Press, 1973)

Plowden, Alison, *Danger to Elizabeth: The Catholics under Elizabeth I* (New York: Stein and Day, 1973)

Potter Lois, *Secret Rites and Secret Writing: Royalist Literature, 1641–1660* (Cambridge: Cambridge University Press, 1989)

Potts, Thomas, *The Trial of the Lancashire Witches*, ed. G.B. Harrison (London: Peter Davis, 1929)

Prior, Roger, 'The Life of George Wilkins,' *Shakespeare Survey*, 29 (1976)

Pritchard, Arnold, *Catholic Loyalism in Elizabethan England* (London: Scolar Press, 1979)

Prothero, G.W. (ed.), *Select Statutes and Other Constitutional Documents Illustrative of the Reigns of Elizabeth and James I* (Oxford: Clarendon Press, 1913)

Prouty, C.T., *George Gascoigne: Elizabethan Courtier, Soldier, and Poet* (New York: Benjamin Blom, 1966)

Prynne, William, *Histrio-Mastix*, ed. Arthur Freeman (New York: Garland, 1974)

Quaife, G.R., *Godly Zeal and Furious Rage: The Witch in Early Modern Europe* (London: Croom Helm, 1987)

Questier, Michael, *Conversion, Politics and Religion in England, 1580–1625* (Cambridge: Cambridge University Press, 1996)

—— 'Loyalty, Religion and State Power in Early Modern England: English Romanism and the Jacobean Oath of Allegiance,' *The Historical Journal*, 40 (1997)

Quintrell, B.W., 'The Practice and Problems of Recusant Disarming,' *Recusant History*, 17 (1985)

Raines, F.R. (ed.), *A Description of the State, Civil and Ecclesiastical, of the County of Lancaster about the Year 1590* (Manchester: Chetham Society, 1875)

Rambuss, Richard, *Spenser's Secret Career* (Cambridge: Cambridge University Press, 1993)

Razell, Peter, *William Shakespeare: The Anatomy of an Enigma* (London: Caliban, 1990)

Rebholz, R.A., *The Life of Fulke Greville* (Oxford: Clarendon Press, 1971)

Renold, P. (ed.), *Letters of William Allen and Richard Barrett, 1572–1598* (London: Catholic Record Society, 1967)

Reynolds, E.E., *The Field is Won: The Life and Death of Saint Thomas More* (London: Burns and Oates, 1968)

Rhodes, Dennis, '*Il Moro*: An Italian View of Sir Thomas More,' in Edward Chaney and Peter Mack (eds), *England and the Continental Renaissance: Essays in Honour of J.B. Trapp* (Woodbridge: Boydell, 1990)

Rose, Elliot, *Cases of Conscience: Alternatives open to Recusants and Puritans under Elizabeth I and James I* (Cambridge: Cambridge University Press, 1975)

Rosen, Barbara (ed.), *Witchcraft in England: 1558–1618* (Amherst: University of Massachusetts Press, 1991)

Rowlands, Marie (ed.), 'Recusant Women, 1540–1640,' in Mary Prior (ed.), *Women in English Society, 1500–1800* (London: Routledge, 1985)

—— *English Catholics of Parish and Town, 1558–1778* (London: Catholic Record Society, 1999)

Rowse, A.L., *Raleigh and the Throckmortons* (London: Macmillan, 1962)

—— *Shakespeare's Southampton* (London: Macmillan, 1965)

Sams, Eric, *The Real Shakespeare: Retrieving the Early Years, 1564–1594* (New Haven: Yale University Press, 1995)

Sayce, R.A., *The Essays of Montaigne: A Critical Exploration* (London: Northwestern University Press, 1972)

Schmidgall, Gary, '*The Tempest* and *Primaleon*: A New Source,' *Shakespeare Quarterly*, 36 (1986)

Schoenbaum, Samuel, *Shakespeare's Lives* (Oxford: Clarendon Press, 1970)

—— *William Shakespeare: A Documentary Life* (Oxford: Oxford University Press, 1975)

Schrickx, Willem, '*Pericles* in a Book-List of 1619 from the English Jesuit Mission and Some of the Play's Special Problems,' *Shakespeare Survey*, 29 (1976)

Scott, Sibbald David, 'A Book of Orders and Rules of Anthony Viscount Montague in 1595,' *Sussex Archaeological Collections*, 7 (1869)

Scott, William, 'Macbeth's – And Our – Self-Equivocations,' *Shakespeare Quarterly*, 37 (1986)

Sedgwick, Eve Kosofsky, *Epistemology of the Closet* (Berkeley: University of California Press, 1990)

Shapiro, I.A., 'Shakespeare and Munday,' *Shakespeare Survey*, 14 (1961)

Sharpe, James, *Instruments of Darkness: Witchcraft in England, 1550–1750* (Harmondsworth: Penguin, 1997)

Sheils, W.J., 'Catholics in a Rural Community,' *Northern History*, 34 (1998)

—— 'Household, Age and Gender among Jacobean Yorkshire Recusants,' in Marie Rowlands (ed.), *English Catholics of Parish and Town, 1558–1778* (London: Catholic Record Society, 1999)

Shell, Alison, *Catholicism, Controversy and the English Literary Imagination: 1558–1660* (Cambridge: Cambridge University Press, 1999)

Shell, Marc, *Money, Language and Thought: Literary and Philosophical Economies from the Medieval to the Modern Era* (Baltimore: Johns Hopkins University Press, 1993)

Shelton, Thomas, *The History of Don Quixote of the Mancha translated from the Spanish of Miguel de Cervantes*, ed. James Fitzmaurice-Kelly (4 vols., London: David Nutt, 1896)

Shepherd, Samuel, *Epigrams Theological, Philosophical and Romantic* (London: 1641)

Shepherd, Simon, *Marlowe and the Politics of Elizabethan Theatre* (Hemel Hempstead: Harvester, 1986)

Shirley, Frances, *Swearing and Perjury in Shakespeare's Plays* (London: Allen and Unwin, 1985)

Shuger, Debora, *Political Theologies in Shakespeare's England: The Sacred and the State in 'Measure for Measure'* (London: Palgrave, 2001)

Sidney, Philip, *A History of the Gunpowder Plot: The Conspiracy and its Agents* (London: Religious Tract Society, 1908)

Siemon, James, *Shakespearean Iconoclasm* (Berkeley: University of California Press, 1985)

Simmel, George, *The Sociology of George Simmel*, trans. and ed. Kurt Wolff (Glenco, Ill.: The Free Press, 1950)

Simonds, Peggy Munoz, *Myth, Emblem, and Music in Shakespeare's 'Cymbeline'* (Newark: New Jersey University Press, 1992)

Simons, Eric, *The Devil in the Vault: A Life of Guy Fawkes* (London: Frederick Muller, 1963)

Simpson, Richard, 'What was the Religion of Shakespeare?' (3 parts) *The Rambler*, 9 (1858)

—— 'The Political Use of the Stage in Shakespeare's Time,' *The New Shakspere Society's Transactions*, 2 (1874) *Edmund Campion* (London: John Hodges, 1896)

Sinfield, Alan, *Faultlines: Cultural Materialism and the Politics of Dissident Reading* (Oxford: Oxford University Press, 1992)

Sirluck, Ernest, 'Shakespeare and Jonson among the Pamphleteers of the First Civil War,' *Modern Philology*, 53 (1955)

Sisson, C.J., 'Shakespeare's Quartos as Prompt Copies, With Some Account of the Cholmeley Players and a Shakespeare Allusion,' *Review of English Studies*, 18 (1942)

Skura, Meredith Ann, *Shakespeare the Actor and the Purposes of Playing* (Chicago: Chicago University Press, 1993)

Slights, Camille Wells, *The Casuistical Tradition in Shakespeare, Donne, Herbert, and Milton* (Princeton: Princeton University Press, 1981)

Slights, William, *Ben Jonson and the Art of Secrecy* (Toronto: Toronto University Press, 1994)

Smith, Irwin, *Shakespeare's Blackfriars Playhouse: Its History and Design* (New York: New York University Press, 1964)

Smith, John, *The Complete Works of Captain John Smith*, ed. Philip L. Barbour (3 vols., Chapel Hill: University of North Carolina Press, 1992)

Smith, Lacey Baldwin, *Treason in Tudor England* (London: Jonathan Cape, 1986)

Smith, Bruce R., *Homosexual Desire in Shakespeare's England: A Cultural Poetics* (Chicago: Chicago University Press, 1991)

Smith, Thomas, *De Republica Anglorum*, ed. Mary Dewar (Cambridge: Cambridge University Press, 1982)

Somerset, Anne, *Unnatural Murder: Poison at the Court of King James* (London: Weidenfeld and Nicolson, 1997)

Southern, A.C. (ed.), *An Elizabethan Recusant House: The Life of Lady Magdalen Viscountess Montague, 1538–1608; Translated from the Latin of Dr. Richard Smith by Cuthbert Fursden, O.S.B. in the year 1627* (London: Sands, 1954)

Southwell, Robert, *An Epistle of Comfort to the Reverend Priests* (St-Omer: 1616)

—— *The Poems of Robert Southwell, S.J.*, ed. James McDonald and Nancy Pollard Brown (Oxford: Oxford University Press, 1967)

—— *An Humble Supplication to Her Majesty*, ed. R.C. Bald (Cambridge: Cambridge University Press, 1953)

Speed, John, *The Theatre of the Empire of Great Britain* (London: 1611)

Spenser, Edmund, *A View of the Present State of Ireland*, ed. W.I. Renwick (Oxford: Oxford University Press, 1925)

Squiers, Granville, *Secret Hiding Places* (London: Stanley Paul, 1934)

Stanley, A.P., *Historical Memorials of Westminster Abbey* (London: 1869)

Stempel, Daniel, 'The Silence of Iago,' *PMLA*, 84 (1969)

Stewart, Alan, *Close Readers: Humanism and Sodomy in Early Modern England* (Princeton: Princeton University Press, 1997)

—— *Philip Sidney: A Double Life* (London: Chatto and Windus, 2000)

Stevenson, Robert, *Shakespeare's Religious Frontier* (London: Routledge, 1958)

Stone, Lawrence, *The Crisis of the Aristocracy, 1558–1641* (Oxford: Oxford University Press, 1965)

Stopes, Charlotte Carmichael, *Shakespeare's Warwickshire Contemporaries* (Stratford-upon-Avon: Shakespeare Head, 1907)

Stow, John, *A Survey of London*, ed. John Morley (London: Routledge, 1890)

Strong, Roy, *The Cult of Elizabeth: Elizabethan Portraiture and Pageantry* (London: Thames and Hudson, 1977)

—— 'England and Italy: The Marriage of Henry Prince of Wales,' in Richard Ollard and Pamela Tudor-Craig (eds), *For Veronica Wedgwood: Studies in Seventeenth-Century History* (London: Collins, 1986)

—— *Henry Prince of Wales and England's Lost Renaissance* (London: Thames and Hudson, 1986)

Sturman, May Winifride, 'Gravelines and the English Poor Clares,' *London Recusant*, 7 (1977)

Sullivan, Ceri, *Dismembered Rhetoric: English Recusant Writing, 1580 to 1603* (London: Associated Universities Press, 1995)

Taylor, Gary, 'William Shakespeare, Richard James, and the House of Cobham,' *Review of English Studies*, 38 (1987)

—— 'Forms of Opposition: Shakespeare and Middleton,' *English Literary Renaissance*, 24 (1994)

—— 'The Cultural Politics of Maybe,' in Richard Dutton, Alison Findlay and Richard Wilson (eds), *Theatre and Religion: Lancastrian Shakespeare*, (Manchester: Manchester University Press, 2003)

—— (ed.), with Michael Warren, *The Division of the Kingdom: Shakespeare's Two Versions of 'King Lear'* (Oxford: Clarendon Press, 1983)

Tenenti, Alberto, *Piracy and the Decline of Venice, 1580–1615* (London: Routledge, 1967)

Thaler, Alwn, *Shakespeare's Silences* (Cambridge, Mass.: Harvard University Press, 1929)

Thomas, Keith, *Religion and the Decline of Magic* (Harmondsworth: Penguin, 1973)

Thomson, Peter, *Shakespeare's Professional Career* (Cambridge: Cambridge University Press, 1992)

Thurston, Herbert, 'Catholic Writers and Elizabethan Readers: Father Southwell the Euphuist and Father Southwell the Popular Poet,' 2 parts, *The Month*, 83 (1895)

—— 'William Shakespeare and Robert Southwell,' *The Month*, 108 (November 1911)

Trevor-Roper, Hugh, 'The Anti-Dukes of Northumberland,' *Journal of Anglo-Italian Studies*, 2 (1992)

Trotman, John William, *'The Triumphs over Death' by the Ven. Robert Southwell, S.J.* (London: Manresa Press, 1914)

Turner, Celeste, *Anthony Munday: An Elizabethan Man of Letters* (Berkeley: University of California Press, 1928)

Ungerer, Gustav, 'An Unrecorded Performance of *Titus Andronicus*,' *Shakespeare Survey*, 14 (1970)

Urquhart, Margaret, 'Was Christopher Simpson a Jesuit?' *Chelys*, 21 (1992)

Waddington, Raymond B., 'The Iconography of Silence and Chapman's Hercules,' *Journal of The Warburg and Courtauld Institutes*, 33 (1970)

Wait, R.J.C., *The Background of Shakespeare's Sonnets* (London: Chatto and Windus, 1972)

Walsham, Alexandra, *Church Papists: Catholicism, Conformity and Confessional Polemic in Early Modern England* (Woodbridge: Boydell and Brewer, 1993)

—— *Providence in Early Modern England* (Oxford: Oxford University Press, 1999)

Warner, George, *The Voyage of Robert Dudley to the West Indies, 1594–95* (London: Hakluyt Society, 1899)

Watt, Tessa, *Cheap Print and Popular Piety in Early Modern England* (Cambridge: Cambridge University Press, 1991)

Waugh, Evelyn, *Edmund Campion* (Oxford: Campion Hall, 1935)

Wayne, Valerie (ed.), *The Matter of Difference: Materialist Criticism of Shakespeare* (Hemel Hempstead, 1991)

Weeks, William, *Clitheroe in the Seventeenth Century* (Clitheroe: Advertiser and Times, 1887)

Weimann, Robert, *Shakespeare and the Popular Tradition in the Theater: Studies in the Social Dimension of Dramatic Form and Function* (Baltimore: Johns Hopkins University Press, 1978)

Wells, Stanley, 'By the Placing of his Words: Shakespeare's First Close Critic,' *Times Literary Supplement*, September 26 2003

Weston, William, *The Autobiography of an Elizabethan*, trans. Philip Caraman (London: Longmans, 1955)

White, Paul Whitfield, *Theatre and Reformation: Protestantism, Patronage, and Playing in Tudor England* (Cambridge: Cambridge University Press, 1993)

Whitfield, Christopher, 'Some of Shakespeare's Contemporaries at the Middle Temple,' *Notes and Queries*, December 1966

Williams, Hugh Ross, *The Gunpowder Plot* (London: Faber and Faber, 1951)

Wills, Gary, *Witches and Jesuits: Shakespeare's 'Macbeth'* (New York: Oxford University Press, 1995)

Wilson, Arthur, *The History of Great Britain, Being the Life and Reign of King James the First* (London: 1653)

Wilson, Ian, *Shakespeare: The Evidence* (London: Headline, 1993)

Wilson, Richard, *Will Power: Essays on Shakespearean Authority* (Hemel Hempstead: Harvester, 1993)

—— 'Shakespeare and the Jesuits,' *Times Literary Supplement*, December 19 1997

—— (ed.) *Julius Caesar: A New Casebook* (Basingstoke: Palgrave, 2002)

—— (ed.) with Richard Dutton, *New Historicism and Renaissance Drama* (Harlow: Longman, 1992)

—— (ed.) with Richard Dutton and Alison Findlay, *Region, Religion and Performance: Lancastrian Shakespeare* (Manchester: Manchester University Press, 2003)

—— (ed.) with Richard Dutton and Alison Findlay, *Theatre and Religion: Lancastrian Shakespeare* (Manchester: Manchester University Press, 2003)

Wilson, Scott, 'Racked on the Tyrant's Bed: The Politics of Pleasure and Pain and the Elizabethan Sonnet Sequence,' *Textual Practice*, 3 (1989)

Wilson, Violet, 'Shakespeare and a Yorkshire Quarrel,' *North American Review*, 219 (1924)

Wood, Diana (ed.), *Martyrs and Martyrology* (Oxford: Blackwell, 1993)

Wood, Michael, *In Search of William Shakespeare* (London: BBC, 2003)

Woodbridge, Linda, *The Scythe of Saturn: Shakespeare and Magical Thinking* (Urbana: University of Illinois Press, 1994)

—— (ed.) with Edward Berry, *True Rites and Maimed Rites: Ritual and Anti-Ritual in Shakespeare and His Age* (Urbana: University of Illinois Press, 1992)

Worden, Blair, 'Shakespeare and Politics,' *Shakespeare Survey*, 44 (1992)

—— *The Sound of Virtue* (New Haven: Yale University Press, 1996)

Wotton, Henry, *Life and Letters of Sir Henry Wotton*, ed. Logan Pearsall Smith (2 vols., Oxford: Clarendon Press, 1907)

Woudhuysen, Henry, *Sir Philip Sidney and the Circulation of Manuscripts, 1558–1640* (Oxford: Clarendon Press, 1996)

Wright, T., *Queen Elizabeth and Her Times; A Series of Original Letters* (2 vols., London: 1838)

Yachnin, Paul, *Stage-Wrights: Shakespeare, Jonson, Middleton and the Making of Theatrical Value* (Philadelphia: University of Pennsylvania Press, 1997)

Yates, Frances, *Astraea: The Imperial Theme in the Sixteenth Century* (Harmondsworth: Penguin, 1977)

Zagorin, Perez, *Ways of Lying: Dissimulation, Persecution, and Conformity in Early Modern Europe* (Cambridge Mass.: Harvard University Press, 1990)

Index